LABOR
ECONOMICS

Paul Sultan

UNIVERSITY OF SOUTHERN CALIFORNIA

HENRY HOLT AND COMPANY
NEW YORK

To

My Mother

and the Memory of

My Father

Foreword

Textbooks and more encyclopedic treatises in the fields of labor economics and labor relations have flowed from the presses in abundance during recent years. Nor is this surprising. Bewilderingly rapid economic and social changes have taken place since the end of World War II, as well as during the decade and a half preceding 1945; the role of government in economic life has both changed in character and assumed enlarged proportions. Developments in, and refinements of, theoretical analysis have, in this interval, been numerous and substantial. The consequence has been the production of texts and treatises that have enriched the study of labor in America.

Professor Sultan's well-written book deserves a cordial welcome because it is characterized by rigidity of theoretical analysis, skillful use of the newer research materials, mastery of institutional material, presentation of controversial issues in nondogmatic manner (and yet without evading the taking of positions), provocative use of quantitative material, and desirable organizational features.

Some of the ends attained by this book may be enumerated with a little more particularity. The section on "Dynamics of Collective Bargaining" presents skillfully the basic issues in the bargaining process, the dichotomy between power and principle in our economy, and the frequent difficulty in reconciling separate value systems in the labor market. There is, as there should be in a labor economics treatise, heavy emphasis on economic theory. The chapters on mercantile, classical, and contemporary wage theory should stimulate students to look into the original sources, and the treatment of unionism and of the influences on union growth is mature and properly balanced. Professor Sultan's distinction between wage problems in an underemployment situation and wage adjustments in a relatively full-employment situation is sharply drawn and is developed in workmanlike manner, and his thesis that unemployment has been one of the basic forces accounting for the character of union growth is persuasively presented. Both supporters and detractors of Keynesian economics will want to think with, as well as against, the analysis in Chapter 23, with its several aptly designed charts. The issues of wage policy in periods of depression are developed penetratingly, and the discussion indicates the many intricacies involved in relating the wage level to economic activity. The matter of the public interest in industrial relations is lucidly presented, and enough appears in various chapters, even if not in a separate section, to give students and instructors a basis for probing the important area of social security.

Labor economists, like economists in general, are endowed with traditional predisposition to disagree among themselves over this point or that when new and substantial works appear; and probably this book will prove no exception to the general rule. Possibly some of the features of Professor Sultan's *Labor Economics* that may be provocative of wholesome argument have been suggested in the foregoing paragraph. The organization of the book, with its early emphasis upon unionism (Section II) is in accordance with recent textbook trends, and while some instructors may feel that the treatment of the economics of wage and employment would better precede the discussion of unionism and the dynamics of collective bargaining, that is a matter of opinion. Professor Sultan's organizational structure is clearly defendable on a considerable number of grounds, and instructors who wish to do so can, of course, base their earlier discussions upon the material in the " Economics of Wages and Employment " section. Many other thoughts are suggested to a reader of the manuscript of this book, but it must suffice here to say that the study of labor economics will benefit appreciably by the publication of this book and that it will receive, I believe, a hearty welcome from those working in this field.

ROYAL E. MONTGOMERY
Cornell University

Acknowledgments

Within this text, I have pointed to the difficulty of untangling from any product the specific contributions made in its creation by the co-operating factors of production. The attempts to acknowledge the assistance given me in the creation of this text brings home the reality of this argument with new force. And while it is difficult to determine " who did what," it is possible to mention just a few of those persons who offered me direct and indirect assistance.

First, I would like to acknowledge the encouragement given to me by Professors Joseph Crumb, George Drummond, and Robert Clark at the University of British Columbia, an interest sustained by those professors guiding my graduate work at Cornell University, Professors Royal E. Montgomery, Harold Reed, George P. Adams, Jr., and N. Arnold Tolles.

My associates at the University of Buffalo, including among others, Joseph Shister, Harold Somers, Bill Hamovitch, Art Butler, and Jack Kaufman, provided a testing ground for almost all of my existing pre-dilections. I am particularly appreciative of the encouragement and generous guidance given me by Joseph Shister for research in the labor field and the freedom he extended to me in both the selection and treatment of labor courses taught in his department.

In the preparation of this text, I hold Professor Royal E. Montgomery responsible for the launching of this project and am most grateful for the continuing guidance he offered me throughout. Several other colleagues have given generously of their time to review certain sections of an early draft, including Professor Herman Krooss of New York University, Bill Hamovitch of Queens College, and Don Gordon of the University of Washington. Albert J. Zack of the AFL–CIO public relations department indicated several improvements for the AFL–CIO organizational chart. Both Carl Bagge and John Balluff, attorneys on the staff of the Santa Fe Railway, offered spirited criticisms of my treatment of " Right to Work " legislation. My participation in the summer Institutes of Business Economics provided for by the Santa Fe Railway at the University of Southern California gave me the opportunity to review with this group much of the discussion of this text. Reaction was often critical, but always fair, friendly, and constructive.

My severest critics proved to be Henry and Stella Falk, who pointed up the inadequacies of early drafts with an enthusiasm and vigor which I can confess now was rather dismaying. They must have established a new precedent for " in-laws," for they appeared more interested in protecting the student from the inadequacy of my authorship than their daughter from the inadequacies of her husband. The text reflects, more than the reader can appreciate, the benefit of this generous assistance. On the technical side, Ruth Halvorsen proved a patient typist with unbelievable skill in deciphering both garbled copy and tapes.

Finally, I must not neglect the large number of writers whose contributions I have freely and gratefully cited and quoted throughout. Considerable stress has been given to journal articles because of my personal conviction that these contain a rich source of information not always adequately explored by the undergraduate student. My obligation to the authors, editors, and publishers of both texts and journals will be immediately apparent to even the most casual reader.

For those errors of commission and omission which inevitably make their unwelcomed appearance, I alone am responsible.

P. S.

March 1, 1956
Los Angeles, Calif.

Contents

IV. The Public Interest and Industrial Relations: A Review of Labor Legislation

V. The Economics of Wages and Employment

Prologue

The irate employer pointed his finger to his employee: " Harris, I've cancelled your hospitalization and sick-benefit policy, closed out your old-age retirement account, cleared your case with the union, given proper legal notice to the Unemployment Insurance Bureau, and had a check drawn for your vacation credit, cost-of-living bonus, severance pay, and accumulated salary, including overtime. You're fired! " This caption to a *New Yorker* cartoon provides an interesting commentary on the present state of labor-management relations, for it reveals the several roadblocks created by both the union and the government to unemployment.

Traditionally labor texts have seized upon the various problems facing the worker — not the least of which was unemployment — as the point of departure for their discussion. Following the analysis of the impact of inadequate wages, erratic employment, child labor and so on, labor texts then turned to the threefold solutions to these difficulties. First labor's solution was seen in the organization of unions and the evolving process of collective bargaining. Second, management's solution was seen in enlightened personnel policies which would meet the basic needs of the work force. And third, the government's solution was seen in minimum wage laws, unemployment insurance, social security, factory legislation, and other statutes to regulate the behavior of both unions and management.

This pattern was upset somewhat by a new vogue for " labor economics," but no sooner had the vogue been established when it was modified by texts which stressed the importance of union institutionalism, labor politics, and industrial sociology. The organizational structure of this text offers no radical departure or surprising innovations from these recent trends, but attempts rather to effect a blending of the old with the new and the theoretical with the institutional. The viewpoint throughout is predominantly " economic," but the analysis has been spiced slightly with historical and sociological references. Just as we shall argue that the union holds no monopoly in the *solution* of labor problems, so must we admit that the economist holds no monopoly in his *analysis* of the labor market.

The text is divided into five major sections, each with its individual design and theme. In Section I, our purpose shall be to gain some perspective on the development of a labor market. Our analysis here will be predominantly historical, for we shall attempt to discover those forces which made possible the unique and novel structure for marketing the labor service that we enjoy today. Chapter 2 will review the sources of labor force growth, and Chapter 3 will indicate the performance of this market mechanism by revealing the changing pattern of real wages that labor has received. Our section will conclude with a review of the labor market, not as perceived by the economist, but as perceived by the worker himself.

In Section II, we shall analyze the " why " and extent of union organization. This analysis will be both descriptive and theoretical and cover such issues as the size of the bargaining unit, racketeering in unions, civil liberties within unions, and so on. Our section will conclude with a general survey of theories of unionism, covering the important contributions offered to us by Marx, Commons, the Webbs, Perlman, Hoxie, Tannenbaum, and Lindblom.

In Section III we turn to unionism in action. We shall begin with a survey of attitudes of both labor and management regarding the purpose and impact of collective bargaining. We shall then discuss the major issues that arise during the bargaining session, examining each of these in terms of the viewpoint of organized labor, management, and the public. Following the review of the agenda of the bargaining session, we shall contrast the role and determinants of " power " with " principle " in bargaining. Our section will conclude with a review of alternative criteria for wage adjustments, and the wider impact of the union on such economic parameters as hourly earnings, productivity and distributive shares.

In Section IV we turn to the public's response to labor-management relations. The government has the responsibility for evolving and making explicit the " rule of the game " in the tussle of pressure groups for economic gain. We shall trace the evolution of legislative and judicial attitudes from the conspiracy doctrine to the Taft-Hartley law.

In our final section we shall attempt to step behind much of the union institutionalism described in previous chapters and analyze those economic forces, including those ideas of the economists themselves, which have had a significant impact on labor-management relations. Of paramount importance to labor is, of course, the possibility of interruptions in the stream of its income payments arising from unemployment. Much of our wage theory is not characterized by the shift from imperfect to more perfect truths, but rather in the substitution of one set of values for another. Wage theories, like old soldiers, never die but just fade away. But unlike old soldiers, they have a habit of becoming revitalized in an appropriate economic environment. We can understand much about the present by studying the speculations of economists in the past. Our section will conclude with an analysis of labor in a fully employed economy.

While it is fashionable to view the problem of labor today from a multicausal or " pluralistic " viewpoint, our discussion throughout is related to several basic propositions. First, it is suggested that labor market organization, especially when Western economies could be described as "backward areas," did little to satisfy the basic needs of the individual worker. Unionism arose because of labor's disappointment with the philosophy of individualism. Second, it is argued that unionism today has embraced completely the orthodox concepts of acquisitiveness. But to many, group organization is viewed as a more effective device for getting "more" than individualism. Third, group organization has created philosophical and economic issues today which are largely unsolved. Solutions are generally rooted in an appeal to "reasonableness" or "fairness," phrases and concepts usually ill-defined or undefined but usually sufficiently flexible to convince each person of the self-righteousness of his own viewpoint. It is relatively easy to secure agreement on the definition of a "competitive" wage, but not on the content of a "fair" wage. Fourth, the worker gains a degree of independence and control through union membership, but membership imposes some restrictions on the worker. Maintaining a degree of equality in the distribution of freedom between the worker and his union, and in turn between the union and management, is the counterpart for the constant search for equality of bargaining power. Our society continues to grope for this optimum combination of distribution of freedom which will provide distributive justice, maximum production, full employment, and stability. Fifth, one of the basic stabilizing mechanisms of a competitive society is the prospect that any factor of production, including labor, can price its services out of the market. If we continue to embrace the notion that the government has the responsibility to maintain full employment regardless of pressures on the industry cost structure, we must search for new stabilizing devices.

I

The Impact of Economic Change
and the Evolving
Labor Market

1

Origins and Emergence
of the Labor Market

This is a book about the labor market. This market is certainly the most important within our economic system, for the consequences of forces operating within it determine the economic well-being of close to 70 million workers. Indirectly these forces have a profound impact on the morale and economic health of the total population. It requires no poetic license to say that the labor market is the focal point for most economic activity: It reflects not merely a slice of reality, but mirrors the major substance of society itself.

But, surprisingly enough, a labor market economy as we know it today is a rather novel experiment in economic organization. When viewed in the broad perspective of history, it is very new indeed. For example, if we were to consider the evolution of civilization from 3000 B.C. to the present time as a twenty-four-hour day, the free labor market is hardly more than forty-five minutes old. It is the very novelty of this new adventure in social and economic relationships which provides the point of departure for this text.

In this chapter we shall show how the shift from the slave system and status organization of labor to the free market structure was abrupt and, for the most part, unanticipated. This transition, paralleling the industrial revolution itself, permitted the tremendous release of man's personal initiative and energy as well as the intensive exploitation of natural resources. The resulting new market organization made possible a spectacular increase in production and material wealth. The technological revolution created a chain reaction affecting every facet of life. Older institutions and customs crumbled under the pressure of these new forces, changing in turn the very core of social and economic relationships. In this chapter, we shall survey briefly the impact of this change.

As we shall indicate later, the union movement has not evolved in spite of, but because of, the dynamic character of capitalism's growth. Union growth has been spontaneous and is, in effect, a defense mechanism against the effects of change. Today, some lament that the union movement reflects society's attempt to "escape from freedom." But unions are not designed to escape from freedom, or even from change; they desire mainly to escape from the uncertainty and insecurity so often associated with change. Thus, by understanding change, we can better understand unionism. And by understanding the origins of the labor market, we can better understand the origins of unionism.

The Slave System in Pre-Christian Cultures

Historically, slave labor has been the most common means for getting work done. If we go back to the cradles of civilization in Egypt, Greece, Israel, and Syria, we discover our best examples of the slave labor economy. In these early cultures one of the most important fruits of military conquest was the number of slaves which were captured and enlisted for manual work. In these ancient cultures, then, slavery was a normal state of affairs. Had not the great philosopher Aristotle explained that slavery was rooted in human nature? "Native distinctions of quality exist such that some persons are by nature gifted with power to plan, command and supervise, and others possess merely capacity to obey and execute." [1] Eventually different levels of social status developed within the slave labor work force. The skilled workers were on occasion permitted to organize as an association, not to exact economic advantage, but to extend their own cultural enrichment and increase their contributions to the gods and to the state. [2]

These early civilizations did not collapse so much from the internal rebellions of labor dissatisfied with its slave status, but rather because they were weakened by the dissipation of resources and energy in military conflict. Slave labor represented the hands operating the economic machine, and success in military conflict was necessary in order to assure a continuing and adequate labor supply. The endurance of these early civilizations suggests, however, that labor was adjusted to its lowly status without experiencing a sense of personal outrage. To the slave, individual wealth and freedom were unattainable. They were, therefore, concepts that had little significance in his life. [3]

[1] As paraphrased by John Dewey, *Human Nature and Conduct* (New York, Henry Holt and Co., 1922), p. 109.

[2] As one historian explains, in the Grecian culture "Slaves and other non-citizens did manual work. The Greek band of associates was a social and religious, not an economic form of grouping. . . . Its members did not need to 'protect their own interests' for these were sufficiently protected by custom and the constitution of society. . . . They did not need to raise prices for they were working not for riches but for honour and a livelihood, and prices were fixed by immemorial custom." Alfred Zimmern, *The Greek Commonwealth* (New York, Oxford University Press, 1915), pp. 256–276.

[3] A somewhat different form of the slave society existed among the Inca civilization in Peru. Members of the Inca society could not add to their possessions, advance one

The Status System of the Middle Ages

The slave system evolved slowly into a status system during the Middle Ages. During this period labor's position was dictated by religious and monarchic authority. Society was held together by a system of mutual responsibilities and obligations. Compliance with this status system did not depend on the force of the whip so much as on the universal dominance of the church. Thus, the growth of Christianity and the triumph of church law did not change the basic structure of society but rather gave moral purpose to man's status. A laborer was not expected to roam the economy as a free agent, to exact for himself as much economic benefit as he could. He was still deeply enmeshed in an authoritarian system, and the church gave this authority its blessing. As R. H. Tawney, in his classic study, *Religion and the Rise of Capitalism*, explains, the lord, peasant, craftsman, and warrior " were to be sublimated into service, vocation and chivalry, and the ritual [of the church] which surrounded them was designed to emphasize that they had undergone a re-dedication at the hands of religion. Baptized by the Church, privilege and power became office and duty." [4]

With a single code dictating the content of moral behavior, society had a common standard which could be used to determine the justice of every act and, furthermore, to establish benchmarks for measuring " just " prices and " just " wages. It was only when the authority of the church was weakened that man could disagree about the content of such justice. But economic circumstances were for the most part on the side of the church during the Middle Ages, for the stability of economic life made it possible to determine, within fairly precise limits, the costs of production for all commodities. Such costs could, in turn, be related to the usual requirements of the individual worker for adequate subsistence. If prices were established on the basis of predictable and " just " labor costs, how would it be possible for individuals to accumulate wealth? And if it were possible, was it *proper?* The indictment of the church against wealth-getting seemed quite clear: The man who makes money out of the market must be wicked, for if one profited by exchange, it could only be at the expense of the other party to that exchange. Was it not clear that one

hair's breadth on the social scale, marry, or even be unemployed without permission of the state. No man could become rich and no man could become poor: " It was the object of the Incas to infuse into their subjects a spirit of passive obedience and tranquility, a perfect acquiescence in the established order of things. In this they fully succeeded. . . . and no people could have appeared more contented with their lot, and more devoted to their government. . . . The astonishing mechanism of the Peruvian polity could have resulted only from the combined authority of opinion and positive power in the ruler to an extent unprecedented in the history of man." William H. Prescott, *The Conquest of Peru* (New York, E. P. Dutton & Co., Everyman Edition, 1909), p. 26.

[4] (New York, Mentor Book, The New American Library, 1950), p. 28.

man's wealth could only be increased by another man's poverty? "Just price," the safeguard against extortion, protected the consumer but it also thwarted the hope for rapid industrial growth. The clerics solemnly agreed that "Neither the Church of Christ, nor a Christian Commonwealth, ought to tolerate such as prefer private gain to the public weal or seek it to the hurt of their neighbours."

Few dared challenge the mandates of the church. When John Ball in 1381 declared that "At the beginning we were all created equal" and that it was "the tyranny of perverse men which has caused slavery to arise, in spite of God's law," Ball was properly hanged, drawn, and quartered. And when Abelard listed some one hundred and fifty propositions of the church which flatly contradicted one another, he was condemned and disgraced for such heresy. The sterility of the period is often attributed to the absence of new adventures in philosophy or political theory or to the vigorous and universal dissent against all dissent. But this ultimate source of weakness of church law proved, for a time, to be a source of its strength. The fear of eternal damnation was real, and the coercive power of the church to save or condemn man was readily used to consolidate its dominance over society.

The rationale of the church for the status structure of society was plausible enough. Just as the body must coordinate the functions of the heart, mind, sword, and hand, so must the functioning of the larger organic unit — the feudal manor — rest on the interdependence of the priest, baron, soldier, and serf. The church, then, provided the unifying influence; it gave coherence and meaning to man's humble existence. For labor to rebel against its status was as rational as for one to inflict a blow on one's own head.

The life of the serf was often hard and wretched, and his major consolation was that "celestial happiness would surely compensate for his earthly misery." His entire family usually lived in a single hut, with a portion reserved for domestic animals. The routines of his work day were carefully prescribed by custom, tradition, and the authority of his lord. He lived at the subsistence level and could face starvation if such natural disasters as storms or floods should destroy manor crops. The peasant remained largely illiterate, highly superstitious, and politically helpless. We should not forget, however, that even though the European continent was characterized by low productivity and political turmoil, the feudal manor did provide a pocket of relative security for the peasant.

While the Middle Ages are usually described as the "dark" or "dormant" stretch of European economic history, the seeds for commercial change were planted in this period, largely during the Crusades, and these seeds were slowly germinating beneath the soil of feudal institutionalism. The Crusades led to the criss-cross of highways throughout Europe and stimulated the tastes of Western man for Oriental luxuries. Symptomatic of this change was the growing number of "merchants, students, minstrels, buffoons, pilgrims, pedlars, friars, masons, scribes, pardoners, cheap-Jacks — all wandering freely from place to place, to give the medieval scene everywhere the same gaudy variety."[5] Towns began to appear, but these were more often than not "congested huddles, dark, unkempt, filthy, and foul-smelling with a turbulent and often vicious life of their own. . . ."[6] The town, however, provided a safety valve for abuses on the manor. It was not unknown for a lord, hoping to increase his opportunities for salvation as he lay on his deathbed, to free a serf from his slave status. Other serfs who were not granted their freedom often slipped away to the town.

The growth of commerce resulted in the parallel growth of guilds. These were organizations designed to stabilize prices, maintain quality standards, and impose apprenticeship regulations for various trades. While these guilds were often quasisocial in nature, they served the economic function of regulating the labor supply and gave more security to workers increasingly apprehensive of insecurity.[7] Often the personal relationship between the master-craftsman and the journeymen within the guild dissolved into an impersonal and antagonistic struggle when the area of competition for the products the guild produced widened, when the pressure of the market for cheap goods increased. As Ralph E. Turner describes the new labor markets in medieval western Europe: "In the towns the workers usually dwelt in miserable suburban hovels. In mining areas they lived in 'company towns.' When seeking employment, they assembled in churchyards, where masters went among them selecting 'hands' according to their needs." And when unemployment increased, workers "were generally forbidden to assemble in large numbers or to carry heavy tools that could be used as weapons."[8]

Looking back, it is difficult to typify the vast stretch of economic history running from A.D. 300 to 1500 in any single phrase, but we should remember that the feudal manor did provide the peasant with one condition in his working life lacking in the new labor markets — a defined (if humble) status. As the labor sociologist Frank Tannenbaum has aptly explained:

[5] As described by Herbert J. Muller, *The Uses of the Past: Profiles of Former Societies* (New York, Oxford University Press, 1952), p. 239.

[6] *Ibid.*, p. 239.

[7] "The guilds tried to control the labor supply by defining the conditions of entrance into the craft. They regulated wages, hours, prices, quality, and tools to be used. They sought equality for each member; they protected members from undue competition and from injury; and they strove for stability. They kept out 'foreigners.' They tried to secure complete control over their own parochial market. . . ." Frank Tannenbaum, *A Philosophy of Labor* (New York, Alfred A. Knopf, 1951), p. 19.

[8] "Economic Discontent in Medieval Western Europe" from "The Tasks of Economic History," *Journal of Economic History*, Supplement VIII (1948), p. 93.

Membership in a guild, manorial estate, or village protected man throughout his life and gave him the peace and the serenity from which could flow the medieval art and craft. The life of man was a nearly unified whole. Being a member of an integrated society pro-tected and raised the dignity of the individual, and gave each person his own special role. Each man, each act, was part of a total life drama, the plot of which was known and in which the part allotted to each was prescribed. No one was isolated or abandoned.[9]

But commercial change could not be restrained. New alliances were be-ing forged as sovereign kings attempted to widen their spheres of influ-ence. Men of commerce, previously carrying on their activities of dubious respectability, now acquired enormous influence.

Capitalism and the Protestant Ethic

Materialism was sweeping through Europe. Could it be reconciled with church law? The Catholic church, to use Muller's phrase, was " never so naive as to believe that morality would be promoted, and the good so-ciety achieved, by glorifying the profit motive." [10] But as we shall see the inexorable forces of economic change required not only an accommodat-ing reorganization of political forms, but a reinterpretation of religion itself. The sweeping popularity of the Protestant ethic laid the foundation for capitalist development. It was Martin Luther who acquired the title: "Father of Revolutions," and yet, ironically, this was the man who de-clared that " The brute populace must be governed by brute force." How can we account for this strange paradox? [11]

[9] *Op. cit.*, p. 30.

[10] *Op. cit.*, p. 251.

[11] Even today society demands constant reassurance about the ethical foundation for individualism, laissez faire, and competition. It is as though we were haunted with the suspicion that Christianity and capitalism do not fit one another as hand and glove. Capitalism is often exposed to the barbs from both its friends and foes for its " irre-ligious " foundations. Can we take seriously J. M. Keynes' statement that "Modern capitalism is absolutely irreligious, without internal union, without much public spirit, often, though not always, a mere congeries of possessors and pursuers"? Is our economy accurately described by R. H. Tawney as "that whole system of appetites and values, with its deification of the life of snatching to hoard, and hoarding to snatch, which now, in the hour of its triumph, while the plaudits of the crowd still ring in the ears of the gladiators and the laurels are still unfaded on their brows, seems sometimes to leave a taste as of ashes on the lips of a civilization which has brought to the conquest of the material environment resources unknown in earlier ages, but which has not yet learned to master itself . . ."? (*Op. cit.*, p. 235.) Many economic historians have condemned the " seamy side " of progress, the staggering costs that the industrialization process exacted from society and the vulgar nature of the economic man. Today, for example, we are confronted with the charge that, while having solved the problem of production, we have yet to determine the pur-poses for which this production should be used. Having mastered the difficulty of getting what we want, we have yet to be happy with what we have. It was the phi-losophy that man existed for riches, and not riches for man, that consumption existed

It should be appreciated that Luther was not attempting to sanction commercialism. Strange as it may seem, it was Luther's basic conservatism which led him to condemn the laxity and corruption of the church. Indeed, he had no desire to approve any relaxation of the Christian ethic as the standard around which all commercial activity must be judged, for commercial activity was, to him, a relapse into paganism. The focal point in his attack was Columbus' observation that " Gold constitutes treasure, and he who possesses it has all the needs in this world, as also the means of rescuing souls from Purgatory, and restoring them the enjoyment of Paradise." But when Luther condemned existing authority by suggesting that man was responsible only to God and not to any existing authority, he delivered a crushing blow to religious, economic and political authoritarianism. " It made for the growth of self-respect and self-reliance, gradually transforming a blind or abject faith in God into an active faith in man. Ultimately it made an incalculable contribution to the cause of democracy." [12] And it provided, too, an incalculable impetus to industrial change.

The issue which disturbed the rising industrial class was the biblical assertion that it would be more difficult for a rich man to get into heaven than a camel to pass through the eye of the needle. Was there substance in the clerical view that the wealthy could not take their gold with them, and even if they could, it would melt? It was Calvin who squarely faced this issue when he posed the question: " Whence do the merchant's profits come, except from his own diligence and industry? " Could not the resources of wealthy individuals be utilized through their dedication to the service of God? Whereas the Roman church, Calvin alleged, encouraged luxury and ostentation, the Reform church settled down to the serious business of frugality and productivity. Success in industrial pursuit represented the reward for productivity. But just as wealth might be the measure of God's pleasure with man's efficiency, so might poverty represent punishment for sloth or laziness. Obviously such a doctrine provided ready justification for extending economic activity, for the evil was not economic activity itself, but rather the hazard that material wealth may be used for purposes of self-indulgence. While this doctrine provided comfort for the economically successful, it had dire implications for the unsuccessful. The poor, humble, and meek might not only fail to " inherit the earth," but their poverty and suffering may be viewed as God's displeasure with their inability to meet the challenge of life. It was un-

to maintain production, rather than production to satisfy consumption, that inspired Ruskin's famous outburst: " There is no wealth but life." As one would expect, it was the church which fought a prolonged but vain rear-guard struggle against the new materialism which swept Europe. We should not imply, however, the disappearance of spiritual values within our culture. The struggle between spiritualism and materialism is fiercer than ever.

[12] Muller, *op. cit.,* p. 272.

doubtedly a perversion of religious philosophy which enabled not a few of those enjoying commercial success to endorse the divine right of property as enthusiastically as they condemned the divine right of kings. Was not their material success evidence of God's pleasure with their wisdom, goodness, and efficiency? [13] By such circuitous reasoning, Adam Smith could write, in 1776: "I have never known of much good accomplished by those who profess to work for the public interest. . . ." With Smith's words, the reasoning had traveled the full circle. The economic man could challenge the existence of the spiritual man, feeling all the while that God was on his side. Thus, through Protestantism, society found a moral sanction for self-interest. As Pope's couplet suggested:

> Thus God and Nature formed the general frame,
> And bade self-love and social be the same.[14]

The Economics of Nationalism

The onrushing current of commercial change inundated the status society of the Middle Ages. When the tide subsided, society had not moved directly to free enterprise individualism, but rather to statism. Mercantilism represents the twilight zone between the status economies of the Middle Ages and the individualism of the nineteenth and twentieth centuries. Mercantilists believed that economic forces, if uncontrolled, might corrupt society. For example, the mercantilist Francis Brewster pointed out in 1702 that " Trade indeed will find its own Channels, but it may be to the ruin of the Nation if not Regulated." The mercantilist Mandeville also reasoned that private vices could be transformed into public benefits, but only by the dextrous management of a skillful politician.[15] Only the state, giving generous guidance to commercial classes, could assure the increase of national power.

It is important to remember that in any nationalist state the orientation for determining the value of labor's production is provided by the state itself rather than by the spending pattern of consumers. In a nationalist (or fascist) regime individual interests and energies are directed to advance the national purpose. As Furniss has written: " Public policy supplants private utility as the touchstone of the laborer's activity." Duty to the state supplants individual aspirations as the motive for labor's activity. Or, stated in other terms, political power rather than purchasing power determines the allocation of resources and the distribution of income. Government policy in the mercantile era was, in effect, to expand the industrial base of the nation and through this, the power of the state, rather

[13] For further discussion see Muller's excellent discussion, *op. cit.*, p. 274.
[14] As quoted by Tawney, *op. cit.*, p. 163.
[15] Both references are drawn from E. F. Heckscher, *Mercantilism*, Vol. 1 (London, Allen & Unwin, London, 1931), pp. 318, 293.

than to improve living standards generally. The low level of wages and consumption provided the painful but necessary foundation for industrial expansion.

Significantly, in the mercantile scheme, national wealth was not determined by simply adding up the total of individual wealth. The profit of the individual could not be identified with the wealth of the nation, for the individual's gain might be the nation's loss. And there could be no question that where individual gain and national gain were competitive, the individual interest must be subsumed to the national interest. Mercantilism was built on the premise that the nation might suffer if the mass of its working population was well off. Furniss explains this paradox: " The present-day economist would find it hard to convince himself that the nation could be rich while its people were hungry or in rags, but, holding a different concept of national wealth, the Mercantilists did not perceive that the poverty of the majority was incompatible with the wealth of the whole; quite the contrary, he came to believe that the majority must be kept in poverty that the whole might be rich." [16]

As we noted earlier, the growth of commerce did not provide for labor's economic emancipation. Instead, liberation from bondage frequently meant a leap to pauperism. Labor was not immediately absorbed into manufacturing employment in the villages and towns and thus the growing " freedom " of labor was often associated with growing pauperism, vagrancy, and unemployment. Mercantile writers usually assumed that such " rogues who infested the kingdom " were men who were " running away " from useful employment, and generally agreed that all labor would be idle if given an opportunity to subsist in idleness. Believing that effective government could solve this problem, the state passed a law providing that " vagrants, beggars and staff-strikers shall be imprisoned till they consent to return home to work." And when this failed to eliminate unemployment and pauperism, they resorted to brutality. The idle were sometimes imprisoned, branded, whipped, mutilated, placed in stocks, and even hung for their crime against the nation.[17] Labor faced some enormous problems as it was cast adrift from the moorings of status and security of the feudal manor. Now, the traditional attitude of the English-

[16] Edgar S. Furniss, *The Position of the Laborer in a System of Nationalism* (Boston, Houghton Mifflin Co., 1920), p. 8. For a more detailed review of the mercantile system, see Chapter 20 of this text.

[17] John Wade wrote, in his *History of the Middle and Working Classes* (London, Effingham Wilson, 1833, pp. 43–44.) that in the reign of Edward VI, " laws were enacted providing that if any person refused to labour and live idly 3 days, he shall be branded with a red hot iron on the breast with the letter V, and be adjudged the slave for 2 years of the person who informed against the idler. And the master is directed to feed his slave with bread and water, or small drink, and such refuse meat as he thinks proper; and to cause his slave to work by beating or chaining him. If the slave absconds for 14 days, he is condemned to slavery for life, and if he runs away a second time, he is liable to suffer death as a felon. These enactments were too severe even for the age, and were speedily repealed."

man toward a stranger was: "Heave half a brick at him." The worker could hardly feel needed and wanted in such a setting.

The political and economic consolidation of geographic units during this mercantile period reflected the extended power drives and influence of the new royal dynasties in England and Europe. Economic nationalism accelerated the absorption of pockets of feudal authority, and this, in turn, made possible the expansion of labor and product markets. Kings, with their intoxicating exuberance for power, subsidized explorations of the new world, encouraged the increase of trade, the development of transportation, and communication. Unification, protectionism, bullionism, and colonialism became the order of the day.

The alliance of the rising merchant class and royalty was an uneasy one, for ultimately the entrepreneurs resented the crown's heavy taxes, autocratic authority, and court extravagances. "By the seventeenth century in England and by the eighteenth century in France, the middle class began to sense that the individual enterpriser's chances for growth would forever remain stunted unless the areas of monarchical privilege were cut down." [18] Political revolutions (including the Puritan and French uprisings) were aimed at providing political institutions conducive and sympathetic to freer economic enterprise.

The attitudes of the government toward the work force reveals an interesting inconsistency, for many laws were both repressive and yet protectionist. The destruction by disease of one half of the working population by the black death in 1348 prompted the government to establish wage ceilings. Later labor statutes carefully defined the wages labor should receive, the hours to be worked, the food labor should eat, and even the clothing it might wear. These statutes provided that wage standards be established by local public officials and that wages reflect local and current living costs. The Poor Laws, first developed from 1536 to 1601, and carried on with varying effectiveness until 1834, required that local parish ministers "urge, exhort, move, stir, and provoke" people to be liberal in contributions toward the comfort and relief of the "poor, impotent, decrepit, indigent and needy people." Regular assessments were made on the community for the support of the growing number of unemployed citizens. When these measures failed, predominantly because of the pervasiveness of competitive pressure, the labor market gradually became an acknowledged reality.

The Growth of the Labor Market

The year 1800 represents a watershed in the development of capitalism, for in the nineteenth century capitalism and the labor market came into

[18] Louis M. Hacker, *The Triumph of American Capitalism* (New York, Columbia University Press, 1947), p. 43.

full bloom. The terms and conditions of employment for labor were, for the most part, to be determined by the haggling process in the labor market, with the outcome depending on the twin forces of supply and demand. Ironically, society became infused with the spirit of free enterprise at that very moment in history when Europe faced a population explosion. Swarms of workers inundated the growing villages and towns. Ortega Y Gasset points to this "gigantic mass," this "torrent," this "heap after heap of human beings dumped on the historic scene" as one of the most significant, yet little appreciated fact in our economic history.[19] For the twelve centuries preceeding 1800 the population of Europe had never exceeded 180 million, but in the next century it had more than doubled. The Hammonds, in their economic history of Britain, concluded: "It looks as if the Peels and the Arkwrights had only to stamp on the ground to turn empty valleys into swarming hives of workpeople." [20]

City population increased for three reasons: Birth rates were increasing, death rates were decreasing, and the enclosure movement was forcing people from the land. Of course, such labor abundance did much to reduce labor's bargaining power. The exhilarating slogan of the new era "liberty, equality, and fraternity" seemed strangely out of tune with the realities of the time. Competitive pressures in the face of excess labor supply caused hungry men to suspect the principles of equality and fraternity and to wonder when, if ever, they would enjoy freedom. It was true that labor had the freedom to charge whatever the labor market would bear, but labor seemed more apprehensive about the employer's freedom to pay as little as the market would bear — or not even hire workers at all.

One of the most imaginative efforts to protect labor's living standard was conceived in 1795 by a group of magistrates in Speenhamland, England. It was decided that every family should receive a "living" wage and that assessments should be made in each community to subsidize all workers unemployed as well as those working but receiving inadequate wages. The plan was widely adopted, but, as one might suspect, faced immediate difficulties. Employers were encouraged to reduce wages, knowing that their work force could secure a subsidy by an amount necessary to provide them with subsistence. And employees were often unwilling to work, preferring subsidized idleness to subsidized employment. A government commission investigated the inadequacies of the Speenhamland system in 1824 and concluded that it was unworkable and tended to corrupt even the most able-bodied workmen. To Karl Polanyi, the

[19] For his analysis of the effect of population growth, combined with new technology and the democratic sentiment, see his study, *The Revolt of the Masses* (New York, W. W. Norton & Co., 1932).

[20] J. L. and B. Hammond, *The Town Labourer* (London, Longmans, Green and Co., 1920), p. 11.

abandonment of this experiment in social welfare spelled the end for any alternative to the free labor market. The great transformation from a status to a market economy was achieved.[21]

The enclosure movement was also accelerated at the turn of the century. Larger farming units were necessary for several reasons: The expanding wool market encouraged the use of land for sheep pastures; British imports of wheat from foreign countries were considered dangerous to England's self-sufficiency, and larger farming units could produce domestic wheat more efficiently than the small units. And land that was enclosed had a market value worth double and triple that of the unenclosed land. The ejected cottars, as noted above, added to the swarms of people searching for employment in the cities.[22] In 1760 about 42 percent of the British population was engaged in farming, and by 1831 this figure was reduced to 28 percent.

There is no lack of evidence of the problems facing labor in the industrial community. Royal Commissions denounced the horrors of child labor, long hours, absence of safety provisions, and the corroding impact of slum life. Poets and writers joined in their condemnation of the new economic philosophy which in theory promised to emancipate all from poverty, but which, in reality, seemed only to hasten the degradation of labor. Robert Dale Owen records his observations in his journey through England in 1815:

> The facts we collected seemed to me terrible almost beyond belief. Not in exceptional cases, but as a rule, we found children of ten years old worked regularly fourteen hours a day, with but half an hour's interval for the mid day meal. . . . In some cases we found the greed of gain had impelled the mill-owners to still greater extremes of inhumanity utterly disgraceful, indeed, to a civilized nation. Their mills were run fifteen, and, in exceptional cases, sixteen hours a day, with a single set of hands; and they did not scruple to employ children of both sexes from the age of eight. We actually found a considerable number under that age.

[21] Karl Polanyi, *The Great Transformation* (New York, Farrar and Rinehart, 1944), particularly Chapter 7.

[22] Arthur Young, a contemporary of the time, was one who denounced the hardships resulting from the enclosure movement. "Go to an alehouse kitchen of an old enclosed country and there you will see the origin of poverty and poor rates. For whom are they to be sober? For whom are they to save? . . . You offer no motives; you have nothing but a parish officer and a workhouse! . . ." From his, *An Inquiry into the Propriety of Applying Wastes*, etc. (London, 1801), p. 13. Karl Polanyi is even more outspoken about this event in history: "Enclosures have appropriately been called a revolution of the rich against the poor. The lords and nobles were upsetting the social order, breaking down ancient law and custom. . . . They were literally robbing the poor of their share in the common, tearing down the houses which by the hitherto unbreakable force of custom, the poor had long regarded as their. . . . The fabric of society was being disrupted; desolate villages and the ruins of human dwellings testified to the fierceness with which the revolution raged." *Op. cit.*, p. 35.

When the arch-conservative of classical economists, J. R. McCulloch, learned of the extent of child labor, he wrote to Lord Ashley in 1833 who was at that time marshaling forces for a campaign to push a ten-hour bill through the British House of Parliament: " I look upon the facts disclosed in the late Report as most disgraceful to the nation; and I confess that, until I read it, I could not have conceived it possible that such enormities were committed . . ." [23] Karl Marx spent much of his time pondering such studies in the London museum, and they undoubtedly confirmed his conviction that capitalism must go.[24]

Most economic historians, regardless of political or economic faith, have been appalled by the hardships confronting labor during the early stages of industrial change. The following summary of the British industrial community by J. L. and Barbara Hammond offers us a brief glimpse of the industrial atmosphere:

> The old English towns were often overcrowded, insanitary, honeycombed with alleys and courts that never saw the sun or breathed the air. . . . they symbolised the absolute dependence and helplessness of the mass of the people living in them. They were not so much towns as barracks: not the refuge of a civilization but the barracks of an industry. . . . these towns reflected the violent enterprise of an hour, the single passion that had thrown street on street in a frantic monotony of disorder. . . . they represented nothing but the avarice of the jerry-builder catering for the avarice of the capitalist. . . . Their towns were as ugly as their industries, with an ugliness in both cases that was a symptom of work and life in which men and women could find no happiness or self-expression.[25]

[23] As quoted by Lloyd R. Sorenson, " Laissez Faire and the Factory Acts," *The Journal of Economic History*, Vol. XII, No. 3 (Summer, 1952), p. 255.

[24] More recently it has been suggested that the usual descriptions of hardship during the industrial revolution reflect an " anti-capitalist" bias and are not substantiated by the facts of industrial history. The thesis is developed in *Capitalism and the Historians* (edited by F. A. Hayek), and a group of essays by T. S. Ashton, L. M. Hacker, W. H. Hutt, and B. De Jouvenal (Chicago, University of Chicago Press, 1954). Hayek writes: "Economic suffering both became more conspicuous and seemed less justified, because general wealth was increasing faster than ever before. But this, of course, does not prove that the people whose fate was beginning to cause indignation and alarm were worse off than their parents or grandparents had been. While there is every evidence that great misery existed, there is none that it was greater or even as great as it had been before." (P. 18.) "There is every reason to remember how miserable the majority of the people still were as recently as a hundred and fifty years ago. But we must not, long after the event, allow a distortion of the facts, even if committed out of humanitarian zeal, to affect our view of what we owe to a system for which for the first time in history made people feel that this misery might be avoidable." (P. 25.) The data on both money and real wage rates show an upward trend during the nineteenth century, with this trend accentuated toward the end of that period. But unfortunately, an improvement in material status after the fact does not reflect the degree of insecurity labor might sense before the fact. The Hayek viewpoint does contain, however, an important element of truth that should be remembered in appraising the discussion of this chapter.

[25] *Op. cit.*, pp. 38–41.

The attempt to measure the effect that industrial change might have had on the happiness of a population is difficult, if not impossible, but Bertrand Russell is one who senses — more by intuition than anything else — that more misery than cheer was created by this industrialization process:

> The industrial revolution caused unspeakable misery both in England and in America. I do not think any student of economic history can doubt that the average happiness in England in the early nineteenth century was lower than it had been a hundred years earlier and this was almost entirely due to scientific technique.[26]

Thus far, we have witnessed how economic change represented a cumulative, spiraling process. Helpless individuals were sucked into the swirling vortex of impersonal market forces:

> Never was a revolution less well understood, less welcomed, less planned. But the great market-making forces would not be denied. Insidiously they ripped apart the mold of custom, insolently they tore away the usages of tradition. . . . The great chariot of society, which for so long had run by gravity down the gentle slope of tradition, now found itself powered by an internal combustion machine. Transactions, transactions, transactions and gain, gain, gain provided a new and startlingly powerful motive force.[27]

In summary, when man became interested in the " right within him," the challenge to the old order became reality. Society shifted from the " Age of Faith " to the " Age of Reason," and having abandoned its subservience to princes and God, searched for new philosophical moorings. Society found them in the presumed wisdom, rationality — and acquisitiveness — of man. But the economic changes continued at a bewildering pace. Intellectual curiosity led to mechanical innovations which increased the welter of machine-produced goods. The changing scene clearly required a new philosophy, or if you like, a new explanation as to what it was all about. If we want to be charitable, we can say that classical economists rose to the challenge and through their analysis " enabled men to perceive beneath the chaos and bewildering complexities of real life that man, after all, may be able to satisfy his own particular needs. . . . Orderliness was generated through the nicely adjusted mechanism of nature without design or conscious control. . . ." [28] But perhaps, if we are to be more candid, the new classical doctrines gave the government a plausible excuse for doing nothing, when it did not know quite what to do.

[26] *The Impact of Science on Society* (New York, Columbia University Press, 1951), p. 22.
[27] As described by Robert L. Heilbroner, *The Worldly Philosophers* (New York, Simon and Schuster, 1953), pp. 24, 25.
[28] F. C. Mills, " Economics in a Time of Change " *American Economic Review*, Vol. 31, No. 1 (March, 1941), pp. 4, 5.

The Growth of Economic Liberalism

In 1776 Adam Smith not only provided the frame, but largely painted the picture for the new economic orthodoxy. While the body of classical economic thought represents a separate study, we may briefly recapitulate a few of its principles which are relevant to the labor market.

The Economic Man and the Invisible Hand. Adam Smith pointed out that the specialization of labor would increase labor productivity, but such specialization was limited by the size of markets. Widening markets would make possible increased production because they permitted, in turn, increased opportunities for labor specialization. But each individual in this process could act in his own self-interest. He need not consciously dedicate his life to working for others, for his own selfish interests would automatically provide for the advancement of society. As he explained, the man who follows his interests " is in this, as in many other cases, led by an invisible hand to promote an end which was no part of his intention. . . . By pursuing his own interests he frequently promotes that of the society more effectually than when he really intends to promote it." [29] Expressed more directly, today we paraphrase Smith by saying simply: " What is good for me is good for you." By Smith's analysis, man need not apologize for his selfish proclivities, for this was the internal combustion machine driving society to material progress.

Individualism and Utilitarianism. The mercantilists believed that poverty represented the best inducement to labor. The classical economists believed that personal prosperity was a more effective inducement to enterprise. Furthermore, individuals should be free to maximize pleasures and minimize pains as best they could. No authority could define the substance of such pleasure, for this was the total of individual utilities. As the utilitarian, Bentham, explained, the community is in effect but a fictitious body composed of individuals. " It is vain to talk of the interests of the community, without understanding what is the interest of the individual. A thing is said to promote the interest, or to be *for* the interest, of an individual, when it tends to add to the sum total of his pleasures: or, what comes to the same thing, to diminish the sum total of his pains." [30] The humanism of this new economic viewpoint was, as we have seen above, in sharp contrast to the mercantile view. Classical writers firmly believed that " What improves the circumstances of the greater part can never be regarded as an inconvenience to the whole. No society can be flourishing and happy of which the far greater part of the members are

[29] *Wealth of Nations* (London, Methuen and Co., 1922 edition), Vol. I, p. 421.

[30] Jeremy Bentham, *Principles of Morals and Legislation* Oxford, Clarendon Press, 1823), p. 3. For a modifying comment on what Bentham actually meant, as contrasted to what other economists have taken him to have meant, see J. Bartlet Brebner, "Laissez Faire and State Intervention in Nineteenth Century Britain," *Journal of Economic History*, Supplement VIII (1948), pp. 59–70.

poor and miserable." Dealing with the mercantile notion that a country can grow rich through low wages, the classical writers reacted: " Perish such riches! " David Ricardo observed that " The friends of humanity cannot but wish that in all countries the labouring classes should have a taste for comforts and enjoyments, and they should be stimulated by all means legal in the exertions to procure them. . . ." [31]

Say's Law of Markets and the Trend Toward Full Employment. Undoubtedly one of the most perplexing problems confronting the un- tutored person viewing the market mechanism was the possibility that the millions of separate decisions might never be sufficiently coordinated to provide for adequate employment, for the production of wanted goods, or for the payment of incomes adequate for subsistence. But producers, to the classical economists, would always take their cue from the way in which individuals spent their money. Therefore the economy would not be exposed to serious overproduction if consumers should suddenly change the *direction* of their spending. Producers and the cooperating factors of production would quickly adjust to the new sources of revenue, adapting production and employment to the change in demand. But what if consumers should decide to cut down their *volume* of total spending? Could not then markets develop unsold inventories and labor become un- employed? Again, the answer was " No." Here the classical economists turned to J. B. Say's Laws of Markets. Supply is demand. Taking first a barter economy, the logic behind this principle was that the buying power of any individual to secure goods produced by someone else was determined by the amount of goods that he himself had to offer in ex- change. Does not then the supply of his goods limit the demand for other goods? Therefore, the greater the volume of production, the greater must be the ability of persons to buy each other's goods. Hence, supply is demand. In a money economy the situation is slightly more complex because goods are exchanged first for money, and then money is ex- changed for goods. Let us assume that the volume of spending is cut in half. If prices and costs are adjusted downward, the smaller amount of money in circulation would do the work of the larger amount. All goods and services could be sold as before. Money in circulation would, in ef- fect, be neutral or would have no effect on the volume of production and employment. If all prices were reduced because of a sudden decline in spending, purchasing power would be redistributed but not destroyed. By such reasoning, classical economists were confident that changes in the amount of spending need not cause unemployment. To recapitulate, the cure for overproduction was actually overproduction itself. If labor, for example, could not sell its services, the solution to unemployment was appropriate wage reductions. By being unemployed, labor then would know that it had priced its services out of the market and the appropriate

[31] As quoted in Heckscher, *op. cit.*, p. 329.

wage flexibility so necessary to maintain full employment could then appear. The equilibrating mechanism bringing wages into line was the experience and privation that arises from unemployment. To try to obscure such simple economic facts from the labor force (by, say, subsidizing workers in their state of idleness) would be no more helpful than throwing a sheet over an infected patient in the belief that if we obscure the abscess from view, he would somehow be cured.

Income Inequality and Industrial Progress. The golden age of classical economic theory is gone, but the ideas and principles of classical theory, while not always in vogue today, are far from dusty museum pieces. Much of classical theory appears anti-labor in tone, but this is undoubtedly an unfair indictment of what was, in a mercantile context, a radically humanitarian philosophy. Conditions in the eighteenth and nineteenth centuries made it self-evident that material welfare could only be enjoyed with the expansion of output, and this in turn required an appropriate combination of the factors of production. Unhappily, labor was in excess supply, and capital represented the bottleneck to the production process. Thus economists, in their obsession to expand production and provide higher living standards for all, stressed capital expansion rather than labor consumption. Parsimony or nonconsumption was a virtue, for only by abstinence could a sufficient portion of income be diverted for vital capital expansion. The unequal distribution of income did not jeopardize this process but rather made it possible. Were not the wealthy those who were able to provide the savings so necessary for investment expansion? In effect, the appearance of indifference to the immediate hardships of low consumption arose simply because of the intensity of their desire to solve the problem. Keynes has offered a succinct statement on this phase of classical thinking:

> . . . Society was so framed as to throw a great part of the increased income into the control of the class least likely to consume it. The new rich of the nineteenth century were not brought up to large expenditures, and preferred the power which investment gave them to the pleasures of immediate consumption. . . . The immense accumulations of fixed capital which, to the great benefit of mankind, were built up during the half century before the war, could never have come about in a Society where wealth was divided equitably. . . . this remarkable system depended for its growth on a double bluff or deception. On the one hand the laboring classes accepted from ignorance or powerlessness, or were compelled, persuaded, or cajoled by custom, convention, authority, and the well-established order of Society into accepting a situation in which they could call their own very little of the cake that they and nature and the capitalists were cooperating to produce. And on the other hand the capitalists were allowed to call the best part of the cake theirs and were theoretically free to consume it, on the tacit underlying condition that they con-

sumed very little of it in practice. The duty of "savings" became nine tenths of virtue and the growth of the cake the object of true religion. . . . And so the cake increased; but to what end was not clearly contemplated. Individuals would be exhorted not so much to abstain as to defer, and to cultivate the pleasure of security and antic-ipation. Saving was for old age or for your children; but this was only in theory — the virtue of the cake was that it was never to be consumed, neither by you nor by your children after you.[32]

Of course today, labor is skeptical that low consumption will, in fact, stimulate high investment. And even if it did, why should labor do any-thing for posterity when posterity has done nothing for it?

Summary and Conclusions

In this chapter, we have briefly surveyed the antecedents to the labor market in order to understand the origin of contemporary labor prob-lems as well as the origin of unionism. As we have noted, classical econo-mists were enthusiastic about the freedom and wealth that could be real-ized by the competitive and individualistic arrangement for marketing the labor service. But others pointed to the disorderly scramble of labor for limited job opportunities and concluded that the application of social Darwinism to economic life was a tragedy of major proportions. Nor did the individual worker like to consider himself isolated, independent, a particle of dust without significance. While the labor market gave man the opportunity to "live dangerously" at the beginning of the nineteenth century, this challenge seemed much like the offer to play a game of Rus-sian roulette. The consequences of failure were frightening and the op-portunities for success, limited. In other words, labor did not readily sub-scribe to the principle "survival of the fittest" for the simple fear that it may not have been among the fittest. From a psychological viewpoint, such fear of failure can create tremendous anxieties, hostilities, and even paralyze one's ability to work effectively. The very pervasiveness of the labor market organization after 1800 created, then, its own reaction. As T. H. Huxley catalogued the shortcomings of such market organization:

> In place of ruthless self assertion, it [society] demands self-restraint; in place of thrusting aside or treading down all competitors, it re-quires that the individual shall not merely respect, but shall help his fellows; its influence is directed, not so much to the survival of the fittest, as to the fitting of as many as possible to survive. It repudiates the gladiatorial theory of existence. It is from the neglect of these plain considerations that the fanatical individualism of our times at-tempts to apply the analogy of cosmic nature to society.[33]

[32] John M. Keynes, *The Economic Consequences of the Peace* (New York, Har-court, Brace & Co., 1920), pp. 19, 20.

[33] From his *Evolution and Ethics*, and quoted by Ashley Montagu, *On Being Human* (New York, Henry Schuman, 1950), p. 22.

While our analysis has stressed the difficulties confronting labor in the process of shifting from one form of economic organization to another, as well as the difficulties confronting labor in the market, it should not be inferred that this market has remained unchanged in the last 150 years, or that labor today enters the market timid and fearful or even as an individual. Indeed, during the golden age of individualism of the nineteenth century, the government was busily violating the basic tenets of classical economic theory by regulating the hours of work, restricting the employment of women and children, prescribing minimum safety standards for industry, imposing minimum wage levels, providing public relief, and so on. The prevailing moving force of the nineteenth century was neither individualism nor collectivism, but the steamrolling effect of industrialism. Society responded quickly by absorbing the advantages of this new industrial mechanism, but it demanded simultaneously that the government take measures to minimize its poisonous by-products. This same pattern was repeated in America. Society paid lip service to individualism while drifting consciously and willingly toward economic and social collectivism. And as we shall see later, out of this welter of change, the organization of the labor movement evolved. Unionism reflected labor's attempts to solve its own problems through its own instrumentality, without violating the tenets of economic orthodoxy.

Because we have paid homage to classical economic philosophy while at the same time cementing our group organizations (to give more effect to our economic goals), we find that a large portion of economic orthodoxy does not square with the economy " as it is." Academicians themselves are split into two camps with one urging that institutions be made to conform to the theories and assumptions of orthodox analysis and the other suggesting that economic analysis describe what " is " rather than what " should be " or " has been." Why have we been so willing to surrender to group organization when this violates the tenets of free enterprise capitalism? A partial explanation is offered by Frank Knight: " The fatal defect of the utilitarian doctrine of maximum freedom as a goal of social policy is its confusion of freedom and power. Its advocates overlook the fact that freedom to perform an act is meaningless unless the subject is in possession of the requisite means of action, and that the practical question is one of power rather than that of formal freedom." [34] Knight is, of course, expressing a sentiment which the untutored mind of the working man had already known to be true. In the market economy it seemed that might made right more often than right made might. It is not surprising therefore that labor should grow interested in constructing its own power instrument as a device for gaining its promised freedom.

Without question the center of gravity of power within society has, in

[34] From his *Freedom and Reform: Essays in Economics and Social Philosophy* (New York, Harper & Bros., 1947), p. 4.

recent times, shifted sharply in labor's direction, a shift sometimes described as from capitalism to laborism. Labor's newly acquired power, while solving some old problems, has created new ones. As we noted above, some look to a solution for current difficulties in a return to the "good old days." Others recognize the impossibility of turning back the clock or altering economic institutions and attempt to find new values, new attitudes, and new behavior patterns as the basis for maintaining industrial peace. Certainly these new times and new institutions require a fresh approach to the labor problem, but we should not neglect the wisdom of the past in attempting to frame wise policies today. Furthermore, much of labor's attitude today is conditioned by labor's experience in the past. We have observed that the broad base for our industrial economy was achieved by breaking some eggs. We cannot now unscramble the omelette. The challenge confronting society is one of adjusting both attitudes and theories to the ever-increasing tempo of change and to control wisely the ever-increasing economic power possessed by pressure groups within our society, not the least being that of the unions.

2

Sources and Size
of the Labor Force

"Labor is not a commodity or article of commerce." This statement embodied in our labor legislation reflects the noble ideal that labor cannot be treated analogously to land, capital, or the many impersonal products of industry. Marketing labor, therefore, must be very different than marketing false teeth, saddle soap or pickles. Yet in the labor market, as in other markets, the forces of supply and demand reveal their pervasive influence. While we can all agree that labor is not an *impersonal* commodity, labor's employment, income, and wage level in the final analysis largely depend on the forces of supply and demand. Put in another way, within very broad limits the bargaining process between workers and employers determines labor's material status and welfare. Platitudes notwithstanding, labor cannot escape the influence of these market forces.[1]

In our previous chapter we discussed the evolution of the labor market. Our plan now is to move the locus of discussion from Europe to America and recount briefly the growth of both the labor market and the labor force in this country. We shall glance briefly at the major sources of labor supply and those factors which contributed to the expansion of the free labor market. We shall find, in effect, that the waves of immigrant labor sweeping into America during the nineteenth century in search of those economic opportunities and political freedoms never enjoyed in Europe played a dominant role in the development of the labor force and the labor market. We shall then turn to the wider problem of population growth and review the cycles and trends of that population participating in the work force. Following this, we shall consider labor's geographic

[1] Today, it is fashionable for the labor economist to conclude that union policy rather than supply and demand determines wage rates. This may in a sense be true, but the establishment of noncompetitive rates has repercussions on both the quantity of labor demanded and the quantity supplied. Thus union wage policy does not "disprove" the existence of such forces or suggest their irrelevance any more than flying an airplane disproves the existence of gravity. And it would be an unwise aeronautical engineer (union) who designs his aircraft (wage policy) on the assumption that gravity (market forces) no longer exists, or can be safely ignored.

mobility and the occupational and industrial allocation of the all-important resource labor. Finally, we shall note the growth of world population and the effect of this growth on world living standards.

The Uneven Supply of Resources: Some Implications

One might be led to believe, on first glance, that the expansion of population need not create serious problems for society, for each person has hands as well as a mouth. Is there not then a " natural " equilibrium between the needs of the mouth and the work of the hands, or between consumption and production? Unfortunately, production is not automatically forthcoming simply because the mouth must be fed, even though the hands are willing to produce: The productivity of the hands depends on the resources and materials made available to them. For example, let us assume that capital is in limited supply or is the " bottleneck " to production, while labor is abundant. The application of additional hands to this fixed supply of capital does not promise a substantial increase in total production. In such a situation the pressure for employment of an ever-larger labor supply crashes into the declining ceiling of diminishing productivity. Stated in another way, if labor cannot work with adequate supplies of the necessary cooperating factors of production, the mere existence of these additional hands willing and able to be productive does not assure that they *can* be productive. While this may seem like an irrelevant construction in terms of the American labor market today, it is far from hypothetical in Asiatic countries now facing excess labor, inadequate capital, and mass starvation.

In summary, the impact of a larger population and a larger labor force cannot be evaluated in a vacuum. We often find that the *relative* growth of capital and labor determines the per capita income of labor. This race between the growth of capital and the growth of the labor force represents one of the most significant contests in any nation's economic development. If capital should expand more rapidly than the labor force, per capita real wages will usually rise. If the labor force should expand more rapidly than the capital to support it, per capita income is likely to decline.[2] In the subsequent chapter our analysis of labor's income will ex-

[2] In this example we have neglected the availability of resources other than capital. Of course, the greater the variety of other resources to support the increase of the size of the work force, the greater the likelihood that labor's productivity (and hence real income) can increase. The growth of the labor force in a labor-scarce economy is likely to result in higher per capita wages for labor. As one student explains, " Where resources are adequate production may increase more rapidly than population . . . the solution to the problem [of world population growth] . . . is clearly through increased production as a direct result of industrialization." He suggests that " a capital investment of 4 per cent of national product would be required to cover a 1 per cent increase in population " if labor standards in underdeveloped areas are not to deteriorate. See Reuben E. Slesinger, " Some Comments on Nonagricultural

plore whether labor has improved its living standard by losing this race with capital expansion.

Mercantilism in America

Bagehot has said "Money will not manage itself." The mercantilists were much more pessimistic in explaining "The economy will not manage itself." As a case in point, the mercantilists said that government must encourage population growth. The expansion of national power could only be effected if the mass of the laboring poor were motivated, under pressure of starvation, to work hard. But such poverty could be achieved only by labor abundance, not by labor scarcity. Colonial America was launched on the rising tide of popularity of such mercantile notions as these. But the colonies were on the "receiving end" of such doctrines. It seldom occurred to England, for example, that the policy of economic nationalism should be exported to the colonies along with its convicts, orphans, kidnaped and indentured servants. In 1772 General Thomas Gage expressed typical British sentiment when he wrote to England: "I [think it would] be for our interest to Keep the Settlers within reach of the Sea-coast as we can; and to cramp their Trade as far as it can be done prudentially. . . ." Colonization was an investment that could only pay off by the growing stream of raw materials shipped to England and the consumption by the colonists of the British manufactured product. In 1774 another Englishman, aghast at the rioting in America on the eve of the Revolution, put the point even more bluntly: "For what purpose were they suffered to go to that country, unless the profit of their labour should return to their masters here?" [3]

Many of the early colonies were actually founded by settlement companies which made generous promises to share profits (as well as to provide housing, vegetable gardens, clothing, and so on) for Europeans willing to pioneer in the development of their chartered lands. Explorations, discovery, and settlement did not, then, reflect so much the unbounding enthusiasm of Europeans for adventure as the cold calculation of royal dynasties that colonies could augment their riches and power.

In modern parlance, the early colonies were "backward" areas, lacking an adequate labor force to promote rapid development. This scarcity of manpower arose in part from British restrictions on the migration of skilled labor to the colonies, restrictions which even extended to the export of textile machinery and blueprints for machinery manufacture. This labor scarcity had the effect of increasing the moral sanctions

Possibilities for Raising the Levels of Living of Underdeveloped Nations," *American Economic Review*, Vol. XLVI, No. 2 (May, 1956), Papers and Proceedings, pp. 329, 331.

[3] Both quotations are drawn from Richard B. Morris' careful study, *Government and Labor in Early America* (New York, Columbia University Press, 1946), p. 2.

against idleness in the New World and encouraging the training of unskilled workers — even slaves — for the craft skills desperately required.
It had the effect, too, of providing for premium pay for those skilled
craftsmen attracted to frontier settlements.

Much of the economic morality current in England was transplanted
to the colonies: As in the old country, idleness was here regarded as the
" parent of all Vices," and plans were established to provide for workhouses so that children might better learn the habits of industry. Colonial
youngsters were taught and believed the aphorisms: " Leisure is the Time
for doing something Useful," and " By the sweat of thy brow thou shalt
eat thy bread." The Puritan morality condemned idleness with almost the
same severity as the Tudor statutes. The idle were punished by whipping
and by fines.[4] Persons unwilling or unable to provide for their own sustenance were regarded with suspicion and hostility. Poor relief was given
reluctantly. In New Jersey the pauper had to wear on the shoulder of his
right sleeve a large blue or red " P " together with the first letter of the
name of the city or county in which he resided.[5]

Sources of Labor Supply in the Colonies

The labor force in colonial America was in large part unskilled and
semiskilled, with close to half having a slave or semislave status. Indentured servants were those who, in exchange for passage to America,
would commit their labor services without wages to an American employer for anywhere from three to seven years. Shipping companies
found importing the labor commodity a profitable venture. On arriving
in America, the labor cargo was usually auctioned off to the highest
bidder. While such indentured servants were not paid wages, their " owners " were required to provide them with food, shelter, and subsistence
during their tenure. A second group, made up of involuntary indentured
servants (most of whom were paupers, convicts, and those kidnaped in
Europe) were also sold for what they could command on the colonial
market.[6] Those not disposed of in this manner were usually purchased by

[4] As early as 1633 an act in Massachusetts fixed the wages for artisans and also ordered
that " noe pson, howse houlder or othr, shall spend his time idley or unpffitably, under
paine of such punishment as the Court shall thinke meete to inflict. . . . the constable
of evy place shall use spetiall care and deligence to take knowledge of offenders in
this kinde, espetially of common coaster, unpffitable fowlers and Tobacco takers. . . ."
[5] See Morris, *op. cit.*, p. 16.
[6] The hardships facing immigrant workers in ship travel to America can be seen
in the accounts of such trips. " One ship sailing in 1730 with 150 emigrants had only
13 survivors. Another sailed in 1745 with 400 Germans, of whom only 50 lived to see
America." (*See* James Oneal, *The Workers in American History*, New York, Rand
School of Social Science, 1921, pp. 34–35.) A London Company received an acknowl-
edgment from Virginia in 1619 that its export arrived: " 100 were children, save such
as dyed on the waie," and included a request for another 100, 12 years of age and
older. In 1627 many ships arrived bringing 1,400 and 1,500 children kidnaped by
'spirits' in European ports. . . ." (*Ibid.*, pp. 59, 60.)

a " soul driver " in a package deal. He would travel through the country with his inventory to market it as best he could. A third group consisted of Negro slaves. The first Negro slaves were brought to Virginia by the Dutch in 1619, but slavery did not spread rapidly in America until around 1650. By 1860 it was estimated that there were 4,442,000 Negro slaves in this country. By 1770 at least one half of the original immigrants were " unfree," indentured, or actually slaves. Many had been victims of kidnapers; others were banished from Europe because of their crimes of vagrancy or petty thievery; still others were deported because of their burden to orphanages and workhouses. Kidnapers, contractors, and slave traders combined to capitalize on the scarcity of labor in the colonies. It is a tribute to these uprooted, dispossessed, and underprivileged people that they proved adequate to the rather grim challenge of the New World by overcoming the obstacles imposed by nature against economic development.

America was soon to burst out of the confines of British mercantilism and assume her own independent status. When Lord Sheffield was explaining that " The only use and advantage of American colonies . . . is the monopoly of their consumption and the carriage of their produce," the colonists were wondering about the uneven reciprocity of such an arrangement. The emergence of commercialism in America led not only to the development of a labor market, but to demands that America be permitted to nourish its own manufacturing process. The colonists were no longer content to be the back yard for British capitalism, nor were they content to confine their commercial enterprise to land speculation and fur trading.

In the early stages of colonial development the opportunities for the division of labor and exchange were very restricted, but the colonists demonstrated amazing ingenuity in providing for their own self-sufficiency. The first inroads of commerce took the form of the " putting out " system, through which an entrepreneur would supply raw materials to various families to be processed in their homes. The merchant-manufacturer was essentially interested in the marketing of these items for profit apart from owning his own capital. The growth of the labor market as we think of it today developed when the middleman provided both the capital and the working plant. The workers were then asked to provide only their labor service.

The Machine Age Develops: Uses of Women and Child Labor

The morality of the colonies did not prohibit but rather encouraged the employment of women and children. Indeed, in 1654, when the burgomaster of Amsterdam had shipped 28 boys and girls (who were living in almshouses) to New Netherland, the vice-director asked that more be sent, "preferably those not under 15 years of age, but those somewhat strong, as little profit is to be expected here without labor." It was reasoned that children were simply "small adults," and could be trained at a tender age to the habits of industry. The *Boston Gazette* of August 14, 1753, described the handsome appearance of "300 spinners, some of them children of 7 or 8 years old and several of them Daughters of the best families among us, with their Wheels at work sitting orderly in three rows . . . on the Common." [7] The child from 8 to 14, if put to useful employment, was considered to be one of the greatest total saving of labor in the country.

In January, 1791, one Samuel Slater opened his factory, employing 7 boys and 2 girls, all between 7 and 12 years of age. This provided a model for other employers. Of the 8,500 persons employed in the cotton mills in Rhode Island in 1831, 3,472 were children under 12 years of age. So productive was child labor that employers sometimes advertised not for men, but for families. The Providence newspaper, *Manufacturers' and Farmers' Journal*, contained a typical advertisement in January 14, 1828: "Families Wanted: Ten or Twelve good respectable families consisting of four or five children each, from nine to sixteen years of age, are wanted to work in a cotton mill, in the vicinity of Providence." Women were also extensively employed in manufacturing, and as competition increased, they suffered abuse and exploitation. It has been estimated that in 1837 there were over 100 occupations in which women were employed with more than 15,000 in the shoe industry of Massachusetts alone. [8] *The Public Charities of Philadelphia* (1829) indicated that women without children in New England employed in the needle trades could earn no more than $58.50 a year and women with children no more than $36.40 a year.

One of the most interesting experiments in the employment of women was seen in the experiments made by the Lowell Manufacturing Company. This "Lowell" system was designed to reduce the stigma of factory employment by introducing an uplift and intellectual climate for its "operatives." In 1836 the Lowell Company stated that it would not "continue to employ any person who shall be wanting in proper respect to

[7] As quoted by Morris, *op. cit.*, p. 517.

[8] E. C. Kirkland, *A History of American Economic Life* (New York, F. S. Crofts, 1936), p. 343. Children were required to work up to 14 hours a day, an abuse that moved Kirkland to observe that "it is not surprising that children had to be struck with water in order to keep them awake. . . ." John R. Commons notes that, "In 1831 in the six New England states and in New York, New Jersey, Pennsylvania, Delaware, Maryland and Virginia, 58.1 percent of all the employees, including hand weavers, in cotton mills, were women and 7 percent were children under twelve years of age. . . . Even in New England in 1832, a committee of the New England Association of Farmers, Mechanics and other Working Men estimated that two fifths of the whole number of persons employed in all the factories were children under 16 years of age . . ." Commons and Associates, *History of Labor in the United States* (New York, The Macmillan Co., 1926), Vol. I, pp. 173–174.

the females employed by the company, or who shall smoke within the company's premises, or be guilty of inebriety or other improper conduct." Girls were to be carefully supervised by " moral " police. Church attendance was compulsory. Foremen in plants were to be married men, preferably Sunday school teachers or men with strong religious conviction. In effect the impression was given that for a young girl to work in the Lowell plant was almost equivalent (from a moral viewpoint at least) to joining a nunnery.[9] Undoubtedly the plant owners reasoned that if high morality represented the cost of securing a cheap labor supply, high morality would be provided. With the intensification of competition, these exalted moral and economic standards (as well as those of economic subsistence) deteriorated. The increased competition of foreign women added to the pressure for low wages and long hours. The *Boston Daily Times* opened an editorial attack on the Lowell system on July 13, 1839, charging that " young girls are compelled to work in unhealthy confinement for too many hours every day; that their food is both unhealthy and scanty; that they are not allowed sufficient time to eat . . . that in consequence they become pale, feeble and finally broken in constitution." The *Times* followed up this editorial with further charges that the girls' morals were being corrupted by a group of young men who methodically enticed them " to infamous places of resort in Lowell and the vicinity and were not returned to their homes until daylight." Needless to say, the experiment was largely discredited by such reports.

The Absence of Feudal Mentality

While not all workers in this colonial period achieved the economic status of which they dreamed, laborers did, nevertheless, acquire a measure of independence, self-confidence, and a psychology of success which served them as a conservative ballast for the hardships they were yet to face. By 1800 the worker did not feel himself " inextricably caught in the meshes of capitalism." Throughout the seventeenth century, his income level had risen substantially above that of his European counterpart. Maryland, for example, reported in 1699 that " The province wants workmen, workmen want not work." John Winthrop records the situation wherein a master, on telling his servant that he saw no prospect of being able to continue paying him his high wages, was told by his em-

[9] Harriet Martineau, writing in 1834 after a tour of the Waltham plant observed that " the girls can earn two and sometimes three dollars a week besides their board. The little children earn one dollar a week. . . . The girls have, in many instances, private libraries of some value. . . . The people work about seventy hours a week on an average. . . . All look like well-dressed young ladies. Their health is good, or rather it is no worse than elsewhere." Quoted in Norman Ware, *The Industrial Worker, 1840–1860* (Boston, Houghton Mifflin, 1924), p. 73. The only fault Miss Martineau found with the mills was the overcrowding of the boarding houses, where girls sometimes slept three in a bed and six or more in a room.

ployee: "Sell more cattle." When the employer asked: "What shall I do when they are gone? " his worker again replied, "You can serve me and get them back." And John Winter wrote from Maine in 1639 that, if the current high rate of wages continues: "The servants will be masters and the masters servants." It is clear that labor in America did not have the feudal background nor serf mentality of its Continental counterpart.

The first two centuries of American economic history were characterized by labor scarcity. But at the turn of the eighteenth century, political and economic unrest in Europe and the widening opportunities in America combined to greatly accelerate immigration to America. Hamilton, in his *Report on the Subject of Manufactures* declared: "To find pleasure in the calamities of other nations would be criminal; but to benefit ourselves, by opening an asylum to those who suffer in consequence of them, is as justifiable as it is politic." The popularity of the sentiment that America was the asylum of the oppressed helped make possible America's amazing economic development in the nineteenth century. In 1840 de Tocqueville prophesied:

> The time will therefore come when one hundred and fifty million men will be living in North America, equal in condition, the progeny of one race, owing their origin to the same cause, and preserving the same civilization, the same language, the same religion, the same habits, the same manners, and imbued with the same opinions, propagated under the same forms. The rest is uncertain, but this is certain; and it is a fact new to the world — a fact fraught with such portentous consequences as to baffle the efforts even of the imagination.[10]

Let us turn now to those factors which made this prophecy a reality.

Sources of Labor Supply: Immigration

Without question the total of 40 million immigrants who came to America from 1820 to the present time represents the largest single force accounting for the characteristics of the American labor force today. While perhaps not more than 70 percent of these immigrants remained here, their contribution to our economic development is incalculable. Their impact on the growth of the labor force is not revealed by the 40 million statistic alone, for an unusually large proportion of these — at least two thirds — were males, and most came to America in their youth.

A modest 8,000 arrived in 1820 when data on immigration were first gathered.[11] Migration to the New World increased substantially after

[10] From Alexis de Tocqueville, *Democracy in America* and cited by Joseph S. Davis, "Fifty Million More Americans," *Foreign Affairs*, Vol. 28, No. 3 (April, 1950), p. 412.
[11] For further discussion and data, see A. J. Jaffe and Charles D. Stewart, *Manpower Resources and Utilization* (New York, John Wiley & Sons, 1951), Chapter 17.

1830 and reached a peak in 1907 when 1,300,000 immigrants arrived in that year alone.

Economic privation alone did not impel all the migration to America. The failure of the several liberal rebellions throughout Europe around 1848 encouraged a new wave seeking relief from the hostile political climate in Europe. Religious persecution prompted others to leave. But the prospects for a new life in America were probably more important in motivating this movement than the hardships in Europe, for the waves of immigration followed rather closely the waves of prosperity and depression in this country and even the seasonal employment of labor within each year. The first major burst of immigration took place from 1847 to 1857 following the general revival of economic activity with the discovery of gold in California. A second burst came from 1881 to 1890 when the economy was shaking off the post-Civil War depression. The final influx developed after 1900. The source of such immigrants changed radically at the end of the nineteenth century. From 1820 to 1890 over 75 percent of the new immigrants were from northwestern Europe, but after 1890 the bulk came from southeastern Europe — from such countries as Austria-Hungary, Italy, Poland, and Russia. This latter group of immigrants gravitated to block settlements of their own countrymen and were less rapidly dissolved in the American melting pot.

Americans have always been torn between conflicting sentiments regarding the need and effect of immigration. Today most of us usually forget that our own presence on this continent is due to the migration here of our progenitors. When labor is scarce, it seems clear that the growth of immigration would be beneficial to the country, but during the prolonged depressions the oversupply of labor appeared to aggravate conditions. Heavy immigration threatened to spread too thin the benefits of American production. Typical of such fear is the statement made by the early American economist, Francis Walker:

> The entrance into our political, social, and industrial life, of such vast masses of peasantry, degraded below our utmost conceptions, is a matter which no intelligent patriot can look upon without the gravest apprehension and alarm. These people have no history behind them which is of a nature to give encouragement. They have none of the inherited instincts and tendencies which made it comparatively easy to deal with the immigration of the olden time. They are beaten men from beaten races; representing the worst failures in the struggle for existence. Centuries are against them as centuries were on the side of those who formerly came to us.[12]

Lest this seem unnecessarily selfish or predatory, Walker went on to explain:

[12] Francis Walker, *Discussions in Economics and Statistics:* "Restrictions of Immigration," p. 447.

Charity begins at home. . . . our highest duty to charity and to humanity is to make this great experiment, here, of free laws and educated labor, the most triumphant success that can possibly be attained. In this way we shall do far more for Europe than by allowing its city slums and vast stagnant reservoirs of degraded peasantry to be drained off upon our soil.[13]

The problem of immigrant labor became particularly acute with the advent of the Oriental immigrant on the West Coast. The Orientals were not welcome, and much pressure was exerted to bar their entry to the country. Congress passed the Chinese Exclusion Act in 1882, which did not exclude the Japanese. Tension continued high on the West Coast against Oriental groups. In 1906 the San Francisco Board of Education placed Chinese and Japanese children in separate schools. Japan protested the decision, and as a consequence a " Gentlemen's Agreement " was reached under which Japan agreed not to issue passports to laborers desiring to go to the United States. In 1924 the Japanese were formally excluded by Congressional action just as the Chinese had been forty-two years earlier. Meanwhile, general pressure began building up throughout the country against any immigration whatsoever. Bills providing for literacy tests were vetoed by Presidents Cleveland, Taft and Wilson, but finally in 1917 such a test became law, in spite of President Wilson's veto. Several laws were passed in the 1920's to restrict immigration further, and in 1929 the national origins standard was developed. By this formula immigration was to be permitted in the proportion of the national origins of people already living in America in 1920, with the total immigration limited to 150,000 in any year. Since 1930 immigrant labor has accounted for an insignificant portion of the total changes in the labor supply. In 1950 the sum of standing national quotas, which are never filled completely, represented only 0.1 percent of our population.[14] Even though migration is a negligible component to the increase of our labor force, its contribution must not be neglected. Many of our most brilliant physicists are refugees from European tyranny. As a case in point, we may well ponder the state of the world today if the anti-Semitism of Germany had not encouraged Einstein to settle in America.

Population Growth: Birth and Death Rates

As the significance of migration to America declines, changes in the natural rate of growth arising from birth and death rates acquire more

[13] *Ibid.*, p. 449. A contrasting view was offered by Dr. Samuel Johnson, the famous British author. He termed Americans as a " race of convicts " who "ought to be content with anything we allow them short of hanging." Quoted in *Social Aspects of Industry*, S. H. Patterson (New York, McGraw-Hill Book Co., 1929), p. 50.

[14] As noted by Davis, *op. cit.*, p. 426. In more recent years there has been a considerable increase in immigration to America, although it still accounts for a small portion of labor force change.

significance. Either a decrease of birth rates or an increase of death rates will decrease the population while, of course, an increase of birth rates and a decrease of death rates will increase its size. In Figure 1 we have

FIGURE 1. Births, Deaths, and Surplus of Births over Deaths per Thousand Population, 1915–1956

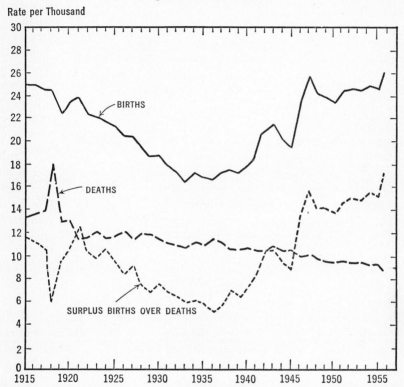

Rate per Thousand

Source: For data from 1915 to 1950 — W. S. Woytinsky and Associates, *Employment and Wages in the United States* (New York, Twentieth Century Fund, 1953). For data from 1951 to 1956 — U.S. Department of Health, *Monthly Vital Statistics,* Vol. 5, No. 7 (September, 1956).

indicated the number of births per thousand of population and the number of deaths per thousand. The difference between these two series reveals the cycle of natural population growth. Most of the fluctuation arises from changes in the birth rate, as the death rate has declined steadily in America from about 14.5 per thousand in 1915–1919 to 9.3 per thousand in 1955. The birth rate, on the other hand, dropped sharply during the depression to a low of 17 per thousand from 1935 to 1939, and during the postwar years it increased very sharply to a high of 26.1 per 1,000 in July, 1956. This postwar expansion of the birth rate, upsetting previous population growth trends, undoubtedly reflects the economic security people enjoy and their confidence in being able to raise families without undue privation. Both the marriage age and median age for maternity has declined while the proportion of the population married has increased. Nor is it any longer true that the rich are getting richer and the poor are having more children, for both the rich and the poor are having more children.[15]

This spectacular growth of the postwar population, with as many as 4,202,000 babies born in 1956, has driven a further spike into the coffin of the stagnation thesis of the thirties. That doctrine suggested that savings found no adequate outlets in investment because, among other things, the population was increasing at a decreasing rate and would soon reach its summit and begin to decline. But today investors are excited again about the prospects of expanding markets and are gearing their current investment decisions to optimistic calculations of society's impending needs. Demographers, through the analysis of the age composition of our inhabitants, are able to speculate about the nature of future population growth. For example, the bulge in population arising since the 1942 boom has created an expansion of demand for various commodities, as these children mature into adults. Consumption has shifted from such items as baby foods, toys, blankets, and school clothing to automobiles and ultimately to housing and home furnishings. By 1962 a new population boom should develop on top of the old one as these youngsters marry and have their own families. In this way, a bulge in the population pyramid of both sexes develops and tends to prolong itself. The stagnationists had predicted the absolute peak of population in America around 1980, but current estimates place the population at 190 million by 1965 and 220 million by 1975. Of course, in the interval between the increase in the birth rate and the time that this upsurge of births permits the expansion of the labor force, increased pressure is imposed on the existing work force for greater output. It is estimated, for example, that the total population from 1955 to 1965 will increase some 20 percent whereas in the same interval, the population available for work may increase by only 6 percent.[16] Even this per-

---

[15] Contrast this view with the rather dismal account of Joseph J. Spengler. "Population Movements and Economic Equilibrium in the United States," *The Journal of Political Economy*, Vol. XLVIII, No. 2 (April, 1940), in which it is suggested that "Present differentials [in the birth rate] appear to be reducing the relative number of persons with I.Q.'s above 115–20 and to be increasing the relative number with I.Q.'s under 80–85," and also that ". . . 75 or more per cent of our population growth is being contributed by about three-fifths of the nation's families who as a group receive only about one-fourth of the national income" (p. 159). Spengler is one of many who predicted in 1940 that "it now appears highly probable that the American population will attain a maximum of about 140 millions in the 1960's; thereafter there will be a decrease of population . . ." (p. 170). The birth rates of high-income groups are now approaching those of lower-income groups, and there seems to be no limit to the future of our population growth if present trends are not suddenly reversed.
[16] Estimates are made by Peter F. Drucker, "America's Next Twenty Years: The Coming Labor Shortage," *Harper's Magazine*, Vol. 210, No. 1258 (March, 1955), pp. 25, 30.

centage increase may be reduced if labor succeeds in its current efforts to reduce the work week to less than 40 hours. There seems as yet little fear that the labor market will be unable to absorb the stream of new entrants, and it is assumed that the ability of our economy to expand production will keep pace with the ever-rising demands of the ever-increasing population. Everyone, from the baby-toy manufacturer to the college president, has reason for optimism.

The Labor Force and Work Force Propensity

Work force propensity is defined as that proportion of the population that is in the work force. It is a ratio of considerable importance, for it indicates the proportion of the producing members of society over the broader number of consuming members. Usually the denominator of the ratio is not the entire population but those persons who are 14 years of age or older.

Movements in and out of the work force, as one might suspect, are induced by a large number of forces. Changes in the proportion of workers in the labor force can arise from changes in the size of the population of nonlabor force age, the changing proportion of women participating in the work force, the changing customs related to the retirement of older workers and the age at which youth enters the work force. These considerations are, in turn, affected by the changing opportunities for employment as well as the need for employment. If we use as our denominator the population over 10 years of age, we find that the proportion participating in the labor force in 1870 was 44.4 percent and this increased to 52.2 percent by 1900. On the basis of a slightly narrower base (the population 14 years of age and over) the proportion working was 55 percent in 1900 and increased only slightly to 56 percent in 1940. During the war years the ratio reached a peak of 63.2 percent participation, but by October, 1956, declined to 59.5 percent. On the basis of an assumed participation rate of the population in the labor force of 58 percent and a projection of population growth, it is expected that the labor force itself will be 88.6 million by 1975.[17]

The slight decline of work force participation since World War II probably reflects the widening of the population at both ends of the age distribution. By 1965, however, the percentage participation should increase, as a larger proportion of the population grows to work force age and as the proportion of female participation gradually increases. The growth of the labor force per year is evidenced by the fact that in the thirties the average annual increment to the labor force was 600,000. From

[17] Estimate made by Gertrude Bancroft, "Trends in the Labor Force" from *Manpower in the United States*, Industrial Relations Research Association (New York, Harper & Bros., 1954), p. 141. For further analysis and data, see W. S. Woytinsky, "The Labor Force," Chapter 23 of his study, *Employment and Wages in the United States* (New York, Twentieth Century Fund, 1953).

1949 to 1954 the increment had increased to 800,000 per year, and by 1965 the projected annual increment will be 1,250,000 workers. Forty percent of this increment, it is estimated, will be women.[18]

Participation in the work force is declining for those from the ages of 14 to 19 and is also declining for those 65 and over. The widening opportunities and need for high school and college training have been major factors in keeping youth out of the work force, and the forced retirement has decreased the participation of the aged. This decline at both ends of the age scale has been more than compensated, however, by the rapid growth of female participation in the work force. In 1890 only 17 percent of the work force was made up of women; by 1940 this had increased to 24 percent. Further female participation was encouraged by the unusual demands for labor during World War II so that nearly one third of all women of labor force age were in the labor force in 1945. It is expected that the participation will continue to increase with estimates placed at 29 percent female participation by 1960.[19] The aging portion of the work force deserves special consideration, not only because of the effect this has on our work force ratio, but also because of the social problems created by age. This is one problem that promises to grow more serious in the future.

Problems of the Older Worker

The age of the work force has been increasing because youth has delayed its age of entry to the labor force and because of the growth of life expectancy, enabling many of the aged to maintain their jobs. The median age of the male work force in 1890 was 33.3, and by 1940 this age had risen to 37.4. But the proportion of men over 65 still in the work force has dropped rapidly. In 1890, 64 percent of these men were employed, while in 1940 this percentage had dropped to about 42 percent. Retirement is often involuntary and has been aggravated by the shift of population from rural to urban centers. On the farm the aging head of the family would still be counted as part of the labor force, but in the city either his retarded efficiency or company policy may disqualify him from the labor force. During the depression many men were squeezed prematurely out of the labor force, and even today employers are reluctant to hire the older worker. Employers fear the added financial burdens under pension plans that arise when older workers are hired and often believe that an early retirement program will increase the opportunity for advancement of younger workers. Some employers are forced

[18] Charles D. Stewart, "Manpower Implications of Changing Patterns of Working Life," *Proceedings* of the Seventh Annual Meeting of the Industrial Relations Research Association (December 28–30, 1954), p. 261.
[19] See John D. Durand, *Labor Force in the United States: 1890–1960* (New York, Social Science Research Council, 1948), pp. 26–27.

to retire workers under union contract provisions.[20] Studies made by the Social Security Board of retired men in seven large cities indicated that only about 5 percent stopped working voluntarily while they were still in good health.[21] Pressure would undoubtedly increase to force the early retirement of workers if unemployment were again to develop. The plight of the older worker would become very acute during any period of declining family income. Nor should we forget that many of the older workers have acquired important attributes, skills, and wisdom which could be of considerable value to industry if greater attention were given to the utilization of this growing reservoir of manpower.[22] In 1900 those persons 65 years of age and older represented only 4 percent of the

[20] Sumner H. Slichter has estimated that the number of workers who would be willing to continue their participation in the labor force, if allowed to, is a million and a half, and that the loss to our economy from such forced retirement for 1950 alone approached some $5 billion. Slichter, "Retirement Age and Social Policy" in "The Aged and Society" (Champaign, Ill., Industrial Relations Research Association, 1950), p. 106.

[21] As cited in Durand, *op. cit.*, p. 36. The University of California study on the *Economic Implications of an Aging Population* provides us with some rather startling data on the employability of the aged. A research staff found that about three quarters of the men over 64 who were not in the labor force indicated they were not well enough to work. Of those well enough to work, there were twice as many who were not interested in working as there were men interested in working. Further, many more of this group retired "voluntarily" than retired for involuntary reasons. In this study the "hard core" of the aging problem is that many of the elderly men are unable to work because their labor skills quickly obsolesced with idleness. Many of these men have most experience in farming, an occupation not readily suited to their re-employment. Close to a quarter of these men were found to have incomes insufficient to support them at bare minimum standards, and it was found that almost half of the males in this category earned no income at all. The income for those who had an education tended to sustain itself at higher levels than for those with limited education. While some of these data are not supported by other research studies, it is probably true that the premature or forced retirement of the aged can quickly contribute to physical and mental deterioration. Studies relying on self-classification may reflect this demoralized state of mind. As Elizabeth Wallace puts it, "Increased leisure may be a good thing, but enforced leisure in the form of unsought unemployment is at any age wasteful and harmful from the point of view of the nation as well as of the individual." For analysis and summary of this study, see "Economic Implications of an Aging Population" by Robert Dorfman, Peter O. Steiner, and Melvin W. Reder, *American Economic Review*, Vol. XLIV, No. 2 (May, 1954), Papers and Proceedings, pp. 634–679.

[22] In an account titled "An Old Man Finds a Job" one ex-writer describes the increasing difficulty he had in securing employment with age: "We (the aging) had one great enemy: the actuarial charts of the insurance companies. Most enterprises of any size have insurance plans for their employees, and insurance companies love only the young and fair." In desperation he finally secured a job as a janitor working for only one sixth of his previous salary, and was advised by his friends that, after all, the secret of success was "to be willing to adapt your prejudices and be willing to honestly evaluate your own potential." With this uncomfortable thought, he was only able to find consolation in the fact that "there is no lean and hungry Cassius waiting in the wings, ambitious for my toga. No assistant looks enviously at my broom and grabs it when I leave the room. My ex-contemporaries now accept me; what their thoughts are, fortunately, I do not know." From *The Reporter* (February 23, 1956), pp. 38–40.

population and by 1950 their numbers had grown to slightly more than 8 percent. Mr. Benson Ford estimated that in 1954 the Ford Motor Company had one retiree for every fifteen active employees, but by 1970 this ratio would increase to one for every seven.[23]

A further index of the problem of aging can be seen in the studies undertaken by the Bureau of Labor Statistics on both the life expectancy of workers and the extent of work force participation expectancy. Paradoxical as it may seem, the average worker spends the same proportion of his lifetime in the labor force (about one third) in 1950 as he did in 1900, and the fact that he now, on the average, enters the labor force at the age of 18 or 19 rather than in his early youth reveals the longer period of work force participation. Actually, individuals today spend a slightly higher number of years in the work force, but the total of man hours contributed during that participation is slightly below the 1900 level because of the decline in the length of the work week. But the increase in the survivorship of labor has expanded more rapidly than the increase in its labor force participation. In 1900 the average period of retirement was only about three years while in 1950 the average period of retirement stretched to six years. It can be assumed that by the year 2000 the average worker may survive in a retired state for a period of nine years.[24] This creates, as we noted above, the twin problems of psychological adjustment to enforced idleness and the economic adjustment usually made necessary by limited retirement income or social security benefits.

In reality, the problems of the aged tend to spill over to those who are middle aged. Government data reveal that the tenure of unemployment tends to be much longer for the person 45 years of age and older than for younger groups, and, further, that three out of every four employers request that public employment agencies do not send them middle-aged applicants. Widening the area of discrimination of course greatly increases the numbers vulnerable to hardship. In 1900 there were 13.5 million men and women over 45 but today there are 47.4 million. By 1975 it is estimated that almost half of the adult population or 64 million workers will be in this middle-age or older group. Industry resistance to hiring such men reflects the fear of higher costs for pension plans, the limited tenure of such persons after they have learned the job, the pressures to promote from within the plant, and the fear that the experienced middle-aged employee often has the illusion that he " knows it

[23] In a speech before the American Hospital Association as reported in *Employee Benefit Plan Review* (October, 1954), p. 42, and quoted by Nelson M. Bortz, "Some Industrial Relations Implications of the Changing Length of Working Life," *Proceedings* of Seventh Annual Meeting of the Industrial Relations Research Association (December 28–30, 1954), p. 269.

[24] These data are taken from Seymour L. Wolfbein's study, "The Changing Length of Working Life," *Proceedings* of the Seventh Annual Meeting of the Industrial Relations Research Association (December 28–30, 1954), pp, 248–255.

all." These possible disadvantages must be counterbalanced with the like-lihood that middle-aged persons are more stable in their work relations with low turnover and absenteeism rates. Discrimination has become so common that two states, Pennsylvania and Rhode Island, have passed " anti-age discrimination laws " banning such items as age limits in labor recruitment advertisements. Probably much can be done to revise pension plans to overcome the resistance employers have to employing this age group.[25]

Seasonal and Cyclical Changes in Labor Force Size

Labor force participation follows both seasonal and cyclical swings related to the changing needs of labor for jobs and the changing needs of the labor market for workers. Taking seasonal variations first, participa-tion usually reaches a low in midwinter and its peak in midsummer, with a typical spread of some 4 million workers from the low to the high. Most of this seasonal employment is confined to students and to farm labor. The high point (June and July) for manpower utilization is 4 per-cent above the winter low, whereas the summer high point or woman-power utilized is 10 percent above the winter low. Most of the seasonally employed men are in the age group of 14 to 24, whereas most of the seasonally employed women are over 25 years of age.[26]

The cycles of prosperity and depression also affect labor force par-ticipation, although available evidence does not suggest any single or clear-cut conclusion on the net effect of such cyclical changes. What forces operate to reduce the number of workers in the labor force during a de-pression? First, with rising unemployment, many workers will decide that an endless search for jobs that do not exist is fruitless. But when they no longer seek work, they are not counted among the unemployed in the labor force.[27] The statistics reveal that the elderly and nonwhite workers are more likely to be affected by such layoffs than the younger and white workers. Furthermore, many youths may decide that there is little oppor-tunity for useful employment and attempt to " ride out " the depression

[25] For more detailed analysis, see Jerry M. Flint's article, "More Companies Shun Jobseekers Over 45, Fret About Pensions," *Wall Street Journal*, Vol. 55, No. 7 (July 11, 1956).

[26] For further discussion and data, see Woytinsky, *op cit.*, pp. 317–321 and pp. 336–347.

[27] One problem in measuring this latter movement is that the unemployed worker may count himself out of the work force in the very nature of the questions asked by the Census. To be in the work force, one must be actively looking for work. As Woytinsky points out: "It is generally agreed that a long and severe depression tends to squeeze marginal workers out of the labor force. After losing their jobs and discovering that they are unwanted by employers, they gradually lose their job attachment to the labor force. Some depend for support on public assistance, others on their relatives. First they lose hope, then spirit; the time comes when they lose their old skills and cease to belong to the active labor force." *Op. cit.*, p. 321.

by extending their education. Many women workers may feel that there is little chance to secure employment, especially if the public is resentful of female employment.

But pressures are also working in the opposite direction during a depression to increase the size of the labor force. While the demand for labor is low, the suppy of labor for this same reason may be very high. As wages are cut and overtime reduced, workers will often attempt to sustain their family income by searching for an extra job. In addition, other family members may be forced to work to supplement income. Students may be compelled, because of economic pressure, to quit school and look for a job. Even the elderly and the marginal workers may face the necessity of searching out employment. Most people cannot forget the need for income simply because the demand for labor has declined. In summary, the lower the earnings, the greater may be the pressure and need for labor force participation. Studies confirm that a decidedly higher proportion of the wives of men in the lower-income brackets are in the labor force compared to those whose husbands are in the higher-income brackets.

The question of labor force participation during prosperity and depression is a vital one, especially when one attempts to appraise the seriousness of unemployment during a depression by reviewing the proportion of those unemployed to the total work force. The problem has stimulated considerable discussion and research, much of it centering around the hypothesis advanced by Wladimir S. Woytinsky in 1940: "During a depression the number of persons seeking jobs tends to outrun the number of persons who have lost their jobs. On the other hand, with progressive recovery the re-employment of usual gainful workers is likely to bring about the gradual withdrawal of additional job-seekers." [28] Clarence Long has attempted to cast doubt on this thesis and indicates his studies reveal that "There was no net influx of desperation work-seekers in the great depression and therefore no flight from gainful labor in the subsequent recovery." [29]

But if poverty increases the numbers searching or hoping for employment, is it also true that prosperity, conversely, reduces labor force participation? Apparently not. Some statistical evidence [30] suggests that better opportunities for employment and higher earnings have done much

[28] See his *Additional Workers and the Volume of Unemployment*, Pamphlet Series No. 1 (Washington, Committee on Social Security of the Social Science Research Council, 1940), and more recently, his study, *Employment and Wages in the United States, op. cit.*, Chapter 24.

[29] See his "Impact of Effective Demand on the Labor Supply," *American Economic Review*, Vol. XLIII, No. 2 (May, 1953), Papers and Proceedings, p. 460. For a review of problems related to measurement, see Don D. Humphrey, "Alleged 'Additional Workers' in the Measurement of Unemployment," *Journal of Political Economy*, Vol. XLVIII, No. 3 (June, 1940), pp. 412–419.

[30] Wolfbein, *op. cit.*, p. 256.

to attract both the young and old to the work force and there seems to be more agreement that prosperity will increase labor force participation than that a depression will reduce it.

Mobility of the Labor Force

The effectiveness in the utilization of labor depends not only on its relative abundance, but also on whether it is available at the time and place it is needed. Classical economists usually assumed that labor, like other factors of production, would be allocated automatically to those establishments where it would be most productive. Growing consumer demand increased sales and profits; these, in turn, made it possible for employers to offer attractive wages to secure a larger labor force. By such seduction labor is pulled into the areas where expanding production is required. Similarly, the decline of consumer demand for a particular product results in unemployment, forcing labor out of such industry. Studies of labor force mobility indicate, however, that labor is not as mobile in a geographic or horizontal sense as theorists would like to believe. Such elements as (a) worker indifference to economic opportunity elsewhere, (b) worker ignorance of such opportunity, (c) the fear that such opportunity, even if known, may not offer the security of the present job, (d) the worker's identification and integration with his community, (e) the costs of such mobility, combine to discourage movement. Studies reveal that a middle-aged person employed at a skilled job over a period of four years or more and owning his own home is likely to be very immobile. If, on the other hand, the worker is young, unskilled, and unmarried, he is generally more willing to consider seriously the advantages of moving to a new labor market.[31]

Historically, there has been considerable movement of the population in spite of the barriers to such movement. Back in 1760 the major portion of the population was located within 100 miles of the Atlantic seashore. By 1950 the population center of America was a little west of Chicago near the 39° latitude. " In a century and a half the center of population has moved about 600 miles westward, at an average speed of four miles a year. The shift was particularly rapid (more than five miles a year) between 1830 and 1890. It then slowed down, especially after 1910 but quickened during World War II." [32]

The mobility of labor in all directions was greatly accentuated by the rapid expansion of demand for labor during World War II, permanently

[31] For detailed discussion, see *Labor Mobility in Six Cities*, prepared by Gladys L. Palmer with the assistance of Carol P. Brainerd, for the Committee on Labor Market Research (New York, Social Science Research Council, 1954), particularly Chapter 6.
[32] W. S. Woytinsky and E. S. Woytinsky, *World Population and Production Trends and Outlook* (New York, Twentieth Century Fund, 1953), p. 91.

altering the contours of labor force distribution. A vast flow of labor developed from the rural areas to all heavy manufacturing and industrial centers, and in the postwar period the reciprocal ebb of manpower away from these areas did not materialize.

The influx of labor into the Middle Atlantic states has not kept pace with the movement to other areas. More specifically, those states which border the Pacific Ocean from Canada to Mexico and those bordering the Gulf of Mexico and the South Atlantic have expanded their payrolls more rapidly than the rest of the country. What explains this centrifugal force driving labor away from the traditional industrial heartland of America? First, the economy is less and less dependent on coal and is utilizing other forms of fuel, more particularly petroleum and its derivatives. This shift has enabled tremendous flexibility in the location of industrial plant sites, especially since oil can be piped at modest cost to almost any area. Similarly, the wider use of hydroelectric power has encouraged many industries to favor the Pacific Northwest.

The other hard core of industrial manufacture, iron, is less tied to the ore sources because of the wider use of scrap metals. Thus the geographic shift of the labor force is, in a sense, determined by changes in production techniques and changes too in the " product mix " making up our total national product. For example, from 1939 to 1952 the expansion of employment in construction led all other industrial sectors with an increase of 120 percent. But the increase of construction employment was over 150 percent in the Pacific states, in the mountain area, and in the West, South, and Central areas. In New England construction employment increased by only 80 percent, and in the Middle Atlantic area it increased only by 76 percent. The expansion of employment in manufacturing too was more rapid in the West and Southwest, especially in California and Texas, than elsewhere. The growth of military bases in many of the Southern and Western states has attracted labor there as has the growth of finance, insurance and real estate activities in Houston, Los Angeles, and San Francisco. The development of atomic energy sites in the West and Southwest has pulled additional workers into these areas, and the sustained growth of the aircraft industry has further stimulated migration to the West Coast. Of course, statistics on population shifts should not suggest that ghost towns are being created in the relatively more mature industrial economies of the East. The center of gravity of our labor force is still in the East, and the shifts of new workers westward reflects a long-term trend which has only recently accelerated in pace.

One aspect of mobility has been the notable decline of labor residence in rural areas and the proportionate growth of the work force in urban areas. Back in 1790 well over 90 percent of the population could be classified as rural, a proportion which had dropped to 85 percent by 1850. But from then on the drift toward the city continued at a very rapid pace so that by 1950 only about 42 percent of the population remained in rural areas. Such migration has, of course, been conducive to the development of a working-class consciousness. City employment encouraged workers to develop a common evaluation of common hazards which were, as we shall see later, essential to the organization of the union movement. The increase in economic interdependence in the city meant that each worker was more vulnerable to economic insecurity. In more recent times, however, the social and economic aspects of city living have been mitigated somewhat by the growth of " suburbanitis." Populations are moving out of industrial centers, and in many cases industry too has moved in the direction of the work force. This development undoubtedly affects labor's attitude toward the union movement. The worker tends to find himself in a more conservative community the farther he moves from the city center.

Trends in the Occupational and Industrial Use of Labor

One final dimension to our kaleidoscopic view of labor force data can be secured by regarding changes in the long-term trends of manpower utilization both occupationally and industrially. In Table 1, the percentage distribution of labor by occupational group for 1910, 1940, and 1950 is provided. The data reveal the basic shift in the structure of our economy. By way of background, in 1910 labor worked some 58 hours a week,

TABLE 1 Percentage Distribution by Major Occupational Groups of Employed Workers: 1910, 1940, 1950

Major Occupational Group	Percent Distribution		
	1910	1940	1950
Total employed	100.0	100.0	100.0
Professional, technical, and kindred workers	4.6	7.9	8.7
Managers, officials, proprietors	24.5	19.5	16.6
Farmers and farm managers	17.3	11.4	7.7
Managers, officials, and proprietors except farm	7.2	8.1	8.9
Clerical and kindred workers	5.5	9.7	12.3
Sales workers	5.0	6.8	7.0
Craftsmen, foremen, and kindred workers	11.7	11.5	13.8
Operatives and kindred workers	14.1	18.9	21.1
Service workers	9.6	11.8	10.1
Laborers	25.0	13.9	10.4
Farm laborers and foremen	11.4	6.9	4.3
Laborers except farm and mine	11.6	7.0	6.1

Source: Gladys L. Palmer and Ann R Miller, "The Occupational and Industrial Distribution of Employment, 1910–50," in *Manpower in the United States: Problems and Policies*, Industrial Relations Research Association, Publication No. 11 (New York, Harper & Bros., 1954), pp. 87, 88.

producing a $556 per capita income (in 1929 dollars). By 1950 the worker was averaging only 42 hours of work per week and enjoying an almost threefold increase of per capita income, measured by those same 1929 dollars. In 1910 the production process required more brawn of labor than it did brains. The two major occupational groups then were " Laborers " and " Managers, officials, and proprietors." Most significant for our purposes is the decline since 1910 of both the farm and nonfarm laborers and the rapid growth today of the machine operator or the man on the production line. We see also that the application of machinery to the farm has reduced the need for farm labor and also the need for farm managers.

The technological revolution has created new (and as yet unsatisfied) demands for men with professional and technical skills. The age of electronics and automation is now bursting on the industrial scene and the pace of innovations is dampened somewhat by the scarcity of technically skilled manpower. Industry today demands an increasing number of engineers, physicists, chemists, electronics specialists, and mathematicians, and these professional areas of manpower utilization will undoubtedly increase in the future.

TABLE 2   Percentage Distribution of Employed Workers
in Major Industry Groups: 1910, 1940, 1950

Major Industry Group	Percent Distribution		
	1910	1940	1950
Total employed	100.0	100.0	100.0
Agriculture, forestry, and fisheries	31.0	18.9	12.4
Mining	2.8	2.1	1.7
Construction	6.1	4.7	6.2
Manufacturing	20.5	24.0	26.3
Transportation, communication, and other public utilities	8.7	7.1	7.9
Wholesale and retail trade	11.8	17.1	19.1
Finance, insurance, and real estate	1.6	3.3	3.5
Business repair services	0.8	2.0	2.6
Personal services	9.8	9.1	6.3
Entertainment and recreation services	0.5	1.0	1.0
Professional and related services	4.7	7.5	8.5
Public administration	1.7	3.2	4.5

Source: Gladys L. Palmer and Ann R. Miller, "The Occupational and Industrial Distribution of Employment, 1910–50," in *Manpower in the United States: Problems and Policies,* Industrial Relations Research Association, Publication No. 11 (New York, Harper & Bros., 1954), p. 90.

Table 2, showing the change in the industrial employment of the labor force, offers further evidence of this technological revolution. The shift since 1910 has been away from the primary industries, such as agriculture, forestry, and fisheries, with stability of employment in mining and construction. But growth has been rapid in the secondary industry, manufacturing, and in most tertiary industries, such as trade, finance, public administration, professional and related services. The decline in personal service employment since 1940 reflects the growing need to economize manpower during full employment. Most families can no longer afford the personal house servant, for the servant may often demand an income comparable to that of the breadwinner of the family.

Our brief panorama of the labor force indicates that labor force size is a major statistic and will continue to be so. But it is a quantity which itself is changing not only in absolute size, but also in terms of its geographic location, occupational use, in terms of its age, sex, and race composition. Obviously a quantum representing close to 70 million individuals is capable of reflecting an endless variety of light rays, but our time and space for turning the kaleidoscope of labor force data is limited. In America population and the labor force have expanded rapidly, and we shall see in the next chapter that, in W. K. Hancock's words " The western miracle of combining a phenomenal increase of population with rising standards of living " is a current reality. But is American experience typical throughout the world? Let us glance for a moment at this world situation.

World Population Growth and Living Standards

One of the most depressing aspects of world living standards is the current population explosion taking place throughout the world—and in particular — in underdeveloped areas. In 1800 the Reverend Thomas R. Malthus attempted to put the serpent back in Godwin's Eden by suggesting that population would tend to expand geometrically and the resources to support it, arithmetically. He insisted that the biological fact of reproduction and the physical fact of diminishing returns combined to depress living standards to their subsistence level. Starvation represented the negative check for such population expansion, while moral restraint provided its positive check. One economist renewed the ancient Hebrew declaration: " When goods increase, they are increased that eat them " with the more direct expression: " With every extra bite of subsistence, a new child is born." Another complained even more forcefully: " Men breed like mice in a barn."

In the Western world Malthusianism has proved of interest mainly to those reviewing the parade of economic theories. Had it not been disproved by technology? Had not Western economies escaped the law of diminishing returns by developing capital and novel techniques to increase food output? And had not birth control retarded the torrent of population growth? The most charitable could say for Malthus only that, by adopting a subjective rather than a physiological definition of subsistence, the more recent slow-down of population growth reflected the aspiration of the Western family for a higher living standard. If actual income should ever reach this aspirational subsistence, family size might again increase. But aspirations always seemed more expansible than income.

The current world population movement has encouraged a rereading and reappraisal of the Malthusian thesis. For example, if the world population in 1950 were to increase by 1 percent per annum, it would reach a point of "standing room only" with one person per square yard (or over 3 million per square mile) in 875 years.[33] Throughout the world today, population is expanding much more than 1 percent per year, and ironically, the expansion is greatest where per capita income is lowest.[34] Most of the underdeveloped areas are estimated to have annual population expansions (for the 1950–1960 decade) of from 1.25 to 2.25 percent.[35] Stated in other terms, if the natural increase of population is more than 30 per 1,000, the population will double in 23 years and quadruple in 46 years. Most underdeveloped areas are currently experiencing a population expansion approximating this 30 per 1,000 ratio and the question must be raised as to whether these "backward" areas can support the mass of new population with a mass of new production.[36] As we noted in the beginning of our chapter, industrialization offers one of the most vital keys to expanded output. But capital expansion involves the reduction of current consumption rather than its expansion. It seems ironic to suggest that the solution to low living standards is even lower living standards, particularly at a time when population pressures are increasing demands for higher consumption.[37]

Ironically, too, the technology of the Western world has done much to aggravate the problem of population pressure in backward areas, for it was the discovery of modern chemicals and drugs, particularly D.D.T., which has enabled native areas to escape the devastating effects of their number-one killer, malaria. It was never before thought that these rela-

[33] As indicated by K. W. Taylor, "Some Aspects of Population History," *Canadian Journal of Economics and Political Science*, Vol. XVI, No. 3 (August, 1950), p. 305.
[34] For analysis, see Joseph J. Spengler, "The Population Obstacle to Economic Betterment," *American Economic Review*, Vol. XLI, No. 2 (May, 1951), Papers and Proceedings, pp. 348–358.
[35] For figures, see Reuben E. Slesinger, "Some Comments on Nonagricultural Possibilities for Raising the Levels of Living of Underdeveloped Nations," *American Economic Review*, Vol. XLVI, No. 2 (May, 1956), Papers and Proceedings, p. 331.
[36] For data on this ratio, see Kingsley Davis, "The Amazing Decline of Mortality in Underdeveloped Areas," *American Economic Review*, Vol. XLVI, No. 2 (May, 1956), Papers and Proceedings, pp. 316–317.
[37] To dramatize the significance of this expansion, Kingsley Davis points out that "The United States, often thought to have established a record in population growth, never had, even in its heyday and with the help of immigration, a faster increase than many of our underdeveloped areas are showing by the sheer excess of births over deaths." *Ibid.*, p. 317.

tively primitive areas could afford the luxury of Western medical care, but a few drugs have worked miracles in reducing death rates at surprisingly low costs.

The future is challenging, especially if one takes the view that poverty and starvation provide the breeding ground for revolutionary ideologies. We face this impressive contrast: In America our major dietary problem is obesity (40 million Americans are overweight); approximately two thirds of the world's inhabitants or 1.5 billion people are suffering from chronic malnutrition. Yet if the 1950 world population of 2.4 billion should expand from 1 to 1.5 percent per year it will reach 4–5 billion by 2000 and 6.5–10.5 billion by 2050. Can technology and productivity pace this increase? And if it cannot, what then? We should not dismiss this problem by simply raising the issue of Malthusianism, for 150 years ago economists were equally pessimistic about the living standards in England. Malthusianism did not discourage industrialization, and we have no reason to believe that what was true for the West in the past could not be found equally true for the East in the future.

3

The Structure and
Trend of Wages

In the United States it is fashionable to judge a man by his performance, and we often conclude a man is worth what he gets and gets what he is worth. In a similar fashion, we appraise the efficiency of our present-day labor market in terms of the results it produces or its performance. Not the least of these results of labor market organization is the income it provides the labor force. In this chapter we shall discuss the importance and general functions of wages to labor, management, and the public. We shall discuss also alternative measures of labor income. Following this conceptual and definitional background, we shall survey the important contours in the progress of labor's money earnings and the extent to which these earnings must be " adjusted " by changes in the cost of living, to determine the buying power of labor's money income. We shall then turn to some of the more important facets of the wage structure in America and conclude with an analysis and appraisal of the share of national income that labor has received. Our analysis will, for the most part, involve statistics. These data should not be viewed as stacks of dry wood, for they represent the bread and butter of the labor force.

Wages: The Worker's View

To labor, adequate income is important not only to provide for adequate daily subsistence but also in a much wider sense to make possible the consumption of goods so necessary to sustain economic activity. Indeed, when workers organize into unions, this sentiment of " enlightened " self-interest acquires enormous significance. For is it not true that without adequate wages or purchasing power, the industrial mechanism would soon grind to a standstill? Is it not true that all production, in the final analysis, must be for consumption? If the wage earner's income is adequate, management would never have any difficulty in maintaining production and employment, for high wages advance society's consumption, industry's sales, and the firm's profits and employment. By securing higher wages, labor advances the economic health of the economy as well as its own health and economic status.

The Rationale for Wage Floors. The issue as to " who should get what " will never be resolved in our society. There is general agreement that everyone born has the right to the opportunity to earn a subsistence income. The idea that society should provide subsistence for its population has a long history and is one that has had special appeal to socialists.[1] The popularity of the sentiment is reflected by government minimum wage laws. By establishing such minimum levels the government, it is reasoned, provides a defense for workers unable to protect themselves. These minimum wage levels act as a defense against a special kind of parasitism of industry. Without them competitive pressures would encourage producers to buy labor at the lowest possible wage rate. While cheap labor may be advantageous to the individual employer, it is hardly an economy for society, for poverty drains not only the energy of the worker but precipitates the associated conditions of slum living, poverty, increased sickness, and so on. The resulting cost to society is not sufficiently compensated by the original savings in wage costs enjoyed by particular employers.

Even though the living wage principle lost its significance with the decline in the influence of the Roman Catholic church, its moral appeal has often been stressed by theologians. In 1891 Pope Leo XIII formulated the doctrine of a minimum living wage in his encyclical " Rerum Novarum ":

> Let it be granted then, that as a rule workman and employer should make agreements, and in particular should freely agree as to wages; nevertheless, there is a dictate of nature more imperious and more ancient than any bargain between man and man, that the remuneration must be enough to support the wage earner in *reasonable and frugal comfort*. If through necessity, or fear of a worse evil, the workman accepts harder conditions because an employer or contractor will give him no better, he is the victim of fraud and injustice.[2]

The inevitable problem is, however, one of defining the substance of " reasonable and frugal comfort " for labor. If the question is to be answered at all, it must be in terms of the value judgments of the person making the response.

John A. Ryan, one of the more recent Catholic proponents of the living

---

[1] Sidney and Beatrice Webb considered the " minimum standard " one of the fundamental forces motivating union behavior. The Webbs quote a union leader in Britain: " It is a vital principle that a man by his labor should live, and notwithstanding all the teachings of political economists and all the doctrines taught by way of supply and demand, a greater doctrine overrides all these, the doctrine of humanity." Sidney and Beatrice Webb, *Industrial Democracy* (London, Longmans, Green & Co., 1902), p. 582.

[2] As quoted by John A. Ryan, *A Living Wage* (New York, The Macmillan Co., 1906), p. 33.

wage doctrine, has pointed to the hazards of relying on bargaining power to distribute goods. Labor may not possess sufficient bargaining power to assure itself a " living " wage. By analogy he poses the situation where a drowning man calls to another for help: " The latter replies: ' I will save you if you pay me a million dollars.' The distressed millionaire prefers life on this hard condition to death without it, and quickly closes the contract. The contract was free, was a source of some gain for both parties, but who would affirm that it was just? " [3] It is in this inequality of bargaining power that Ryan finds the justification for union organization: " Man's natural rights must not be so widely interpreted that the strong, and the cunning, and the unscrupulous will be able, under the pretext of individual liberty, to exploit and overreach the weak, and simple, and honest majority." [4]

From time to time various agencies, including the Bureau of Labor Statistics, have attempted to establish objective standards of " necessary " income for family units. In this context, a subjective standard may be defined in psychological terms by the aspirations, desires, or self-defined needs of the family. The so-called objective standards, on the other hand, are based on the physiological needs of the family, with those needs defined by experts. Even objective standards contain subjective elements in the estimates that must be made of clothing, housing, medication, and other needs of the family.[5]

---

[3] Ryan, *op. cit.*, p. 36. He quotes with approval Comte de Mun's statement to the French Chamber of Deputies: " Liberty does not consist in a theoretical right, but in the possibility of exercising it. The power to be free, in a regime which puts the workingman's life at the mercy of supply and demand; which exposes himself, his wife, and his children to the hardships of a competition that knows no moderation; which sets no limit to his exploitation except the interests of those who employ him — the power to be free in such conditions, when the need of subsistence is so pressing as to permit of no waiting, no choice, no hesitation, does not exist and consequently the laborer is not free." *Ibid.*, p. 298.

[4] *Ibid.*, p. 64.

[5] Various benchmarks developed for objective standards are:

(a) *The Poverty Level:* This is a state of submergence, a level at which even the prudent expenditure of family income does not provide for adequate subsistence. Families living at the poverty level are characterized by undernourishment, overcrowding in slum conditions, inadequate household furnishings and clothing. They face the constant problem of sickness or other emergencies with no resources or savings. A large percentage of the group most likely to be found at the poverty level are some of the racial minorities, such as the Puerto Ricans, Indians, Negroes, and " wetback " Mexican immigrants. Department of Commerce figures indicate that there are some 12 million family units with a cash income of less than $2,000 a year, representing 25 percent of American families.

(b) *The Minimum of Subsistence Level:* This standard provides for the physical and material upkeep of the family but is in no way adequate for contingencies. Any emergency may result in reductions of income allocated for basic subsistence.

(c) *The Minimum Health and Decency (or Subsistence plus) Level:* Families in this group can provide for physical subsistence and also have income sufficient for some elementary social necessities. Such " luxuries " may include medical attention, extra carfare, insurance, and a small portion for recreation, clothing, and education.

In 1947 the Bureau of Labor Statistics published the "City Worker's Family Budget" designed to define not a "mere existence level nor a luxury level, but a modest but adequate standard of living for the city worker's family." This budget is based on the assumption that the typical wage earner has a wife, a boy 13 years of age, and a girl 8 years of age. Rather than construct the theoretically normal or "desirable" pattern of consumption expenditures, analysis was made of the purchases of the working-class families. With appropriate weights established by items actually purchased, it was then possible to price the commodities entering into such budgets. Regional budget studies have been developed by pricing these commodities in 34 cities in America. The distribution of families into the various planes of living will depend, of course, on whether the nation as a whole is enjoying prosperity or suffering a depression. These minimum budget figures are sometimes employed in collective bargaining, especially if unions can prove that labor income is inadequate for "subsistence." [6]

Alternative Views of Labor Income. Money wages alone do not determine labor's living standard, for they must be related to the current consumer price index. It is not, in other words, the money that labor earns but rather the goods and services that this money will command on the market place or the "real" wage that is significant. We should, though, be aware of several of the limitations of this concept. First, it is obviously impossible to determine the cost of living for each and every family, since each family purchases different items or has a different budget. The government consumer price index attempts to indicate changes in costs for the average family, but no family is in fact "average." Moreover, buying habits change from time to time. More recent revisions of the consumer expenditure pattern give weight to such items as television sets, automatic washers and dryers, baby-sitting fees, and so on, but the index weights are not revised as quickly as the pattern of expenditure. A third difficulty is that prices vary from region to region, and the national consumer price index may not reflect local living costs. A fourth difficulty is determining an appropriate base for the index and appreciating how the percentage change of any index is a function of the height of the base. For example, the 1947–1949 base for the consumer price index obviously shows much smaller percentage changes in the current price level than one rooted in a 1939 base. The problem is particularly difficult because of the common tendency to impute normal conditions to the base year. For example, percentage changes in wages

(d) *The Comfort Level:* At the comfort level the family is able to afford a decent home or apartment and have reasonably adequate funds for such items as insurance, education, vacations, health maintenance, and amusements. It is the level to which most American families aspire, and one that many family units in America have reached.

[6] For fuller discussion, see Chapter 15.

compared to changes in the consumer price index are only as meaningful as the relationship of wages to prices in that base year.

A second method for calculating labor income is to treat the family, rather than the individual worker, as an earning unit. The logic of this approach is obvious, for in many families the father's income is supplemented by contributions from the employed son, daughter, or wife. Actually, most of the extra workers are women. Of the 22 million workers boosting family incomes in 1953, 15 million of these were women and about 5 million were the sons of the family head. The main breadwinner may, in addition, hold a part-time job apart from his regular employment. In isolated cases the main family earner may hold two full-time jobs.

These secondary workers make a significant contribution to family income. In a study made by *Fortune* in 1954, 55 percent of all nonfarm families then received more than $4,000 cash income (after taxes) with 43 percent of all families in the $4,000 to $7,500 class.[7] Taking the 41 million families in the United States in 1953, about 17 million had at least one earner in addition to the family head. Some 42 percent of all families, then, relied to a varying degree on this extra income.[8]

A third facet of labor income is the greater amount of leisure that labor has secured for itself. If labor demands a shorter work week for the same pay, this is an alternative to maintaining the same work week with higher pay. In 1900 the normally scheduled hours of work each week was around 60. In the last 100 years it is likely that the length of the working week has been cut almost in half. While labor used to work from sunup until sundown (and up to 16 hours a day), today it is more usual for labor to work an 8-hour shift (or slightly less than this) for 5 days a week. Another way of measuring the increased amount of leisure enjoyed in America is by noting that in 1900, about 40 percent of the population was in the labor force, working approximately 60 hours a week or a third of all their

---

[7] "The Rich Middle Income Class," *Fortune* (May, 1954). Of the 20 million families in America headed by workers (craftsmen, operatives, laborers, etc.), 9 million were (in 1954) in this $4,000 to $7,500 class and another 2 million are in the over $7,500 class. Almost 60 percent of all the family units with incomes of $4,000 to $7,500 (after taxes) or the middle-income group were represented by "workers." Taking the $4,000 to $7,500 group alone, 70 percent of those family heads who are classified as service or unskilled workers had supplementary earners in the family to put them into this category. Almost 50 percent of the semiskilled family head workers have supplementary income earners, and this same proportion holds for the clerical and sales group. Almost a third of the skilled family head workers had supplementary workers. In other words, taking the nonfarm families in the middle-income group alone, about 40 percent of the workers and nonworkers alike in this group were only there because someone besides the family head was working — at least part of the time. Supplementary earners are important to all income groups.

[8] All data from *Fortune* article, pp. 95–99, 193. It is interesting to speculate to what extent a recession would squeeze the second breadwinner from employment. Should this happen, the effect is likely to be very pronounced in the market, especially for the large growth of industry built up to supply the semiluxury demands of this middle-income group.

living time. For the population as a whole, about 13 percent of all "living time" (40 percent workers × 30 percent of working time) was consumed in active labor. Today it is estimated that the percentage of the population's living time spent on the job is down to 9 percent.[9] Rough estimates have been made to indicate that American labor has taken about 65 percent of its increase in production in higher wages, and about 35 percent in the form of leisure.[10]

Wages: Management's View

Apart from their function as income to workers and purchasing power for consumers, wages are also significant as costs to employers. Much of the controversy between labor and management is rooted in these two aspects of wages: labor has the "wages-as-income" orientation and management the "wages-as-cost" viewpoint. It is clear that if wages are increased without relation to adjustments of employer's sales, prices, or production, the burden of the wage increase will fall on either the employer's income, on some of the other factors of production employed, or (if employment is reduced) on the workers themselves. It is understandable that management usually resists any motion for a substantial wage increase. A cost increase is usually a firm commitment by the company to its labor force, while the revenue or sales required to cover those costs may be highly variable. Any evaluation of the ultimate impact of wage adjustments must be related to possible changes in labor productivity, market prices, sales, and so on. Management is understandably reluctant to be tied to a rigid cost structure when all else is in a state of flux. Let us glance briefly at a few benchmarks which management must consider in appraising the impact of wage adjustments.

While labor is interested in its take-home pay (and what it will buy),

---

[9] Estimated by Daniel Seligman: "The Four Day Week: How Soon?" *Fortune* (July, 1954), p. 81. Seligman notes the reactions of several business leaders to the 5-day week instituted by Henry Ford in his plant in 1926. John E. Edgerton, president of the National Association of Manufacturers, stated: "I regard the five-day week as an unworthy ideal. It would be an economic faux pas, imposing further penalties upon industry and undermining our social structure. So, let the emphasis be turned from leisure to work for all, from rights to obligations, from agitation to education. More work and better work is a more inspiring and worthier motto than less work and more pay. . . . It is better not to trifle or tamper with God's laws. . . ." Judge Elbert Gary, board chairman of U. S. Steel: "The commandment says, 'Six days shalt thou labor and do all thy work.' The reason it didn't say seven days is that the seventh is a day of rest, and that's enough." James Carey Martien, president of the Baltimore Association of Commerce: "Mankind does not thrive on holidays. Idle hours breed mischief." An unidentified company president quoted by the NAM: "It would mean a trend toward the arena. Rome did that, and Rome died." Economic writing in the nineteenth century contains ample quotations lamenting the hazards of increased leisure for the work force.

[10] For the basis of such estimates, see Seligman's article, *op. cit.*

management is vitally concerned with its per unit labor cost. These costs, in turn, reflect the output of labor.

Labor Productivity

Interest in labor productivity, or the ratio of physical production divided by man-hours, has grown rapidly in recent years. Labor scarcity as well as the high cost of each man-hour has forced management to make every effort to increase labor output. The ratio is important, too, for unions often point to increases in labor output as justification for wage increases. The suggestion that wages should follow or parallel the productivity of labor is not, of course, novel to our generation, for most of the early incentive wage plans developed out of the recognized advantage of relating the pay of the worker to his output. But the concept of labor productivity is very slippery. One problem is to develop an appropriate single physical production index for a firm which processes a diverse number of products. How should one weigh, for example, the production of automobiles with the production of tractors, or the production of a pretzel-making machine with that of a coke dispenser? Just how should one record the improvements of quality of the product from year to year? And how should one calculate labor productivity, for example, when mining has been diverted from the production of high-grade ore in small quantities to the extraction of low-grade ores in large quantities? Should labor productivity be determined in terms of the ore finally extracted or the total tons of material moved by labor? [11] Should labor productivity include the supervisory personnel, the maintenance worker, the salaried workers, and the salesmen? Obviously the selection of man-hours may be completely arbitrary, and it would be just as logical (although perhaps not quite as helpful) to calculate output per unit of capital, or per acre, or per foreman, as the output per man-hour of labor. To argue that one ratio is more valid than the other is equivalent to reasoning that distances should be measured in feet rather than meters. It is also evident (though sometimes forgotten) that changes in output per man-hour often take place independently of variation in the exertions of labor employed.[12] A further

[11] Several of the difficulties in calculating labor productivity are explored by W. Duane Evans, Chief, Division of Industry Economics, BLS, in W. S. Woytinsky's and Associates, *Employment and Wages in the United States* (New York, Twentieth Century Fund, 1953), Chapter 7, "Productivity and Wages."

[12] Typical sources of changes in labor productivity are described by the Bureau of Labor Statistics: In the production of bolts productivity may depend in part on the speed and efficiency of screw machines; in electrical instruments productivity is partially determined by the skill and efficiency of labor. In coal it may partially be determined by the size, shape, and location of the coal vein; in canned goods it may be determined by the quality of the crop which in turn determines the amount of culling and sorting required. In wheat it may be related to such things as sunshine and rainfall. Within the plant itself improvement in productivity may be traceable

popular misconception is that one cannot logically impute the increase in production to labor just because labor productivity has increased. Simply using man-hours as the denominator of this ratio does not isolate the contributions of the nonlabor factors to changes in the numerator of the ratio. There is no simple way yet devised for determining just what part of the total output results from the work of labor and what part from the interaction of other cooperating factors. Certainly labor productivity figures do not tell us this.

Because of the difficulty of combining physical production of various factors into one index, employers may prefer to calculate the *value* of the firm's output, and divide this by the man-hours involved in the production of such goods. Such analysis simplifies the problem of combining a number of participating physical units and is often more relevant an index from management's " ability-to-pay " viewpoint. It is possible, for example, that the *physical* productivity of labor may increase, while the *value* of that output is decreasing. Wage demands related to changes in physical productivity can usually be absorbed during a period of rising prices because the value of output may increase in proportion to (or even more rapidly than) physical supply. But wage demands related to physical productivity during a period of declining prices may be meaningless for the value of output may decrease as the total of physical output increases.

Unit Labor Costs

A third alternative is to divide total physical production by the total wage bill to indicate per unit costs. The resulting ratio is of importance in both economic theory as well as in practical business operations. Labor often contends that increases in wage rates need not result in any increase in per unit labor costs, for such costs will be absorbed in rising labor productivity. The wage adjustment must be deflated or inflated by the changes in physical production; deflated if physical production increases and inflated if it decreases.

Product Wages

A further important ratio is that of the money wage rate to the wholesale price of the goods being produced. A direct comparison of money

to additional investment of capital for machinery and equipment, more extensive or more efficient use of power, improvement in plant layout, work flow or work techniques, improvements in supervision and management, sounder design of products or improvements of jigs or fixtures resulting from departmental engineering. All these factors may operate in addition to the efficiency or application of the individual worker. See George E. Sadler, " Productivity Program of the Bureau of Labor Statistics," *Sixth Annual Conference on Research in Industrial Relations* (Minneapolis, University of Minnesota, May 9, 1950), p. 1, and the BLS, " Productivity Measurement: A Tool for Evaluating Production Efficiency." Mimeographed.

wage earnings to the consumer price index (or the cost of living) reveals the real wage for the worker, but the comparison of wage costs to the employer's own wholesale prices is, of course, more meaningful to the employer. Recognition of the importance of this relationship to the employer has encouraged a few experiments in formally tying wage rates to product prices, but such sliding-scale arrangements have usually proven unpopular, especially from the labor viewpoint when product prices began to slide downward. An even more distilled wage cost ratio is that of the per unit labor cost to the per unit wholesale price. Even this ratio may not always reflect wage pressure on the particular employer, for the tight margin of per unit wage costs to prices may be compensated by a large volume of sales. In the final analysis probably the most significant ratio is the total wage bill related to firm income. We shall later view some data on the distributive share labor has received from total income.

Before we turn to the actual data on labor's material progress, we should be familiar with the concepts employed by the government in developing such information.

Alternative Measurements of Labor's Income

Average Hourly Wage Rates. This rate, generally a negotiation issue in the collective bargaining process, indicates the money income a worker receives for each hour of work. The base excludes any consideration of premium pay arising from piecework, bonuses, and income earned through overtime. It is the base measure of the price of one hour of labor. The use of the hour as a unit of time is important in determining take-home pay, for many of the salaried employees paid by the week are less likely to experience adjustments of pay either for absenteeism or for overtime work. Under an incentive plan the wage rate reflects the pay for each unit of production.

Average Hourly Earnings. Hourly earnings more directly represent the take-home income that labor receives. It is determined by dividing total weekly earnings by the total hours actually worked by the labor force.[13] This index of earnings rather than of wage rates is provided by the Bureau of Labor Statistics because hourly earnings can be calculated from data on payrolls and man-hours of employment. Hourly earnings

---

[13] Monthly compilations of data on average hourly earnings and average weekly hours of work in manufacturing industries were begun by the Bureau of Labor Statistics in 1932 and subsequently carried back as far as 1909. The *Monthly Labor Review* publishes data on average weekly hours, average hourly earnings, and average weekly earnings for 135 industries and 20 major groups of industries as well as for durable and nondurable goods groups, and for all manufacturing. The data are based on monthly reports from some 35,000 cooperating establishments and cover both full- and part-time production workers who worked or received pay during any part of the pay period ending nearest the fifteenth of the month. Vacation hours are included as time worked, and vacation pay is included as pay earned.

reflect income arising from shift differentials and alterations in incentive pay. Even change in the composition of the work force can change hourly earnings. For example, if low-paid workers are laid off, the reduction of work force will increase the hourly earnings for those remaining. Similarly, if industry hires a large number of unskilled workers, women, or students at reduced rates, this will decrease average hourly earnings.

Weekly Earnings. Weekly earnings reflect the income labor receives during the week rather than for an hour. This measure can be developed in three main ways:

(1) *Full-time weekly wage rate*
$$= \frac{(\text{wage rate}) \times (\text{standard hours per week})}{\text{production workers on payroll}}$$

(2) *Full-time weekly earnings*
$$= \frac{(\text{average hourly earnings}) \times (\text{standard hours per week})}{\text{production workers on payroll}}$$

(3) *Average actual weekly earnings*
$$= \frac{\text{weekly payroll}}{\text{production workers on payroll}}$$

One and two above are more likely to reflect " theoretical " rather than actual earnings. The full-time weekly wage rate (1) is found by multiplying the wage rate (rather than earnings) by the standard, going, or customary length of the work week which may or may not accurately reflect the actual length of the current work week. The full-time weekly earnings (2) are somewhat more representative in that average hourly earnings (rather than wage rates) are multiplied by the standard work week referred to above. The actual weekly income of the work force (3) is derived simply by dividing the actual payroll by the number on the work force. Obviously, the latter concept has the advantage over (1) and (2) in revealing changes in the length of the work week. A further problem in each of these ratios is to determine just what persons should be counted as production workers or included in the denominator. If all part-time workers are included in the work force, this will deflate the weekly earnings' figure. If such part-time workers are included, the index reveals the effects of " unemployment within employment " or the effect of partial unemployment (or part-time work) on earnings.[14]

Average Annual Earnings. Average annual earnings are derived by dividing the total actual annual payroll by the number of production

[14] The Bureau of Labor Statistics secures payroll data each month for both full- and part-time production workers who worked or received any pay during any part of the pay period ending nearest the fifteenth of the month. Payrolls as reported to the BLS include employee contributions for old-age benefits, unemployment insurance, and group insurance. Not included are the estimated value of free rent, fuel, and other payments in kind. Bonus payments, unless earned and paid regularly each pay period, are excluded.

workers on the payroll. Here again the statistician is confronted with the difficulty of determining just who should be counted as a member of the work force. Should only " active " or full-time members of the work force be included? Or should the unemployed (but attached) workers be included? During the depression some felt that annual earnings data should be determined by dividing total earnings by the total number of workers (whether employed or not) attached to industry, in order to reveal the total impact of unemployment on all workers. The reasoning behind this was the belief that average annual earnings mean little if such earnings are only enjoyed by a portion of the work force, but today data are usually developed on the basis of those active members of the labor force actually employed. In more recent periods of high employment there has been less demand and less need to deflate any of these figures by inclusion of the " attached unemployment."

As we have seen, labor's earnings can be measured by the hour, day, week, month, or year and such earnings may be divided by actual hours, normal hours, full-time employees, or full- and part-time employees combined. Each of these concepts has its advantages and limitations, and one must be aware of what is being measured to avoid confusion. The following statement indicates how the different indices account for substantial differences in the take-home pay of the worker.

> . . . during World War II the average gross weekly earnings of factory workers went up 77 percent, but only one-fifth of this increase resulted from basic rate increases. One-third resulted from increased hours and extra pay for overtime, and one-third came from the wartime upgrading of workers from unskilled to semi-skilled jobs, from increased output under incentive or bonus systems and the transfer of workers from low wage to high wage industries. In October, 1945, a few months after the close of the war, gross weekly earnings had declined almost 13 percent, although hourly wage rates had increased 1 percent during those few months.[15]

With these limitations of statistical data in mind, let us turn to the several measures of labor's income levels.

The Record: Changes in Money Wages, Living Costs, and Real Wages

Any survey of long-range trends must be interpreted cautiously because of the difficulty of securing consistent and accurate data over a long period of time. As one might expect, industrial classifications are splintered, statistical techniques refined, size of samples changed, and so on, as

---

[15] Florence Peterson, *Survey of Labor Economics* (New York, Harper & Bros., 1951), pp. 259–260.

the economy itself has grown more complex. Consequently, much of our data represents the splicing together of separate studies. The following data should not be analyzed for the detail of any one year but only in terms of the general trends they reveal.

FIGURE 2. Indexes of Money Wages, Cost of Living, and Real Wages, 1840–1890
1860 = 100

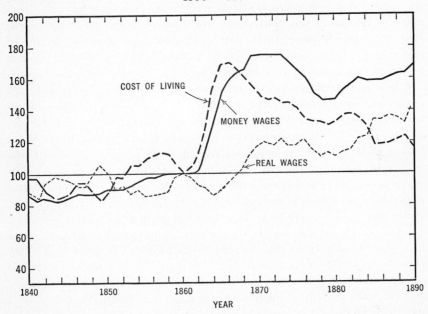

Figure 2 shows the path of the index of money wages, the cost of living, and real wages from 1840 to 1890.[16] Before reviewing the data, what factors account for changes in the real wage? The real wage rate, or what money wages will buy, is most frequently utilized as the best single index of changes in labor's living standard. Changes in real income can be caused either by changes in money wages *or* changes in the cost of living. Real wage rates do not, of course, reveal unemployment. During a de-

[16] In Figure 2 money or "nominal wages" were calculated by Rufus S. Tucker, "Real Wages Under Laissez Faire," *Barron's Weekly* (October 23, 1933), pp. 6–7. This index represents an average of the Aldrich committee's average of daily rates (converted to an hourly basis) with a composite index compiled by Carl Snyder. The cost of living index is actually a wholesale price index weighted in terms of estimates of consumption. The index, designed by R. P. Falkner for the Aldrich committee, omits those items for which consumption items are not available and such items as rent. It is most likely to be deficient in periods of rapid change, for wholesale prices are generally more elastic than retail prices. The real wage rate, as noted above, is derived by dividing money wages by the cost of living. These data are taken from the study by Woytinsky and Associates, *op. cit.*, pp. 582–583.

pression the cost of living index usually declines sharply. As a consequence, the real wages often increase, but this is significant only for those who are still employed. For this reason an increase of real wage rates cannot in itself indicate an improvement in the material living standard for all labor. Conversely, during a period of growing prosperity money wages often lag behind prices, causing a reduction in the level of real wages, but this is often associated with an expansion in the level of employment. In the former depression situation real wage rates may increase while (because of spreading unemployment) the total of wage payments or the wage bill may decrease. In the latter prosperity situation the decline of real wages may be associated with an expansion of employment, so that the total wage bill may actually increase.

It is only possible to secure fragmentary evidence of labor's real wage rate prior to 1840, and the data in Figure 2 following 1840 is rather speculative. During the Civil War it is apparent that prices did increase sharply, and it is likely that wage increases did not fully pace the price adjustments. Living costs generally moved downward from 1820 to 1850 with the notable exception of 1830 to 1837, a period of wildcat banking culminating in the financial panic and crisis of 1837. Alvin Hansen's study of real wages indicates that real average hourly earnings had increased from 41 in 1820 (base 1913 = 100) to 51 in 1830,[17] but in 1840 the real wage index was still 51. As we can see by the data in Figure 2, real wages did fluctuate considerably from 1840 to 1864, from a low in the latter year of 86 (with 1860 = 100) to a high of 105.1 in 1849. There was no discernible upward trend of real wages until 1864, and from this date on they increased rather steadily. A plateau of real wages was reached between 1870 and 1876. Much of the increase in real wages from 1865 to 1876 may be attributed to the downward movement of prices during the interval with farm prices, in particular, declining. We see that real wages again increased from 1880 to 1890. While we are viewing here the average of real wages, it must not be assumed that all labor groups shared the gains of real income equally. Undoubtedly the enormous supply of immigrant labor flooding into the country prevented many of the unskilled workers from gaining as much as the highly skilled craftsmen. We should also remember that a portion of the gains which labor received was shorter hours.

Figure 3 provides us with more reliable information on real wages, money wages, and cost of living movements from 1890.

From 1890 to about 1917 we observe a rather remarkable constancy of real wage levels. While the cost of living was about 38 percent higher in 1913 than in 1896, money wages followed the changes in the consumer price index rather closely. It is likely that real wage rates did not keep

[17] See Alvin H. Hansen, "Factors Affecting the Trend of Real Wages," *American Economic Review*, Vol. 15, No. 1 (March, 1925), p. 32.

pace with the growth of production from 1899 to 1919.[18] Inflation, wartime demands on the national product, and the reduction of the work
week may help explain the relatively stable real income for labor in this
period.

After 1920 real wages increased rather sharply, reflecting increases in
productivity. The mass production technique popularized in the automobile plants was spreading to other industries. Scientific management was

**FIGURE 3. Indexes of Money Wages, Cost of Living, and Real Wages, 1890–1947
1926 = 100**

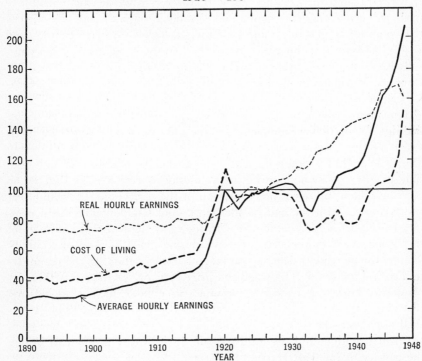

taking hold as an " enlightened " management began applying the laws of
science to industry. New attention was being focused on the optimum
speed of machinery, the location and design of plant, machinery, and tools
as well as the scientific allocation of manpower. Incentive plans became
popular to encourage increased productivity. The growth of labor's real
income undoubtedly diminished hostility between labor and management.
Restrictions on immigration contributed, too, to a tightening of the labor
supply so that the competition of employers for the more limited supply
of workers encouraged upward wage adjustments.

During the depression real wage rates continued to increase, but it was

[18] One indication of the growth of industry during this period can be seen in the fact
that value added by manufacturing increased from $4.6 billion in 1899 to almost $24
billion in 1919. This latter figure is undoubtedly augmented by the postwar inflation.

an increase engendered more by the collapse of prices than by the increase of money rates.

> . . . the great decline in total labor income during the first three and a half years of the depression and the tragic impairment of standards of living was due to the shortening of the working week of those employed and to the tremendous loss of real average earnings per active member of the working class consequent upon widespread unemployment. . . .[19]

It was estimated that, taking the work force as a whole, this unemployment reduced average per capita real earnings enough to wipe out not less than one third — possibly more — of the gain achieved between 1890 and 1930. The turning point came in 1933, when the economy began a painfully slow economic recovery. From 1933 to 1936 real average weekly earnings in manufacturing increased by 18 percent, and real hourly earnings about 16 percent.[20]

The improvement of labor's real wages gained momentum in recent decades. Of particular significance is the increase in real hourly earnings (as in Figure 3) and real weekly earnings (as seen in Table 3) during World War II. This improvement of living standards was only made possible by the enormous increase in production during World War II, an increase which followed the absorption of the reserves of idle manpower and resources with the end of the depression. Undoubtedly union pressure for higher wages, combined with the tight labor market and the fact that prices were supposedly " frozen " during much of the war, contributed to the increase of labor's real income in this period. In the reconversion period the removal of wage and price controls led to the startling expansion of both wages and the consumer price index, the net result being that real wage rates in 1947 were actually below their 1944 level. As we shall note later, this postwar inflation played a critical role in labor management agitation, and the industrial unrest in turn did much to inspire the passage of the Taft-Hartley law.

More accurate data on gross average weekly earnings and net spendable weekly earnings of production workers in manufacturing are provided in Table 3. Here we can trace the effects of taxation on take-home pay as well as the influence of the change in the price level. Gross weekly earnings are deflated by the 1947–1949 base of the consumer price index and by year-by-year changes in the price index relative to this base. We observe that real weekly earnings reached a plateau in 1944 and then remained level or even sagged during postwar inflation. By 1949 real weekly earnings began their upward trend. These figures roughly parallel those

[19] Harry A. Millis and Royal E. Montgomery, *Labor's Progress and Some Basic Labor Problems* (New York, McGraw-Hill Book Co., 1938), p. 117.
[20] Leo Wolman, " The Recovery in Wages and Employment," National Bureau of Economic Research, Bulletin 63, p. 12.

for real hourly earnings. Since 1939, the earnings level per hour of work almost tripled, while the cost of living almost doubled, leaving an increase of real hourly earnings of close to 50 percent.[21]

TABLE 3 Gross Average Weekly Earnings and Net Spendable Weekly Earnings of Production Workers in Manufacturing

(In Current and 1947–1949 Dollars)

Year	Gross Weekly Earnings	Real Weekly Earnings	Net Spendable Average Weekly Earnings			
			Worker with No Dependents		Worker with three Dependents	
			Current Weekly Earnings	Real Weekly Earnings	Current Weekly Earnings	Real Weekly Earnings
1939	$23.86	$40.17	$23.58	$39.70	$23.62	$39.76
1940	25.20	42.07	24.69	41.22	24.95	41.65
1941	29.58	47.03	28.05	44.59	29.28	46.55
1942	36.65	52.58	31.77	45.58	36.28	52.05
1943	43.14	58.30	36.01	48.66	41.39	55.93
1944	46.08	61.28	38.29	50.92	44.06	58.59
1945	44.39	57.72	36.97	48.08	42.74	55.58
1946	43.82	52.54	37.72	45.23	43.20	51.80
1947	49.97	52.32	42.76	44.77	48.24	50.51
1948	54.14	52.67	47.43	46.14	53.17	51.72
1949	54.92	53.95	48.09	47.24	53.83	52.88
1950	59.33	57.71	51.09	49.70	57.21	55.65
1951	64.71	58.30	54.04	48.68	61.28	55.21
1952	67.97	59.89	55.66	49.04	63.62	56.05
1953	71.69	62.67	58.54	51.17	66.58	58.20
1954	71.86	62.60	59.55	51.87	66.78	58.17
1955	76.52	66.82	63.15	55.15	70.45	61.53
1956 (Jan.)	78.55	68.54	64.74	56.49	72.07	62.89

The real weekly earnings above are calculated by dividing the gross weekly wage figure by year-to-year adjustments of the Bureau of Labor Statistics' index of consumer prices. The base for the consumer price index is 1947–1949 = 100. Real weekly earnings are, therefore, actual earnings expressed in terms of constant 1947–1949 dollars.

The Bureau also provides data on "net spendable average weekly earnings," which is the gross weekly earnings less federal social security and income taxes for which the worker is liable. The last four columns above reveal how the differential tax rates affect the actual and real weekly earnings of the worker with no dependents and the worker with three dependents.

Source: Monthly Labor Review Vol. 79, No. 6, (June, 1956), Table C–2 and Table C–3, p. 742.

Changes in the Wage Structure

The single index of money earnings in manufacturing of Figure 3 should not obscure the fact that this over-all average represents highly

[21] For further discussion and data, see Lloyd G. Reynolds and Cynthia H. Taft, *The Evolution of Wage Structure* (New Haven, Yale University Press, 1956), p. 319.

divergent trends of wage movements for particular manufacturing firms. The diversity of the pattern of wage movements has stimulated considerable discussion and controversy, first, as to the actual extent of such dispersion, and, second, on the forces that account for the pattern that has appeared. One might expect an almost random distribution of wage adjustment because of the highly decentralized or fragmentized process of wage determination and the complexity of pressures operating on each wage adjustment process. These pressures have been grouped under two general headings: those which reflect the " administered " decisions of both the company and the union and those reflecting market forces. Within this first group of forces the company may be following a uniform policy for handling wage adjustments and may be tied to the pattern of the community; it may be influenced by the custom or traditions of the firm. It may reflect the " political " pressure on the union leader to secure wage concessions that match those secured by other major unions. These administered forces reflect, in other words, the conscious decisions of collective agencies to shape the wage structure and levels in a predetermined manner. Such policy can only emerge or be of significance where institutions are of sufficient size to implement their decisions. The second or alternative approach is to consider the wage pattern evolving from the pressure of market forces, rather than from administered policy. In effect, the pressures of supply and demand determine the wage rates, for neither the union nor management can " fly in the face " of these forces. This dichotomy is unfortunate, for it is founded on the misleading assumption that decisions made by consolidated groups do not operate *through* supply and demand. In reality, man is a part of nature, and his institutions or groups are integral parts of the market mechanism. Decisions are made, it is true, that cannot always be reconciled with market pressures but the organization of groups does not reflect the aspiration to *ignore* supply and demand. It reflects the simple desire to control, influence, or even " be " the fountain of those pressures.[22]

The major difficulty in reviewing the actual facts of wage structure development is the multiplicity of data that can be analyzed, or more specifically, the multiplicity of comparisons of wage ratios that can be made. In the simplest case we may take one job title and compare the diversity of payments for that job within a given labor market or throughout the country. A third dimension is added by comparing single job-wage diversity through time. The permutations and combinations of ratios increased substantially when one examines the hierarchy of rates for all occupations. The character of interoccupational wage differentials can be

[22] An example of a " conscious " policy decision and the forces of demand and supply co-existing and interreacting is seen in John L. Lewis's statement: " We decided it was better to have a half-million men working in the industry at good wages and high standards of living, than it is to have a million working in the industry in poverty and degradation." Cited by E. R. Wickersham, *Industrial and Labor Relations Review* Vol. 6, No. 4 (July, 1953), p. 601.

measured by establishing the range of pay from low to high, the median or some other average of pay, and the ratio of all job pay to unskilled pay. These structures can, in turn, be compared both spatially and temporarily.

TABLE 4　Comparison of Average Hourly Earnings of Male Unskilled Labor for 1923, 1939, and 1946 and for Production Workers, 1955

Industry	1923		1939		1946		1955	
	Hourly Earnings	Rank	Hourly Earnings	Rank	Hourly Earnings	Rank	Hourly Earnings	Rank
Printing, newspapers and magazines	.540	1	.623	10	1.005	9	2.50	1
Rubber	.522	2	.673	3	1.222	1	2.09	4
Automobile	.496	3	.797	1	1.161	2	2.29	2
Paint and varnish	.494	4	.627	8	.959	11	1.66	15
Iron and steel	.484	5	.638	6	1.080	4	2.02	6
Chemical	.477	6	.694	2	1.082	3	1.99	7
Wool	.470	7	.524	16	.956	12	1.39	17
Foundry and machine shops	.469	8	.629	7	1.068	5	1.98	8.5
Agricultural implements	.450	9	.654	5	1.055	6	2.07	5
Leather and tanning	.442	10	.557	11	.935	15	1.81	13
Paper and pulp	.442	11	.540	13	.939	14	1.94	10
Printing, book and job	.442	12	.543	12	.998	10	2.13	3
Paper products	.435	13	.531	15	.868	19	1.83	12
Electrical manufacturing	.428	14.5	.669	4	1.036	7	1.88	11
Meat packing	.428	14.5	.624	9	1.021	8	1.98	8.5
Cotton (north)	.403	16	.494	17	.890	17	na	
Furniture	.390	17	.536	14	.900	16	1.61	16
Lumber and mill	.369	18	.479	18	.948	13	1.69	14
Boot and shoe	.367	19	.434	20	.577	20	1.35	18
Hosiery and knit goods	.356	20	.458	19	.872	18	1.33	19

Source: Sumner H. Slichter, "Notes on the Structure of Wages," *The Review of Economics and Statistics*, Vol. XXXII, No. 1 (February, 1950), p. 89. These data were derived by Slichter from the National Industrial Conference Board, "Wages and Employment in the United States, 1914–1936," pp. 56–185; *The Conference Board Economic Record*, Vol. II, No. 10 (March 28, 1940), pp. 120–132; *The Conference Board Management Record* (October, 1946), p. 339. Data for 1955 are from the *Monthly Labor Review* and cover production workers rather than male unskilled labor. Descriptions of industrial sectors from 1955 to earlier years are not strictly comparable.

Table 4 reveals one phase of the evolving wage structure. Twenty industries are arranged or ranked in terms of the level of their wage payments in 1923, 1939, 1946, and 1955. The relative positions of one industry's earnings with the others is thus revealed by the changing "rank" that industries have from year to year. What causes this shift of status from year to year? Many factors have a potential influence: First, a strong union may pursue vigorous campaigns for higher labor earnings, although this may in part be minimized by sympathetic wage adjustments in those plants and for those industry sectors hoping to avoid unionization. Second, labor productivity varies tremendously from plant to plant and from year to year, and one might guess that advances in labor's economic status are related to its productivity.[23] Such productivity may give rise to higher profits for management, and these, in turn, may enable management to pay higher wages. A further force may be the degree of concentration of various industries. If an industry is in an imperfectly competitive product market, the discretion it has over price adjustments may enable it to make concessions to labor, with at least a portion of the incidence of these wage concessions being absorbed by the public in higher prices. Or, looking at the opposite side of the coin, the more intensive the competition in the product market, the more likely it is that increase in labor productivity will result in lower product prices rather than higher money wages for labor.[24]

Let us turn from this brief survey of the ranking interindustry wage levels to the dispersion of interoccupational wage structure. When one considers very broad categories first, it appears that manual workers have gained considerably over the white-collar workers. During the depression the relative security of the several salaried occupations did much to enhance the prestige and economic status of the white-collar job, but during World War II a new premium was placed on the services of the man on the production line, the man who could produce those items desperately required for the war effort. This pressure for output created an up-

[23] This has been the thesis advanced by John T. Dunlop (in " Productivity and the Wage Structure," printed as a chapter in *Income, Employment and Public Policy*, New York, W. W. Norton, 1948, pp. 341–362). Dunlop explains: " The inter-industry patterns of changes in average hourly earnings over substantial periods is to be explained fundamentally in terms of the following factors: change in productivity, change in output, proportion of labor costs to total outlays, competitive conditions in the product market, and the changing skill and occupational content of the industry " (p. 360). Sumner Slichter has found (" Notes on the Structure of Wages," *Review of Economics and Statistics*, Vol. XXXII, No. 1, February, 1950, pp. 80–91) positive correlations existed between the ranking of various industries' average hourly earning structure of the male unskilled workers to the value added by manufacturing per man-hour, the value of product per man-hour; the ratio of payrolls to income from sales and the ratio of net income after taxes to sales. These correlations, for the most part, support the Dunlop position. Arthur M. Ross and William Goldner (in a further study of " The Interindustry Wage Structure," *Quarterly Journal of Economics*, Vol. LXIV, No. 2, May, 1950) indicate that " Dunlop's theoretical model is plausible enough, but unfortunately he does not offer much statistical support " for it (p. 256). They stress the influence of unionism and employment on the wage structure. Joseph W. Garbarino follows up Dunlop's analysis with further analysis of correlations of output per man-hour and earnings and concludes that the resulting increase of earnings with labor productivity reflects both the company's ability to pay higher earnings from enlarged output and the more or less automatic adjustments of labor income to productivity when labor operates under incentive systems.

[24] For a statistical analysis of the influence of these several forces, see Garbarino's, and Goldner's, Dunlop's, and Slichter's studies cited above.

heaval in the relative earnings position of the manual worker to the white-collar worker which has not been restored. In 1939 the average annual earnings per full-time employee in finance, insurance, and real estate was 129 percent of the manufacturing average, but by 1950, their earnings had dropped to 99 percent of the manufacturing average.[25] A second major trend for these larger occupational classifications has been the marked lag in farm labor wages. The cataclysmic decline of farm prices and income in the depression resulted in a substantial decline of farm wages. Data suggest that farm wages are about twice as sensitive as manufacturing wages in a depression. This can be explained in part by the return of unemployed workers to the farm for subsistence during the depression and the source of farm labor found in the relatively larger size of farm families, but the drain of farm labor to the cities during World War II did not result in reciprocal farm wage increases.

Occupational wage differences over time have, for the most part, been diminishing. One study of the ratios of the skilled labor wage earnings to unskilled earnings in manufacturing reveals a steady decrease from a median ratio of 205 in 1907 to 155 in 1947.[26]

What forces account for this decline? Again, no single force is at work, and hence no single explanation can account for the movement. Among those which are probably important are (a) the reduction of the swarms of unskilled labor coming into the country arising from the restrictive immigration laws of the twenties. The flood of immigrant labor, largely unskilled, served to depress the lower end of the wage scale. (b) There has been an expansion of educational opportunities and the vertical mobility of the work force. Labor has had unusual opportunities to acquire job skills through the availability of vocational training. Advancement within the labor force may " dry up " candidates for unskilled jobs. The GI Bill program has accelerated the acquisition of job skills and training of the new entrant to the labor force. As such training becomes widespread, a new competitive standard is established for the entire labor force. (c) Many of the new employment opportunities in the age of " automation " do not require the years of apprentice training. The worker on the production line or the machine operator can quickly acquire job skill, and such upward mobility of the work force reduces the availability of unskilled, low-paid labor. (d) The continuing experience of full employment has enabled workers to be much more selective in taking jobs. They can afford to reject those jobs which are arduous, unpleasant, that obviously require little skill. Why take a low-paying job when more interesting jobs can be had at higher pay? Since certain manual jobs must still be performed, employers are often forced to make generous wage

[25] For discussion, see Reynolds and Taft, *op. cit.*, pp. 320–321.
[26] Harry Ober, " Occupational Wage Differentials, 1907–1947," *Monthly Labor Review*, Vol. 67, No. 2 (August, 1948), p. 130.

payments for such labor. (e) A significant effect on the wage structure is the habit of labor to demand flat " across-the-board " wage increases. If a 20-cent per hour wage increase is given to the employee making $1.00 an hour as well as the employee making $2.00 an hour, the percentage increase for each is not the same, and the percentage differential between the two jobs is thereby reduced. The popularity of flat pay increases rather than percentage increases has probably been a dominant force leading to the narrowing of wage differentials. (f) Wage escalation arrangements that provide for uniform cost-of-living adjustments and productivity adjustments also serve to narrow percentage differentials for the same reason that a general or flat wage increase does. (g) Government minimum wage laws can also exert pressure on the lower end of the wage structure.

In summary, there is a tendency for wage differences to be narrowed, especially when the differential is measured by the percentage difference between the low- and high-paying job. Of course, the absolute dollar-and-cent spread between the low- and high-paying job has not disappeared, and in many instances it has actually increased. With a general increase of all wage rates, this absolute differential loses considerable significance. A fifty-cent spread between the $1.00 an hour janitor and $1.50 electrician is much more significant than the fifty-cent spread between the $2.00 janitor and $2.50 an hour electrician.[27]

The role of differentials in the growth of the economy can now be outlined roughly: When a nation begins industrialization, the attraction of high wages are necessary to induce the agricultural labor force into the manufacturing centers. During the phase of industrial growth wage differentials are important in allocating labor to the changing patterns of demand, but their over-all level must be sufficiently low to make possible capital investment. Unions gain general support to protect the living standards of " submarginal groups," and the egalitarian principle gains increasing popularity. As the industrial economy matures, it is again appreciated that the trend toward narrowing differentials has proceeded to dangerous limits; it is undermining the morale of skilled workers and reducing the supply of labor interested in acquiring job skills. Both the unions and employers reappraise the problem and are again willing to offer percentage wage increases in order to restore historic differentials. A cumulative cycle is established, with its origin in the pressure to raise up the lower end of the income scale. This is followed in time with a pressure to maintain traditional wage differentials.[28]

It is often thought that the continuing reality of wage differentials es-

[27] For data on the absolute differences between low- and high-skilled jobs, see Ober's article, cited above. For percentage and absolute increases of straight-time hourly earnings for various time intervals from 1933 and 1946, see Ross and Goldner, *op. cit.*, pp. 264, 268.

[28] An outline similar to this is suggested in Reynolds and Taft, *op. cit.*, pp. 355–356.

tablishes the sterility of classical wage theories. It was the classical presumption that changes in demand would reflect themselves in changes in product prices, sales, profits, and ultimately in the demand and wage for labor. Labor would thus be constantly shifting to those occupations where its pay and productivity could be maximized. While under static conditions this process would continue until wages were more equal, the fact that differentials have persisted hardly disproves such analysis. In a dynamic expanding economy changes in demand usually take place more rapidly than wages and labor mobility can adapt to them. The dog, in effect, never catches up with the waving path of the bicycle. This does not disprove the fact that the dog is chasing the bicycle. Similarly we cannot disprove static classical wage theory by pointing to the dynamic character of economic development.[29]

Endless facets of the wage structure and sources of wage differentials exist. Racial minorities often receive lower pay than other groups. Female employees often receive less than male workers. The young and old worker receive less than the middle-aged worker. Geographical differences also exist, with the South's urban wage level approximately 15 percent below that of the Northeast, and the Northeast's, in turn, approximately 15 percent below that of the Far West's. Small industry generally pays less than large-scale industry. The country employee often receives less than the city worker.

The Share of Wages to National Income

One final measure of labor's material progress is the share of income labor has received. Our investigation of the facts of this problem shall be reserved for Chapter 16, but we can anticipate those results by indicating that over time labor's distributive share has remained amazingly constant. The constancy of this share has induced one labor economist to speak of the twentieth-century " statistical wages fund " concept, to replace the somewhat disreputable wages fund concept of the nineteenth century.[30] It would indeed be surprising if the total complex of forces left the over-all share of labor just about the same year by year and yet this seems to be the case. But the stability of over-all proportions does not indicate stability of the labor share in component industries. Because there are at

[29] Donald E. Cullen uses the gross average annual earnings for the eighteen Census years from 1899 to 1950 to examine the dispersion of the annual earnings structure, and finds a " definite secular stability " in the dispersion of wage differentials. He suggests high profits may lead to a cumulative process of expanding efficiency, research, innovation, higher productivity, and ever-higher wages. See his study, " The Interindustry Wage Structure: 1899–1950," *American Economic Review*, Vol. XLVI, No. 3 (June, 1956), pp. 353–369.

[30] See Martin Bronfenbrenner's excellent discussion: "The Incidence of Collective Bargaining," *American Economic Review*, Vol. XLIV, No. 2 (May, 1954), Papers and Proceedings, p. 295.

least five basic concepts of national income, we have again a series of alternative ratios that can be utilized to reveal the changing share going to labor. Several of these series suggest a slightly upward trend in the distributive share going to labor. This increase in labor's distributive share could be accounted for by:

The "ratchet" effect of declining prices and stable costs. During a depression labor costs are often notoriously sticky, and the collapse of industry prices can force the redistribution of income in labor's favor. But the movement is asymmetrical in the sense that labor does not lose as much of its share in the succeeding prosperity as it lost in the previous recession.

Government price controls and hard money policies. Monetary policy can impose a ceiling on price increases. Should industry face "hard" markets in the sense that consumer spending will not absorb price increases, the pressure of wages will force a redistribution of real income in labor's favor. Periodic intervals of hard money can operate like a rachet as described above to provide for periodic increases of the share going to labor.

Government taxation. Taxation by the government, reflecting the popularity of the majority to "soak the rich," can effect the redistribution of these distributive shares — especially when account is made of the benefits reflected by government services.

Elasticity of substitution. If capital innovations are labor-using rather than labor-saving, the intensification of the investment process may actually increase the proportions of income going to labor rather than decrease it.

The changing structure of the industry. The secular decline of farming activity has reduced the sources of entrepreneurial income, while increasing the volume of wage payments, as ex-farmers take jobs in the city. In 1900 about one third of the labor force was engaged in agriculture and from 1947 to 1951 this proportion was down to 13 percent.

It is also possible to explain the increase in labor's share by looking at those factors accounting for the decline in the volume of payments to other factors. But this would divert our attention from labor.

Summary and Conclusions

Our chapter has revealed that there are diverse concepts and measures of wage payments. Even more diverse is the pattern of wage adjustments. This diversity reflects the high degree of autonomy in the wage bargaining process as well as the unique combinations of factors which can influence each of these "atomized" wage bargaining sessions. A look at the trend of real wage movements reveals that labor has secured genuine improvement in its real income, and while the rate of improvement has been uneven, it has for the most part been upward. Our data suggest that the labor market has " delivered the goods." But, of course, labor's welfare has more than this one wage dimension, and our review of employment trends (or the continuity of the *receipt* of real income) will be taken up in Chapter 22.

Over time, wage differentials have tended to narrow somewhat, although this narrowing process is not common to every industry. A wide variety of differentials exists within the wage structure, reflecting union pressure, varying experiences of labor productivity, industry profits, the degree of competition in the product market, and so on. Actually, the unskilled worker has received percentage increases in his wage rate that are much more substantial than those being paid to the highly skilled worker. The narrowing of such differentials complicates the recruitment problem of industry for skilled workers.

The pattern of wage adjustments has had a profound influence on the outlook of the American worker, and as one might suspect, many laborers feel they have a vested interest in both their job and the capitalist structure. In Chapter 1 we reviewed the growth of the market economy and some of the problems such organization posed for the worker in the marketing of his labor service. In Chapter 2 we reviewed the growth of this market in America, with particular focus on the labor supply side of that market. In this chapter we have stressed the substantial but diverse improvement in labor's material status. In our following chapter we shall attempt to gain some insight into the social and psychological aspects of the work force.

It is the attitude of the individual worker that accounts for the movement of these aggregate statistics. Let us turn to those more nebulous attitudes which give the labor " mass " its velocity.

4

The Worker and the
Working Class

The interreactions of changing ideas and institutions have produced the labor class as we know it today. In this chapter we shall turn from the institutional aspects of the labor market and review briefly the socio-economic profile of the work force itself. The attitudes and perspectives of labor represent the hard core of the labor problem. As Rexford G. Tugwell once explained:

> The attempt to direct the economic system toward human welfare without understanding human nature would be quite as futile as the attempt to cure disease without a preliminary study of physiology, or to do — what no skilled worker will defend — work in any material without an intimate understanding of its composition, its workability, and its amenability to different modes of manipulation . . . The economists' obligations to understand the substance and workability of the endowments and capacities of men is correspondingly heavy. . . .[1]

Clearly any analysis of the economics of the labor market would be incomplete without a study of labor's propensities, instincts, and impulses.

We shall address ourselves to the following questions: What institutional and psychological factors have encouraged and discouraged the development of a labor class consciousness? In what way is a class consciousness the outgrowth of institutional conditions or simply the perception of groups of people of their own status? What is the communist view of the class structure, and how does it contrast with the democratic view? What institutional factors have contributed to the fluidity of the American class structure? What types of classes exist in America?

Following our discussion of the class structure, we shall turn to the individual worker and examine briefly his motivations. For what does the individual worker strive? How important is money to him? What are his basic occupational " likes " and " dislikes "? But we cannot consider the worker only as an individual. No man in our society is an island, and no

[1] Rexford G. Tugwell, "Human Nature in Economic Theory," *Journal of Political Economy*, Vol. 30, No. 3 (June, 1922), p. 344.

worker can be isolated from the mores of the work force. Therefore, we shall conclude the discussion of this chapter with a brief appraisal of the impact that group organization has on the individual, first from an economic viewpoint and then from a psychological or behavioral viewpoint. The tendency toward collectivism or "groupism" has genuine psychological and social foundations as well as economic justification. This analysis will provide the logical point of departure for the next Section of this text: the growth of the union movement.

The Growth of Class Consciousness

The word "class" in our vocabulary has almost subversive connotations, for it was Karl Marx who dramatically described the division of society into two warring camps: the bourgeoisie and the proletariat. To Marx this division inexorably followed capitalist development. The capitalists owned the means of production, while workers had only their labor service to offer in exchange for their subsistence wages. Marx held that the wider use of machinery would reduce the number of workers that could be profitably employed. And as the wage bill became an ever smaller portion of the total product, labor's misery and poverty would increase. Such poverty would condition a class consciousness, and this would spark the revolution, culminating ultimately in the dictatorship of the proletariat. It is not surprising that some workers living in poverty — feeling helplessly and hopelessly trapped by market forces — are so willing to believe they are the victims of the inexorable laws of capitalist development. It is also not surprising that many students of labor history have pondered the development of class consciousness in America to determine to what extent, if any, this dramatic thesis may have some validity. As the late Joseph Schumpeter observed, the economist finds it exceedingly difficult to "resist the temptation to enliven his presentation with something that fascinates most of his readers — in other words, to stoke his sputtering engine with the potent fuel of the class struggle." [2]

We have already related the personal contact between apprentice, journeyman and master craftsman in the production process of a preindustrial society. In the handicraft stage of economic development, pride in the skill of manual labor provided a vital satisfaction to workers. Even in the later "putting-out" system, the producing unit was an integrated whole, providing stability and status to each worker. The corroding effects of industrial change have already been mentioned in Chapter 1. The widening of markets and the intensification of competi-

[2] From his *Imperialism and Social Classes* (Village Station, N. Y., August M. Kelley, 1951), p. 138 and cited in part in *Class, Status and Power: a Reader in Social Stratification*. Edited by Reinhard Bendix and Seymour Martin Lipset (Glencoe, Ill., The Free Press, 1953), p. 76.

tion made possible the specialization of labor and an enormous increase in productivity. But the individual worker became inextricably entangled in an industrial mechanism over which he had no control. He acquired an impersonal "cog" status. He was, in effect, a badly designed single-purpose machine. Specialization required exchange in the monetary sense and the instability of the exchange process (or if you will, wide fluctuations in total spending) revealed how intimately each worker's material welfare was dependent upon impersonal market forces.

When the gears of the industrial mechanism were smoothly meshing, its productivity was prodigious, and each worker adjusted to the new monotony of the machine age, comforted by the improvements of his material status that it made possible. It was only when the machine ground to a standstill that individuals fully sensed their helplessness. The reduction in the size of the total product, together with the complete interruption of the share which had previously gone to the now unemployed, provoked a re-examination of the new industrial relationships.

Prior to 1930, the study of the class structure in America had been largely neglected. Management had proven its ability to deliver the goods and capitalism had "taken care" of labor. As sociologist Daniel Bell points out:

> The temporary victory of one group, the business class, at the end of the 19th century, brought with it an attempt to identify democracy with the narrower category of "free enterprise." But the depression broke the crust of ideological unity and revealed the manifold conflicts beneath.[3]

The depression of the thirties, then, created new antagonisms. Labor resented its unemployment and the indignity of the fruitless search for employment. These frustrations induced a new "labor class" consciousness. Unwilling to accept the blame itself for its frightful economic plight, labor projected the blame to other "classes." While the shadow of Marx's thesis lurked in the background, sociologists approached the work force with some novel questions: "Do you feel there is a rich class and a poor class in America?" "To which class in America do you belong?" The responses revealed a unique consciousness in America — not simple proletariat and bourgeois groupings, but a class structure much more complex and subtle than Marx had postulated.

Class as Subjective or Objective Reality

It goes without saying that the United States — like all other societies — is made up of individuals. But the complex interdependence of individuals in a highly developed capitalist society prevents them from assert-

[3] "America's Unmarxist Revolution," *Commentary* (March, 1949), p. 209.

ing any effective degree of economic isolationism. Economic philosophy notwithstanding, the American economy is probably more accurately described as a group economy than one characterized by individualism.[4] At best, we might say our economy is characterized by individualistic groups.

One popular approach to classes in our society is to group its citizens in terms of some measurable standard, such as occupation or income. Since stratification is inherent in any society characterized by a division of labor, the distinctions of task and reward provide a useful basis for measuring the existence of classes. The existence of stratification does not, in itself, prove an awareness of those distinctions or the development of a class consciousness. Thus it must be remembered that a class structure is not revealed by institutional stratification alone, but by the perceptions individuals have about class. Class structure, in the final analysis, is what people *think* it is, not what occupational and income distributions might suggest. Thus, a complementary approach is to define class only in terms of the subjective identifications of the work force itself. This subjective development of a class consciousness is more likely to arise where a group enjoys a common heritage, has a sense of identification to a common cause, when individuals have a sense of belonging to the group, and above all, a common awareness of the necessity of group membership. More often than not, the cohesive influence is the existence of some challenge to that group, or its members.

Two further observations suggest the importance of the distinction between class as an objective and subjective reality. First, the *objective* determination of class stratifications often concentrates on the status individuals have in the *production* of goods and services. Is the hod-carrier in the same " class " as the banker? The *subjective* determination of class structure on the other hand, is often perceived by viewing the *distribution* of income. Usually, but not always, the person with considerable objective status in the production process is able to enjoy the reinforcing status of high income from the distribution process. Thus the level of money income is a critical benchmark for determining status or class alignment.[5] Second, the communist will argue that the classless society

---

[4] The concept of a power-bloc economy has gained increasing popularity in recent times. See, for example, John K. Galbraith, *American Capitalism: The Concept of Countervailing Power* (Boston, Houghton Mifflin Co., 1952). J. B. S. Hardman also suggests that ". . . we have become a nation of substantial groups of the citizenry, each identified and practically unified by 'clear and present' special interests and desirous of having those interests realized . . . and the Nation is really becoming ever more a confederation of power blocs, contending, coalescing, cooperating, making war or peace with one another as the case may be." From his " The Power Motivations of the American Labor Movement," *Monthly Labor Review*, Vol. 76, No. 3 (March, 1953), p. 260.

[5] For related discussion, see Max Weber: *Essays in Sociology*, translated by H. H. Gerth and C. Wright Mills (New York, Oxford University Press, 1946), pp. 180–195. Talcott Parsons has suggested that money is the measuring rod for success: " Like office, its primary significance is as a symbol of achievement. But it owes its special

will ultimately be achieved when the subjective foundations for class consciousness are eliminated. The tasks in their classless society will still be dissimilar, but the distribution of the product in terms of " need " is presumed to eliminate any perception of class and, in turn, any need for class conflict. The democrat, on the other hand, will argue that American society is classless because income is not an important or single determinant of status. As T. H. Marshall explains, " It follows that there are two main roads to the classless society. One leads through the abolition (as far as possible) of the social differences between individuals – which is roughly the way of communism – and the other proceeds by rendering all differences irrelevant to social status – which is roughly the way of democracy." [6]

In summary, people work at different jobs for different incomes. The sociopsychological interpretation given to these inequalities reflects the degree of our class consciousness. Let us examine some of the conditioning forces of class consciousness in America.

Horatio Alger and the Open-End Class Structure

The American is often pictured as an individualist, a democrat, being both egalitarian and utilitarian. He lacks the heritage of feudalism and serfdom of Europe. The unexplored opportunities of the American West encouraged all Americans to believe in the equal opportunity for success. As early as the 1820's, Hegel observed that the firm demarcation of classes did not exist in America " for it has the outlet of colonization constantly and widely open, and multitudes are continually streaming into the plains of the Mississippi. By this means the chief source of discontent is removed. . . ." [7] In 1893 Frederick Jackson Turner advanced his famous thesis that the territories of the West served as a safety valve for industrial unrest and prevented the consolidation of classes in the East:

> Whenever social conditions tended to crystallize in the East, whenever capital tended to press upon labor, or political restraints to impede the freedom of the mass, there was this gate of escape to the free conditions of the frontier. . . . Men would not accept inferior wages

prominence in that respect to certain peculiar features of our social system. . . . The measures of achievement are technical and specific for each particular field. Hence it is difficult to make comparisons . . . except in money. . . . There is an income hierarchy which, on the whole, corresponds to that of direct valuation. . . . Furthermore, within any particular group, it is fairly adequate as a criterion, since the more highly valued jobs are also the best paid jobs." From his " An Analytical Approach to the Theory of Social Stratification," *The American Journal of Sociology,* Vol. XLV, No. 6 (May, 1940), p. 857.

[6] *The Nature of Class Conflict,* edited by T. H. Marshall (Ledbury, Eng., Institute of Sociology, Le Play House, 1938), p. 98.

[7] As cited by Louis M. Hacker, *The Triumph of American Capitalism* (New York, Columbia University Press, 1947), p. 201.

and a permanent position of social subordination when this promised land of freedom and equality was their for the taking. . . .[8]

But more than the frontier contributed to the fluidity of the American class structure. The flood of immigration created new demands that had to be satisfied by immediate industrial expansion. A premium was placed on the person who could produce rather than on the one who could boast of title and background. The spiraling expansion of demand (together with its constant shifts) had its counterpart in the scramble of men to mobilize American resources. Our industrial history could be characterized as a game of musical chairs, with the participants being added along with more chairs, but both in uncertain amounts. The music occasionally stopped, but the resulting hardships simply induced an even greater resolve and effort for success.

Probably one of the most unusual manifestations of this unique philosophy was the widespread popularity of the 135 novels written by Horatio Alger. The popularity of these novels reveals the extent to which the American public in the late nineteenth century was hypnotized by optimism. Interestingly enough, these novels in their original form were not about the industrious slum child pitted against the adversity of the city and raising himself by his bootstraps through hard work. Rather the hero was usually a farm boy who, after the death of his father (and with his mother and family to support), travels to the city for employment. The privations and low wages prevent escape from his humble lot, in spite of his unbelievable Puritan virtues of hard work and thrift, but success is reached — by some accident — as he saves the infant being dragged to certain destruction behind wild horses or rescues the child drowning in the bay. The rich parents offer the young hero a better job and success seems assured for the future. These novels reflected the " rags to riches " prospects which fired the imagination of their 50 million readers. To be cynical about the opportunities of achieving success in America through hard work was about equivalent to doubting the existence of God. As the early American economist, Richard T. Ely explained:

> If you tell a single concrete workman on the Baltimore and Ohio Railroad that he may yet be president of the company, it is not demonstrable that you have told him what is not true, although it is within bounds to say that he is far more likely to be killed by a stroke of lightning. . . .[9]

The flood of immigrant labor added to the opportunity for vertical mobility, for the native American was better able to bid for advancement

---

[8] As cited by Hacker, *ibid.*, p. 201.
[9] As quoted by R. Richard Wohl, " The 'Rags to Riches Story': An Episode of Secular Idealism," in *Class, Status and Power*, edited by Reinhard Bendix and Seymour Martin Lipset (Glencoe, Ill., *The Free Press*, 1953), p. 393.

than the relatively unskilled immigrant. Paradoxical as it may seem, when the torrent of immigration was later reduced to a small trickle, the scarcity of labor also encouraged the upgrading and promotion of labor. In a similar way the comparative differential infertility of the wealthy created a social and economic vacuum which enabled the skilled and gifted children of the manualist class to bid successfully for promotions. One of the most significant factors contributing to the prospects of vertical mobility has been the availability of public education (and in more recent times the wider opportunities for college training) for millions of children. Parents often shift the unfilled expectations of their own lives to their children. Rather than grieve over their own disappointments, they are more often determined to give their children the opportunities for success that they lacked. This "equality of opportunity" arising from extended higher education facilities has done as much in the twentieth century to reduce class consciousness as the availability of land did in the nineteenth century.

Some Data on the Class Structure

Since classes reflect what people think about their interpersonal relationships and status, what standards are utilized to determine membership in various classes? In one study of 95 unionists in the textile town of Paterson, New Jersey, the respondents mentioned money and wealth twice as many times as all the other factors put together, and over three times as much as the next most important factor, "occupation." [10] Interestingly enough, about half of these workers classified themselves as members of the "working" class, about 22 percent as members of the "middle" class, and only about 13 percent as members of the "poor" class. About one third felt that class inequalities were increasing, while one half felt they were decreasing. These responses, it must be remembered, are from union members.

The various studies undertaken often reveal that the type of response varies with the status of the respondent. For example, it is generally found that the lower-income groups place much more stress on money as a criterion of class membership, while those groups with money stress family and education.[11] The fact that different groups in our society offer different responses suggests, too, the importance of defining one's status and prospects realistically. If the very low-income group constantly aspires to a substantial increase of income which is never realized, the continuing experience of failure may prove dangerous psychologically and

[10] J. G. Manis and B. N. Meltzer, "Attitudes of Textile Workers to Class Structure," *The American Journal of Sociology*, Vol. LX, No. 1 (July, 1954), Table 2, p. 32.

[11] For detailed discussion, see Richard Centers, *The Psychology of Social Classes: A Study of Class Consciousness* (Princeton, Princeton University Press, 1949), Chapter 6.

socially. Thus, those on the lower end of the occupational scale are likely to have much more moderate aspirations for future success, to consider their prospects of vertical mobility limited, to anticipate only modest improvement of their pay, and so on.[12]

In Richard Centers' study, he gave his sample four alternative classes to designate as their own. These were (1) upper class, (2) middle class, (3) working class, and (4) lower class. Over half of the respondents identified themselves with the working class and 43 percent with the middle class. Only 3 percent considered themselves members of the upper class and 1 percent members of the lower class.[13] We see then that the bulk of the American public considers itself to be neither rich nor poor, although the predominance of the "working class" identification runs counter to other studies which had dramatized the "middle class" consciousness of the American public.[14]

In more recent times the technological revolution has required the expansion of a new middle class, a group with semiprofessional and professional job responsibilities. This group is the fastest growing within our class structure and includes such occupations as clerical employees, technical engineers, technicians, a wide variety of professions, and a substantial number of white-collar workers. This middle class serves as a bulwark against the polarization of the class structure. Many members of this class have one foot in the camp of management and the other in the working class. For the most part they are hostile to the idea of union membership because of their conviction that they enjoy certain prospects for advancement.

In summary, it would appear that the American worker is class con-

[12] This same pattern is often passed from the parent to the children, so that children of poor parents, too, have much more modest goals than those coming from, say, professional families. For example, the college student coming from a professional family is likely to have much more optimistic plans for the future, as well as higher predictions for his earnings potential than the student from a "lower" class family. Furthermore, the former student is much more likely to "live dangerously," to adopt an "all or nothing" attitude in the struggle for economic success, while the latter is more likely to place a premium on security.

[13] *Op. cit.*, p. 77.

[14] In a more modest study undertaken by Seymour Lipset and Joan Gordon, an attempt was made to determine some of the differences between the union and non-union members' attitudes toward society. It was found that where the father was engaged in a manual occupation, the sons were much more likely to be union members than nonunion members. If the son was engaged in a job requiring the same degree of skill as his father, he was more likely to become an active union member. Similarly, membership in the union varied directly with the total proportion of the job career spent in manual occupations. It was also found that the union member had less faith than the nonunion respondent in his ability to hold his job should a depression develop. While this was not a national survey, it suggests that the continuing experience of a manual occupation, especially if passed down from father to son, leads to union membership. The nonunionist is more likely to demonstrate middle-class values, while the unionist will possess a working-class viewpoint. "Mobility and Trade Union Membership," appearing in *Class, Status and Power, op. cit.*, pp. 491-500.

scious but not in the sense suggested by Marx. Marx's class consciousness often arises from the realization of individuals that their ability to advance out of their own class is very limited. Interpreting such possibilities realistically is vital for the stability and mental health of the individual, for it avoids constant disappointment and frustration. Of course, many rationalizations are offered for inequalities. Many low-income people feel: "Most wealthy people happened to be born to their desirable estate; others happened to stumble on good fortune, as witlessly as the child in the fairy story stumbles on a pot of gold." [15] These economic indexes of income and wealth are usually related to occupational status, and money is an important measuring stick of class status. But most consider that income differentials are necessary economically, and many still entertain the hope that they — or their children — will enjoy an improved economic status in the future. Similarly, inequality is seen as a necessary device to encourage or motivate people to work. One worker put it this way: "The people who have money own business and the rest of the people work for them. If there were no rich people, whom would the poor people work for?" [16] And when a group of 95 unionists were asked whether they regarded the class structure as permanent in America, 53 said it was "inevitable and desirable" while only 18 said it was "inevitable and undesirable." We conclude that Marx has been found wrong, not alone because of the substantial improvement of working-class living standards, but because labor in America does not perceive itself to be exploited by any "anti-working class bourgeois dictatorship." As one economist put it, Marx knew that the American worker would have problems, but what he did not know is that these would be "parking" problems.

We have suggested that money provides a vital measuring stick for class status in America. Our analysis will now examine the role of money and the motivations of the individual worker.

Money and Worker Motivations

Economics is defined as the "wealth-getting" and "wealth-consuming" activities of man. The bulk of all economic analysis is rooted in the assumption of income maximization and the corollary assumption that acquisitive impulses are capable of providing substantial benefits to all of society.[17] Since the worker is a part of this economic universe, he too, is assumed to have a strong impulse to get ahead. This maximizing prin-

[15] Katherine Archibald, *Wartime Shipyard* (Berkeley, University of California Press, 1947) and reproduced in part in *Class, Status and Power, op. cit.*, p. 401.
[16] Manis and Meltzer, *op. cit.*, p. 35.
[17] For an interesting account of the origins of these concepts, see Alfred F. Chalk, "Natural Law and the Rise of Economic Individualism in England," *The Journal of Political Economy*, Vol. LIX, No. 4 (August, 1951), pp. 332–347.

ciple as a human trait has, in recent times, come under attack. First, it is argued that acquisitive norms have been "induced" and are not the "natural" or native impulses of man. Second, some studies appear to show that reliance on financial incentives generally releases but a small fraction of the energy of the worker. Third, the worker is more se-curity conscious than wage conscious, and this is taken as proof of his relative disinterest in money and acquisitive goals. Evidence is offered, too, that the individual worker in reality is more concerned about main-taining his status and prestige in the group than maximizing his money income. Let us review the merit of each of these arguments briefly.

Is Acquisitiveness a Natural or Acquired Instinct? It is undoubt-edly true that our behavior is conditioned by society's expectations that individuals be successful in a pecuniary sense, but it is difficult to refute the charge that these are "unnatural" values and that the individual is unnatural in responding to them. The argument against acquisitiveness as an inborn impulse is put in its simplest form by William F. Whyte, who explains: "Man is not born loving money. He has to learn to love it. This learning takes place in varying degrees in various parts of the world . . . in our society too, the response to money is a learned re-sponse; nor is it uniform. . . ."[18] To Whyte, even the employer is trapped by society's expectations that he behave in an acquisitive manner.

> According to the folklore or economics, the American businessman is a single-minded individual motivated almost exclusively by his desire to make a profit. Anyone who seeks to explain the behavior of the businessman in those terms will go hopelessly off the track. As we see him, the businessman while much interested in profit making is also a man of strong "moral" sentiments . . . . he has very strong feel-ings about the "right" and "wrong" ways of behaving and these feelings are only incidentally connected with profit making. On vari-ous occasions in our research we have observed executives who are quite willing to take economic losses in order to uphold a moral posi-tion in which they believe. Of course, this position is rationalized as being necessary for a greater economic gain *in the long run*. But this should not mislead us. In our culture, the businessman feels compelled to justify his behavior in terms of economic logics even when those logics have little to do with the factors that gave rise to the behavior.[19]

To Whyte, the employer is more concerned about being "right" than being "rich." It is doubtful, however, that this dichotomy produces a split personality in the employer, for the Protestant ethic has enabled many employers to point to their pecuniary successes as evidence of their moral and righteous behavior.

[18] From *Money and Motivation, An Analysis of Incentives in Industry* (New York, Harper & Bros., 1955), p. 210.

[19] "Semantics and Industrial Relations," *Human Organization*, Vol. 8, No. 2 (Spring, 1949), p. 4.

It is true, however, that in many of the so-called " backward areas," a wage increase for native workers often results in the labor force working fewer hours. This does not disprove the acquisitive nature of man in a native state, for often such people are not aware of the variety of goods that can be acquired by the use of money. Without developed markets they are not aware how additional funds can advance their material living standard.[20]

The anthropological studies of primitive communities offer inconclusive evidence on whether man is, in " raw nature," more acquisitive than cooperative, more selfish than generous. Neither a clear capitalistic or communistic pattern is uniformly revealed.[21] It is true that many native tribes share their wealth equally. One obvious reason for such equality is that very often there is little income to be distributed, and most tribes operate on the principle that a minimum of subsistence should be available to all members of their community. In many tribes the generosity of the wealthy member was not without ulterior motive. The ability of any individual to be generous was often a measure of his personal accomplishment and dignity, and in many instances those who received gifts were under tremendous pressure to reciprocate by giving even more to the donor. Thus " giving " rather than " getting " has been an important motive for the activity of native tribes. Frequently, though, it appears that the giving was motivated by a greed for prestige rather than a charitable impulse. Even in our own society a great deal of the acquisitiveness of man is justified in terms of the generous distribution of income made by wealthy philanthropists. The model of the economic man does not preclude this generous impulse. The act of philanthropy does not,

[20] This point is developed by Wilbert E. Moore, *Industrialization and Labor* (Ithaca, N. Y., Cornell University Press, 1951). In his paper, "Labor Attitudes Toward Industrialization in Underdeveloped Countries," Moore explains: " The effectiveness of wage incentives is relative to the availability of goods and services in the market that form part of the effective wants of workers. This is essentially a common-sense static principle. But it is quite limiting, and failure to recognize it accounts for some of the exasperation of observers of 'irrational' natives. The worker in an undeveloped area is typically not accustomed to expect, or even to aspire to, any considerable raising of ceilings on his consumption and social position. And there are many wants typically not satisfiable by market mechanisms. So we have both limited demand and limited supply." *American Economic Review, Proceedings*, Vol. XLV, No. 2 (May, 1955), pp. 162–163.

[21] Paul Einzig, in his study *Primitive Money* (London, Eyre and Spootiswoode, 1949) suggests that many primitive tribes displayed both a communist and capitalist impulse. He writes, " laisser-faire does not truly represent the primitive character. The fact is that the predominant majority of primitive communities had controlled economies and savages were found to be guided by self-interest to a much less degree than modern men. . . . [p. 28] . . . on the other hand . . . what is often loosely described as original Communism very often amounted in reality to ownership by the chief of the tribe and not common ownership by members of the tribe. Indeed, while in many instances the prevailing system in primitive communities is distinctly Communistic, in other instances private ownership is carried to extremes unknown in the most highly individualistic modern communities . . ." (p. 29).

in itself, prove that the individual is not motivated by competitive behavior to *acquire* that wealth.[22]

Is the Financial Incentive the Most Important? The second criticism — financial incentives fail to release but a small portion of labor's energy — contains a degree of truth, but it does not disprove the thesis that such incentives may still be the strongest single positive inducement to labor in our society.[23] The argument is usually rooted in the examination of workers operating under a wage incentive system. The work group holds production to that level where they are able to enjoy " expected " premiums. If individual earnings are out of line, this will indicate loose rates have been set and encourage management to develop some engineering pretext to restudy the job and set a tighter rate. As a consequence of this experience, the worker realizes that earnings must be kept in line. The individual in this situation must either go along with the group norm or face ostracism. The fact that such a norm exists, and that usually all workers conform to it, does not however disprove the general interest of all labor in making more money. What happens in fact is that workers, with uncanny intelligence, determine what can be safely earned without upsetting the rate structure. The effort to keep earnings within these limits simply reflects the drive to maximize income in the long run rather than indulge in a short-run money grab. In other words, maximum effort and productivity today may not lead to maximum income tomorrow. Thus, while certain individuals could increase their earnings today by increasing their output, the fact that rate busters are the exception rather than the rule does not discredit but rather reinforces the arguments for acquisitiveness of the labor force. It is certainly misleading to conclude, as does William F. Whyte, that ". . . the theory on which the whole incentive program is based [acquisitiveness] apparently applies only to a small fraction [the rate busters] of the population. . . ."[24] The key to workers' behavior is indicated by William Gomberg:

[22] Lionel Robbins, in his defense of the " economic man," complains of the narrow misconceptions held of the economic man's behavior: " The general absurdity of the belief that the world contemplated by the economist is peopled only by egotists or 'pleasure machines' should be sufficiently clear from what has been said already. . . . So far as we [the economists] are concerned, our economic subjects can be pure egotists, pure altruists, pure ascetics, pure sensualists or — what is much more likely — mixed bundles of all these impulses." From *An Essay on the Nature and Significance of Economic Science*, 2d ed. (New York, The Macmillan Co., 1940), pp. 94, 95, 97.

[23] As J. N. Keynes explans: " For while it is true that our economic activities are subject to the influence of a variety of motives, which sometimes strengthen and sometimes counteract one another, it is also true that in economic affairs the desire for wealth exerts a more uniform and an indefinitely stronger influence amongst men taken in the mass than any other single motive." From his *Scope and Method of Political Economy* (London, Macmillan and Co., 1891), p. 115.

[24] From *Money and Motivation* (New York, Harper & Bros., 1955), p. 212.

The important thing to remember in this connection . . . is the fact
that the workers soon grasped the secret that the fundamental purpose
of the wage incentive payment plan was not to encourage labor's unrestrained productivity but to keep the engineer's plan in balance!
For the record shows that the workers adjusted their future production to match the wage design that the company wanted. . . .[25]

Is Security Rated Higher Than Increased Income? The third criticism against the pecuniary interests of labor is the charge that labor is
more interested in security than high wages. Again, however, this tends
to support rather than disprove the importance of income to labor. It is
true that many of the studies of worker goals reveal their primary interest in security. In Lloyd Reynolds' study, *The Structure of Labor Markets,* he confronted one sample of workers with the following question: [26]

> " Suppose you had a choice on your present job of getting a wage in-
> crease or getting a guarantee of steady work throughout the year;
> which would you take? " Several possible amounts of wage increases
> were then mentioned by the interviewer in an attempt to determine
> the worker's " point of indifference." Fifty per cent of the workers
> replied that they would take the guarantee of steady employment
> under any circumstances. An additional 23 per cent said that they
> would take the employment guarantee unless the wage increase was
> very large, i.e., 25 to 100 per cent above their present wage. The re-
> maining 27 per cent said that they would prefer the wage increase.

In January, 1947, *Fortune* magazine conducted a survey of men to determine how security conscious they were. The results appear on page 89.
The tabulations presented do not discredit the income maximizing principle. Rather they are quite consistent with it. Income is not a static concept, but a flow. The appraisal of the value of any job depends in large
part on the future *flow* of revenues anticipated from that job. Obviously
any insecurity or possibility of interruptions in the flow of income will
radically affect the present value of that income stream.

**Does the Worker Value Approval by His Group Above Increased
Income?** The final criticism — that the individual is more concerned with
his group membership and status — than his income level is, in part, dealt
with by our previous analysis of the class structure of America. As Whyte
again explains the argument: " Offer them [labor] a financial reward
for behavior that damages their relations with other men, and you can
hardly expect them to respond with enthusiasm." [27] This argument too

---

[25] *A Trade Union Analysis of Time Study* (Chicago, Science Research Associates,
1948), pp. 181–182.
[26] (New York, Harper & Bros., 1951), p. 86.
[27] William F. Whyte, "Economic Incentives and Human Relations," *Harvard Business Review,* Vol. 30, No. 2 (March–April, 1952), p. 73.

Question: Here are three different kinds of jobs. If you had your choice, which would you pick?

Type of Job	Total	Profes- sionals, Executives	Salaried Employees	Factory Workers	Union Members
	percent	percent	percent	percent	percent
A job which pays quite a low income but which you are sure of keeping	48.2	25.5	42.3	59.9	56.0
A job which pays a good income but which you have a fifty-fifty chance of losing	22.8	32.0	27.3	20.9	23.7
A job which pays an extremely high income if you make the grade but in which you lose almost everything if you don't make it	23.8	35.5	26.8	16.9	17.8
Don't know	5.2	7.0	3.6	2.3	2.5

contains an element of truth, for we must certainly disbelieve Pinkerton's boast that he could hire one half of the labor force to destroy the other half. There are limits to which labor and unions will not go in their drives to maximize labor income — even though many a company official at collective bargaining sessions has often wondered just where that limit might be. But high income, more often than not, tends to reinforce one's prestige and social status, and the values of society have been sufficiently molded to the acquisitive drives so that neither labor nor employers often have to apologize or have a guilt complex about economic success.

In summary, we cannot agree with Whyte's observation that "The economic man theory has been so thoroughly discredited through research that it would be tedious to go over that ground again." [28] The worker is acquisitive and desires high income not only today, but a high and constant stream of income for the future. He may protest that he does not like money — only his wife does — but his interest in getting " more " cannot be lightly dismissed. The enthusiasm of most American labor to work overtime, and even to take a second job, reveals the force behind this drive to improve one's material status. The worker is not readily deflected from such a drive by such philosophical observations as T. N. Whitehead's that "It is only in a sick society that satisfaction is measured

[28] "Organization and Motivation of Management," *Industrial Productivity*, Industrial Relations Research Association (December, 1951), p. 101.

in terms of money and purposeful activity is counted a disutility." [29] Workers will often reply to this: "You can't buy money with happiness."

Our discussion has indicated the important influence that the labor group can have over the behavior of the individual worker. Let us review briefly some of the more important facets of individual-group relationships.

The Group: Its Social and Psychological Significance to the Individual

Many of the economic problems of the labor market reflect themselves in the psychological and social considerations confronting the worker. Thus, the relationship of the worker to the group — and his response to group pressures — is the focal point of industrial sociology and psychology.

The individual worker may not fear failure itself so much as the loss of status in the eyes of his community associated with that failure. He must above all measure up to the expectations of those about him in order to win their continuing devotion, support, and respect. As Erich Fromm explains:

> Since man cannot live doubting his identity, he must, in the marketing orientation, find the conflict of identity not in preference to himself and his powers but in the opinion of others about him. His prestige, status, success, the fact that he is known to others as being a certain person are a substitute for the genuine feeling of identity. This situation makes him utterly dependent on the way others look at him and forces him to keep up the role in which he once had become successful.[30]

Because of this pressure, the individual worker is likely to be, in a very real sense, what those around him expect him to be. This desire to conform to the expectations of those around him will be particularly strong if the individual feels that he could not succeed " on his own " in the market place. This need for approval represents one of the most important sources of support and power for the union movement. The union will often presume to represent or mirror all worker attitudes. To reject membership in the union is tantamount to rejecting the association of your co-workers. The pressure that group sentiment has over the individual can hardly be exaggerated, and it provides us with clues to much

[29] "Human Relations Within Industrial Groups," *Harvard Business Review*, Vol. 14, No. 1 (1935), p. 1.

[30] Quotation taken from Karl de Schweinitz and Kenneth W. Thompson, *Man and Modern Society, Conflict and Choice in the Industrial Era* (New York, Henry Holt and Co., 1953), p. 384.

of labor's behavior. One student of the labor problem, working along with workers, testified:

> It is to be confessed that as a laborer I became a fairly expert loafer — that on many jobs, here and abroad, *the longer I worked, the less I did!* The more skilled I grew as a craftsman, the more efficient I became as a dissembler, expert in giving the *appearance* of diligence without delivering the actuality thereof. The reason was that by no other way could comradeship with the others be obtained — and such comradeship was essential to the purpose in hand. To get close to them every newcomer had, willy-nilly, to obey the whispered admonitions — yes, the threats — which kept coming until he finally slowed down to a rate which made motion all but invisible! [31]

The struggle to be accepted as " one of the gang " has grown rapidly. In David Riesman's analysis the individual may be classified as either " inner-directed " or " other-directed." The essential difference of these two types is that the inner-directed person lives by internal values and goals even though by doing so he may not enjoy the approval of all society, the community or the work force of which he may be a member.[32] The " other-directed " person, much more common today, seeks comfort through his acceptance by others, but he finds that such acceptance is possible only through his willingness to conform to the values of the group. The stress of much popular education today is in adjustment, of peaceful coexistence, of compromise or blending in with the group. Such analysis helps us to understand labor union relations. A hard core of unionized workers usually can exert enough pressure on new workers to encourage their union participation. The new worker, insecure in his role within the social system of the plant, may hope that by joining the union he can increase his acceptance, status, and security with his fellow workers.

As a capstone to our discussion of class structure, individualism and " groupism," let us briefly catalogue some of the major " dislikes " and

[31] Whiting Williams, *Mainsprings of Men* (New York, Charles Scribner's Sons, 1925), p. 114.

[32] The inner-directed man, according to Riesman, takes the view that while others cannot protect him against self-criticism, self-criticism can protect him against others. He is job-minded and work conscious, dedicated to the proposition that through hard work one can succeed. The more usual " other-directed " man is people- rather than work-minded, looking to the approval of others rather than to himself for assurances and security. He characterizes the " other directed " office worker as one spending most of his time ". . . exchanging office gossip ('conferences'), making good-will tours ('inspection'), talking to salesmen and joshing secretaries ('morale'). This person is liked for his recreation and loved for his vices." Undoubtedly this picture of the office worker could be applied to many in the work force today: Congeniality rather than efficiency determine success and status. For further discussion see *The Lonely Crowd* (Garden City, N. Y., Doubleday & Co., 1954), especially pp. 19, 20, 149–151, 162.

" likes " of the work force. Motivation and morale are not unitary concepts, and while we have stressed the importance of money to labor, this does not preclude, as we have observed, the operation of other forces. Our check list will indicate the multiple problems and the multiple interests of the worker.

A Check List: What the Worker Dislikes

One of the major problems confronting the worker is the humility of hunting for a job and more specifically, the tragedy of not finding one. To search for employment when jobs are extremely scarce can be a most demoralizing experience. Each failure to find employment reinforces the worker's suspicion that his labor service might be worthless.

A second major problem confronting him is the fear that, even though employed, he may soon become unemployed. The fact that thousands of workers are willing to participate in a spontaneous walkout because one worker is fired for an apparently inadequate reason indicates labor's determination to protect its employment security. Such a discharge is often interpreted as a direct and personal threat to each worker.

A third major fear of labor is that of instability and uncertainty related to changes on the job. From time to time overtime work may be eliminated, workers may be reassigned to new jobs involving different responsibilities, production standards may be changed, and so on. There are innumerable potential points of friction which unnerve the worker. The union gives the worker a mechanism for the orderly representation of his grievances and provides a channel for expressing his fears.

Finally, the worker may become disturbed by the nature of his work. Especially in the mass production industries, the worker may be performing a single, repetitious, wearisome job week after week, year after year. The production line grinds on, and the worker is under constant pressure to keep up with it. One auto worker testified, " The work isn't hard . . . it's the never-ending pace . . . the guys yell ' hurrah ' whenever the line breaks down . . . you can hear it all over the plant." Another worker stresses the repetitiveness of the operations: " It's not a matter of pace. It's the monotony. It's not good for you to get so bored. I do the same thing day after day; just an everlasting grind." And another worker complains: " The job gets so sickening — day in and day out plugging in ignition wires. I get through with one motor, turn around, and there's another motor staring me in the face." [33] It is true, of course, that some

[33] These quotations are taken from Charles R. Walker and Robert H. Guest, " The Man on the Assembly Line," *Harvard Business Review*, Vol. 30, No. 3 (May–June, 1952). The authors suggest various solutions to minimize job monotony including: (1) social interaction breaking the monotony; (2) enough operations on their particular jobs to give variety to it; (3) opportunity to work back up the line and give the worker a " breather "; (4) opportunity to alternate one set of operations with another

workers enjoy repetitive work, but probably most resent unrelieved monotony and the continuing pressure of the production line. In such a situation the worker is depressed by a sense of anonymity.

These dissatisfactions explain, in part, the role the union can play in industry. Through his union the worker is attempting to acquire some control over his environment and to acquire some self-determination. The worker is a citizen in his community but a subject in industry. Since income is so necessary before the worker can enjoy his political freedom in the community, the demands made on him in industry are much more significant than the problems of his government. Stated in another way, the worker is necessarily more concerned about his status as a subject in industry than his status as a citizen in society.

The Positive Forces: What the Worker Wants

It is usually easier to locate the sore spots aggravating labor than it is to pinpoint labor's positive goals or any goal beyond that of eliminating labor's grievances. One early classification of human behavior suggested that the goals of labor were made up of: First, the wish for gain and fear of want; second, the hope of reward of a noneconomic kind (approval) or the fear of disadvantage of a noneconomic kind (e.g., punishment); third, sense of honor and fear of disgrace; fourth, the impulse to activity and exercise of power; and fifth, the motive of duty and fear of conscience. Again, we return to the point that maximizing income is not usually inconsistent but rather makes possible the achievement of most of these goals.

Another way of approaching the problem of motivation is to assume that all workers are interested in status and prestige and then attempt to analyze the determinants of such status. According to sociologist Talcott Parsons, status is determined by (1) membership in a kinship unit, (2) personal qualities, (3) achievements, (4) possessions, (5) authority, and (6) power. At least five of these six categories are considerably influenced by one's income, and as Parsons himself explains, " Perhaps at no time in history have such a large proportion of a great population been ' on the make ' as in the United States of the early twentieth century." [34] Certainly the labor movement is no exception to this general rule. We should not be startled to learn that men in overalls have motives which are largely similar to those of the rest of the community.

Undoubtedly the demands imposed on labor by our society have changed radically in the last fifty years, as have labor's values, attitudes,

set of different character; (5) opportunity to alternate jobs with other workers within the same section; (6) a long time cycle encompassing a larger number of operations than usual and of a more interesting character (p. 79).

[34] " An Analytical Approach to the Theory of Social Stratification," *The American Journal of Sociology*, Vol. XLV, No. 6 (May, 1940), p. 859.

and behavior in the labor market. During the frontier stages of industrial development the capital scarcity and labor abundance forced the worker to adopt a morality rooted in the virtue of hard work. Erich Fromm has offered us a profound observation in noting that: " In order that any society may function well, its members must acquire the kind of character which makes them *want* to act in the way they *have* to act. . . ." [35] Benjamin Franklin laid down the morality of the nineteenth century by stressing that the way to wealth was " as plain as the way to market. It depends chiefly on two words: industry and frugality. . . ." The prevailing attitudes of a few generations back are reflected in a notice posted in a Salt Lake City bank on April 11, 1864, for the benefit of its employees:

NOTICE TO EMPLOYEES

Bank opens at 7 A.M. and closes at 8 P.M. except on Saturday, when closed at 9 P.M. This is in effect the year 'round.

Employees are to sweep floors, dust furniture and office shelves, and remember, " Cleanliness is next to Godliness." Each clerk to bring in one bucket of water and one scuttle of coal.

Any employee who smokes Spanish cigars, uses liquor in any form, gets shaved at the barber shops or frequents pool halls or public dance halls, will give his employer every reason to suspect his integrity and all-around honesty.

Men employees will be given one evening off each week for courting purposes. Two evenings each week, if they go regularly to church and attend to church duties. After any employee has spent his 13 hours of labor in the office, he should then spend his leisure time in the reading of good books.[36]

Today we enjoy the sweeping benefits of automation. Work itself involves less physical strain, and the standard of living rises to ever higher levels. Labor has become acutely consumption rather than production conscious. But the changes in the production process involving a high degree of specialization and the employment of hundreds of thousands of men in some large plants has left the individual worker believing that his individual effort in no direct way affects his economic status. Furthermore, as production is machine-controlled, he quickly abandons any illusion he had about increasing his own efficiency or output. In spite of and even because of these changes in technology, the traditional fear of insecurity is still with the worker. In previous decades he worried about " poverty in the midst of poverty," but today he fears the possibility of

[35] " Individual and Social Origins of Neurosis," *American Sociological Review*, Vol. IX, No. 4 (1944), p. 381.
[36] As reproduced in the *Los Angeles Mirror-News* (Friday, February 11, 1955).

"poverty in the midst of plenty." Nor is the American worker satiated with his growing income, for he is participating in a constant race to keep up with the ever-rising living standards in the community. If over-production occurs, it will not arise from any lack of labor's will to consume, but rather from its lack of ability to buy.

Multiple Loyalties and the Worker

Is the worker more loyal to his union or his company? If the worker is loyal only to his union, he is likely to endorse all of its actions and perhaps even subscribe to the establishment of a strong labor party to reinforce the goals of the union. On the other hand, a worker with dual loyalties is much less likely to subscribe to any single political or economic reform policy. If the worker feels he is getting a square deal in the plant and has reasonable opportunity for getting ahead, he is not usually for the union 100 percent. Even if the worker is anti-employer, he is not likely for that reason to be anti-capitalist. If the union movement is altering the basic structure of our capitalist system, it is not by conscious policy. Any such effect is rather the inadvertent by-product of policies which are designed for other purposes. Indeed the success of unionism in America does not depend on its challenge to the "American way of life" but rather by the extent to which it is admitted as an integral part of the conservative scene. In George Bernard Shaw's apt phrase, "Trade unionism is not socialism; it is the Capitalism of the Proletariat."

Paradoxical as it may seem, recent studies of worker loyalty indicate that the individual worker is often equally enthusiastic about *both* his union and his company. Frequently the worker who offers most active support for the union is the same person most loyal to his company. Ross Stagner reported that:

> The climate, whether favorable or hostile, tends to embrace both company and union. . . . The workers do not accept the inevitability of conflict, nor do they accept the necessity of binding themselves to one group or the other. They accept the status of dual allegiance and, at least under normal conditions, seem to experience no internal stress as a result.[37]

Rev. Theodore V. Purcell's study of packinghouse workers indicated that many workers saw no conflict between labor and management. ". . . unlike a few labor and management leaders, the rank and file workers want both their company and union to coexist. If their leaders recognize this desire, at least one source of industrial conflict should be diminished."[38]

[37] "Dual Loyalty in Modern Society," *Monthly Labor Review*, Vol. 76, No. 12 (December, 1953), p. 1274.
[38] "Dual Allegiance at Swift & Co., Chicago," quoted in the *Monthly Labor Review* (December, 1953), p. 1277.

It may seem puzzling that the worker can be strongly for both management and labor, but it is not surprising that the inevitability of conflict thesis should be rejected by both labor and management. What labor desires is simply a "fair" share of income, reasonable security, and a chance to see that labor is given "fair" treatment by management. The bulk of disputes in industrial relations result from attempts to define and make explicit differing concepts of fairness and equity, but seldom do the issues relate directly to the value of capitalism as a method of organizing economic activity. As Clark Kerr has rightly observed, "We may find that the greater hope for democracy lies with a multiplicity of allegiences — to self, family, union, church, employer, and government . . . the great danger is not that loyalties are divided today but that they may become undivided tomorrow." [39]

[39] *Monthly Labor Review* (December, 1953), p. 1273.

II

Unionism: Determinants and Characteristics of Growth

5

The Struggle to
Organize Labor

We indicated in our previous section that group organization was the collective response of individuals to their common problems. The history of union development provides us with a fascinating case study of this principle in operation. Unfortunately we do not have space to discuss all those economic changes which created new problems for labor in America, but it will be immediately apparent from our discussion in this chapter that the impulse for labor organization evolved from the realization of the individual that he could not solve his economic problems alone. Thus, the growth of unionism provides a significant symptom of the general frustrations and disappointments of individual workers, as well as an interesting index of that shifting balance of power between labor and management caused by economic change.

Labor in the Frontier Economy

During the colonial era the eastern settlements were small patches on this vast unexplored continent. Living on the fringes of this unknown quantity enabled many of the pioneers to contemplate the riches that its exploration and settlement might provide. This setting induced many individuals to acquire a spirit of adventure and a psychology of success. It was like entering a gambling casino with a quantity of blue chips: success could not be guaranteed but at least the possibility of success existed for anyone with the gambling spirit. Nor was there much of the labor market organization as we think of it today.

The organization of labor first took the form of quasi-guilds in such trades as shoemaking, carpentering, printing, and baking. Craftsmen in these trades were interested in protecting the standards of their profession and the quality of their product. These organizations were fraternal in character and were often made up of both journeymen and master craftsmen, or employees and employers. Dues were collected, mostly for modest welfare benefits for any member's family in distress. Employees and employers worked together, belonged to the same club, and shared common views of common problems.

Prior to 1800 there were occasional instances of labor unrest, and we have fragmentary evidence of early strikes (or " turnouts " as they were then known) in this colonial period. In 1636 a group of fishermen were reported to have mutinied; in 1676 the cartmen refused to remove dirt from New York City streets; in 1768 journeymen tailors of New York struck because of inadequate wages; in 1778 printers in that city also struck for similar reasons, as did the shoemakers and journeymen printers in Philadelphia in 1779. These reflect isolated disputes, and most strikes were spontaneous rather than carefully planned by labor's fraternal organizations. For the most part strike action was viewed as a rather futile effort of crackpot elements within the work force to cause trouble. The challenge in America was that of increasing production or the size of the income pie rather than indulging in premature disputes over its distribution. Most Americans had only contempt for any " foreign ideology " which might encourage labor organization. This sentiment became all the more apparent when the judiciary, with untroubled simplicity, transplanted the common law conspiracy doctrine from England to America. The press, too, with the eloquence of Elizabethan prose, failed to understand how any employer " having the soul of a man within him can submit to such degradation " as union organization. The public usually considered militant union members as part of the lunatic fringe of society.

Early Experiments with Union Organization: 1800–1837

After 1800 America became caught up in the process of economic development that was sweeping Europe, and the early fraternal organizations of labor became increasingly concerned with economic issues.

The quickening pace of immigration around 1815 increased the number of unskilled workers willing to attempt the job of the skilled artisan. When manufacturing processes became more widespread, the opportunities and economies of using such labor multiplied. The hostility toward both the First and Second Banks of the United States led to intervals of wildcat banking, with pronounced inflation from 1814 to 1816 and especially from 1830 to 1837. Workers began to suspect that through such inflation the unholy alliance of business and bankers had conspired to deprive the common worker of the fruits of his labor. The price list (or wages) negotiated by friendly association did not keep pace with inflation. With the depression that swept Europe following the Napoleonic wars, European nations began dumping their surplus products in America, aggravating the problem of unemployment and depression.

The union movement grew, then, out of the turmoil and turbulence of economic development. The widening of the market and the " lengthening" of the production process resulted in the loss of personal contact between employer and employee. Perhaps it is no exaggeration to suggest that unionism in America was launched in 1817, when one society of journeymen interrupted its meeting to request that employers leave. It then passed a resolution stating that " the interests of the journeymen are *separate* and in some respects *opposite* to those of the employers." [1]

In the 1820's economic changes gave impetus to union growth, but many of the newly organized agencies were quasi-political in nature. In 1827 the first city central or association of unions was formed in Philadelphia to support, among other things, the carpenter's strike for a 10-hour day. The carpenters had made the radical suggestion that the working day begin as late as 6 in the morning and end as early as 6 in the evening, with an hour off for breakfast and lunch. Employers pointed to the "temptations and improvident practices" that such idleness would produce.

> We fear and dread the consequences of such a measure upon the morals and well being of society. We cannot believe this project to have originated with any of the faithful and industrious Sons of New England, but are compelled to consider it an evil of foreign growth, and one which we hope and trust will not take root in the favoured soil of Massachusetts.[2]

The early association of Philadelphia unions was titled the Mechanics' Union of Trade Associations and this, in turn, gave birth to the Working Men's Party, alleged to be the first labor party in the world. It endorsed the spirit of Jacksonian democracy, demanded reduction of the monopoly power of business, the decrease in the distillation of "ardent spirits," reform of the money, prison, and militia systems, and the elimination of imprisonment for debt. Basically, they pressed for "an enlarged diffusion of views and real intelligence among the mass of the people." The Working Men's Party collapsed under the rising tide of criticism which charged that its members were agrarians, atheists, and free lovers. Its utopian leaders had proposed various reform schemes for labor's welfare. Thomas Skidmore advocated the redistribution of property, with the redivision to be accomplished at a state auction at which all adults would have equal rights to bid. Robert Dale Owen, son of the British cotton manufacturer Robert Owen, felt Skidmore's plans too radical and advocated instead a system for providing equal instruction, food, and clothing to all children at public expense so that everyone would have equal opportunities for advancement in America. George Henry Evans modified the more

[1] Cited in Selig Perlman, *A History of Trade Unionism in the United States* (New York, The Macmillan Co., 1922), p. 5.
[2] As cited in John R. Commons and associates *History of Labor in the United States* in Vol. 1, Part I, "Colonial and Federal Beginnings to 1827," by David J. Saposs (New York, The Macmillan Co., 1921), p. 160.

radical proposals of Skidmore by concentrating on the need for distributing the land resources of America, and his agitation gave momentum to
the homestead movement. Factionalism between Owen and Skidmore
accelerated the disintegration of the Working Men's Party.

In the 1830's President Jackson's feud with Nicholas Biddle of the
Second Bank of the United States led to a new era of wildcat banking.
The rapid rise in the cost of living sharpened the economic orientation
of labor organizations. Benevolent trade associations transformed themselves into trade unions, concentrating on problems of rising prices, sweatshop conditions, abuses of apprenticeship conditions, and the employment of children, women, unskilled and prison labor. The inflation was
particularly serious when money earnings were modest. It has been estimated that in the thirties, a cotton factory operator might earn about
$2.19 a week, a seamstress about $1.25 a week. Women might receive
wages of 12 cents a day. Several of the growing cities developed federations of local unions, usually called City Trades' Unions, and as inflation spread, their agitation increased. The *New York Times*, in April,
1836, complained: " The barbers have struck, and now all that remains
for editors is to strike too." [3] The public became increasingly concerned
with the general labor agitation, and in 1835 the *Philadelphia Gazette*,
reporting on street parades and mass meetings observed:

> " The times are completely out of joint. . . . Our streets and squares
> are crowded with an idle population. Some manifestations of violence
> have already taken place. . . . Our buildings are at a stand and busi-
> ness generally is considerably impeded." The labourers, cordwainers
> and carpenters organized processions and marched through the streets
> of the city with fife and drum and flags bearing the inscription " From
> 6 to 6." [4]

By 1836 food prices were double their 1833 level, but the inflation culminated in the crisis and panic of 1837.

Humanitarianism: 1837–1848

The serious depression that followed the economic crisis of 1837 cut the
ground from under bread and butter unionism. When the foundation for
labor's bargaining power was lost, many workers became interested in
the more ambitious projects to restructure the entire organization of the
economy. The intention was not to secure a " fair day's pay for a fair
day's work " within the labor market, but rather to eliminate the labor
market. But no single blueprint for reform gained uniform support, and

---

[3] As cited in Foster Rhea Dulles, *Labor in America* (New York, Thomas Y. Crowell,
1949), Chapter 4, p. 54.
[4] Commons and Associates, *op. cit.*, Vol. 1, Part III, " Trade Unionism," pp. 390–1.

about as many panaceas were proposed as there were degrees of frustration. This was the heyday for the intellectual and the reformer. It is quite likely that the popularity of various utopian schemes sharpened the contrast between the reality of depression and the intensity of hope held by many immigrants to America. Slum conditions in New York City, for example, had grown scandalous. The immigrant could rent his lodging — straw on the cellar floor — for two cents a night, or sleep without the straw for one cent. America became the nursery for various utopian experiments because ". . . the immigrants from feudalism and famine in Europe were finding in the crowded American cities new misery and new hard masters. And the Socialist movement both relieved the congestion and revived the disillusioned political thinkers." [5]

Orestes A. Brownson preached the spiritual richness of transcendentalism, through which labor could rise above the problems of the cruel world by viewing life as a challenge, a game that must be played with determination and vigor, with the spiritual ability to transcend present obstacles no matter how overwhelming they may appear. Albert Brisbane popularized the writings of Charles Fourier, a plan to evoke the essential harmonies of the universe. Fourier felt that society must be reorganized into small groups called phalanxes.

Others turned to producer cooperatives as the solution for labor's difficulties. Horace Greeley urged the extension of profit-sharing techniques, while George Henry Evans advocated a "new agrarianism" to distribute the natural rights of life to man, including light, air, water and soil.[6] Reform was in the air. Emerson, in a letter to Carlyle, wrote: "We are all a little wild here with numberless projects of social reform, not a reading man but has a draft of a new community in his waistcoat pocket." [7] Let us look briefly at a few of these reform measures.

The British reformer, Robert Owen, had championed the thesis that if employers would care for their workers as they did their capital, they would enjoy substantial returns. His own successful cotton mills in England became models of enlightened management. But Owen was disillusioned with the failure of the British government to establish factory reforms, and concluded that Europe was diseased beyond hope. He consequently departed to America to found a model community, New Harmony, in Indiana. On July 4, 1826, he advanced his "Declaration of Men-

---

[5] As described by Edmund Wilson, *To the Finland Station* (Garden City, Doubleday and Co., 1953), p. 101.

[6] Such an argument gave encouragement to the government to accelerate its distribution of lands in the West. In 1852 it was pointed out that 1½ billion acres of land were yet to be disposed of, and at the previous rate, it would require from 400 to 900 years to make this complete. The slogan "Vote Yourself a Farm" led ultimately to the Homestead Act of 1862.

[7] Quoted in H. U. Faulkner and T. Kepner, *America: Its History and People*, 5th ed. (New York, Harper & Bros., 1950), p. 572.

tal Independence " from the three great oppressors of humanity: Private Property, Irrational Religion, and Marriage. It is not surprising that his program appeared dangerously radical in " unspoiled " America. His unrestricted invitation for membership in his model community attracted an undesirable assortment of drifters. New Harmony lasted only three years, and Owen returned to England disillusioned with the prospects for his " once-and-for-all " program of labor reform.

The Frenchman Charles Fourier also drafted a plan for a utopian community which inspired several American experiments. Fourier was conditioned by Rousseau's philosophy that mankind is naturally good and is perverted only by evil institutions. Thus, he believed that if people in their formative years were taught the right things, they could be rendered universally happy and good. His model community would depend on private capital. The problem of distribution in his community would be solved by a scientific formula: Capital would receive 25 percent of the product, while five twelfths was to go to labor and three twelfths to talent. Each person could be assigned the job he preferred most to do, so that everyone would be happy. " Two problems which had troubled him — why boys love dirt and how refuse of the community was to be got rid of — were found to solve one another reciprocally: the boys were to dispose of the refuse." [8] Because Fourier did not have sufficient funds to establish his model Phalanx community, he publicized the fact that he would be home at noon every day, ready to discuss his project with any rich person interested in financing it. While the rich person never turned up, the idea excited the imagination of the American Albert Brisbane. Horace Greeley, editor of the *New York Tribune*, gave generous space to the discussion of Fourierism and the publicity proved so successful that more than forty phalanx groups were established. The founders were, in their words, " desirous of escaping from the present hollow-hearted state of civilized society, in which fraud and heartless competition grind the more noble-minded of our citizens to dust." Most phalanxes were short lived.

The more moderate demands of George Henry Evans replaced those of Thomas Skidmore, with the slogan, " Vote Yourself a Farm." George Henry Evans reasoned that since man lives, he has the right to be, and the right to be implies the right to the materials of nature necessary for existence. These materials include light, air, water, and soil. Parting with Skidmore's philosophy, he considered liberty, labor, capital, and education as acquired or derived rights. Since people's existence was rooted in their right to the soil, public land must be distributed freely to those who wanted to cultivate it. This program had obvious appeal, and its supporters formed the Agrarian League and later the National Reform Association.

[8] As cited by Wilson, *op. cit.*, p. 90.

Even the producer cooperatives which had grown popular proved fragile and often failed because of inadequate capital, the lack of skilled leadership, and the pressure of competition. Prevailing morality was cited in the case against cooperatives: " *The attempt to improve on the divine law is not ridiculous* . . . it is absurd and blasphemous. If men cannot live and get along as God has arranged and ordained, they can get along in no other way." [9]

National Labor Organization and the Civil War

Interest in the various reform programs began to fade with the revival of economic activity around 1848. During the latter half of the century the tempo of industrial activity increased rapidly, especially after the Civil War. Railroads were busy spreading a network of communication and transportation facilities to bind the economy together with ribbons of steel. Such industrial barons as Gould, Vanderbilt, Rockefeller, Carnegie, Hill, and Morgan established vast industrial empires. The corporate structure of enterprise became an increasingly effective device for gathering the tremendous funds necessary for industrial expansion.

The growth of the national markets at the turn of the mid-century encouraged the establishment of trade unions national in scope. From 1856 to 1866 twenty-six national unions were organized. These new unions dedicated themselves to getting more income, maintaining apprenticeship regulations, improving working conditions, reducing the hours of work, securing closed-shop agreements, and so on. Many catered to the partisan interests of particular skilled labor groups. After the Civil War many workers supported the anti-deflationary program of the Greenback party. This party proposed that the government print an adequate supply of money to reduce the cost of money or the interest rate to the workingman. Labor could then afford to invest in capital and share in American prosperity.[10] Farmers also subscribed to this platform as an anti-deflationary measure, for low farm prices in the post-Civil War period had reduced farm income.

The growth of national markets required that labor organize all sectors of the labor force. Without such national organization any single employer accepting the union scale might be exposed to the destructive

[9] Commons, *op. cit.*, p. 571.

[10] The mechanics of the Greenback party philosophy are rather involved. It was assumed that the government war debt could be used to furnish more money. " This was to be done by reducing the rate of interest on the government bonds to 3 percent and by making them convertible into legal tender currency and convertible back into bonds, at the will of the holder of either. In other words, the greenback currency, instead of being, as it was at the time, an irredeemable promise to pay in specie, would be redeemable in government bonds. If a government bondholder could secure slightly more than 3 percent by lending to a private borrower, he would return his bonds . . . for greenbacks." As explained by Perlman, *op. cit.*, pp. 51, 52.

competition of employers operating with nonunion labor. The new national unions began to negotiate trade agreements which would bind all employers in particular trades, and this in turn accelerated the growth of national employer associations to deal with labor.

Unions campaigned for the "union label" and insisted on its use in order to encourage the public to purchase only union-made goods. The boycott became a common labor weapon. Strike funds were accumulated.

The employers fought back with their own associations, often requiring new workers to sign agreements specifying that they would not join a union or participate in a labor dispute. Employers also circulated blacklists naming employees who were unionists and trouble makers. In 1866 the National Labor Congress, or National Labor Union, convened as an organization presumably representing all labor, skilled and unskilled (as well as farmers). This national movement was predominantly reform minded, concentrating on consumer and producer cooperatives, the need for the 8-hour day, currency and banking reform, the restriction of immigration, the establishment of a department of labor, and so on.

By 1872 the movement had become transformed into the National Labor Reform party, but its efforts to name a candidate for the president were bungled, and the organization quickly lost its influence as a political party. By 1878, however, the National Greenback Labor party won considerable support polling over a million votes and electing fourteen representatives to Congress. The unemployment, characteristic of the seventies, took much of the steam out of business unionism, and labor turned, not to utopian reform as in 1837, but to radicalism and violence.

Violence on the Labor Scene: 1870–1890

On January 13, 1874, a meeting was called in New York City at which the mayor was to speak regarding the current problems of unemployment, but the meeting was canceled without notice. When a crowd assembled, unaware of the change of plans, they were charged by the police. The *New York Times* simply explained: "The persons arrested yesterday seem all to have been foreigners — chiefly Germans or Irishmen. Communism is not a weed of native growth." [11]

The doctrines of Marx were receiving increased attention in America, and the decision to move the headquarters of the Communist International from Europe to New York City added to the nervousness of the American public. It was significant that at this Tompkins Square riot, a youth named Samuel Gompers observed the violence and sensed the futility of conflict in labor-management relations. In the seventies the Molly Maguire organization terrorized the coal fields. This secret organization, made up for the most part of anti-British Irishmen who had

[11] Quoted by Dulles, *op. cit.*, p. 116.

migrated to America, was designed to punish autocratic employers. Members operated on a secret cell basis, intimidating foremen, destroying property, and even murdering those who abused their members. The Pinkerton detective agency finally was able to plant James McPharlan in the Molly Maguire organization by having him pose as a desperate fugitive. McPharlan's evidence convicted twenty-four Maguire members, ten of whom were hanged for murder.

The July, 1877, railroad strike spread through all lines east of the Mississippi and local newspapers expressed fear that this was not a strike, but a labor revolution. Federal troops were required to restore order in West Virginia. A battle developed between state militia and strikers in Baltimore, in which twelve persons were killed. In Pittsburgh the situation got even further out of hand, for local militia refused to take part in the combat, and units from Philadelphia were dispatched to the scene. In the battle which ensued twenty-five persons were killed. The angry mob seized the railroad station, setting it afire, and burned 2,000 cars, machine shops, grain elevators, 2 roundhouses, and 125 locomotives. The militia retreated across the Allegheny River. Local newspapers characterized the strikers as " hoodlums, rabble, bummers, looters, blacklegs, thieves, tramps, ruffians, incendiaries, enemies of society, brigands, rapscallions, riffraff, felons and idiots . . ." while other headlines described Pittsburgh as a city completely sacked and in the hands of a howling mob of Communists.[12]

The Haymarket Square riot in Chicago in May, 1886, did not involve so many people but was equally sensational. The anarchist branch of the Communist International had its headquarters in Chicago and was headed by Johann Most.[13] It had about 2,000 members, mostly German and Polish immigrants. When a strike for the 8-hour day at the McCormick Harvester plant involved a clash that killed four workers, the Black International of the Chicago anarchists issued a pamphlet announcing a meeting to protest these deaths. It contained the words: ". . . to arms we

[12] For a vivid account of this violence, read Chapter VII of Dulles' absorbing book, *Labor in America, op. cit.*

[13] The Congress of the International Workingmen's Association met at the Hague in 1872. The anarchist faction, led by Bakunin, had shown such strength that Marx moved the General Council to America. Bakunin was devoted only to one idea: revolution, and the revolution must destroy all traditions, institutions, and classes. Above all, the group that foments the revolution should not attempt to impose its own political organization from above on the people; any organization must be spontaneous; it must arise from the people themselves. It is clear that this latter sentiment does not conform with Marxism. In one account of Bakunin's attitude, the story is told that Bakunin was traveling from Paris to Prague and " happened upon a revolt of German peasants, who were making an uproar around the castle, not knowing what to do. Bakunin got out of his conveyance, and, without wasting any time to find out what the dispute was about, formed the peasants into ranks and instructed them so skilfully (he had been an artillery officer in Russia) that by the time he resumed his seat to continue his journey, the castle was burning on all four sides." From Edmund Wilson, *To the Finland Station,* (Garden City, N. Y., Doubleday and Co., 1953), pp. 267–268.

call you . . . to arms." Three thousand workers gathered at Haymarket
Square, but the weather was cold and the crowd was apparently dissipat-
ing when 200 police arrived to break up the meeting. Someone hurled a
bomb into the ranks of the police, and in the ensuing battle three policemen and four workers were killed. The public was outraged, and eight
anarchists were arrested and charged with murder. While no evidence
was available as to who had tossed the bomb, seven of the leaders of the
International were sentenced to death. A new uproar was created when
Governor Altgeld of Illinois commuted some of the sentences to life
imprisonment.

The Rise and Fall of the Knights of Labor

In December of 1860 nine tailors decided to form a secret organization.
Little did they realize that sixteen years later, their organization would
have over 700,000 members and be described as the most potent force in
the American community. The spectacular rise to power of this organization was almost as sudden as its collapse. What were the moving forces
behind this new union? The preamble of the Knights of Labor affirmed:
" We mean no conflict with legitimate enterprise, no antagonism to necessary capital." The Knights of Labor is our best example of " reform-
minded " unionism popularizing the " one big union " ideal. The Knights
of Labor hoped to unite all labor into one large organization, regardless
of trade, regional location, or status. Because of the unhappy history of
the Molly Maguire organization, the Pope forbade membership of all
Catholics in the Knights of Labor. In 1881, however, the union decided to
forego its secrecy and its membership then increased rapidly. Its first
leader, Uria S. Stephens, was educated for the ministry while its second
leader, Terence V. Powderly, had studied law and was mayor of Scran-
ton. The organization avowedly set out to prevent the unjust accumulation of power and wealth. Its methods for achieving this goal were, first,
education, second, reform legislation, and, third, mutual benefits. The
strike was a weapon of last resort.[14] When Powderly succeeded Stephens
to leadership in 1878, he considered that producer and consumer cooperatives would provide the solution to labor's difficulties. Labor could
escape " into self-employment through cooperation." One hundred and
thirty-five cooperatives in all were established, and early successes reinforced Powderly's conviction that such cooperatives would ultimately
supplant the wage system.

[14] Typical of the philosophy of the Knights of Labor is the reaction of Powlerly to
the suggestion that he support the demand of labor for the 8-hour day. Powderly
suggested that rather than have the Knights of Labor participate in any parade for
such an issue, it would be more appropriate to have his many locals conduct an essay
writing contest on the advantages of the 8-hour day, and winning essays would be
published simultaneously on George Washington's birthday.

The spectacular growth of the Knights followed its dispute with the major industrialist, Jay Gould and the Wabash Railway. Gould had systematically fired those workers who were members of the Knights, but when the Knights threatened a strike against the company and a boycott of all Wabash rolling stock (affecting 20,000 miles of railway), Jay Gould yielded and revoked his policy, sensing that a strike would be inexpedient at that time. The country was amazed by his decision and his announcement that he would "always endeavor to do what was right" for labor. The *New York Sun* published a rather exaggerated picture of Knights of Labor power: "Five men in this country control the chief interest of 500,000 workmen, can at any moment take the means of livelihood from 2½ million." Membership expanded rapidly after this success, but a strike in the following year on the Southwest system proved disastrous for the Knights. Gould hired strikebreakers and refused to negotiate. Five thousand miles of railway were affected, but after a few months of sporadic violence the workers admitted defeat and returned to work. From this time on the influence and prestige of the Knights of Labor declined almost as rapidly as it had grown.

The decline of the influence of the Knights of Labor should not be attributed only to the failure of the southwestern railroad strike. The organization attempted to appeal to all workers — including farmers and small merchants — and the diversity of its membership's interests undermined the structural unity of the Knights. It provided for a large degree of centralization of control, but this was of no significance when in critical moments the ranks rejected the orders of the general command. Many of the producer cooperatives organized by the Knights faced financial difficulties and many failed. The public hostility toward the anarchists in the Haymarket riot of 1886 spilled over against the Knights of Labor. The public feared all unions were essentially destructive, no matter how welfare minded they alleged to be. The ultimate weakness of the Knights was the failure of the rank and file to subscribe to its idealism — or its refusal to believe that the welfare of one rested in the welfare of all and that sectional interests must on occasion be submerged if necessary to advance the welfare of the whole. The leadership of this union turned the corner toward utopian goals and found that the mass of workers it presumed to be leading had not turned the corner with it.

Business Unionism Sinks Permanent Roots

At the time that the Knights of Labor began to fade, a new federation of labor, based on different principles of organization and a contrasting philosophy, emerged. The Federation of Organized Trades and Labor Unions of the United States and Canada provided the foundation for what was later called the American Federation of Labor. The triumvirate, Adolph Strasser, Ferdinand Laurrell, and Samuel Gompers conceived the wider organization from the core of their own union, the International Cigar Makers' Union. It was to be an organization much different than that of the Knights of Labor. These gentlemen understood the need for expediency: " Necessity has forced the labor movement to adopt the most practical methods." The Federation distrusted utopian reformers, Communists, and even Socialists. It talked less about morals and more about practical matters. The American Federation of Labor was truly federal in character. Many students of labor history attribute its continuing success to the high autonomy of its various pockets of skilled craftsmen. Like other unions preceding it, the Federation included in its program the extension of educational opportunities for children, the prohibition of child labor under 14; the need for uniform apprentice laws, prison reform, the 8-hour day, and so on. But its main purpose and function was to negotiate a trade agreement with industry with the best possible terms for labor. The great offense against the labor union was " dualism," or dissension within each pocket of organization. Gompers realized that dissension might easily develop if the union became a part of any political machine or became involved in any grandiose scheme for social reform. In politics he constantly recommended that the Federation pursue the policy of " rewarding its friends and punishing its enemies " but such action could cut across traditional party lines and should do so if necessary. As the labor student, Selig Perlman, observes, the success of this form of organization was rooted in the fact that it appreciated the basically sectional interests of each labor group:

> . . . the principle of craft autonomy triumphed chiefly because it recognized the existence of a considerable amount of group selfishness. The craftsman . . . wished to use his superior bargaining strength for his own purposes and evinced little desire to dissipate it in the service of his humbler fellow worker.[15]

The Knights of Labor, with diminishing prestige and influence, was openly critical of the American Federation of Labor. Powderly again stressed that the craft workers of the AF of L could not hope for much progress if they left the unskilled workers behind. The Knights appealed to the AF of L to "annex your grand army and powerful corps to the main army that we may fight the battle under one flag," but the invitation was refused. In spite of this interunion rivalry, in spite too of the attacks made on the Federation and Gompers by the Socialists and Communists, and in spite of resistance of employers, the Federation enjoyed a continuing increase of membership. It was not until the financial panic of 1893 that its permanency was fully realized. Membership remained at the modest level of 275,000, but the fact that the depression had not crushed the

[15] Perlman, *op. cit.,* p. 122.

union established a new precedent in union history. Unionism no longer appeared as a fair-weather enterprise.

Industry Counterattacks: *Carnegie and Pullman*

The fact that the new unions of the American Federation of Labor had survived economic crisis did not mean that American industry considered unions a permanent part of the industrial scene. Two violent strikes in the 1890's revealed the determination and the potency of management's resistance to unions. These were the strikes in the Carnegie Steel Plant in Pittsburgh, and the national rail strike that had its origins in Pullman, Illinois.

In 1892 the most powerful union within the Federation, the Amalgamated Association of Iron and Steel Workers (with over 24,000 members) was negotiating a contract with Carnegie Steel. The appointment of H. C. Frick to represent the company in negotiations created considerable concern, for Frick had the reputation of being a bitter opponent of labor. Negotiations collapsed, and even before the men walked out of the plant, Frick had arranged with the Pinkerton detective agency to provide 300 men as " plant guards." The union became furious, charging that Frick had not been bargaining in good faith. News later leaked out that Frick had planned to tow strikebreakers up the river to the Carnegie plant in Pittsburgh under cover of darkness. The men on the barges were armed with Winchester rifles, and the union members lined the riverside to do battle. The fight lasted from 4 in the morning until 5 in the afternoon. The workers spread oil on the river and set fire to it and fired a small cannon on the strikebreakers from behind their improvised barricade of railway ties. After a half dozen on both sides had been killed and many more seriously wounded, the would-be guards surrendered. Six days later, however, 8,000 state militia marched into the Homestead plant to protect any strikebreakers willing to work. The strike continued until midwinter when, on November 20, the union admitted defeat. One of the largest unions in America had been crushed.

A further outbreak of violence developed in the company town of Pullman in 1894. Wages had been reduced several times, and the workers felt that their rents — paid to the company — should also be reduced to ease the burden of reduced income.[16] Eugene V. Debs had recently organized the American Railway Union, which was having its convention in Chicago at the time of the Pullman dispute. Debs was reluctant to involve his relatively new industrial union in the dispute and asked Pull-

---

[16] Dulles describes the conditions as being desperate in the town; of more than 5800 employees, more than half had been laid off; wages were cut from 25 to 40 percent and without rent reductions. One worker received a pay check, after deductions, of two cents.

man to arbitrate his differences with his workers. When Pullman rejected the suggestion, the American Railway Union began a boycott of all Pullman cars. Within a few days 40,000 miles of track were affected. The railroads then attached Pullman cars to railway mail cars, and by such a device the federal government immediately became involved in the dispute. President Cleveland announced that " If it takes every dollar in the Treasury, and every soldier in the United States to deliver a postal card in Chicago, that postal card should be delivered." When federal troops arrived in Chicago, violence and disorder developed in the proportion of the 1877 railway strikes, and total destruction amounted to over $80 million. A sweeping injunction was issued by the federal court restraining the American Railway Union and Eugene V. Debs from further strike action, and when the strike did not cease, Debs and other officers of his union were arrested for contempt. When the strike lost its leadership, the union cause was doomed. Debs spent six months in jail, but in the process he became a martyr of labor's cause. When he returned to Chicago, he was greeted by a crowd of 100,000 people. Debs had become disillusioned with the prospects for unions in a capitalist economy and following this experience became an advocate of socialism.

1900: A New Era with Old Problems

A new spirit of liberalism swept America at the turn of the century. The government became interested in social reform, " trust busting," slum clearance, public health, and restricting the employment of women and children. Samuel Gompers was an active participant in the National Civic Federation, an organization which attempted to find the middle path between the anti-union radicalism of some employers and the extreme left-wing element of the union movement. Union membership meanwhile shot up from 800,000 in 1900 to 2 million in 1904, and Samuel Gompers enjoyed the fruit of many years of organizational effort.

But labor-management relations were still punctuated with incidents of violence and open conflict. A prolonged strike developed in 1902 by the United Mine Workers. When the union proposed that differences between it and the companies be arbitrated by the National Civic Federation, the spokesman for the coal mine operators, George F. Baer, issued a statement which gained immemorial fame. Baer pointed out that " anthracite mining is a business and not a religious, sentimental or academic proposition " and further affirmed, " The rights and interests of the laboring man will be protected and cared for — not by the labor agitators, but by the Christian men to whom God in His infinite wisdom has given the control of the property interests of this country . . ." [17] After five months of striking, the dispute was finally settled by an award of a presidential commission.

[17] Cited in Dulles, *op. cit.*, p. 191.

The National Association of Manufacturers, which had been organized in 1895, began a campaign to discredit labor unions by an open-shop offensive in 1903. Probably the most shocking instance of management resistance to unionism developed in 1913 in the Colorado Fuel and Iron Company strike at Ludlow, Colorado. The tent camp of striking workers was attacked by the militia and burned to the ground. The indiscriminate machine gunning of the workers' families resulted in the death of eleven children and two women. The public understandably became aroused over this brutality, and a government commission was appointed to investigate the circumstances of the strike and the responsibility for this violence. John D. Rockefeller, owner of the company, insisted that the battle against unionism must continue: " It was upon a similar principle that the war of the Revolution was carried on. . . . It is a great national issue of the most vital kind."

The efforts of Gompers to advance the cause of " pure and simple " unionism and establish its respectability in the eyes of the American public were somewhat thwarted and complicated by the mushroom growth of a new left-wing union organized in Chicago in 1905, the Industrial Workers of the World. This new union was made up of the excitable Western Federation of Miners, the Socialist Labor party led by Daniel de Leon, and the Socialist party led by Eugene V. Debs. Its members, often called " wobblies," showed little aversion to violence, for their goal was to eliminate the wages system. Their most successful strike was in the textile industry in Lawrence, Massachusetts, but in 1913 they became involved in a prolonged and bitter struggle in the Paterson, New Jersey, silk mills. Following considerable violence, this strike was broken, and the membership of the IWW decreased after that. When the IWW opposed participation of the United States in World War I, the organization was dubbed, " Imperial Wilhelm's Warriors." The bulk of its leadership was arrested and sentenced to long jail terms for sedition.

The war proved a great boon to union organization. The government was anxious to secure the continuing cooperation of labor in increasing war output. Labor was invited to participate in the councils of government (along with management) in making certain that production could expand uninterrupted by industrial disputes. In April, 1918, the tripartite National War Labor Board was established to settle all industrial disputes that were not resolved by other means, and this board evolved principles for settling disputes which later became an integral part of labor legislation. The board specifically recognized the right of labor to organize and bargain. Management was ordered to negotiate with its employees, but it was not compelled to recognize representatives of unions who were not themselves in the employ of the company.

Union leaders enjoyed a new sense of security during the war period, but they were quickly disillusioned in the postwar period when the tolerance of unions by both the government and employers faded. In 1919

President Wilson called a National Industrial Conference to try to evolve some permanent principles for industrial peace, but the conference broke up on the issue of " inside " versus " outside " union representation, the employers clinging to the proposition that they would not negotiate with any labor representative not employed in their own company. A new wave of Americanism swept the nation, epitomized by the general sentiment that the only " one big union " that should be tolerated in America was that whose symbol was the stars and stripes. Industrial unrest provoked public hostility. In 1919 a general strike erupted in Seattle which tied up the community for five days, with over 60,000 workers involved. In Boston the police struck when nineteen policemen were fired for joining the American Federation of Labor. One of the largest postwar strikes developed in the steel industry when 350,000 men quit work in nine states. In the ensuing violence twenty persons were killed, and the interchurch report of the dispute declared that the United States Steel Company was " too big to be beaten by 300,000 workers."

The Roaring Twenties: Unionism on the Defense

Contrary to earlier experiences of the nineteenth century, union influence and membership declined during the prosperity of the twenties. Employers began their active anti-union campaign with considerable success. They projected an " American Plan " in Chicago in 1921, arguing that the traditional values of America were those of rugged individualism rather than collectivism. Employers warned the public against the dangers of subversion inherent in the union movement. They also stressed union racketeering and the tyranny of labor bosses. They made unionization difficult by circulating blacklists, by securing yellow-dog contracts, by using plant spies to gain information on labor agitators.

While management was increasingly hostile to unions, it became considerably more enlightened in its attitudes toward labor. It impressed the workers with management's appreciation of their individual problems and attempted to reinforce the harmony of interests of labor and management. In one sense union organization was being killed by management's kindness.

Scientific management was also the new vogue in industry. Labor was allowed to share in the increases in productivity by the adoption of wage incentive systems, and these higher incentive earnings again weakened the propensity for union membership. Furthermore, the dilution of craft skills weakened the traditional craft basis for unionism. The skilled craftsman now tended to become a semiskilled machine operator; and more important, a person could be trained to take his place in a relatively short period of time. In the new era of welfare capitalism, profit-sharing schemes also became popular. It was not surprising that in this interval company unions should grow rapidly; by 1926 it was estimated that over 1,300,000 workers belonged to such organizations. Not until the mid-thirties did the government declare company-dominated unions to be illegal. In the twenties it appeared to be the company and not the union that was " delivering the goods " to labor.

There was also a tendency for those industries in which unionization was better established to decline or migrate. This was particularly true of clothing manufacture and New England textiles. The growth of the manufacturing industry in the South was not accompanied with a pro-portionate growth of union membership in that area. In addition, eco-nomic activity in the twenties placed less stress on primary production and more on secondary and tertiary activities. Consequently, the num-ber of professional services and white-collar workers increased, and these workers proved difficult to organize. The industrial wage earner, the so-called " proletariat " of the work force, represented 42.4 percent of those gainfully employed in 1920, but this proportion had declined to 37.9 percent by 1930.

Management also organized many labor-management cooperation com-mittees in order to secure the participation and support of labor in in-creasing efficiency. Such committees did much to satisfy the worker's search for recognition. The American Federation of Labor was forced to admit the logic and need for increased production but claimed that labor-management cooperation committees established outside the orbit of the union (and indeed quite independently of the union) would tend to usurp the union's functions. In effect, they would tend to increase the company domination of the work force, for representation on the com-mittees was not through nomination by the union or election by the workers, but through the appointment by the employer.

It is not surprising that labor should again develop an interest in pol-itics. In the spring of 1924 Senator Robert M. La Follette became the in-dependent presidential candidate and was supported in his campaign by the railway unions and the rank and file of the American Federation of Labor. He received the somewhat reluctant endorsement of Samuel Gompers. La Follette advocated public ownership of the nation's water power, railroads, conservation of natural resources, aid for farmers, tax reduction of moderate incomes, downward tariff revision, and remedial labor legislation. He received 5 million votes (one sixth of the votes cast). Following this unsuccessful bid for power, the third-party movement collapsed.

The Depression Decade: Unionism on the Offense

One cannot fully appreciate the impelling forces behind union organ-ization in the thirties without taking into account the economic climate of the nation in the stagnant thirties. Within a few years after 1929 real incomes were reduced 30 percent, manufacturing had declined almost 50 percent, and unemployment had increased to unheard of proportions. Labor's initial reaction to such change was more one of disbelief than antagonism. Labor seemed more stunned than roused to any immediate and imaginative reform program. But disillusionment slowly developed regarding the capacity of market forces to cure their own evils, and a new cynicism developed regarding the harmony hypothesis of welfare capitalism. President Hoover stressed the importance of maintaining faith and optimism in the capacity of the nation to recover from the setback and appealed for general business optimism. President Roosevelt, in a similar vein, declared that the nation had " nothing to fear but fear itself." But how was the change in the public psychological climate to be established? The new Democratic administration, coming to power in 1933, began a series of experiments in the belief that positive action of some kind was better than inaction. The New Deal developed slowly becoming much more a political and economic philosophy after the fact than before the fact. It seemed clear that even the Democrats were not certain just what ought to be done. They agreed only that something should be done.

In 1932 the Norris-La Guardia Act restricted the use of the injunction in labor disputes and made yellow-dog contracts unenforceable in the courts.

The first body of legislation in the thirties that gave legal inducement to labor organization was the National Industrial Recovery Act of 1933. This act provided that price codes for various industries be established in order to prevent cumulative delation, but Section 7(a) specified that where price codes were established, employees had the right to organize and bargain collectively through representatives of their own choosing without interference, restraint, or coercion on the part of employers. Most employers felt it would be more appropriate if workers were organized on company lines, rather than through outside unions. It has been estimated that from 1932 to 1935 the number of company-dominated union members increased from 1,200,000 to approximately 2,500,000 members.

Probably the largest single boost to union activity came with the passing of the Wagner-Connery Labor Relations Act, commonly called the Wagner Act, in 1935, and its validation by the Supreme Court in 1937. Under the provisions of this act, the question as to whether unions were to be recognized by the employer was determined by the majority wishes of the work force. Employers were required to bargain " in good faith " with certified unions and a series of " unfair employer practices " were enumerated, including the domination of the union by any employer. To interpret and enforce the provisions of the law the National Labor Relations Board was established. In case of defiance of the Board's orders, the issue could be taken to the courts to secure compliance.

Structural and personality elements within the labor movement combined with favorable labor legislation to encourage the mushroom growth of unions in the thirties. John L. Lewis, as head of the United Mine Workers, felt that the American Federation of Labor was giving inadequate attention to the need for organizing the mass production industries along industrial lines. At the convention of the Federation in 1934, fourteen resolutions were advanced on the issue of craft and industrial unionism. A compromise resolution was evolved, in which the Federation reiterated the need for craft organization, but directed the Executive Council to issue charters for national unions in the automotive, cement, aluminum, and any other mass production industry necessary to "meet the situation." It was to inaugurate a campaign to organize the iron and steel industry " at the earliest practical date."

At the Atlantic City convention of 1935 the industrial union faction charged that the Federation leadership had ignored the spirit and letter of the 1934 resolution and proposed the resolution. ". . . It is the declared purpose (of the AF of L) to provide for the organization of workers in mass production and other industries upon industrial and plant lines regardless of claims based upon the question of jurisdiction." This resolution was rejected by the convention, and to John L. Lewis, this was tantamount to the rejection of industrial unionism. Following the convention, Lewis invited eight of the officers and representatives of the industrial unions within the American Federation of Labor (representing approximately 900,000 workers) to meet with him to discuss common problems. They formed the Committee for Industrial Organization, and when news of this meeting reached President William Green, he demanded the immediate dissolution of the Committee. The Committee ignored the order and suggested instead that it would provide one third of a $1 million fund to organize the steel industry if the rest of the AF of L unions would provide the rest. The offer was rejected by the AF of L, and on July 15, 1936, the Executive Council of the AF of L met to hear charges that the Committee was guilty of " fomenting insurrection " and of acts " constituting rebellion." The officers of the committee were ordered to stand trial, but the accused persons refused to appear. On September 5, 1936, the dissident unions were suspended from the AF of L, and by October 25, 1937, the Committee decided, after a failure to reconcile their differences with the AF of L, to establish a permanent Congress for Industrial Organization. This rivalry between the CIO and AF of L gave new impetus to labor organization as each scrambled to enlist the support of the unorganized. New organization techniques were employed, including the use of the sound-truck blasting such statements as: "The President Wants You to Join a Union." The research division of the CIO provided data on wage and earning levels, company profit, and so on to give persuasive arguments for union organization. Newspapers were published, pamphlets distributed, rallies and meetings held, all to convince the workers of the advantages they would enjoy, if organized. The campaign to organize mass production industries was highly successful, and by 1941 most major employers had not only recognized unions as the bargaining agent of their work force, but many had accepted closed-shop contracts giving the union a high degree of security, and a guaranteed membership. The continuing success of the Democratic party at the polls seemed to insure labor a continuing favorable political and legal climate in which to operate.

World War II and After: Unions Consolidate Their Position

The tempo of union activity and organization did not decrease during World War II. The dramatic increase in the demand for labor did much to give an economic foundation to labor's bargaining power, reinforcing the strength unions had found in favorable government legislation and general public sympathy. As the nation faced World War II, the government was still firmly dedicated to the proposition that labor should have the freedom to organize in order to assure a more equal balance of bargaining power.

World War II provided an interesting case study of unions in a full-employment economy. It became immediately evident that the total demand for labor would soon outstrip the supply, and a wage-price spiral appeared immanent if collective bargaining was to continue free and unrestrained. But the government could not afford strikes or any interruptions in the production process. It seemed clear that the government would now have to define " fair and equitable " conditions for labor contracts. The economic complications of over-full employment were presumably to be solved by making the process of collective bargaining a political rather than economic problem.

Prior to United States intervention or involvement in World War II, President Roosevelt, in March 19, 1941, created the tripartite National Defense Mediation Board. The Board's function was to propose a fair and acceptable solution to a conflict. It was not to gear its decisions to the economic power of each party to the dispute or, in other words, to give to the lion the lion's share. The mediation board immediately became involved in union security issues and evolved the compromise proposition between the demand on the part of unions for closed-shop provisions and the desire of employers to avoid any such union security clause by providing the " maintenance of membership " agreement. The collapse of the Mediation Board followed the disagreement over the issue whether the United Mine Workers should secure union-shop contracts in all bituminous coal mines operated by the steel companies.

Before this difficulty could be fully appreciated, the attack of Pearl Harbor led to participation in World War II. On December 13, 1941, President Roosevelt issued a call for a conference on labor and management representatives and requested a voluntary no-strike and no-lockout pledge for the duration of the hostilities. On December 17, 1941, such a conference was held, and both labor and management rose to the President's challenge. It was also recommended that a tripartite War Labor Board be established to settle those disputes which might otherwise lead to a deadlock or strike, and on January 12, 1942, such a board was established. The power of this board was complete and final, and when compliance was not forthcoming, the disputes were referred to the President. The President could order seizure of the plants and during the war forty plants were seized by the government. When the Board terminated its activities on December 31, 1945, it had handled about 20,000 labor disputes, and in about 800 of these a strike had followed the ruling of the Board. The Board attempted to resolve disputes on a "case by case" basis, evolving in a sense a new common law of industrial relations with each decision.

The major exception to the effective operation of this machinery developed early in 1943 when John L. Lewis defied the War Labor Board in the coal strike. The public considered a coal strike unthinkable and was stunned when the coal miners walked off their jobs on Lewis' orders. Even the threat of seizure did not resolve the dispute, for the miners rejected the order of their "commander-in-chief," President Roosevelt, to return to the mines. Lewis simply pointed out the difficulty of "mining coal with a bayonet." The public was enraged and the aroused Congress quickly passed, in June, 1943, the War Labor Disputes Act or Smith-Connally Act, over the President's veto. This act gave statutory authority for the President to seize plants, made it a criminal offense to instigate, direct, or aid a strike in a seized plant, and outlawed strikes in privately operated war plants until thirty days' notice had been filed and a strike vote taken to indicate whether the workers desired to strike. Such legislation was clearly contradictory to the no-strike pledge given by labor, since it provided for a vote to determine whether the workers wanted to strike.

Avoiding interruptions in production was just one facet of the labor-management problem. The other was to avoid a wage-price spiral. During the initial phase of the war period it was assumed that a program of voluntary restraint would provide sufficient stability, but as the inflationary trend became more pronounced, a definite control policy was necessary. The Little Steel Formula was evolved on July 16, 1942, providing for a maximum of a 15 percent wage increase from the January, 1941, base. In October, 1942, the War Labor Board was given responsibility for the wage stabilization program. It attempted to impose, from time to time, stringent limits on wage increases, but its policies were basically a " defense in depth " rather than a rigid wage ceiling.

In the postwar period it was hoped by the President that labor and management might extend their no-strike, no-lockout pledge, so that the readjustments from a wartime to peacetime economy could be more speedily established. On November 5, 1945, President Truman called a Labor-Management Conference in order to find a working relationship between labor and management, but neither side could see much value in the continued no-strike, no-lockout pledge. Philip Murray, president of the CIO, recommended the return to free collective bargaining, " to cushion the shock to our workers, to sustain adequate purchasing power, and to raise the national income." Management, too, seemed equally willing to escape wartime restrictions.

Employers demanded revisions of the Wagner Act in order to restore a more equal balance in labor-management relations. Labor representatives, on the other hand, refused to admit the need for any change in the Wagner Act, but this was a position that neither the public nor the Congress seemed willing to share.

A new period of industrial unrest developed in the 1945–1946 interval. There had been some decline in employment in 1945, although much less than economists had predicted. The readjustments, however, necessitated a cutback on the hours worked per week and these resulted in a decline in weekly earnings for labor. The rash of strikes that followed demobilization and the postwar inflation did even more to convince the public that irresponsible unionism must be restrained by new legislation. The Taft-Hartley Act became law in June, 1947, over the President's veto, and a new phase of labor-management relations was initiated.

6

Influences on
Union Growth

The several episodes of union development described in the previous chapter are much like single snapshots taken from a motion picture. Since it is impossible to reproduce *all* the events in the development of the union movement that are of significance and interest, it is generally necessary to relate those few events, selected from the chronology of history, to a central thesis or theme to indicate their particular significance. In our last chapter this central thesis or hypothesis was that changes in the economic environment accounted for changes in the growth of unionism. In this chapter, we shall review this argument (and a few alternative ones) more carefully. We shall analyze various influences for union development: (1) the influence of the economic cycle, (2) the influence of the product and labor market, (3) the influence of the strong leader, and finally (4) the influence of legislation and judicial interpretation.

Following this presentation of the "why" of union growth, we shall briefly discuss the geographic dispersion of union growth and some of those occupational considerations which will influence the nature of unionism's future growth.

Before embarking upon our analysis of why the union movement has grown in the manner that it has, let us glance at the data on such growth. In Figure 4 we see the figures for the absolute volume of union membership from 1897 to 1955. The free-hand trend line again indicates the strong upsurge of union membership after 1935. The significance of union membership growth can better be appreciated if it is analyzed in terms of labor force size. Because of the importance of the percentage of workers organized, the index of "real" union membership is indicated in Figure 5. "Real" union growth is revealed by dividing the changing union membership by the changing size of the work force.

For the most part, the patterns of actual and real union membership follow each other rather closely, except for the twenties and early thirties. The relative lag in real union growth in those years was occasioned by the more rapid growth of the labor force without a corresponding growth of union membership.

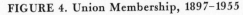

FIGURE 4. Union Membership, 1897–1955

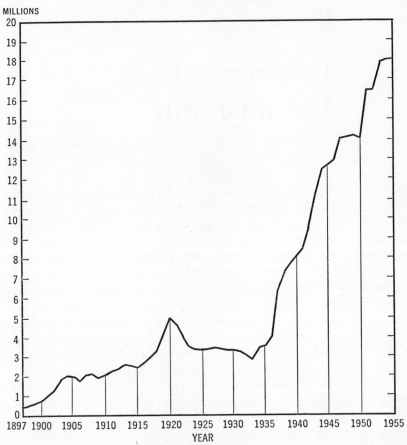

Source: Data from 1897 to 1950 are taken from Bernstein's study, "The Growth of American Unions," *The American Economic Review*, Vol. XLIV, No. 3 (June, 1954). Bernstein's data are secured from Leo Wolman's analysis, but from 1949–1953 Bernstein makes a projection of union growth based on AF of L data. The data utilized from 1951 to 1955 are based on Bureau of Labor Statistics estimates but may not be strictly comparable with earlier years. The data for Figure 4 include the Canadian membership.

The percentage representation of the union in the labor force as a whole is often taken as a measure of union influence. Here again, however, one must be cautious, for the impact of the union is likely to be more pervasive than the percentage figures indicate. First, employers with unorganized plants are sensitive to the progress made by the unionized workers. Unless they match the benefits provided in union plants, their employees may develop an interest in organizing to help maintain their relative position. Gains in one are, therefore, often transmitted like electrical impulses to the other. Thus statistical " discrepancies " between

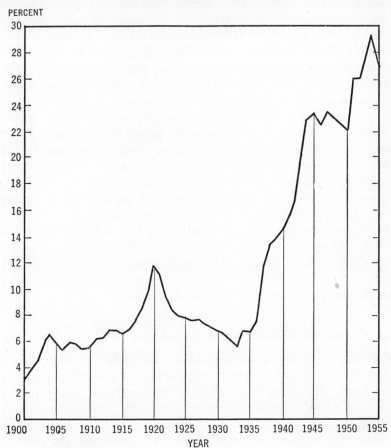

PERCENT

YEAR

Source: See Figure 4 Source.

The estimates of "real" union membership can be compared with Bernstein's and others made by the Bureau of Labor Statistics.

Year	Bernstein Estimate	BLS Estimate Percent of Total Labor Force	BLS Estimate Percent of Nonagricultural Workers
1949	22.9	22.4	33.0
1950	22.1	22.0	31.9
1951	24.4	24.3	33.8
1952	25.2	24.0	33.0
1953	26.8	25.2	34.2
1954	na	25.1	35.3

The BLS estimates exclude from union membership totals the Canadian members of the American internationals who totaled 933,000 in 1954. Figure 5 data include the Canadian membership.

unionized and nonunionized workers are not too meaningful when used
to prove or disprove the influence of the union. Second, the civilian
labor force figure includes those not normally classed as employees, such
as professional, proprietary, and managerial persons. If these are not
counted as part of the organizable force, we find that not one out of four
members of the labor force is unionized, but that one out of three
organizable members of the labor force is unionized.[1] In a general summary of these data we see that 1935 represents a turning point in the trend
of union development. Taking the earlier period first, we see in Figure 5
that in 1900, a mere 3 percent of the labor force was organized. A peak
in the proportion of workers organized was reached in 1920 when approximately 12 percent of the work force had joined unions. But by 1933
the proportion of union membership had declined to less than 6 percent.
From 1900 to the early twenties, then, we may characterize union growth
as having an upsurge, centered around World War I, but this growth was
quickly dissipated in the prosperity of the twenties and the depression of
the early thirties. In the second period, from 1933 on, the proportion of
union membership increased in almost every year, with spectacular
growth through the late thirties and early forties.

The Economic Cycle as a Determinant of Union Growth

For many years labor economists have generally believed that there was
a tendency for unions to expand during periods of prosperity and to contract during periods of recession. The arguments for the sympathetic
pattern of union and economic growth are fairly obvious, and only recently has it been suggested that the correlations of union membership to
several of the more important economic parameters are very poor. The
decline of unionism during the prosperity of the twenties and its growth
in the depression of the thirties seems to stand this thesis on its head.[2]

The Wave Characteristic of Union Growth. Before we examine the
logic of this argument, let us turn to an explanation of union growth —
which we have dubbed the " wave theory " — that came before this more
formal and sophisticated cyclical theory. The wave theory is not so much
an independent theory of union growth as an observation of the nature of
its growth. Briefly, it suggests that unions have grown in the manner of
waves lapping on the shores of the unorganized labor force. But the tide
of organization is rising. With each successive wave the proportion of organized workers increases, but with each successive recession the decrease

---

[1] For discussion and data, see Benjamin Solomon, "Dimensions of the Union Growth,
1900–1950," *Industrial and Labor Relations Review,* Vol. 9, No. 4 (July, 1956),
p. 546.

[2] For a critical analysis of this cyclical approach see Irving Bernstein, "The
Growth of American Unions," *American Economic Review,* Vol. XLIV, No. 3
(June, 1954), pp. 301–318.

of union membership is not as great as the preceding increase. Richard T. Ely observed in 1886:

> A reaction appears to have set in, but a change will come again, and the unions and various associations will once more report an increasing membership. The progress of the labor movement may be compared to the incoming tide. Each wave advances a little further than the previous one; and he is the merest tyro in social science, and an ignoramus in the history of his country, who imagines that a permanent decline has overtaken organized labor, whatever his talents or acquisitions may be in other respects.[3]

A similar viewpoint was expressed by Samuel Gompers in 1904: " From the formation of the first *bona fide* trade union movement in modern times, it has grown with each era of industrial activity and receded to some degree with each industrial depression, but in each recurring revival in industry the degree of growth has been greater . . . than its immediate predecessors."[4] In more recent times Joseph Shister has pointed out that the union membership follows a cyclical pattern, with asymmetry in the progressive cycles. He attributes this asymmetry, first, to the fact that the longer the worker is a union member, the less likely he is to abandon his membership even if he becomes unemployed. The worker may maintain his union membership (a) because of anticipated re-employment, (b) to avoid the costs of paying an initiation fee again, or (c) to show his loyalty to the union. Seniority provisions which promise preferential consideration to the long-term member in rehiring will also encourage such workers to stick with the union. Figures 4 and 5 substantially support this " wave " characteristic of union membership expansion.

Unemployment and Price Factors in Union Growth. Let us consider now whether union membership has paralleled the economic cycle: There is, of course, no single measure of a business cycle, for it is made up of movements of employment, production, the cost of living, wholesale prices, income, and so on. Generally these parameters of economic activity move in sympathetic directions, but this is not always the case. Taking first the level of unemployment, it can be reasoned that when unemployment is high, the employer is in position to exact the degree of labor efficiency and cooperation he demands. Employees appreciate the desperate situation the employer is in, not because they want to share his problems and responsibilities, but rather because they realize that failure to cooperate might cost them their jobs. The employer is in no mood for compro-

[3] Richard T. Ely, *The Labor Movement in America* (1886), p. 90 and quoted in Millis and Montgomery, *Organized Labor* (New York, McGraw-Hill Book Co., 1945), p. 79.

[4] Proceedings of the 24th Annual Convention of the AF of L 1904 and quoted by Horace B. Davis, " The Theory of Union Growth," *Quarterly Journal of Economics*, Vol. 55 (August, 1941), p. 620n.

mise agreements with the unions. He must have output at all costs, and a challenge to this drive is met with the blunt statement that any obstruction will jeopardize the economic welfare of all. Management can use such a situation to undermine or weaken the union and often has. Management cannot openly discriminate against workers for union membership, but disapproval of union activity may be subtle and effective. The worker, anxious to preserve his job, may fear that loyalty to the union will be construed as hostility to the employer. With widening unemployment, the union loses much of its bargaining power for the threat to strike loses its sting. The union loses prestige when members sense how ineffective the union is in dealing with their plight.

During a period of expanding employment the shoe is on the other foot. Employers, anticipating an ever-tightening labor market, are anxious to appease their work force. Wage and other concessions are made to maintain their present work force and attract new members. Nor is management reluctant to give the union credit for negotiating such benefits. Workers securing jobs join the union without fear of reprisals and regard membership dues a sound investment. The union may also negotiate a union-shop contract which reduces the selling job of the union to secure new members.

Price changes, too, may also explain why unions contract during depressions and increase during prosperity. During a depression two price-induced forces weaken the impulse to union support. First, the employer, knowing that he cannot shift any part of the burden of worker demands on to the public because of declining prices, stiffens in his resistance to union demands. Second, the worker still employed is likely to enjoy substantial increases of real income because of the price deflation. This advantage would tend to curb his desire to demand increases of money wages, and even soften his resistance to modest cuts in money income. During the period of prosperity, these forces operate in reverse to encourage union growth, especially as the increase in the cost of living reduces real wage rates. Workers feel genuinely aggrieved because of the decline of living standards, especially when total production is increasing. The union is quick to capitalize on this dissatisfaction. Further, the employer may feel reasonably confident of his ability to shift at least a portion of the burden of higher wages on to the public by higher prices.

As we mentioned above, the fact that unionism declined in the twenties and expanded in the thirties suggests that these economic forces do not operate as directly to affect union growth. Irving Bernstein, following his study of the correlation of membership with the cost of living, employment, wholesale prices, and industrial production, reaches the conclusion that " The conventional monocausal explanation for fluctuations in union membership, the business cycle, is without general validity." [5]

[5] *Op. cit.*, p. 317.

But we cannot neglect the influence of such economic variables on the basis of poor correlation alone. For example, the *intensity* of economic change appears to be related to membership growth.

The Intensity of Economic Change and Union Growth. One might suspect that the *cumulative* growth of prosperity and business optimism

TABLE 5 Direction of Change of Union Growth with Changes in Various Economic Variables: 1901–1948

Total Number of Years of Increase *in Various Parameters of 3% or More Per Year*

Variable	Total Number of Years *Increased* by 3% or More	Number of Years Unionism INCREASED		Number of Years Unionism DECREASED	
		Actual	Real	Actual	Real
Cost of living	19	18	16	1	3
Wholesale prices	21	18	15	3	5
Employment	23	15	13	8	9
Production	28	17	16	11	11
Total	91	68	60	23	28

Total number of years of Decrease *in Various Parameters of 3% or More Per Year*

Variable	Total Number of Years *Decreased* by 3% or More	Number of Years Unionism INCREASED		Number of Years Unionism DECREASED	
		Actual	Real	Actual	Real
Cost of living	6	1	0	5	5
Wholesale prices	9	4	2	5	5
Employment	6	2	2	4	4
Production	14	8	6	6	7
Total	35	15	10	20	21

Source: Data derived from Bernstein's study, "The Growth of American Unions," *American Economic Review*, Vol. XLIV, No. 3 (June, 1954), pp. 303, 304, 312.

is conducive to union expansion just as cumulative depression discourages union growth. It is likely that the business outlook is, in large part, determined by the extent to which economic indexes move upward or downward. In Table 5 we have analyzed the change in both actual and real union membership from 1901 to 1948, but only for those years when the cost of living, wholesale prices, employment, and production increased by 3 percent or more. The 3 percent figure is an arbitrary selection, but it is a benchmark which might distinguish the rather minor changes from those which are significant. Table 5 indicates that more often than not, union growth was positively associated with these changes. This suggests, then, that the pace of change is an important determinant of union growth.

Further support to the thesis that the economic climate has an important bearing on union growth can be found in unemployment figures. In each of the twelve years that unemployment diminished from 1929 to 1950, actual union membership in all of these years increased. On the other hand, in the eight years when unemployment increased, actual union membership increased in four years and decreased in four years. This lends rather conclusive support to the role we have assigned unemployment in explaining union growth, and it also supports the thesis advanced by Ely, Gompers, and Shister that union growth is likely to be asymmetrical.

The " Market Contour " Approach to Union Growth

Both the characteristics of the product market and the labor market can explain, in large part, the character and degree of unionization at any point of time. This explanation of the effect of market forces is not, of course, inconsistent with our discussion above but is rather complementary to it. What are some of these market contours that affect unionization and in what way may changes in these contours offset union growth?

The resistance of management to unionism may vary directly with the proportion of labor costs to total costs. It may vary with the availability of substitutes for products that union labor is producing, whether such substitutes are produced by unionized labor, whether the consumer demand for the product is highly elastic or inelastic, whether the entire industry is unionized or only part of it, and so on.

The worker's impulse to join a union, on the other hand, may be affected by his feelings of insecurity, by his feeling that he is dropping behind in his relative income position with other workers, his annoyance with management, the sentiment within the rest of the work force regarding the union idea, the history of resistance to unionism offered by management, the organizing techniques employed by the union, the distance between the worker and his employer (geographically, functionally, socially, and psychologically), the dispersion of workers in the plant and industry, the proportion of male to female workers (female workers are likely to be less militant than male workers), the ethnic and racial composition of the labor force, and so on. It is obviously difficult for the union to organize the small scattered plants with relatively few workers, with those workers sometimes performing semimanagerial functions along with management. These institutional factors have led some to predict that the union movement has already reached its saturation point, and the attempts to further extend union membership will offer rapidly diminishing results at the expense of ever-increasing costs to unions.[6]

As we noted in Chapter 2, the increased technology, specialization, and expansion of production in our society has involved an increase in the proportion of the labor force engaged in service trades, white-collar pursuits, and skilled technical occupations. The technical, professional, and administrative workers, including engineers, chemists, architects, accountants, artists, editorial and technical writers, photographers, technicians, specialists, government workers, teachers, nurses, librarians, numbering over 3.5 million persons, are difficult to unionize. Those who help advertise, sell, service, and distribute the products of industry, including office and field workers, account for another 7.5 million persons, who are often skeptical of the value of unionism for them.[7] Many of these workers are individualists, convinced that everyone is master of his own destiny and succeeds through his own vigorous efforts. The nature of their work often involves considerable initiative, originality, authority, and responsibility, which encourages their identification with management. Many of these have enjoyed considerable educational background, so while they are not openly intolerant of the production workers, they do not mingle freely with them. Nor are they attracted to the union movement, associated in their mind with " laborers."

A further aspect of the growth of union membership is the character of technological change in industry, which, of course, affects the quality and functions of labor required by industry. Fewer unskilled workers are in demand and even the number of semiskilled machine operators may be reduced as automation is extended within the plant. With a decreasing proportion of labor costs to total costs, management can afford to be liberal in its wage policies, for the increment of total costs of a generous wage policy may not be substantial. The average investment in plant, machinery, and inventory per worker in America is roughly $7,500, but in some industries, such as chemicals, this investment runs as high as $25,000 per worker. The volume and value of such capital investment is likely to increase rapidly and continually in the future.

Union Leadership and Union Growth

The American union movement has never suffered a lack of interesting and dramatic personalities, and to many the strategy, skill, and ambition of these leaders does much to explain the growth of unionism. The

[6] For an interesting discussion, see Daniel Bell, " The Next American Labor Movement," *Fortune* (April, 1953).

[7] These figures are contained in Robert K. Burns' study, " Unionization of the White Collar Worker," American Management Association, Personnel Series, No. 110, and reproduced in Shister, *Readings in Labor Economics and Industrial Relations* (Philadelphia, J. B. Lippincott Co., 1951), p. 56.

"strong-man" approach to history has lost much of its vogue in recent times, mainly because we have seen the extremes to which fascist dictators in Europe would go to aggrandize personal power, and because we dislike thinking of people as a malleable mass that can be manipulated at the whims of the strong leader. There is, unfortunately, sufficient evidence to suggest that very frequently the rank and file of union members reject active participation in union affairs, and it is out of such apathy that the unscrupulous leader finds the opportunity to build his own power apparatus within the union.[8]

Because the union leader is located on the apex of union power, he is most frequently the focal point for attack by both employers and the public. Criticisms usually allege that it is not that American workers are corrupt, but simply that they have been duped by unscrupulous, Godless, power-hungry leaders. As a case in point, even the idealistic leadership of the Knights of Labor could not escape the full fury of public criticism: One newspaper reported a meeting by stating " The worst element was out last night to hear a kid-gloved, oily-tongued, slip-faced demagogue hold forth in an incendiary, blood-curdling speech on the rights of the horny-handed workmen." The account went on to explain that the labor leader was a:

> Communist, Socialist, Molly Maguire, incendiary blood-and-thunder spouter, hungry-looking loafer, a sinister-faced wretch whose company could be dispensed with in this community, a fellow whose appearance suggested a recent visit to the penitentiary; a fellow who violently gesticulated and frothed at the mouth for half an hour without saying anything; a blatherskite who had the audacity to stand before a body of workmen to tell them of their wrongs, while he himself was dressed in a suit of broadcloth. Such creatures should be treated as they deserve by the honest toilers and sent out of town in a suit of tar and feathers. . . .[9]

Undoubtedly, much of this resentment against union leadership arises because of the skill with which the public feels that labor leaders exploit industrial unrest and dissension. The union leader plays his most dramatic

[8] In developing the " personality" theory of union growth two factors must be kept in mind. First, it is impossible to either prove or disprove the influence of the leader in any empirical manner for, like other hypotheses of the social sciences, we cannot set up a controlled experiment to evaluate the development of the union movement in, say, the absence of John L. Lewis' influence. In this sense, our analysis is predominantly speculative. Second, it is difficult to determine to what extent the leader is in effect leading or just capitalizing on the peculiar nature of forces existing at any moment. Undoubtedly the man and institutions interact on one another: the leader both leads and is led, shapes institutional development, and is, in turn, shaped by institutions. On balance, it seems doubtful that we can consider leadership a completely independent variable as the cause of union growth.

[9] As quoted by Eli Ginsberg, *The Labor Leader* (New York, The Macmillan Co., 1948), p. 44.

role during turmoil, for it is his function to cement or coalesce the work group into an effective power unit.

> A crisis . . . precipitates new problems that demand immediate solution. The new situation and the fact that it must be handled expeditiously give the leader his chance. At such times the old structure loses much of its inflexibility and the pressing reality facilitates changes that would not have been tolerated during stable periods. . . .[10]

The economic crisis of the thirties, for example, created tremendous opportunities for union leadership. It is significant that John L. Lewis's fame spread during the crisis of unemployment in the thirties and during the emergency of World War II, rather than in the predepression period of the twenties or the postwar decade of the fifties.

Let us consider the background of some of our union leaders. Traditionally, a leader has been fictionalized as a wild-eyed, bushy-haired, thick-skulled, foreign-born agitator, loyal to Russia, intoxicated with Communist ideology, and dedicated to the destruction of the American way of life. The few case studies of union leadership suggest, however, that this picture is grossly distorted. Back in 1927 Pitirim Sorokin classified the biographic material contained in the *American Labor's Who's Who*, for 1925.[11] He came up with some tentative observations: Comparing place of birth to present residence, Sorokin found that the Middle Atlantic area was a center of influx for labor leaders, that the West, North, and Central were centers of exodus for such leaders. The West seemed to spawn a great proportion of labor leaders who had not been permanently absorbed in labor leadership in their home area. A surprisingly high proportion of union leaders were, however, foreign-born — 32.7 percent (compared with a proportion of 13.2 percent foreign-born for the population as a whole). Sorokin used a socio-occupational class scale to determine the occupational status of the fathers of such leaders and found that the larger portion of leaders came from the managerial and business classes rather than from the unskilled and occupational groups. He further found that one half of the national union leaders held college degrees, while only 20 percent of the lesser officials were college graduates.

In a more recent study by C. Wright Mills and Helen S. Dinerman, a shift in the characterization of the labor leader is clearly indicated.[12] In 1940, 10 percent of the United States population had a college education, while 25 percent of the AF of L leadership and 33 percent of the CIO

[10] *Ibid.*, p. 16.
[11] "Leaders of Labor and Radical Movements in the United States and Foreign Countries," *American Journal of Sociology*, Vol. 33, No. 3 (November, 1927).
[12] *The House of Labor*, edited by J. B. S. Hardman and Maurice F. Neufeld (New York, Prentice-Hall, 1951), Part 1: The American Labor Movement, Section 2: Leaders of the Union.

leadership were so educated. Only 11 percent of both the leadership of the AF of L and the CIO were foreign-born, with slightly smaller percentage of foreign-born union leadership than the percentage of foreign-born persons for the total population. However, the labor leader group contained more people who were native white with foreign or mixed parentage. This later study found that the majority of the labor leaders were from the working force itself, with about six out of ten coming from laboring homes, mainly at the foreman and skilled-labor levels, three out of ten from the free enterprise class of farm owners, large and small business owners, and independent professionals, and one out of ten from the new middle class of salaried professional and white-collar workers.[13] About three quarters of the union leaders had been working as wage earners before becoming union officials.

There is considerable difference between the personality traits of the local union leader and the head of the international. If we consider this smaller group, we see some interesting profiles. Outstanding of course is the personality of John L. Lewis, who long ago learned to implement the advice given by Charles de Gaulle for those seeking power: ". . . the prestige [of the leader] requires mystery because men little revere what they know too well . . . in the plans, the manner, the movements [of the leader] there must be an element which other men cannot capture, which intrigues, moves them, keeps them breathless. . . ." [14] Lewis has succeeded in keeping his own union rather " breathless," but in a most autocratic manner. The officers of twenty-three of the union's thirty districts are appointed by Lewis and can be removed by him. Lewis defends this procedure by " business expediency " and the simple statement that elections cost time and money, and that, after all, he is a better judge of ability than the rank and file.[15] Such autocracy has contributed to a degree of order in the coal industry and some coal mine operators fear the disorganization that may result with his demise. Lewis's dramatic personality has won for him continued attention in the press. During the thirties he was second only to President Roosevelt in the coverage of his activities by the press. His membership swears by him, and the public has a strange fascination for his courage and biting bombast.

But these traits of national union leadership do not encourage social recognition. Indeed, the union leader is fairly low in the scale of social acceptance. In a painfully candid analysis of Lewis's social status, one writer explains:

[13] Hardman and Neufeld, *op. cit.*, p. 30.
[14] As quoted in *Fortune* (August, 1954), p. 48.
[15] As noted by *Fortune* (November, 1954), p. 80. The last time Lewis was challenged was in 1944 when Ray Edmundson, an appointed officer, raised a demand for autonomy in Illinois. After being removed from office by Lewis, he was denied admission to the convention on the ground that he had neither held office in the union nor was he a worker in a mine.

The head of a miners' union may use Shakespearian English, enjoy an upper class income (and the dubious privilege of paying high taxes), wield tremendous power, and even have a son rising to professional (physician) levels; yet socially the labor leader is regarded as a miner, although occasionally he is invited out in the upper social circles because of a host's desire for novelty.[16]

One study indicates that in thirty-one important universities, there was only one union leader among 728 trustees; by 1950 only four labor leaders had received honorary degrees from American universities, and of the 42,500 entries in the 1950–1951 edition of *Who's Who in America*, only 84 were labor leaders, compared to 8,700 businessmen and 2,920 clergymen.[17] This rejection by the community undoubtedly contributes in no small way to the belligerence of the union leader. This possibility is suggested by Imberman's analysis:

> Close up, a local union head crying into his Scotch at night in a lonely bedroom in a Detroit hotel is not an easy sight to forget, especially when he has been under tension all day directing a strike against a large corporation and at night, exhausted and a little inebriated, his thoughts revert to his daughter who was virtually forced to drop out of her college sorority weeks ago when it was discovered that her father was a labor leader and social ostracism followed. The impotence of the father to deal with such a situation is not unrelated to the fury with which he pursues his strike ends.[18]

Of course, the lack of recognition may in part be explained by the fact that the number of prominent union leaders in this country is no larger than 500. But it is still disillusioning for such leaders to realize that they have the income and generous impulses requisite for community status but are more often feared than respected.[19]

[16] A. A. Imberman, "Labor Leaders and Society," *Harvard Business Review*, Vol. 28, No. 1 (January, 1950), p. 55.

[17] Orme W. Phelps, "Community Recognition of Union Leaders," *Industrial and Labor Relations Review*, Vol. 7, No. 3 (April, 1954), pp. 421–422.

[18] *Op. cit.*, p. 58.

[19] Space limitations preclude any personality profiles of our important union leaders. For further discussion, see the cover story on George Meany, *Time*, Vol. LXV, No. 12 (March 21, 1955) and the cover story of Walter Reuther, *Time*, Vol. LXV, No. 25 (June 20, 1955). Other references of interest include K. Eby, "The Expert in the Labor Movement," *American Journal of Sociology*, Vol. 57 (July; 1951); C. Wright Mills, "The Trade Union Leader: A Collective Portrait," *Public Opinion Quarterly* (Summer, 1945); G. Strauss and L. R. Sayles, "Occupation and the Selection of Local Union Officers," *American Journal of Sociology* (May, 1953); A. L. Gitlow, "Union Rivalries," *Southern Economic Journal* (January, 1952); and A. W. Gouldner, "Attitudes of 'Progressive' Trade Union Leaders," *American Journal of Sociology* (March, 1947). Books on this subject include C. Wright Mills, *The New Men of Power: America's Labor Leaders* (New York, Harcourt, Brace and Co., 1948) and J. A. Weschsler, *Labor Baron: A Portrait of John L. Lewis* (New York, Wm. Morrow and Co., 1944).

The national leader not only faces the hostility of the community, but the opposition to the maintenance of his competitive position in the hierarchy of union leadership. It must be remembered that the rank and file's standard for successful leadership is not represented by moderation or statesmanship in collective bargaining, but the benefits it gains for the membership compared with concessions gained by other union leaders. Thus McDonald of the Steelworkers Union must secure gains that compare favorably with those of Reuther of the Automobile Workers. This competition has a membership as well as a wage dimension. The rambunctious campaigns of the Teamsters to increase their membership has probably antagonized other unions almost as much as it has employers, for some leaders complain that Beck is " Organizing the Organized."

In summary, the leader of the national union enjoys privileges and honor but it does not isolate him from criticism and the loneliness of success. The union leader can never relax, for even within his camp there are others eager to replace him. The few circumstances described help explain the aggressive nature of union leadership and why they are so anxious to extend memberships. Membership is an index of their own ability and success.

The Legal Climate and Union Growth

The laws of the land are undoubtedly among the more important determinants of union growth, for these provide the basic rules for the collective bargaining game. We may visualize two alternative approaches to the labor problem: struggle and bargaining within the economic arena, in which labor and management contend with the favorable and unfavorable elements of supply and demand, and the competitive struggle in the political arena, in which the government may be called on to help either contender. To foreign observers, one of the perplexing aspects of American unionism has been its reluctance to make greater use of its political influence. When George Meany was approached by a British trade unionist (also a member of the Labor party) with the question, " When are you Yanks going to wake up and form a political party? " Meany replied: " When collective bargaining yields as little for us as it does for you, we may have to form a political party." [20] But this does not deny the influence of labor legislation. The protests of organized labor over the Taft-Hartley Act testified to labor's appreciation of this point.

It is rather " old hat " to point out that the union cannot deliver the vote of its members, and more recently union leaders themselves have appreciated the multiple loyalties and interests of their members. The union cannot secure the partisan support of its own members to a political platform that is only pro-union.

[20] Recounted in *Time* (March 21, 1955), p. 23.

Because the pattern of labor legislation will be reviewed in Section IV, we shall not attempt to recapitulate that discussion here. We might note here, however, that the tremendous upsurge of union membership followed the Wagner Act in 1935, and particularly the 1937 validation of the act by the Supreme Court. Of particular significance was the provision of the Wagner Act which made the certification and recognition of a union an issue to be resolved by the balloting of the workers themselves rather than resolved by a test of strength between employers and employees. Employers were required to bargain in good faith with the accredited representatives of the majority of the labor force. Furthermore, an explicit list of unfair employer practices were enumerated to protect the worker from discrimination by the employer because of his membership in the union.

Another factor which contributed to the rapid growth of unions has been the negotiation of union security provisions. Three major forms of union security provisions have been negotiated in the past. The closed-shop provision requires that the new employee become a union member as a condition of employment. The union-shop provision, as distinguished from the closed shop, requires that the new employee become a union member within a stated period of time after taking up employment in the plant, generally thirty days. A third provision, the maintenance-of-membership ruling, requires that all those workers who elect to remain in the union within a stated escape period, must remain union members for the duration of the contract. It is apparent that such provisions may account for the rapid growth of union membership, especially during a period of rising employment. The closed-shop provisions were outlawed under the Taft-Hartley law, and in an earlier form of that law, the negotiation of the union shop was made somewhat more difficult. It is possible that a fair portion of workers are union members not because they want to be. Because of union security provisions, new workers may never have had an opportunity to make a choice in the matter.

Theories of Union Growth: A Summary Statement

A complex of forces affects the nature and direction of union growth in this country. While today it is the vogue to speak of a " pluralistic " theory of union growth (in which there is an interplay of social, political, psychological, and economic forces), we have reasoned that many of these basic forces at work are economic in their nature, even though they have such things as " leadership " or " legislative " manifestation. Of course, ascribing economic change as a moving force does tell us much of the story, for economic forces themselves are multiple and diverse and above all do not produce any single or highly uniform reaction by the work force.

FIGURE 6. Union Membership

(a) Union membership as a percentage of nonagricultural employment

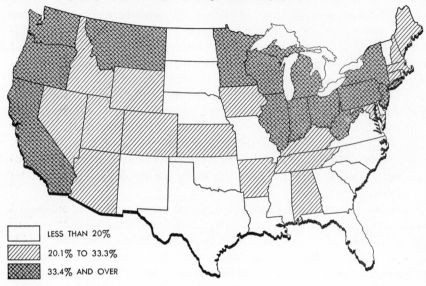

LESS THAN 20%

20.1% TO 33.3%

33.4% AND OVER

(b) Union membership (in thousands) by state

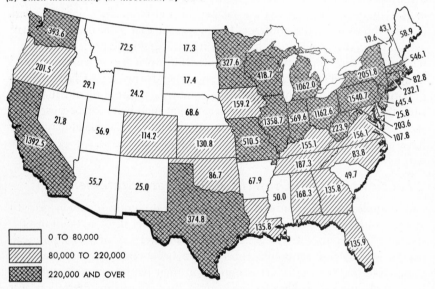

0 TO 80,000

80,000 TO 220,000

220,000 AND OVER

(c) **Percentage increase in union membership, 1939-53**

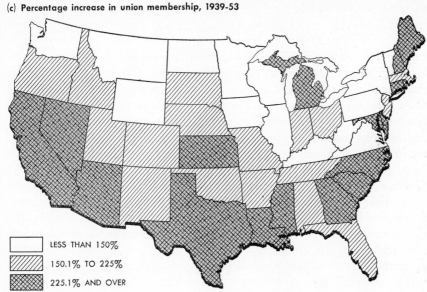

LESS THAN 150%

150.1% TO 225%

225.1% AND OVER

Source: Adapted from data by the National Bureau of Economic Resource.

Our data have indicated a startling upsurge of unionism since 1935. This growth has been caused, to use Daniel Bell's apt phrase, " by eruption, extension and enforcement." The eruption phase is explained by labor's loss of job opportunities and general economic instability: The public and government become more tolerant of the union idea, and the workers support unionism with greater enthusiasm. The extension phase develops from the proximity of unorganized workers to organized workers and the ensuing osmosis of the union idea within the work force from the union core to ever-widening perimeters. The enforcement phase arises from those union security provisions which require workers to join the union within a stated period of time.

There is considerable disagreement as to whether the various influences discussed will operate with the same intensity as they have in the past. Union growth may be likened to a horse leaping over successively higher hurdles; there is good reason to suspect that some of the hurdles ahead represent substantial obstacles to further rapid growth. Before examining the prospects of union growth for the future, we shall consider the geographic dispersion of membership today.

The Geographic Dispersion of Union Membership

From discussion of the reasons for union membership we would guess that the industrial areas of America would have a higher membership than the predominantly rural states. An examination of Figure 6(a) shows the breakdown by states of union membership as a percentage of the non-agricultural population. We see that the industrial East and North Central regions have the highest proportion of unionized workers in the country. But a second growth cone is found on the West Coast, including the states of California, Oregon, and Washington. States surrounding these areas also have a moderate proportion of their nonagricultural work force organized. If we consider the actual rather than the " real " union membership, we find again that the largest numbers of union members are in the East, North Central, and the West Coast, and Texas too must be added to the areas of large membership. This dispersion is seen in Figure 6(b). In Figure 6(c) we see the percentage changes from 1939 to 1953. This chart reveals the result of the union's drive to organize the South, for the band of largest percentage increase is clearly centered in the southern states. The percentage growth, however, is all the more spectacular in these areas simply because of the modest unionization in 1939, the year from which these percentage changes were calculated. It will be observed, for example, that even though Texas enjoyed a percentage increase of union membership of over 225 percent from 1939 to 1953, it was still an area in which less than 20 percent of the nonagricultural labor force was organized.

A factor not revealed by these figures is that the predominant number of the nonunion labor force is still located in the North. For example, the four northern states with the largest number of nonunion workers were New York, Pennsylvania, Illinois, and Ohio (in that order), and these together with California contained a total of over 12.7 million of nonunion workers. The five southern states with the largest number of nonunion workers are Texas, North Carolina, Missouri, Georgia, and Virginia (in that order), having an aggregate total of only 5 million nonunion workers. Thus, the drive for union membership will have to concentrate both in the North and South as well as in the West if union organizing goals are to be realized.[21]

Prospects for Future Union Growth

The public no longer views organized labor as the youthful innocent David facing the powerful and oppressive tyrant, management. The public is likely to support the underdog in any combat, but the suspicion is spreading that unionism is now the tail wagging the dog or that it is, in other words, a power center capable of seriously disrupting industrial activity. As Daniel Bell has observed, " Public opinion, that amorphous and highly manipulable animal, is today distinctly edgy about unions.

[21] The data on union membership are derived from a National Bureau of Economic Research Study on this project, undertaken by staff member, Leo Troy.

Talk about 'Big Labor' has had its effect on a suspicion of union purposes." [22]

The data on union membership suggest that the pace of growth leveled off somewhat after 1945.[23] It remains to be seen what effect the merged organizational plans of the AFL–CIO will have on future union membership. Certainly, unions have not abandoned their drive to widen their membership, and the consolidation of efforts to organize the unorganized will undoubtedly result in a larger membership. But unions still face some rather substantial obstructions, rooted mainly in the public concern that union power may already be overextended. What forms might these obstructions take?

First, unionism in large part evolved because of industrial insecurity. There exists a fairly strong possibility that the political inexpediency of tolerating unemployment on any large scale will do much to reduce the social unrest that arose in the past from economic disorganization. Second, pressure has built up in recent years for " right to work " legislation in various states, to restrict union security provisions on the ground that the worker should have the " right " to employment even if he is unwilling to join a union. Undoubtedly much of the union membership expansion in the war and postwar periods arose from rising employment in plants where existing union security provisions enforced an almost " automatic " expansion of union membership.

Probably, though, the character of the labor force and its utilization are more important than public sentiment in determining the future of union organization. The index of the total work force is not a completely satisfactory denominator for calculating real union membership, for this work force includes the self-employed persons or, in fact, all persons who work — regardless of their trade or profession — for an income. As we noted in Chapter 2, the labor force has undergone several important structural changes, including the decline of the farm proprietors and the expansion of the " white-collar " groups. Therefore, the union " potential " for organization, if we include within it the white-collar workers, has expanded. One calculation reveals that the portion of the labor force that might have been organized in 1900 was only 49.0 percent, but in 1950, this had increased to 72.5 percent.[24] Another view of this realloca-

---

[22] "The Growth of American Unions," by Daniel Bell, *Proceedings,* Industrial Relations Research Association (December, 1954), p. 235.

[23] Irving Bernstein points out that union membership in 1947 was 14,119,000 and in 1952 was 15,912,000. The percentage of union membership over the total labor force was 23.5 in 1947 and 25.2 in 1952. But Daniel Bell points out that if deductions are made for the number of Canadians that are members of American unions, and if the real union membership is calculated only on the basis of wage and salary employees in nonfarm establishments (excluding the self-employed), the ratio of union membership was 31.7 percent in 1947 and only 30.9 percent in 1952.

[24] From Benjamin Solomon, "Dimensions of Union Growth: 1900–1950," *Industrial and Labor Relations Review,* Vol. 9, No. 4 (July, 1956), p. 546. Solomon excludes

tion of labor is that in 1900 the white-collar sector comprised 20.8 percent of the union potential, while in 1950 it made up 35.5 percent of this potential.

We can see, then, that the future of unionism in large part depends upon the susceptibility of the white-collar worker to unionization. In 1950 less than one sixth of the approximately 16 million white-collar workers were organized. The group is difficult to organize for reasons already discussed. Many such workers are located in jobs essentially local in character. For example, most retail stores have only local markets, and many of the employees have a local orientation which discourages support of unionism. Retail clerks are seldom aware of wage structures in other markets, and perhaps are not concerned as much as other members of the labor force about wage differentials of other labor markets. Furthermore, organizing such workers is painfully slow and expensive as they are often located in scattered business establishments.[25] The cost of contacting a scattering of small establishments is substantial, and the lack of communication of such workers with other persons similarly situated reduces their perception of the " group " solution to their " group " problems. There is, therefore, a lack of physical as well as psychological cohesion among such workers. A further difficulty is that many of the unorganized live in small towns most frequently characterized by economic conservatism. Unionism faces a hostility in many rural communities.

Many of the unorganized, particularly in the white-collar groups, are young women, who do not view labor force participation as a permanent way of life. They are working simply to fill in time until they become married, or if married, simply to supplement the husband's earnings in order to meet the initial costs of setting up a household or to meet some extraordinary expense. Their outlook is not conducive to union membership.

While the weight of evidence suggests the increasing costs and difficulties for widening membership, there are forces at work which will minimize some of these difficulties. The application of automation to the

---

from the organizable labor force such groups as farmers and farm managers; farm laborers and foremen; managers, officials, and proprietors (except railroad conductors and postmasters), private household workers; among professional, technical and kindred workers – physicians and surgeons, lawyers and judges, clergymen, dentists, funeral directors, therapists and healers, optometrists, chiropractors, veterinarians, and osteopaths; among service workers, except private household – boarding- and lodging-house keepers, housekeepers and stewards, policemen and detectives, sheriffs and bailiffs, marshals and constables, midwives; among sales workers – real estate agents and brokers, hucksters and peddlers, auctioneers. . . . The self-employed and unpaid family classes of workers were, for the most part, also excluded. The most questionable of these exclusions would be the farm worker.

[25] This problem is general to much of the unorganized labor force, not the white collar group alone. A UAW survey showed that 97 percent of the still unorganized plants within the union's jurisdiction have less than 250 workers each and 63 percent have less than fifty workers each. Noted by Bell, *op. cit.*, p. 234.

office or the greater use of electronic equipment gives many workers a semitechnical status which frequently encourages unionism. Furthermore, the narrowing difference in earnings of the white-collar worker and the union worker would tend to increase interest in union membership, even though many employers try to avoid this possibility by giving tandem raises to all workers when the union secures wage boosts for its members.[26]

[26] As a case in point, the new Engineers and Scientists of America, a loose federation made up of fourteen independent engineers' associations, has been organized. The causes for membership in such an organization are (1) the erosion of status brought about by mass employment of engineers, (2) the multiplication of hierarchal levels. (3) the failure of employers to utilize engineering skills, (4) the narrowing of wage differentials, as well as wage distortion arising from the tightening labor market. "Reward on the basis of merit, not on the basis of scarcity, is one of the chief demands of the engineers." For discussion, see "Organized Engineers," *Fortune* (June, 1954), pp. 68, 70.

7

The Structure of Union
Organization

In Chapter 6 we traced the development of unionism. In this chapter our purpose will be to develop a second dimension to this picture by providing a cross-section of the extent and characteristics of unionization today. We shall examine the extent of union organization for various sectors of the economy and then appraise the functions and purposes of the various components to this aggregate organizational structure. We shall look first at the local, its leadership, purposes, and basic problems. In this discussion we must be ever mindful of the traditional conflict between the craft and industrial principle of organization, even though this distinction is of less significance in recent times. Turning from the local, we shall consider the wider functions of the nationals and internationals, of which the local is usually a part. Here we shall again appraise the problem of power and democracy within these large federations.

The latter section of this chapter will be concerned with the background for the merger of the AF of L and the CIO. December 5, 1955, is often taken as a watershed in the structural growth of unionism, for the merger of these two organizations at that time gave America a single labor organization with a membership of over 16 million and revived again the fear of trade union monopoly power. On closer inspection we shall see that the merger is not the monolithic agency that its organizational chart might suggest. This large federation contains within it a complex of divergent forces. We shall analyze, then, the structure of the merged organization and some of the basic difficulties it faces.

A Planetary View of Unionism: Some Basic Data

At the beginning of 1955 approximately 18 million workers belonged to American unions. Approximately 10.9 million of the total was accounted for by the original membership of the American Federation of Labor, while the Congress of Industrial Organizations accounted for 5.2 million members. Unions not affiliated with the AF of L or CIO included another 1.8 million. Slightly more than a million of this 18 million total, however, were outside the United States, mostly in Canada. Almost 3 million union members were women, who represented only one seventh of all the women in the labor force.

The core of union structure is not the much publicized AFL–CIO organization, but its national and international components. America has approximately 200 nationals and internationals, and even those affiliated with the AFL–CIO have a high degree of autonomy from the parent federation and independence from each other. These organizations are of uneven size, for 124 (with fewer than 50,000 members each) number only 1.5 million of the total union membership, while the 6 larger unions (with over 500,000 members each) account for a total of over 6 million members, or one third of the total union membership. Another way of appreciating the disproportionate strength of a few of these internationals is to note that more than half of the total of 77,000 locals in America are affiliated with 19 unions.[1] At least 125,000 collective bargaining agreements have been negotiated on behalf of organized labor.[2]

While the American Federation of Labor originally seized upon the craft principle of union organization, a principle long considered " correct " for the American scene, industrial unionism is the type more common today. Only 26 of the 123 national unions in the AF of L were industrial, compared with 22 of the 30 national unions of the CIO, but an examination of the *membership* of the merged organization reveals that only about one third belong to craft unions, while two thirds belong to those organized or functioning on an industrial basis.

The policies of these nationals vary considerably. For example initiation fees vary from 65 cents to $250. All unions together collect a total of some $457 million dollars in dues; approximately one half of this goes to the national or international headquarters. The remainder of this is kept by the locals to meet local expenses. Provisions for such issues as strike authorization, strike votes, contract authorization, qualifications for membership, racial restrictions and discrimination provisions, methods of electing union officers, procedure for discipline, and so on vary considerably from union to union.[3]

[1] Looked at in slightly more detail, these 19 large nationals contain approximately 40,000 locals. If we take the 80 smaller nationals, each with less than 100 locals, we find that together they contain a total of 3,000 locals, or only 4 percent of the total. Data are from William Paschell, " Structure and Membership of the Labor Movement," *Monthly Labor Review* Vol. 78, No. 11 (November, 1955), p. 1237.

[2] *Ibid.*, pp. 1231–1239.

[3] For a detailed discussion, see James J. Bambrick, Jr., and George H. Haas, *Handbook of Union Government Structure and Procedures* (New York, National Industrial Conference Board, 1955); Thomas C. Fichandler, " Collective Bargaining " from Woytinsky's study, *Employment and Wages in the United States;* the *Monthly Labor Review* article, " Size of Labor Unions in the United States " (July, 1950), and the " Extent of Collective Bargaining and Union Recognition," 1946, Bulletin No. 909 of the Bureau of Labor Statistics, 1947.

TABLE 6　Proportion of Wage Earners under Union Agreement by Industry, 1946, 1944, 1938

Industry	Degree of Unionization		
	1946 (percent)	1944	1938
Agricultural equipment	80–100	Large proportion	Almost no agreement
Aircraft and parts	80–100	Large proportion	Almost no agreement
Aluminum	80–100	Almost all	Large proportion
Automobiles and parts	80–100	Almost all	Large proportion
Breweries	80–100	Almost all	Almost all
Carpets and rugs, wool	80–100	n.a.	About half
Cement	80–100	About half	Large proportion
Clocks and watches	80–100	Large proportion	Almost no agreement
Clothing, men's	80–100	Almost all	Almost all
Clothing, women's	80–100	Large proportion	Almost all
Electrical machinery	80–100	Large proportion	Large proportion
Furs and fur garments	80–100	Almost all	Almost all
Glass and glassware	80–100	Almost all	Moderate proportion
Leather tanning	80–100	Large proportion	Moderate proportion
Meat packing	80–100	Large proportion	Moderate proportion
Newspaper printing and publishing	80–100	Large proportion	Almost all
Nonferrous metals and products	80–100	Almost all	About half
Rayon yarn	80–100	Large proportion	Large proportion
Rubber	80–100	Large proportion	Large proportion
Shipbuilding	80–100	Almost all	About half
Steel, basic	80–100	Almost all	Large proportion
Sugar	80–100	Large proportion	Moderate proportion
Actors and musicians	80–100	Almost all	Almost all
Airline pilots and mechanics	80–100	Almost all	n.a.
Bus and streetcar, local	80–100	Large proportion	Large proportion
Coal mining	80–100	Almost all	Almost all
Construction	80–100	Large proportion	Large proportion
Longshoring	80–100	Almost all	Large proportion
Maritime	80–100	Large proportion	Large proportion
Metal mining	80–100	About half	About half
Motion-picture production	80–100	Almost all	Large proportion
Railroads	80–100	Almost all	Almost all
Telegraph	80–100	Almost all	Moderate proportion
Trucking, local and intercity	80–100	Large proportion	About half
Book and job printing and publishing	60–79	About half	Large proportion
Canning and food preserving	60–79	Moderate proportion	Moderate proportion
Coal products	60–79	Large proportion	Moderate proportion

TABLE 6 (continued)

Industry	1946 (percent)	Degree of Unionization 1944	1938
Dyeing and finishing textile	60–79	Moderate proportion	Moderate proportion
Gloves, leather	60–79	About half	n.a.
Machinery, except agric. and elec.	60–79	Large proportion	Large proportion
Millinery and hats	60–79	Large proportion	Large proportion
Paper and pulp	60–79	Large proportion	Moderate proportion
Petroleum refining	60–79	About half	About half
Railroad equipment	60–79	About half	n.a.
Steel products	60–79	About half	n.a.
Tobacco	60–79	About half	Moderate proportion
Woolen and worsted textiles	60–79	About half	Moderate proportion
Radio technicians	60–79	Large proportion	n.a.
Theater: stage hands, motion picture operators	60–79	Large proportion	Moderate proportion
Baking	40–59	About half	About half
Chemicals (excluding rayon yarn)	40–59	Moderate proportion	Almost none
Flour, grain products	40–59	About half	Moderate proportion
Furniture	40–59	About half	Moderate proportion
Hosiery	40–59	About half	About half
Jewelry and silverware	40–59	Large proportion	Moderate proportion
Knitwear	40–59	n.a.	n.a.
Leather, luggage, handbags, novelties	40–59	About half	Moderate proportion
Lumber	40–59	About half	Moderate proportion
Paper products	40–59	Moderate proportion	Moderate proportion
Pottery, including china	40–59	About half	n.a.
Shoes, cut stock and findings	40–59	About half	About half
Stone and clay products except pottery	40–59	Moderate proportion	n.a.
Bus lines, intercity	40–59	About half	About half
Light and power	40–59	Moderate proportion	Moderate proportion
Newspaper offices	40–59	Moderate proportion	Moderate proportion
Telephone	40–59	Moderate proportion	Almost none
Beverages, nonalcoholic	20–39	n.a.	n.a.
Confectionery products	20–39	Moderate proportion	Almost none
Cotton textiles	20–39	Moderate proportion	Moderate proportion
Dairy products	20–39	Moderate proportion	Moderate proportion
Silk and rayon textiles	20–39	Moderate proportion	About half

TABLE 6   (continued)

Industry	Degree of Unionization		
	1946 (percent)	1944	1938
Barber shops	20–39	Moderate proportion	Moderate proportion
Building service and maintenance	20–39	Moderate proportion	Almost none
Cleaning, dyeing	20–39	Moderate proportion	Moderate proportion
Crude petroleum and natural gas	20–39	Moderate proportion	About half
Fishing	20–39	Moderate proportion	Moderate proportion
Hotels and restaurants	20–39	Moderate proportion	Moderate proportion
Laundries	20–39	Moderate proportion	Almost none
Nonmetallic mining and quarrying	20–39	Moderate proportion	n.a.
Taxicabs	20–39	Moderate proportion	Moderate proportion
Agriculture	1–19	Almost none	Almost none
Beauty shops	1–19	Almost none	n.a.
Clerical and professional except trans., commun., theater, and nwsp.	1–19	Almost none	Almost none
Retail and wholesale trade	1–19	Almost none	Almost none

Source: The 1946 data of Table 6 are derived from Bulletin 909 of the BLS *op. cit.,* p. 2, the 1944 data from the *Monthly Labor Review,* April, 1944, and the 1938 data from the *Monthly Labor Review,* March, 1939.

In the 1950 Bureau of Labor Statistics study of some 7,500 collective bargaining agreements, it was found that slightly more than a third of these covered less than 100 workers each. Three fourths covered less than 500 workers and about one in ten covered 1,000 or more workers. Only one out of every 100 included 10,000 or more workers.[4]

The Bureau of Labor Statistics has categorized various industrial groups in terms of their " degree " of unionization for the years 1938, 1944, and 1946. These statistics have served as a jumping-off point for most research designed to reveal differences between the union and nonunion sectors of our economy. The degree of unionization is one of the few devices for measuring union influence; but the Bureau's classifications are only approximations, and the data in Table 6 are cited here only to suggest the general areas of " high " union organization with those of " little " unionization.[5] As we see in Table 6, industries which have most successfully re-

[4] *Monthly Labor Review* (July, 1950), pp. 113–114.
[5] Kirk R. Petshek, in " Research on Extent and Scope of Collective Bargaining," Industrial Relations Research Association, papers presented December 28–29, 1952, explains the limitations of such data. " The BLS used to publish figures of contract coverages by industries, from agreements and other sources. This series has been

sisted unionism include agriculture, clerical and professional workers, retail and wholesale trades, laundries, building service and maintenance trades. The industries most highly unionized from 1938 to 1946 include aircraft, aluminum, automobiles, cement, electrical machinery, men's and women's clothing, and newspaper printing and publishing. It should be remembered, however, that the number of workers covered by union agreements is not the same as union membership. Except under union-shop conditions, agreements cover nonmembers as well as members employed within the given bargaining unit. On the other hand, some union members may be working in unorganized plants, and many civil service employees and teachers are members of unions but are not covered by union agreements. These data indicate the general success of union activity in the various fields, and there is a rough correlation between workers covered by union agreement, and those who are union members.

TABLE 7   Percentage of Nonagricultural Wage and Salaried Employees Organized 1930, 1935, 1940, 1947

	1930	1935	1940	1947
All nonagricultural industries	10.9	13.1	24.5	30.7
Manufactures	8.8	13.3	34.1	41.9
Transportation, communication, and public utilities	23.4	26.4	48.2	64.2
Building	54.3	56.5	65.3	74.6
Mining, quarrying, and oil	21.3	54.4	72.3	84.0
Services	2.7	3.1	6.7	8.8
Public service	8.3	8.5	10.2	11.9

Source: Data developed by Leo Wolman for the National Bureau of Economic Research's study, *A Half-Century of Union Membership*, contained in Wolman's article, "Concentration of Union Membership," Industrial Relations Research Association, *Papers* presented December 28–29, 1952, p. 216.

It is easier to perceive the trends of union organization for major industrial sectors in the Table 7 data developed by Leo Wolman. While Wolman cautions that such classifications are subject to a large margin of error, the figures indicate the significant increase of unionization in the manufacturing sector. In 1929 membership in building and transportation accounted for more than half of all union membership, but by 1947 manufacturing totaled nearly half of the union membership. The expansion of the automobile, steel, and machinists' unions gave tremendous momentum to industrial unionism. If we relate unionism to "production workers" only, we find that unionism represented 52 percent of all production

discontinued some time ago as not reliable enough. The coverage was too uneven" (p. 221, note). Page 223 of his paper does include some further "fragmentary" classifications of industries in terms of their coverage by collective agreements.

workers in manufacturing in 1947 (68.3 percent in metals, and 62.1 percent in clothing).

The diversity of the pattern of union growth reflects the multiple, and sometimes conflicting, forces impelling workers to organize. As we noted before, the proportion of workers organized in any industry depends on such forces as the history of the union, whether the membership is composed of highly skilled craft workers or semiskilled machine operators, whether there is intense competition among various unions themselves for representation of a given group of workers, whether the industry in which the union operates is one facing an expanding or declining market, whether job characteristics are changing rapidly because of automation and so on. Because of the diversity of these forces, it is not surprising that success has varied considerably from union to union. In our review of some of the major characteristics of union organization, it should be kept in mind that what may generally be true may not be an accurate description of any particular union.

The Local

The local is an organization which contrasts in several vital respects with the upper layers of administrative machinery serving it. In large industrial centers, several locals often operate side by side within the framework of their national union. The local is the front line of unionism because of its daily contact with management. And playing a crucial role in this front line, is the shop steward. This official is elected (but sometimes appointed) by the workers themselves to represent labor in various matters arising on the job. In contrast with European practice, shop stewards are usually paid by the company for time spent on grievances and their adjustment. Management usually believes that such representation helps to expedite satisfactory settlement of the day-to-day grievances. In this sense stewards are viewed as the " loyal opposition " within the plant. Any person desiring to advance himself within the union movement will often find that serving as a shop steward is a valuable and necessary apprenticeship. Such experiences as meeting with management, evaluating worker grievances, and winning and maintaining the confidence and support of the work crew are invaluable to any union officer. Whether daily labor-management relations are amicable or hostile depends frequently on the skill and tact of the steward. An inept steward can create havoc by misrepresenting management's statements, by pushing poor grievances for settlement, and by encouraging dissension. A skilled steward will carefully screen worker grievances to make certain that only strong cases are pushed to settlement and can earn a reputation for integrity from both labor and management.

Some unions, particularly in the building, clothing, and metal trades, employ a local business agent. This is a full-time union employee, paid by the union, and usually not working as an employee of the company. He often participates in the settling of shop grievances, assists in contract negotiations, maps out strategy for increasing and maintaining union membership, and so on. He can acquire considerable power and prestige because of his full-time interest and influence in labor-management relations. In the eyes of management, the steward and the business agent often represent the union, but the business agent is usually a person with considerably more skill and confidence than the steward.

The local may elect, or the executive officers of the local may appoint, both a negotiating committee and a grievance committee. The task of the former committee is to formulate demands prior to the negotiations of a new contract. The demands may arise at union meetings, and in this sense, be formulated by the rank and file themselves. Or they may be framed by the negotiation committee and submitted to the rank and file for its approval prior to negotiations. As a third possibility, the committee may prefer to keep the substance of the demands to itself so as to have more flexibility in dealing with management, and perhaps in this way suffer less loss of prestige in the eyes of the membership if the targets of the union are not met. The negotiation committee will usually be chaired by the president of the local and will include the business agent and any of the " walking " delegates from the national or international office having time to sit in on the negotiations.

Usually the members are given the opportunity to formally approve of the settlement reached by their negotiating committee. In many cases, however, the approval of the contract is usually assumed to be forthcoming, especially if the negotiating committee is enthusiastic about the concessions secured.

In the National Industrial Conference Board study of almost all nationals and internationals in this country it was found that over half of the union constitutions did not formally specify that the membership of the union must vote on the acceptance or rejection of negotiated agreements. It must not be assumed, however, that the absence of this provision in the union constitution precludes the practice of membership approval from being generally followed. The details of the NICB study are revealed in Table 8 on page 150.

To what extent must the local bargaining committee secure approval of the national to new contract provisions? Here again, the NICB study revealed that close to one half of union constitutions (representing about 46 percent of union membership in this country) provided for some form of national approval of union contracts. Only 5.7 percent of the constitutions (representing 3.7 percent of union membership) specifically indicated that national approval was not required. This may suggest, however, greater national control than in practice exists for close to a quarter

TABLE 8   Membership Voting in the Authorization of Contracts
(Declared Membership in Thousands)

Provision	No. of contracts	Per- centage	Declared Membership	Per- centage
Total Unions	194	100	17,514	100
Require a secret ballot vote by members to ratify contract	6	3.1	362	2.1
Require a membership vote but do not specify that it be secret ballot	25	12.9	2,639	15.1
Membership vote not required by union constitution	98	50.5	9,724	54.5
Union does not enter into collective bargaining contracts (Civil Service Unions)	19	9.8	797	4.5
No contract authorization provisions in the constitution	46	23.7	3,993	23.4

Source: National Industrial Conference Board study, *Handbook of Union Government, Structure and Procedures*, Studies in Personnel Policy, No. 150 (1955), p. 51.

of all contracts in the NICB study had no provisions which pertained to this issue.[6]

Participation in the union movement, it is often boasted, is based on voluntarism. Spontaneous interest is alleged to be the cement which binds the union together, but a review of the attendance of members at regular meetings suggests that much of the glue which originally accounted for the participation and cohesion of union membership is losing its adhesive quality. Attendance at those local meetings (usually held once a month) where members are not fined for nonattendance is usually estimated to average about 5 percent of the membership. Many factors contribute to this poor attendance record. First, the worker faces the competition of other interests, including television entertainment (many locals avoid holding union meetings on boxing or wrestling nights) and do-it-yourself projects. The home owner may find endless distractions in developing his garden, making improvements in his house. A further distraction from union attendance is the growing habit of families to shop in the evening. Furthermore, the worker may have to travel a considerable distance to get home from his job and is not disposed to hurry the evening meal in order to return to the union meeting in the city. And his own material comforts contribute to a conservative outlook. Perhaps because of the very economic success of his union, the worker's perception of the need for his participation and support of the union is less urgent.

Finally, union meetings are often neither interesting nor entertaining. Many local presidents have despaired in trying to develop programs which will encourage attendance and have resorted to offering door prizes, serv-

[6] For further data and analysis, see Bambrick and Haas, *op. cit.*, pp. 49–54.

ing beer before and after meetings, having a guest speaker, showing films, and so on in order to attract attendance. Because these inducements often fail, some locals maintain good attendance by fining absentees. Thus far this seems to be the best single device for encouraging participation, but fining creates its own problems for workers resent being forced to attend meetings. It might be added parenthetically, that it is usually the non-participant who complains about how the union is controlled by an inside clique. Such persons usually rationalize their nonparticipation by reasoning that even if they did attend the meeting, they would not have any chance to buck the clique that runs the show.

With this background, one can begin to appreciate the problems facing the local president. He is elected to office and in order to maintain his position, must do what he can to placate the constantly soaring expectations of the membership. Since there is no end to the problems demanding solution, the local leader is bound to bear the brunt of considerable criticism. Nor are local presidencies usually full-time salaried jobs. While representing workers at grievance proceedings, however, presidents may be paid by the company, or jointly by the company and the union. They usually receive a modest expense account or a bonus of a few hundred dollars at the end of the year as a payment for their services. Such local leaders often become bitter about the lack of support and understanding they receive from the rank and file, and there is considerable turnover in men holding this office.

One of the problems of the local union government is, paradoxically, the degree of democracy exercised by the rank and file and the insecurity of the local officer.[7] This insecurity of tenure by men holding this office is explained by Philip Taft:

> At the local level, contests for office are frequent and the rule . . . Not only are officers at this level affected by the normal ambition of members to hold office, but the members are aware of the performance of full-time officials who engage in negotiations and handle grievances. . . . Defeat of local officers is not unusual. . . . Turnover of local officers, rejection of contracts by the membership, and the fear of union negotiators that their recommendations may not be accepted are illustrations of democracy at work within unions. . . . Anyone who has observed negotiations with employers or acted as an arbitrator knows that union officers are highly sensitive to the wishes of their members, and frequently show genuine fear of thwarting their will.[8]

[7] Sometimes the local leader is too close to the scene of daily labor-management relations to get the desired perspective for reaching sound decisions. Joseph Shister points out that, "The local leadership, less experienced and more emotionally embroiled in the plant situation than the national leaders, is likely to encourage work stoppages even where the union cannot succeed." *The Economics of the Labor Market* (Philadelphia, J. B. Lippincott Co., 1949), p. 90.

[8] "The Internal Characteristics of American Unions," *The Annals of the American Academy of Political and Social Science,* Vol. 274 (March, 1951), p. 100.

Furthermore Taft questions whether this grass-roots or town-hall democracy of the local always contributes to stability and efficiency in labor-management relations: Taft explains:

> In a sense there can be too much democracy in union affairs. A form of organization guaranteeing the membership against the arbitrary acts of union officials is necessary, but at the same time neither the union nor the employer will profit if the officer becomes a puppet ready to jump at the demands of any vociferous group in the organization. Unless the leadership has sufficient authority to say " no " to demands it regards as unreasonable, it will have to respond to every whim of the rank and file. Unions in which officers are forced to bend to every wind that blows through the membership are those in which discipline is low and dissatisfaction high.[9]

The problem of democracy within the local is not its absence, but rather that its excessive exuberance may serve to destabilize labor-management relations. The local leader is not likely to abuse power, for he may not have much power to abuse. Joseph Kovner states the situation very pointedly: " Special action must be preserved to suppress local democracy; in the national, it takes special action to preserve it." [10]

It may seem paradoxical to describe the apathy and inertia of the rank and file on one hand and problems arising out of grass-roots democracy on the other. It must not be forgotten that the political problems of the local mirror those of all political institutions. In civic affairs the citizenry tends to be inactive but critical of its government. It is vocal and active when its own particular interests are affected and indifferent when its welfare is not directly involved. So it is with the union. The apathy of the rank and file is not necessarily permanent, for the membership can quickly and spontaneously develop a highly militant viewpoint. The membership may grow outraged if it feels that its representatives are not doing the job expected of them. When issues are particularly crucial, such as one involving the formulation of wage demands or a strike vote, the rank and file is likely to show intense interest. The local leader must, therefore, be alert to agitation lest it lead to cumulative discontent and his downfall. On the other hand, the more docile and inactive the rank and file, the greater the opportunity for stable, peaceful, and responsible union leadership. Unfortunately, such a situation also expands the opportunity for corruption and bureaucracy of union leadership.

The National and the International

The trend over time has been toward the centralization of control of American unions. As we noted above, the local leader is not often the

---

[9] " Understanding Union Administration," *Harvard Business Review*, Vol. 24, No. 2 (Winter, 1946), p. 248.

[10] "Union Democracy," *Papers*, Industrial Relations Research Association, 1952, p. 226.

focal point of either power or corruption. He is too close to the scene to escape the scrutiny and criticism of the general membership. As we move farther away from the rank and file, the opportunities for taxation without representation increase, and it is here that the critics of unionism are often able to level their most telling criticisms. Of course, some coordination of union policies is, from the labor viewpoint, necessary. And with the widening of the area of competition in our society, it has been necessary for labor to construct fences of ever-widening perimeters around its jobs. As labor and industrial mobility increased, the need for uniform policies over a widespread geographical area became increasingly apparent. Uniformity develops for another important reason: the content of a fair or reasonable labor-management policy is often difficult to define, but a " fair " policy in the worker's mind is usually thought to be one that is " uniform " for workers similarly located.

The parent organization encompassing the locals scattered throughout the country is known either as the national or international union in the United States, depending upon whether its participating locals exist only within the confines of this country or also include affiliated locals outside the nation's boundaries, as in Canada. As far as structure and organization, a national and international union are one and the same. For the purposes of our discussion, we shall use the term " national."

The national provides many useful services for the local. Besides coordinating policy for all locals, it is able to pool the resources of a larger group of labor for research.[11] It can develop and provide highly skilled negotiators for locals. It can build up a strike fund to help any particular local in distress or to subsidize all members in time of a general walkout or lockout. It can publicize labor's demands in the local press. Such demands will be considered seriously because they represent the sentiments of a group with power to implement their desires. The national usually evolves the constitution which serves not only to define the responsibilities of each local, but of the national itself. This constitution becomes the law of the local, and it is a law which the national usually has the power to enforce. As Joseph Shister has observed, " The local leadership only *executes* the law of the union; it does not *make* the law. It is the national unit which is primarily, though not exclusively, responsible for the formulation of most union laws." [12]

The national may also evolve wage policy to be followed by each of the locals in negotiations or actually undertake the negotiations itself. The

[11] Of the 199 international unions surveyed by the BLS in 1955, 96 reported they had research directors and 81, education directors. The recent growth of collectively bargained health, insurance and pension programs has created a demand for personnel to develop policy and explain existing plans. Close to half of the surveyed unions had personnel related to various social insurance programs. See William Paschell " Structure and Membership of the Labor Movement," *Monthly Labor Review* (November, 1955), pp. 1238-1239.

[12] *Op. cit.*, p. 82.

Steel Workers Union, for example, has a wage policy committee composed of representatives of important locals throughout the country. This committee meets prior to negotiations to advise the president and the executive officers of the union on strategy to be followed in negotiations with the company. The president and his staff will then sit in with the leaders of the key locals in securing agreements with the key company. Once an agreement is secured from one company, it tends to set the pattern for the rest of the industry. The national staff may then move on to assist in the negotiations with other large companies. Concessions by particular locals which tend to break the pattern are frowned upon by the national office, especially when such concessions tend to weaken the uniformity of gains won in the initial agreement. In some cases, however, concessions may be granted to smaller companies facing financial difficulties.

The national also provides relevant data that can be used by the local in preparing demands at local bargaining sessions. It may provide training facilities for shop stewards and union leaders to enable them to handle grievances and to present cases before arbitration more effectively. The national usually publishes a newspaper which provides a clearinghouse for information of the activities of locals throughout the country and encourages the growth of an *esprit des corps* within the union.[13]

A portion of the dues paid by the rank and file is assigned to the national, and such funds may be helpful in times of distress for member locals. The national is also better equipped to exert pressure politically, as their leaders tend to become well-known national figures, speaking for labor before public and official meetings and hearings. National officials may testify before Congressional committees on such matters as labor legislation, social security, and housing. Because of the stature and influence of national leaders, they are likely to be of a different cast than local leaders and more conservative than the rank and file itself. The president and his executive staff, which may be composed of several vice presidents and a secretary-treasurer, are full-time officers, sometimes earning attractive salaries.[14] In some instances, national presidents have engineered rather substantial salaries for themselves, and many of the rank and file

[13] Of 199 national unions surveyed by the BLS in 1955, 166 issued publications, most of these appearing monthly. See Paschell, *op. cit.*, p. 1239.

[14] In a CIO pamphlet, " The CIO: What it is and What it Does," published June 1, 1951, details were provided regarding the annual salary of highest paid officers for some 30 of their nationals and internationals. The highest paid official was the president of the Steel Workers, receiving $25,000. The Textile Workers Union president received $16,000, the Retail, Wholesale and Department Store Employees $12,500, and Communications Workers of America, $13,200, the Amalgamated Clothing Workers, $15,000, and the Automobile Workers, $11,250. The bulk of the other " highest salaries " were in the range of from $5,000 to $10,000. These figures do not reflect the expense accounts which undoubtedly many of these officials enjoy together with other supplementary benefits.

are not reluctant to see their own elected president as well off financially as the president of the company in which they work. While he often speaks of the needs of labor, he himself often lives comfortably, drives a good car, has luxurious headquarters, and so on.

The powers granted the national officers are usually specified in the constitution, but the parliament of the national is the convention, usually held every year or every two years. At these conventions, the officers are generally elected — or in most instances — re-elected to their positions. One of the long-standing criticisms of labor organization is the tendency for the executive officers to enjoy a continuing tenure of office. Such tenure is usually made possible when the president himself appoints the nominating committee.

There are several alternative constitutional provisions that guide the election of national officers, and as noted above, these most frequently provide for the election of the president by the convention. The representation of convention delegates generally gives greater voice to the smaller locals than to the large city locals. For example, a union of over 1,000 members may have a maximum of four delegates, while those with less than 100 members have one delegate. By such regressive weighting several small local unions can outvote a local with a large membership. In the NICB study of national constitutions, it was found that, of the 137 unions that provided for the nomination and election of the national president by convention delegates, only 18 of these (or 6.5 percent of the total membership analyzed) provided for secret balloting. Voting by a show of hands or by a roll call is likely to reduce the chances of a revolt on the floor against existing officers. It has often been thought that the wider use of the referendum and a general membership vote on all important issues [15] (rather than the use of the convention) would encourage interest and participation of the rank and file, as well as make the election of officers and development of union policy more democratic. This may not always be the case, however, for where the union is large and is made up of locals spread throughout the country, it has been found difficult for any " opposition " candidate to gain sufficient reputation or support to be elected to national office. The incumbent officer is always better known, and his control of the union machinery may discourage any would-be opposition candidate from attempting to win such an election.

The length of tenure of union officers is another factor which weakens the opportunity for a vigorous opposition party within the union. It may discourage young men from aspiring to top office, as well as discourage the locals from developing policy in opposition to that of the national. Very frequently the president appoints the credentials committee for conventions. This committee evaluates the status of delegates attending the convention and by this instrumentality any delegation that has plans

[15] For further discussion and data, see Bambrick and Haas, *op. cit.*, pp. 72–77.

to stage a rebellion against the existing executive officers might be dis-
enfranchised. Isolated cases of flagrant violations of democratic procedures are not too difficult to discover. The investigations of racketeering
on the New York waterfront revealed evidence that some locals had
not held elections for a 15-year period, while other locals had not
met for a period as long as 10 years. The Tobacco Workers International
did not hold a convention from 1900 to 1939, and in this interval any
local that clamored for a convention simply lost its charter.[16] As one
student of union democracy has observed, the "Power over individuals
(by the national) is given by vague clauses in union constitutions prohibiting 'improper conduct,' 'disturbing harmony of meetings' or 'in-
subordination' or 'for just and sufficient cause.' At the very worst, a rival
faction may be outlawed by labeling it a dual union movement." [17]

One of the basic and certainly unresolved issues within the union
movement is to reconcile free speech and union security. As a matter of
practice, the president of the international usually dominates the executive board, and the board in turn usually dominates the convention. The
average delegate has the limited task of hearing and approving reports,
of voting for or against the re-election of existing officers. Whether the
union in this setting is democratic or not depends in large part on the
personality and quality of its leadership.[18] The threat of dualism is often
considered ample justification to give the president sufficient authority
to take emergency measures against any particular local. For example,
the constitution of the Musicians Union gives extensive power to President James C. Petrillo:

> The president may annul and set aside the constitution, by-laws, stand-
> ing resolutions, or any portion thereof, excepting such which treat
> with the finances of the organization, and substitute therefore other

[16] For an excellent review, see Joel Seidman, "Democracy in Labor Unions," *Journal
of Political Economy*, Vol. LXI, No. 3 (June, 1953), and his book, *Union Rights and
Union Duties* (New York, Harcourt, Brace and Co., 1943).

[17] "Democracy in Labor Unions," *op. cit.*, p. 227.

[18] As Seidman, in his study *Union Rights and Union Duties* (*op. cit.*) explains: "If
he (the union president) is lustful for power or possesses an ego that craves flattery,
he may build a machine that crushes democracy. He sets the tone at national gather-
ings, and may so weight the atmosphere against dissent and so identify opposition
with treason that only an unusually fearless delegate may dare to express disagreement on an important issue. If the president is unusually intelligent, if he possesses
democratic instincts, if he has faith in the capacity of the membership instead of an
exaggerated estimate of his own ability and the role of leadership, he will encourage
delegates to express their opinions even when he thinks they are wrong, and create
an atmosphere of intelligent discussion and free interchange of ideas. He will introduce the concept of the loyal opposition that disagrees, not because of subversive
motives, but because of a different and honestly held conception of the union's best
interests. He may consciously use the convention, with its committee discussions and
floor debates, as a training ground and school for younger members. Needless to
say, there are few union leaders, as there are few men in any walk of life, who
possess this breadth of vision" (p. 50).

and different provisions of his own making; the power to do so is hereby made absolute in the president when, in his opinion, such orders are necessary to safeguard the interests of the federation, the locals or members. . . .[19]

The opportunity for abusing such a provision is self-evident, and it is obvious to all that the democratic nature of the union structure at this level depends on the personality of the president, the confidence he has in his own administration, together with his willingness to permit the rank and file to review fully, and express its reactions to, the record of his administration. The difficulty is even more obvious when one appreciates that the basic function of the union is not to provide a town hall for discussion, but to exact benefits from the employer through the exercise of bargaining power.[20]

We must not forget that the power of the national office is designed primarily for constructive purposes. There are many instances of intervention of the national office to investigate and expose fraudulent or gross mismanagement of union funds by local officers, or instances of intervention to break up harmful factional disputes between opposing groups within the union, or instances of intervention to stop a local wildcat walkout in defiance of the contract. The fact that power centers exist in the national office does not preclude opportunities for its constructive use.

In most unions the national has the authority to either (a) suspend, (b) place into receivership, or (c) revoke the charter of a local union. Placing the union in receivership is generally an emergency measure designed to prevent further mismanagement or abuse while the situation is being investigated. While there are instances of union locals being in receivership for an extended period, it is generally an emergency measure that is quickly terminated. When a local is suspended, there is generally no stated time interval for the suspension, and in many unions such suspensions are declared by the executive board rather than by a presidential order. The third alternative, revocation of the local's charter, is, of course, even more serious, as it implies a more or less permanent break of the local from the national.[21]

[19] As cited by Frank C. Pierson, " The Government of Trade Unions," *Industrial & Labor Relations Review*, Vol. 1, No. 4 (July, 1948), p. 606.

[20] " It goes without saying that unions should protect their members against oppression, and due process and fair trials for those charged with violating union regulations are absolutely essential. However, a union is not a debating society; it is a powerful organization, and unless the union officer can guide and sometimes even impose his trained judgment, industry is sure to be bedevilled by avoidable controversies. In other words, if the union leadership is sound by other criteria, long tenure of office may be an asset both to union and management." Taft, " Understanding Union Administration," *op. cit.*, p. 253.

[21] For further discussion, see Horace B. Davis, "Receivership in American Unions" *Quarterly Journal of Economics*, Vol. LXVII, No. 2 (May, 1953).

The Convention

Because the convention represents the supreme governing body of the national, convention meetings do much to shape the national's policies and character. The convention represents the final court of appeal in disciplinary actions. It usually elects the national officers; it has the power to impeach union officers for malfeasance; it has authority to amend the union constitution; it determines the amount of dues that members pay, the qualifications for membership. In effect, the convention can " legislate " or make and alter union law.

A little more than a third of all nationals meet in convention every two years, while a little more than a quarter meet each year. Statistics further reveal that the larger the national, the more likely it is that it will hold its conventions biennially rather than annually. Thus only about 11 percent of the union membership is represented by nationals having annual meetings, 23 percent by nationals having meetings every two years, and 28 percent by nationals having meetings every four years. This does not reflect the impulse of the larger organizations to " escape " from meetings of local union representatives, but rather the desire to minimize the cost and energy involved in planning and attending such elaborate meetings. Because costs have grown rather substantial, especially as the unions themselves have increased in size, the general inclination is to hold conventions less frequently, and to reduce the number of delegates representing the locals.

Between the meetings of the regular convention, an executive board is usually responsible for the day-to-day affairs of the national. This board is usually elected by the convention itself and made up of the national's executive officers (the president and the secretary-treasurer) and a varying number of vice presidents. The executive board may be called upon to authorize collective bargaining contracts or even sanction the strike of some local. But its power is limited by the constitution, and it cannot undertake to change the constitution without the consent of the convention.[22]

Union Revenue

One of the common misconceptions of all unions is that they are set up by a few labor bosses for the benefits to be derived from taxing labor.

[22] It has sometimes been held that the less common form of executive board, one made up not only of the executive officers but of elected representatives of the membership, is more democratic and less likely to be dominated by the president. But in some instances, the dependence of the membership representatives on income arising from special assignments of the national president weakens their resistance to the policies of the president. Those executive representatives whose salaries are provided for by the constitution may be in better position to exert an independent judgment on the policies of the president.

While the total revenues of all the unions are considerable, individual union income is certainly modest when compared to any of our major corporations.[23] The NICB study found 75 union constitutions which contained some provision on the minimum monthly dues that members must pay, $2 being the most common minimum. Of 36 constitutions which provided a maximum amount, this figure was most frequently $5, but in the instance of the AF of L, Air Lines Pilots, if individual pilot incomes reached between $19,000 and $20,000, they could be required to pay as much as $25 a month.[24] In the NICB study of constitutional provisions for initiation fees, $5 was the most frequently mentioned minimum and $10 was the most frequent maximum.

Craft versus Industrial Unions

Traditionally, the craft versus industrial form of organization has been a focal point in labor's organizational struggles. It was an issue at the end of the nineteenth century in the clash between the Knights of Labor and the AF of L. It became a burning issue again in the mid-thirties and led to the splintering away of several industrial unions from the AF of L to form the CIO. The American Federation of Labor's organizing strategy had been simply to mobilize the power of the workers with special skills. As the mass production techniques gained momentum, it seemed clear that a wider basis for organization was necessary. Strength was not to be found by threatening to deprive the employer of particular skills but rather in the threat to deprive the employer of all workers (and if possible, to prevent the employer from hiring substitute labor). Today the distinctions between craft and industrial union are less meaningful, for craft unions have drifted into industrial or semi-industrial unions, and often industrial unions have become multiple craft unions.

We may note this blending of organizational form by treating the craft and the industrial unions as extreme poles on a grid. On the one hand, the craft union is composed of a restricted number of highly skilled workers performing a single operation. Next to it, the amalgamated craft union has a less exclusive membership, for all members are not performing

[23] In a survey conducted by Nathan Belfer, in 1949 of 107 of the larger nationals, Belfer found that the 53 nationals responding had a combined membership of 10 million and a combined total net worth of $265 million. The wealth of the union was correlated more with its age than size of membership. Only one union, the Brotherhood of Railroad Trainmen, had assets approximating as much as $50 million. As E. E. Witte points out, " 780 corporations had assets greater than $50 million. . . ." Data on net worth of the international do not include, however, the net worth of the locals. For discussion see Belfer, "Financial Resources of Trade Unions," *Journal of Political Economy*, Vol. LVII, No. 2 (April, 1949), pp. 157–161, and E. E. Witte, "The Role of Unions in Contemporary Society," *Industrial and Labor Relations Review*, Vol. 4, No. 1 (October, 1950), pp. 3–14.

[24] See Bambrick and Haas, *op. cit.*, p. 29.

a single task, but jobs that are interrelated (yet skilled) in their nature. A modified craft union exists where the members are not only performing somewhat different tasks, but not all of them are necessarily skilled. A semi-industrial union is one where there is no distinction regarding the degree of skill required to perform the job, but membership is exclusive in that only production workers are included. As we approach the other pole, the industrial union is made up of all workers in the plant so that the basis for the organization is the type of industry itself. Even here organization can be somewhat widened as a sort of "catchall" to include workers other than those employed in a particular industry. The classic example of such union organization is District 50 of the United Mine Workers, which includes chemical workers, railroad workers, and even dairy farmers. If such a principle of organization were carried to its logical conclusion, we would have the "one big union" principle for organization where all labor, regardless of the industry in which it is working, belongs to one large labor organization. Such a labor organization is often visualized as one that could best dramatize class warfare, with the general strike as its major weapon. But not all attempts at organizing the one big union are motivated by economic and political subversion. The old Knights of Labor is a case of "one big union" dedicated, not to the forceful overthrow of the capitalist system, but rather to the peaceful evolution, through education, of a cooperative society.

Does the merger of the CIO and the AF of L into a single giant labor organization mean that labor has returned to the "one union" principle of organization? While such a conclusion may appear self-evident, it is erroneous. First, the merger does not provide for the physical blending of all labor groups into a single national or international organization. Rather, all nationals and internationals maintain their identity within the merged organization. The principle of "federation" provides a degree of central coordination and protection commensurate with the maximum amount of local autonomy. The autonomy of the national and international is maintained in the merged movement as it was in the traditional AF of L and CIO governments when each was a separate agency. By analogy it may be viewed as the swapping of two umbrellas — covering the activities of the many nationals and internationals — for a single umbrella. Of course, this consolidation gives much more force to united political and economic action but beneath the umbrella, nevertheless, the diversity of structural organization remains.

Background to the Merger of the AF of L and CIO

As will be recalled from our discussion of union history, the original split between the AF of L and CIO had its origin in the 1934 convention of the AF of L, when John L. Lewis, of the United Mine Workers, urged that more attention be given to organization of the mass production industries. His dissatisfaction with AF of L policies led to the floor fight in the 1935 convention, at which time it was made clear that the bulk of AF of L members still favored the craft basis for union organization. Eight nationals then formed a " committee " for industrial organization. With the ultimate failure of efforts to reconcile their differences with the AF of L, the Committee for Industrial Organizations was formally established in 1936. This group displayed new energy and imagination in extending organization, and by 1937 the CIO had more members than the AF of L. The Federation then accelerated its own drive for membership and by the early forties had again pulled ahead of the CIO in membership. Besides the differences over craft and industrial unionism, the two agencies had other distinguishing features. The CIO tended to look to political pressures for union benefits. Had not the Wagner Act legislation in large part enabled its rapid growth? The CIO opposed racial discrimination and racketeering and favored a slightly greater central control over nationals and internationals than the older American Federation of Labor. The Federation tended toward a more neutralist political position, believed its basic strength lay in the autonomy of its component parts, and was nervous about the political liberalism of its CIO counterpart. Of course, the personalities of John L. Lewis and William Green (president of the Federation) go a long way to explain the widening gap between the two agencies. Each was anxious to increase his power and prestige and neither leader had faith in, nor respect for the other.

In 1939 President Roosevelt urged a consolidation of the two labor groups, but negotiations were again unsuccessful. It was not until the November, 1940, convention of the CIO (when John L. Lewis stepped down because of the re-election of President Roosevelt) that the opportunities for merger improved. But internal factionalism within the CIO weakened the CIO's bargaining position, as did the AF of L's expanded membership. Early in 1942, John L. Lewis again entered the scene by dramatically proposing the merger of the two organizations, but this move was interpreted by many as an attempt to embarrass his successor, Philip Murray. Lewis's hostility toward the CIO increased and in October, 1942, Lewis formally withdrew his UMW from the organization.

The next move developed in the spring of 1947, following the rather pronounced swing of the country to the right and the growing hostility of the public to organized labor. Again, however, the CIO was rather fearful of unsettled jurisdictional issues between it and the AF of L, and the AF of L was fearful of the vigorous political activity of the CIO. By 1950, however, both groups were in a more conciliatory mood. The AF of L had established its Labor's League for Political Education, admitting the need for political pressure. The CIO, during 1949 and 1950, had expelled eleven of its unions on charges of Communist domination. This did much to reconcile AF of L leaders to a merger. In December, 1950, a United Labor Policy Committee was organized representing all major labor organizations to give uniform representation to labor's problems during the Korean war crisis. While this agency was dissolved in mid-1951, its success encouraged further serious negotiations for unity.

In the fall of 1952 the coincidental death of both William Green and Philip Murray provided a fresh opportunity for unity discussions. George Meany was quickly elected head of the American Federation of Labor, but a bitter contest developed for leadership of the CIO. Allan S. Haywood, executive vice president of the CIO (who had the support of the steel workers and several other smaller unions) and Walter Reuther, head of the UAW, both campaigned for the presidency. Reuther received some 3 million votes to Haywood's 2.6 million. Hostility had meanwhile developed between David J. McDonald, who succeeded Murray as president of the Steel Workers and Walter Reuther. Reuther was under pressure to effect quickly a merger to stall any disaffiliation of the United Steel Workers to the AF of L, or to a third independent union movement.

The CIO insisted, however, that prior to the merger the AF of L eliminate racketeering, accept the CIO concept of industrial unionism, oppose racial discrimination and agree to machinery to eliminate jurisdictional strife.[25] The fact that the AF of L had in 1953 revoked the charter of the crime-ridden International Longshoremen's Union impressed Reuther with the new vigor of the AF of L in ridding itself of the stigma of corruption. The negotiation of a no-raiding agreement (that went into effect January 1, 1954, for a period of 2 years) removed one of the most serious obstacles to unity. A final merger agreement was developed February 9, 1955. Both federations formally adopted the merger early in 1955 and on December 5, 1955, the merger became official.

The Structure of the AFL–CIO

As one would expect, the structure of the merged organization reflects both that of the AF of L and CIO, but the over-all picture resembles the AF of L structure more than that of the CIO. Figure 7 provides the major organizational features of the merged union. Before reviewing this structure, let us first note the stated purposes of the merged organization.

The Preamble and Purpose of the AFL–CIO. Traditionally, the preamble to union constitutions provides the philosophical frame of reference for union activity. The preamble of the AF of L constitution, developed in 1881, reflected the complex of humanitarianism and sense of oppression of organized labor in the late nineteenth century while that

[25] For a detailed discussion, see Joel Seidman, "Efforts Toward Merger: 1935–1955," *Industrial and Labor Relations Review*, Vol. 9, No. 3 (April, 1956), pp. 353–370.

FIGURE 7. Organization of AFL-CIO

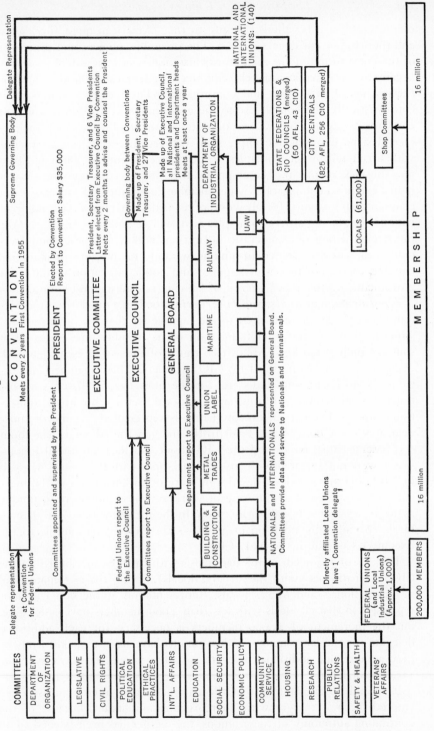

of the youthful CIO alluded simply to the "American quest for liberty and the struggle for equality. . . ." The preamble, objects, and principles of the constitution of the merged organization reveal the extent to which organized labor has completely embraced those ideals considered to be the essence of orthodoxy and conservatism. The merger commits itself enthusiastically and completely to the growth and perfection of the free enterprise system. The twelve-point statement of objects and principles provides the unmistakable impression that organized labor is concerned with bread-and-butter principles, to be realized through " pure and simple " business unionism. The union is " for " improved wages and shorter hours, extended unionization, wider membership in the Federation, greater economic opportunity for all workers regardless of race, creed, color or national origin, legislative principles that will advance society's welfare, the strengthening of democratic institutions and world peace and freedom, peaceful coexistence of unions without raiding or jurisdictional conflict, the sale of union-made goods and public education of the labor movement, and the wider interest of labor in registering and voting.

The Locals, Nationals, and Internationals. If we move from the bottom of our organizational chart to the top, we see that the organizational structure rests on the solid foundation of its membership, estimated at some 16 million workers. About two thirds of this is represented by AF of L members and one third by CIO members. These members are organized into locals, and locals are, for the most part, affiliated with nationals or internationals. In this sense, the local itself has no direct connection with the Federation, except that it is represented by one or more delegates at the convention. Prior to the merger, the AF of L had about 900 federal labor unions and the CIO about 100 local industrial unions. These were not affiliated with any national, only with the parent AF of L or CIO governing body. These locals were often " nationals in the making " or composed of a scattering of workers whose jobs were so unique as not to warrant national organization. In the merger about 1,000 of such locals (having a membership of 200,000) are directly responsible to the Executive Council of the AFL–CIO.

The AF of L joined its 108 nationals (with their 50,560 locals) to the CIO's 32 nationals (with their 10,672 locals), giving the aggregate total of 140 nationals and 61,232 locals. Representation at the convention is regressive in that all locals with less than 4,000 members have 1 delegate, but the increment of 25,000 members is necessary for each additional delegate for the large unions. When unions have over 175,000 members, they acquire one additional delegate for each 75,000 members over the 175,000 total.

It should be emphasized that the nationals (and internationals) have entered the new merger with their organizations intact. Because of the continuing autonomy of these unions, the merger has been likened to an assembly of business concerns into a Chamber of Commerce or a National Association of Manufacturers. This analogy probably exaggerates the looseness of the Federation's organizational structure, but it should be remembered that these nationals maintain a large degree of independence. Their actions are pivotal and their importance should not be buried by the several layers of the organizational hierarchy above them.

The merger agreement also provided for the merger of local, territorial, regional, and state central bodies within two years of the date of the adoption of the constitution. These state and local bodies pay an annual fee to the merged organization, and each is entitled to one delegate at the biennial convention.

Of considerable significance is the creation of the Department of Industrial Organization which, in effect, permitted the CIO to maintain much of its organizational structure within the AF of L. Furthermore each department like the Department of the Building and Construction Trades, the Department of Metal Trades and, significantly, the Department of Industrial Organization, is permitted to maintain its state and local councils. The function of these regional councils is to coordinate the organizing, collective bargaining, strike, lobbying, educational and political activities of unions that have joined each department. As one writer notes: " How the local and state councils of the Industrial Union Department will be able to avoid duplication of effort in relation to the merged local and state central bodies is difficult to imagine. . . ." [26]

The Departmental Organization of the AFL–CIO. As noted above, the department feature of the AF of L has been retained. The department is, in reality, a subdivision of the Federation based on the functional grouping of nationals (and internationals) with joint interest. The assumption is that where an area of common interest exists between and among nationals, greater interunion cooperation might be affected by association in an appropriate department. The Building and Construction Trades Department and the Metal Trades Department were established in 1908, the Railway Employees Department in 1909, and the Union Label Trades Department in 1911. Within the framework of the AF of L, these departments had established regional or local councils to coordinate the activities of various unions in various regions. In some instances the loyalty to the council has seemed greater than the loyalty of particular locals to their own national. The constitution of the merged Federation contains the provision that " No department, local council or railway system federation of the same shall enact laws, rules, or regulations in conflict with the laws and procedures of the Federation . . . ," and any local, to enjoy representation in a department, must maintain its affiliation with a national (or international) union. These departments have, in the past, held their own conventions pe-

[26] As noted by Maurice F. Neufeld, " Structure and Government of the AFL–CIO," *Industrial and Labor Relations Review,* Vol. 9, No. 3 (April, 1956), p. 383.

riodically, and the department itself is governed by an executive council composed of a president, secretary-treasurer, and several vice presidents. Such councils have on occasion represented unions in negotiations, have established methods for handling jurisdictional problems for competing members, have shown considerable interest in labor-management cooperation and the need for developing more harmonious relations between employer and employee. It is sometimes suggested that since such departments often cut across craft lines, they provide the advantage of industrial organization to craft unions.

One of the distinctive innovations of the merger, to repeat, was the addition of the Department of Industrial Organization. Membership in this department is sought by many semicraft unions, who see through such participation much wider areas for the recruitment of new members. When the Teamsters' Union decided to join this department, President Meany charged that a fair portion of the Teamster membership was not industrial in character and that he alone would determine what proportion of the Teamster membership could be represented in this department.

The widespread membership leads to the speculation that it might serve as the largest single pressure group within the merged Federation, giving the CIO core a basis for spreading its influence and policies to the Federation as a whole. In his speech before the Executive Board of the CIO on February 24, 1955, urging adoption of the merger agreement proposed by the Unity Committee, Walter Reuther explained:

> I would like to make this one thing clear. I think it would be very unfortunate and rather tragic if people had the feeling that this Council of Industrial Organizations was going to provide us the base for building a kind of power bloc inside of a united labor movement. I personally am not willing under the slogan of labor unity to start out on the basis of power blocs. Let's go in with one dedication to the whole labor movement, and let us integrate ourselves with the total movement. . . .[27]

What in effect happened was that some 35 former AF of L nationals, including building trade unions, joined the Industrial Organization Department to bring the membership in this department to over 7 million. This maneuver reduced the likelihood that the original CIO unions would maintain their partisan viewpoint within the structure. This department began its organization with a treasury of over $1 million and makes a separate assessment on a per capita basis on all nationals which affiliate with it. Walter Reuther heads this department, and its secretary-treasurer is James B. Carey. It has twelve vice presidents.

The Convention. Let us now work from the top down of our organization chart. Here we see that the convention, meeting every two years, is

[27] "The New Beginning," The CIO, Pamphlet No. 268, p. 18.

the parliament of labor. Representation of the national at the convention is contingent upon the organization receiving a " certificate of affiliation " at least one month prior to the convention itself, and no person can qualify as a delegate who is not a member in good standing in the union he is representing. The secretary-treasurer has the task of determining the delegation permissible from each union, based on the per capita tax paid by the union to the national (or international). Fairly strict control over the agenda of the convention discussion is maintained by the president. The president appoints the various committees prior to the convention to discuss, study, and make recommendations on issues which should be considered by the convention as a whole. All resolutions and recommendations that are to be made by delegates must be received thirty days prior to the convention, and all such resolutions must have the support of the member organization making them. Upon receipt of the resolution, the president is authorized to classify the nature of the contents of the resolution and refer such resolution to the appropriate committee which in turn reports to the convention. Under certain circumstances, new business may be allowed from the floor, but again these resolutions are referred to the Executive Council. It is understood that if such resolutions are to be accepted, they must be unanimously adopted by the convention.

At the first 1955 convention the centralized control and organization of activities became immediately apparent. Over 4,500 guests and 250 newspapermen were present in addition to the 1,500 union delegates. Only a single microphone stood on the floor for the use of the delegates.[28] Because of its unwieldy nature, and the fact that the convention will meet only every second year, provision is made for the executive staff to handle the day-to-day problems of the federation.

The Executive Staff. The two executive officers are George Meany, president, and William F. Schnitzler, both AF of L men. These are full-time officers carrying the administrative responsibilities for the AFL–CIO staff. The president, as of 1956, received a salary of $35,000 a year and the secretary-treasurer $33,000 a year. All officers are members of affiliated organizations, and all are elected by the majority vote of the convention. The locus of power of the merged Federation, to the extent that one can speak of such a locus, undoubtedly rests with the president, for it is his function to supervise all the affairs of the organization, to preside at conventions, to call meetings of the Executive Council, to interpret the constitution between meetings of the Executive Council, to appoint, pay, and direct (or even suspend) union organizers or representatives or other employees of the Federation. His appointment of the various committees to process recommendations made prior to the convention gives him further control over the substantive issues to be discussed at the convention. The secretary-treasurer must report to each of the affiliated nationals four

[28] As noted by Neufeld, *op. cit.*, p. 378.

times a year on the financial status of the Federation, and the books of the Federation must be audited at least twice a year.

The Executive Council. While the two executive officers handle the day-to-day affairs of the union, the Executive Council, made up of these two officers and twenty-seven vice presidents, must meet at least three times a year, and it has the " power to direct the affairs of the Federation and to take such actions and render such decisions as are necessary and appropriate to safeguard and promote the best interest of the Federation. . . ." The Council is required to " watch legislative measures directly affecting the interests of the working people." It has the authority to make rules which are consistent with the Constitution and directives of the convention. It has the power to conduct investigations either by itself or with appointed committees " of any situation in which there is reason to believe that any affiliate is dominated, controlled or substantially influenced in conduct of its officers by any corrupt influence or if policies are consistently directed towards either Communist, Fascist or totalitarian movements." The teeth, to implement the findings of such committee investigations, are provided by the constitution. The Council has " authority upon a two-thirds vote, to suspend any union found guilty of a violation of this section. Any action of the Executive Council under this section may be appealed to the convention, provided, however, that such action shall be effective when taken and shall remain in full force and effect pending any appeal." [29]

It is the further responsibility of the Executive Council to encourage the unionization of the unorganized without discrimination against race, color, creed, or national origin. It also has the important power to grant a charter to a new national or international, but again the council is permitted to delegate this responsibility to the president. The granting of such a charter must, however, " be based upon a strict recognition that both craft and industrial unions are equal and necessary as methods of trade union organization " (Article 3, Section 7). The power to revoke a charter of any national or international is limited, however, to the convention, and here a two-thirds majority roll call is necessary to sanction such a revocation.

The Executive Committee. Because a full meeting of the Executive Council is not easily arranged, and because of the size of this organization, provision is made for a separate Executive Committee, made up of the president and secretary-treasurer together with six vice presidents. The vice presidents are selected from the twenty-seven vice presidents of the Executive Council by the convention itself. This group meets every two months and advises and consults with the President on policy matters. The all important Executive Committee can constitute itself as the " Credentials " Committee for convention attendance or appoint a group to per-

[29] Article 8, Section 7.

form this task. The appeals from the decisions of the Credentials Committee lie with the floor of the convention. Most issues are resolved by oral expression or a show of hands, but if 30 percent of the delegates so demand, a roll-call vote will be held.[30] It is clear that the constitution is set up in such a way as to maximize the control over the convention by the president so that explosive, disorderly or highly controversial discussion can be avoided. The conventions of both CIO and AF of L (as separate organizations) revealed the drama and conflict that can arise within the parliament of labor, especially on such crucial issues which occasioned the clash between John L. Lewis and William Green over the function of industrial unionization, and the battle within the CIO over the revocation of the charters of Communist-dominated unions.

Committee Organization. The president has authority to appoint standing committees, each dealing with an important problem area of the Federation. The fact that the president of the Federation appoints such committees increases his authority and influence, for such committee reports undoubtedly reflect the viewpoints of its appointed members. The Committee on Legislation is designed to implement the policies of the Federation in federal, state, and local governments. The Committee on Civil Rights is designed to implement " at the earliest possible date " the principle of nondiscrimination within the union; the Committee on Political Education is established to encourage the political education and interest of all union members to participate in the voting privilege and responsibility. The Committee on Ethical Practices is designed to help the Federation keep free " of any taint of corruption or communism." The Committee on International Affairs concerns itself with the relationship of the Federation to the international trade union movement as well as international affairs that affect labor. The Committee on Education is assigned the task of developing not only union educational programs, but the educational level of all Americans. The Committee on Social Security provides " guidance and information " in the fields of social insurance and welfare, while the Committee on Economic Policy recommends those policies which will best promote prosperity, full employment, and the full utilization of all our resources. The Committee on Community Services is designed to stimulate the participation of union members and locals in community affairs including participation and cooperation with the projects of social agencies in each community. The Committee on Housing advises on all matters relating to housing, while the Committee on Research reviews and appraises all the research activities of the Federation so that

---

[30] Sir Walter Citrine, of the Trades Union Congress of Great Britain, observed of the Resolutions Committee of the AF of L: ". . . apparently you have a sort of demolition squad in the form of a Resolutions Committee that succeeded in making that explosive material — embodied in some of the resolutions referred to the committee — rather harmless." As cited by Clyde Dankert, *Contemporary Unionism in the United States* (New York, Prentice-Hall, 1948), p. 80.

adequate research data is available to the Federation. The Committee on Safety and Occupational Health recommends ways of promoting national health and safety. The Committee on Veterans' Affairs keeps all locals informed of the rights and benefits available to veterans and proposes measures to protect those rights. Finally, the Committee on Public Relations attempts to improve the relationships of the Federation to the public by keeping the public informed of the goals and policies of the Federation. The wide variety of committees, together with the topics with which each committee deals, suggests the broader interests of the union movement. These indicate that the Federation is no longer willing to be pictured as a pressure group interested only in narrow partisan goals. Increasingly, it interprets its own goals in terms of the general welfare of the American community, as well as the civil rights of its own members.

One of the most important committees is the Department of Organization, headed by John W. Livingston, a vice president of the United Automobile Workers. This department has tremendous responsibility and will undoubtedly spearhead the organizational campaigns of new unions. Several problems, however, confront this vital section, for the Industrial Union Department also assumes responsibility for extending the organization of industrial workers and the Executive Council too assumes responsibility for encouraging union expansion and chartering new unions. The overlapping of interest and enthusiasm in this all important area is even more apparent when it is realized that none of the 140 nationals and internationals have abdicated their responsibility to extend their own membership.

The Jurisdictional Problem. It is the task of the president of the merged organization to minimize or eliminate, where possible, conflicting jurisdictions " by the process of voluntary agreement or merger between the affiliates involved," but no national or international was asked at the time of merger to surrender any of the rights or characteristics of its organization that it enjoyed within the framework of either the CIO or AF of L. If the president cannot secure agreement in a jurisdictional dispute case, he reports the difficulty to the Executive Council, which will hear the testimony of the union officers involved in any dispute. If either union should fail to abide by the decision of the Council, the dispute then can be taken to the convention for appropriate action.

One of the major obstacles to the merger has been the desire of each national to expand its membership, even at the expense of other nationals affiliated with the same federation. Typical of the sentiments of union leadership to such an issue is that expressed by David J. McDonald, when he accepted the presidency of the United Steel Workers of America union in March 11, 1953. He declared, " Now listen, please: Don't come around crying to me about the intrusion of other unions into what you consider to be our jurisdiction. Don't come crying to me. Let the other unions come crying to me." While McDonald affirmed that he was not talking about raiding but only of organizing the unorganized, his sentiment reflects the traditional enthusiasm most leaders have for expanding their union membership. The CIO had established an "Organizational Disputes Agreement" to minimize and, if possible, eliminate jurisdictional disputes within the CIO, while the AF of L had established its own Internal Disputes Plan. Prior to the merger it was necessary for both unions to agree to a common approach in eliminating such raiding, and they reached the "No Raiding Agreement," October 15, 1954. The intent of the merged Federation is to consolidate these three no-raiding plans into permanent and enduring machinery to eliminate all costly jurisdictional disputes.

8

Union Institutionalism

Five major phases of union activity have been selected for investigation in this chapter: (1) the admission policies of unions, (2) judicial procedures within unions, (3) racketeering in unions, (4) left-wing unionism, (5) unions in politics. These topics in no way provide an exhaustive list of union activities, but they do represent issues of general public interest and concern. And while all these topics are interrelated in one way or another, it is hoped that the reader will not condemn unions for "guilt by association" because we precede our discussion of the interest of unions in national and local politics with surveys of racketeering and communism within unions. These issues have been selected for discussion because they bring into sharp focus the continuing difficulty of maximizing that degree of freedom the individual worker acquires by giving continuous support *to* his union, with that degree of freedom he acquires by asserting his independence *from* the union. This theme will become even more apparent in our analysis of the collective bargaining process in Section III.

The Admission Policies of Unions

Should the union's perspective include the welfare of all the labor force or only that of its own membership? The admission policies of unions often hinge on the answer given to this question. It is immediately apparent that if the union can successfully construct a fence around a limited supply of labor, or if it can, in other words, acquire a monopoly position in the sale of a limited supply of labor, its opportunity for maximizing membership wage rates is much improved. This strategy has its roots in the guild system of the Middle Ages, and even today it acquires significance when the labor supply is rapidly expanding relative to its absorption, or when the demand for labor is stable and declining. If the union pursues an "exclusionist" policy with regard to the total labor force, it may be able to reduce the number of workers with ration coupons or claimants for job opportunities. The fewer the workers, the greater the income they can enjoy.

However logical this reasoning may be, it overlooks some conflicting forces. First, unions have learned that they advance into the territory of high wages with exposed flanks if a large portion of the labor force (possessing equivalent skills) remains unorganized. The competition in the product market for goods produced by cheaper nonunion labor has immediate repercussions on the union employer, and these pose limits to the goals of union employees. It is necessary for union workers to either adapt themselves to competitive conditions or organize the unorganized. This latter alternative has been the most frequent solution to the difficulty, and thus unions have a pragmatic interest in extending the unionization of their own and allied trades. Second, the union itself will view its strength in terms of its membership, for dues-paying members provide the necessary life blood to the organization. The union must pay its way, and this task will become easier if the overhead of a union administration is spread over a large rather than a small number of members.

Unhappily, the economic justification for restrictionism has blended in many instances with a prejudice against those of certain political beliefs, national origin, race, religious beliefs, and color. For example, the four large railway unions bar Negro persons from membership in the parent unions. While these unions, together with that of the AF of L Postal Transport Association, account for only a total of 442,197 members, the hardship produced by their discrimination can neither be overlooked nor condoned. The unemployment ratios for Negro workers and other racial minorities, for example, is always larger than that for the total work force.

Union constitutions provide a variety of " conditions " for union membership. The bulk of unions quite naturally specify that candidates for membership must be employed in a craft or in an industry under the union's jurisdiction. Twenty-seven nationals (representing almost 10 percent of all union members) have established a " fraternal " system for admittance, through which the applicant must be accepted by a formal vote of the membership, while twenty-five nationals (representing almost 5 percent of all union members) provide for an apprenticeship system. The most frequent apprenticeship period is four years, although the Friendly Society of Engravers and Sketchmakers requires a seven-year apprenticeship. Not only does such apprenticeship serve to reduce the supply of skilled labor in particular trades, but limitations are also placed on the number of apprentices that shall be trained.[1] Apprenticeship regulations are most frequently found in the building, printing, and metalwork trades.

[1] While the International Association of Machinists (AF of L) permits the membership of " production workers," its constitution stipulates: " Every shop which employs three or more journeymen may have one apprentice and may have one additional apprentice for every ten journeymen employed." As cited by James J. Bambrick, Jr., and George H. Haas, *Handbook of Union Government, Structure and Procedures* (New York, National Industrial Conference Board, 1955), p. 60.

In isolated instances unions attempt to restrict membership by charging high initiation fees. A further device has been to issue temporary " permit " cards to nonunion members to enable them to work from week to week on a fee basis. This device has encouraged corruption (the " kickback " or " rake-off ") at the local level, and most nationals oppose the use of the permit card by their locals.

In Table 9, we see those exclusion policies of unions which are aimed at particular groups:

TABLE 9   Constitutional Provisions Regarding Union Membership

Constitutional Provision	No. of Unions	Per- centage	Declared Membership (in thousands)	Per- centage
Bar all persons (foremen, supervisors, and employers) who have power to hire and fire	35	18	3,383	19.3
No provision	159	82	14,130	80.7
Total	194	100	17,514	100.0
Bar all Negroes and other racial minorities	5	2.6	442	2.5
No provision	189	97.4	17,072	97.5
Total	194	100.0	17,514	100.0
Constitution specifically declares that all persons regardless of race, creed, or color (if otherwise qualified) *are eligible* to union membership	39	20.1	4,321	24.7
No provision	155	79.9	13,193	75.3
Total	194	100.0	17,514	100.0

Source: James J. Bambrick, Jr., and George H. Haas, *Handbook of Union Government Structure and Procedures* (New York, National Industrial Conference Board, 1955), pp. 62–63.

It is understandable why many unions deny membership to those persons with the managerial function of hiring and firing. Restrictions are also sometimes imposed against any person who is a member of another union. Fifty-six unions, covering a declared membership of 6,190,044 members specifically state that no Communist or other subversive is to be admitted to membership, and many constitutions have been changed to eliminate the statement that no discrimination should be made against applicants on the basis of their political beliefs because of the general fear of Communist membership.[2] A United Mine Workers' constitutional provision indicates those " subversive " elements which cannot qualify for membership: " Any member accepting membership in the Industrial

[2] Bambrick and Haas, *op. cit.,* p. 61.

Workers of the World, the Working Class Union, the One Big Union, or any other dual organization, or membership in the National Chamber of Commerce or Ku Klux Klan, or in the Communist Party, or Fascist, Nazi or Bund organizations, shall be expelled from the United Mine Workers of America. . . ."

What is the legal status of provisions which deny union membership to certain workers? There is no clear court precedent which establishes the legal right of a worker to membership in a union, and most of the test cases have evolved around discrimination against a worker who is already a member of the union. In 1944 the Supreme Court of California had ruled that a union enjoying a closed shop was not entitled to such an agreement so long as it refused to admit Negroes on the same basis as whites.[3] The Taft-Hartley Act has outlawed the closed shop as well as " excessive or discriminatory " initiation fees. Section 8(b)(2) of the Taft-Hartley law further prohibits a union from inducing an employer to discriminate against any employee who has been denied membership for any reason other than refusal to pay the organization's customary initiation fees and dues. By this regulation a union cannot force an employer to exclude a Negro worker from employment if the union refuses to admit him to membership. Several states have passed fair employment practice laws which make it an offense to discriminate against persons because of race, creed, national origin, or ancestry.

But discrimination undoubtedly continues to exist, particularly in the railroad industry, where the decline of employment has probably added to the pressure to maintain it. Some railroad unions admit Negroes to membership, but have organized separate auxiliary bodies for them. The National Mediation Board of the railway industry has concluded that certification will not be established for bargaining units separated on the basis of race or color. When membership is permitted, often discriminatory policies are negotiated by the union which work against the Negro element within the union, and occasionally unions deny the responsibility for representing the Negro element within their organizations.[4] Chief Justice Stone, in dealing with such a case, pointed out that, " The statute [the Railway Labor Act] does not deny to . . . a bargaining labor organization the right to determine eligibility to its membership " and raised the question whether a Negro worker, excluded from membership in a union, can be adequately represented by that union in negotiations with the employer. While this may suggest that a vigorous stand has been taken against discrimination, Aaron and Komaroff concluded from their study

[3] Noted by Frank C. Pierson, " The Government of Trade Unions," *Industrial and Labor Relations Review*, Vol. 1, No. 4 (July, 1948), p. 599 from *James v. Marinship*, 25 Cal. (2d) 721, 155 P. (2d) 329 (1944).

[4] For a documentation of these abuses, see Benjamin Aaron and Michael I. Komaroff, " Statutory Regulation of Internal Union Affairs: *Illinois Law Review*, Vol. 44, No. 4 (September–October, 1949) and Vol. 44, No. 5 (November–December, 1949.)

of the railroad industry: ". . . the agencies responsible for the administration of the Act have only made matters worse by their pious policy of hearing, seeing, and speaking no evil." [5] Of course, one might argue that instances of racial discrimination have been so rare as not to require legislative action. It is probably true that there are much fewer examples of racial discrimination within unions outside of the railroad industry.

Undoubtedly legislation will help to reduce the interracial tensions and discriminations found in our society, and the unions themselves are in most cases moving rapidly toward greater tolerance. The CIO and the International Ladies Garment Workers (within the AF of L) enjoyed an excellent record of tolerance, and some nationals within the AF of L had levied fines in instances of racial discrimination by their locals. It is significant that in the merger agreement between the AF of L and CIO, principle 2(b) of the merger states:

> The merged federation shall constitutionally recognize the right of all workers, without regard to race, creed, color or national origin to share in the full benefits of trade union organization in the merged federation. The merged federation shall establish appropriate internal machinery to bring about, at the earliest possible date, the effective implementation of this principle of non-discrimination.

Disciplinary and Judicial Systems within the Union

Any organization professing to be democratic must permit the free expression of its individuals and permit minority groups the freedom to convert their convictions into majority sentiment. It is further necessary that fair judicial processes be established to judge those accused of not conforming to its laws. The union is primarily an agency to increase the power behind labor's demands for improvement of its material status: The struggle to get " more " supersedes any other drive or issue. In such a setting the exercise of civil liberties, freedom of speech, or open criticism of union officers can readily be interpreted as being tantamount to treason or sedition. The union leader expects and demands uniform support in time of crisis and when such support is not forthcoming is as indignant and outraged as any military officer who, in the face of a perilous mission, finds his troops openly posing the question: " Is this trip necessary? "

Simply to say that the union is a power mechanism does not exempt it from the scrutiny of those concerned with the rights of individual workers and the abuses of union leadership which violate individual rights.

[5] They further point out that "Strangely enough, while frequently threatening to revoke the certification of any union whose internal policies included a refusal to grant equal status to all employees in the bargaining unit for which it was the exclusive representative, the Board has not once, in over 14 years, found the facts of any case sufficiently clear to require such action on its part." *Ibid.*, pp. 438–440.

This problem is no less important simply because it is often difficult to distinguish the legitimate expressions of minority opinion from divisive sentiments that undermine union effectiveness.[6]

A large part of the difficulty arises because of the absence in most unions of any continuing two-party system. While elections for officers may provide for lively campaigns and active participation of all members, especially at the local level, there is no permanent " loyal opposition " to continually challenge the wisdom and the policies of existing officers. Indeed, as we have already observed, the whole concept of " loyal opposition " is likely to be construed as a contradiction of terms. The notable and classic exception to this generalization is, of course, the International Typographical Union. This is the oldest union in the United States, and since 1898 we have seen a continuing contest between its two parties, the Progressives and the Independents, for leadership of the union. The union also employs a referendum system for electing its international officers, and every presidential candidate has faced opposition for election since 1916.[7]

Because this organization is unique, it is apparent that union conditions are not generally conducive to the two-party system. The hostility toward union leadership discourages any overture to " institutionalize " dissension. While a two-party system could serve as a check against the more widely reported abuses of power within the union, it must not be assumed that a democratically operated union is one that is necessarily more moderate, especially if one measures moderation in terms of the demands made on the employer. On the other hand, we see the unhappy development of autocracy within the International Pressmen's Union, an organization in the same field as the ITU. The death of its president, George Berry, in 1948 prompted a Congressional investigation of the

[6] We return to this rather obvious point. When Arthur J. Goldberg of the CIO wrote on " Civil Rights in Labor-Management Relations: A Labor Viewpoint " (*The Annals*, May, 1951, Vol. 275), he by-passed discussion of the absence of the two-party system within most unions but emphasized that any freedom the individual worker acquires is not based on his ability to jeopardize the collective action of labor, but rather his willingness to participate in such action: " It may seem paradoxical, but it is nevertheless a basic truth that the liberty of the individual is best secured by the practice of collective action. It is only by the joining together the individuals employed in any given plant or industry that some measure of equality of bargaining power can be achieved. This measure of bargaining power is fundamentally the only thing that gives labor an element of freedom in the labor management field " (p. 149).

[7] *The Typographical Journal*, the monthly union newspaper, publishes articles from both parties. The vitality of the democracy within this union is evidenced by the fact that the union membership has voted in over 500 referenda since 1889 to approve or disapprove suggested union policies. Out of 24 referenda to increase the salary of international officials since 1900, the increase has been defeated 17 times. Local unions have independently put forward 27 referenda and 18 of these have passed. In recent elections an average of 73 percent of all members voted on such issues. See Seymour M. Lipset, " Democracy in Private Government: A Case Study of the International Typographical Union," *The British Journal of Sociology*, Vol. III, No. 1 (March, 1952), pp. 47, 48.

union, and this revealed that Berry had misappropriated at least $200,000 of the International's funds. It was difficult to untangle and classify those investments by Berry of union funds on behalf of the union from the investments he made of union funds on behalf of Berry. Under Berry's regime many locals were denied the right to choose their own officers. Various locals were suspended for opposing the decisions of the International.[8]

Turning to the more general problem of disciplinary procedures, most constitutions explain in varying detail the types of prohibited offenses, the process for judging them and the punishment stipulated, such as reprimands, fines, suspensions or expulsions from the union. As one would expect, the union constitution is a sufficiently elaborate doctrine without adding to it a catalog of all the potential crimes of its members or punishments for infraction of its rules. Most contain a brief statement of the types of prohibited offenses. These often reflect the character of the industry and the past experiences of the union. The Lithographers Union, for example, forbids the use of chromic acid in making lithographic plates because of its hazards to health; the International Ladies Garment Workers denies membership to those with " contagious and loathsome or dangerous disease "; the Teamsters Union prohibits the ". . . assaulting or injuring of a general officer or organizer . . ." and the International Association of Machinists will punish those refusing to do " rough or dirty work "; the Airline Dispatchers expel members for " intoxication "; the Marine Cooks will expel members for obtaining transportation by false representation; the Locomotive Firemen and Enginemen's constitution reflects nineteenth-century morality with the threat of expulsion for those indulging in " immoral practices, wife abandonment, or improper treatment of family "; the Progressive Miners will expel any member ". . . taking a star and gun for the purpose of using them against the interests of organized labor. . . ." [9]

Most constitutions contain a blanket clause of an all-inclusive nature, forbidding such behavior as " misconduct," " acting against the interests of the union," " acts discrediting the union," " undermining the union," " creating dissension," " acting collusively with any employer or his agent to the detriment of the international . . . ," " willfully slandering any union officer," and " gross disloyalty." It is precisely because the content of unbecoming conduct may not be known before the fact that the individual union member may find himself vulnerable to disciplinary action.

[8] Seidman points out that " since 1928, Local 4 of the Printing Pressmen of Chicago has been headed by an administrator appointed by the national officers, and for an even longer period Local 3 in the same city has been under such control." *Union Rights and Union Duties* (New York, Harcourt, Brace and Co., 1943), p. 25.

[9] These examples are drawn from Bambrick and Haas, *op. cit.*, pp. 65–66, and Clyde Summers, " Disciplinary Powers of Unions," *Industrial and Labor Relations Review*, Vol. 3, No. 4 (July, 1950), pp. 492–493.

These provisions are not deliberately vague; they exist simply because of the difficulty of enumerating potential misbehavior. And there are good and sufficient reasons for some form of discipline within the union: the union must protect its reputation and responsibility by reprimanding members who, through their behavior, disgrace it. It must be able to enforce contracts which it has negotiated by punishing those members who flaunt the contract; it must have some defense against that unscrupulous element which might abscond with union funds; and it must have a defense against those who are deliberately attempting to discredit the union by planting false rumors or making malicious charges. The difficulty arises when the protestations of members are well founded as in situations of gross mismanagement. Free discussion cannot flourish if members are prevented from " impugning the motive of officers " or " circulating materials to union members without approval of union officers." Some classic cases exist where union officials have made sweeping use of these vague clauses to stamp out legitimate criticism. In some cases when the entire local was up in arms against corruption in the ranks of the international, the international has simply revoked the charter of the local.[10]

When an individual is charged with misconduct by a union, it is usually necessary that the charge be put in writing, that the individual be informed of the charge, and that the machinery be promptly set in motion to evaluate the charge. In most instances a committee of union members is elected by the union or appointed by the president to hear both sides of the case. On some occasions the executive officers of the union perform this function. In almost every situation the evidence is gathered following the cross examination of persons involved, and a summary of findings is then reported to the full membership meeting. It is usually the task of the membership to vote on innocence or guilt, and if the party is found guilty, to determine the nature of the punishment. While the constitutions declare that a " fair and impartial hearing without delay " should be provided, the hearings do not always conform to judicial standards. More often than not they are held in a highly emotional or charged atmosphere, resulting in the accusation that they are more in the nature of star-chamber proceedings. The hostility of the unions against the " formalism " of law is revealed by the fact that a few constitutions forbid representation by a lawyer as legal counsel for any participant in a dispute. These proceedings, essentially informal in their nature, probably leave much to be desired. They have been criticized by both the American Civil Liberties Union, and by such sympathetic students of the labor

---

[10] For discussion, see Summers, *op. cit.*, pp. 498–508. In the NICB study of union constitutions, only one of 98 constitutions contained a provision which stated: ". . . nothing herein . . . shall in any way infringe the right of the member to criticize any action or policy of the international administration or local union administration. . . ." Bambrick and Haas, *op. cit.*, p. 67.

movement as Philip Taft, Clyde Summers, Frank Pierson, Benjamin Aaron and Michael Komaroff.[11]

The accused who is found guilty by the local still has the recourse to appeal the decision to the national. If the president of the national sustains the local, the case can usually be appealed to the Executive Board, and ultimately to the convention itself. On occasion the cases have been taken into the courts. The courts have usually required that the complainant exhaust the machinery within the union before assuming jurisdiction, and are likely to appraise the behavior of the individual in terms of the content of the union constitution and contract.

Instances of union disciplinary procedures are relatively rare, with the large bulk of cases arising in temporary suspensions for nonpayment of dues. The hazards of serious abuse are much reduced, for following the Taft-Hartley Act, the union cannot compel the employer to fire any employee for any reason other than nonpayment of dues. While the field of union discipline is characterized with vagueness and uncertainty, union officers are more anxious to retain and extend existing membership, than to reduce it by expulsions.

Racketeering and Unionism

In the Spring of 1956, when the New York *Daily Mirror* labor reporter Victor Riesel stepped on to a busy New York City street, an assailant threw acid into his eyes. The press and public were outraged by the audacity and viciousness of the crime. When medical reports indicated that Riesel had lost the sight of both eyes, the FBI intensified its search for the culprit. The thug was soon found dead, with a bullet in the back of his head. The FBI arrested a half-dozen ex-convicts who

[11] For example, see Philip Taft, "Judicial Procedure in Labor Unions," *Quarterly Journal of Economics* (May, 1945); American Civil Liberties Union, *A Bill to Amend the National Labor Relations Act*, submitted to the Senate Committee on Labor Education (February, 1947); Frank Pierson, "The Government of Trade Unions," *Industrial and Labor Relations Review* (July, 1948); and Clyde Summers, "Disciplinary Procedures of Unions," *Industrial and Labor Relations Review* (July, 1950 and October, 1950). Benjamin Aaron and Michael I. Komaroff, in their excellent study, "Statutory Regulation of Internal Union Affairs" (*op. cit.*), stress the importance of state and federal law in preventing violations of individual civil liberties within the union. Most attention to this problem has been given by New York courts, which have established the following standards: The member must be given written notice of charges before trial and the charges must clearly reveal the nature of the alleged offense. The hearing must be held at the proper time and place. The member must be given the opportunity to confront his accusers and to hear the testimony against him. He may testify in his own defense and call witnesses in his own behalf. The trial must be conducted in good faith before a regularly authorized union tribunal and in accordance with constitutional procedures. No member of the trial body may be an interested party to the case. Only properly authorized penalties may be imposed. For documentation of these principles and discussion, see page 662. The authors stress that it is "startlingly apparent" that these standards are not universally recognized by courts.

were alleged to have masterminded the attack. *The cause:* Riesel had been testifying freely about racketeering in unions. *The result:* an alarmed public demanded that the criminal element within the union movement be crushed. To suggest that unionism suffers from " guilt by association " in this respect is certainly an understatement. Top union officials have grown increasingly nervous about the rising tide of criticism leveled against unions and are taking steps to clean their own houses before legislation does it for them.

While the criminal element is but a very minor portion and corruption is a rare incident in labor-management relations, the steady trickle of reports about corruption are having a corroding effect on union status. Needless to say, such reports provide fascinating copy for the tabloids. Let us review a few such news stories:

When racketeer William Bioff was introduced to Nicholas M. Schenck, president of Loew's Inc. (which operates the Loew chain of theaters and produces Metro-Goldwyn-Mayer motion pictures) by George E. Brown (president of the International Alliance of Theatrical Stage Employees and Moving Picture Machine Operators) back in April of 1936, Mr. Schenck was startled when Bioff got to the point of the interview with his simple observation and demand: " I'm the boss . . . and I want from the movie industry $2,000,000." It was not until May, 1941, that both Brown and Bioff were indicted under the Federal Anti-Racketeering Law for extorting over $1,500,000 from the movie industry [12] and that the connection between Willie Bioff and the Al Capone gang became known. By testifying freely of his associations in the underworld, Willie Bioff was paroled. But in the winter of 1955 Willie Bioff (attempting to live out his life in seclusion) touched the starter of his automobile. A blast of dynamite ended his life.

Of more recent interest has been the struggle to oust the criminal element from the International Longshoremen's Association, in New York, a drama that received national attention in the award-winning movie, " On the Waterfront." There was more truth than fiction in this story. As Daniel Bell describes the situation:

> . . . you are in a rough, racket-ridden frontier domain ruled by the bull-like figure of the " shaping boss." Here brawn and muscle, sustained where necessary by baling hook and knife, enforce discipline among a motley group. . . . Here one finds kickback, loansharking, petty extortion, payroll padding, tribute on cargo, bookmaking, numbers, theft and pilferage — and murder — a commonplace of longshore life. In such an atmosphere, rumor is rife and facts prone to exaggeration. Waterfront gossip insists, for example, that Cock-eye Dunn,

[12] And another $1,250,000 by a 2 percent assessment of the membership. Ironically, George E. Brown was a vice president of AF of L from 1936 and was responsible with other members of the executive council to enforce the anti-racketeering resolution adopted by the 1940 convention.

head of three federal A.F. of L. locals before his execution in Sing Sing in 1949 for killing a recalcitrant hiring boss was responsible for thirty-seven murders. "We should be careful," states Bill Keating, onetime assistant district attorney and former counsel to the New York Anti-Crime Committee, "and put the figure at thirteen." [13]

It is estimated that organized theft on the New York waterfront amounted to some $30 million per year, with exorbitant loading charges adding another $10 million. While loading and unloading has traditionally been a minor expense for ocean shipping, today longshoring accounts for 50 percent of the ship's total expense in moving cargo.

The opportunities for "holding-up" unionism arose simply because the difference between profit and loss for shipping companies was the speed with which they could secure a quick "turn-around" or fast loading and unloading. Similarly, the congestion created when trucks attempt to pick up cargoes from narrow piers and streets adds to the delay truckers face in getting goods to their consumers. The organization of the pier made possible the exploitation of the situation. Shippers could secure cooperation and avoid delays by a payoff, and truckers could go to the head of the line to load up by paying a "hurry-up" fee.

In November, 1952, the New York State Crime Commission disclosed that more than one hundred union officials regularly received gifts and payoffs from the major stevedoring concerns. About 30 percent of the port's ILA officials had criminal records. The hearings were so damaging that the AF of L revoked the charter of the ILA and tried to organize a substitute union. Meanwhile President Ryan and other union officials were indicted on charges of larceny and extortion.

The organizing attempts of the AF of L "reformed" waterfront union were not successful. In its coverage of the 1953 developments, *Fortune* explained, "Terror plays a role. On Pier 32, controlled by muscleman Albert Ackalitis, a hiring boss who went over to the AF of L was drowned. Accidental or not, his death is looked on as a warning. Two AF of L hiring bosses who replaced Anastasians in Brooklyn quit after they were beaten up. The AF of L has been unable to find local men willing and able to become leaders." [14] In a supervised election in the fall of 1956 the AF of L was still unable to wrest control of the waterfront from the ILA. Congressional investigations of labor racketeering in the spring of 1957 served to draw attention from longshoring to the Teamsters' Union, when startling allegations of corruption within this union received national publicity.

Unfortunately, the building, and service trades too have been found vulnerable to racketeering. Building contractors are often required to meet deadlines in construction and may be required to pay a penalty if

[13] "Some Aspects of the New York Longshore Situation," Industrial Relations Research Association, *Papers* presented December 28–30, 1954, p. 298.
[14] "The Polluted Port," *Fortune* (December, 1953), p. 66.

not able to finish the job in the alloted time. The employer is then vulnerable to a strike threat, for any delay may prove ruinous.[15]

In 1943 a student of this problem, Joel Seidman, concluded that " The failure to oust racketeers (from unions) is due to no lack of available remedies, but to the indifference or fear of union members and employees, or to the political influence that racketeers possess. It is a disgrace to the labor movement, however, that racketeers should so often be tolerated until the government intervenes." [16] His sentiment is equally true today.

On the question of corruption, Walter Reuther has observed that it is up to the labor movement itself to establish effective procedures for ferreting out the criminal and corrupt element within unions:

> . . . if the labor movement did not create internal machinery to clean up its own house with a stiff broom, then we could get repressive legislation, and anti-labor forces would do the job with a meat axe and try to destroy our labor movement in the process.[17]

The merged AFL–CIO is increasingly sensitive to the charge of corruption within its ranks, and it will undoubtedly extend its efforts to rid legitimate unionism of this minor, but ugly blemish.

Communism and American Unionism

To many the specter of Communist infiltration into American unions is seen as a greater problem than that of corruption, for at least the ex-

[15] For a discussion of problems in the trucking industry, see "Beck's Bad Boys," *Fortune* (May, 1954 and December, 1954). In a speech given April 26, 1954, Dave Beck, president of the International Brotherhood of Teamsters in Chicago, explained: "If there is any proof of labor racketeering (in our union), I recommend the district attorney or the prosecuting attorney go in and seek an indictment, give him and every other man the right to have his counsel of defense, his opportunity to cross-examine and put under oath those that accuse him. . . . Congressmen have said, 'Mr. Beck, why don't you throw these men out of your union that are accused?' Accused — not even indicted much less convicted of anything and I say to them, 'You don't have to go over to Minneapolis or Detroit to find someone to throw out, why the hell don't you start throwing them out in Congress. . . .'" Report of the first annual meeting of the Central States Conference of Teamsters, pp. 9 and 10.

[16] *Op. cit.,* p. 118.

[17] "The New Beginning," an Address by Walter Reuther, Pamphlet No. 268, CIO (April, 1955), p. 16. Reuther contends, in a philosophical vein, that some forms of corruption arise, not because of the union leader's inherent intent to do wrong, but because of the pressures of our society: "We live in a society in which the acquisition of material wealth and personal gain is considered the measurement of success. In a society with an acquisitive philosophy it is perfectly understandable how a labor movement can become corrupted, and it becomes corrupted when you apply within the labor movement the standards of personal conduct that are accepted as perfectly proper in the business community. When a businessman makes a fast million dollars, he is looked to as a real sharp, successful businessman. But when a labor leader makes a fast buck, he is corrupt" (p. 17). Reuther appears to be confusing the legitimate revenues of management with corruption. Certainly the corrupt businessman stands as condemned as does the corrupt union official.

tortionist is willing to work within the framework of the free enterprise system, while the doctrinaire Communist is only interested in the destruction of that system and the "expropriation of the expropriators." Communism is not a recent threat to independent unionism in this country, and we shall try to cast the problem it poses in its historical perspective. Public concern about this issue seems to run in cycles, with peaks of apprehension in postwar periods. Today, however, with the consolidation of the world largely into two ideological camps, we can anticipate a continuing " plateau " of concern over this issue.

Actually, it is possible to impute the pure and simple bread and butter characteristics of the American Federation of Labor to its resistance to both the political agitation of the Lasalle Socialists on the one hand and the cooperative schemes of the Knights of Labor on the other. It must be remembered that the immigrants Adolph Strasser and Samuel Gompers, (who formed the American Federation of Labor) were " reared in the cradle of radicalism." They were aware of the practical obstacles to both utopian and scientific socialism. To them, the union was solely an economic agency to deal solely with economic issues.

Even before the turn of the century, the Marxists could not make up their minds whether it was better strategy to " bore from within " existing unions or to set up " dual " unions. Socialists attempted to gain control of the Knights of Labor, but their influence declined with the large growth of that organization in 1885. In 1893 socialist members of the AF of L submitted an eleven-point resolution to their convention, which included the controversial tenth point declaring that the organization pledged itself to " collective ownership by the people of all means of production and distribution." Gompers engineered the defeat of this motion in the 1894 convention, and in revenge the socialists engineered the defeat of Gompers as president of the organization. However, his re-election in the following year represented a complete route of socialist unionism within the AF of L.

Various splinter groups of left-wing unions formed the Industrial Workers of the World in 1905 on the premise that the cause of revolution could be better advanced by establishing a separate dual union movement. This group " scoffed at the opportunist radical advocacy of peaceful and gradual penetration of the existing unions and gradual capture of the state in order to dethrone capitalism." The spectacular growth of the IWW within the decade of its inception encouraged many radicals to believe that dual unionism was justified.

The formation of the Third Communist International in 1919 after the Russian Revolution, revitalized the efforts of Marxists to communize the American labor movement. William Z. Foster was destined to play a leading role in this drama. He became convinced that syndicalism of American industry could be achieved by boring from within existing labor movements. His doctrine was criticized by the revolutionary IWW as being, ironically, " dualism " or competing with the more valid form of revolution represented by the IWW. But when the prestige of the IWW collapsed, this technique gained new attention. In 1921 Foster organized the Trade Union Educational League, which proposed the re-organization of the American union movement on industrial lines. Members of the League were to serve as the growth cone for the ultimate control of major unions within the American Federation of Labor. Foster's proposals were catapulted into national prominence when the Moscow Congress on International Communism decided, in 1921, that attempts should be undertaken to unify revolutionary activities within trade unions. Although Communists held the bread and butter unions in contempt, they felt that the AF of L could be subverted to revolutionary goals. The League assaulted with vigor unions in the railroad, construction, printing, and clothing trades, with mixed success. Perhaps most dramatic was the control the Communists gained over the International Ladies Garment Workers Union. In 1926 this union called a strike which proved disastrous. After twenty weeks its treasury of $3.5 million was depleted, and the union was discredited and crushed.

The AF of L was quick to see the challenge of Communist infiltration and was desperately anxious to avoid the stigma of communism. It urged that the American government refuse recognition of the Soviet Union, and " expulsionism " of left-wing members from AF of L nationals became the order of the day. Philip Taft summarized the period:

> In no union, except the rather small Furriers' union, were the Communists able to win control. They were swept out of influence and by 1928 the Communists had been virtually squeezed out of every organization of labor. This was done by the trade unions themselves.[18]

When it became apparent that the penetration of Communist elements within existing unions was not succeeding, the Communist party decided to switch back from " boring within " to dualism. To implement this change of strategy, they dissolved the Trade Union Educational League and established in its place, the Trade Union Unity League. They attempted to establish new unions in coal, steel, textile, clothing and other areas of industry and manufacturing, but these efforts were largely unsuccessful. In this brief interval, from 1928 to 1933, the Unity League provided a vital training for Communist organizers. Their experience and skill was soon utilized (especially by industrial unions) during the ground-swell growth of membership in the last half of the thirties.

During the New Deal the Communist party again returned to the strategy of boring from within. Many of the older AF of L unions were

---

[18] " Communism in American Trade Unions," Industrial Relations Research Association, *Proceeding* (December 28–30, 1953), p. 19.

well versed in the strategy and technique of Communist infiltration so that Communists had less opportunity to "isolate the bureaucracy" of the union away from the rank and file. On the other hand, the industrial unions were usually willing to utilize those vigorous and spirited organizers who had gained valuable experience in the now defunct Trade Union Unity League. These agitators found it relatively easy to penetrate the new unions and locate themselves in strategic positions. David Dubinsky, having observed the destruction of the larger part of the International Ladies Garment Workers Union in the 1926 strike, cautioned John L. Lewis against using these left-wingers. But Lewis was confident he could control this minority within his union, and replied to Dubinsky: "Who gets the bird, the hunter or the dog?" [19]

But the Communist element was not to be so easily dislocated, for they had established a firm contact with the rank and file, and became highly skilled in the techniques of maintaining worker support. Taft estimates that at one time about fifteen of the new international industrial unions within the CIO were under Communist domination, while others estimated that by 1944, the Communist core dominated about twenty international and numerous local unions.

International tensions and the personality of John L. Lewis were the forces which shaped Communist party strategy in the early phase of World War II. When the Nazi-Soviet nonaggression pact was signed in 1939, the isolationist John L. Lewis received warm support from Communists within the CIO. Even after Lewis's resignation in 1940, this element continued to give support to Lewis rather than their new CIO leader, Philip Murray. But on June 21, 1941, the situation instantly changed. Germany began her invasion of Russia. To Communists, Roosevelt was no longer the imperialist warmonger but our beloved commander-in-chief, behind whom all must unite. Philip Murray, as he himself describes it, "was dragged by these same citizens [the Communist element in the CIO] from the bottomless pits of hell and lifted to a veritable sainthood." [20] Needless to say, Lewis was now alleged to be a member of the Fascist, anti-working class dictatorship.

Following World War II, the CIO leadership became increasingly nervous about the Communist elements within its organization. Walter Reuther began an intensive and successful campaign to oust the Communists from the United Automobile Workers. In 1948 and 1949 the battle lines were developing within the CIO to resolve the issue of Communist penetration in other affiliated internationals. By 1949 the Communist-dominated United Electrical Workers Union suspected that the

[19] This incident is described by Albert S. Epstein, of the International Association of Machinists, in his discussion of Taft's paper cited above, p. 33.
[20] As cited by Gordon F. Bloom and Herbert R. Northrup, *Economics of Labor Relations* (Homewood, Ill., Richard D. Irwin, 1954), p. 67.

break with the CIO was inevitable and, following the defeat of the right-wing slate of officers, the executive board of the UEW secured emergency powers to expel members who might engage in raiding or secession activities. Philip Murray, now secure in his position as president of the CIO, decided to move swiftly. The CIO adopted a constitutional amendment at its 1949 convention which declared ineligible to serve, either as an officer or as a member of the executive board, any individual: " Who is a member of the Communist party, any Fascist organization, or other totalitarian movement." Further power was granted to the CIO executive board to refuse to seat at convention, and to remove from office, any member of the executive board and to permit the board to disaffiliate, expel, or take other " appropriate action " against any national or international which does not conform with CIO policies. Ben Gold, president of the Communist-dominated Fur Workers, declared the amendment to be an " anti-American, anti-democratic, anti-labor move," and Harry Bridges of the Longshoremen and Warehousemen declared: " They say the issue is communism. The real issue is they don't want opposition. You can vote, but when you do make sure you vote right." [21]

The United Electrical, Radio and Machine Workers of America and the United Farm Equipment and Metal Workers of America were expelled from the CIO at the 1949 convention, and nine more Communist-controlled unions were expelled in the 1950 convention. Following the expulsion of the UEW the CIO immediately established its own rival organization to capture the membership of the UEW, the International Union of Electrical, Radio and Machine Workers. While this new union captured about two thirds of the UEW membership, the UEW organization still remains a potent force in the electrical industry and denies that it is led or dominated by Communists.

Postwar efforts to apply federal legislation to this problem included Section 9(h) of the Taft-Hartley Act, which required union officers to file non-Communist affidavits in order that the union might enjoy the use of the National Labor Relation Board procedures. The union officer must state that he is not a member of the Communist party or affiliated with such a party, and that he does not believe in, and is not a member of, or supports any organization that believes in or teaches, the overthrow of the United States government by force or by any illegal or unconstitutional methods. Some unionists have declared that such provisions make second-class citizens of union leaders, for they alone, and not employers (nor the bulk of other citizens) are required to sign such a statement in order to carry on their jobs. The provision may have doubtful effect, since some of the known Communists have pursued the " resign and sign " tactic. In September, 1950, for example, Ben Gold announced his resignation from the Communist party in order to sign the non-Communist

[21] Quotations are drawn from Aaron and Komaroff's study cited above, pp. 631–633.

affidavit but declared: "I resigned from the Communist party but I do not give up my belief in true democracy." [22]

Basic to this issue of communism in unions is the problem whether special legislation should be enacted to thwart the purposes of the Communist party. Such legislation raises questions as to how one might define a Communist, and how one might define Communist activities within the union. One must remember that the attempts to regulate union affairs by governmental authority constitutes a threat to traditional freedoms. The paradox of democracy is that it " lives dangerously " inasmuch as the freedom of expression of minority sentiment provides the potential for a minority to crush democracy itself. If one feels that the " clear and present danger " to the American way of life is represented by the Communist minority, then emergency control and legislation can be justified by the courts. In this context, however, if the danger is considered to be continuing, so then will the infringement of civil rights be continuing. There is no single or ready answer to this issue, for it involves the careful weighing of alternatives, each of which carries with it serious hazards. The difficulty is appropriately summarized by Benjamin Aaron:

> It seems to me that what we need is not new legislation, but more, much more, objective inquiry, discussion and reflection. We are not engaged in a simple game of cops and robbers, a game in which virtue and wickedness are clearly defined and in which the sole problem is how to catch the " bad guys." Our problem is the terribly complex and never-ending one of reconciling the need for national security with the American promise of individual freedom.[23]

Labor in Politics

The equality of the individual at the polls is not equivalent to his equality in the market place. A basic tenet of political democracy is that each citizen should have equal influence in determining the policies of the government. But in the economic area, such egalitarian principles are considered unnecessary and perhaps even dangerous, for equal influence in the market place would imply equal purchasing power and perhaps even equal bargaining power. It is precisely because of the relative weakness of labor's bargaining power in the economic arena that labor has, on occasion, turned to the tempting alternative of political action. If influence is to be measured by votes alone, should not the greater number of workers compared to employers offer labor a tremendous tactical advantage? Indeed, since the numbers are in such obvious imbalance, how could employers offer any effective resistance to labor's political demands?

[22] Cited by Benjamin Aaron, "Statutory Regulation of Internal Union Affairs: The Control of Communism," University of California, Los Angeles, Fifth Annual Conference on Labor, p. 396.

[23] *Ibid.*, p. 412.

There are forms and degrees of labor participation in politics. First, labor could organize an independent labor party to give clear expression to labor's goals. The Labor party of Great Britain established a clear precedent for such action. A second alternative is to subscribe to revolutionary political action. This alternative lost much of its significance in America when Communists themselves could not agree on the appropriate role of political action.

The third form of political activity involves "nonpartisan political action," or a continuing interest of the union movement in politics without becoming an integral part of any party machine. This has been the alternative most popular to American unions. As the 1901 AF of L resolution stated: "Stand faithfully by our friends and *elect* them. Oppose our enemies and *defeat* them; whether they be candidates for President, for Congress, or for other offices, whether Executive, Legislative or Judicial."

The American Federation of Labor began to lobby in national politics in 1895 by appointing representatives in Washington. It was rather distressed by the fact that when, in 1906, the Executive Council submitted a list of labor's grievances to Congress together with a list of needed reforms, Congress ignored the petition. This prompted the AF of L to participate actively in the 1906 campaign, and the Nonpartisan Political Campaign Committee that spearheaded labor's activities in election continued its activities. Gompers felt that while economic forces represented the main "fulcrum of power" in the American scene, many economic decisions were made in a political climate that could affect the outcome of these decisions. The interest of the AF of L in politics was increased in 1921 when a large legislative conference committee was established to secure measures from Congress sympathetic to the labor movement.

Even though the principle of nonpartisan action gained wide support, the union movement has, from time to time, flirted and sometimes even embraced the activities of a particular party. The National Labor Union had attempted to organize a National Reform party back in 1872, but this party failed as a political organization. The Greenback party gained considerable support from both farmer and labor groups in the election of 1880. Henry George came close to winning the mayoralty campaign for New York City with a Labor party support in 1886. Labor parties sprang up in many of the New England, the Middle and Northwest states during this period and gained considerable support. An American Labor party was established in Chicago in July 1920, with fifteen state labor parties already organized, and in 1922 a Communist-controlled Federated Farmer-Labor party appeared. In 1922 various railway unions created the Conference for Progressive Political Action to encourage nonpartisan politician activity. The acid test for labor and socialist parties developed in 1924, when most labor groups endorsed LaFollette as presidential candidate on the Progressive party ticket. Even the AF of L endorsed

LaFollette but pointed out that this action did not signify "a pledge of identification with an independent party movement or a third party, nor . . . support for such a party, group or movement except as such action accords with our nonpartisan political policy." [24]

LaFollette's poor showing at the polls discouraged the third-party movement. Four years earlier Tammany Hall Boss Charles F. Murphy is alleged to have declared: "We don't need a Socialist Party. If the people of New York want Socialism, then Tammany Hall will give it to them." [25] Indeed, it appeared that labor was content to let the traditional parties represent its interests. So firmly had the AF of L embraced the economic philosophy of free enterprise, that even with the initial shock of the great depression, it was not prepared to support government intervention on the grounds that intervention violated the principles of free enterprise and jeopardized the freedom of the individual to solve problems on his own. It might further weaken the inclination of workers to turn to collective bargaining to solve their problems. As late as 1932, the AF of L opposed social reform legislation including such measures as unemployment insurance, but when the numbers of unemployed increased to disastrous proportions new attitudes crystallized.

In 1935 many AF of L and CIO unions united to form the Labor's Nonpartisan League to encourage the re-election of Roosevelt in 1936. The International Ladies Garment Workers Union had suggested the establishment of a third labor party at the 1935 convention of the AF of L, but this motion received little support. In the 1932 election, which swept Roosevelt into power, the Socialist party under Norman Thomas received a little better than 2 percent of the popular vote and the Communist party about .02 percent of the vote. The Nonpartisan League spawned the American Labor party in New York State, which gave its vigorous support and helped re-elect Governor Lehman and President Roosevelt in 1936. Right- and left-wing elements within this party split in 1944, with the right-wing forces establishing a new Liberal party.

Even within the framework of Labor's Nonpartisan League, controversy developed when, in 1938, William Green, as president of the AF of L, charged that the group was being manipulated and dominated by CIO leaders. He urged that all AF of L representatives withdraw. Such antagonism is understandable when one appreciates the split between the AF of L and the CIO which had just taken place and the rapid successes of the CIO in expanding industrial unionism. Even within the AF of L itself there was some disagreement on the policies and political

[24] As cited by Henry David, "One Hundred Years in Politics," in the *House of Labor*, J. B. S. Hardman and Maurice F. Neufeld, editors (New York, Prentice-Hall, 1951), p. 93.
[25] As cited by Max M. Kampelman, "Labor in Politics," Industrial Relations Research Association, 1952, p. 184.

strategy pursued by the long-established Nonpartisan Political Campaign Committee of the AF of L.

As noted previously, it must not be thought that all labor is Democratic nor can all workers be counted upon to support a pro-union program. In one study of presidential elections since 1936 it was estimated that about 60 percent of all AF of L members and about 70 percent of all CIO members vote Democratic. These ratios have remained remarkably stable.[26] While labor lobbyists represent the largest single pressure group in our society, their strength is minimized by the fact that the union cannot "deliver the vote" on any particular issue or to any particular candidate. Thus, effective political campaigning by the union requires pressure upward on the Congress, as well as downward on the rank and file. For example, John L. Lewis's condemnation of President Roosevelt was not enough to turn organized labor away from its support of Roosevelt, nor were the combined efforts of the CIO and AF of L to defeat the co-author of the Taft-Hartley Act, Senator Robert Taft, successful in the Ohio elections in 1950.

The CIO, encouraged by its successes in industrial organization, approached political action with considerably more enthusiasm than did the AF of L. In the summer of 1943 the Political Action Committee of the CIO was organized, but its chairman, Sidney Hillman, reaffirmed the ancient principle of working within the framework of existing parties.

Labor continued to have little interest in third-party movements after the war. Philip Murray, as leader of the CIO, remarked that third parties as panaceas are "our greatest indoor and outdoor national sport" and:

> We in the organized labor movement do not become alarmed over these manifestations; we regard them as pure Americana and weigh them on the scale of practicality. It is for this reason that we have discarded at this time and for the foreseeable future all proposals to establish in the United States a third political party.

The participation of labor in politics was obstructed, somewhat, by Section 313, under Title III, of the Taft-Hartley Act, which prohibits corporations and unions from making contributions or expenditures in connection with any election to national office. Unions have charged that such legislation is discriminatory since it does not restrict contributions by the National Association of Manufacturers or the American Medical Association to political parties. As a consequence, unions have had to distinguish support of "educational" activities from contributions to particular candidates or parties and have only been able to pass on the voluntary contributions from workers. Unions are still free to inform its members on legislative issues and about the voting records of Congressmen.

[26] These figures are quoted in "One Hundred Years in Politics," *op. cit.,* p. 106.

The 1955 merger of the AFL–CIO involved structural changes as well as strategy refinements for union political activity. The newly organized Committee on Political Education, usually referred to as the COPE, represents an integration of the CIO's Political Action Committee and the AFL's Labor League for Political Education. With its inception, George Meany was named chairman of the committee; James McDevitt of the LLPE and Jack Kroll of the PAC were named co-directors. In the AFL–CIO constitution, the COPE has the responsibility to provide "sound political education" for its members as well as to encourage all workers to register and vote.

The advantages to the union movement of uniform political action are readily apparent. With over 15 million members in the AFL–CIO, it is possible to undertake a single drive for political-education funds. Leaders of the merged organization can speak with more authority and influence because they represent one of the largest single blocs of voters in the country. A single program prevents overlapping of jurisdiction, making possible a greater economy of effort in political campaigning as well as giving more force to any campaign to secure labor's support.

The techniques of political education employed by the COPE in the 1956 elections suggest the growing importance to organized labor of political developments. First, the COPE conducted a widespread campaign to get union members registered so they would be able to vote. Secondly, it undertook to raise funds for political education by asking for a $1.00 contribution from each member. Theoretically, this could have netted $15 million, but the COPE's target was $3 million. Thirdly, a widespread campaign was undertaken to inform members of the previous voting records of candidates. Tabulations were made of the "right" and "wrong" votes of candidates and these were widely circulated.[27] In addition, information was provided through the newspapers of many nationals and internationals. Television and radio broadcasts also provided information. Speeches and telephone calls, together with door-to-door canvassing, were undertaken to increase registration; arrangements were made to provide for baby-sitters and transportation on election day.

It is, of course, impossible to determine the effect this had on the voting record. It should not be forgotten that an estimated 60,000 full-time staff personnel are employed by all unions with the AFL–CIO organization, and this number represents an effective core of persons usually able to articulate with enthusiasm the union viewpoint.

The COPE is fully aware of the difficulties confronting it. It does not

---

[27] Considerable reliance was placed on the distribution of these pamphlets through the mails because it had been found in prior elections that, when the distribution of political pamphlets was left to the locals, poor attendance and indifference reduced their circulation. In addition, by using the mails, it was hoped that the housewife, often suspicious of the union, might develop a sympathy and understanding of the union's political goals.

presume to deliver the vote. As Walter Reuther himself explained: " I have only one vote. I control no one else's vote. I never claimed that I have." As we pointed out above, the failure of the determined 1950 campaign of the union movement to unseat Robert Taft as senator of Ohio suggests that a highly militant union effort to secure rank-and-file support is not always successful, especially when the issues are confined only to unionism. In this campaign Senator Taft enjoyed a majority of 430,000 votes in spite of (and in the opinion of some, because of) organized labor's efforts to engineer his defeat.

Union strategists have attempted to meet this difficulty by widening their perspective on political issues. While it is true that the union movement has always been interested in issues relating to schooling, social security, housing, minimum wages, and legislation affecting collective bargaining, today the COPE takes an active interest in such problems as migrant labor, defense spending, natural gas, farm price supports, uses of atomic energy, immigration laws, tariff policy, foreign aid, and so on.

One observation is clear to all: the paper merger of the political arm of the AFL and CIO does not, in itself, produce uniformity in the political sentiment of union members. There still exists a divisive and heterogeneous quality to labor's vote. Family traditions, racial origin, and religion — these are often found to be the tap roots shaping the individual's political loyalties. In this sense, the attempt to establish a uniform policy for all organized labor may accentuate rather than minimize difference in political conviction. The Teamsters, for example, are more interested in unhampered enterprise, while the Garment Workers are more interested in social reform and civil rights. As a case in point, we saw considerable controversy in the meeting of the General Board AFL–CIO in the fall of 1956 before it reached the decision to formally endorse the Democratic party in the presidential and congressional elections.

A further difficulty confronting the COPE is that, in leaning entirely on the Democratic party, they must contend with the conservatism of the Southern Democrats. As the union movement itself is growing increasingly conscious of the need for greater racial and religious tolerance, the clash with Southern elements within the party may grow more apparent. In the 1956 campaign Arthur Larson, then Undersecretary of Labor, attempted to exploit this difficulty by pointing out, " The only time a Democratically-controlled Congress is ' liberal ' is when a strong Democratic President is able to override the traditional independence of Congress and impose the executive will, as in the period 1935–38." [28] The argument is that since many of the committee chairmanships are established on a seniority principle and since, within the Democratic party, the Southern Democrats have accumulated considerable seniority, a Democratic Con-

[28] "Why Labor Should Vote Republican," *Harper's Magazine* (September, 1956), p. 74.

gress would be substantially less liberal than a Republican Congress. It is doubtful if many union leaders are persuaded by the logic of this argument.

Undoubtedly, the increased interest of organized labor in politics is a healthy step because partisan education is better than no education, and there is certain little danger in contemporary America that the individual worker will be deprived of the opportunity to hear and read both sides of important campaign issues.

9

Capitalism and Unionism

In Section I we analyzed those difficulties created for the individual worker by the evolution of capitalism and by the creation of the labor market. In Section II, we noted that unionism was, in a sense, the response of labor to the challenge posed by industrialization, or more specifically, by the impersonal, immutable, and unpredictable behavior of market forces. Today, on the one hand unionism is praised as an institution dedicated to man's most noble purposes. On the other hand it is considered to be an institution appealing only to man's base instincts, corrupting labor's moral fiber and disrupting the smooth " clock-work " mechanism of the capitalist economy.

In appraising the role of unionism in the broader setting of capitalism, labor students too are not at all agreed on its ultimate impact. John R. Commons considered it to be the " reaction and protest against capitalism " while G. D. H. Cole views it as the " child of modern capitalism." In other instances the union may be viewed as a device for " breaking through " the pervasive competitive pressures of the market that might otherwise drive labor's income down to subsistence levels; it may be viewed as an institution to restore to the worker some sense of dignity and status; it may be viewed as a device to provide the worker with a degree of independence and control over his job territory; or it may be viewed as a device to restore some social purpose and identification to the worker.[1] Whatever its function, however, the impact of unionism on capitalism cannot be denied, and this impact is not less important because it produces multiple and conflicting responses; nor is it less important because we have diverse and contradictory analyses of union influence. In this chapter we shall review seven theories of unionism offered by seven economists. This discussion should provide us with a more discerning perspective for appraising the collective bargaining process in Section IV.

[1] For a critical discussion of the alleged shortcomings of these traditional views, see Clark Kerr and Abraham Siegel, " The Structuring of the Labor Force in Industrial Society: New Dimensions and New Questions," *Industrial and Labor Relations Review*, Vol. 8, No. 2 (January, 1955), pp. 151–168.

Karl Marx: The Revolutionary Viewpoint

Karl Marx applied Hegel's dialectic philosophy to economic development. Hegel had pointed out that ideas evolve through the original statement of a central thesis, which in turn is challenged by an " antithesis." Through this struggle of the old and new, a synthesis is formed but at the very moment of its fruition is again challenged by a new antithesis. Marx reasoned that economic development was but another application of Hegel's dialectic principle, with the class conflict as one of its manifestations. In the final stages of class warfare the proletariat would triumph over the bourgeoisie, and ultimately the final synthesis would be achieved in a classless utopia. This is very much a deterministic theory of economic change, for by its logic we are today on the escalator to revolution. Marx was persuaded that the inexorable forces of history could not and would not be denied; that the union movement could play an active, but essentially ancillary, role in the inevitable drift toward revolution.

Marx's theory of exploitation was built upon the labor theory of value, originally developed and generally supported by classical economists. It stated in essence that labor created all value. Capital was congealed or embodied labor in that labor created capital, and capital was by such reasoning simply a transformation of labor. As capital depreciates or wears out with its use in production, its labor power " rubs off," as it were, in the final product. Under capitalism and its " legal fiction " of private property, capitalists acquire the legal right to the flow of income of capital, not because of any labor they themselves contribute to the production process, but merely because they own capital.[2] Marx scorned the necessity of the private ownership of the means of production and denied that its destruction would undermine men's motivations to work. He noted that nine-tenths of the population in capitalism did not own private property and ". . . if being deprived of private property made man universally lazy, bourgeois society ought long ago to have gone to the dogs through sheer idleness; for those of its members who work acquire nothing, and those who acquire anything do not work." [3]

The rate of exploitation was, in Marx's scheme, the volume of surplus value (total value of product — labor's wage) over the wage bill, while the rate of profit was the surplus value over the wage bill *plus* capital and raw material expenditures. The capitalist would attempt to increase

[2] As G. D. H. Cole points out, "Ownership is not a creative act, but a claim to share in the results of the creative acts of others . . . no social system can make either things or the fact of ownership into positive agents of creation. The fact that ownership confers a recognised claim to appropriate value does not constitute the owner a creator, though of course he may be a creator if he works as well as owns." *What Marx Really Meant* (New York, Alfred A. Knopf, 1934), p. 220.

[3] From the *Communist Manifesto*, as reproduced, in a *Handbook of Marxism* (New York, International Publishers, 1935), pp. 40–41.

the volume of surplus value by substituting capital for labor, or by reducing the wage bill while maintaining or expanding the level of production. But while the *rate* of exploitation is thus increased, the increment of capital costs could reduce the rate of profit. Or alternatively, if the capital supply is increased while the surplus value remains the same, the rate of return of capital, or profit, will decrease. Here Marx felt he had found the basic contradictions of capitalism: the expansion of capitalism would permit a more rapid pace of labor exploitation by displacing labor, but this same process would tend to reduce the rate of return or profit of industry, leading to industrial crisis. Capitalists tried to help themselves by increasing labor's hours of work without increasing labor's pay, but this could only be a temporary palliative.

Marx also assumed a continuing existence of the reserve army of unemployed labor, weakening labor's bargaining power and enabling management to maintain its exploitation of labor. Paradoxical as it may seem, successful union pressure for higher wages would simply accelerate the pace of capital substitution for labor, diminishing the demand for labor, and enable even more exploitation.

It is significant that Marx could not make up his mind whether the real living standard of the worker would improve under capitalism. In the *Communist Manifesto*, he wrote:

> The modern labourer . . . instead of rising with the progress of industry, sinks deeper and deeper below the conditions of existence of his own class. He becomes a pauper, and pauperism develops more rapidly than population and wealth. . . . the bourgeoisie . . . is unfit to rule because it is incompetent to assure an existence to its slave within his slavery, because it cannot help letting him sink into such a state. . . .[4]

In his *Capital*, written twenty years after the *Manifesto*, Marx still claimed that the working class was bowed beneath a system in which "abject poverty, oppression, slavery, degradation, and exploitation increase."[5] In his *Capital* he is not so certain that living standards must fall during the growth of capital. If production is increasing rapidly, could not both wages and profits, consumption, and investment, increase together? While Marx was less dogmatic on this point, he felt that any increment of real income was but a crumb from the capitalists' table. Given continuous unemployment, wages would gravitate around the subsistence level, and increases in production would then only increase the degree of exploitation of labor. As Marx explained, "To say that the worker has an interest in the rapid growth of capital means only this: that the more speedily the worker augments the wealth of the capitalist, the larger will be the

[4] As reproduced in the *Handbook of Marxism, op. cit.*, p. 36.
[5] *Capital*, Vol. 1, p. 342, as quoted by Georges Sorel, *Reflections on Violence* (London, Allen & Unwin, 1915), p. 147.

crumbs which fall to him, the greater will be the number of workers that can be called into existence, the more can the mass of slaves dependent upon capital be increased." [6] Even though the material living standards may be slightly improved, it " does not abolish the antagonism between his interests and the interests of the capitalist. Profits and wages remain as before, in inverse proportion." He added, " We dare not believe them [the bourgeois economists] even when they claim that the fatter capital is the more will its slave be pampered." Capital formation increases the degree of specialization of labor, dilutes job skills, and intensifies the competition among workers for jobs. The net result is that " the forest of outstretched arms, begging for work grows ever thicker, while the arms themselves grow even leaner." [7] Marx was determined to blast the classical economists' axiom that " capital sets labor in motion," and more specifically, that the benefits received by the capitalist would inevitably promote the welfare of the working class. As Joan Robinson describes the Marxian view, " Any concession which the capitalist makes to the worker is the concession which the farmer makes to his beasts — to feed them better that they may work the more." [8] But if the improvements in living standards were substantial, does not this destroy the foundation for dissatisfaction?

If improvement in labor's living standard is an accepted fact, can Marx build his case on " relative " exploitation by claiming that the *proportion* of the final product labor receives is continually reduced? Cole leans heavily on this alternative: " The view that Capitalism degraded the general condition of the poor in the advancing industrial countries is based on sentimentalism, and not on an objective study of the facts . . . His [Marx's] exploitation is to be measured not by what he [the worker] receives, but rather by what he fails to receive. . . . Men feel rich or poor, not absolutely, but in relation one to another and to the available supply of wealth." [9] Our data of labor's distributive share do not support Marx.

One of the serious problems facing Marxists in American unionism was the permeation of the bourgeois philosophy within the ranks of the working class. Communists have indulged in considerable head-shaking and lament over this turn of events. They constantly proclaimed that the " Gomperses " must be expelled from the union movement, for these are

[6] Karl Marx, *Wage, Labour and Capital* (New York, International Publishers, 1933), p. 39.

[7] *Ibid.*, pp. 40, 47, 48.

[8] *An Essay on Marxism Economics* (London, Macmillan and Co., 1947), p. 3.

[9] Cole, *op. cit.*, pp. 48, 49. Cole goes even further to emphasize that " Marx's theory of exploitation does not involve, but explicitly contradicts, the view that the rise of Capitalism has made the lot of the labouring class as a whole absolutely worse." (*Ibid.*, p. 49.) But later, Cole contradicts himself and inadvertently reveals the contradiction of Marx by stating: " This interpretation [of only a relative decline of labor's share] is plainly inconsistent with Marx's own words. He does quite explicitly prophesy for the poor a fall in the standard of living, and not merely a failure to improve it in proportion to the increase in capitalist wealth." (*Ibid.*, p. 109.)

the "agents of the bourgeoisie," the "labor lieutenants of the capitalist class," "the bourgeoisified workers," "anti-socialist," "counterrevolutionary" in goal. Bread and butter unionism was especially suspect, for if it were successful in capturing back from the capitalists some of labor's surplus value, this might, to use Lenin's words, cause "temporary decay" in the working-class movement.[10]

As the split between "Gomperism" and "communism" widened, Gompers blasted the socialists openly:

> According to my opinion, professional Socialism accompanies insta-
> bility of judgment or intellectual undependability caused by inability
> to recognize facts. The conspicuous Socialists have uniformly been
> men whose minds have been warped by a great failure or who found
> it absolutely impossible to understand fundamentals necessary to de-
> veloping practical plans for industrial betterment.

Again, he told socialists: "Economically you are unsound; socially you are wrong; industrially you are an impossibility."

The Marxists were quick to pick up the challenge and exchanged insult for insult. They charged that while Gompers "made a swing or two" at understanding Marxian theory, he "missed completely." This was because to them "Gompers was forever a child, he was bewildered, he was uninformed, and he loved to roll in the vast seas of meaningless patriotic verbiage." [11] His fundamental error, in the Marxist view, was his attempt to build reform on the shifting foundations of capitalism. "To lay a foundation you have to have something to lay it on. The quicksand of 'Americanism' will never succeed in doing anything else but swallow the proletariat." [12] Gompers' method and philosophy was, in effect, "nothing more than the ripest fruit of a bourgeois, liberal mind." They added that ". . . after all, Gompers was in essence the chairman of the board of directors of a great corporation, the A. F. of L. To undermine capitalism was to undermine his own organization and his life's work. 'Trade Unionism pure and simple' is merely another way of saying 'company unionism.'" [13] When Gompers died in 1924, the Communists announced hopefully: "Gompers is dead; now let us kill Gomperism!" [14]

[10] Samuel Gompers's statement in 1913 before the United States Commission on Industrial Relations is often cited as the essence of "Gomperism": "The intelligent common-sense workmen prefer to deal with the problems of today, the problems with which they are bound to contend if they want to advance, rather than to deal with a picture and a dream which they have never had, and I am sure will never have, any reality in the actual affairs of humanity. . . ."

[11] George Simpson, "Sam Gompers: Misleader of Labor," *The American Mercury*, Vol. XXXIII, No. 130 (October, 1934), p. 186. These criticisms of Gompers are taken from Simpson's study.

[12] *Ibid.*, p. 188.

[13] *Ibid.*, p. 190.

[14] For an analysis, see John Spargo, "The Passing of Gompers and the Future of Organized Labor," *The North American Review*, Vol. CCXXI (March, 1927), p. 407.

Our analysis of the class structure in Chapter 4 indicated the weakness of Communist ideology as an explanation for American unionism. The American worker has developed an effective ideologic defense-in-depth against its doctrine, and the support given to free enterprise by most Americans has, as one British observer pointed out, acquired a " deeply sincere, quasi-religious moral attitude, as little susceptible to rational argument as the Hindus' aversion to killing cows." If this word picture is correct, Americans can feel doubly secure, for most unionists deny any " rationalism " let alone plausibility in the Marxist argument. Marx's proclamation: " Let the ruling classes tremble at a Communist revolution. The proletarians have nothing to lose but their chains. They have a world to win. Working men of all countries, unite! " is a call to arms strangely out of tune with American sentiment and brings only a wry smile to the face of the typical worker rather than a flush of anger.

John R. Commons: The Institutionalist Viewpoint

John R. Commons, " father " of labor institutionalism, academician and advisor to the national and state governments on labor issues, was a friend to American labor. Labor organization, he pointed out, faced an uphill struggle because of the heterogeneity of the early immigrant labor force, the boon of early universal suffrage, and the dilution of labor's job skills arising from industrialization. But competitive pressures necessitated organization, even though it was difficult to find a basis for coalescing diverse groups. Individualism had to give way to groupism, for the individual worker was not as free as management. The worker could not as lightly surrender his job as the employer could readily dismiss the worker.

The tendency toward group organization was not confined to labor alone, for Commons saw that economic pressure groups were becoming the " occupational parliament of the American people, more truly representative than the Congress." [15] A single monopoly posed a genuine hazard for society, but two-sided collective action could be viewed as a phase of " collective democracy." The organization of groups, however, required adaptability or modification of traditional concepts. No one group must become dominant, and each group must avoid surrendering its authority to the government. On the other hand, the government could not adopt a laissez-faire attitude. He explained:

> The businessmen and economists did not really mean all that they said about *laissez faire*. They were speaking to England and France, the most powerful governments in the world. . . . What businessmen and economists really meant by *laissez faire* was: prevent everybody else at home and abroad from doing as *they* please, in order that we may do as we please with what we claim as our own. [16]

[15] From his *The Economics of Collective Action* (New York, The Macmillan Co., 1950), p. 33.
[16] *Ibid.*, pp. 82–83.

Because individualism had given way to " corporationalism," the basic function and responsibility of the government was to attempt to maintain a balance of bargaining power between contesting groups. It was no longer possible to depend on the equilibrium that theorists had indicated would evolve in an atomistic and competitive society because of the absence of atomism in economic relationships. As has been explained by Commons:

> If American democracy is " saved," it will be saved by collective economic organization of corporations and labor unions. Instead of the traditional equilibrium between equal individuals of economic theory, the alternatives today are between an economic government based on balance of power between self-governing corporations and unions, and a suppression of both organizations, or their leaders, by military power.[17]

This solution is deceptively simple, but Commons had sufficient experience with the problems of labor legislation to appreciate how difficult it was to define " equality " in a legislative and judicial sense. Evolving such standards of reasonableness represented, to Commons, the major challenge of our time. He was not willing to lean on market-determined standards, for his concept of " reasonable " value must take precedence over " market " value. In the final analysis reasonable value was just what the courts said it was.

Commons was apparently looking for some kind of ground swell of morality in society which would make the concept of reasonable value self-evident to all.

> If the nineteenth century is the culmination of three centuries of the scientific revolution, the twentieth century, beginning with two world wars, is pre-eminently the century of an ethical revolution to correct the world massacres resulting from the triumphs of " science." For the scientific revolution consisted in dropping both the divine will and the human will from the restraints of ethical investigation, and reducing not only physical nature but also human nature to a blind war of atoms, molecules, protons, electrons, statistics, quanta, and a bloody struggle for existence and survival.[18]

In effect, Commons firmly believed that the problem of the twentieth century was to recognize the collective nature of human behavior. We live in a group economy and predicating policy decisions on the basis of atomistic competition is unrealistic and unwise. The key to establishing working relationships between groups is in stabilizing social behavior; in effect, to " create security of expectations " for the individuals and groups. This stabilized relationship is only possible when we have defined the limits to the discretionary action of groups. The rules define the status of individuals and groups. Such rules reflect the social valuations of the

[17] *Ibid.*, p. 263.   [18] *Ibid.*, p. 166.

various groups and are rooted in the " reasonableness " of both individuals and groups. " Reasonableness relates essentially to the question of how much disparity of economic power is tolerable in agreements over prices." [19] Commons is not disturbed by the growth of union power, for this is but one facet of collectivization of persons within the framework of capitalism. The problem created is one of redefining the relationships of group with group. Commons does not advocate the destruction of " imperfectly competitive " pressure groups, but rather the search for their common area of interest so that " mutuality " and working rules may be established. Neither does he appear disturbed by the growth of government regulation and control but is most anxious that the government does not monopolize the power that rests within the various groups. We must, in the final analysis, hope that people will be sufficiently intelligent and " reasonable " to develop working rules.

Commons' analysis is, of course, rooted in his faith in the collective bargaining process:

> Now I go further than I did 25 years ago and contend that the preservation of the American economic system against a totalitarian world, and against its own internal disruption, consists mainly in the collective bargaining between organized capital and organized labor, as against government by the traditional political parties.[20]

Robert F. Hoxie: A Sociological Interpretation

Hoxie is credited with advancing a multicausal and multifunctional explanation of unionism arising from the stress he gives to the influence of the changing institutional conditions. This milieu or culture in which the union exists reflects juridical, ethical, esthetic, religious, as well as other standards of society and is the key to his theory of unionism. As Hoxie explains:

> It must never be forgotten that the present is a product of the past, and in a sense is the past; that our ideals, standards and institutions are largely inheritances, undergoing slow modification by present forces; that as individuals and groups we are largely hereditary products — bundles of instincts, habits, propensities, tendencies, preconceptions, prejudices — the product of past struggles with environment.[21]

Because through time institutions and the standards by which society judges the union are constantly changing, the problems that labor faces also vary. There is nothing universal, everlasting, or immutable about

---

[19] As cited by Parsons, " John R. Commons' Point of View," *The Journal of Land and Public Utility Economics*, Vol. 18, No. 3 (August, 1945), p. 258.
[20] *Op. cit.*, p. 262.
[21] *Trade Unionism in the United States* (New York, D. Appleton & Co., 1920), p. 20.

existing institutions or their standards, for history reveals that to society nothing remains absolutely right or sacred: ". . . rights are merely the crystallized will of the group or groups dominant at a particular time, about which there is nothing absolute or sacred . . . everything is open to examination and is to be judged solely by its effects . . ." [22]

Just as the force of institutional change explains the cause of group organization, the union itself becomes the result: " Workers similarly situated economically and socially, closely associated and not too divergent in temperament and training, will tend to develop a common interpretation of the social situation, and a common solution of the problem of living." Because of this, labor does not cling to any single philosophy or program of action. Although labor is usually more concerned with matters of employment, wages, and hours, working conditions, and so on, the group psychology which develops reflects the temperamental characteristics of the group as well as the problem it faces. " Environment is practically the sole, and economic environment the chief, formative force, and unionism is again regarded as a series of successive adaptations of one and the same thing to the changing environmental conditions." [23] The test of such policies which the union finally adopts will not be determined by its logical consistency but rather by the question: " Does it work as a unifying and dynamic group force? "

The diverse principles of organization are revealed by the four " functional " unionism types Hoxie describes.[24] (1) *Business unionism* is trade rather than class conscious, interested in high wages, shorter hours, and better working conditions, relying mainly on collective bargaining to achieve its goals. It tends to be inclusive rather than exclusive as far as membership is concerned and exerts continuing pressure on leadership to deliver the goods. (2) *Friendly or uplift unionism* is idealistic, stressing the need to elevate the moral and intellectual life of the worker. It stresses the dignity of man, the need for cultural education, the importance of leisure, and deplores the vulgar scramble for subsistence in a market economy. It is easily encouraged to support panaceas or utopian reform programs. (3) *Revolutionary unionism* following the call to action sounded by Marx, is essentially class conscious and hopes to speed the ultimate collapse of capitalism. It operates by provoking strikes, sabotage, and agitation. (4) *Predatory unionism* subscribes to no economic philosophy

[22] *Ibid.*, p. 27.

[23] *Ibid.*, p. 65.

[24] "If . . . we dispense with narrow preconceptions and face things as they actually are, and are becoming, it is impossible to say that unionism as such is artificial or natural, revolutionary or conservative, violent or law-abiding, monopolistic or inclusive, boss-ridden or democratic, opposed to industrial progress or favorable to efficiency, the spontaneous outgrowth of legitimate needs or the product and tool of selfish and designing individuals. In short, there is unionism and unionism. But looking at matters concretely and realistically, there is no single thing that can be taken as unionism *per se*." (*Ibid.*, p. 36.)

except the insatiable thirst for " more." It is ruthless, often boss-ridden and corrupt. This is subdivided into two groups — (a) hold-up and (b) guerilla unionism.

Hoxie felt there was little to fear from left-wing unionism in this country, and he regarded the IWW as an object " more of pathetic interest than of fear." These unions tended to neutralize their effectiveness, for they could not always agree on the role of the union in its march toward revolution. Should the workers' uprising be spontaneous or planned? Should unions combine for general strikes, or concentrate on guerilla warfare? Further splits developed between those favoring direct action and those favoring political action.

Hoxie fully sensed the difficulties of union administration faced with the hostility of the employer, the courts, and the public. Union membership frequently had the illusion that management was enjoying enormous profits which could be tapped for generous wage increases if only their negotiating committee had sufficient skill in the bargaining process. This pressure within the ranks put union officials on the spot, leading frequently to frustration and resentment. " There is too, a constant drain of leaders by corruption and by politics. Here is a great weakness of unionism — it dies at the top. . . ." [25]

In a more philosophical context, Hoxie refused to condemn the union for violating basic American rights, for he reasons that " every group or class can have its rights in proportion to the power to enforce its claims." [26] Hoxie believes that most existing standards reflect group powers and that, in effect, the interests of dominant groups usually " masquerade " as the respectable standards for all society.

Hoxie was critical of existing labor codes, for he felt they were usually rooted in individualism, making freedom and the sacredness of the individual contract the touchstones of absolute justice.

> I simply know that the law as it is is not in harmony with the spirit of the age . . . it tends to be a system based on logic rather than on life. . . . as such our law is individualistic rather than socialized. It postulates the individual as the center of the universe and does not recognize fully the existence of social groups and group relationships . . . except to deny their normal existence. It knows no society apart from the aggregation of individuals and no social welfare apart from individual welfare.[27]

Hoxie seems to have had several thoughts regarding the inevitable outcome of union organization. He suggests that collective bargaining is a step toward full labor control, an entering wedge which can abolish the profits system and substitute in its place industrial democracy. The union

[25] *Op. cit.*, p. 180.   [26] *Ibid.*, p. 200.   [27] *Ibid.*, pp. 214, 216, 217.

movement, in this context, is not an instrument of peace but an instrument in the process of control.

In another context he points out that unions do not usually understand the impact of their own demands. " They *feel*. But as always in working class movements the rationale of the demand of the movement has had to be worked out for them by middle class minds." [28] But the third party — " the people " or the consumers — are not happy about the prospect of labor's dominance in society. And it is this third party which can save the day, for it advances its own concept of social justice and represents the " true social will." It is capable of acting as mediator and arbiter between warring groups:

> With the growth of knowledge of social affairs and the increase of social interaction fostered by democracy, this third party will gradually absorb control of the warring classes and ultimately absorb them. The social will will then be supreme, and social harmony will prevail.[29]

He offers a sort of " pendulum theory " to explain this principle: " The individual consciousness of the seventeenth and eighteenth centuries; the group consciousness of the nineteenth; and the social consciousness of the twentieth century " is the cycle of historical evolution of man's organization.

> In the first stage, individualism is rampant. The individual seeks only or mainly his own well-being, unconscious of a larger whole. The contest is between individual and individual. Then, gradually, groups with common interests develop. The consciousness of the individual is enlarged. He sees his interests in the interests of the group. Group standards arise. The individual is subjected to them. Then comes contest between groups. Finally social consciousness emerges. The individual identifies his good with the good of the whole; social standards and social control arise. Social well-being is consciously sought and to an extent attained. But all the while, conditions, needs, relationships, problems, terms of welfare, are changing. The standards of social welfare set up gradually cease to fit needs; the system of social control, becoming invalid, hampers progress. There is a revolt. Old standards and systems of control are broken down. Individualism is again idealized and becomes rampant. Then the process of socialization begins again.[30]

The multicausal theory of union growth provides then multiconsequences. Hoxie's analysis, revealing profound insight into the forces behind the labor movement, cautions against dogmatism. To Hoxie, the immediate task of society is to find workable " rules of the game," to discover, if possible, the specific minima and maxima for union behavior or the range within which " social right " and justice lie.

[28] *Op. cit.,* p. 279.   [29] *Ibid.,* p. 368.   [30] *Ibid.,* p. 205.

Selig Perlman: Job Consciousness Unionism

Perlman feels that the union movement was subject to three separate influences and the direction of union development would be determined by which of these were dominant. The first force was the "resistance power of capitalism" or the "will to power" of the entrepreneurial group. The outlook and philosophy of the entrepreneurs revealed their optimism and confidence in being able to deliver the goods to the American worker. But their success depended on their ability to maintain a division of labor between labor's "manual" functions and their own managerial functions. The second force was the "manualist" sentiment of the workers, reflected in their concern with the scarcity of employment opportunities and their limited control over working conditions. The third influence was that of the "intellectual," and especially that group which wanted to alter the structure of our capitalistic system. To the intellectual the labor movement was an "abstract mass in the grip of an abstract force." Most intellectuals had a tendency to overestimate labor's "will to change," and underestimate the ability or "will of resistance" of the employer group. How would labor fare under these conflicting pressures?

The resistance power of capitalism is not determined by the militant strength of the employer when in combat with the worker, but rather by the employer's own basic efficiency. The capitalist system is a highly complex economic apparatus, and the employer group realizes that the welfare of all society rests on its responsible and intelligent management of this machine. Labor senses the difficulties of this task and is not eager to assume the responsibilities of management. Furthermore, the worker tends to be pessimistic because of the scarcity of his own economic opportunities. The employer, as we noted above, is an eternal optimist. " To him the world is brimful of opportunities that are only waiting to be made his own." [31]

The employer's confidence in his ultimate success increases the effectiveness of his resistance to worker control. Even if the individual worker is not convinced of the necessity for a distinct division of labor between employer and employee, the American public is. The labor movement cannot flaunt " public sentiment " successfully:

> Briefly, if the century-long experience of American labor as an organized movement holds any great lesson at all, that lesson is that under no circumstances can labor here afford to arouse the fears of the great middle class for the safety of private property as a basic institution . . . any suspicion that labor might harbor a design to do

[31] Selig Perlman, *Theory of the Labor Movement* (New York, The Macmillan Co., 1928.) p. 239. This study was republished in 1949 — Village Station, N. Y., Augustus M. Kelley. All citations are from the original text.

away altogether with private property, instead of merely regulating its use, immediately throws the public into an alliance with the anti-union employers.[32]

Because of the social and economic conservatism of the American public, labor must accept a moderate economic platform.

Other factors in America served to weaken the development of the labor movement. These include the lack of psychological cohesiveness of the wage-earning class, the opportunities of the West, the characteristically American fluidity of economic society, the lack of class consciousness, and the gift of the ballot to the worker. Every segment of society was permitted to share the "American success story," but this abundant consciousness began to fade with the settling of the West, the loss of the frontier, and the intensification of industrial activity. Workers became acutely aware of the scarcity of job opportunities and thus "job-conscious" unionism evolved. Before we explore this thesis, let us consider the impact of the intellectual.

The labor force was, to the anti-capitalist intellectual, the raw material out of which evolution or revolution of society might be shaped. Labor was "in the center of vision" of rival ideologies. But the intellectual's efforts have not been confined to labor alone. "He has been busily indoctrinating the middle class . . . thus helping to undermine the important prop of capitalism and to some extent even the spirit of resistance of the capitalists themselves."[33] But from the very beginning, the intellectual has had a hard time of it in America.

> No intellectuals, in the true sense of the word, presided at its [the union movement's] birth. . . . American labor has always been prone to identify itself in outlook, interest and action with the lower middle class, the farmers, the small manufacturers and businessmen. . . . The harmony between the self-interest of the individual pursuing his private economic aid and the general public interest proved a real and lasting harmony in the American colonies and states. . . .[34]

The red thread running through Perlman's thesis is that labor in America has faced a "scarcity" of opportunities. The union, in effect, "undertakes to parcel it [job opportunity] out fairly, directly or indirectly, among its recognized members, permitting them to avail themselves of such opportunities . . . only on that basis of a 'common rule.'"[35] This assignment was difficult because unions faced their own problem of survival. Because of the peculiar characteristics of the American scene, "The overshadowing problem of the American labor movement has always

[32] *Ibid.*, pp. 160, 161.
[33] *Ibid.*, p. 5.
[34] *Ibid.*, pp. 154, 157–158.
[35] *Ibid.*, p. 242.

been the problem of staying organized. No other labor movement has
ever had to contend with the fragility so characteristic of American labor
organizations. . . ." [36] American unions could not always be " hard hitting," for they lacked inherent strength and support. Appreciating their
weakness, unions were persuaded to accept the more modest or limited
objectives of " wage and job control ":

> . . . They found that a labor movement became proof against dis-
> integration only when it was built around the job. . . . it grasped the
> idea, supremely correct for American conditions, that the economic
> front was the only front on which the labor army could stay
> united. . . . during depression, labor's strategy should be thoroughly
> to dig in on the same economic front, awaiting the next opportunity,
> which was certain to come, for advancing further.[37]

This target proved appropriate and plausible for the American economic philosophy. The corporation had acquired enormous power to
control the destiny of the worker. The public was willing to believe that
the union was simply a defense mechanism to assist the worker in meeting this power.[38] In this setting, the purpose of labor was not to achieve
revolution, but to advance the shop rights for its members. These were,
to the worker, " identical with ' liberty ' itself, since thanks to them, he has
no need to kowtow to foreman or boss, as the price of holding his job.
And, after all, is not this sort of liberty the only sort which reaches the
workman directly and with certainty and that can never get lost *en route*,
like the ' broader ' liberty promised by socialism? " [39]

What is the future of the union movement in Perlman's scheme of
things? It is true that the union movement is a challenge to the existing
order and may at times, through its political influence, stage a " revolt."
The resistance power of capitalism is not determined alone by its wealth
or influence, but rather by its " good healthy blood." [40] The union movement is not, however, dedicated to conflict, but rather to the simple proposition of acquiring " more." In this drive unions cannot fail to appreciate
that higher living standards are derived largely from higher production.

> And as unionism takes more and more of a hand in running the pro-
> ductive process, it comes to depend for guidance less and less on a
> dogmatic anti-capitalist philosophy, but more and more on prag-
> matic faith in industrial government through a cooperation of equally
> indispensable " functional " classes.[41]

[36] Perlman, *op. cit.*, p. 162.
[37] *Ibid.*, pp. 196, 197.
[38] *Ibid.*, p. 215.
[39] As quoted by Lyle W. Cooper, "Theories of the Labor Movement, As Set Forth
in Recent Literature," *Quarterly Journal of Economics*, Vol. XLIII (November,
1928), p. 161.
[40] As quoted by Perlman, *op. cit.*, p. 309.
[41] *Ibid.*, p. 317.

In effect, Perlman is not distressed about the future of the union movement, for with growing power will come growing responsibility.

Sidney and Beatrice Webb: A Socialist Interpretation

The Webbs not only helped found the Fabian study group, which spawned the Labor party in Britain, but provided a treatise explaining both why the organized labor movement behaved the way that it did and how it might behave to advance the cause of socialism. Basic to their socialist philosophy was the conviction that a government-controlled and a private sector of industry could exist peacefully side by side. The boundary line between these sectors varied from time to time and from socialist to socialist. They also warmly embraced the concept of democracy. Not only did they advocate peaceful parliamentary reform to achieve socialism, but believed that democracy should not be confined to politics alone. In the future society must accept industrial or economic democracy.

The Webbs felt that the basic difficulty confronting labor was that market demand might not always absorb the labor supply. Organized labor could meet this problem in one of two ways: It could attempt to organize pockets of the labor force (and exclude all others) in an attempt to secure employment and wage benefits for particular sectors of the work force. This approach was described as the " restriction of numbers " principle. It does not solve the general labor problem, but it appeals to the vested interests of sectional groups of the labor force. This philosophy characterized the early craft organization of labor in America as well as some craft unions today.

The second approach is to support the "common rule " principle. Minimum standards must be provided for the total labor force and indeed for all society. This approach finds moral sanction in the doctrine of the " living wage."

To the Webbs, much of union behavior could be explained by the separate philosophies of various unions, and in particular instances, the difficulty unionists themselves faced in trying to reconcile these dual and conflicting impulses.

Let us examine the " restriction of numbers " approach first. To the worker his job is his capital, and he feels as strong a right to this vested interest as the employer does to his property rights. " The trade by which we live is our property, bought by certain years of servitude, which gives to us a vested right. . . ." [42] Whatever the emotional basis for this sentiment, the Webbs felt certain it would have to be modified because of the contemporary " passion for progress " or the need to constantly adapt job functions in a dynamic economy. A second aspect of this approach was that unions must operate through demand and supply

[42] Sidney and Beatrice Webb, *Industrial Democracy* (London, Longmans Green & Co., 1920 edition. First published in 1897), p. 564.

rather than in spite of them. While labor's effectiveness in controlling demand may be limited, they could secure advantages by restricting the labor supply in certain sectors. The beauty of this approach was that it could hardly be criticized by those versed in economic orthodoxy. " The great captains of industry, though genuinely alarmed at the Trade Union pretensions to share in the profits of good times, found it difficult to refuse this application of their own Doctrine of Supply and Demand." [43] A drawback to this restrictive approach was that it could create distortions and contrasts in labor class welfare which labor itself could hardly sanction. For example, the unorganized with weak bargaining power might work up to 70 hours a week for a pittance, while those highly organized might work 33 hours a week for handsome wages. As the Webbs explain: " 'Supply and Demand' is throwing the bread of their children into a scramble of competition, where everything is decided by the blind and selfish struggles of their employers. . . ." [44]

Because of the shortcomings of the exclusionary aspects of labor organization, unions have drifted toward the " common rule." Every citizen of the community should be assured a living wage. Such a doctrine appeals of course to human sentiment, but it is only " tentatively " accepted by society. The vested-interest approach has its political counterpart in individualism and conservatism; the " common rule " approach stresses collectivism and socialism. The Webbs cite three techniques to extend the principle of common rule: mutual insurance, collective bargaining, and legal enactment. Under mutual assistance workers attempt to diminish their insecurity by setting up reserve funds, from which sick benefits, out-of-work benefits and so on, may be paid. Collective bargaining involves the negotiation for increased wages and fringe benefits. The strike enforces these demands when necessary. Through such bargaining rules are jointly determined for labor-management relations to apply for the duration of the contract. Through legal enactment labor invokes political pressure to secure its aims.

In describing the collective bargaining process, the Webbs point out that the range within which the actual agreement is established has an upper limit set by the mobility of capital and a lower limit set by the mobility of labor. When union demands become oppressive, management has the option of quitting or moving. Similarly, if wage conditions become oppressive for the worker, it is assumed that at some point the workers will move or quit. On balance, it appears that the worker's alternative may be more limited than that of management. Because labor is less mobile, it has less bargaining power.

Many of labor's difficulties are rooted in the nature of the competitive system. They arise, not because the employer is vicious, but rather because he is exposed to competitive pressures, which may be likened to

[43] The Webbs, *op. cit.*, p. 576.   [44] *Ibid.*, p. 587.

an inverted pyramid converging on labor at the bottom. On the top, the consumer buys where prices are lowest. Retailers are compelled to buy from wholesalers whose prices are lowest. The pressure is then on the wholesaler, who in turn transmits it to the manufacturer and ultimately to the workers. Wages must be lowered. The unions, surveying the electrical impulse of competitive pressures from the consumer to the worker, conclude that they must somehow insulate labor from these pressures. In essence, the union is designed to take the worker " out of competition."

In this context it is clear why employers are motivated to advance technology. Through innovations the employer can offer a better product at a lower price perhaps without reducing wages. But technology works a hardship on workers too, for workers have a vested interest in the " old way " of manufacturing. They are naturally reluctant to approve of any innovation which causes them to become unemployed.

One thing is clear to the Webbs: Labor cannot afford to sit back and assume that market forces will take care of its welfare. They specifically reject the notion that, just as the government can do the workers no good, the employer can do the workers no harm.[45] To drive home their point, they quote Edgeworth's famous observation: ". . . the one thing from an abstract point of view visible amidst the jumble of catallactic molecules, the jostle of competitive crowds, is that those who form themselves into compact bodies by combination *do not tend to lose but tend to gain.*" [46]

How can the union protect the worker from competition? Protection is to be found in the establishment of a national minimum of income payments that employers must meet. Such a floor will not end competition, for employers will then give increased attention to technology to secure competitive advantage. The Webbs are firmly convinced that " where labor is cheapest, progress will be slowest " and that labor and indeed, the entire community, should not be required to subsidize business inefficiency by means of low wages and by the derived costs to the community of poverty. " Every time the Common Rule is achieved . . . through Collective Bargaining or Legal Enactment, it knocks another nail in the coffin of the least intelligent and worst-equipped employers in the trade." [47]

What is the future of the labor movement? The Webbs hope for the widening of democratic relations to include economic as well as political decision-making. Needless to say, employers are not willing to concede that giving labor a greater voice in industry is either necessary or con-

[45] The Webbs quote with approval the American economist, Francis Walker: " If the workman from any cause does not pursue his interest, he loses his interest, whether he refrain from bodily fear, from poverty, from ignorance, from timidity, and dread of censure, or from the effects of bad political economy which assures him that if he does not seek his interest, his interest will seek him." (*Op. cit.*, p. 649.)

[46] *Ibid.*, p. 650

[47] *Ibid.*, pp. 728, 792.

structive: "The captains of industry, like the kings of yore, are honestly unable to understand why their personal power should be interfered with, and kings and captains alike have never found any difficulty in demonstrating that its maintenance was indispensable to society. . . ." [48] But democracy is a principle that cannot be contained within political boundaries: "The democratic idea which rules in politics has no less penetrated into industry. The notion of a governing class, exacting implicit obedience from inferiors, and imposing upon them their own terms of service, is gone, never to return. Henceforward, employers and their workmen must meet as equals. . . ." [49]

The Webbs point out, however, that the worker must not forget his responsibilities to the community. He is a citizen first, and a trade union member second, and it is in his capacity as a citizen that the worker must decide between the rival forms of social organization. The Webbs believe that labor will subscribe to the egalitarian principles of the "common rule." But any lasting, constructive social reform must be rooted in the support and understanding of the large mass of the laboring population.

> In the administration of society Knowledge and Capacity can make no real and durable progress except by acting on and through the minds of the common human material which it desired to improve. It is only by carrying along with him the "average sensual man," that even the wisest and most philanthropic reformer, however autocratic his power, can genuinely change the face of things. . . . [50]

Frank Tannenbaum: The Sociopsychological Viewpoint

Tannenbaum explains that union growth is no accident but inherent in the process of capitalism's growth. The essential feature of medieval society was that man enjoyed a sense of belonging and a sense of security through the protection of the manor and the guild. The worker's life was part of a unified whole. However elaborate the regulations controlling wages, hours, prices, quality, and tools to be used and however modest his living standard, the worker's sense of identification with society was a vital and necessary part of his life.

With the Industrial Revolution the individual was left to his own resources, and this posed a frightening challenge. If the individual was to be "self-made," his economic success measured his intrinsic worth. Capitalism held out the promise of material success, but it did not deliver it to all. The market place served as a testing ground to sort out the efficient

---

[48] *Op. cit.*, p. 841.

[49] *Ibid.*, p. 841. The latter portion of this quotation is cited by the Webbs from Stirling's book, *Trade Unionism*, published 1869, p. 55.

[50] The Webbs, *op. cit.*, pp. 844–845.

from the inefficient, the productive from the unproductive, the valuable from the valueless. Capitalism could only promise that success would be more likely to come to those who worked hard and diligently, but actual success was always a matter of conjecture. Life became a lottery.

It was true that the individual was free in the sense that he was no longer bound up by the status system of the Middle Ages. But now that the individual was thrown on his own resources, he was isolated and faced competition from all sides. He was often overwhelmed with his sense of individual helplessness. Tannenbaum points out that the commodity status given labor was implicit in classical theory. " The political theorist and the economist were deeply impressed by the breakdown of matter into atoms, and they proceeded to do the same to society. Men were interchangeable, equal, unrelated, and subject to manipulation. They ceased to be human." [51]

How does the trade union movement fit into this scene? The essence of Tannenbaum's viewpoint is contained in the following paragraph:

> Man has to belong to something real, purposeful, useful, creative; he must belong to his job and to his industry, or it must belong to him. There is no way of permanently separating the two. What gnaws at the psychological and moral roots of the contemporary world is that most urban people, workers, belong to nothing real, nothing greater than their own impersonal pecuniary interests. To escape from this profound tragedy of our industry society is the great issue of our time, for a world in which neither the owner nor the worker is morally identified with his source of income has no principle of continuity. No institution can survive in a moral vacuum. For the working the trade union has represented an unwitting attempt to escape from this dilemma.[52]

Union membership does not, in itself, satisfy all the needs of the worker, but it is an instrument of power to give the worker a sense of general security in the labor market. In effect unionism is designed to increase labor control over the market. This interest in security is akin to the " job consciousness " described by Perlman, but Tannenbaum feels that the effort for labor to gain control of the job through union activity has sweeping implications for society.

The union, it should be noted, does not operate from values different than those of management, for management too is often happy to escape from competition into collusive or monopolistic arrangements, willing to divide up markets in its search for stability and security. The union is not less inspired by the acquisitive drive than management. " The trade

[51] Frank Tannenbaum, *A Philosophy of Labor* (New York, Alfred A. Knopf, 1951), p. 53.
[52] From " The Social Function of Trade Unionism," *The Political Science Quarterly*, Vol. LXII, No. 2 (June, 1947), p. 176.

unions may not have taken over all of the implicit value judgments of the
free market economy or have been aware of all its sanctions, but they
took over those that they understood and that they could use." [53]

What then is the problem that unionism poses for society? The drive
for labor control, in Tannenbaum's mind, is not related to the skill or
sense of responsibility of labor to produce more. In other words, unions
demand " more " without fully facing up to the reality that they must be
responsible for producing the augmented income they desire. The acquisitive drives of rival bargaining groups create problems of reconciling
the sum total of all demands to the total flow of production. " Trade
unionism is often monopolistic, restrictive, arbitrary, often at war within
itself, costly, and in contradiction of all theories of a free unrestricted
market. So is the corporation." [54] All this is, to Tannenbaum, rather
ironical.

> We have here a curious outcome of the free market that began by
> describing labor as an impersonal, fluid, pecuniary, unmoral com-
> modity. The fact that the laborer was denied the morally associative
> relationship, which he needed, forced him to construct an instrumen-
> tality that in the long run has accumulated enough power to disrupt
> the very society of which it is a part.[55]

Charles Lindblom: An Alarmist Approach to Unionism

Wage pressures of American unions are not inspired by an " anticapi-
talist " ideology. Rather unions are much concerned with the survival
and prosperity of the industry in which they operate. Thus " business
unionism " conceded that free enterprise capitalism is a permanent and
desirable structure. As Arthur Ross explains: " If capitalism is supplanted
in the United States, it will not be over the wage issue." [56]

In a highly controversial book, *Unions and Capitalism*,[57] Charles Lindblom has indicated that he does not share Ross's optimism regarding the
mutual survival of both capitalism and unions. Briefly, Lindblom fears
that capitalism cannot survive union growth. What is the basis for his
pessimism?

Lindblom does not believe that the undermining of the capitalist system is the result of the conscious revolutionary philosophy of workers.
The irony of the situation is rather that the average worker and his union
are dedicated to the free enterprise system. While the acquisitive drive
of organized labor is consistent with the philosophy of free enterprise, it

---

[53] *A Philosophy of Labor, op. cit.,* p. 160.
[54] " Social Function of Trade Unionism," *op. cit.,* p. 176.
[55] *Ibid.,* p. 184.
[56] *Trade Union Wage Policy* (Berkeley, University of California Press, 1948), p. 10.
[57] New Haven, Yale University Press, 1949.

poses the major challenge to capitalism's survival: "Little wonder that it is rarely perceived that unionism in the U. S. now is as revolutionary in consequence as it is conservative in intention." [58] Wage demands produce either inflation or unemployment and to a degree that the capitalist system cannot tolerate.

In effect, unions represent blocks of bargaining power designed to increase wages. As the strength of the union is increased, it is better able to implement its wage demands. The collapse of capitalism does not loom because of the deadlock through strikes, but rather in the size of labor's demands: ". . . the wage rate is not merely adrift, having broken from its moorings. It has been torn loose by unionism and moves with union power behind it. . . ." [59] In effect the market mechanism cannot restrain such union pressure. The basic difficulty is that the union is dedicated to the conservative goal of acquiring "more, more, more, now," and management resistance is buckling under this pressure.

Theorizing about wage rates and invoking principles of wage determination represent a disguise for union opportunism. Labor is particularly careful to avoid accepting any doctrine which implies union responsibility for unemployment.

> Workers do not believe that unemployment in their skill, industry, or market proves wage rates too high. It might be thought that unemployment would provide as good a criterion for ability to pay or productivity. Actually, unions wisely refrain from using anything so dangerous. They can believe that a shortage of workers justifies a wage increase without ever agreeing that unemployment calls for wage reduction. [60]

Capitalism is threatened because, given full employment, labor has both the desire and power to demand more.

Of course, in traditional equilibrium analysis, if wages are increased above "competitive" levels, labor is priced out of the market. Unemployment increases and as the bargaining power of labor and unions is reduced, wages may return to their competitive level. But Lindblom does not view unemployment as an immediate threat to union power. "Only in the long run in relatively vigorous competition will unemployment actually materialize to the degree necessary to limit union monopoly," [61] and presumably the damage of labor's demands may be realized by that time. Furthermore, employers themselves have not formulated an intelligent policy to meet the acquisitive drives of unions. As more and more workers are unionized, the employer finds the supply of nonunion labor diminishing. He faces the alternative of paying the union rate or hiring no workers. The more widespread the wage bargain, the more likely the

[58] *Ibid.*, p. 20. [60] *Ibid.*, p. 34.
[59] *Ibid.*, p. 25. [61] *Ibid.*, p. 75.

concession from management and thus cost structures move up for the whole industry.

The escape open to the employer is price increases, but this method of absorbing the wage increase creates the new problem of inflation. If, however, prices cannot be increased, unemployment looms as an immediate and serious challenge to capitalism. Furthermore, wage pressure obstructs business investment and the ability of management to meet this problem by increasing labor productivity.

> From now on unionism will be an increasingly great hazard to profitable investment. Further, management faces a " shrinking domain " in its ability to allocate resources effectively. The continuing challenge to management prerogatives diverts management's attention away from production efficiency to the struggle of power, jeopardizing the " organizational stability " of the corporation. And labor cannot always be dissuaded by the argument that wage increases lead to price increases, with little or no improvement in real living standards resulting. For with sectional wage bargains, particular workers will stand to gain in the interval. They can still gain more as workers than they lose as consumers. . . .[62]

Lindblom does not see a solution for the problem in wage and price controls, for the government is confronted with the difficulty of finding satisfactory criteria for a correct wage policy. Here " the problem is a matter of both ignorance and conflict of interests. . . ." [63] A solution to the problem seems to be blocked at every turn. Nor does Lindblom favor the outlawing of industry-wide bargaining, for he is not convinced that this would significantly reduce union power. But the monopoly problem is not confined to unionism alone even if the competitive system is saved by protecting it from labor monopoly: ". . . hypothetically, it is possible to save competition from unionism only to have it die at the hands of corporate monopoly. Those who think this is a probability may wish to give up competition at once. . . ." [64] Unhappily, Lindblom does not offer us a solution to the difficulty that he poses.

To summarize, Lindblom charges that the union is a monopoly; secondly, the monopoly power of the union enables it to challenge management's freedom to manage, and worse, to impose wage demands which presumably outstrip the growth of production. The increase in per unit labor costs imposes an intolerable strain on management. Two alternatives may then follow. Under a tight money policy (or a stable price structure) the safety valve of the wage pressure is unemployment. Alternatively, if management is allowed to pass on the incidence of the wage increase in higher prices, ensuing inflation results.

[62] *Unions and Capitalism, op. cit.,* p. 198.
[63] *Ibid.,* p. 209.   [64] *Ibid.,* p. 233.

Is the dilemma confronting society as serious as Lindblom paints it? It is quite possible, for example, that the level of wage demands may keep pace over the long run with the growth of production and this would stabilize per unit labor costs, and not necessarily involve either inflation or unemployment. It is also possible to find a solution in alternating small doses of inflation and unemployment. Neither need destroy capitalism, for have not such fluctuations characterized our economy in the past? The analysis does suggest, however, the need for establishing principles around which to judge the impact of labor, and more specifically, establishing standards for wage increases: "The immediate obstacle," Lindblom stresses, "is the lack of satisfactory criteria by which a public authority could set wage rates. Public control will founder on this reef." [65]

[65] *Ibid.*, p. 247.

III

The Dynamics of Collective Bargaining: The Process and Its Impact

10

The Ideological Framework
and Institutional Scope of
Collective Bargaining

In Chapter 9 the discussion of seven alternative theories of unionism was designed to reveal some of the philosophical implications of unionism when cast in the setting of the free enterprise system. While the abstractions of these theories appear to explain little of the day-to-day collective bargaining process, we should not forget that the success or failure of collective bargaining ultimately depends on society's reactions to and judgments of unionism. The public view, in turn, rests on a philosophy that is largely derived from the sentiments of the moral philosopher and the social scientist. In effect, the institution of unionism cannot escape the value orientations of the society of which it is a part, any more than society can escape the value orientations of its philosophers. As we move closer to the collective bargaining process, these interrelations become even more apparent.

Our assignment in this chapter is twofold: First, we shall review the philosophies of labor and of management as they approach the collective bargaining process. Following a brief thumbnail sketch of this two-valued orientation, we shall turn to an analysis of the public viewpoint by establishing four major categories of public thought. The rationale for this "multiple-orientation" approach is the dictum that: "It is not for social scientists to adopt one value orientation and to deal with the matter under study exclusively within that frame of values."[1] The second and major portion of the chapter will review the structure of bargaining representation and the advantages and disadvantages of the broad versus narrow base for labor representation. This latter section will provide an institutional base upon which to evaluate these alternative approaches to the bargaining process, as well as a foundation for our later discussion of issues in the bargaining process.

[1] As stated by Arthur Kornshauser, Robert Dubin, Arthur M. Ross, *Industrial Conflict* (New York, McGraw-Hill Book Co., 1954), p. 5.

Management's Philosophy and the Bargaining Process

Management's philosophy is rooted in the irrefutable axiom that society must first produce that which it would consume. While the theoretical implications of this argument will be examined in Section V, we should note here the pervasive appeal of this common sense notion. The basic task of management in a free enterprise system is to allocate resources in such a way that its own profit is maximized. In a competitive society this income maximization goal would encourage the optimum allocation of all resources: All factors would be put to work where they would be most productive; all individuals would be maximizing both their incomes and their pleasures. To obstruct management in this goal or to deny it the freedom to maximize its profits would be obvious folly. Unionism, on the other hand, concentrates on the "fair" distribution of the product. Because ethical norms do not provide a unique definition of such fairness, management argues that endless quarrels over the distribution of the product would only deflect energy from the basic task of increasing the size of the product. The best solution to the dispute over "fair shares" is simply to make the pie so large that minor adjustments in the position of the carving knife are of no serious consequence.

In this sense, management pictures itself as the major architect of capitalism. It is not only the protagonist of free enterprise, but by its own actions, has actually demonstrated the efficacy of this system of economic organization. Management is for capitalism; the union is for socialism or statism. Management is for individualism; the union is for collectivism. Management is for openly facing the rigors of competition; the union is for building a cushion of security. Management is for increasing the size of the national product and is therefore production-minded; the union is for increasing its share and is therefore consumption-minded.

Because of these divergencies, management usually considers itself not only to be the "trustee of wealth," but also the trustee for our economic way of life. Certainly it does not take seriously any charge of labor exploitation. Many of labor's complaints arise simply because of its inability to appreciate that the vicissitudes of the market are often beyond the employer's control. Furthermore, the worker fails to appreciate that his individual day to day performance must ultimately determine management's ability to pay him ever-higher wages. Thus, management's interest in higher output and lower per unit labor costs, technology and automation, higher sales and larger profits stem from a more general purpose than simply advancing its own welfare. Management is the protector of the free enterprise system and, paradoxical as it may seem, through its hard-headed decisions is advancing the material welfare of the work force. These moral qualities in the self-image of management reveal its desire to secure the "approbation of legitimacy" from society. Stated in other words, the earnestness of management in advancing economic orthodoxy as the only valid economic philosophy for capitalism is symptomatic of its desire to be reassured that the public welfare is its particular trust, that human welfare and human rights inevitably evolve from management efficiency and property rights.

Union's Philosophy and the Bargaining Process

The scars of the great depression still remind labor that "automaticity" and laissez faire are twin economic concepts that can result in the twin disasters of unemployment and government indifference to unemployment. Labor today argues that the likelihood of economic success depends not alone (or even in any significant way) on its application and enthusiasm in performing its tasks for management, but rather on the wisdom and responsibility of management. If employers fail to provide workers with the security they deem indispensable, the responsibility for economic welfare is then shifted, by default, from the employer to the government. The union is a device to provide the worker with that advancement, security and self-determination which was not his when he faced the employer as an individual. The union exists because market forces cannot be trusted to provide for labor's continuing material welfare. The union exists because employers too are unable always to provide adequate welfare for the workers. In summary, the union exists because workers dare not trust the continuity or permanence of either management's charity or wisdom. The union is, in effect, a power mechanism to provide for distributive justice in an economy where neither market forces nor management can be relied upon to do the job. The union is the "watchdog" for labor's welfare.

The Public's Philosophy and the Bargaining Process

We have seen then, two poles of economic philosophy. To the individualist, unionism violates the basic tenets of classical economic doctrine; it violates the spirit of the frontier; it violates the inspiration provided by the Horatio Alger stories; and as we shall soon see, for many years it violated the law. To the unionist, the dogmatic individualism of management is as outmoded as a pre-Adam Smith pamphlet. To deny the need for labor association in the present market economy is to deny one of the plainest facts of life. The public's reaction to the incompatibility of these philosophies is often, "a plague on both your houses." This does not mean, however, that the general public is neutral, or that its values have no effect on the collective bargaining process. Because it is difficult to distill the essence of public philosophy touching controversial issues, it may be regarded as a spectrum with an infinite blending of values. Let us briefly review four bands of color on this philosophical spectrum.

The Division of Functions' Approach to Bargaining

In the range of attitudes less sympathetic to unionism is the one which stresses the importance of managerial prerogatives, the need for freedom of action in management, and the vital role that private property plays in our economy. Management's job is to manage, to assume the risks of enterprise, to allocate resources, to secure venture capital, and so on. Labor's job is to cooperate with management in implementing management's directives. The efficiency of the team rests on labor's willing and enthusiastic response. If labor fails to accept its responsibility, or worse, threatens management's freedom to manage, productive efficiency is jeopardized. If the hands reject the order of the brain, industrial paralysis or chaos will develop.

As long as unions feel they have a vested interest in any issue which affects job security and labor income, they pose a constant challenge to managerial control. The compartmentalization of functions can only be sustained when labor is convinced that management is fulfilling labor's expectations. Since management performance can never completely satisfy labor's soaring expectations, unions demand the right to bargain over an ever-widening range of issues. The union is thus seen, not only a threat to managerial prerogatives, but indirectly a threat to the institution of private property itself.

Those holding such fears often interpret every concession to labor as a threat to prevailing institutions. As early as 1818, a justice of the peace in Sidmouth, England wrote: " I am convinced from what I see and hear in every direction that the lower classes are radically corrupted. An advance of wages or prices for work done, as I have before intimated, is a mere stalking horse. . . . Their aim is revolution." [2] Often the courts constituted themselves the ordained agents for nipping in the bud the dangerous radicalism of the working man. As one early British magistrate phrased it, if the distressed workers could only be separated from the influences of demagogues and disappointed reformers, they would be found " extremely well behaved, and always thankful for a very moderate pittance of parochial relief." [3]

The press and the public too have often needled management about

[2] Quoted by Harold J. Laski, *Trade Unions in the New Society* (New York, Viking Press, 1949), pp. 115–116.

[3] Arthur Aspinwall (ed.), *The Early English Trade Unions* (London, Batchworth, 1949), p. 273. Quotation dated August 17, 1818, and published in Laski's study, *op. cit.*, p. 116.

the hazards of accepting unionism. The *New York Journal of Commerce,* in the mid-nineteenth century carried this item:

> Who but a miserable, craven-hearted man, would permit himself to be subjected to such rules, extending even to the number of appren- tices he may employ, and the manner in which they shall be bound to him, to the kind of work which shall be performed in his own office at particular hours of the day, and to the sex of the persons employed, however separated into different apartments or buildings? [4]

The encroachment by unions on management prerogatives is likely to be more feared where labor-management relations are strained in a sort of " armed truce " than where relations are harmonious and cooperative.[5] Where companies recognize the union as a permanent and constructive institution, unions are less concerned about union versus management " rights." In this situation such controversies as do arise, both in negotiat- ing the contract and processing grievances, reflect day-to-day problems rather than an ideological conflict over rights. The National Planning Association study on the causes of industrial peace revealed that success- ful labor-management relations are characterized by a management " be- ing willing to discuss anything, by being willing to state its position frankly, by putting its cards on the table, while insisting upon its responsi- bility to the owners for the conduct of the business. . . . Most of the studies point out that the question of management prerogatives has not been an important issue." [6]

On our scale of ideologies, however, considerable support is given to the fear that the union in its capacity as a " right changing " institution, is upsetting the traditional balance of power within our society, and that this upheaval will have profound implications on our economy.

---

[4] From Stevens, *New York Typographical Union No. 6,* pp. 240–241, and quoted by Neil Chamberlain, *Collective Bargaining* (New York, McGraw-Hill Book Co., 1951), p. 24.

[5] Frederick H. Harbison and John R. Coleman provide us with some quotations re- flecting this militancy. One company official cautions: " Management must neither surrender nor share its responsibility to manage. Management initiates policy. In very limited areas, the union may properly question management actions. But we must never let unions get into the position of sharing in making decisions. The union is not part of management; it is really a barnacle on the hull of the company. Manage- ment's job is to minimize the union's obstruction of efficient production. The com- pany should negotiate with unions on as few issues as possible. Unions need to be put and kept in their place." Another company official contributes his views: " You can get nothing from a union. It constantly asks for more, more and still more — but it never gives anything in return. The best thing for an employer to do is just to minimize his collective bargaining losses and hold on for the next onslaught." *Goals and Strategy in Collective Bargaining* (New York, Harper & Bros., 1951), pp. 22, 24.

[6] As described by Douglas McGregor, " The Influence of Attitudes and Policies," Chapter 4 in the *Causes of Industrial Peace Under Collective Bargaining,* edited by Clinton S. Golden and Virginia D. Parker (New York, Harper & Bros., 1955), p. 35.

The " Maintain Competition " Approach to Bargaining

Allied to the " division of functions " approach discussed above, but somewhat more sophisticated in its argument, is the claim that we must, at all costs, maintain competition within our society. It is contended that the union movement in effect represents a deviation from competitive norms which could ultimately prove disastrous to the free enterprise system. Like the cleric who finds the solutions to all temporal problems in a " return to religion," so do supporters of this viewpoint find the solution to most of our economic problems in a return to competition. The most articulate spokesman for this viewpoint was Henry Simons who reasoned that:

> A community which fails to preserve the discipline of competition exposes itself to the discipline of absolute authority. . . . An obvious danger in collectivism is that the vast powers of government would be abused in favoritism to particular producer groups, organized to demand favors as the price of maintaining peace, and available to support established authorities against political opposition. Adherence to competitive, productivity norms is, now or under socialism, a means for avoiding arbitrariness and, to my mind, the only feasible means.[7]

The multiple problems that arise from group organization and the negotiation of " noncompetitive " wage rates were made explicit by the courts with the application of the conspiracy doctrine against labor in the early nineteenth century. The content of the argument has not changed much since that time. High wages could injure the public by forcing it to pay higher prices; it could injure the employer by reducing his profits and motive for production; it would frustrate the employer's efforts to expand investments; it would create unemployment; and it would depress wages in the nonorganized sectors of the work force as unemployed workers searched for jobs.[8]

We cannot treat the anti-union monopoly sentiment as an antiquated museum piece. Current newspaper editorials still demand that the public receive some protection against abusive union monopoly power. Typical

[7] Henry C. Simons, " Some Reflections on Syndicalism," *Journal of Political Economy* (March, 1944), pp. 1, 25.

[8] The application of the conspiracy doctrine against the group-organization of labor alone was indeed bewildering to labor. One of their labor journals explained: " Shall all others, except only the industrious mechanics, be allowed to meet and plot; merchants to determine their prices current, or settle the markets, politicians to electioneer, sportsmen for horse-racing, and games, ladies and gentlemen for balls, parties and banquets; and yet these poor men be indicted for combining against starvation? " From Commons and Associates, *History of Labor in the United States* (New York, The Macmillan Co., 1921), p. 141.

of such sentiment is that of Donald R. Richberg, (co-author of the Railway Labor Act in 1926) voiced in March, 1947:

> . . . despite these weaknesses in labor unions, which have newly come into their monopolistic powers, they have made it evident in the past year (in the one year of 1946 it has been made very clearly evident) that we have been nourishing the growth of economic monsters that are capable of vast destruction. Even before they have reached maturity they have shown that they are able and willing to rule or ruin our commerce and are able and willing to paralyze our industry to achieve their selfish aims. We have ample evidence that these economic monstrosities can, by industrial paralysis, render the government impotent to protect the American people at home or to serve them faithfully in international relations. . . . Such a private power cannot be successfully regulated. It cannot be tolerated. It must be destroyed.[9]

The charge of " monopoly " invokes fears of money-hungry union officials and equally predatory rank and file exerting their coercive power to exploit both management and the public. The monopoly charge is also raised on the controversial " right to work " issue where it is often charged that unions are exerting monopoly power to coerce the helpless worker into the union. The problem of monopoly has both an industry as well as union side to it, and too few persons apply their anti-monopoly convictions with equal vigor against both labor monopoly and management monopoly. We dare not, of course, abandon the vital role of competition within our society but we must regard with some reservation the claim that all problems can be solved by " returning to competition," especially in the absence of any program which demonstrates just how this is to be accomplished.

The " Equality of Power " Approach to Bargaining

To those sensitive to the reality of coercive power in the labor market, no argument is more appealing than the need to maintain a balance of power between contesting groups in the labor market. It was this reasoning which provided the necessary sanction for the favorable labor legislation developed in the 1930's.

[9] " Industrial Disputes and the Public Interest " (Berkeley, Institute of Industrial Relations, University of California, March, 1947), p. 57. Philip Murray replied to the accusation of union monopoly in the following manner: " Labor still has a monopoly on all the ramshackle houses in the slums of our great cities. . . . Labor has a monopoly on the wards of too many unkempt charity hospitals. . . . a monopoly or near monopoly on inadequate medical treatment, on fear of unemployment, and on a million ' tin Lizzies ' that will be paid for in three years if not attached because a few installments cannot be met." *CIO News* (January 2, 1950), p. 4, and quoted in Domenico Gagliardo, *Introduction to Collective Bargaining* (New York, Harper & Bros., 1953), p. 525.

That labor had unequal power is an observation as old as it is valid. In 1776 Adam Smith stated:

> We rarely hear . . . of the combination of masters, though frequently of those of workmen. But whoever imagines, upon this account, that masters rarely combine, is ignorant of the world as of the subject. Masters are always and everywhere in a sort of tacit, but constant and uniform combination, not to raise the wages of labour. . . . To violate this combination is everywhere a most unpopular action, and a sort of reproach to a master among his neighbors and equals. . . . Masters too sometimes enter into particular combinations to sink the wages of labour . . .

The champions of labor organization have usually used this imbalance as the main justification for their cause: As Horace Greeley explained in 1853:

> We believe that unregulated, unrestricted competition — the free trade principle of " every man for himself " and " buy where you can buy the cheapest " — tends everywhere and necessarily to the depression of wages and the concentration of wealth. Capital can wait — Labor cannot but must earn or famish. Without organization, concert and mutual support, among those who live by selling their labor, its price will get lower and lower as naturally as water runs down hill.[10]

Horace Greeley did not believe that either management or labor should unilaterally have power to designate wage levels and working conditions, but a bargain struck between equals " will usually be just about right."

Most labor students have, in recent times, been quick to stress the economic justification for labor organization. Labor economist Lloyd Reynolds declares simply: " In general, the alternative to collective bargaining is no bargaining." [11] Harold Laski points out that labor individualism can in no way be reconciled with corporate collectivism: " The notion that a worker should be free to dispose as he will of his labor belongs to an era of individualism which has now no longer any historical meaning, and has had none since the rise of the factory system." [12] William Leiserson explains that prior to the protective labor legislation of the Wagner Act " all that the employees had was a right to try to organize if they could get away with it; and whether they could or not depended on the relative economic strength of the employers' and employees' organizations." [13] The role of power in this bargaining process is pointedly stated by Felix Morley:

[10] Horace Greeley's contributions are found in the *New York Daily Tribune* (April 13, 1853), and quoted by Chamberlain, *op. cit.*, pp. 27–28. For further discussion of this point see Chapter 18.

[11] *Labor Economics and Labor Relations* (New York, Prentice-Hall, 1949), p. 169.

[12] *Op. cit.*, pp. 150–151.

[13] *Right and Wrong in Labor Relations* (Berkeley, University of California, 1938), pp. 24–27.

The employee simply does not hold the cards. The hazards of life make it necessary for every business to be organized in such a way that no individual is indispensable. Because he is not indispensable, . . . the individual employee, no matter what his competence, is unable to negotiate effectively on working conditions as an individual. The threat of discharge has him bound. " Take it or leave it " is the ace of trumps in management's hands.[14]

In the words of the union member, " Employers understand only one language — the language of the strike." [15]

In a definitional sense, being for " equality " of power is more nebulous a goal than being for " competition." Should equality of power be measured by the equality of damage that one party can inflict on the other? Is equality determined by the price impact of a wage adjustment? More specifically, do we have equality of bargaining power between labor and management today? The varying response to these questions reflect, not the rejection of the equality of power ideal, but the absence of agreement as to what equality actually is.

The " Industrial Constitution " Approach to Bargaining

The daily policy decisions of the corporation do not reflect the majority decisions of its employees, nor for that matter the majority sentiment of its shareholders. If industry is autocratic by tradition, can it be democratized by the collective bargaining process? In this context we shall not view industrial democracy in the extreme sense of syndicalism or worker control, but in terms of the formal representation given to labor through the bargaining process.

To many labor students the contract negotiated by the union is labor's constitution, making explicit industrial law and defining the rights and duties of both labor and management. It provides formal sanction to labor's rights. Should disagreements arise, recourse may be had to grievance machinery and usually, in the final analysis, to arbitration. On the job, the contract becomes the worker's " Bill of Rights." [16] This approach

[14] " The Meaning of Economic Liberalism," *Wage Determination and the Economics of Liberalism* (Washington, Chamber of Commerce of the United States, January 11, 1947), p. 9.

[15] For analysis of the workers' viewpoint, see Harbison and Coleman, *op. cit.*, p. 28.

[16] ". . . collective bargaining itself is justified not only by protecting the rights of labor but also by extending that diffusion of power which strengthens democracy. Collective bargaining has been, and remains, a brake against the exercise of absolute authority to hire and fire and otherwise determine conditions of employment. . . . Indeed, collective bargaining can introduce into industrial management a number of safeguards that may be likened to our constitutional system of checks and balances. If political government requires constitutional protection against the arbitrary use of power, so too, does industrial government." S. T. Williamson and Herbert Harris, *Trends in Collective Bargaining* (New York, Twentieth Century Fund, 1945), p. 241. Edward T. Cheyfitz writes in a similar vein: "Collective bargaining is not a mere signing of an agreement granting seniority, vacations and wage increases. It is not a

appeals to most students of labor relations, for the collective bargaining process is viewed as a contest to establish "favorable rules" for the administration and utilization of the labor force during the contract year. By establishing such rules the likelihood of managerial abuse, favoritism, nepotism, or unfavorable discrimination is greatly narrowed. We must not forget, however, that management usually maintains control over its vital "hiring and firing" functions which, in the last analysis, provide management with the authority and discretion necessary to maintain and increase plant efficiency. While the contract may be viewed as an extension of democracy, it is more in the nature of a treaty between the ruler and his subjects, outlining the scope of permissible management and union behavior, than a declaration providing universal suffrage. By political analogy, the worker is still more a "subject" than "citizen" of the plant. The true locus of labor's power is not found in its "political freedom" in industry but in its bargaining power. Stated in other terms, the worker is not granted any political "right" to a favorable contract, but such privileges as are secured by the contract reflect the power and skill of his representatives at the bargaining table.

Our discussion thus far has indicated that the public does not view the collective bargaining process with a single frame of reference. Its sympathies are often divided. Because of the importance of public support, both labor and management attempt to identify their sectional interests with the general welfare. They pose as champions of the public. While Charles Wilson spoke the essence of economic orthodoxy when he explained that he believed that what would be good for General Motors would necessarily be good for America, the public uproar over this statement led the CIO to offer their allegedly contrasting philosophy: "What is good for America is good for the CIO." The struggle to win public approval and support continues, and in a very real sense it represents the "balance wheel" in the power struggle between labor and management.

One of the most troublesome aspects of the collective bargaining process is that it involves negotiations of power blocs or groups. Before we turn to the variety of issues arising between contending groups, let us briefly recapitulate the degrees of consolidation of the bargaining process and the advantages for both labor and management that this provides.

The Extent of Consolidation of the Bargaining Process

The complex structure of our economy is reflected in the diversity of the bargaining structure. The simplest form of bargaining exists when a

mere sitting around the table discussing grievances. Basically, it is the democratic joint formulation of 'company policy' on *all* matters that directly affect the worker in the plant. Collective bargaining is self-government in operation. It is the projection of policy by management with labor given a right to be heard. It is the establishment of factory law based upon common consent." *Constructive Collective Bargaining* (New York, McGraw-Hill Book Co., 1947), p. 35.

single employer faces a single union to negotiate a single contract. Looking only at the employer side of the coin, Table 10 suggests some of the alternative forms of representation, considering both alternative employer and alternative areas of representation:

TABLE 10   Alternative Areas of Employer Representation in Collective Bargaining

1. Single shop: single employer
2. Single department: single employer
3. Single plant: single employer

4(a) Multiple plants within city: single employer	(b) Multiple plants within city: multiple employers
5(a) Multiple plants within region: single employer	(b) Multiple plants within region: multiple employers
6(a) Multiple plants: corporation and nation-wide: single employer	(b) Multiple plants nation-wide: multiple employers

The employer may engage in collective bargaining on a single-plant basis or, if he owns more than one plant, on a multiple-plant basis. Similarly, an employer association may represent city-wide, regional, or industry-wide units. Obviously the bargaining process becomes increasingly consolidated the greater the size of the single employer or employer association and the wider the representation of the union.

The number of persons covered by agreements which are national in scope is not large. The 1947 Bureau of Labor Statistics study estimated that somewhat more than 4 million workers were covered by collective agreements negotiated with groups of employers. Of the seven industries listed in Table 11 as having national agreements, only coal and glass employ a substantial number of workers.[17] In Frank Pierson's study, railroads are added to the list of industry-wide bargaining, extending the importance of this form of bargaining.[18] But since 1950, the pressed and blown glassware industry — the classic case of national multiemployer bargaining and a model for responsible and peaceful labor management relations almost since its inception in 1888 — began to crumble. By 1952 the employer association in this industry was a bargaining agent for only a small group of machine plants employing about one fourth of the union's membership.[19]

[17] "Collective Bargaining with Associations and Groups of Employers," *Monthly Labor Review*, Vol. 64 (1947), p. 398.

[18] "Prospects for Industry-Wide Bargaining," *Industrial and Labor Relations Review*, Vol. 3, No. 3 (April, 1950), p. 349. Pierson explains that of the total number of employees covered by industry-wide agreements, approximately 90 percent are in but two industries — coal and railroads (p. 353.)

[19] For an interesting analysis of the rise and fall of multiemployer bargaining in this industry, see Gerald G. Somers, "Pressures on an Employers' Association in Collective Bargaining," *Industrial and Labor Relations Review*, Vol. 6, No. 4 (July, 1955), pp. 557–569.

TABLE 11   Area of Bargaining with Associations or Groups of
Employers, by Industry, 1947

Industry-wide or National Bargaining	Regional Bargaining	Local Area Bargaining (Within a City, County, or Metropolitan Area)
Coal mining	Canning and preserving foods [a]	Baking
Elevator installation and repair	Dyeing and finishing [a] textiles	Beverages, nonalcoholic
Glass and glassware	Fishing	Book and job printing and publishing
Installation of automatic sprinklers	Hosiery	Building service and maintenance
Pottery and related products	Leather (tanned, curried, and finished) [a]	Clothing, men's [b]
Stoves	Longshoring [a]	Clothing, women's [b]
Wallpaper	Lumber [a]	Confectionery products
	Maritime	Construction
	Metal mining	Cotton textiles
	Nonferrous metals and products except jewelry and silverware [a]	Dairy products
	Paper and pulp	Furniture [b]
	Shoes, cut stock and findings [a]	Hotel and restaurant
		Jewelry and silverware
		Knit goods
		Laundry and cleaning and dyeing
		Leather products, other
		Malt liquors
		Meat packing
		Newspaper printing and publishing
		Paper products, except wallpaper
		Silk and rayon textiles
		Steel products, except stoves [b]
		Tobacco
		Trade [b]
		Trucking and warehousing [b]

[a] There also is some bargaining on a city, country, and/or metropolitan area basis.
[b] There also is some bargaining on a regional and/or industry-wide basis.

Source: Adapted from *Collective Bargaining with Associations and Group Employers,*
Bulletin No. 897 (Washington, Bureau of Labor Statistics, 1947), p. 399.

Table 12 indicates the breakdown of bargaining between single-employer and multiemployer units, both for the number of contracts negotiated and the number of workers covered. Contract-wise, we see that the single-employer contract outnumbers the multiemployer contract 4 to 1, but in terms of worker coverage, the single-employer contract out-numbers the multiemployer contract only 2 to 1. As one might expect, most multiemployer contracts cover a larger number of employees than do most single-employer contracts. While these figures are derived from a sample study of over 3,000 contracts for " all industries," the BLS breakdown of the data between the manufacturing and nonmanufacturing sector reveals an interesting contrast. Only 11 percent of all contracts in

TABLE 12   The Structure of Bargaining Units

Units (based on sample of all industry)	Percentage Distribution by No. of Contracts		Percentage Distribution by Workers Covered	
Single-employer bargaining units, total	80		67	
Single plant		68		28
Multiplant		12		39
Multiemployer units, total	20		33	
National				4
Regional				6
Local				23
Total	100		100	

The figures for the distribution of workers covered by multiemployer units (the lower right of our table) are not identical with those developed by Frank C. Pierson. Pierson's minimum estimate of workers covered in each of these forms of multiemployer bargaining puts slightly less weight on city or local area bargaining. Taking the multiemployer classification as 100 percent, he finds 26 percent of workers are covered in industry-wide agreements, 23 percent by region-wide agreements, and 51 percent by city or local agreements. See his break-down of data in "The Prospects for Industry Wide Bargaining," *op. cit.*, pp. 350–353.

Source: U.S. Bureau of Labor Statistics, *Monthly Labor Review*, Vol. 71, No. 6 (December, 1950), p. 697, and also reproduced in Daugherty and Parrish, *The Labor Problems of American Society* (Boston, Houghton Mifflin Co., 1952), pp. 512, 514.

manufacturing represented multiemployer negotiations, while this same ratio was 42 percent for the nonmanufacturing sector. In terms of work-ers covered, only 20 percent of the workers in manufacturing were cov-ered by multiemployer negotiations, while 62 percent of workers in nonmanufacturing were covered by multiemployer negotiations. This indicates that multiemployer agreements were much more common in the mining, transportation, retail and wholesale trade, services, and con-struction trades, than in manufacturing.

The form of bargaining seems to follow regional characteristics. In New England and the South fewer than 10 percent of the bargaining units were of the multiemployer form, whereas on the Pacific coast and in the Mountain States, approximately 48 per cent of the agreements were of this form. This suggests that growing industries are more susceptible to the standardization of bargaining procedures. It is not surprising that the number of multiemployer bargains should be much higher for those unions which were originally AF of L members than those which were CIO unions. When the union embraces the entire work force of the firm, there are less compelling reasons for widening the area of representation to other employers. Even though approximately a third of the employees covered by collective agreement in this BLS study secured their agreement's through multiemployer negotiations, we see in Table 12 that these agreements are not typically national in scope. The bulk of bargaining with more than one employer is on a regional, city, county, and metropolitan area basis. Studies further reveal that the union seems to favor the multiemployer form of bargaining somewhat more than does management.[20]

A bargaining technique more common than multiemployer negotiations is where the union and a single employer negotiate a key contract which serves as a model for the rest of the industry. Such pattern following may operate to cover a particular city, a particular region, or even be national in scope. The pattern may be confined to a single craft, to a single industry, or cut across industry lines. While these are conceptually concise perimeters, in reality the scope of pattern following is difficult to contain, especially when a union has flexible jurisdictional limits and negotiates with a large number of employers in diverse trades. The pressure for pattern following becomes immediately apparent when it is appreciated that prevailing standards are probably the most popular benchmark for equity in contract adjustments. Furthermore, pattern following provides the union with the tactical advantage of presenting uniform demands on employers without the employers themselves being formally organized to present a united front against the union. Thus, a single employer may be selected by the union to establish the " key " bargain because of his record of reasonableness in negotiations, because of his high revenues and profits (and hence ability to pay), or because of his known anxiety to avoid a work stoppage. We have, in effect, wage leadership and wage following in the same way that some firms pursue the practice of price leadership and price following. The impulse to conform to the pattern is usually overwhelming.

Following the pattern, though, is no proof of any coercive demand on the part of the international that this be done. As one small employer explained, the fact that his plant was located in an area of pattern following forced him to do likewise. " How will it be possible for a small fabricator to employ men at any substantial amount less than his next

[20] Of a total number of 87 firms surveyed by W. S. Woytinsky and his associates, it was found that 45 or almost one-half preferred bargaining by a single company, 24 preferred bargaining through local employers' associations or committees, 9 preferred in industry-wide bargaining, and 7 said it would depend on circumstances. Two had no preferences. See W. S. Woytinsky and Associates: *Labor and Management Look at Collective Bargaining* (New York, Twentieth Century Fund, 1949), p. 13.

door neighbors are paying? " [21] Of course, the marginal employer would most often be vulnerable to any uniform upward cost adjustment. Leo Wolman explains that industry-wide and pattern bargaining

> . . . has been going on for only a few years, but it has already had far-reaching effects on the wage structure of the country. In the steel and automobile industries long-standing wage differentials in favor of plants situated in small towns and rural communities and of small and new businesses have been eliminated. . . . The process of attrition is inexorable and the lag between regions and types of business is steadily narrowing. . . ." [22]

Bills have been introduced into Congress which would have limited bargaining units in a geographical sense to a 50-mile radius, or which would make it an unfair labor practice for a parent union to force an affiliated local to settle for contract terms prescribed by the parent body. Because of this public concern, let us briefly review the major advantages and complications that the consolidation of the bargaining process provides for both labor and management. Several of the advantages for the union will be similar to the disadvantages for the employer, and we must be ever mindful that both labor and management may share jointly in the advantages of consolidated bargaining at the expense or disadvantage of the public.

Expanding the Area of Bargaining: The Union Viewpoint

The resistance of a particular employer to a wage demand will depend on his calculation of what effect a wage increase will have on his competitive position in the industry. If he knows that all his competitors are to be subjected to a similar cost increment, he is less likely to fear the deterioration of his competitive position and will, therefore, be more willing to grant the union demand. A pattern of wage adjustments is more likely to lead to a pattern of price and adjustments, and through such general wage and price adjustments, the union is more likely to be successful in advancing its gains.[23] The opportunity for shifting the incidence

[21] As noted by George Seltzer, "Pattern Bargaining and the United Steel Workers," *Journal of Political Economy*, Vol. LIX, No. 4 (August, 1951), p. 330.

[22] As quoted by Seltzer, *op. cit.*, p. 319.

[23] This may be particularly true in an oligopolistic industry characterized with the kink in particular employer product demand curves. The demand curve is thought to be elastic above existing price because of the fear that, if a single employer raises his price, none of his competitors will follow him up in such an adjustment. The employer will resist wage increases, for he cannot shift any of the incidence of the wage increase on to the public. If a pattern or uniform wage adjustment faces all employers, each is likely to anticipate that the other will raise price. The demand curve for the product is thus seen to be less elastic, and the opportunity for raising the price, to shift at least part of the wage burden to the public, becomes a reality.

of a wage increase to the public will depend on the elasticity of the product demand, and in most instances, the industry must weigh carefully the effect on total sales that price increases produce.

A second advantage of uniform negotiations and/or pattern following is tactical: Through multiemployer and industry-wide bargaining the union may be in a position to completely stop production. The potential damaging effect on the employers and on the public at large is likely to engender immediate and strong reaction to strike. There is less likelihood for development of a painfully long strike or that kind of endurance test that the union is less likely to win. If an industry-wide tie-up brings the government into the dispute, the union may secure a more advantageous settlement than might otherwise be secured. When the issue is no longer economic but political, the public authority is likely to be sensitive to the political repercussions of any settlement it endorses or recommends.

Thirdly, such bargaining provides several administrative advantages. Besides being represented by expert and seasoned negotiators, research staffs can gather data; intelligent analyses can be made of union costs, industry profits and sales, and so on. The technician is likely to play a greater role in the bargaining process and may suggest decisions which are economically sound. Furthermore, the decisions reached by the bargaining agents may have such widespread effects that the negotiators are likely to sense a new status and appreciate the need for industrial statesmanship.

A fourth advantage is the economy that such procedures involve. The centralized bargaining sessions represent a considerable economy of man-hours in the bargaining process. The uniform agreement may be easier to enforce. Certain key issues may be resolved through arbitration, and the precedents set by such awards may serve as a common law for the entire industry and reduce the possibility of future misunderstanding.

A fifth advantage is political. Each union leader in the atomized bargaining situation is likely to feel the intense pressure to keep up and improve upon the pattern being negotiated by competing unions. With an industry-wide contract, such political pressures are much reduced; the danger of comparisons, (and their political repercussions) are minimized. In this climate the union may be in a better position to negotiate a contract with an eye to the economic needs of the industry and the public, rather than the political consequences of not doing as well — or better — than competing unions. A further valuable role of the national in securing multiemployer agreements is that the national can discipline local unions for wildcat walkouts or other behavior in violation of the contract. The national officers are more completely aware of the importance of adhering to the letter of the law and the provisions of the contract. Pressure from the head office may represent a useful face-saving device for local officers who become embroiled in a dispute from which they might not otherwise be able to retreat gracefully. The national, in this context, may police the contract. In the bargaining sessions themselves, the union representatives often have a wider perspective than local representatives, and are therefore able to reach settlements which could not be so readily secured by the " steamed-up " local representatives.

A sixth advantage is psychological. The work force is likely to interpret a uniform or standard wage rate for key job classifications throughout the industry as a " square deal." Discrepancies that develop within the wage structure, based on sectional bargaining, can be a divisive factor within the work force and union itself. Animosities, jealousies, and conflict may develop, having an adverse effect both on the political stability of the union and the morale and productivity of the workers.

A seventh advantage of such bargaining is its egalitarian appeal. Such bargaining is likely to reduce the dangers of sweatshop conditions for isolated portions of the work force in industry. The workers in a weak bargaining position, because of determined employer resistance, now secure greater support in their united demands against all employers.[24] The sum total of bargaining power for labor resulting from such united effort probably increases in greater proportion than is indicated by the number of workers represented in the bargaining unit.

Finally, multiemployer bargaining provides labor with the equalizing influence in facing management. As Franklin D. Roosevelt, Jr., declared:

> Modern industrial unionism has not created a labor monopoly power; it has only succeeded, in part, in reducing the absolute monopoly which the employers had enjoyed in these industries for so many years. . . . Compare the $11 million total assets of the United Steel Workers of America, held in behalf of over a million union members, with the $1,541 million assets of the Bethlehem Steel Corporation and $3,140 million assets of the United States Steel Corporation. Contrast the $14 million total assets of the United Automobile Workers of America with the $3,671 million assets of the General Motors Corporation. Does the $175 billion in total current assets owned by American corporations — including $30 billion in cash and $20 billion in United States Government bonds alone — give the impression that it is the workers who have been extracting an extortionate share of the national income? [25]

[24] " The industry-wide and regional bargaining in which the clothing industry engages has not stifled competition; this industry is one of the most sharply competitive in the United States. It does strive, however, to eliminate the sweatshop and the outmoded practice whereby one employer seeks to compete against the other by depressing the wages and working standards of helpless working men and women." Remarks by Franklin D. Roosevelt, Jr., in the House of Representatives, February 19, 1953.

[25] Remarks before the Committee on Education and Labor with reference to H.R. 2545, and reproduced in the transcript of the proceedings of the 83rd Congress, first session, House of Representatives, February 19, 1953.

By such reasoning, to pulverize the union movement into smaller bargaining units might seriously undermine labor's bargaining power and the collective bargaining process itself.

But multiemployer and industry-wide bargaining poses some problems for the union too. First, the centralization of the bargaining process is likely to remove the vitality of participation in policy formation and bargaining at the local level. The fewness of representatives relative to the size of the labor force reduces the grass-roots nature of the bargaining session. This, in turn, raises the possibility that local unions may suspect that they are being " sold down the river " by their bargaining representatives. Furthermore, a national agreement may neglect the problems of the single marginal firm, some of which may consider quitting operations because of the wage pressure. The loss of employment is not likely to be greeted with enthusiasm by the workers involved, however well-meaning the intentions of union representatives. The problem may be minimized by adjusting a national agreement to fit the needs of particular employers. But the danger in permitting such flexibility is, that should these modifications to the master agreement become numerous, the stabilization of interemployer wage relationships may be undermined. A further difficulty for the union may be that, while it may have gained in the consolidation of its bargaining efforts, so will management establish its counterpart bargaining agency. Power is increased for both parties. As one union leader explained the bargaining process: " We think this is guerilla war. Advance where you can, retreat where you must — but don't allow them to get you lined up on one long front. We want to keep employers apart." The employer association has tremendous resources for the hiring of economic and legal experts to represent them at the bargaining table; they may also accumulate considerable sums for research and public relations to put across to the public the justification for industry's resistance to union demands.[26]

Expanding the Area of Bargaining: The Employer Viewpoint

Consolidated bargaining may assist the employer who would otherwise have low resistance to union pressure. It should be remembered, however, that the employer with the least bargaining power is not necessarily the marginal producer but is just as likely to be the financially successful

[26] Everett M. Kassalow points out: " In many instances, rhetoric has given way to, or at least, is supplemented by the written brief bristling with facts and figures. The union or management seeks to enforce its position by economic logic, which may sway the public and/or government officials. As a consequence, the table-pounder's place is, to some extent, usurped by the ' professional ' — the research expert and the lawyer." " New Patterns of Collective Bargaining " from *Insights into Labor Issues*, edited by Lester and Shister (New York, The Macmillan Company, 1948), p. 127.

operator. Paradoxical as it may seem, the financially weak employer has new-found power in the very fact that he is weak, for he has less " territory " to surrender to the union. He poses the genuine threat to abandon his operations should union demands add to his difficulties. The strong employer may seek refuge behind this weak employer by pointing out to the union the dangers of bankrupting marginal producers. One manager explains the advantages of group bargaining in the following terms:

> " If we ever tried to negotiate individually it would be murder. And we'd ruin ourselves and everyone else in the industry. Thank God we have an association." Another explained: " Industry-wide bargaining is the best for our industry. And I believe it's best and fairest for most industries, provided all groups are properly represented. It's the only way the little fellow can have an equal chance with the big fellow. The big manufacturer could afford to give concessions that would cut the little man's throat." [27]

The procedure, as we noted for the unions, has the advantage of administrative simplicity; it encourages and generally makes financially possible the hiring of experts, such as lawyers, statisticians, and economists. It is likely to lead to more responsible decisions for the industry as a whole. The breakdown of discussions may be less likely because both parties appreciate the serious effects the industry-wide stoppage may have, not only to each party, but in terms of injury (and subsequent hostility) of the public. If the recourse to the use of force is rather frightening (as, for example, the prospects for hydrogen war in international relations), the search for peaceful solutions is greatly increased. It also permits a uniform interpretation of the standard contract together with greater ease of enforcement. The expansion of the bargaining unit may even permit the hiring of a permanent umpire to resolve disputes for the industry.

This method does pose some serious hazards for participating companies too. As we noted above, a single employer operating on a very narrow profit margin may find that the agreement negotiated by his association is disastrous.[28] Plant technology, profit margins, sales, expecta-

---

[27] Quoted in W. S. Woytinsky and Associates, *Employment and Wages in the United States* (New York, Twentieth Century Fund, 1953), p. 248.

[28] The National Labor Relations Board has ruled that members of such associations are not exempt from the obligations to bargain in good faith with the union representatives; resigning from the employer association which negotiated the contract does not invalidate the contract nor reduce the employer's obligation to adhere to that contract. In determining the scope of the bargaining unit, the NLRB has reasoned that the employer's participation in joint negotiations is the determining factor (see the Plumbing Contractors Association of Baltimore, Inc., 93 NLRB 1081), and it is not necessary that he agree in advance to be bound by any contract which may be jointly negotiated (Whiz Fish Products Co., 94 NLRB 198). In another case the Board ruled that the employer's expressed intention to pursue an individual course of bargaining in the future, was not offset by an interim agreement which extended

tions for the future, the proportion of labor costs to total costs, per unit labor costs, and so on, vary widely from plant to plant so that a horizontal wage adjustment, if applied equally to all employers, will not have a similar impact on all employers. Unless the union is willing to adapt its master contract to fit local needs, the hardships worked on particular employers may be serious indeed. However, George Seltzer, in his careful study of the policies of the United Steel Workers of America as one of our dominant examples of pattern bargaining, reaches the conclusion that the charge of " labor monopoly " is unsupported by the facts. Furthermore " . . . the anticipated effects on marginal firms have been avoided by the willingness of the union to modify and adapt its policies to fit special circumstances. . . ." [29]

A further problem is giving adequate and equal representation to the participating companies. How much weight should be given to the large employer with large profits as contrasted to the small employer with small profits? The heterogeneous nature of price-cost structures, technology, product mix, intensity of competition and so on, often make it extremely difficult to secure a common area of agreement. Bargaining on an individual basis may provide a very necessary degree of flexibility and freedom required by individual employers. As one company manager explained: "By all means [I prefer] the local officers. They are familiar with the problems and are much better able to represent the workers and also know the company's problems and are responsible for them. There has been a great difference when the international officers come into the picture. We are much more likely to settle with local men. The international officers use a standard formula which does not apply in our case." And another spokesman put it this way: " We prefer the local officers — no question about that. The international officers cannot know the problems as well; their personnel is not big enough and their interets are too scattered. On the occasions when they do come in, they can't contribute much." [30]

One final disadvantage of such multiemployer bargaining is that collusive action among employers could lead to Congressional action. The Department of Justice may take antitrust action against employers and unions who cooperate to establish uniform and restrictive policies for their industry.

---

the terms of the last joint contract but which was executed and signed by the employer on his own behalf (Milk Dealers of Greater Cincinnati, 94 NLRB 11). Furthermore, an employer will not be permitted to change his course from joint to individual action during the term of an existing contract, because this would not make for that stability in bargaining relations which the Act seeks to promote (W. S. Ponton of N. J., Inc., 93 NLRB 924). For discussion see the Sixteenth Annual Report of the NLRB, (Washington, U.S. Government Printing Office, 1952), pp. 103–104.

[29] Seltzer, *op. cit.*, p. 331.

[30] Quotations from Woytinsky, *Employment and Wages in the United States, op. cit.*, p. 252.

The Expanded Bargaining Unit: The Public Interest

The main fear of the public in the expansion of industry-wide bargaining, is that the joint collusion of labor and management may provide both parties benefits at the expense of the public. With no one to represent the public at the bargaining table, it may come out a poor third. Inflation is much more likely to ensue in such an arrangement. Similarly, the very hazard of industry-wide strikes crippling the economy increases the possibility of government intervention in labor relations.

On the other hand, such bargaining has distinct advantages for the public. The administration of government policies during periods of overfull employment and depression on such issues as wages and prices permits the government to put its finger on certain key power centers in the economy for purposes of stabilization. The growth of the power of both labor and management creates its own problems, but it creates opportunities too.

It is quite likely that the single master agreement for each industry will not become a common feature of collective bargaining in the foreseeable future, for the divisive pressures and interests of both employers and employees represents the hard rock capable of grounding most plans for uniformity.[31]

[31] As a case in point, the diversity of forces and the diversity of responses of labor and management to similar forces are revealed in Gerald Somer's study on the resurgence of "individualism" in the glass industry (*op. cit.*, p. 569). For a contrasting view, see the study by Kenneth M. McCaffree, which explains how technology, mobility, and bargaining power are encouraging the widening of the bargaining unit from a local to regional basis in the construction industry. "Regional Agreements in the Construction Industry," *Industrial and Labor Relations Review*, Vol. 9, No. 4 (July, 1950), pp. 595–609.

11

Issues in the
Bargaining Process: 1

Labor organizations developed because of labor's conviction that unless it controlled its total supply it had little *quid pro quo* in the bargaining process. Through effective organization workers could threaten to strip management of all employee services; the consequences of such a possibility required that management consider seriously and carefully labor's demands. The growth of collective bargaining represents, in effect, the triumph of the notion that labor should be able to negotiate from a position of strength, and that a " fair " settlement is more likely to evolve from the give-and-take between equal powers than when either party is dominant.

It was Tallyrand who advised Napoleon that you could do almost anything with the point of a bayonet but sit on it. Today, it must be conceded that the creation of power blocs has not provided society with the industrial peace it desires. Before we examine more carefully the determinants of bargaining power between labor and management, and the alternative reliance of " principle " for dispute settlement, let us review briefly several of the issues often arising at the bargaining table. In this chapter, we shall provide a capsule summary on a few of the procedural problems related to union representations, including the determination of the appropriate bargaining unit and the meaning of bargaining " in good faith." With this foundation we shall turn to specific issues, including negotiations involving the prerogative issue and wage issue.

Procedural Aspects of Union Recognition

Historically, a considerable number of strikes in America were fought over the recognition issue, or the union's attempt to force management to recognize and negotiate with it. As we shall later see in our discussion of labor legislation, the Wagner Act of 1935 substituted political determination for this economic contest to resolve the issue of union recognition. It set up provisions to enable workers to vote on whether they wanted a union or not, and if so, which union would become the certified bargaining agent. The appealing proposition to abandon economic coercion to resolve this issue created, however, a new set of problems. The National Labor Relations Board (NLRB), established to administer the act, had then to resolve a host of collateral problems, as just what " majority " support of the workers was, who should be eligible to vote in such elections, where, when, and how the elections should be conducted, for how long the union certification should be binding, and whether employees were being intimidated by specific acts or words of management prior to and during such an election.

The Board evolved a series of decisions, forming a sort of common law to guide both labor and management on such issues. The Board rulings have been modified to conform to legislative changes of the Taft-Hartley Act. They also reflect the changing viewpoint arising from the shifting composition of the Board. When dominated by Democratic appointees, the Board tends generally to be more sympathetic to the union, while a Board dominated by Republican appointees tends to sympathize with the employer.[1]

In practice, an employer has the legal right to refuse to recognize any union which he feels does not have the majority support of the workers. If the union is intent on securing recognition, it can petition for an investigation by the NLRB. Following the Board's study of the situation, it can recommend either a withdrawal of the petition or that both parties consent to an election. If disagreement should arise regarding the bargaining unit, a formal hearing may be held and a report made to the Board. The Board will then determine whether an election should be held or the case dismissed. Eligible voters generally include those not employed in the current payroll period because of illness, vacation, or temporary layoff, and in various test cases, probationary employees, part-time employees, strikers, and workers wrongfully discharged have also been eligible to vote. Voting is, of course, secret. It is generally conducted on company property and supervised by the Board's agents. Certification of the union generally removes all doubt of the union's majority status for a year.

It is illegal for an employer to attempt to prejudice the outcome of such an election by intimidation or coercion although the extent to which the employer should be entitled to " freedom of speech " in voicing his views about unionism presents a continuing problem for the Board. The Board has ruled that the union could not place a sound truck, emitting electioneering material to those voting, that employers could not take

[1] As the Republican appointee to the Board, Albert Beeson, explained: " There's been a great shift in board thinking. But there had to be one. When you've been veering off the road for some length of time, it may seem like a sharp reversal to get yourself back on the road." As reported in *Fortune* (October, 1954), p. 67.

photographs of employees and union organizers distributing union literature, and that the employer could not threaten to remove his plant or
intimate that his employees would become unemployed if they supported
a union. More recently, however, the Board has permitted an employer
to interview workers individually to determine their attitudes toward
supporting a union attempting to gain recognition. Under previous
Boards such interviews would probably have been regarded as intimidation.

Involved as these problems may appear, they are certainly not as complex as the task of the Board in determining the appropriate bargaining
unit. The Taft-Hartley law attempted to resolve once and for all the
somewhat shifting impulses of the Board in determining appropriate bargaining units by offering the Board the following directives: [2]

> 1. Professional employees may not be included in a unit of non-
> professional employees, unless a majority of the professional employ-
> ees vote for the inclusion in such a unit.
> 2. No craft unit may be held inappropriate on the ground that a
> different unit was established by a prior Board decision.
> 3. Plant guards, who enforce rules for protection of property or
> safety on an employer's premises, may not be included with other
> employees.

Obviously the decision made regarding the composition of the bargaining unit will often control the results of an election. If only a pocket of
the workers appear to support the union, a rather wide perimeter for the
bargaining unit may reduce the chances for a union victory in the poll.
Similarly, clashes develop in large industrial units between craft unions
attempting to represent particular trades within the work force and industrial unions hoping to represent the bulk of all workers. Obviously,
the wider the industrial unit, the greater the likelihood that the indus-
trial-type union will be selected compared to the craft-type union.

It has been charged that the Board's selection of larger bargaining units
encouraged the growth of unionism and union monopoly power. On the
other hand, the more recent tendency of the NLRB to favor the smaller
bargaining unit is criticized as the deliberate " Balkanization " of labor-
management relations, tremendously complicating and dangerously weakening collective bargaining. Thus, the decision regarding the appropriate
unit cannot be untangled from the issue of craft versus industrial representation. The decisions made by the Board involve an interpretation of

[2] Section 9(b) of the Taft-Hartley Act. Section 2(3) expressly excludes from the
term "employee" as used in the act, any individual employed as an agricultural
laborer, or in the domestic service of any family or person at his home, or any individual employed by his parent or spouse, or any individual having the status of an
independent contractor, or any individual employed as a supervisor, or any individual
employed by an employer subject to the Railway Labor Act, as amended from time
to time.

public policy and hit the very nerve centre of the vested interests of particular unions.

The Board has developed the following criteria as a basis for its decisions: (1) the extent and type of union organization of the employees involved; (2) any pertinent history of collective bargaining among the employees involved; (3) similarity of duties, skills, and working conditions of the employees; and (4) the desires of the employees. The Board has generally taken the view that it will not disturb a well-established bargaining pattern unless there are compelling circumstances for doing so, but the history of the bargaining relationship will not control if it is inconsistent with other standards.

In attempting to define a craft skill deserving separate representation, the Board has stated that such craft workers, to qualify for such status, must have undergone extensive training or apprenticeship. It must be further clear, too, that the craft unit is doing work requiring skills sufficiently distinct from those of production employees. They must generally function as a cohesive unit in their own shop under separate supervision. But even so, the Board has on occasion granted craft status to the traditionally craft groups, even though these often do not have craft skills. Such groups include truck drivers, powerhouse operators, foundry workers, and so on. A further standard was to take into account the wishes of the workers themselves. If two units appear " equally appropriate," the board may order a self-determination or " Globe election." [3] This most commonly arises where one union is seeking an industrial unit that includes a group of craft employees which another union is seeking to represent separately. In these cases the ballots of the craft employees are segregated and counted separately. If a majority of them vote for the union seeking the craft unit, they are ordinarily accorded separate representation, but if they vote for the union seeking the industrial unit, they are ordinarily included in the unit.[4] This procedure was modified in 1944 by the General Electric formula.[5] The Board then held that it would entertain representation petitions from craft members included in a larger industrial unit when it could be shown that (1) the craft employees involved constituted a " true " craft and not a mere dissident faction and (2) the craft members maintained their identity throughout the period of bargaining upon a more comprehensive unit and protested their inclusion in such a larger bargaining unit. During and after World War II the Board usually decided that a stable and responsible history of bargaining on an industrial basis should outweigh any craft desires for separation from the industrial unit. In 1948 the National Tube Company de-

---

[3] The name is derived from the case in which the rule was first established, Globe Machine & Stamping Co., 3 NLRB 294 (1937).

[4] *Sixteenth Annual Report of the National Labor Relations Board*, p. 92.

[5] General Electric Co., 58 NLRB 57 (1944).

cision further reinforced this position by stressing the "integration" needs of the mass production industries. By using the integration principle the Board viewed the extent to which all plant operations are interdependent and integrated and concluded that deviation from plant-wide bargaining would have adverse effects on production and the effectiveness of employment representation. This standard has been employed in denying separate craft representation to groups in the basic steel, lumbering, and basic aluminum industry. However, in the above cases, the NLRB has been willing to permit the severance of boiler-room operators in an aluminum plant and the severance of patternmakers in a steel plant not primarily engaged in the basic manufacture of steel. In 1954 the American Potash Case revived concern over "Balkanization," and paradoxical as it may seem, employers have grown increasingly nervous over craft separatism. As *Fortune* explained:

> . . . more and more employers, faced with the vexing problem of negotiating with five, six, or even a dozen craft unions, each competitively seeking greater advantages and differentials over the others, have reversed their stand. They now long for the day when only one union represented the workers, and the union leadership, not the employers, faced the political problem of deciding which interest-group demand ought to be given priority in wage bargaining. . . .[6]

Employers found considerable reason for alarm in the Hamilton Paper Company case, too, for here some nine craft units, (some employing as few as two workers) were carved out of a fifty-six man work force.

These issues suggest just a few of the difficulties created by government intervention in the bargaining process. Government rules presumably rest on concepts of public interest and fairness, which are not susceptible to clear definitions. Board decisions have been flexible, but it is likely that while decisions to splinter bargaining units reduce the threat of labor monopoly, these decisions create new problems for both labor and management. Sectional bargaining will increase the hazards of jurisdictional strikes and encourage belligerent wage demands because of intensive competition between unions attempting to demonstrate their effectiveness at the bargaining table. It can also greatly complicate management's problems in dealing with its work force, in establishing a rational wage structure, in establishing uniform work regulations, merit plans, and so on.

Bargaining in " Good Faith "

Once a union is certified as the bargaining agent for a group of workers, management and the union are compelled to bargain in good faith

[6] *Fortune* (May, 1954), p. 53.

with each other. This mandate to bargain in good faith does not require that concessions or compromise solutions be found while bargaining. Rather, it indicates an obligation to hear the demands of the other party in the bargaining session and to participate in discussions in the hope that settlement of disagreements can be resolved peacefully. But the Board has stated, by way of clarification:

> Mere participation in meeting with the Union and protestations of willingness to bargain do not alone fulfill the requirements of Section 8(a)(5) and 8(d) of the [Taft-Hartley] Act, for these only are the surface indicia of bargaining. Bargaining in good faith is a duty on both sides to enter into discussions with an open and fair mind and a sincere purpose to find a basis for agreement touching wages and hours and conditions of employment.[7]

Obviously, it is extremely difficult to determine precisely what represents bargaining in food faith, but the Board has proceeded on a case by case method in an effort to evolve guiding standards.

For example, the Board will attempt to determine the motive of either the employer or the union behind their overt acts or statements. If it appears that the action of the employer is designed to weaken or destroy the union, or represents an attempt to circumvent the union by dealing directly with workers, the Board is likely to charge bad faith. The content of bargaining in good faith is, of course, crucial when an impasse in bargaining is reached. The Board has observed, however, that "The course of bargaining cannot be expected always to be smooth nor to be governed by the rules of a polite debating society. . . . Angry arguments, criticisms, and accusations between the negotiators . . . have their place in the process of collective bargaining."[8] Of course, a stalemate on, say, the wage issue, does not exempt either party from attempting to find compromise solutions on other issues. Neither employers nor unions are less likely to face the charge of bad faith if, in spite of the stalemate, both parties have made proposals and counterproposals for settling disagreements. It is also important that employer as well as union representatives have adequate authority to make responsible decisions for their respective bodies. Furthermore, the Board must appraise the history of bargaining and background in attempting to ascertain the absence of good faith. For example, if the employer refuses to supply data upon which incentive standards have been established, but has given sincere encouragement to the union to make its own independent study, the NLRB is less likely to interpret this as a refusal to bargain in good faith, compared to the situation where the establishment of the plan has been

---

[7] Southern Saddlery Co., 90 NLRB 1205, quoted in the *Sixteenth Annual Report of the National Labor Relations Board*, op. cit., p. 203.
[8] Elwell Parker Electric Co., 75 NLRB 1046.

completely unilateral and is an issue which management refuses to discuss with labor.

The concept of good faith in bargaining can be used to characterize the spirit with which both parties enter collective bargaining. It is a phrase that often enters into the discussions themselves for, as one participant to a bargaining session observed ". . . accusing a man of bad faith is sometimes a legitimate bargaining tactic, too." Edward Peters, in his down-to-earth study of the *Strategy and Tactics in Labor Negotiations*,[9] draws a worth-while distinction in defining " good faith " in bargaining: " Undesirable bargaining practices make for poor relationships between the parties, but they do not necessarily violate the rules of the game. The parties, in order to gain short-range advantages, do many unwise things which intensify conflict in the long run. But there is a vast difference between a short-sighted action and an unethical one." To Peters, the unethical tactic reflects lack of good faith in bargaining.[10] Again, however, it remains the basic task of the National Labor Relations Board to define the substance of that ethic.[11]

The Prerogative Issue and Bargaining

Often the contract is silent on the issue of prerogatives, but such silence cannot obscure the continuing power struggle between labor and management. We noted earlier that labor's interest in widening the area of negotiable issues is not a product of its radicalism, but simply reflects its desire to deepen its cushion against insecurity. What are the " fringe " areas of union probing? They include a desire to control or regulate company hiring policies, promotion policies, the content of the " fair day's work," investigation of the techniques of rate-setting employed by the company, analysis of the company's job evaluation plan, the general wage structure, the company's incentive plan, restraints on company discipline, and firing policies. On many such issues the union's right to challenge management's decisions is recognized, although labor representatives are not usually given any formal role in the shaping of company policy. But the steady growth of union pressure and power has resulted in a rather subtle, but nevertheless substantial, shift in the boundary line between labor and management prerogatives. Indeed, the issue of relative rights has been so frequently disputed that the boundary line distinguishing management prerogatives resembles the goal line in the football sta-

[9] New London, Conn., National Foremen's Institute, 1955.

[10] *Ibid.*, p. 209.

[11] For an account of cases which have been ruled by the Board to reflect lack of " good faith " in bargaining, see *Labor Course* (New York, Prentice-Hall, 1957), pp. 4104–4107, 4116–4119. Because of the variety of circumstances surrounding each case, it is difficult to establish self-evident standards.

dium after the spirited defense of the home team, with first down and goal to go. It is difficult to find the line at all.

What are the consequences of such union power? One student of industrial relations indicates that thus far unions have been able to employ their power only defensively, in a real sense negatively:

> They can make demands upon others, but they cannot initiate. They may play a critic's role, but not the actor's. Behind their search for increased authority in the business sphere lies the realization that their great growth of power has not fully been recognized, for it is given no constructive role. It provides as yet an imperfect means of self-expression, for it is held in reserve to be exercised only when challenged or challenging.[12]

But even so, the original interest of workers in such traditional topics as "wages, hours, and working conditions" has been so extended as to cover every facet of plant management. Defining management's prerogative for such issues as determining "proper" working conditions is not easy. For example, one dispute before the War Labor Board in World War II over working conditions for long-distance truck drivers contained sixty-two points, one of which related to the quality and character of the mattress in the sleeping units and another to where the second or relief driver should sleep while his mate is at the wheel.

The reluctance of management to discuss a certain issue often results in a protest to the National Labor Relations Board for an administrative decision of its appropriateness for collective bargaining. The Board has ruled that such issues as merit increases, the right of the union to demand confidential wage data for analyzing merit wage increases, the future re-employment of laid-off employees, the size and composition of the shop committee selected to handle grievances, the elimination of rest or lunch periods, are among those topics properly part of the collective bargaining process.

Management tries to buttress the case for its resistance to union claims by pointing out the dangers to the labor force itself, if management were not free to manage. If we define private property as " the right to derive an income on the basis of the ownership and use of property," the challenge to management's freedom to use its property as it sees fit is often interpreted as a challenge to the institution of private property itself. In addition, it is argued, the union does not appreciate the implications of what it asks. When unions demand the right to formulate policy on such vital issues as determining the speed of the production line, they can inadvertently face an explosive political problem within the union. Worker may then be pitted against worker in controversy over proper managerial

[12] Neil W. Chamberlain, *The Union Challenge to Management Control* (New York, Harper & Brothers, 1948), quoted in J. Shister, ed., *Readings in Labor Economics and Industrial Relations* (Philadelphia, J. B. Lippincott Co., 1951), p. 177.

policy. Labor may no longer be united in its common resolve to secure increased benefits from management.

A substitute for formal union intervention in the area of production and efficiency is collaboration. Management sometimes establishes advisory boards of workers to help solve the various problems facing the company. While historically unionists have feared that such joint-consultative boards might weaken unionism, such cooperation does not involve any serious challenge to management control.

Management sometimes attempts to defend its rights by including in its contract a provision like the following:

> The Union agrees that the products and types of products to be manufactured, the establishment or discontinuance of extra shifts and specific jobs; the means of manufacturing (including the use of labor-saving techniques and machinery); the price of the products; the determination of financial and accounting policies; the identity and character of all customers and suppliers; the mills or departments to be operated; the production required of each mill or department; the determination of the job content; the judgment as to the ability of an individual to handle a particular job; and the assignment of individuals to various shifts all be solely and exclusively within the responsibility and prerogatives of the company and not subject to grievance procedure or arbitration.

A second, more general provision is occasionally included:

> 1. The Union recognizes that the management and operation of the Company's business is vested solely with the company.
> 2. The union recognizes and agrees that except as expressly limited by the provisions of this agreement, the supervision, management, and control of the company's business, operations, and plant are exclusively the functions of the company.[13]

It is evident that management does not treat this prerogative issue lightly and while it is reluctant to speak of its "inalienable rights," it senses a deep responsibility, stewardship or trusteeship to the equity owners of the corporation and to the workers themselves. Freedom to manage is identified with the survival power of industry and the more belligerent the union in circumventing management's freedom, the more determined is the demand to "hold the line," but management personnel does not agree just where the line should be placed when prerogatives are analyzed in terms of specific issues.[14]

[13] From C. Wilson Randle, *Collective Bargaining Principles and Practices* (Boston, Houghton-Mifflin, 1951), p. 136.

[14] For further discussion, see John G. Turnbull, "The Small Business Enterprise and the Management Prerogative Issue," *Industrial and Labor Relations Review*, Vol. 2, No. 1 (October, 1948), pp. 33–49.

The Wage Issue in Collective Bargaining

The targets of organized labor differ from union to union, from time to time, from region to region, from industry to industry, and so on, but the uniform interest of all workers in getting " more " is common to all unions in all places at all times. Such general interest in wage gains gives coherence and order to what otherwise could be regarded as the patch-work pattern of union behavior. Because of the importance of this issue, let us subdivide it into several of its more important parts:

Competition and Administered Wage Rates. In our earlier discussion we stressed the pervasive influence of market forces and noted that through collective control of the labor supply, labor aspired to manipulate these same forces to its own benefit. In effect, labor can hope to maximize its wage rate or the " price " of labor by either contracting its available supply, or encouraging the expansion of its demand.

How can unions influence the demand for its services? The " Union Label " Department originally established within the American Federation of Labor was designed to make the American public conscious of union-made products and encourage their purchase. Unions have often attempted to assist their employers by advertising the products their members produce. They have, on occasion, opposed tariff reductions if these threatened the home market and their own wage structure. Unions have also objected to the imposition of selective credit controls on particular industries because of the dampening effect this had on industry sales and its unfavorable repercussions of the employer's demand for labor. In effect, the manipulation of labor demand often requires the manipulation of consumer demand, and unions have often been quick to appreciate the harmony of interest they have with employers in stimulating market demand and sales.

Turning to the supply side of the market, the controls that labor can effect operate in a more direct and predictable manner. If the union can create an artificial scarcity of the labor supply by restrictive admission requirements, apprenticeship regulations, and so on, they may be able to command higher wage rates by reason of that scarcity. Establishing such artificial scarcity can, however, be difficult and ineffective if unemployment is general. Labor is much more likely to be successful in wage negotiations if there is a *general* scarcity of all workers. If, for example, the aggregate labor demand exceeds the supply of workers, employers will be competing with each other for the limited supply, or " pirating " each others workers by volunteering higher wage payments. It is little wonder that unions are interested in the over-all employment level, for labor scarcity is a basic determinant of union bargaining power, particularly over wages.

If an employer refuses to adjust wages in terms of prevailing patterns during a time of general labor scarcity, he is likely to find that his labor force is melting away, and realize how unsound it is not to keep his wage structure " in line." But apart from the recruitment and turnover problem, inadequate wage payments may also encourage the union to pose the threat of a strike.

Two coercive elements are thus present in viewing wage pressures arising from adjustments of labor supply. On the one hand, a single employer may gradually lose his work force because of workers enjoying alternative employment opportunities at higher wages in the same labor market. Or he may temporarily lose all his work force as the consequence of a strike. Either alternative can prove costly, and the company may actually minimize its losses by readily agreeing to a substantial wage increase. The "staying power" of workers during a strike will determine the effectiveness of the walkout and influence management's calculation as how best to minimize its costs in the face of union wage demands.

While we have stressed that the contraction of the labor supply — either gradually or suddenly — can improve labor's wage rates, it should not be thought that wages can advance without limit. While labor mobility (sudden or gradual) provides a lower limit to wages, so does capital mobility provide an upper limit. The employer is not usually under any legal compulsion to stay in business, and if his prospects for profits are so diminished by oppressive wage demands, he is usually entitled the last freedom of folding his business. The mobility of capital will, in itself, depend on alternative uses of investment funds. During the depression many employers operated at negligible profits or they absorbed losses in order to keep their plant and labor force intact for better times. The willingness of management to absorb those losses reflected the absence of alternative profitable ventures as well as the battered but not crushed hope that recovery was just around the corner.

We return again to the point that the success of the union in securing a given wage level does not disprove the influence of demand and supply. A classic case is John L. Lewis's success in negotiating higher wages in the coal industry at the cost of complications both for the employers and union members. We should not be misled into concluding that John L. Lewis would fail a course in basic economics. As early as 1925, in his book *The Miner's Fight for American Standards*, John L. Lewis explained that union wage policy was aiding the industry to cure itself of " too many mines and too many miners " and was ridding the industry of " uneconomic mines, obsolete equipment, and incompetent management." He reasoned, therefore, that " any concession of wage reductions will serve to delay this process or reorganization, by enabling the unfit to hold out a little longer." [15]

[15] From Carrie Glasser, "Union Wage Policy in Bituminous Coal," *Industrial and Labor Relations Review*, Vol. 1, No. 4 (July, 1948), p. 609.

The range within which wage rates are negotiated is all the more broad the less competitive are the product and labor market. For example, in an oligopolistic or imperfectly competitive industry, pressure to raise wages may result in price adjustment and/or a drive on the part of management to reduce " overhead." It is not impossible that some other factor of production in the same plant will ultimately bear part of the burden of the wage pressure. Similarly, the fact that labor is not mobile permits the union considerable opportunity to raise wages without fearing that the employer will be swamped with job applicants. Such immobility and imperfection of competition permits, therefore, the adjustment of wages without the immediate repercussions that one might anticipate from drawing " noncompetitive " wage rates above the points of intersection of highly elastic labor demand and supply schedules.

Wages and Employment as Competing Goals. Economists have often assumed that at any point of time the employer's demand for labor was inversely related to the price of labor: The higher the wage rate, the fewer men the employer could profitably hire; the lower the wage rate, the larger the employment. The logic of this argument is convincing in static analysis, but the labor market is more dynamic than static. We shall see in our discussion in Section V that it is hazardous to assume constancy in the position of the labor demand schedule in order to predict the employment effect of a wage change.

We have noted that wages cannot be increased without limit, that labor can price its services out of the market. Because of this possibility, wage and employment relationships are of vital concern not only to the professional economist, but also to unions, management, and the general public.

In negotiations for higher wage rates the employer is anxious to avoid a firm commitment to a high wage cost structure when the elasticity and position of the demand curve for his product is uncertain. The employer will attempt to project future trends of company income on the basis of immediate experience, but he can never be certain that unanticipated developments may reverse favorable expectations. The more pessimistic the business outlook, the more contracted will be the employer's demand for labor or the more elastic will be his demand for labor in the face of a wage increase. Needless to say, because wage adjustments are binding for the contract period, yet revenues can be determined only after the fact, the employer will often decide it is good strategy to adopt a pessimistic view for the future during wage negotiation. One company representative confided the reason for his gloom during negotiations: " I wasn't authorized to be optimistic." Unions, for similar tactical reasons, are incurable optimists at the bargaining table. In spite of managements' protestations and prophecy of layoffs, the union frequently makes the deliberate decision to " live dangerously," knowing that no one can be certain what the immediate future prospects for the company are and what the employment repercussions of the wage demand will be.

This should not obscure the fact that when particular companies are threatened with their survival by wage demands, the union is forced into a painfully sobering decision. The company in such a situation will usually offer to show its books to the union's auditors and make it clear that the issue is now one of mutual survival. Many examples are available of instances where unions have foregone anticipated wage increases (and even accepted temporary wage cuts) in order to give management some breathing space. These are often considered to be isolated cases but probably seem so only because two decades of high employment have greatly reduced the occasions requiring such a union policy.[16]

As one might expect, if the prospect of a layoff rather than a complete shutdown is imminent, the high seniority union members are more inclined to disregard the risks of high wages than the low-seniority employee. The union is interested, in effect, in not only maximizing the hourly wage rate but in the aggregate " take-home " pay of its membership. Thus, it is concerned not only in the numbers employed in the plant (for this is usually a direct determinant of the wage bill as well as union membership), but also in the hours of work and the prospects for overtime pay. If a wage increase results in only minor or no reductions in the labor force, the total take-home pay will be increased.

Most of the above discussion relates to wage increases during prosperity. During a depression the union fights a defensive action, clinging desperately to the existing wage structure for fear that piece-meal cuts will prove to be cumulative and aggravate the economic problems not only for those employed, but also for the entire economy. The rigidity of wage rates, however, does not imply a rigidity of per unit labor costs. During a depression or during periods of intensified competitive pressure, management is likely to attempt to effect substantial increases in productivity per worker in order to absorb the pressure of stable wage costs. Failing this, the other major safety-valve for management is to lay off workers.

[16] We must be cautious then, in accepting without reservations Lloyd Reynolds' observation that " There is little evidence that union leaders think in terms of a demand curve for labor, or that they try to estimate the effect of different wage levels on the volume of employment in industry." *Labor Economics and Labor Relations* (New York, Prentice-Hall, 1953), p. 382. A static or declining employer demand for labor forces the union to consider this problem. This is not to deny that on occasion the union will force an employer out of business, but usually when this happens, the union leaders have had ample opportunity to consider the agonizing alternatives of employment for their members at low wages, or no employment. For an interesting account of union leadership strategy in the face of this problem, see Edward Peters, *Strategy and Tactics in Labor Negotiations* (New London, Conn., National Foremen's Institute, 1955), Chapter 4. The union's negotiating representative in this example concluded: ". . . better lose the place than have the headaches that'll come from settling under the scale . . ." (p. 52).

Wage Standards: Reasons or Rationalizations. In their approach to the wage issue union and management both generally orient their data, claims, and counterclaims to well-recognized standards or principles for wage adjustments. While we shall later analyze the merit of these many standards, we should note here the self-righteousness that each party often assumes in approaching negotiations. With a little imagination each party can justify almost any position it takes by some principle, and discussions often become particularly embittered when they involve the abstract views of justice. Such standards as ability to pay, prevailing practices, the living wage, the cost of living, productivity, and so on, become battle standards in partisan debate. It is often alleged that the union " acts first and thinks afterwards," and in the wage issue formulates its demand first and then window-dresses it with impressive principles. Of course, the union is no exception to the general practice of advancing one's particular goals with the childlike innocence and faith that these are in reality for society's benefit. It would be difficult for even the participants themselves to determine which of these wage standards were " instrumental " or inherent in their own value systems.[17]

Union Politics and the Wage Drive: A Digression on Arthur Ross's Thesis. One of the most provocative studies of union behavior has been that provided by Arthur Ross's *Trade Union Wage Policy.*[18] Ross feels that it is no longer possible to explain the determination of wages by supply and demand alone, when the determinants of supply and demand can be manipulated by collective organizations within our society.

The reason for our interest in Ross's thesis here is the focus he offers us on union politics and the wage bargain. Briefly, he argues that the union leader is necessarily wage conscious but cannot afford to contemplate the employment effect of a wage bargain even if this were possible. The union, as a political agency, is more interested in its own survival. Thus it is more concerned with the " membership effect " of a wage adjustment than its employment effect. Further, the worker determines the fairness of the wage bargain not by the absolute level of his real or money income, but rather by how this compares with other incomes in the plant, industry, community, and nation. The union leader is under pressure to keep up with the pattern of rates being negotiated by other unions. " Orbits of coercive comparison," established by the rank and file, pose a constant threat to the political security of the leader.

The union must make the decision regarding appropriate wage policy. The corporate goal is to maximize profits, but the union goal is to maxi-

[17] For an analysis of the " intricate blend of the quest for immediate selfish advantage and ultimate social values," see Werner Hochwald, " Collective Bargaining and Economic Theory," *Southern Journal of Economics*, Vol. XIII, No. 3 (January, 1947), pp. 228–246.

[18] University of California Press, Berkeley, 1948.

mize the more nebulous economic "welfare" of its members. "Profit can be measured in one dimension. 'Economic welfare' is a congeries of discrete phenomena — wages, with a dollar dimension; hours of work, with a time dimension; and physical working conditions, economic security, protection against managerial abuse. . . ." [19] The problem of defining welfare is difficult but this is the task of union leadership. For example, should a union pursue a wage increase if it results in a decrease in the number of workers employed and a reduction of the total wage bill? Ross is inclined to believe that the union leader must always favor upward wage adjustments, even in the face of the argument that unemployment may result. In reality, no one can predict with certainty the employment change that may result from the wage adjustment. Furthermore, if unemployment should develop, no one can attribute this to the wage factor alone.

What factors upset the alleged inverse relationship between wages and employment? First, a wage adjustment may be associated with changes in labor productivity, so that we cannot be certain that per unit costs and money wage rates move in the same direction. Second, we cannot be certain how prices will respond to wage adjustment. For these reasons, it is impossible to predict with certainty any dire consequence of the upward wage adjustment. Further, an increase in wages may concurrently cause unemployment *and* an increase of union membership, for workers may be attracted to the high paying industry.

Finally, the most potent force determining union policy is the attitude of workers; whether members feel they are getting a raw deal or a square deal: "The stenographer who celebrated jubilantly when she received an increase of $10 a month is disillusioned upon finding that an office mate received $15." [20] The comparison may be based on concessions granted to other workers, whether in the same plant or in the same trade. By such a flexible standard even the highly paid worker might find some basis for charging inequity in his own wage payment. This explains the pressure on the union leader to keep up with the pattern of wage adjustments. "It is very difficult for a union official to forego a wage increase or to consent to a wage cut, or to recommend to his constituents that they do so. Union leaders rarely lose their jobs for being too militant, but often for being too conciliatory." [21] Understanding union attitudes in wage negotiations is not to be measured by the degree of "responsibility" in the wage advance demanded by the union. Using the "employment" criterion as a standard for measuring the responsibility of a wage demand is, to Ross, highly unrealistic. "Although economic considerations are approached with great solemnity and argued with a fine show of confidence, they are not conclusive in the making of the bar-

[19] Ross, *op. cit.*, p. 27.
[20] *Ibid.*, p. 51.   [21] *Ibid.*, p. 91.

gain. The employment effect becomes a symbol in the service of partisan debate, and not a useful test of policy." [22] This is a convincing theme, but we must not forget that whatever the indeterminacy of the connection between wage adjustments and employment, the level of unemployment (however caused) is a highly important determinant of union power, and power a determinant of union policy.

The wage structure and job evaluation. While we talk frequently of " the " wage rate negotiated by the union, this is a short-hand expression for the " wage structure." Actually the union negotiates for a pattern of wage adjustments. Relative adjustments (apart from the absolute size of adjustment) provide one of the most sensitive issues in collective bargaining.

If we assumed that management paid workers as little as they had to, changing conditions of supply and demand would soon create substantial distortions in the plant wage structure. Indeed, many firms that lack a formal wage policy, or pay only the " necessary " wage to recruit " necessary " employees soon find that they have created administrative problems for themselves and serious morale problems for their employees.

Unions have often capitalized on these distortions. Frequently the union will argue that such inequities must be eliminated by bringing the bulk of workers in line with the higher-paid jobs. The most usual form of this strategy is to argue that the income of the lowest-paid employees is insufficient to provide adequate subsistence. In subsequent negotiations the union may reverse itself and stress the morale (and even recruitment) problems arising from the narrowing of differentials between the unskilled and highly skilled workers and then press for improvements for the upper end of the pay structure. By such " whip-saw " tactics or by working on one flank at a time, the union is able to raise the entire wage level.

Management has attempted to defend itself against this tactic, as well as against the inevitable moral problems arising from wage distortions by adopting job evaluation systems. A job evaluation plan is designed to provide some rational basis for wage differences in the plant. Basically, it is erected upon the principle that some standard other than supply and demand should determine the pay that particular job titles receive. A separate value system is constructed to determine proper wage differentials, and this value system usually includes consideration of such variables as experience, working conditions, education, and skill required to perform each job. It is a plan to allocate a given wage bill in such a way as to satisfy both the worker's and management's sense of fairness.

The establishment of a job evaluation program begins with a careful examination of job titles and job descriptions. Usually a committee is formed to determine what benchmarks should influence the relative

[22] *Ibid.*, p. 93.

importance of each job. What weight should "working conditions" be given relative to the "skill" of the job? Each of the half dozen bench-marks are weighted, and then each job is assigned points in terms of the selected standards. It is particularly important, of course, not to assign a high number of points to a job because it is known to be highly paid, for the purpose of job evaluation is to construct a measuring stick to evaluate the existing pay structure. It is often wise to process such jobs through a committee so that discrepancies in judgments can be carefully reviewed and reconciled. Management must explain carefully to labor the intent of such a program and why labor cooperation is so vital. On occasion union participation in the point-assigning job evaluation process is con-sidered to be a most valuable device for securing labor support for ad-justments that may be necessary. Once the point assignments have been made, these can be cross-checked graphically with the pay actually of-fered each job. The scatter distribution indicates those jobs which, accord-ing to this new value system, are overpaid and underpaid. A free-hand or mathematically derived line may be drawn through the distribution, with a plus and minus range around this central trend to indicate those jobs which are out of line. Traditionally, management has found it un-wise to attempt to lower the rate for overpaid jobs. It tries to get such wages in line by refusing the regular increment to these when general wage increases are granted, by eliminating the job, by transferring em-ployees to other jobs with a pay equivalent to their old rate and hiring new workers to perform the old job at the adjusted rate. Usually those with underpaid jobs receive increments to bring their wages into line.

What are the difficulties created by such a plan? First, no one suggests that the procedure is scientific, but represents a pooled judgment of what wage differentials "should" be. Obviously workers will be skeptical of any standard that suggests they are being overpaid and are often sus-picious that management has "cooked" the procedures to discriminate against particular groups. The political problems created by union par-ticipation are immediately apparent, for as noted above, the plan is not established to elevate the general wage level but only to adjust rates. Since such adjustments can create resentment, the union itself may be split over approval of the plan. The union further fears that such a plan is really a disguised defense-in-depth against wage increases, for manage-ment will no longer entertain rate adjustments providing preferential treatment to particular job titles. Unions have further argued that such a plan — since it is designed to pay the "task" rather than the man — pro-vides management with the opportunity to misallocate labor. Management can pay a highly skilled man a low rate because he is performing a low-rated job.

Evaluations plans pose some difficulties for management too. Most serious is the fact that evaluated rates may not permit management to recruit adequate manpower for particular jobs. The scarcity of technical manpower, for example, has forced management to pay wages above the established rates (called red-circle rates). And the more management by-passes the evaluation program to recruit new workers, the less meaningful is job evaluation. Yet even the best-designed job evaluation program cannot "fly in the face" of supply and demand. If the general wage structure in the plant is higher than prevailing wages, management is less likely to face this difficulty. But all firms cannot pay wages higher than those prevailing in the labor market.

Wage Incentives and Collective Bargaining. At the turn of the century Frederick Winslow Taylor argued that labor worked at much less than at full capacity because of labor's inherent laziness and labor's group-dictated laziness. Taylor did not excuse management from the laziness charge either, and he proceeded to demonstrate that if management had the energy to develop and apply scientific methods to industry, it could provide enormous increases in production. Specifically, Taylor recommended that in order to get men over their dead center of underproduction, increased rewards would have to be offered them.

The contrast of earnings of workers paid by the day and those paid by incentives is noted in Figures 8 and 9 on page 260. Earnings under an incentive system will increase once a production norm is reached. Under the more usual payment-by-time plans, earnings do not vary (in any contract period) to changes in daily output. The significance of changes in the level of production on per unit labor costs related to these two systems can be seen in the right-hand section of Figures 8 and 9. While per unit labor costs level off with each added unit of production under an incentive plan, they continue to decline as the "overhead" of the daily wage is spread over more and more units under payment-by-time. The question can then be raised: Why should management ever bother with incentive systems? The answer lies in the fact that if workers operate at production level X (as in Figure 9), the per unit costs of labor under time payment remain high. If management is unable to control the organized resistance of workers to output (as is certainly often the case) the labor costs relative to output pyramid. If, however, workers can be persuaded to work to level of production Y, per unit costs are decreased. An incentive plan, therefore, is designed to provide for increased output with the promise that worker's earnings will vary directly with that output. The worker no longer feels that his extra efforts result only in higher profits for the company, but that he is working for himself in that he can share directly the benefits of his own higher productivity.

It is significant that Lenin, while condemning Taylorism as a plan which reveals the decadence of bourgeoise capitalism, was quick to study and apply the techniques of scientific management to Russian industry. It provided a basis for maintaining some balance between labor's produc-

FIGURE 8. Earnings and Per Unit Labor Costs under Incentive Plan with Guaranteed Base

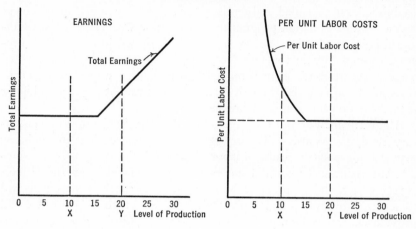

FIGURE 9. Earnings and Per Unit Labor Costs under Payment by Time

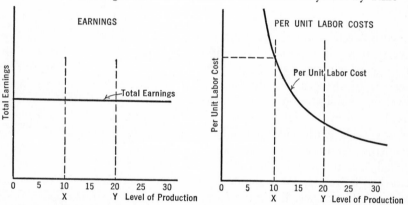

tion and income, and a most valuable source of motivation when traditional motivations for labor (*viz.*, the fear of becoming unemployed) were minimized. Undoubtedly management's interest in such plans in our economy will increase if our own economy continues to provide high levels of labor employment.

But this plan, too, provides many sources of controversy and friction between labor and management. While we cannot undertake an analysis of all the difficulties, let us briefly catalog a few objections of organized labor to such plans.

First, individual wage incentives pit worker against worker. Discrepancies in earnings from worker to worker and from job to job result in hard feelings and break down the *esprit de corps* of the union. Antagonisms develop against those workers who " break " the rates. Hourly workers supplying the production line or others not on incentive naturally resent the higher earnings of those incentive workers " on the line."

Second, the union charges that industrial engineering techniques have not yet eliminated judgment in rate setting. What worker should be selected for timing the normal rate? What procedure should be used to " correct " raw data so that it will be normal? What allowances should be made for fatigue? In other words, what is a " normal " level of production for the " normal " worker? Rate setting requires that this unhappy question be answered, and it is not surprising that labor and management should disagree over the standard management establishes. The production-earnings ratio may be too tight.

Third, unions fear that if workers succeed in earning " too much," management will cut the rate. In order to avoid this possibility, many contracts stipulate that rates will be adjusted only where fundamental engineering changes in method require a new job process. Even so the union will charge management with fabricating changes in work methods to cut down worker earnings. This fear of rate cutting explains why workers often insist that earnings be kept in line.

Fourth, the union fears that the incentive system reduces the worker to a cog status in the plant. He is no longer able to work at a leisurely pace, and older workers in particular are fearful that they may be unable to reach the production standards established by the company.

The techniques used by the industrial engineers to set rates are often complex, and union leaders resent the technical arguments used by management to support the rulings of their engineers. Furthermore, the intelligent appraisal of rate-setting methods requires that the union have some basic knowledge of the rate-setting techniques. While some unions – particularly the International Ladies Garment Workers Union – have established their own industrial engineering department, union representatives are often frustrated by the alleged pseudo-scientific arguments of management.

While not many unions have demanded participation or an equal voice in the rate-setting process, they have insisted on the right to challenge management's decisions. Wage incentive plans provide management with an unusual opportunity to expand output and stabilize per unit labor costs, but an incentive system will not manage itself, and management must always be on the alert to handle the day to day grievances that inevitably result from distortions in the earnings structure.

12

Issues in the
Bargaining Process: 2

In the bargaining process the competing goals and aspirations of labor and management are joined. The points at issue involve much more than wages and while it would be difficult to catalog the large assortment of nonwage issues, several have been selected for review in this chapter. We shall be concerned with guaranteed annual wage plans, seniority, union security, automation, production controls, and the hours of work.

The Guaranteed Annual Wage and Supplemental Unemployment Benefit Plans

The contract negotiated between labor and management is unlike most contracts in that only the price for labor is specified and not the quantity of labor that management will buy. Thus, the contract stipulates the wage rate but not the wage bill. Needless to say, a contract which stipulates both the minimum wage rate and the minimum employment level is radically different from one that stipulates the minimum wage rate alone. Because labor costs are often the largest single cost that management must meet, and because of the unpredictable nature of sales, any contract which would commit management to a wage bill rather than wage rate has been considered by management to court disaster.

Labor's recent increased interest in the guaranteed annual wage plans reflects labor's continuing concern with the possibility of unemployment. While such stabilization plans have had a long history, today they are still in the experimental stage and cover only a small percentage of the work force. In the past these schemes were usually developed by a paternalistic management. One pioneering wage stabilization plan in the wallpaper industry ran from 1894 to 1930. The vogue of enlightened management in the twenties encouraged further experiments with wage stabilization, but almost all schemes were found to be unworkable with the collapse of industry revenues during the thirties. In the mid-thirties, however, the federal government took steps to encourage states to establish unemployment insurance schemes. States passing unemployment compensation legislation meeting certain minimum requirements of the federal government were entitled to recapture 2.7 percent of a 3 percent payroll tax levied by the federal government for unemployment insurance.

Several factors account for the interest of organized labor in wage stabilization plans in recent times. First, and most important, is labor's continuing concern about unemployment. Even if the over-all employment level is " high," no single group of workers can be guaranteed continuing employment. A 3 percent level of unemployment may not represent a serious national problem, but if you are (or may be) among the 3 percent unemployed, your perspective immediately changes. Secondly, the existing unemployment insurance provisions do not provide adequate subsistence for the unemployed. Such benefits vary considerably from state to state as do the duration of benefits and the qualifications for insurance. Furthermore, the experience-rating provisions in many state plans permit employers to secure a payroll tax reduction when they can demonstrate that they have stabilized employment or are not contributing to the drain of the pooled unemployment fund reserve. Experience rating, unions charge, often encourages employers to devious devices to prevent deserving claimants from securing necessary unemployment relief. And the payments made by most states represents a steadily declining proportion of regular earnings, so that unemployment involves genuine hardship and hardly even a basic ration.[1] A further, although probably minor, reason for labor interest is the desire to secure benefits that will not immediately exert pressure on the price structure. Labor is often blamed for the wage-price spiral, and fringe benefits resulting in deferred wage payments are possibly less inflationary — or at least thought to be — than direct wage payments.

Interest in employment stabilization was revived during World War II when the United Steel Workers demanded the sanction of the War Labor Board for a guaranteed annual wage plan. The Board denied approval of such proposals, but recommended that the President appoint a fact-finding board to study the feasibility and implications of such programs.

[1] As Under-Secretary of Labor Arthur Larson testified, " To the extent that the benefit structure falls short of the half-of-average-wage, six-month pattern, it is probably failing to do the economic job that is nowadays expected of it. . . . The economic job is not done if the benefit level provides only the barest starvation-prevention subsistence, and forces a man to forfeit the goods he is buying on installments and perhaps lose even his house." " The Economic Function of Unemployment Insurance," *Proceedings* of the Industrial Relations Research Association (December 28–30, 1954), p. 156. Speaking on the same platform, Seymour Harris testified: " Here is a program that covered only one-quarter of the cost to labor of unemployment in a year of modest unemployment even after almost 10 years of unparalleled prosperity. Even in 1953 the maximum of benefits averaged $27 per week; the average weekly benefit, $23.58; the average potential duration, 22 weeks, the average duration of benefits, 10 weeks. . . ." " Economics of the Guaranteed Wage." *Ibid.*, p. 169.

Murray W. Latimer headed up the study, and the 1947 Latimer report provides the foundation for much of the current discussion for employment stabilization. The Steel Workers have continued to express their intent to ultimately negotiate such a contract, although other unions — namely the United Automobile Workers — have taken the initiative in pressing for it.

The 1955 contract of the United Automobile Workers with the automobile industry did contain Guaranteed Annual Wage provisions, although these are more realistically termed " SUB " (Supplemental Insurance Benefits) rather than " GAW." The union pursued the tactic of divide and conquer by negotiating first with the Ford Motor Company. By 1955 the union had assembled a war chest (reportedly of some $25 million) and the overtime work prior to negotiations probably enabled much of the rank and file to build up an emergency reserve in case a strike developed. But most important in the outcome of negotiations was the crucial competitive race between Ford and General Motors for an increasing share of the auto market. Henry Ford II himself explained that the settlement was " forced upon us by the competitive situation in the industry." [2]

In the plan negotiated with the Ford Company the company agreed to contribute into a trust fund at the rate of 5 cents per hour for each employee, until the fund reached approximately $55 million. The size of the trust fund was calculated by formula from average payroll data and involved an annual contribution by the Ford Company of some $15 million until the " 100 percent trust fund position " was attained. In the contract with General Motors it was estimated that the annual contribution of the company would run to some $40 million per year with a trust fund ceiling of some $150 million. When these funds reached their maximum level and as long as they were not drained by layoffs, further contributions to them are not required. Most important, the contribution at the rate of 5 cents an hour per worker is the sole and maximum financial liability of the company. With this limited liability provision, many proposals are much less frightening to employers.

A complicated procedure was devised to determine benefit payments. Every worker had to have one year of seniority to be eligible for benefits. Credits are earned by the number of weeks each worker is on the company payroll, and laid-off employees are eligible for payments after a waiting period of one week. The worker will continue to receive payment until his " credits " with the fund are exhausted. The rate at which the credits are canceled varies from worker to worker (depending on each one's seniority) as well as on the proportion of the existing fund to the total maximum fund. The lower the seniority and the lower the cash po-

[2] As quoted in the First National City Bank *Monthly Letter* (New York, July, 1955), p. 76.

sition of the trust fund, the more quickly are the worker's credits canceled by each week of benefit that he receives.[3]

Several features of the payment level are significant. First, the total of benefits approximates about 60 percent of his regular take-home pay, *including* unemployment compensation. In effect, the payments are supplements to unemployment insurance, and all else being equal, the cash drain of the reserve fund would be less the larger the unemployment insurance payment the worker receives. Under present provisions the maximum benefit period under ideal conditions would be 26 weeks. In effect, the worker is not guaranteed an annual income, but assured of the opportunity to receive supplemental payments from a company trust fund for half a year to increase his income to almost two thirds of his regular take-home pay. Secondly, laid-off employees, in order to qualify for payments, must also be eligible for state unemployment compensation. Thus employees who have been fired or those who go on strike would not usually be covered.

Union spokesmen have often noted that each guaranteed wage plan must be tailored to local industry conditions. Most plans that are proposed limit the company's liability to contributions (at a predetermined minimum rate) in building up a trust fund or drawing account, from which deductions are made during a layoff. In the United Steel Workers' proposal for a GAW made to Alcoa in 1953 it was proposed that the Steel Workers be offered a weekly guarantee of 30 times the employee's standard hourly rate. For example, if the hourly rate was $1.905, the employee would receive $57.15 each week. If unemployment compensation was $30.00, the company-financed trust fund payment would be $27.15. In this hypothetical case the employee would receive approximately two thirds of his regular earnings. Generally, the benefits received exclude incentive pay earnings, overtime, and shift premiums, so somewhat less than two thirds of gross earnings (inflated for such reasons) would be received by the unemployed worker.

We noted previously these proposals do not guarantee wage payments for the year. But as Henry Ford has admitted, the concessions of the automobile industry in 1955 represented a "step down the road." Probably demands will continue to be made to widen the benefits secured in a recent contract.

What are the advantages and disadvantages of such benefit plans? Looking at the advantages from the worker and union viewpoint first, it promises a greater measure of security against unemployment — and a greater degree of sustenance if unemployed. The union argues that industry can still do a great deal to minimize its seasonal use of manpower through

[3] For discussion, see Philip W. Cartwright, "The Economics of the UAW–FORD Contract," *The American Economic Review*, Vol. XLV, No. 5 (December, 1955), pp. 932–937.

product diversification, expanding warehouse facilities, and educating the public in an effort to iron out the uneven pattern of consumer spending. As a case in point, Walter Reuther has suggested that the automobile industry provide a sliding scale of diminishing car prices to encourage purchases in slack seasons, but the industry in effect offers this by adjusting trade-in allowances. Management will, nevertheless, be under increased incentive to stabilize employment because of the opportunity to reduce its wage tax (of 5 cents an hour) to zero. It is somewhat ironical that union leaders have been critical of the way in which experience rating has been "used" by employers to deprive workers of their legitimate benefits, when such experience rating was originally established to encourage employers to secure reduced tax rates by stabilizing employment. However, union spokesmen indicate that the increased payroll tax required by SUB plans provides more genuine incentive for payroll stabilization, and that the "marginal" cost of rehiring a worker is much reduced because of the employer payments to idled workers.[4] One of the undesirable features of unemployment compensation is that states have undertaken to compete with each other in order to attract industries by reducing payroll taxation. If fairly uniform SUB plans are negotiated for an industry, this may tend to minimize such interstate competition. Employers will also be more interested in expanding unemployment insurance because of the opportunity they may have to escape SUB demands, or to reduce the cost incidence of SUB plans if granted to the work force. It has been charged that the plans are designed to delay technological development, but union spokesmen have vehemently denied this charge. Basically, it is hoped that management will time the introduction of new machinery to avoid layoffs. Union objections are not "against" the level or rate of automation. The unions simply insist that innovations be timed to minimize the hardship and dislocation of the labor force.

Unions further resent the implication that such plans would encourage workers to be idle. Management spokesmen have been reluctant to characterize the work force as being either cheaters or loafers, but rather indicate that the American worker is always hopeful of getting "something for nothing;" is always searching for a "deal" or "bargain." If SUB plans permit workers to be idle, so much the better. Isolated instances exist, unfortunately, where workers have abused the unemployment insurance provisions by vacationing while presumably searching for em-

---

[4] Nat Weinberg, research director for the UAW explained, "It is common knowledge in the automobile industry . . . that workers laid off by one company while another is hiring will not be employed by the latter because of their probable return to work with their original employer. This is true even where the 'employers' are different plants of the same multiplant corporation. Continuance of this practice is most unlikely once wage guarantees become effective since employers in the same area will be able to minimize their aggregate liabilities by hiring each other's laid-off workers." From "Discussion of Guaranteed Annual Wage Plans," *Proceedings* of the Industrial Relations Research Association (December 28–30, 1954), p. 189.

ployment. But we must be careful not to condemn any plan outright because of its possible abuse by a small number of workers. Nat Weinberg drives this point home with unusual candor.

> . . . no one assumes, because fire insurance will pay off in full, that all of us are likely to become arsonists to raise quick cash when we want it. We rely on the police department to catch and punish those guilty of arson. The innocent are not penalized. . . . It is worse than immoral for industry to use its own failure to provide sufficient employment opportunities as an excuse to punish all workers for the potential sins of an infinitesimal minority. Why not put all bankers in jail because some have been convicted of embezzlement and others may abscond tomorrow? [5]

Others, like Seymour Harris, point to the rapid re-employment of the mass of unemployed men during the World War II emergency as further evidence that few men prefer idleness to employment.

A further advantage of the scheme is its counter-cyclical or " built-in-stabilizing " features. In effect, the payment of supplemental payments during layoff will tend to buoy up consumer purchasing power at a critical moment. Manpower layoffs which reduce labor's purchasing power may result in a cumulative cycle of unemployment and reduced industry sales. While SUB reserve funds are modest (when viewed in terms of the aggregate expenditures of our society), the spending they permit may come at a strategic moment to sustain business sales and optimism. Related to this same argument is the possibility that the more secure the work force, the more continuous will be its expenditure for consumer goods. Expressed in more technical terms, studies suggest that the more certain workers are of the *permanence* of their increased income, the higher is their marginal propensity to consume, or the increment of consumption related to that income increase.

Finally, it is reasoned that SUB plans will prove profitable for industry. It will reduce labor turnover and, more than this, will eliminate those work restrictions of the labor force rooted in labor's fear of unemployment. Once the worker no longer feels the pressure to preserve his job, his productivity will rapidly increase.[6] Workers are less likely to resist technological changes, less determined to negotiate or cling to make-work

---

[5] "Analysis of Some Arguments Against the Guaranteed Annual Wage." A supplement to the Industrial Relations Research Association papers (December 28, 1953).

[6] Fred H. Blum, in his study, " Guaranteed Wages and Work-Satisfaction," points to the favorable experience of the Hormel meatpacking company with its guaranteed annual wage: "Output per man-hour is about 50% higher . . . than in the rest of the packing industry. In 1951, for example, the average Hormel worker earned over 30% more than the average worker in the packing industry while working an average of 34.4 hours per week instead of 41.5 hours. Wage costs per unit of output are about the same for the Hormel company as for the other major companies in the industry." *Proceedings* of the Industrial Relations Research Association (December 28–30, 1954), pp. 307–8.

rules, and less concerned about seniority provisions. It is further suggested that labor mobility need not necessarily decline through the negotiation of such provisions. In industries characterized with seasonal unemployment, the pool of casual or seasonal workers that will be required to service such industries will be reduced, and this in turn will encourage the migration of workers to other industries where employment is stabilized throughout the year.[7]

While these advantages are attractive, SUB plans involve complications too. First, employers fear that such plans will not eliminate unemployment, but actually contribute to it. Employers will be reluctant to hire new workers lest they become part of their fixed operating costs. Since industry sales can never be guaranteed, how can employers guarantee their wage bill? The only " safe " policy will be one that minimizes the wage bill, and more particularly, minimizes the number of workers hired. Furthermore, the added cost increment will, other things being equal, reduce the number of workers that can be profitably hired. This problem may be more serious for the declining industry or for very young industry with uncertain markets and uncertain revenues.[8] If we assume that the economies of large scale are necessary to absorb the wage tax, might not such plans represent serious obstructions to the small struggling plant and encourage the consolidated power of the larger corporation? In effect, it is feared that employers will expand employment only as a last resort. Isolated pockets of unemployment will develop; workers will find it increasingly difficult to " break into " a plant to secure initial employment.

Thus, it is charged that SUB plans offer less protection to the very workers who need it most. In particular such seasonal industries as construction may find such a plan unworkable, simply because of the unavoidable employment instability of the industry. The paradox of the plans is that they are most workable in those plants which have less need for the plan, and less workable in plants which have most need for them. The National Association of Manufacturers puts it this way: " If the ' guarantee ' is comprehensive — the number of employees covered must be limited. If the coverage is comprehensive — the ' guarantee ' must be limited. If both the ' guarantee ' and the coverage are limited — the GAW

[7] For analysis of some of the economic implications, see Werner Hochwald, " Guaranteed Wages " *The American Economic Review*, Vol. XXXVII, No. 3 (June, 1947), pp. 303–319.

[8] Union spokesmen reply to this criticism by indicating that only the worker with one full year of seniority qualifies for benefits and this will give management considerable elbow room in its employment decisions. But it is the worker without the protection of seniority that is most concerned about the hazard of a layoff, and the more elbow room management has in this respect, the less the SUB solves this basic difficulty. The union also reasons that in a declining industry, the natural labor turnover, retirements, and so on should enable industry to reduce employment in proportion to the decrease in its need for manpower.

provides little ' protection ' to anyone." [9] Just as unions have revised their arguments about the ability of employers to minimize unemployment (to avoid the cost incidence of these plans), employers have now switched to the previous union position to argue that unemployment generally arises through forces beyond the individual employer's control. "Layoffs are generally a reflection of business conditions and other factors which are either beyond the control of management or essential to more efficient operation." [10] Furthermore, it is feared that the cost increment of the payroll tax, arising at a time of layoffs, will aggravate rather than cure employment. When layoffs are necessary, management should enjoy cost relief rather than added cost pressures. Even union spokesmen admit that the plan cannot be considered in any sense a panacea for cyclical unemployment but feel it could prevent a bad situation from deteriorating and can supplement other devices to stabilize our economy.

Management also fears that the increase of worker benefits to two thirds of regular take-home pay will discourage worker's enthusiasm to search for jobs.[11] Another more technical difficulty is the administration of such plans. Should the plans be jointly administered by both unions and management, and if so, what effect would this have on rulings regarding eligibility and so on? Furthermore, complications would immediately arise if the industry should adopt more liberal standards for unemployment benefits than are established by the state board administering the unemployment compensation. A further difficulty arises when states rule any worker ineligible for unemployment compensation if he receives supplemental income payments from any source. The revisions of state laws to permit such supplemental payments have reduced this immediate hazard to SUB plans.

Probably one of the most serious difficulties is that the plan does not offer equal protection to all workers in that under existing seniority provisions, all workers do not feel equally vulnerable to unemployment. It offers preferential benefits to the younger low-seniority employee, and can be construed as a transfer payment from high- to low-seniority workers. Not only may this create resentment within the union, but workers often are much more interested in money in the hand than the possibility of funds in some indefinite period in the future. The plan, in effect, may stand the seniority system on its head, with high-seniority workers aspiring for a layoff in order to get some of the " gravy." On the other hand, the guarantee of wages should permit management a

[9] "Questions and Answers About the Guaranteed Annual Wage " (New York, National Association of Manufacturers, March, 1955), p. 10.

[10] *Ibid.*, p. 5.

[11] For some fragmentary evidence on this problem, see Emerson P. Schmidt, " Private Guaranteed Wages and Unemployment Compensation Supplementation," *Proceedings* of the Industrial Relations Research Association (December 28–30, 1953), pp. 107–108.

little more flexibility in dealing with difficult seniority problems, for if management is committed to a fixed wage bill, it would seem reasonable that management should have increased discretion in allocating labor within the plant to support that wage bill.

Because of these several difficulties, it is not likely that SUB plans will spread rapidly throughout American industry. It is more likely that increased attention will now be given to the inadequacy of State Unemployment Compensation plans. But with limited liability provisions, accepting such a plan is not disastrous for an employer. Employers, in effect, simply offer a " forced-savings " service to their employees. Workers may not always appreciate this, especially if they do not anticipate unemployment. As we indicated earlier, the plan does not always appear practical to those industrial sectors where it is most needed, and it is most feasible in those sectors where it is least necessary.

Seniority

The purpose of seniority provisions is to establish a clear and uniform rule to guide management in decisions related to promotion, layoff, rehiring, transfers, and assigning work shifts. The single rule advocated by unions is that the length of service be the paramount guide to the company when making such decisions. While the seniority principle is basically a buffer against management abuse, it can be justified in other terms. For example, one can reason that the length of service is roughly correlated with the experience and skill of the operator apart from the worker's cumulative contribution to the plant, so that preference for the long-term service employee over the short-term service employee has economic as well as ethical justification. Seniority, in effect, represents the attempt to secure a mechanical, impartial standard to minimize the abuse possible in unilateral management decisions on such vital matters as promotions and layoffs.

It is not surprising that management often protests and resists the adoption of seniority provisions, for the difference between a successful and unsuccessful business in some measure may rest on the employer's ability to discriminate against the inefficient worker in favor of the efficient. It should not be assumed, however, that under most seniority clauses management must give complete weight to the length of service of employees. There is straight seniority, in which length of service is given paramount consideration, but most plans are " modified " or " flexible " in the sense that seniority is a controlling factor if ability and efficiency of the workers competing for the job are assumed to be equal.

Rightly or wrongly, workers believe they have a property right in the job, and this right is reinforced as the worker contributes a greater portion of his life to it. Unlike GAW plans, seniority discriminates against those workers who have short-term service in favor of those who have long-term service, and thus it is not primarily a device to protect the union as a whole, but rather a certain portion of its membership. It does not, for example, eliminate the hazards of unemployment, but shifts the incidence of that hazard from the long- to short-service employee.

The perimeter for the seniority plan may be the entire multiplant company, a single plant, the individual department or job. The scope of such plans is of no small consequence to both management and the work force. If the company or plant is the seniority unit, it means that workers have a greater opportunity for bidding for jobs that cut across department lines. This may prove an advantage for management in that the work force may become more flexible or possess more diverse talents, but during a period of layoffs the " bumping " by old-time workers of younger workers is likely to be much more extensive than if seniority is on a departmental or job basis. Such bumping may lower both the morale within the plant and the efficiency of the work force. Using the wider unit will give greater protection to the older worker, for the layoffs would have to be substantial before the old timers could be affected. Seniority on a departmental basis permits a long-term service worker in one department to be laid off before a short-term service worker in another department.

What are some of the advantages and disadvantages of seniority? First, as noted above, workers feel that seniority plans provide them with protection from discrimination. It may be that the foreman, who enjoys the delegated powers of management, has " pets " or relatives to whom he gives preferential treatment. Management, in making its decisions to demote, suspend, or discharge workers, is exposed to all the limitations of human nature, and labor argues that issues so vital to it should not be left to the random whims or guesswork of management.

The plan, though, has disadvantages for the work force and the union too. First, and perhaps most important, it is likely to create a political cleavage within the union, dividing the long- and short-term employees. Secondly, there are many administrative headaches related to the seniority plan which may confound the union as much as management. The workers are naturally concerned with protecting their rights to their jobs, but often in competition with other workers. It is awkward for union officials to pick sides in such disputes. Many of the grievances lead to expensive arbitration proceedings. Does a worker lose his seniority if he is laid off, if he is irregular in his attendance at work, if he is in the armed services, if he is absent for a considerable period of time? In effect, many of the issues related to the seniority cannot be anticipated at the time the seniority agreement is reached and plague both management and the union during the life of the contract. Problems are multiplied if there is a merger of two companies and two seniority systems are integrated. Or if any attempt is made to alter the appropriate unit for calculating seniority, the work force may immediately be thrown into two separate hostile camps, one camp fearing the loss of previous security, the other anticipating an increase of security by " reform " measure. The threatened loss of seniority can also be a powerful weapon in the hands of management. If a strike develops, management may find it possible to resume operations with nonunion members. If the strike is lost, the old workers may have to return to their jobs with the status of new employees. The settlement of a strike may be much more complicated if management has promised employment security for the strikebreakers, and is unwilling to violate those promises by re-employing union strikers with full seniority.

From management's viewpoint the seniority system poses rather obvious problems too, the most important being management's reduced ability to promote on the basis of ability and efficiency. To management the system is mechanical and expensive, for it protects the inefficient worker as well as reducing the incentive of the young, ambitious, and skilled new employee. In addition, bumping within the plant may create difficulties for management. If a plant-wide seniority system is used, all the workers become immediately concerned with any layoffs: All jobs are tied in to each other, and the fluctuation in the level of employment, while affecting only the low-seniority workers, will involve a shift of job functions of many in the plant. For example, when the Goodyear Tire & Rubber Company had to drop 1,295 employees in the midwinter of 1954, they had to make 3,458 changes in job assignments. A spokesman of the International Harvester Company described an even more serious dislocation than this: " We found that it averaged ten to twelve moves before an employee actually left the plant. Each employee bumped downward has to get three days' notice, and it took two to three weeks before someone left the plant. Labor costs in piecework increased 25 per cent." [12] Of course the more limited the seniority unit, the greater the opportunity to dampen the bumping cycle — the wider the seniority unit, the greater the protection to the older worker, but the greater the disruption of plant activity arising from the bumping process. The Goodyear Company pointed out that bumping creates serious production problems as employees do not know how long they will hold their jobs before being bumped by a man with more seniority. The company cited numerous instances where as many as three workers have " passed through " on a job in a single day.[13]

Management, nevertheless, enjoys some advantages from such a system. First, the secure worker may be a more efficient worker. His morale and productivity are high, for he does not fear personal discrimination, nor worry from day to day whether he will be employed. He does not fear working himself out of a job. He will be anxious to reward the company

[12] From " The Bumpy Road," *Fortune* (March, 1954), p. 69–70.
[13] *Ibid.*, p. 72.

by doing a fair day's work in return for the stability of employment he enjoys. Management will be much more selective in securing new workers; employers will be anxious to examine new recruits carefully to determine their experience, education, and decide whether they will be compatible with company personnel and policies. Such a screening may provide a more satisfactory long-term employment relationship. A further fruitful by-product of union interest in seniority has been the development of more formalized " merit-rating " plans. Such plans make explicit those factors which management feels should control promotion or advancement within the company, and again as such judgments are pooled or systematized, the less likely it is that workers will be exposed to personal discrimination. Labor turnover in a plant with seniority is likely to be less than in a nonseniority plant. Even the laid-off worker is not likely to search for employment elsewhere immediately but hope for re-employment in his old plant. Labor turnover is, of course, a very expensive item for management, and such turnover is likely to increase during a period of high employment when employers are attempting to " pirate " each other's labor force. The seniority system is one effective device for reducing such costs, for a man does not lightly surrender his seniority, even if the pay in the plant across the street is higher.[14]

Union Security

Union security contracts define the status of the union with reference to the work force. It may appear strange that the union should attempt to clarify its own relationship with the work force via an agreement with management, but this is precisely what a union security clause does. The drive to secure such a provision reflects the traditional insecurity of the union in the face of the hostility of the employers, the courts, and in some instances of the rank and file itself. It also reflects the drive of other unions for membership. Unions are, therefore, anxious to formally establish the sovereignty and permanence of their organization. Such provisions are primarily for the protection of the union as an institution, but are justified as a means to a more important end: the security

[14] In Lloyd Reynolds' study of a sample of unemployed workers in the 1948–1949 recession, he found that two thirds of the sample had been unemployed three months or less. " Each worker was asked whether he would like to go back to work for his previous employer. . . . In . . . cases where it was applicable, however, 87% of the workers said they would like to go back to their previous jobs, and 50% believed that they would actually be able to do so. Those who wanted to go back but did not believe they would be able to, fall into two main categories: (1) Workers with very low seniority. As one man said, ' Well, they've laid off up to eight years now, and I've only got eighteen months. I don't think they'll get back down to me for a long while.' (2) People whose work record has been unsatisfactory and who didn't think the company would want them back." *The Structure of Labor Markets, Wages and Labor Mobility in Theory and Practice* (New York, Harper & Bros., 1951), pp. 81–82.

of the individual worker. In effect, they are designed to make the union secure and through union security, make the worker secure.

Conceptually, there are several alternative relationships that might be established between the union and the company. On one extreme, the now illegal yellow-dog contract required new employees to agree that during their term of employment they would neither join a union nor participate in any strike action. Historically, management in America has often pursued a nonunion shop policy. The employer would hire only nonunion workers, but no commitment was made by the latter which would prevent their joining a union if they should subsequently decide to. This arrangement, too, is now largely defunct. The 1935 Wagner Act made it an unfair management practice to discriminate in any way against a worker for his membership or activities in a union. Today management cannot declare it will not hire any active union supporter.

A third relationship is the open union shop. In this situation the company recognizes the union as the representative of all the workers. Not all the workers are compelled, however, to join the union, and thus union and nonunion members work side by side. Under the law management cannot discriminate against individual workers for nonmembership or for membership in the union, and the union must equally represent all workers, whether members of the union or not. A fourth form of organization is the preferential shop, in which the company agrees to give preferential treatment to union members in hiring and in making layoffs. In such an arrangement management inquires at the union hall to determine if union members are available for work. If the union fails to supply such workers, the employer is then free to go into the market and hire any worker that he pleases. In some situations in the past the nonunion workers could keep their jobs only until the union found a worker to replace him. Such discrimination against the nonunion man was also applied to layoffs. Union hiring halls have continued to operate in several industries even though the Taft-Hartley law outlawed them. They are permitted if the hiring hall does not discriminate against nonunion members.

A fifth form of union security is the union shop, the most common form of union security provision today. Under this provision management agrees to require all new employees within its existing labor force to join the union after a specific number of days, generally 30 to 60 days. The employer is free to hire whomever he wants, but all workers are then required to join the union as a condition of employment after the expiration of the specified interval. A sixth form is the "maintenance-of-membership" union security clause. In this provision, the company agrees to permit all workers to decide for themselves whether they want to join the union or not. They are usually given a 15-day escape period in which those who are currently union members can resign. But once the decision is made to join the union, such members are required to maintain that membership as a condition of employment for the duration of the contract. This form of union security was developed by the War Labor Board during World War II as a compromise between the closed-shop demands of the union and the open-shop demands of the employer.

FIGURE 10. Union Security Provisions in Collective Bargaining Agreements: 1946, 1949–1950, and 1954

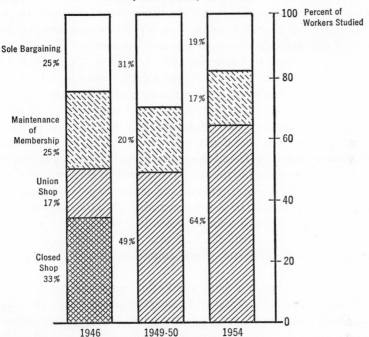

Source: Rose Theodore, "Union-Security Provisions in Agreements, 1954," *Monthly Labor Review*, Vol. 78, No. 6 (June, 1955), p. 655.

A further form of union security is the closed shop. Under this provision the worker must be a union member as a condition of employment. The closed-shop provision was outlawed by the Taft-Hartley Act, and prior to the 1951 amendments of that law restrictions were placed on the negotiations for the union shop.[15]

[15] Under the original provisions of the Taft-Hartley Act unions were required to have a referendum, conducted by the National Labor Relations Board, to determine the majority sentiment of all workers on the union-shop issue. In such elections, those voting "yes" for the union shop had to be a majority, not of all those voting, but of all workers in the plant. Thus, if a person did not vote, this represented a "no" vote for the union shop. If the majority did approve of the union shop, then and only then would it be possible for the union to negotiate for this. Of course, the employer was under no compulsion to meet the demand simply because the majority of the workers wanted this provision. It was found that in over 90 percent of the elections, the workers were in favor of the union shop, and hence in 1951 this provision of the law was amended so that elections are no longer required.

An additional union security provision, with as yet very limited application, is the " agency shop," which requires that all employees pay dues to the union but does not compel workers to join the union. Each of these forms of union security may be modified somewhat from contract to contract. For example, the major steel agreements in 1952 stipulated a maintenance-of-membership provision which required each new employee to sign an application for membership in the union, with the option of canceling the application between the fifteenth and thirtieth day of employment. If not canceled, union membership became binding for the length of the contract. Some union-shop provisions stipulate for some degree of preference in hiring for union members. " Usually the union was permitted to refer union members for job vacancies who would be considered with other applicants on the basis of their qualifications." [16]

In Figure 10 we see the recent changing pattern of union security provisions. In 1946 the last BLS study of union security before the Taft-Hartley Act indicated that about 33 percent of all workers under agreement were covered by closed-shop provisions. But by 1950 union-shop provisions absorbed almost the same proportion of such workers as were previously covered by both closed- and union-shop provisions. We can see that by 1954 the degree of union security was extended, with close to two thirds containing union-shop clauses. In this same year about 75 percent of the agreements had checkoff provisions which required the employers to deduct union dues from employees' pay for transfer to the union.[17]

While labor has made a determined effort to repeal the Taft-Hartley Act, unions are now diverting their attention to the threat of " right-to-work " laws which, in effect, invalidate and make illegal various forms of union security provisions. In 1939 Wisconsin amended its " little Wagner Act," declaring that two thirds of the employees of a plant must vote for union security provisions before it could become part of a labor-management contract. Colorado and Kansas followed in 1943, Colorado requiring a three-quarters affirmative vote of the employees in the collective bargaining unit, and Kansas requiring a majority of the workers to vote in favor of the union security provision. In 1947 New Hampshire passed a similar law, requiring a two-thirds affirmative vote. In 1944 Florida and Arkansas amended their state constitutions to outlaw all union security provisions, and in 1947 Arizona, Nebraska, and South Dakota followed suit. By 1957 eighteen states had taken some action to restrict union security provisions, and on January 3, 1949, the Supreme Court validated the right of any state to curtail arrangements making membership in a

---

[16] Rose Theodore, " Union-Security Provisions in Agreements, 1954," *Monthly Labor Review*, Vol. 78, No. 6 (June, 1955), p. 651.

[17] These data are contained in Rose Theodore's study cited above. The BLS studied 1,716 collective bargaining agreements in effect in 1954 covering 7.5 million workers.

labor union as a condition of employment.[18] As can be seen by the states involved in such legislation, right-to-work legislation is more popular in the South than in the East or West. The 1955 BLS study indicated that in the Pacific region (California, Oregon, and Washington), 78 percent of the contracts analyzed provided for a union shop. In the West South Central region (Arkansas, Louisiana, Oklahoma, and Texas) only 16 percent of the contracts contained such provisions.

What are the advantages and disadvantages of union security provisions? Taking first the union and the worker viewpoint, the union claims that these security provisions simply require that all workers share equally in the burden or expenses related to union activity, since they all share in the benefits of such organization. In effect, they eliminate the " free rider." To reason by analogy, the couple without children contributes through property taxes to the support of schools for those that have children. Similarly, during a war the government enacts conscription laws to be certain of uniform participation or sharing in the risks and burdens of war. It is precisely on this point, however, that the argument is joined by the opponents of union security regulation. The National Association of Manufacturers, for example, has pointed out that it is a false analogy to compare the functions of the union to its members with that of the government to its citizens. " The union argument, if it proves anything, proves too much. If every worker who is supposed to benefit from the activities of unionism ought to be required to join a union, every manufacturer ought to be compelled to join the National Association of Manufacturers, and surely every beneficiary of Christian civilization ought to be forced to join a church." [19] The major complaint then, is that such provisions represent coercion of the individual worker: he is *compelled* to join the union. Addressing themselves to this point, Clinton S. Golden and Harold J. Ruttenberg defend the union position:

> Of course, it's coercion. That's what all the argument is about: the right to force someone to do something against his will. But this is not a legitimate objection to the union shop, as coercion is the fundamental basis of organized society. In fact, civilization can be said to have attained maturity when men became intelligent enough to order their affairs and compel the recalcitrant man, the ignorant man, to submit to certain compulsory rules for the common good of all men. I cannot drive through a red light, although I have enough good sense not to drive carelessly through an intersection; but, because other men lack such sense, for the common good, I am coerced into

[18] *Lincoln Federal Labor Union* v. *Northwestern Iron and Metal Co.,* 335 U. S. 525 (1949).

[19] " The Closed Shop " (New York, National Association of Manufacturers, 1941), and cited in E. Wight Bakke and Clark Kerr's *Unions, Management, and the Public* (New York, Harcourt, Brace and Co., 1948), pp. 126–127.

stopping for a red light, although no cars may be coming from the opposite direction.[20]

To these authors, the essential difference between a democracy and a fascist state is whether the minority or the majority do the coercing and they point out that union security provisions are supported by the majority of the workers.

A second defense of such plans questions whether labor in reality has the right to work. Right-to-work laws operate on the assumption that the worker has the opportunity to work if he should be so inclined, but whether this right exists depends on the number of job vacancies compared with the number of unemployed workers. Unions stress the fact that the labor market is more often a buyer's market than a seller's market, and thus, such freedom to work does not exist. Workers have only "the right to go from employer to employer in search of work." If this argument is valid, it is hardly possible to claim that union security clauses deprive the worker of this right, for labor cannot be deprived of a right which workers do not possess. Of course, a closed-shop provision could deprive a worker of the opportunity to take a job that he knows exists if he cannot or will not join the union, and the hardship worked against him may be substantial. On the other hand, the union, through its organization and through the extension of its economic power, is likely to expand the area of rights of the work force as a whole.[21]

A third defense of union security clauses is that they simply represent the application of the democratic principle of majority rule. If the majority of the workers decide they want the union shop, is it tyranny to permit them to enjoy their collective desires? However, in a democracy, the minority sentiment must be protected and should be free to convert the majority to its viewpoint. As noted earlier, the union member may face considerable risk in challenging union leadership. Of course, any party elected to office can abuse its power and repress criticism, but many fear that giving the union a security clause is an open invitation to abuse. The worker ends up with two bosses, divided loyalties, and dual obligations.

Another argument for union security provisions is that when the union is secure, union leadership can be diverted from the defensive to more

---

[20] *The Dynamics of Industrial Democracy*, Harper & Bros., New York, 1942, from a passage cited in Bakke and Kerr, *op. cit.*, p. 132.

[21] Indicating the opposite viewpoint, J. C. Gibson, attorney for the Santa Fe Railroad explained: "Right-to-work laws do not purport to create new rights but only to protect fundamental rights from invasion through imposition of compulsory unionism as a condition of employment. They do not directly create any jobs, but by helping to keep the economy free and by keeping opportunities open, they inevitably in the long run lead to more and more chances for employment." "Legislative Restrictions Upon Union Security Agreements," an address before the Section of Labor Relations Law, *American Bar Association*, Philadelphia, Pa., August 23, 1955.

constructive efforts. Such leadership may attempt to increase worker efficiency, campaign for reductions of waste, labor turnover, absenteeism, tardiness, and so forth. In addition, the union leader may be sobered by his power and demonstrate his responsibility. He will not only be anxious to support the contract, but will have new sources of power for enforcing it. There is less danger of wild-cat walkouts and other violations of contracts. A further advantage to the company is that leadership will no longer be under pressure to provide the rank and file with a continuing series of dramatic concessions from management. A politically insecure union leader may lean over backward in his defense of the worker's position, and he may dramatize grievances and even exaggerate the plight and hardships of the workers so that the membership will be conscious of his efforts on their behalf. With union security granted, a more stable, mature leadership can develop, able to scrutinize worker grievances objectively rather than in terms of political expediency.

As we noted above, the passage of " right-to-work laws " in eighteen states has revived interest in the union security issue. Much of the controversy centers around Section 14 (b) of the Taft-Hartley Act which provides: " Nothing in this Act shall be construed as authorizing the execution or application of agreements requiring membership in a labor organization as a condition of employment in any state or territory in which such execution or application is prohibited by state or territorial law." In other words, the tolerance of union security contracts under federal legislation shall not deny the validity of state laws which outlaw union membership as a condition of employment.

Supporters of organized labor have introduced several bills into Congress to strike Section 14 (b) but without success. The amendment in 1951 to the Railway Labor Act permitted the negotiation of the union-shop contract, state legislation notwithstanding. Five employees of the Union Pacific Railroad Company initiated legal action because of their refusal to join a union, and on May 21, 1956, the Supreme Court unanimously upheld the constitutionality of the 1951 amendment. Eleven workers of the Santa Fe Railroad, seeking protection of the Texas right-to-work law, argued for their constitutional right to employment in spite of their refusal to join the union, but the Texas Supreme Court upheld the 1951 amendment to the Railway Act. Thus, railroad unions are free to negotiate a union shop which is binding in spite of state right-to-work legislation.

What are the arguments advanced by management in resisting the demands for union security provisions? First, it is charged that compulsory union membership denies labor its basic freedoms assured under the Fifth and Fourteenth Amendments. The " right " to work assumes the freedom to select among alternative of working and not working, and this freedom is limited by the refusal of a worker to join a union. The courts have previously stressed how precious were these rights to a job: They invalidated post-Civil War legislation which would have deprived professional employment to those supporting the Confederacy; they have protected the rights to employment of Chinese laundrymen in San Francisco; they have protected the jobs of foreign language teachers in the hysteria following World War I; they have protected the rights of Japanese fishermen to their occupation off the Pacific Coast after World War II. Justice Charles Evans Hughes in the Truax case of 1915 pointed out that " It requires no argument to show that the right to work for a living in the common occupations of the community is of the very essence of the personal freedom and opportunity. . . ."

Management has also reasoned that union security provisions may be treated analogously to the yellow-dog contract, for each denied the worker the opportunity to employment unless he joined, or did not join the union. As the president of the Santa Fe Railroad, Fred G. Gurley explained:

> They said that it (the " yellow-dog " contract) enabled the employer to use his freedom of contract to destroy the freedom of choice of the employee in joining an organization. They said it violated his right of association. I think they were quite right and I am glad they succeeded in securing the passage of statutes which outlawed the practice.[22]

By similar reasoning President Gurley argued that unions today were attempting " to turn the clock back " by restricting the freedom of choice of workers regarding union membership.

A further argument is that compulsory union membership is not consistent with the principle of majority rule because unions are not characterized with a two-party system and do not encourage (or always tolerate) dissension within the ranks. Many union constitutions and membership oaths forbid participation in a dual union movement. Freedom to distribute circulars or other literature critical of union officers is also circumscribed. Thus it is argued that compulsory union membership is not an extension of democracy, but may actually weaken it. One of the restraints of union behavior is its necessity to maintain the voluntary support of the rank and file and prevent desertion. The discipline provided by labor's freedom to join or not to join is a necessary check on union authority. Management fears that union security clauses in the absence of traditional checks and balances will extend union power at the expense of the worker's individual freedom.

The argument that the union should demand the support of all workers securing the benefits of union organization, in the same way that a government expects support for its administration by taxation of the pub-

[22] Address before the annual meeting of the Chamber of Commerce of the United States, Washington, D. C., May 3, 1955, pp. 5–6.

lic, is met with the observation that the union is not a sovereign state, nor can the union legitimately assume the tax powers of the state. Union leaders often delight in showing the parallel to unionism and the closed shop resulting from the standards imposed by the medical association or the law association. One lawyer denies the validity of such a comparison. " A lawyer is an officer of the court and as such liable to close supervision and restriction. His practice of law is a privilege and not a matter of right. In states with integrated bars, the organizations are not private associations but official government bodies." [23]

Another awkward issue is raised with the restrictions imposed by unions, particularly in the railroad industry, against equal participation of Negro union members. J. A. McClain points out that the union security clause can force a railroad employee to apply for membership, but at the same time he may then be rejected for membership or forced to be a " free rider " by union action. It is paradoxical that any worker should be compelled to try to join a union or lose his job.

Finally, it is agreed that unions — for their own best interests — do not need union security clauses. Almost all of the railroad industry is unionized and became unionized in the absence of union security clauses. Similarly, it is argued that there has not been any significant discrepancy in the rate of union growth in states with right-to-work statutes compared to those without them. There can be little doubt that many workers intuitively resent being compelled to join unions and would probably be more loyal union members if they had the opportunity to make the voluntary choice in the matter.

In summary, the union argues that the worker is only free in the sense that union organization widens the control and influence of the worker. As an individual, the worker has only the freedom to refuse to work on managements terms. Management, on the other hand, suspects that so much public attention has been given to the struggle between union and management as to deflect attention away from the equally important struggle between the worker and the union. Freedom of association and the right to work are basic freedoms but under union security clauses the worker cannot enjoy *both* his freedom of association and his right to work. In exercising this former freedom in deciding not to join a union, he may sacrifice the latter freedom, the right to a job. The union charges that management's interest in the individual workers' welfare is charitable, but workers should be permitted to look after themselves without such indulgence. Unions suspect management interest is simply a circuitous and disguised device to weaken the solidarity of the union, to undermine union power at the bargaining table. Probably few issues reveal the blend of principle and pragmatism in labor-management relations.

[23] J. A. McClain, Jr., " The Union Shop Amendment: Compulsory ' Freedom ' To Join a Union," *American Bar Association Journal* (August, 1956). Reprint, p. 6.

Automation

In his book, *Seventy Years of Life and Labor*, Samuel Gompers recalls as a child in London, the hardships worked on the silk weavers by the creation of silk-weaving machinery:

> No thought was given those men whose trade was gone. Misery and suspense filled the neighborhood with a depressing air of dread. The narrow street echoed with the tramp of men walking the street in groups with no work to do. Burned into my mind, was the indescribable effect of the cry of these men, " God, I've no work to do. Lord strike me dead — my wife, my kids want bread and I've no work to do." Child that I was, that cry taught me the worldwide feeling that has ever bound the oppressed together in a struggle against those who hold control over the lives and opportunities of those who work for wages. That feeling became a subconscious guiding impulse that in later years developed into the dominating influence in shaping my life." [24]

Today there is little impulse to smash machinery and there are probably few workers wishing themselves dead because they lack employment. But the reality that machinery can and does replace men still poses a serious threat to many American workers.

The automation problem has been catapulted into national prominence for a little more than a decade. To some, automation simply represents the intensified tempo of industrial change and poses few problems that were not inherent in the industrial revolution. Others insist that new phrases are necessary to describe what is essentially a new process. Each day we hear more talk of automation, cybernetics, servomechanisms, analogue and digital computers, feedback mechanisms, and so on. As we learn of the seemingly endless capacities of machines to control, regulate, inspect, reject, even to " think " and " memorize," we can easily imagine a sort of science-fiction fantasy world created by this robot revolution, with the robot controlling man more than the man controls the robot. The Industrial Revolution was characterized by the application of power to machinery; automation is characterized by the application of electronic control devices to both power and machines. The Industrial Revolution was characterized by men making machines that in turn made machines; automation is characterized by men supervising machines which regulate the operation of other machines. It involves human supervision over the work of electronic brains which in turn harness and control mechanical muscles. Machines watch, control, operate, discriminate, count, inspect, gage, test. In the Industrial Revolution, man achieved a " cog " status in that he had to work *with* the machine and was in a very real sense *part* of the machine. Through automation, man liberates himself from this

[24] New York, E. P. Dutton & Co., 1943, pp. 4–5.

status. His function is to control the control mechanism, to feed information and instructions into machines by cards or tapes, and to stand by for mechanical breakdowns that may never come.

The phrase automation was coined by D. S. Harder of the Ford Motor Company to describe " the automatic handling of discrete parts between progressive processing operations." Whether we agree that this is simply a new phrase for an old process, automation is having widespread effects on our economy and labor-management relations. Automation operates in three separate (although not independent) areas: Automation can be thought of as the " Detroit " process of integrating machines with one another to provide a continuous flow of production " untouched by human hands." Relating the operation of one machine to another by the use of belts, hoses, and chutes in a preconceived and predetermined manner has been found to be particularly successful in the oil, flour-milling, and chemical industries. Machines are simply linked together into a continuous operation to provide a production *flow* rather than a simple " batch " of goods. This can be called " link " automation in that it involves the linking together of machine operations. For example, the General Electric appliance plant in Louisville has automatic conveyor lines which are part of an 8.5-mile system that eliminates moving heavy parts by hand in stove assembly operations.[25]

A second area of automation is " feedback " automation where electronic control mechanisms regulate the operations of the machine. Feedback mechanisms operate in the same way that a thermostat controls room temperature by affecting the operation of the furnace. They are sometimes likened to the closed circuit of the human nervous system. Feedback exists " when information about the output at one stage of a process is returned or fed back to an earlier stage so as to influence the process and hence change the output itself." [26] Feedback is thus a self-corrective mechanism, but designed to control a wide variety of factors such as temperature, speed, thickness, or any other tolerance required in the production process. A third type of automation can be called computer automation, for it involves the use of data-processing machinery. Computers are creating a revolution in the recording, tabulation and analysis of data. These devices are particularly significant for the office worker, for there seem to be few clerical tasks that these machines cannot handle with enormous rapidity. All three phases of automation have one feature in common: they substitute human operations with mechanical operations, human judgment and control with electronic judgment and control. They are, in effect, substitutes for human labor.

We see constant references to the miracles of production achieved by

[25] For photographs and discussion, see *Time* (March 19, 1956), pp. 98–106.
[26] Edgar Weinberg, " A Review of Automatic Technology," *Monthly Labor Review*, Vol. 78, No. 6 (June, 1955), p. 640.

these ingenious machines. Traditionally, the single lathe was operated by an individual, but now multiple lathes have been created, controlled by electronic gaging devices to provide workmanship to closer tolerances than was possible by human hands. The Cross Company has installed a "sectionized transfermatic," which is, in effect, a line of machine tools 350 feet long, performing 555 machining operations on engine cyclinder block castings.[27] Today dial telephones account for some 85 percent of all calls and close to 60 percent of all long-distance calls. The Bureau of Census is utilizing electronic data processing machinery to cut the costs of its current population surveys in half. Railroads are automatizing freight yard handling and the dispatching of freight cars. Mines are using longer, faster moving and larger capacity belts, sometimes dubbed "rubber railroads" to speed the shipment of materials. An automatic filling machine will package semisolid tins of baby food at the rate of 800 per minute. Even college professors have been haunted with the prospects of nationally televised lectures.

What is it that accounts for the widespread interest in automation? First, and most obvious, is the continuing scarcity of manpower and the related high labor costs (and inefficiency) related to this bottleneck in the production process. One employer estimated that for each $5,000 he invested in capital he could displace one worker. The profitability of such substitution depends, of course, on the relative cost as well as the relative performance of both the machine and the worker. One employer explains why he is anxious to make the substitution.

> Now men by definition are difficult and tricky things to play around with. You have to have employee-relations men, time-study men; you have training and educational directors; you have personnel men, washroom men, cafeteria men. That all costs money. My point is this: that if we could take some of the money that we are spending in trying to ease the pain of our assembly-line personnel, and apply that money for some research to get the men out of there entirely, we would be far better off in the long run.[28]

Like many labor-management issues there are two sides to the automation question too. Let us briefly look at some of the major advantages it provides. Most significant, automation promises rather substantial increases in labor productivity. No labor official has gone on record opposing technological development, for everyone appreciates that higher living standards can only be achieved by increased output. If per capita productivity for nonfarm employment increased from 2 to 3 percent,

[27] Edgar Weinberg, "An Inquiry into the Effects of Automation," *Monthly Labor Review*, Vol. 79, No. 1 (January, 1956), p. 6.
[28] Statement by Dr. J. J. Brown in *Fortune* and quoted by Robert Bendiner, "The Age of the Thinking Robot, and What It Will Mean to Us," *The Reporter* (April 7, 1955), p. 15.

this would provide for an addition of $54 billion by 1965, or an increment of income on a per capita basis of more than $287 in that year. Both labor and management are lyrical in picturing potential improvements, but labor usually stresses that sustained improvements are only possible as long as markets are available to absorb the increased output. This, in turn, is contingent upon labor receiving a " fair share " of increased industry revenues. Productivity gains may be granted by lowering prices or by raising wages or a combination of both methods; either could give labor the increase in real wages it desires. It is also argued that unemployment need not be a serious problem, for like all technology a host of secondary or complementary investments are built up to support innovations. In other words, one innovation will encourage a pattern of others, which in turn expands the over-all demand for labor. Displacement in one industry is usually associated with expanding employment opportunities in other industries.[29] Many fears arise simply because of the facility of measuring the volume of displaced labor and the relative difficulty of measuring the opportunity for expanded employment opportunities elsewhere.

Another advantage of considerable interest to labor is the opportunities automation provides for reducing the length of the work week. But one authority on automation cautions against regarding automation as the " panacea for all troubles culminating in the seven day weekend." [30] It is further argued that automation will result in the general upgrading of the labor force as new labor skills are demanded. Workers will be required to acquire a cross-section knowledge of electronics and hydraulics, as well as basic mechanics, and with increased skill and responsibility will come higher pay.

Apart from these direct economic improvements, workers will be separated from the routine and unhealthy aspects of industrial manufacture. They will more likely be separated from noxious fumes, from dangerous materials, and enjoy increased safety and reduced strain and tension on the job.[31]

Management, too, will be less tied to the population centers in plant location, for they will have less need to recruit large numbers of workers. With the mobility of power (such as piped gas) and with limited but highly specialized manpower requirements, new plants can be located away from the heavily industrialized centers.

[29] For discussion of this point, see Gerry E. Morse's discussion of " Automation, Productivity and Industrial Relations," *Proceedings* of the Industrial Relations Research Association (December 28–30, 1954), pp. 139–141.

[30] John Diebold, " Integrating Automation into Our Economy," *Monthly Labor Review* (May, 1955), p. 526.

[31] For discussion of the health aspects of automation, see Dr. C. Richard Walmer, " Workers' Health in an Era of Automation," *Monthly Labor Review* (July, 1956), pp. 819–823.

But these advantages must be weighed against the problems of auto-mation, not the least of which is the general fear and anxiety of labor related to the uncertainty of its job status and function. Any innovation which threatens the source of livelihood, whatever its economic justifica-tion, is regarded with fear. Labor suffers " automation jitters " or the fear of machine displacement. It is true that as long as employment levels are generally high the problem of securing re-employment is not usually serious, but re-employment is more a reality after the fact than a cer-tainty before the fact, and this uncertainty leads to tensions and anxiety. Several companies — particularly insurance companies — which have in-stituted the use of electronic data processing machines, maintained con-stant and detailed communication with their work force regarding the nature of the change and the reasons for it. Employees were promised that there would be no downgrading or layoffs as a consequence of the change.[32] It is true that the basic motive for automation is to reduce labor cost, and the reality of labor displacement can hardly be avoided. But management hopes that such reduction of the work force can be absorbed by the normal attrition of the labor force. While this may be possible in a plant that does not hire additional workers, it hardly solves the prob-lem from the viewpoint of the economy as a whole when close to a mil-lion new workers each year must somehow secure useful employment.

It was suggested that the over-all impact of technology should not be a net reduction, but rather net increase in the demand for labor because of (a) the increase in the labor required to produce automated equip-ment and (b) the increase in the demand for labor to produce supporting or secondary capital. Fragmentary data and speculation have not been very reassuring. " Electronics output in 1952 was 275 per cent higher than in 1947, but was produced by only 40 per cent more workers." [33] And there is some suspicion that automation will not set in motion a wave of sec-ondary capital expansion. Walter S. Buckingham explains:

> Automation does not promise to create as much secondary investment as have some of the earlier developments in technology. The intro-duction of the automobile and the resulting increase in primary in-vestment in that industry stimulated a wave of investment in the oil, rubber, and construction sectors of the economy. In this respect, automation probably will not make the far-reaching investment im-pression on the economy that the introduction of and later improve-ments in automobiles, railroads, and canals, for example created.[34]

[32] See " Adjustments to Automation in Two Firms," *Monthly Labor Review*, Vol. 79, No. 1 (January, 1956), Case Study 2, and Wesley S. Bagby, " The Human Side of Electronics," *Systems Magazine* (July–August, 1956), pp. 13–14.

[33] BLS data cited by Bendiner, *op. cit.*, p. 17.

[34] " Industrial and Economic Implications of Automation," *Monthly Labor Review* Vol. 78, No. 5 (May, 1955), p. 521.

Other students have indicated the possibility of the creation of depressed areas arising from the sudden obsolescence of plant equipment because of innovations developed by competitors. Plants may be abandoned because of the competitive pressure these innovations make possible, working a serious hardship for pockets of the labor force. Labor fears too that more often than not automation will involve a downgrading rather than upgrading of labor, with lower rather than higher wages. The "middle class" within the occupational structures will disappear as demands for labor on both ends of the job skill scale increase. Unions too may face the impact of weakened bargaining power because of the changed attitude of the "semitechnical" worker, the splintering of industrial unions into smaller craft units as each technical group attempts to organize around its unique skills. Quarrels may develop over proper union jurisdiction as labor's "job mix" or job functions change. Furthermore, management will insist on more liberal interpretation of seniority clauses or wider units for labor force allocation to minimize layoffs, and such adjustments create thorny problems for both the union and management.

There is, however, no reason for panic in the face of automation. Changes are revolutionary, but they are made gradually. While some assert that the automated age is already with us, others point to the technical difficulties related to any wholesale reorganization of the production process. Detailed experiments must be undertaken. Many machines are tailor-made to perform specific functions. This often requires as much as five years (or even more) before a labor-saving device is put into operation. Many industries, especially the smaller ones, will be discouraged by the substantial costs of such equipment as well as the necessity of maintaining the constant flow of production. During a period of economic uncertainty broadening the base of fixed-capital charges may appear unnecessarily reckless, for any decline of demand with high "break-even" points could be disastrous. Furthermore, automation must overcome not only the resistance of the workers, but the resistance in the upper echelons of management. The reorganization of production often involves a reorganization of management, and middle management often resists change with as much determination as the workers themselves.

The time lag in installing such equipment provides management with an interval to pave the way for the equipment's introduction. Maintaining communications with the rank and file is most important. The union position has not been to resist these innovations, but that management plans these in such a way as to consider the "human equation," and to minimize dislocation. Labor urges that it receive higher pay to permit proportionate expansions of labor income with labor output. It stresses the importance of retraining, either on the job or in cooperation with local schools. It stresses the need for shorter hours to absorb the increased labor productivity in this way. It stresses the importance of extra consideration to the plight of the older worker who may have difficulty in securing re-employment. It strives for a lower retirement age, expanded unemployment compensation benefits, the implementation of the guaranteed annual wage, and dismissal pay. Finally, it is often suggested that the United States Employment Services be expanded to assist workers trapped by such technology. Subsidies might be given to workers for training, and to encourage mobility to other centers of expanding employment. One consideration stands above all others: the ability of the economy to absorb displaced labor depends on the over-all level of employment and the prospects for business expansion. The hardships of automation would become painfully apparent if the economy faced widespread unemployment.

Production Control and Make-Work Rules

Related to the problem of automation are the restraints exercised by the work force on total output. It has already been pointed out that workers themselves may resist working to optimum capacity because of inherent laziness. Or it may reflect a group-dictated behavior pattern — to win the approval and respect of the group, one must conform to the group-definition of a "fair day's work," and one violates such group values at his peril. Restrictions on output do not arise simply because of labor's spiteful or malicious nature but because of a well-grounded fear that they may work themselves out of a job. Such fears may seem groundless after two decades of high employment; however, they still have considerable force.

Production control and make-work devices often reflect labor's ingenuity. As the following newspaper account indicates, one German carpenter hoped to guarantee full employment for himself in a rather unusual way:

> *Bonn, West Germany, April 5, 1955* — A dead carpenter's device to keep himself in business still worries police and the fire brigade in the Mauerkirchen District near here, because it makes farm houses burn down with ominous regularity. The carpenter, Johann Bernhofer, hanged himself in a prison cell two years ago at the age of 77 after police had learned about his trick of building timing devices into houses, so they would burn down after a certain period. Bernhofer, according to police records, designed his device during the early 1930's because he feared the depression and slackening building activity might force him out of a job. In all chimneys he helped construct, he built in a panel of wood, which would burn through slowly and then expose a trigger that would fire the house.[35]

Sumner Slichter, in his definitive work, *Union Policies and Industrial Management,* has described nine principle "make-work" categories de-

[35] News item in *Los Angeles Times* (Wednesday, April 6, 1955).

veloped from time to time by unions:[36] (1) Limiting daily or weekly output; (2) indirectly limiting the speed of work; (3) controlling the quality of work; (4) requiring time-consuming methods of doing the work;
(5) requiring that unnecessary work be done or that work be done more
than once; (6) regulating the number of men in a crew or on a machine
or requiring the employment of unnecessary men; (7) requiring that the
work be done by members of a given skilled craft or occupation; (8) prohibiting employers or foremen from working at the trade; (9) retarding
or prohibiting the use of machines and labor-saving devices.

To what extent are these various alternatives explicitly incorporated
into the working rules, the agreements between labor and management?
The incidence of such " codes of ethics," " principles of conduct," " bylaws," or " codes to insure just protection " varies considerably from industry to industry, but they are more likely to be found in the seasonal
industries or where employment is unstable. A number of classic illus-
trations often receive publicity in the press so that it should not be necessary to catalog numerous examples of these restrictions and agreements.
From time to time, bricklayers were forbidden to lay bricks with both
hands or more than a certain maximum number of bricks per day; ap-
prenticed plumbers are often not allowed to use a journeyman's tools;
painters are sometimes limited in the size of their brushes and restricted
against the use of sprayers and rollers; longshoremen have been restricted
in the size of their slings in loading and unloading ships; carpenters have
been limited in the use of power tools; printers have insisted on the dupli-
cated setting of " bogus " matrices for advertising and other printed material; the musicians' union has on occasion insisted that broadcasting stations sending out recorded music or transmitting " live " musical programs
originating in other cities hire an orchestra to " stand by "; motion picture operators have demanded that two operators work for each projec-
tor; railroad unions have insisted on " full-crew " laws or that extra firemen be employed in diesels where the fireman has little if any function;
theatrical stage employees have required a minimum size crew for each
performance whether needed or not; painters have been required to work
over with dry brushes the seats, cabinets, and other articles already finished at the factory; electrical workers have refused to install switch-
boards or other wiring unless factory wiring was torn out and the whole
job redone by union electricians; and so on.[37] What are the effects of such
practices, regulations, and agreements? Do they offer genuine protection
against insecurity for the worker? Can they prevent employment from
decreasing in a declining industry?

Most of these measures increase the wage costs of business. Such pres-

[36] Washington, Brookings Institution, 1941.
[37] These several examples are drawn from Carroll R. Daugherty and John B.
Parrish, *The Labor Problems of American Society* (Boston, Houghton Mifflin Co.,
1952), pp. 347–350.

sure may induce (a) higher prices for the product and/or (b) further technological change in an effort to minimize the proportion of labor costs to total costs. In the first case, a portion of the incidence of the make-work rule is shifted to the consuming public. If consumers are particularly sensitive to price increases, or if they have alternative sources of supply, they are likely to cut down on the volume of consumption. It would follow that the employer would not be able to maintain his volume of production, and unemployment may result. Thus, the attempt on labor's part to increase or stabilize employment produces just the opposite result. If the demand for some product is particularly inelastic, labor can " hold up " the consumer via the price increase and secure some benefits. Or labor may " exploit " the other factors of production, *viz.*, management may be compelled to rebudget funds intended for other costs and divert them to meet the added labor costs. Such success may be temporary, and it is clear that in a declining industry the union is likely to be fighting a losing battle in insisting on make-work regulations. Make-work rules hasten, rather than postpone, the decline of the industry. In the railroads, for example, the determination of the union to maintain " full crews " and their reluctance to alter work rules which would economize on labor cost has intensified the decline of employment in that industry. The railroads face intensive competition from private trucks, private automobiles, buses, and airplanes. In effect, if the work rules reduce the company's ability to earn higher revenues, they reduce the company's ability to pay higher wages and sustain the level of employment.[38] In several industries workers have appreciated the competitive nature of the market and have understood that work rules which reduce labor efficiency or add to the wage bill unnecessarily are short-sighted. It can only be hoped that such understanding will become more general, and that the fear of unemployment will be much less justified by the continuing experience of high employment.

Hours of Work

Labor does not usually secure all of the gains of productivity in the form of higher real wages but divides the increment with increased leisure. Labor's drive for a shorter working day is as old as labor organization itself. The Puritan virtue of working 16 hours a day to strengthen

---

[38] H. D. Wolf in his study of "Railroads" in *How Collective Bargaining Works,* edited by H. A. Millis (New York, Twentieth Century Fund, 1945), points out that in 1938 train and engine service employees are shown as having been paid $452 million for 498 million hours. However, they are shown as having actually worked only 403 million hours, payment for which amounted to $366 million. Here is a difference of 95 million hours between those worked and those paid for, involving payment of $86 million. Wolf explains how this discrepancy is created by the various rules and regulations in the railroad industry for counting railroad labor time.

one's moral fiber came to be regarded with considerable suspicion, especially when the work was arduous and hazardous. Labor has based its claim for the 10-hour day, the 8-hour day, and more recently the 6-hour day (or 30-hour week) on the proposition that only through leisure could workers fully enjoy the fruits of their labor. In more recent times labor's interest in the shorter work week has been supported by the claims that it would (1) provide a greater opportunity to balance ever-expanding labor productivity with ever-expanding labor consumption; (2) provide labor with an opportunity to increase its education and training and enable management, the public, and the worker to profit from acquired skills; (3) increase the health of the worker (A worker with additional leisure is less likely to suffer fatigue on the job. This will contribute to industrial efficiency, cut down on accident rates, and increase the over-all occupational life-expectancy of the worker.); (4) attract additional workers into employment, including married women and students who will be better able to handle domestic and academic assignments along with full-time employment; (5) provide labor with the opportunities for dual employment (Many workers on a reduced work schedule may be able to handle two jobs.).

The ability of management to reduce the length of the work week without reducing income requires, of course, substantial improvement in labor productivity. Traditionally, management has opposed such work reduction because of the pressure it creates on industry costs. It was often argued that the profit management enjoyed was only secured during the "final hour" of labor's employment, the balance of the working day creating revenues necessary for meeting the other costs of production. To reduce the working day from 12 to 11 hours might, therefore, wipe out management profits and lead to the ruination of industry. Karl Marx pointed to the interest of employers in extending rather than contracting the work day as a device to increase the exploitation of the proletariat.

It has been estimated that for the past one hundred years labor has acquired about 50 percent of increased productivity in higher wages and the other 50 percent in increased leisure. From 1920 to 1950, however, the increment has favored higher wages, with about 60 percent of the productivity increment going to wages and about 40 percent to leisure.[39] The standard of the work week is more likely to be altered in spurts, reflecting a union drive for reduced hours, increased leisure arising from work-sharing during mass unemployment, and the less intensive utilization of manpower following wartime mobilization.

As we noted in Chapter 2, the reduction in the hours of work has been one of the major benefits of industrial technology; per capita living stand-

[39] Clark Kerr, in his discussion of Charles D. Stewart's paper, "Economic Growth: The Shortening Work Week as a Component of Economic Growth," *American Economic Review*, Papers, Vol. XLVI, No. 2 (May, 1956), pp. 218, 219.

ards have doubled for each generation even though, over the last one hundred years, the length of the work day has been cut almost in half. Current proposals to establish a work week of 4 days are often greeted with grim foreboding. It is feared that such a move might cut down the efficiency of the worker and dangerously increase the costs of industry. The substantial cost burden will not be confined only to those firms with a high wage bill. It will be serious where industry has invested heavily in capital. When such heavy investment requires continuous operations, the 4-day week may require the employment of staggered shifts which, in turn, often involve premium pay. Or if labor secures the 6-hour day (and machinery must be utilized on a round-the-clock basis to justify its purchase) management must then hire three premium-pay shifts rather than two, as well as absorb the considerable costs in setting-up time and other delays arising when a new shift takes over from the old.

Such considerations as these have proven effective obstacles to the reduction of the work week in the past. As late as 1923, the steel industry was operating with a " 13 out of 14 " system, with labor getting one day off every two weeks and working from 10 to 12 hours per day. We noted the clamor that arose when Henry Ford introduced the 5-day week in the automobile industry in 1926: His move was considered a violation against the laws of economics and God's admonition to labor 6 days and rest on the Sabbath. Looking back over our economic history, industry was generally operating on a 10-hour day by the end of the nineteenth century, and the 8-hour day became widespread during World War II. The next major break came with the great depression, when employers often took the initiative in reducing the length of the work week in order to share limited job opportunities. The reduction of the work week, in this setting was not usually associated with constancy of weekly earnings. In 1938 the Fair Labor Standards Act established the 40-hour work week as normal and required that employers pay time-and-a-half for overtime. During World War II the actual working hours per week rapidly climbed to 48, and the existence of the 40-hour norm for labor permitted many workers to enjoy substantial overtime increments in their take-home income. Today, the 40-hour week is again the standard of actual work hours in most industry.

In recent years the discussion of the 4-day week (or 30-hour week) has gained considerable attention. In the heat of the presidential campaign in 1956 Vice-President Nixon declared that the 4-day week could be a reality for labor in the not too distant future. Walter Reuther has gone on record as saying that the reduction of the work week would be the next major bargaining target of the United Automobile Workers, and several union spokesmen have expressed similar interest in additional leisure. More often than not, these pronouncements evolve from conferences and conventions of unions concerned with technology and automation. The wage policy boards of many nationals have placed demands for increased leisure at the top or near the top of the agenda for future bargaining sessions.

But, as we noted above, the capacity of industry to absorb the reduction in the length of the work week, along with stability (or increased) weekly earnings, depends on the rate of growth of labor productivity. In order to examine the cost incidence of increased leisure, let us take the existing hours and weekly earnings in manufacturing during 1955. Dividing the actual hours into actual earnings reveals average hourly earnings. The following scale suggests by how much average hourly earnings must increase if the length of the work week is reduced while total weekly earnings are constant:

TABLE 13   Effect on Hourly Earnings in Manufacturing When Work Week Is Reduced But Weekly Earnings Held Constant

	Average Weekly Hours	Gross Weekly Earnings	Average Hourly Earnings	Index of Hourly Wage Increase When Weekly Earnings Constant
1955:	40.7	$76.52	$1.88	100
With Weekly Hours:	40		1.91	101.6
	39		1.96	104.2
	38		2.01	106.9
	37		2.07	111.2
	36		2.13	113.3
	35		2.19	116.5
	34	(constant)	2.25	119.7
	33		2.32	123.4
	32		2.39	127.1
	31		2.47	131.4
	30		2.55	135.6

In Table 13 hours are reduced from the 1955 level of 40.7 to 30. As the smaller number of hours is divided into the gross weekly earnings of $76.52 for 1955, it is possible to determine the increase in average hourly earnings necessary to keep gross weekly earnings at the 1955 level. In the final column, the increase in the hourly earnings level is provided in an index form, with 1955 = 100. It can now be seen that a reduction of the work week to 30 hours, all other things being equal, involves an increase of some 67 cents per average hourly earnings, or an increase of 35.6 percent of earnings above the 1955 level. If such a reduction in hours were to be accomplished over a 10-year period, it would require an annual increase in hourly wages of from 5 to 8 cents per hour. Such an adjustment could probably be absorbed by productivity increases, but the "average" productivity gains for manufacturing should not obscure the widely varied productivity experience for particular manufacturing firms. It should be remembered, too, that unions are not likely to be content with stable weekly earnings. Obviously, a demand for both increased leisure and income will compound the cost pressure for industry.

Organized labor is not unaware of these realities, and there is considerable discussion of alternative methods for increasing leisure. It has been suggested, for example, that labor might prefer to work 4 days a week, but 10 hours per day. This has the advantage of reducing weekly commuting time, a considerable element in such areas as Los Angeles. But studies suggest that labor productivity drops off sharply beyond the 8-hour limit. It has also been proposed that labor might work 7 hours (and ultimately 6 hours) a day for 5 days a week, but again management points out that the set-up time may prevent a worker from making a sufficiently substantial contribution in any 6-hour day. A third alternative is to extend the length of week-ends, perhaps on an every-other-month basis, and more frequently as labor productivity permits. Or it may be possible to extend the total length of vacations with pay from 2 to 3 or 4 weeks, and in some cases to 8 weeks. On January 19, 1957, David J. McDonald suggested to the Western Regional Conference of his United Steelworkers Union that they negotiate for a 3-month paid vacation, to be granted to production workers every 5 years, in addition to regular vacation benefits. Such a scheme, McDonald affirmed, would serve as a brake against "machines replacing workers." [40] A moment's contemplation will suggest the infinite number of ways in which increased leisure could be offered to workers.

The contemplation of the delights of increased leisure will undoubtedly gestate into concrete plans in the near future. But such an interest does not overshadow the persistent interest of labor in higher pay, and it is not likely that labor will sacrifice earnings for leisure if ever confronted with the need to choose between the two. Indeed, the interest in leisure cannot be taken as evidence of labor's lack of interest in higher pay. The reduction in the length of the work week during a time of labor scarcity will force management to resort, increasingly, to overtime labor service, and such overtime pay will provide labor with a welcomed bonus to regular earnings. Within the next 10 to 15 years labor will certainly secure advances in this direction. Granted continuing high employment, labor will have the bargaining power to secure some concessions, especially if productivity and price adjustments enable management to make such concessions without impairing profits. If, in the unlikely event our economy should face a serious recession, labor will turn to the government for legislation to reduce the "normal" work week as a device to minimize the incidence of unemployment.

It can be seen that the prospects for increased leisure have innumerable ramifications, some economic, others social. Some sociologists have ex-

[40] As reported in the *Los Angeles Times* (January 20, 1957), p. 18.

pressed a little apprehension about the possible repercussions of having the " man of the house " home for 3 days a week. It is possible that some workers will be able to take on additional part-time work or even hold down two full-time jobs. Housewives and students may be better able to participate in the labor force on a full-time basis because of the reduced demands a 30-hour week would make on their time. Beyond these considerations, the reduction in working hours will probably do much to take the sting out of working. Labor sociologist Nelson N. Foote describes the "junior welfare state" that many corporations represent:

> There is already a profusion of such on-the-job benefits which apply mainly to executive and white-collar ranks but are spreading rapidly downward. Executive development programs, conferences, coffee breaks, " economic education," house publications and industrial recreation illustrate their range. And the growth of high life on the expense account illustrates the amount of money they can soak up. The line between work and play on the job get's dimmer every year.[41]

Our discussion in this chapter has covered several of the diverse items appearing on the collective bargaining agenda. Interest in all such topics does not, of course, characterize all bargaining sessions. The changing " package " of demands made by labor reflects the strategy of union leaders to fire the imagination of the rank and file with concessions not yet contemplated. It is also designed to keep management on the defensive, to have it fight only a rear-guard action in the face of steady union pressure for " more." The success unions have in securing their bargaining goals does not only reflect the merit of their demands, but the underlying persuasiveness of union power. With this sampling of bargaining topics, let us turn to the strategy of the bargaining process.

[41] Nelson N. Foote, discussion on " The Shortening Work Week as a Component of Economic Growth," *American Economic Review*, Papers, Vol. XLVI, No. 2 (May, 1956), p. 228.

13

Power and the
Bargaining Process

George Bernard Shaw once remarked that to most Americans, there were few problems that could not be solved with a well-placed "sock on the jaw." Certainly most of us enjoy the conviction that ultimately right must make might, that injustice carries with it the seeds for its own destruction. However implicit in our philosophy is the power play between good and evil, justice does not triumph through a Gandhian tactic of passive resistance but through the mobilized power of aroused individuals intent on securing justice. In labor-management relations, too, the strike represents the "sock on the jaw." The force of evil is pitted against the force of good, and, needless to say, each side is anxious to establish the virtue of its position or to pose as "the good guy." It must not be thought, however, that the use of economic coercion is a novel phenomenon confined only to labor-management relations. It has its roots in early civilizations and is common throughout the world today. Nor is striking confined to production workers alone, for in the past strikes have been undertaken by such as hangmen, fishermen, football players, undertakers, geisha girls, and teachers.

In this chapter we shall review the elements that contribute to this coercive power in labor-management relations. We shall briefly view the freedom to strike as a device to encourage peaceful settlement and then analyze some of the more important determinants of the bargaining power as well as some of the more important causes of strikes. Our chapter will conclude with historical data on strikes, together with a brief discussion of the manner in which such strike data has correlated with prosperity and depression.

The Strike

Strikes, in the public mind, are often thought to be the outburst of unrestrained or undisciplined workers or the conspiracies of ruthless union leaders. Whatever their source, they are thought to be essentially negative and destructive in their impact. While it must be admitted that a strike is injurious, this should not obscure the utility of the freedom to strike. Collective bargaining cannot be free when parties to that process do not have the right to disagree with each other. It is precisely because a stalemate can be injurious that the strike represents a force conducive to agreement and compromise. The more frightful the costs of disagreement, the more impelling are the reasons for searching for a working compromise.[1] By analogy, in international relations the notion has gained ground that there is no alternative to peace, for the destruction of nuclear warfare is unthinkable. Ironically, it is when both parties are unable to test their relative strengths by a show of force that disagreements are accentuated. Stated in terms of labor and management, when the government restricts the freedom of labor and management to disagree with each other, relations often become more disagreeable.[2]

A further utility of the strike is that it may "clear the air." It is impossible to determine precisely how much good has been accomplished by such strike action, just as it would be to determine the benefits of international conflict. A continuing domestic cold war can exact frightful costs from both industry and the worker that a strike might avoid. While

[1] In the succinct statement by Bakke and Kerr, it is explained: "Implicit in the whole process [of collective bargaining] is the ultimate resort to force. Nearly all bargaining takes place under the implicit if not explicit threat of a strike or a lockout. The threat of warfare, backed by both the ability and willingness to fight, is the primary bargaining weapon of each side. The alternative of no bargain at all is constantly before the parties. The final question asked is whether it is better to settle at a specific figure than to fight. The greater the relative capacity of a party to fight, the greater the relative capacity to bargain to a conclusion acceptable to that party. The results of the process depend on how iron the hand as well as how silken the glove." From *Unions, Management, and the Public* (New York, Harcourt, Brace and Co., 1948), p. 354. In somewhat more emphatic terms, Charles Gregory makes the same point: "The backbone of collective bargaining has always been economic coercion, which includes union recourses like strikes, boycotts, and picketing, as well as employer recourses like shutdowns, lockouts and farming out work. Naturally a good deal of collective bargaining takes place around a conference table, but those who believe that such parliamentary procedure is all there is to collective bargaining are just kidding themselves. Possibly the word 'bargaining' is a misleading term for this whole process, and terms like 'hold up' or 'starve out' may be more accurate." From *Labor and the Law* (New York, W. W. Norton and Co., 1949), p. 387.

[2] This problem becomes more obvious when a government nationalizes an industry. In Communist nations, for example, strikes are often described as "counterrevolutionary" activities. In Britain's nationalized industries one Yorkshire miner observed: "Union leaders are in the unenviable position, after years of 'boss-bashing,' in which the miner was always right, of having to prove to their members that the boss can be, and now almost always is, right." The Secretary of the Trades Union Congress suggested in a 1947 broadcast that when the consultative machinery was perfected in nationalized industries, the question of strike action would become "almost entirely theoretical." The identification of union leadership with company management does not eliminate the problem of disagreement; it may actually aggravate it. Workers may strike against both the company *and* their union leadership. For discussion, see K. G. J. C. Knowles, *Strikes: A Study in Industrial Conflict* (Oxford, Basil Blackwell, 1952), Chapter 2, Section IV, pp. 90–98.

justifying strikes for this reason may be considered analogous to indulging the child in his tantrum (on the assumption that he will be a better-
adjusted child after the experience), there can be no doubt that in many
situations the strike serves as a safety valve, and that after the strike,
workers return to their jobs with a fresh perspective on the importance
of their income and the importance of getting along with management.
Finally, the strike can be justified as a legitimate expression of a legitimate freedom. The right to work, as we indicated earlier, exists only
when the worker has the freedom *not* to work. Legislation and restrictions on such freedom are always exposed to the hazard that they may be
ignored. The police power of the state must be careful not to reveal its
own impotence.

While the American public does sanction the use of force to rectify
serious abuses or grievances, it does not approve of the use of force for
its own sake. In this sense, it is distinctly hostile to the party who is trying to " pick a fight." Thus in labor-management relations the issue as to
who takes the initiative in the use of economic coercion profoundly
affects the direction of public support. Are strikes taken at labor's initiative more common than lockouts taken at management's initiative? Who,
in other words, initiates most industrial conflict?

A strike is a concerted action on the part of labor to quit work in order
to interrupt or delay the employer's flow of production. A lockout, in
contrast, is action initiated by management in which workers are refused
admittance to the plant because of their refusal to accept the terms management suggested for continued employment. Initially the Bureau of Labor Statistics attempted to differentiate between strikes and lockouts, but
such classifications tended to become nonoperational. If an impasse in
negotiations is reached, management often confronts the workers with
a " take it or leave it " proposition. If the work force elects to " leave "
the offer, a strike is called. Regardless of the substantive issue involved,
the initiative to quit work is usually taken by labor. Even if a walkout is
management-inspired, it is still commonly considered a labor strike, and
unions have often protested that the responsibility for such strike action
is unfairly laid at labor's doorstep. The *appearance* is established that labor is the aggressor, that management is striving to keep the peace. The
fact that more often than not management is content with the *status quo*
means that unions are always exposed to the charge of being the " dis-
turbers of the peace."

Such anti-strike sentiment has understandably been supported by management. In 1903 David M. Parry, former president of the National Association of Manufacturers, explained: " The spirit of the mob has
brooded over the country during the last year as it has never brooded before, and in looking for the cause I ask you not to overlook the labor agitator, the chief ranter against law and the worst firebrand of anarchy

with which we are now afflicted." [3] Organized labor had to learn and re-spect this fear of violence before unionism could be accepted. Gompers devoted much of his energy to impress upon the American public the respectability and peaceful intent of the organized labor movement. He explained: "Language fails me to express how earnest are the organized laborers in their desire to avoid and to reduce the number of strikes." [4] So obvious was the loss incurred by strikes that in the Commissioner of Labor's Third Annual Report of 1887 tables were provided indicating not only the number of strikes, but the number of days required, at increased wages, to recover the loss of income during the strike.

While the public is fascinated by the drama that unfolds with a power play, it cannot sanction the resort to force when efforts have not been made to find peaceful solutions to differences. The view is commonly held that the very survival quality of democratic institutions rests on the ability of reasoning men to reach reasonable (and peaceful) solutions to their differences. In this context the strike is seen as a return to the law of the jungle. The morality of our society rejects the use of force when its application arises, in turn, from the rejection of reason, or the rejec-tion of principles that would make dispute settlement possible. It is often difficult, however, to find peaceful alternatives to the use of force within the framework of established principles of labor-management relations simply because the principles themselves are frequently at issue in the dispute. Stated in another way, it is often difficult to make reference to the rules of the game in settling disputes peacefully when the rules them-selves may be an issue causing disagreement. [5]

The relationship between power and freedom has always posed chal-lenging philosophical issues and thorny practical problems for society. A

---

[3] Quoted by Griffin, *Strikes, a Study in Quantitative Economics* (New York, Co-lumbia University Press, 1939), p. 89, from Parry's speech "Mob Spirit and Organized Labor," in an address delivered at Chautauqua, New York, August 13, 1903.

[4] Quoted by E. T. Hiller, *The Strike* (Chicago, University of Chicago Press, 1928), p. 212.

[5] Cyrus Ching pointed out that some of the bitterest controversies in collective bar-gaining arise over the question of principle itself. He declared: "Don't be so darned sure you're right; be careful about taking positions on 'matters of principle.' By standing on so-called principle, labor and management have cost the American econ-omy many millions of dollars in strikes and lost production over the years. A lot of things that once were thought to be principles are found later not to be principles at all, but merely obstacles in the path of developing proper collective bargaining rela-tionships. There are, of course, some which should be strictly adhered to. But Dr. Hadley, one-time president of Yale, once said that he had found that 'principles' with most people were merely re-arrangements of their prejudices." (*Review and Reflections*, New York, B. C. Forbes & Sons Publishing Co., 1953, pp. 167–168.) As the Webbs observed in 1890: "In the really crucial instances – the issues relating to the conclusion of a new agreement – habitual and voluntary recourse to an umpire may be expected, we think, only in the unlikely event of capitalists and workmen adopting identical assumptions as to the proper basis of wages." *Industrial Democracy* (London, Longmans, Green, 1902), p. 237.

few statements from some of our more thoughtful citizens reveal the nature of these issues. On the one hand, we have the position taken by Justice Holmes (in a letter to Sir Frederick Pollock): "As between two groups, each equally convinced with the righteousness of its own cause, I see no ultimate arbitrament but force." In a tactical sense, the determination of only *one* party in a dispute not to use force (while the other appears ready to use it) obviously weakens its bargaining power. Furthermore, the willingness to resort to force is often interpreted as the measure of the one's conviction in the justice of his cause. Taking a rather deterministic view, Justice Holmes suggested that the "test of truth is its ability to establish itself in the competition of the market." A contrasting view is offered by Donald Richberg:

> The proposition that economic justice cannot be obtained except by leaving men free to coerce and intimidate one another is absurd on its mere statement. If force must be the final arbiter of any dispute, then the underlying principle of a civilized society compels us to establish a *public* force controlled by a *public* law as the arbiter and to prohibit the use of *private* force and the application of any *private* law to dictate the decision.[6]

We must not slip into the easy position that we can safely deprive private pressure groups of their freedom to pursue their own interests as best they can. This temptation must be resisted for public regulation is not always an effective substitute for private force.

We must, however, continue to sanction the use of "reason" and "compromise" in the give and take of the bargaining session, or those alternatives to the use of force. Alfred North Whitehead stated:

> The worth of men consists in their liability to persuasion. . . . Civilization is the maintenance of social order by its own inherent persuasiveness as embodying the nobler alternative. The recourse to force, however unavoidable, is a disclosure of the failure of civilization either in the general society or in a remnant of individuals.[7]

Our argument here is only that the freedom to *apply* force provides an impelling motive to both labor and management to "keep the peace." This value is described by William H. Davis in the following terms:

> . . . in the last fifteen minutes of big controversies it is the right to strike or the threat of a strike, the possibility of a strike, that is the instrument with which the controversy is settled. It is always present at the conference table. It is the thing that puts a limit on unreason

---

[6] *Industrial Disputes and the Public Interest* (Berkeley, Institute of Industrial Relations, University of California, 1947), p. 60.

[7] Quoted by William H. Davis, "Collective Bargaining and Economic Progress," from *Industrial Disputes and the Public Interest* (Berkeley, Institute of Industrial Relations, University of California, 1947), pp. 8, 9.

and it is the thing that holds the parties in the last fifteen minutes to the full responsibility of making their own decisions. And without that responsibility you do not have collective bargaining.[8]

In effect then, the freedom to disagree represents a check against unreasonableness, and encourages us to accept that " nobler alternative " of persuasiveness.

The Determinants of Bargaining Power

Basically, the relative power of labor compared with that of management depends on the importance of continuing cooperation of each party. Management offers labor an income, and labor offers management its labor service. Both are equally necessary to the continuous flow of production, but labor's need for employment and income may not necessarily balance management's need for labor. It is in this concept of *relative* need that we find the basic determinant of power.

Several formulations have been developed to describe the content of such relative power. In one formulation the bargaining power of labor is said to be the need of management for the labor service minus labor's need for employment. If labor's need is greater than management's, management has superior bargaining power. In somewhat more refined terms, the " net " bargaining power of labor is determined by the following formulations:

$$\begin{array}{c}\text{Labor's}\\\text{Bargaining}\\\text{Power}\end{array} = \left[\begin{array}{c}\text{Labor's Desire}\\\text{for Leisure}\end{array} \; plus \; \begin{array}{c}\text{Management's Desire}\\\text{for Labor's}\\\text{Service}\end{array}\right] \; less$$

$$\left[\begin{array}{c}\text{Management's}\\\text{Desire}\\\text{to Reduce}\\\text{Wage Payments}\end{array} \; plus \; \begin{array}{c}\text{Labor's}\\\text{Desire}\\\text{for}\\\text{Wage Payments}\end{array}\right]$$

In this context a labor force that was subsidized during a strike (so that it could well afford to be idle) and not anxious to secure re-employment would have superior bargaining power, especially if management were desperately anxious to secure the re-employment of labor and had abundant funds for such purposes. Or conversely, management's bargaining power would be maximum if labor had little stomach for enforced idleness, was desperately anxious for income, and if management were indifferent about re-employment of labor and treasured rather highly those revenues which might otherwise be paid out to labor. Of course, relations are not likely to be characterized by these extreme conditions, but rather by the subtle combinations of these needs.[9]

[8] *Ibid.*, p. 12.

[9] These considerations are developed from formulations provided in Alfred Kuhn's interesting analysis, *Labor, Institutions and Economics* (New York, Rinehart & Co., 1956), pp. 129–130.

FIGURE 11. Relative Bargaining Power Between Labor and Management: The Union and Management Cost of Agreeing Compared to Their Cost of Disagreeing

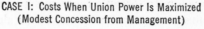

CASE I: Costs When Union Power Is Maximized
(Modest Concession from Management)

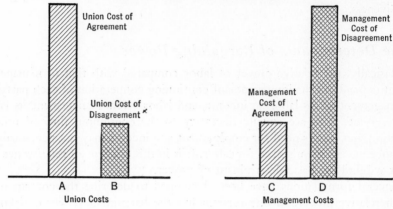

CASE II: Costs When Management Power Is Maximized
(Generous Concession from Management)

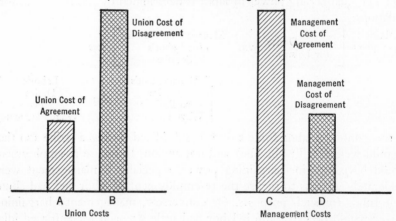

Probably a more direct way of viewing the power balance is to determine the relative "costs" to labor and management of not agreeing with each other, relative to the costs that arise when they do agree. Power is, in this sense, determined by the damage that one party can impose on the other as a consequence of the stalemate. But a certain cost or damage may also arise as a consequence of the agreement. The union leadership may face the charge that they "sold out" to management in not securing more; management may face the cost of a higher wage bill. Bargaining power evolves, then, from the relative costs of disagreement for each side, relative to their costs of agreement. The complex of costs will depend on the content of the proposed settlement, and it will be seen that the more generous the company offer, the stronger management's bargaining power and the weaker is the union. The more niggardly the offer, the stronger will be the union's bargaining position.

In Figure 11 some hypothetical union and management costs of agreeing and disagreeing to a particular wage settlement are suggested. Such costs may not always lend themselves to precise calculation, but whether measurable or not, the consequences of accepting or not accepting any package settlement must be carefully weighed at the conference table.

The analysis may be refined by viewing additional cost ratios. Table 14 indicates several situations in which union bargaining power would be maximized:

TABLE 14   Maximization of *Union* Bargaining Power

Figure 11 Designations	Ratio	Size of Ratio for Maximum Union Power
A/B:	$\dfrac{\text{Union cost of agreeing}}{\text{Union cost of disagreeing}}$	High ratio provides maximum union bargaining power.
C/D:	$\dfrac{\text{Company cost of agreeing}}{\text{Company cost of disagreeing}}$	Low ratio provides maximum union bargaining power.
A/C:	$\dfrac{\text{Union cost of agreeing}}{\text{Company cost of agreeing}}$	High ratio provides maximum union bargaining power.
B/C:	$\dfrac{\text{Union cost of disagreeing}}{\text{Company cost of disagreeing}}$	Low ratio provides maximum union bargaining power.
$\dfrac{\text{A/B}}{\text{C/D}}$:	$\dfrac{\text{Union cost of agreeing/disagreeing}}{\text{Company cost of agreeing/disagreeing}}$	High ratio provides maximum union bargaining power.

In order to reduce the abstraction of this analysis to more concrete terms, let us review some costs facing labor and management.

A. *Union Cost of Agreement*

1. The prestige of the union bargaining committee and leadership may be weakened greatly if the final settlement is much less than what the rank and file expected.
2. The effectiveness of the union in future bargaining sessions may be weakened if the union agrees to wholesale concessions on its part after making initial high demands.
3. The prestige of management may be much increased if it has willingly complied with wage demands. The credit given to the union may be weakened if it appears the union was pushing its way through an open door in getting concessions.

4. The work force may be lulled into a false sense of security. A peaceful settlement of the issue may reduce labor's militancy and conceivably weaken labor's bargaining power in subsequent negotiations.
5. The morale of the work force may be reduced because the concession pattern may not conform to the pattern gained by other unions or by other workers or may not compensate for changes in living costs, productivity, and so on.

Such costs may appear rather nebulous, and many are more likely to concern union leadership rather than the rank and file. If the union has not been able to keep pace with the general pattern of wage concessions, this may signal the restless minority into action. A competing faction within the union may make an appeal for new leadership.

B. *Union Cost of Disagreement*

1. The cost measured in terms of the loss of wages during the strike.
2. The cost represented by the deterioration of public relations between the union and the public. As other industries in the area are affected, charges of union " irresponsibility " are likely to increase.
3. The cost of growing bitterness in labor-management relations. The strike may cause management to stiffen its attitude toward organized labor. If the conciliatory attitude by management led to a strike, management may conclude it is the wiser strategy to display firmness.
4. The cost of loss of union membership. If unemployment continues, workers may drift into other jobs. Workers may drop their union membership or delay payment of union dues because of insufficient income.
5. The hazards of competitive unions. Another union or new elements within the old union may charge that the leadership had bungled negotiations, leading to the current strike.
6. The cost of restrictive government legislation. The government may actually intervene in the strikes. In a national emergency it may provide for injunctive relief or a " cooling-off " period. Strikes encourage anti-labor legislation.
7. The cost to the individual workers in resuming operations. The loss of business to the company may reduce the ability of the workers to secure subsequent benefits. It may take several months or even years before the company might hope to regain its present competitive position.
8. The deterioration of plant relations. When work is resumed, much hostility may characterize plant relations; the strike may leave a heritage of bitterness, reflecting itself in low plant morale and productivity.

To this list can be added a rather endless series of indirect repercussions. On the other hand, the employer too faces the problem of minimizing his burdens either by accepting the inevitability of the strike, or providing for a concession to labor which would prevent such a walkout.

C. *Company Cost of Agreement*

1. The increment to the wage bill. Actually, this increment will depend on employment policy. The wage bill may be less because of the need to reduce the size of the work force. The added cost may also reflect itself in higher per unit labor costs. If the company attempts to pass some of the increment of the wage cost on to the consuming public, the company must then determine whether the total value of sales will be higher after the wage increase.
2. Problems related to pressure by stockholders and the board of directors. If the wage pressure results in a reduction of profit volumes, managerial decisions may be challenged by the board of directors. The earnings position of the industry may be affected, with long-run consequences on the capacity of the corporation to float new stock issues and reduce its ability to attract venture capital.
3. The strengthened prestige of the union. If the concession results from determined union pressure, the wage increase may be viewed by the workers as the consequence of successful and united union activity. As the prestige of the union is strengthened, the company may find itself confronted with even more consolidated union bargaining pressure in subsequent negotiations.
4. Social problems may be created for employers within the industry if one employer appears more liberal in his wage concessions than others.

D. *Company Cost of Disagreement*

1. The loss of revenues during the period of interrupted production.
2. The permanent loss of customers to competitors during the strike.[10]
3. The ill-will created within the work force during the strike period resulting in inefficiency, low morale, and even sabotage with the return to employment.[11]
4. The injury to public relations within the consuming community and within the working community. The publicity given to unrest may

---

[10] The loss of both customers and revenues may be minimized if the employer succeeds in farming out work to other employers. Or if he can continue to supply the market from inventory, the cost of disagreement is greatly minimized.

[11] The union increases the pressure for management concessions by indicating the nature of labor force expectations and the consequences if these expectations are disappointed. As Alfred Kuhn explains, "Some union leaders have exploited this factor, trading good will for a fat concession, only to repossess the good will in time for the next session of bargaining." The extent to which the union can induce high and low morale is, however, limited: ". . . good will cannot be turned on and off indefinitely, because the union's alternate exhortations to its members first to love and then to hate the company will meet diminishing returns." *Op. cit.,* p. 132.

stigmatize the product somewhat, especially in the eyes of union members.

5. Injury to plant machinery and equipment. This is possible through enforced idleness and inadequate attention to maintenance.

6. The possibility of government seizure and repressive government legislation, limiting the freedom of employers in dealing with labor-management problems.

Again, this list is far from complete, but it reflects some of the problems confronting management. The interpretation given by management to labor's demands will depend, of course, on the size and implications of those demands. For example, issues which are seen as an invasion of management prerogatives are often subject to bitter dispute, not because of their immediate increment of cost or inconvenience to management, but because they set a dangerous precedent which may, in the long run, dangerously weaken management's freedom to manage.

We may now contrast our hypothetical costs in Figure 11 by contrasting Case I with Case II. In Case I a rather small concession is made by the company. Because of its size, the union's cost of agreeing to it is greatly increased. Accepting it would be a blow to union prestige and to labor's faith in the efficacy of its union. Indeed, the minor concession may become a stimulus for union unity and action or is seen as proof that a strike is necessary. The company, on the other hand, will find that the cost of agreeing to a modest wage increase is not serious, but the likely cost of a prolonged strike is. Modest concessions, considering all variables, are likely to shift the balance of bargaining power to labor.

The appraisal of management's concession will depend in part on the original bargaining goal of the union. Union leadership faces two problems: the resistance from above, or management's desire to offer as little as possible, and the push from below, or the demands of the membership to get as much as possible. It is possible that the union leadership will try to minimize both pressures by formulating demands that will simplify its task. The economy of effort can only be realized when workers have modest expectations. The more ambitious the demands of the union, the greater the cost to it of failure, and the greater the incentive for management to cause that failure.[12]

[12] This point is made by Lloyd Reynolds: "Union leaders probably follow the principle of economy of effort in pressing for wage increases. There is no indication that they try to get much above the minimum which they judge necessary to keep the members satisfied with the union and its present leadership. There is no indication that they try to maximize the wage level, the wage bill, or any other quantity. The reason may be that, as the size of the wage demand increases, employer resistance grows steadily while the added advantages *to the union as an organization* diminish. Union leaders must make an implicitly marginal calculation of the point at which they should stop." (*The Structure of Labor Markets, Wages and Labor Mobility in Theory and Practice*, New York, Harper & Bros., 1951, p. 236.) Within our conceptual framework, the union will attempt to secure a wage which will minimize both its cost of agreement and the company's cost of agreement.

On the other hand, if management makes a generous offer and is only a cent or so apart from the union's original demand, the enthusiasm for a strike will, for that reason, be much diminished. Management will have acted in good faith. Furthermore, the increment of income that might be secured through a prolonged strike is hardly significant. The public may feel that union negotiators have been unreasonable and arbitrary. The possibility of a strike becomes a popular target for criticism not only by management but by the workers themselves. The cost of disagreement by the union is increased just as the cost of disagreement for the company is reduced, for the company will pay heavily even in the absence of the strike. Thus, the refusal by the union of the last generous offer of the company may be construed as good reason for the company to meet the union head-on with force. In making a generous offer, then, the balance of bargaining power is likely to shift from labor to management. This preliminary outline of the determinants of bargaining power provides us with a framework for analyzing the implications of the length of the strike, the types of strikes, and also the chance for success of various strikes.

The Duration of the Strike and Bargaining Power

As the duration of a strike is extended, it is likely that workers will suffer much more than management. Usually the individual worker has less financial reserves and less opportunity to live on credit. The continuing family demand for sustenance cannot be ignored as sources of income and credit dry up. Many strikes collapse as soon as the Christmas season approaches as the pressure for an income is then overwhelming. The recent growth of consumer credit further complicates labor's position in a war of attrition, for labor's fixed costs in retiring multiple obligations imposes immediate pressure on the family should there be any reduction or loss of income. The employer, on the other hand, is better able to withstand the strike, for after the initial adjustment the burden of continuing strike action may not grow appreciably. Hence, unless there is a relatively quick settlement, the opportunity for labor's victory decreases. Labor can hardly hold out indefinitely, and management may prefer to close the plant, permanently if necessary, rather than to settle on labor's terms. Because the strike is a trial of endurance, it is important for the union that the strike be timed when the employer is most anxious to secure continuing and expanded output. A strike during a recession may even be welcomed by management as a device to dispose of accumulating inventory, with the blame for unemployment shifted to the union and its leaders. The proportion of strikes that succeed generally varies directly with the degree of prosperity in the economy.[13]

[13] *The Handbook on Trade Union Methods*, produced by the International Ladies' Garment Workers Union (New York, 1937) explained: "Back in 1914 the theory

Before leaving our discussion of strike costs to both labor and management, we should note that a separate calculation of cost can be developed for the economy as a whole. Certainly the social cost of the strike is usually much greater than the sum total of labor and management costs, for a continuous ripple of side effects develops. The interdependence of the production process means that the impulse of dislocation is quickly shifted to many parts of the economy. Producers who supply goods to the struck industry will lose their market, and other industries suffer from the decline of expenditures by the families of striking workers. It is, of course, precisely because of these wider effects that the government has attempted to improvise national emergency legislation to minimize public inconvenience.[14]

In a rather ambitious attempt to categorize and quantify those costs which are most serious to the public, Neil Chamberlain and Jane M. Schilling, in their study *The Impact of Strikes*,[15] outline how the " market necessity," the " stock " or inventory effect, and the substitutability effect vary from day to day as the strike is prolonged, and varies for both those directly and indirectly involved in the dispute. These students attempt an industry-by-industry appraisal of the cost of major strikes in order to provide some objective standard for public policy in strike-control measures. They conclude that " any satisfactory strike-control program must allow a large measure of administrative flexibility, simply because strikes cannot be classified in advance by degree of public effects, because even within the same industry or firm the nature of effects varies with underlying conditions. . . ."[16]

We mentioned earlier the determination of each party to a dispute to establish the justice in the public mind of its cause. Such public sentiment represents a rather effective balance wheel in dispute settlement. As E. A. Ross expressed this pressure: " It is not so much the dread

---

was advanced that the best time to strike was in the slow season on the ground that the workers could afford to strike then without losing any income. While it is true that if a strike came in the slow season the workers would not lose, neither would the employers. They could afford even better than the workers to keep their factories closed. The term 'strike' means 'to hit'. And the only time we can 'hit' is when the employer has merchandise to turn out." (P. 37.)

[14] There is considerable controversy as to whether many strikes really represent serious national emergencies. Taking the negative view, Edgar L. Warren declared: "Forty percent of those strikes which have attracted nation-wide attention during the past thirty-six years were in industries where 'necessary goods and services' were not involved. Another 24 percent did not result in a 'dangerous curtailment of supplies' because they were in industries where the product could be stock-piled and stock piles were never entirely exhausted. . . . Only in the field of public utilities and transportation do we find instances of strikes which come within the definition of national emergencies, and even these industries produce few real crises." "Thirty-Six Years of 'National Emergency' Strikes," *Industrial and Labor Relations Review*, Vol. 5 (1951), pp. 12–15.

[15] New York, Harper & Bros., 1954.

[16] *Ibid.*, p. 253.

of what an angry public may do that disarms the modern American, as it is sheer inability to stand unmoved in the rush of totally hostile comment to endure a life perpetually at variance with the conscience and feeling of those about him." [17] Because of the pressure of such opinion, Neil Chamberlain has undertaken a study of public attitudes toward the strike.[18] While public opinion certainly remains rather amorphous or nebulous, unions have grown increasingly concerned about public approval simply because they have learned the consequences of public disapproval. Few union leaders have been so rash as John L. Lewis in defying an outraged public. The public can afford the reaction: "A plague on both your houses" but neither party can usually afford the reaction: "The public be damned."

Some Causes of Conflict

Beyond the consideration of the cost of agreement and disagreement are the purely tactical aspects of bargaining. The skilled negotiator is one who understands his opponent well, who has an intuitive sense of timing, who has a persuasive manner and insight into psychology and economics, and who appreciates the advantages and hazards of bluffing as techniques in the bargaining strategy. Generally the bargaining begins with the total package the union requests exceeding by a considerable margin that which it actually hopes to secure. The basic task of the bargaining process is for management to determine the "true" minimum expectation of the union and for labor to determine the "true" maximum concession from the company. Each party will attempt to smoke out the other, while obscuring its own final or real bargaining position. More often than not, the apparent gap between union expectations and management concessions remains substantial until the pressure of impending strike action forces some give and take. Both parties eye each other nervously as the strike deadline approaches, but neither party may be willing to make concessions. The more difficulty each side has in gracefully retreating from original positions, the greater the possibility of a deadlock.

To recapitulate, the basic task in bargaining is to determine just what the gap is between both parties, and attempt if possible to bridge it. Artificial positions are taken by both sides simply to create the illusion of compromise. But one of the causes of strikes arises when one party miscalculates the strategy of the other. For example, the union may operate on the assumption that the company is bluffing. It may order the strike to establish its determination to win its demands and to "smoke

[17] E. A. Ross, *Social Control* (New York, The Macmillan Co., 1901), p. 105 and quoted by Neil W. Chamberlain, *Social Responsibility and Strikes* (New York, Harper & Bros., 1953), p. 30.
[18] *Social Responsibility and Strikes,* cited above.

out " management. But if management's stated maximum concession is its actual maximum, the strike becomes a war of attrition. The union's tactical error may not be realized until the strike is extended. Precisely because of this danger, many unions and companies have decided that it is better strategy to make a firm decision and a firm statement on their expectations, and shift from these demands only slightly during negotiations. While such " once and for all " statements may not appear conducive to the give and take of discussions, they serve to minimize the confusion of bargaining arising when both parties search for real positions.

In this sense the strike can be viewed as a device to " test the market." The willingness of the company to meet union demands may never be known until the situation has actually been put to the test. This point of view was well expressed by William Graham Sumner:

> Strikes are not necessarily connected with violence to either persons or property. Violence is provided for by the criminal law. Taking strikes by themselves, therefore, it may be believed that they are not great evils; they are costly, but they test the market. Supply and demand does not mean that social forces will operate of themselves; the law, as laid down, assumes that every party will struggle to the utmost for its interests — if it does not do so, it will lose its interest. Buyers and sellers, borrowers and lenders, landlords and tenants, employers and employees, and all other parties to contracts, must be expected to develop their interests fully in the competition and struggle of life. It is for the health of the industrial organization that they should do so.[19]

In this same context it is important to appreciate that the willingness of the union to strike is not tantamount to its dedication to strike action. The willingness to resort to militancy does not prove that one is more interested in war than peace. As John Mitchell (the predecessor to John L. Lewis as president of the United Mine Workers) explained: ". . . it can no more be said that trade unions desire strikes because they are equipped for them than that the United States desires war because it has an army and navy. . . ."[20] The final positions of both labor and management will depend in part on the willingness of each party to contemplate a deadlock and the ability of each party to sustain successfully a war of attrition.

Alternative Forms of Striking

The strategy of inflicting damage on the company can take diverse (and sometimes, perverse) forms. The union may attempt to tie up the

[19] Reproduced in Bakke and Kerr, *op. cit.*, p. 408.
[20] *Organized Labor* (New York, American Book and Bible House, 1903), p. 299.

entire industry; it may attempt to strike one employer at a time, intensify-
ing productivity and output in the nonstruck firms to increase the speed
with which the struck firm might lose its competitive position; it may
attempt to damage the company by rotating the workers on strike, by
increasing absenteeism, refusing to work overtime, and so on. The union
may strike one plant with the balance of union members supporting the
striking workers. Various forms of indirect pressures can be developed.
The union may urge a product boycott of all consumers of goods produced by the struck plant; it may urge that other unions refuse to handle
" hot " items coming to or from the struck plant. Transportation workers are in a particularly strategic position to lend support to striking
workers by refusing to cross a picket line or handle such goods. Prior to
the legislative restrictions of the Taft-Hartley Act, unions would sometimes attempt to establish a strike against a second employer not directly
involved in the dispute, but one who was doing business with the first
employer in whose firm the dispute developed. Such indirect pressure,
arising from the withdrawal of labor from firms doing business in which
the primary dispute arose, is called a secondary strike. When labor is only
remotely connected to the issues of the primary dispute, but nevertheless
walks off the job in protest, we have a sympathy strike.

One of the most dramatic forms of strike action occurs when all unions
and all workers participate in a general strike. Often such labor unity
reflects political instability and revolutionary inspiration, but such strikes
have been few and far between. In 1919 a general strike spread throughout Seattle for six days, but this strike was less a Bolshevist outburst than
a protest against the deterioration of labor conditions following World
War I. In that same year a general strike continued for six weeks in
Winnipeg, Canada, as a protest against labor conditions there. In May of
1926 the British labor movement began a general strike to protest the
lockout of coal miners, with over 3 million workers involved. None of
these strikes were classified as successes for the labor movement, although they did dramatize the problems confronting labor. The wholesale interruption of economic life creates new fears of irresponsible
union leadership, and in many instances swings public sentiment in sympathy with the anti-union employers.

The sit-down strike became popular during the late thirties, especially
during the mass organizational campaigns of the labor movement. The
effectiveness of this form of strike is suggested by the following description of a sit-down strike in 1936:

> Friday, the 13th of November, 1936, was an ominous day for the
> General Motors Corporation (of Flint, Michigan). The auto union
> had been ploddingly building its membership in Fisher I. On the eve-
> ning of the 12th, hundreds of workers went to a store across the

street which had been rented by the union and signed application cards. The next morning three welders came to work to find their time cards missing from the rack. That meant, as they would be told upon inquiry, that they had been fired. A fourth union man protested to the foreman. He too was fired. As he was being paraded through the plant to the gate, he passed Bud Simons, torch solderer for G. M. and torch bearer for the union in Fisher I.

"Where are you going, Sam?" Simons inquired.

"You come along, too, Bud," the foreman said.

Simons complied, but as he walked the length of the belt-line his glance communicated a message. Each worker wiped his hands on his overalls, turned from the moving row of Chevrolet bodies and joined in a sit-down strike. The news spread throughout the plant. By the time Simons had reached the end of his "last mile" seven hundred men were idle. A committee of workers hastened after Bud Simon and the foreman. They met in the office. Simon noted the arrival of the committee and turned to the plant manager.

"Mr. Parker," he said, "you are now talking to a union."

While the manager was recovering from his surprise, the sitters were formally voting, *vive voce*, they would not resume work until the discharged men had been returned to their jobs. And they insisted also that they be paid for the time they had been "sitting." After slight deliberations, both demands of the men were met and work was resumed — but not until the lesson of the power of the auto union had been driven home.[21]

The sit-down strike may not be as spontaneous as described in this situation, but rather carefully planned by union leaders. During the thirties detailed instructions were often given to the work force regarding their behavior during such a strike. Plans were sometimes established for the election of shop committees to maintain discipline, for the election of pickets, for the restraint of any damage to property, and for the flow of goods including food and adequate bedding for the workers.

Contact committees maintained communications with strike headquarters, a particularly difficult task where police or militia barred persons from entering the plants. Picket or patrol committees check on all doors, gates and approaches to the plant; they ferreted out the violators of the universal rules against smoking or drinking alcoholic liquor in the plants. . . . This committee also had the right to examine food, blankets, or notes which wives or other relations might deliver for the sitters. Visitors, excepting sympathetic fellow unionists in time of possible attack, were barred. . . . The committee served the meals where possible using company cafeterias. . . . In some plants, educational committees flourished, but more often the strikers

[21] Edward Levinson, *Labor on the March* (New York, Harper & Bros., 1938) and reproduced in Bakke and Kerr, *op. cit.*, p. 410.

favored the efforts of the entertainment committees which provided shows, dances, and music. Almost every large factory held by sitters produced a band, sometimes only an accordion and a mandolin. . . .[22]

The tactical advantage of the sit-down strike was that it dramatized the plight of the worker to the public, reduced the possibility that the employer could secure strikebreakers to resume operations of the plant, and required that the employer take the initiative in " removing " the workers. If violence developed, it would appear as though the employer had taken the initiative, for the intent of the sit-down strike was not to destroy company property, but to be certain that it could not be operated by strikebreakers during the strike.

The turning point in the popularity and success of sit-down strikes came with the Supreme Court decision in the case of the National Labor Relations Board versus the Fansteel Metallurgical Corporation. On February 27, 1939, Chief Justice Hughes delivered the majority opinion of the Supreme Court, indicating that the discharge by the company of the sit-down strikers was justified because the employees had not used the remedy provided by the Wagner Act. The principle that labor should not take the law into its own hands by occupying the land and property of the owners of industry is one that the public unanimously supports today. Any action, regardless of its economic or tactical advantage, is likely to lose its effectiveness if it does not enjoy the support of the public or the courts.

Because labor has a new responsibility — the protection and care of intricate and expensive machines — it also has a new power. A mechanical breakdown of the machine may result in delayed production in the entire plant in addition to the costs of repairs. If labor feels aggrieved, it can often effect subtle and yet effective methods of sabotaging plant production. Management may find it impossible to trace the responsibility for such sabotage to any one person. The danger of this form of labor retaliation to management policies is very real and cannot always be solved by tighter supervision or more exacting quality control standards. The best check against abuse is to develop within the worker a feeling of responsibility to management and the positive motivation to do a good job.[23]

[22] From Levinson, *op. cit.*, pp. 175–179.

[23] J. B. S. Hardman, *American Labor Dynamics* (New York, Harcourt, Brace and Co., 1928), describes how striking workers decided to return to work in a shirt plant as " scabs," under union orders. Company officials felt that they had broken the strike. " But curious letters began pouring in from a number of cities. Somehow or other most of the shirts happened to be put together in a queer sort of way. Where one sleeve wasn't longer, the other was shorter; the collar was invariably too tight and the neckband a size or a half its own junior. The matching of colors was rather impressionistic. And dealers were enraged at the carelessness with which their orders were filled. The company seemed to have been bent on sending things nobody wanted." (P. 135.)

Sabotage may occur when workers misplace tools, permit imperfect work to slip by, or operate machinery in an abusive manner to speed a breakdown. Workers may decide to give more careful inspection to every product upon which they work. In some cases workers may decide to obey every work rule to the letter of the law, causing near chaos in the plant. Eliminating this type of sabotage is all the more difficult for usually labor will deny any intent to interrupt production. Louis Adamic recalls learning of the value of such sabotage from IWW or "wobbly" members:

> Sabotage, this dark, invincible, terrible Damocles' sword . . . hangs over the head of the master class . . . sabotage, as we practice it, is a more powerful injunction against their machinery. In vain will they invoke old laws and make new ones against it – they will never discover sabotage, never track it to its lair, never run it down, for no laws will ever make a crime of the " clumsiness and lack of skill " of a scab who bungles his work . . . There can be no injunction against sabotage. No Policemen's club. No rifle diet. No prison bars.[24]

Because of the increasing value and complexity of modern technology, management is making every effort to provide the workers with concrete evidence of their fair-minded policies. Certainly sabotage on the job can often be more harmful than the absence of the worker from the job.

Historical Data on Strikes

The annual frequency and impact of strikes has been measured in terms of (a) the number of strikes that develop, (b) the men involved in strikes, (c) the man-days lost through strike action, (d) the proportion of the labor force involved in strike action, and (e) the loss of production and wage payments because of the strike action. Further studies have been undertaken to correlate the number and duration of strikes with changes in the price level, the work force, union membership, the business cycle and so on. In Table 15, we have a breakdown of work stoppages from 1881 to 1955 in terms of the number of work stoppages, the number of workers involved, and the number of idle man-days. The exact number of workers involved in strikes from 1916 to 1926 is not known, but Table 15 provides a rough estimate for the interval.

The peaks of these data represent years of considerable industrial unrest. Among the stoppages of 1886 were the Chicago Haymarket riot and the strikes of the Missouri Pacific Railroad. The drive for the 8-hour day brought strike figures to a new peak in 1890. A further peak was reached in 1903 because of the organizational drives of the American Federation of Labor. The war boom accelerated strike activity to a new peak in

[24] Louis Adamic, *Dynamite: The Story of Class Violence in America* (New York, Viking Press, 1934), p. 376.

TABLE 15 Work Stoppages: 1881–1955

| Year | Work Stoppages | | Workers Involved | | Man-Days Idle | | |
	Number	Average Duration	Number in Thousands	Percentage of Total Employed	Number in Thousands	Percentage of Estimated Working Time	Per Worker Involved
1881	477	14.0	130				
1882	476	24.0	159				
1883	506	22.7	170				
1884	485	33.4	165				
1885	695	33.0	258				
1886	1,572	25.6	610				
1887	1,503	22.9	439				
1888	946	22.3	163				
1889	1,111	28.8	260				
1890	1,897	26.6	373	4.2			
1891	1,786	38.4	330	3.6			
1892	1,359	25.7	239	2.5			
1893	1,375	22.6	288	3.2			
1894	1,404	35.6	690	8.3			
1895	1,255	22.5	407	4.4			
1896	1,066	24.0	249	2.8			
1897	1,110	20.1	416	4.3			
1898	1,098	24.7	263	2.6			
1899	1,838	16.7	432	3.9			
1900	1,839	25.4	568	4.9			
1901	3,012	32.1	564	4.6			
1902	3,240	27.9	692	5.4			
1903	3,648	32.0	788	5.9			
1904	2,419	39.1	574	4.3			
1905	2,186	25.4	302	2.1			
1906–1913: data not available							
1914	1,204						
1915	1,593						
1916	3,789		1,600	8.4			
1917	4,450		1,230	6.3			
1918	3,353		1,240	6.2			
1919	3,360		4,160	20.8			
1920	3,411		1,460	7.2			
1921	2,385		1,100	6.4			
1922	1,112		1,610	8.7			
1923	1,553		757	3.5			
1924	1,249		655	3.1			
1925	1,301		428	2.0			

Table continues

TABLE 15 *(continued)*

Year	Work Stoppages		Workers Involved		Man-Days Idle		
	Number	Average Duration	Number in Thousands	Percentage of Total Employed	Number in Thousands	Percentage of Estimated Working Time	Per Worker Involved
1926	1,035		330	1.5			
1927	707	26.5	330	1.4	26,000	0.37	79.5
1928	604	27.6	314	1.3	12,600	0.17	40.2
1929	921	22.6	289	1.2	5,350	0.07	18.5
1930	637	22.3	183	0.8	3,320	0.05	18.1
1931	810	18.8	342	1.6	6,890	0.11	20.2
1932	841	19.6	324	1.8	10,500	0.23	32.4
1933	1,695	16.9	1,170	6.3	16,900	0.36	14.4
1934	1,856	19.5	1,470	7.2	19,600	0.38	13.4
1935	2,014	23.8	1,120	5.2	15,500	0.29	13.8
1936	2,172	23.3	789	3.1	13,900	0.21	17.6
1937	4,740	20.3	1,860	7.2	28,400	0.43	15.3
1938	2,772	23.6	688	2.8	9,150	0.15	13.3
1939	2,613	23.4	1,170	4.7	17,800	0.28	15.2
1940	2,508	20.9	577	2.3	6,700	0.10	11.6
1941	4,288	18.3	2,360	8.4	23,000	0.32	9.8
1942	2,968	11.7	840	2.8	4,180	0.05	5.0
1943	3,752	5.0	1,980	6.9	13,500	0.15	6.8
1944	4,956	5.6	2,120	7.0	8,720	0.09	4.1
1945	4,750	9.9	3,470	12.2	38,000	0.47	11.0
1946	4,985	24.2	4,600	14.5	116,000	1.43	25.2
1947	3,693	25.6	2,170	6.5	34,600	0.41	15.9
1948	3,419	21.8	1,960	5.5	34,100	0.37	17.4
1949	3,606	22.5	3,030	9.0	50,500	0.59	16.7
1950	4,843	19.2	2,410	6.9	38,800	0.44	16.1
1951	4,737	17.4	2,200	5.5	22,900	0.23	10.3
1952	5,117	19.6	3,540	8.8	59,100	0.57	16.7
1953	5,091	20.3	2,400	5.6	28,300	0.26	11.8
1954	3,468	22.5	1,530	3.7	22,600	0.21	14.7
1955	4,320	n.a.	2,650	n.a.	28,200	0.26	n.a.
1956	3,800	n.a.	1,900	n.a.	33,000	0.30	n.a.

From W. S. Woytinsky and Associates, *Employment and Wages in the United States* (New York, Twentieth Century Fund, 1953), p. 655.

Data on duration of strikes from 1880 to 1905 from John I. Griffin: *Strikes, A Study in Quantitative Economics* (New York, Columbia University Press, 1939), p. 87.

Total employed workers as used here refers to all workers except those in occupations and professions in which there is little union organization and seldom strikes. *Monthly Labor Review*, Ud. 78, No. 5 (May, 1955), p. 539 and Vol. 80, No. 2 (February, 1957), Table E, p. 264.

n.a.: Not available.

1917, and another peak was reached in 1919. In that year 367,000 steel workers walked out in an unsuccessful attempt to win union recognition and 425,000 bituminous coal miners struck to secure a wage increase.[25] Following several years of relative industrial peace during the twenties and early thirties, a new wave of industrial unrest developed in 1936 and 1937. Union recognition was the main issue in almost three out of every five stoppages in 1937.[26] A further strike wave developed in 1941, but strikes then declined rapidly because of the war crisis. During the war strikes were short-lived, but their duration and number increased sharply after World War II. Both 1919 and 1946 appear as peaks in strike studies, and this suggests that strikes become widespread in readjustment periods when labor hopes to maintain and extend the benefits secured during the period of high employment.

The over-all interpretation of strike statistics is complicated by the fact that there are many alternative methods of measuring strikes. But strikes must be evaluated in at least three dimensions: the total number of strikes developing, the total number of workers involved in such disputes, and the average duration of the dispute.

One interesting attempt to call attention to this multidimensional aspect of strike data is made by John V. Spielmans.[27] He takes the number of workers involved in a dispute and divides this into the total of man-days lost by workers. The quotient gives us an average duration of the strikes. He then plots on a horizontal scale the number of workers involved and on the vertical scale the average length of the strike. The area of the resulting rectangle is the total of man-days lost. (He records separately the number of disputes accounting for the totals.) " The resulting profiles, with the varying width and height of their several rectangles, looking now like a towering Manhattan skyline, now like the low silhouette of a battleship, give by themselves a vivid numerical account of the strike history of the country during the last sixteen years." [28] The narrower and higher his profiles, the fewer the number of workers involved but the longer the duration of the strike, suggesting greater intensity of the struggle. A low flat profile indicates widespread participation in strikes of short duration. He finds that from 1927 to 1943 America has moved from the " skyscraper " strike (with few workers involved but of long duration) to the " flat " strike in 1943 (with a large number

[25] From Thomas C. Fichandler, "Work Stoppages," Chapter 21, in W. S. Woytinsky's study, *Employment and Wages in the United States* (New York, Twentieth Century Fund, 1953), pp. 284–286.

[26] *Ibid.,* p. 286.

[27] "Strike Profiles," *The Journal of Political Economy*, Vol. LII, No. 4, December, 1944, pp. 319–339. For criticisms of his methodology and alternative expository devices, see K. G. J. Knowles, *Strikes: A Study in Industrial Conflict* (Oxford, Basil Blackwell, 1952), pp. 152–153.

[28] *Ibid.,* p. 332.

of workers involved for short duration). Profiles are developed for various nations, as well as for the various issues involving the strike, and in terms of whether the strikes were won by management or labor.

In general most of the strike indexes reflect a peak during World War I, with a slump in both the number of work stoppages and workers involved (as well as man-days idle) during the twenties and the early thirties. But a gradual upward trend began again in 1933 for both work stoppages and workers involved, although the total of man-days idle did not increase substantially until 1946. The year 1946 is, in all respects, an unusual year in strike history. Strikes developed in January and February of that year involving the steel, automobile, electrical, and meat-packing industries, and the tide of strike action did not subside until June. Over 116,000,000 idle man-days were caused by strikes, and over 4.6 million workers were involved. The total of working time lost by such unusual strike activity did not, however, account for more than 1.43 percent of the total of working time.[29]

The data of Table 16 and 17 provide a breakdown of causes of industrial dispute. Originally the United States commissioners had classified strikes in terms of 65 causes, but as the volume of data required and collected by the government increased, it was necessary to broaden such classifications. Eighteen major classifications were developed to explain the cause of strikes, and these in turn were summarized in three groups: wages and hours, union certification, and miscellaneous. Table 16 represents data developed by John I. Griffin from 1880 to 1937. More recent BLS data covering 1935 to 1955 are provided in Table 17.

Data on the number of strikes tend to follow the growth of the trade union movement.[30] Workers involved in strikes hit a peak in 1919, and union membership reached its peak in 1920. During the twenties both union membership and workers involved in strikes declined rather steadily. Union membership increased sharply after 1933, as did the number of workers involved in strikes. But the number of workers involved in stoppages increased much less rapidly than did the growth of union membership. Some consolation can be found in the fact that after World War I, the number of workers involved in strikes exceeded union membership while after World War II strikers represented only a fraction of union membership.[31]

[29] For discussion of data and trends, see Joseph P. Goldberg and Bernard Yabroff, "Analysis of Strikes: 1927–49," *The Monthly Labor Review*, Vol. 72, No. 1 (January, 1951), pp. 1–7.

[30] For a comparison of the workers involved in strikes and union membership, see Figure 47, Chapter 21 in Woytinsky, *op. cit.*, p. 291.

[31] The highest number of working days lost by strike action (as a multiple of union membership) from 1927 to 1947 occurred in 1946 when the average union member was off 7.8 days. Previous high years were 1927 with 7.3 days and 1933 and 1934 with 5.9 and 6.0 days respectively. The average working days lost per union member

TABLE 16   Numbers of Strikes Broken Down into Percentage
Distribution of Major Causes: 1880–1937

Year	Wage Increase	Wage Decrease	Hours	Other
1880	62.5	10.0	0.9	24.9
1881	67.7	12.1	5.7	21.4
1882	59.3	16.1	4.0	24.9
1883	50.9	26.3	2.3	25.7
1884	35.9	38.2	3.8	29.8
1885	44.2	28.7	3.4	30.0
1886	53.5	9.5	20.1	32.8
1887	42.8	12.0	12.5	40.5
1888	32.9	22.3	9.7	42.9
1889	36.4	22.6	9.3	41.0
1890	40.0	10.9	13.5	44.2
1891	37.1	11.8	10.8	50.4
1892	37.4	13.0	10.7	47.2
1893	32.3	26.5	7.8	40.8
1894	36.8	26.9	3.8	38.1
1895	50.7	18.9	4.7	35.6
1896	38.2	19.4	5.2	48.3
1897	45.9	20.3	5.9	38.5
1898	47.3	15.7	6.5	40.4
1899	53.3	6.1	11.4	45.4
1900	52.9	6.1	16.5	45.7
1901	42.0	4.6	14.3	53.6
1902	47.1	4.1	13.9	52.0
1903	47.8	3.7	16.7	52.0
1904	33.8	8.4	9.9	61.8
1905	39.1	5.4	11.0	56.7
1906	47.1	2.0	11.5	37.1
1907	52.1	2.7	10.5	34.5
1908	33.3	11.3	6.2	49.0
1909	47.5	4.4	5.4	42.4
1910	51.9	4.1	5.9	38.0
1911	45.3	4.9	8.1	41.6
1912	53.2	2.9	7.7	36.0
1913	51.8	4.7	6.6	36.7
1914	32.5	11.3	5.9	50.1
1915	43.6	8.1	6.6	41.4
1916	59.5	1.1	3.7	35.5
1917	56.9	.9	4.1	37.9
1918	60.4	1.2	2.9	35.3
1919	53.4	2.5	4.2	39.7
1920	58.6	4.7	2.2	34.3

Table continues

319

TABLE 16   (*continued*)

Year	Wage Increase	Wage Decrease	Hours	Other
1921	9.7	43.7	14.0	32.4
1922	23.6	28.6	3.2	44.4
1923	44.2	3.3	1.4	50.9
1924	33.4	11.5	2.0	52.9
1925	33.5	10.0	1.0	55.2
1926	40.7	5.3	2.3	51.5
1927	29.1	9.3	2.6	59.0
1928	21.8	12.4	1.6	64.2
1929	24.2	14.0	2.2	59.6
1930	16.8	25.7	1.1	56.4
1931	12.6	42.4	1.1	43.9
1932	14.5	50.6	.6	34.3
1933	41.5	13.3	.6	44.6
1934	32.3	6.5	.7	60.5
1935	23.2	12.5	2.2	62.1
1936	25.9	7.9	1.3	64.9
1937	27.9	1.4	.6	70.1

Total percentages for some years exceed 100 as strike causes are tabulated under more than one cause for certain strikes.

Source: John I. Griffin, *Strikes, A Study in Quantitative Economics* (New York, Columbia University Press, 1939), pp. 76–77.

Paul Douglas attempted to analyze whether the union sector was more prone to strike than the nonunion sector of the labor force by looking at strike statistics from 1881 to 1921.[32] He undertook to compute the propensity of unions to strike by calculating the percentage of union strikes over union members, compared to the ratio of nonunion strikes over nonunion members. He discovered that the possibility of union members becoming involved in a strike was, on the average for the forty-year period, approximately twenty times as great as for the nonunion members. While no recent data on this thesis exist, it would seem that there is a greater likelihood that organized labor will strike than unorganized workers. One must be cautious, however, in imputing direct interdependence between unionism and strikes. Both union membership and strikes may increase during a period of business prosperity. The causal factor operating on both union membership and strikes may be the state of the economy. This possibility will be examined in somewhat more detail below.

for this 1927–1947 interval was 3.0 each year. See Arthur M. Ross and Donald Irwin, "Strike Experience in Five Countries, 1927–1947: An Interpretation" *Industrial and Labor Relations Review*, Vol. 4, No. 3 (April, 1951), p. 332.

[32] "An Analysis of Strike Statistics: 1881–1921," *Journal of American Statistical Association*, Vol. 1, XVIII (1923).

TABLE 17   The Number of Strikes Broken Down into the
Percentage Distribution of Causes: 1935–1955

Year	Wages & Hours	Union Organization	Other Working Conditions	Union Organization Wages & Hours	Interunion or Intraunion Matters
1935	37.9	47.2	14.9		
1936	35.1	50.2	14.7		
1937	29.9	57.8	12.3		
1938	28.0	50.0	22.0		
1939	26.5	53.5	20.0		
1940	30.2	49.9	19.9		
1941	35.6	49.5	14.9		
1942	46.8	13.7	16.4	17.5	5.6
1943	51.0	9.5	29.3	6.2	4.0
1944	43.3	11.3	36.3	5.0	4.1
1945	42.4	12.6	32.7	7.9	4.2
1946	44.9	14.1	17.6	18.3	4.9
1947	46.3	14.7	18.8	15.1	4.3
1948	50.8	13.4	21.5	9.4	3.8
1949	46.6	15.7	25.0	6.0	5.8
1950	52.8	13.4	22.0	5.6	5.3
1951	44.4	14.4	28.3	4.3	6.9
1952	47.9	11.7	26.9	4.7	6.5
1953	55.5	10.7	22.3	4.0	5.4
1954	49.8	12.4	24.1	4.6	7.3
1955	49.9	12.5	22.3	7.1	6.9

From 1935 to 1941, stoppages primarily over union organization matters but also involving wages and hour issues were classified under "union organization."

From 1935 to 1941, stoppages primarily over interunion or intraunion matters (jurisdictional and rival-union disputes) were classified under "other working conditions." The percentage calculations prior to 1941 are not comparable to those after 1941 because of the larger number of classifications in this more recent period.

Source: Data from W. S. Woytinsky and Associates, *Employment and Wages in the United States* (New York, Twentieth Century Fund, 1953), p. 654 and BLS Bulletins, *Analysis of Work Stoppages* (1951, 1952, 1953, 1954 and 1955).

It has often been suggested that young unions are more prone to strike than old or mature ones. The strike weapon becomes a device for the union to secure recognition, to prove itself to management, and once such recognition is granted and there is a mutual respect for the responsibilities and rights of each other, labor-management relations settle down to a more peaceful co-existence.

The Strike, Business Cycle, and Economic Crisis

Social scientists have been intrigued with the possibility that the changing pattern of economic conditions has induced strikes and that strikes in turn have induced the changing pattern of economic change. Early speculation in this area was provided by Alvin Hansen, whose study of strike data from 1881 to 1919 led him to conclude that " strikes correlate inversely with the business cycle in periods of long-run falling prices, while they correlate directly with the business cycle in periods of long-run rising prices." [33] In more recent times E. H. and D. B. Jurkat have employed monthly data and conclude that there is a high positive association between strikes and the business cycle,[34] and Albert Rees, in his study, " Industrial Conflict and Business Fluctuations," concludes that there is a high " correspondence between strike cycles and the business cycle for the period 1915–38 and very little correspondence for the war and postwar years, 1939–50." [35] Rees's analysis is rooted in the reference cycle of the National Bureau, and is confined to the number of strikes beginning in each month. While the pattern of conformity does disappear in recent decades, Rees points out that there is a clear tendency for the peak in the number of strikes starting each month to precede the peak of the business cycle, and to lag at the bottom turning point of the cycle. " The time between the reference turn (of the cycle) and the strike turn averages four months at the peak and six months at the troughs." These lead-lag relationships are important to those who attempt to uncover some cause and effect in the relationship of the strike to industrial crisis.[36]

If the number of strikes beginning each month declines prior to most economic downturns, this weakens the argument that strikes provoke economic crisis. The British economist, A. C. Pigou, points out, however, that strikes can have an infectious effect on the general prospect for profits:

> It seems plain that, whenever the number of men involved in industrial disputes is larger than usual, this must make *pro tanto* for a decline in the prospect of profit elsewhere, and so in aggregate activity, and that, whenever the number so involved is smaller than usual, there is *pro tanto* an impulse toward industrial expansion. . . . In view of these considerations, there can be little doubt that industrial disputes — or rather excesses and deficiencies in industrial disputes as against the average — are a genuine cause of industrial fluctuations.[37]

[33] " Cycles of Strikes," *American Economic Review*, Vol. XI (1921), p. 620.

[34] " Economic Function of Strikes," *Industrial and Labor Relations Review*, Vol. II (July, 1949), pp. 527–545.

[35] *The Journal of Political Economy*, Vol. LX, No. 5 (October, 1952), p. 373.

[36] Rees suggests that several business series: the number of business failures or liabilities of business failures, series on investment, security issues, contracts and orders, lead the peak of industrial crisis. Downward shifts in these in turn reflect " the changed expectations of businessmen. As the cyclical peak is reached, the more pessimistic expectations may be shared by some union leaders, and strikes fall off." *Ibid.*, p. 381.

[37] *Industrial Fluctuations* (London, Macmillan and Co., 1929), pp. 50–51.

Looking at annual data, strikes reached a very high level in 1919 and the crisis of 1920 followed. Strikes were at a very low ebb prior to the 1929 crash, although there were slightly more strikes in 1929 than in 1928. Strikes increased sharply in 1936 and 1937 prior to the 1937 recession. However, growing industrial unrest did not prevent the World War II boom from developing, and the high volume of strikes in 1946 did not push the economy into a depression, even though a readjustment recession had generally been anticipated by economists. It does not seem likely that strikes play a critical role in causing economic crisis.

Sustaining and Concluding the Strike

We have emphasized how the strike often represents a test of endurance or a war of attrition, but it should not be concluded that collective bargaining ceases because the strike has been called. Indeed, the NLRB has ruled that either party might be liable to an unfair labor practice if it refuses to re-enter into negotiations, even though there may not have been any new promise of concessions prior to the invitations to such negotiations. Throughout the strike both labor and management will often make separate appeals for public support and understanding. Advertisements often appear in local newspapers dealing with the issues involved. The union strikers may secure support from the national union, from other local unions (and even from the public) in the form of cash contributions, and sometimes contributions of food and clothing. Violence must be avoided. As one union handbook explains: " The temptation to ' dare ' the cops is a strong one, but there is no point in alienating them needlessly. They too are workers and often none too well paid. Kidding by pretty girls is perhaps more effective than a truculent attitude." [38] The union side of the story must be presented to the public through photographs and human interest stories:

> Human sympathy is quickened by tales of unnecessary suffering. Play up the mother of six children who gets clubbed and the aged man needlessly beaten. Violations of civil liberty, always inherent in a strike situation, may be exposed, but lay emphasis on the human rather than the legal aspects of the case. . . . Pictures will help to tell the story of the strike to the public — pictures of picket lines, of cops mistreating strikers, of pretty girls who have been arrested, of a worker's home (but see that the kids aren't dressed up for the occasion in all the neighborhood finery). . . .[39]

The union must maintain the morale of the striking union members, keep up the picket line, discourage the use of substitute labor in every

[38] ILGWU, *Handbook of Trade Union Method*, pp. 37–56, and quoted in Bakke and Kerr, *op. cit.*, p. 442.
[39] *Ibid.*, p. 448.

way possible short of intimidation and violence, set up a system of strike benefits, and nail false rumors that may have been planted by employer missionaries. But the union, too, must always be ready to negotiate a settlement and reach a compromise agreement. And when such an agreement is made, it is wise for the union to attempt to dispel as effectively as possible the bitterness created by the strike.

The company faces similar problems during the strike. Management must attempt to sustain its own morale and united front to provide press releases and conduct an effective campaign to win public sympathy and support to justify the company policy in dealing with the work force the way it has. The company must be ready at any moment to resume negotiations and, when these result in agreement, to attempt to re-establish harmonious relations with the work force.

It must be noted that company attitudes toward unionism have changed radically since the mid-thirties, although many union leaders suspect that management's secret aspiration or hidden hope still is to break the union. Most companies are willing to admit that unions are here to stay and simply urge more responsible union leadership and policies. Hence, when a strike develops, management often criticizes the leadership of the union, rather than the principle of unionism itself.

The thirties left a heritage of militancy in labor-management relations. The investigations of the La Follette Committee revealed that many employers were storing sizable arsenals for availability in disputes. Company spies were often used by employers to keep a running account of union activities. Blacklists were often kept by employers to reduce the danger of hiring union agitators and to discourage employees from getting involved in union activity. On occasion it was found that employers had even encouraged violence on the part of the union through planted " missionaries " within the ranks of the union group to win public support to the company viewpoint.

Perhaps the most popularized technique employed in the late thirties for handling a strike was that developed by Mr. Rand of the Remington Rand Corporation, a procedure that was dubbed the " Mohawk Valley " formula. It involved the following procedures. (1) When the strike is threatened, the employer should (a) label the union leaders as agitators; (b) conduct a forced balloting under the direction of foremen in an attempt to determine the representation of the strikers; (c) indicate that only a minority of workers desires the strike; (d) spread press releases indicating that strikers appear to be making arbitrary demands; (e) by threats to move the plant and so on, align a citizens' committee of bankers, real estate owners, and businessmen, who in turn can protest reduction of purchasing power and the effect on property values and community income of any strike. (2) When a strike is called, raise high the banner of " law and order," and secure legal and police weapons against the

union. (3) Call a " mass meeting " of citizens to coordinate public sentiment against the strike. (4) Bring about the formation of a large armed
police force to intimidate the strikers and to exert a psychological effect
upon the citizens. (5) Perhaps most important, heighten the demoralizing
effect of the above measures — all designed to convince the strikers that
their cause is hopeless — by a " back-to-work " movement. (6) When a
sufficient number of applications are on hand, fix a date for an opening of
the plant through the device of having such an opening requested by the
" back-to-work " organization. (7) Stage the " opening " theatrically,
throwing open the gates at the propitious moment. (Along with the
opening provide a spectacle — speeches, flag raising, and praises for the
employees, citizens, and local authorities so that, their vanity touched,
they will feel responsible for the continued success of the scheme.)
(8) Capitalize on the demoralization of the strikers by continuing the
show of police force and the pressure of the citizens' committee.
(9) Close the publicity barrage — on the theme that the plant is in full
operation and that the strikers were merely a minority attempting to
interfere with the " right to work," thus inducing the public to place a
moral stamp of approval upon the above measures. With this, the campaign is over — the employer has broken the strike.

While this procedure was followed in many respects by many employers during the thirties, unions today seldom face such a militant attack
from employers. It is true that management will often attempt to drive a
wedge between the rank and file and union leadership, but management
must, because of existing legislation, be circumspect in its treatment and
statements of labor both prior to and during the strike. The strategy of
management is basically very simple: to convince the work force of the
futility of their demands, of the dangers to industry (and hence employment) of unreasonable demands. By threatening a separation of the
worker from his income, management is hitting the worker where he is
most vulnerable.

A more recent technique of management for dealing with union at the
bargaining table has been labeled " Boulwareism," after Lemuel R. Boulware, vice president of the General Electric Company, the plan's author.
The strategy of the company is to apply the same sales techniques to
their workers as they do to their customers. It implies a tough but firm
policy in dealing with the union, a year-round campaign to convince
workers that they have good jobs and that their supervisors have their
interests at heart.[40]

The procedure followed by companies is this: After studying union
demands prior to negotiation, the company announces and publicizes an
offer which it describes as fair and the best that it will do. If the wage

[40] Stephen K. Galpin, " Boulwareism: C.I.O. Cries Foul as 'Tough But Fair' Wage
Policy Spreads," *Wall Street Journal*, November 3, 1954.

negotiations do not bring any settlement, the company implements the wage increase for all those workers who are not represented by the union. It points out that unless the union accepts the offer, there will be no retroactive wage increase. There is no point in striking, for the offer of the company is final. Even if a strike should develop, the company sticks to its position. The main feature of the plan is to increase the flow of communication between the company and the worker, circumventing the union with the emphasis on the fair aspect of the company concession, and secondly, the determination on the part of the company not to offer the workers more even if they should strike. For each day of prolonged negotiations beyond the deadline of the pay offer, the union work force loses income that it might have enjoyed simply by accepting the company offer. As Boulware explains, it is most important that the union understands that the reasonable company offer is final. " The sooner you tell them what you expect to do and get them to believe it, the better labor relations are going to be." The strike is unnecessary to determine what is right, for the intent of the company (in Boulware's words) is to

> . . . act right, tell employees about it, and tell the community about it. . . . We strive to do right, and voluntarily. . . . We study constantly how we may become more competent to know and do what's right by all the proper standards. We try to have all concerned relieved of any ideas we would ever have to be dragged unwillingly to do what's right in this field.[41]

The union, of course, objects to the unilateral determination of what is right and construes the " take it or leave it " approach of the company as a challenge to collective bargaining. James B. Carey, president of the CIO Electrical Workers Union, has expressed serious concern over such company strategy: " Boulware is an industrial agnostic. I never met a guy who is more of an anarchist. . . . Even after Mr. Boulware goes, he will leave scars it will take years and years to heal." [42]

———

In summary, our chapter has reviewed industrial conflict, that phase of collective bargaining that attracts 95 percent of the public's attention. Yet, ironically, over 95 percent of the collective bargaining contracts are signed each year without a strike. One of the paradoxes of successful and " free " collective bargaining is that each party shall have the freedom to resort to force and yet must be restrained in the exercise of this freedom. There is no visible alternative to the freedom of disagreement as a pervasive device to secure agreement. Both labor and management are necessary as cooperating factors in the production process: mutual survival dictates cooperation rather than conflict.

[41] Galpin, *op. cit.,* p. 1.   [42] *Ibid.,* p. 1.

There is no conclusive evidence to suggest that labor-management relations are necessarily growing more peaceful, although the character of strike action has changed. Certainly there is less violence and militancy. The strike still remains a war of attrition, but instances of tear-gas warfare, police charges into picket lines, and plant destruction are unusual. The peaceful strike has become institutionalized to the point where on occasion management invites union representatives to make periodic tours through the plant to be assured that no attempt is being made to maintain production, and where unions reciprocate with working agreements to maintain the plant capital in working condition so that production might be resumed with the minimum of delay and inconvenience. The increase in strike action following World War II should not be taken as a dangerous trend toward instability, for such unrest is typical of any period of our history characterized by that social ferment arising from demobilization and inflation.

The strike data do suggest that the number of strikes has increased, while the total of man-days lost through strike action — a more valid index of the cost of striking — has decreased. This apparent inconsistency is reconciled by the fact that the more numerous strikes are generally of a shorter duration.[43]

[43] An interesting study of international strike comparisons is undertaken by Arthur M. Ross and Donald Irwin, " Strike Experience in Five Countries: 1927–1947: An Interpretation," *Industrial and Labor Relations Review*, Vol. 4, No. 3 (April, 1951), pp. 323–342. The authors point out that while unionism as a percentage of nonagricultural employees has been much less in America than in Great Britain, Sweden, or Australia, "Union members in the United States have been more prone to strike than those of any of the other four countries" (p. 329). They also conclude that " It is significant that the ratio of lost working time in the United States was higher than in any other country studied . . . the average annual loss per union member was approximately twice that in Sweden and Canada, three times that in Australia, and four times that in Great Britain" (p. 333). Because of the declining strike experience in Sweden and England, the authors are inclined to the view that the organization features of unionism in that country — including a high proportion of unionism, security for the union movement and so on — account for the peace in those countries.

14

The Mechanics of
Dispute Settlement

To indicate — as we did in our previous chapter — that the outcome of the bargaining process depends on the amount of damage that one party can inflict on the other — casts the collective bargaining process in a rather crude context. Fortunately, while power may be the ultimate arbiter of the bargaining process, it is not the *sole* force at work. In this and the following chapter, we shall discuss the more idealistic aspect of the bargaining process: the role of principle. We turn then to the admonitions of George Taylor: "The old wheezes about the 'lion's share to the lions' and about 'charging what the traffic will bear' are fatal rules for wage determination if collective bargaining is to be preserved. Intelligence has to be substituted for brawn at the bargaining table if the determination of wages and other conditions of employment is to remain securely in the hands of industry and labor." [1] We are going to be concerned then, with the role of intelligence or reason in the bargaining process. We should note at the outset, however, that when we abandon the "old wheeze" of charging what the traffic will bear, we move into an area characterized by conflicting ethical norms or contradictory value judgments. Unhappily, the feasibility of securing uniform agreement to principle often seems to vary inversely with the nobility of that principle.

The principles for dispute settlement have acquired enormous significance in recent times. The organization of pressure groups (or the imperfectly competitive character of market organization) has weakened the pervasive influence of competitive pressures. Individuals today are determined to control market forces rather than be controlled by them; they resist accepting a "market-determined" destiny. However, to the extent that groups are able to control market forces rather than be con-

---

[1] George W. Taylor, "Criteria in the Wage Bargain," *New York University First Annual Conference on Labor*, edited by Emanuel Stein (New York, Matthew Bender & Co., 1948), p. 68.

trolled by them, policy in the application of that control becomes increasingly, and sometimes painfully, relevant. Each group feels compelled to define and make explicit its targets and policies. Each group searches for that convincing rationale which will justify both its ends and the means it employs to achieve them. This problem is no more apparent than on issues involving distributive shares. As Lloyd Reynolds has characterized bargaining over the wages issue: ". . . the rates for specific jobs in the plant are determined, within rather broad limits, by managerial discretion or union-management negotiation. A job rate is an administered rate *par excellence*." [2] If one has the power to administer prices and wages, just what responsibilities must be associated with that power? If, to use Ross's phrase, a little decision is merely the choice to be swept along in a stream and a big decision can redirect the stream itself, in what direction should the stream be diverted?

In recent times this question has been posed more frequently: This is because the continuing experience of high levels of employment has created novel problems in the area of labor-management relations. The traditional stabilizing and equilibrating force in a market economy was the prospect that any factor or product might be priced out of the market. The vanishing fears of unemployment have created new sources of instability, which more often than not we hope to resolve by an appeal to reasonableness or responsibility. Again, these concepts are only significant when defined and understood.

Because of the growing importance of this area, we have broken the material into two separate parts. In this chapter we shall deal with the mechanics of dispute settlement concentrating on the techniques of mediation, conciliation, and arbitration.

The Advantages of Not Using Force

The advantages of not resorting to force are both (a) tactical and (b) philosophical. In the former context, there is again something dramatic about two reindeers with antlers locked in combat until death, just as there is of two duelists firing at each other at three paces. But the reality of mutual destruction is as sobering to the participants of the dispute as it might be entertaining to those witnessing it. In this sense, when both labor and management have equal bargaining power, the gain of striking is less apparent to each. It is only when one party is obviously at a disadvantage that coercion can be contemplated to resolve the dispute. This, of course, is simply the application of the balance of power principle to our domestic relations. This is not to suggest that when bargaining power is equal, mutual destruction is certain. However, when the outcome of a dispute is rather indeterminate simply because of

[2] *The Structure of Labor Markets* (New York, Harper & Bros., 1951), pp. 237–238.

equality of power, the justification for securing a peaceful settlement becomes all the more apparent to both parties.[3]

As one might suspect, the party with the less economic power is always more interested in peaceful rather than militant solutions. In terms of a historical perspective, it appears that labor has been more eager to settle differences that arise during and after negotiations by arbitration. This probably reflects labor's belief that it could secure more from arbitration (where the principle involved in the dispute might be given consideration) than by a test of strength. If management does have superior bargaining power, it may be reluctant to submit a dispute to arbitration, for fear that an arbitrator may grant the union more than the union could otherwise secure.[4] The growing interest and use of arbitration today suggests that equality of power is characteristic of labor-management relations.

In our previous chapter we reviewed the philosophical appeal of settlements rooted in understanding and reason. Both parties anxiously outscramble each other in attempting to establish their statesmanlike approach to bargaining as well as to prove their aversion to the use of force. For example, Walter Reuther testified:

> The basic principle is that economic decisions . . . be based upon economic facts and not based upon economic power. . . . We cannot intelligently or rationally find the proper balance between wages, prices and profits unless we know all of the pertinent facts. You can't have collective bargaining with one side of the table blindfolded, nor can you achieve a rational solution to problems if you work within

[3] Cyrus Ching takes exception to this notion. "It is argued that more employer associations should be organized to balance the bargaining power between employers and the big national unions. The reasoning behind this view seems to be well stated by one union leader: 'It is unwholesome for either party to have unchecked power. The union leader who cannot rely on the employer to defend the firm's rights is often on the hot seat, for his membership very soon expects him to overreach on their behalf.' . . . I cannot accept the proposition that meeting unreasoning force with unreasoning force presents a sure pattern for industrial peace. At one time, the whole international system was based on the balance of power; but the world today is pretty well disillusioned on that score. Few people now believe that the balance of power theory can produce international peace. It more often breeds war. . . ." *Review and Reflections: A Half Century of Labor Relations* (New York, B. C. Forbes and Sons Publishing Co., 1953), p. 137.

[4] In a survey of 50 union leaders conducted by the Twentieth Century Fund, W. S. Woytinsky and Associates, *Labor and Management Look at Collective Bargaining* (New York, 1949, pp. 54, 62) it was found that 32 percent favored arbitration in general, while only 11 percent said they opposed arbitration in general. Of 87 management respondents, 28 percent said they favored arbitration in general while 57 percent said they opposed it in general. In a survey of conciliation and mediation in Minnesota it was noted that "The question of attitude was emphasized much more strongly by employers than by unions. Some feeling still persists among a minority of employers that mediators — particularly from the state service — are pro-labor." For discussion, see John G. Turnbull and Clara Kanun, "Conciliation and Mediation in Minnesota," *Labor Law Journal* (October, 1952), p. 682.

an economic vacuum. Yet as long as industry is not willing to lay all the facts on the table so that you can make a decision based upon facts, they, by their unwillingness, commit collective bargaining to the laws of the jungle, where the decision will be made based upon economic power — whoever can get the biggest club and swing it first. . . .[5]

The interest in establishing the principles behind and merit of each case is reflected in the growing research of both labor and management on wage-price relations, industry profits, comparative wages, and so forth. While the data may be discounted at the bargaining table, they can be used to good advantage for distribution to the shareholders, to the rank and file, and to the general public. Labor and management often distribute press releases, bulletins and pamphlets, and sometimes research monographs to the public in support of their cases.[6]

Let us briefly review the mechanics of dispute settlement.

The Conciliation and Mediation Process

Often the words *conciliation* and *mediation* are used synonymously, but a distinction in these terms can be made. The conciliation process refers to the job of " keeping the discussions going " through the activities of a third party. The effort to prolong discussion and negotiation does not, in any way, involve the viewpoint or sentiment of the conciliator. The mediation process represents somewhat more active participation in discussions than conciliation. The mediator will not only attempt to prolong negotiations, but will make specific suggestions from time to time to see if a compromise can be reached. Both federal and state governments rely heavily on conciliation and mediation to maintain industrial peace. In 1952 it was estimated that about 31 percent of all work stoppages in the United States (involving 58.8 percent of workers and 84.3 percent of man-days idled by strike action) were settled by the assistance of government agencies.[7] In the National Labor-Management Conference called by President Truman in November, 1945, representatives categori-

[5] *The Economics of Collective Bargaining* (Berkeley, Institute of Industrial Relations, University of California, 1950), pp. 6–7.

[6] A case in point is the monograph produced by Dr. Jules Backman of New York University in reply to the Nathan report. Nathan outlined arguments to support wage increases for labor, and each of these arguments was analyzed by Backman in a 287-page monograph, titled *Economics of a Fourth Round of Wage Increase; Testimony on Behalf of Steel Companies Before the Presidential Steel Fact Finding Board* (New York, August, 1949). A comparison of Backman's study with Nathan's, *A National Economic Policy,* brings into sharp focus the problems of agreement between labor and management, or more specifically, between labor and management economists, on both economic principle and economic fact.

[7] Kurt Braun, *Labor Disputes and Their Settlement* (Baltimore, Johns Hopkins Press, 1955), p. 48. Well over half of all such disputes were settled with the assistance of the government agencies during World War II.

cally rejected compulsory arbitration as a solution to disputes, but recommended unanimously the use of conciliation whenever agreement could not be reached, and when such conciliation failed, the use of arbitration.

Because of the success of conciliation and mediation and the general support given to this process, the government has long been active in the field. First legislation dealing with conciliation developed in Maryland in 1878. The federal government first became interested in conciliation as a device for avoiding disputes in the railroad industry. The federal government established the United States Conciliation Service on March 4, 1913. Under the provisions of the Taft-Hartley Act in 1947, a Federal Mediation and Conciliation Service was set up independently of the Department of Labor to provide this same function.[8] The Director of this agency is appointed by the President with the approval of the Senate. The service has branch offices located throughout the country and employs approximately 300 commissioners. Usually these conciliators, as the federal agency commissioners are called, enter a dispute at the invitation of one or both of the parties to a dispute. Several states also provide Mediation Boards who perform similar functions. Their representatives are usually called mediators. Interest in the mediation process has been extended since the Taft-Hartley law requires that all governmental levels of the Mediation Service receive notification if a dispute is developing.[9]

Because the mediator or conciliator cannot compel acceptance of any proposal to secure settlement, his major weapon is to remind each party that the consequences of disagreement can only be a costly strike.[10] And it is because the pressure of the strike is most conducive to compromise that mediation is often most successful in an atmosphere of crisis. In more recent times, however, the Federal Mediation and Conciliation

---

[8] Because the Department of Labor was established to "foster, promote and develop the welfare of the wage-earners of the United States . . . ," management sometimes felt that the Conciliation Service, as a division of the Department of Labor, could not provide a neutral service. The 1947 act was designed to meet this criticism by removing the agency from the authority of the Secretary of Labor.

[9] In the Labor-Management Relations Act of 1947, Section 8 (d), Title I, the meaning of "to bargain collectively" is spelled out; Subsection (3) requires that the federal service (as well as any existing state agency) be notified of the existence of a dispute within designated time limits and by the moving party. The federal service may "proffer its services" upon its own motion or upon the request of one or more of the parties to a dispute (Title II, Section 203 [b]). The parties to the dispute "shall participate fully and promptly in such meetings as may be undertaken by the Service under this Act for the purpose of aiding in the settlement of the dispute." Section 204 (3).

[10] As Dr. John R. Steelman, director of the U. S. Conciliation Service, explained: "The minute you make a cop of a conciliator you have destroyed his usefulness. We do not want authority. We believe it to be the very antithesis of the spirit in which really effective conciliation is carried on." *New York Times Magazine* (March 30, 1941).

Service has noted the value of "preventive mediation," a procedure through which the mediator is present prior to the crisis stage of negotiation and tries to prevent a deadlock from developing.[11] A permanent meditator for an industry can often provide invaluable services to a particular firm or industry. He can learn the technical conditions of the industry, the unique personality or human relations problems around which many disputes evolve, and through his experience and insight suggest solutions to issues which might otherwise lead to strikes. The criticism of the *ad hoc* mediator is that he may become involved in the dispute prematurely (so that both sides spend their energy attempting to explain to him the nature of the difficulty rather than attempting to find a solution), or he may become involved in the dispute when the strike is on, with both parties firmly entrenched in their positions.[12]

The government agent participating in these discussions must, of course, be neutral. He must have the appearance and reputation for "objectivity"; he must be a man of integrity, with deep insight into human nature as well as the technical problems of industry. Of course, understanding the technical problems of production may assist him in understanding the nature of the conflict, but his fundamental task is to determine the true cause of disagreement, and this can often be a problem of clashing personalities and principles. His first step will be to gain the confidence of the participants and then listen carefully to each party as each side of the story is told. He may then ask to speak to each party separately. In the semiconfidential atmosphere of the caucus room, he may learn further information and attempt to determine the absolute limit of the concessions by each party. He may then propose a compromise solution, or at least indicate to each party that a stalemate need not develop as long as there is some willingness to compromise.[13]

[11] For a critical comment on the effectiveness of preventative mediation in the absence of the atmosphere of crisis, see Allen Weisenfeld, "Some Thoughts on Labor Mediation," *Proceedings* of the Sixth Annual Meetings of the Industrial Relations Research Association (December 28–30, 1953), pp. 276–283.

[12] The difficulties of such permanent mediators are similar to those of the permanent arbitrator. In fact, it may be difficult to distinguish the mediation and arbitration functions in such a situation. As Julius J. Manson has observed, the plan for using an impartial chairman to mediate disputes "has had varying success because of the industry arbitrator's preference to remain not only above the battle, but in his seat." From his discussion of the paper cited above, *ibid.*, p. 293.

[13] A privately circulated essay, written with tongue in cheek, described the methods sometimes employed by mediators. One method was the "traumatasonic technique" in which the mediator, when confronted by disorder and shouting, whistled with such a "piercing and physically painful sound" that a state of trauma was produced among the parties and the way was cleared to successful mediation of their differences. Among others mentioned was the "multiple confusion technique," in which the mediator, in the process of restating the issues in his own language, created such an "atmosphere of mutual perturbation" that the parties found themselves well advised to get together forthwith. The author found this technique to be particularly effective when the mediator began to outline his own opinions of "some of the

What are the beneficial effects that result from the presence of the mediator or conciliator? First, it may calm down the emotional nature of the discussion. Each side may have been highly belligerent, perhaps resorting to abusive language. Tempers may have been reaching their breaking point. Each side's argument will probably be more objective and less emotional when presented to the mediator and such recapitulation may be conducive to settlement. Secondly, the mediator may serve as a " sounding board " or " crying wall," permitting each side to " let off steam." A sympathetic listener provides invaluable therapy and may contribute to a more conciliatory atmosphere in the discussions. Thirdly, the mediator may offer " face-saving " services. Because the ego, pride, and prestige of the participants to the bargaining session are often involved in the " final " positions they take, it is vital that they be able to retreat gracefully. The mediator can assume the blame for any concessions that are forthcoming; it is easier to make concessions to the mediator than to the coercive pressure of the other party to the dispute.[14]

Despite the hint of compulsion in the Taft-Hartley law, the mediation process is more accurately described as an extension of the collective bargaining process rather than as interference by the government in that process. This does not mean that the mediator cannot be " used " by each party in such bargaining. One party, for example, may be resigned to a strike, but will make a much-publicized appeal for mediation in order to draw the attention of the public to its efforts to avoid the breakdown of negotiations. It may then escape blame for the collapse of negotiations. Similarly, it is not impossible for each side to use the mediator in order to find out the weak spots of the other. While each side attempts to find the " real " bargaining position of the other, the mediator may be used as part of the bargaining strategy to feed misinformation to the opposition on its own real position.[15]

---

more important economic and social implications of the dispute." As described by Frederick H. Bullen, " The Mediation Process," *New York University First Annual Conference on Labor, op. cit.,* p. 113.

[14] In fact, on occasion the mediator has been blamed for the concession. If one representative creates the impression that a concession of " X " cents per hour could be made, the conciliator may sound out the other party on that figure. If the other party agrees to that figure, the first party may then deny a willingness to the " X " cents per hour figure, indicating that this was only tentative. They may then only reluctantly accept that figure because the mediator misunderstood their viewpoint. This technique is, of course, hardly fair to the mediator, and is not a common procedure. It does indicate, though, the extent to which participants will go to " save face " in making concessions.

[15] Edgar Warren indicated that mediation had not been successful in the big disputes involving automobiles, basic steel, and coal mining, and suggested that in some situations, it may be necessary to provide another representative of the mediation service ". . . who happens to have either greater prestige with the parties or a greater familiarity with their problems and their personalities, or it may be an outsider, an *ad hoc* mediator." For his discussion, see *Proceedings* of the Sixth Annual Meeting of the Industrial Relations Research Association (December 28-30, 1953), pp. 288-290.

The Arbitration Process

The notion that industrial strife can be avoided by the resort to arbitration has gained substantial support recently and the widespread use of arbitration has revived interest in the mechanics as well as the principles underlying this technique. Arbitration is the process through which both parties agree to submit to an impartial umpire who will make a decision that both parties agree in advance will be binding. It is important to note that the determination of the decision to arbitrate is voluntary in that usually the consent of both parties is required before a dispute is arbitrated. But once the decision is made to submit the dispute to arbitration, the decision of that arbitrator is binding on both parties. Thus, it might be more accurate to speak of " voluntarily adopted compulsory arbitration," in that the technique is voluntarily accepted but the decision is binding. The essential difference between voluntary and compulsory arbitration is determined by whether either party can refuse to submit differences to arbitration. Compulsory arbitration implies a radical departure from the principles of free collective bargaining, while voluntary arbitration is more readily accepted as a natural extension of free bargaining. One might, in a conceptual sense, also distinguish between compulsory or voluntary " awards," with the latter case permitting either party to reject the decision of the arbitrator. This form of arbitration is unusual today and, as noted above, it is understood that the arbitrator's award shall be technically and legally binding on both parties.

Arbitration can also be analyzed in terms of the composition, responsibilities, and tenure of the arbitrator. A single arbitrator may be selected by both management and labor and his responsibilities terminate when he renders his decision. This is generally called *ad hoc* arbitration. An alternative is to appoint a permanent umpire or arbitrator to service a large corporation or an industry. Estimates again suggest that about 85 percent of contract provisions provide for *ad hoc* arbitration, while only 15 percent call for a permanent arbitrator. The arbitrator who is appointed for a single case has the advantage of providing a fresh perspective to the problem, and because his tenure will terminate with his decision, he may be encouraged to provide a more objective decision than one whose employment depends upon the mutual satisfaction of both parties with his decisions. On the other hand, the permanent arbitrator has the advantage of gaining insight into industry conditions, gaining the confidence of both parties to the dispute and the opportunity to establish his integrity. He can blend his arbitration functions with those of mediation to minimize misunderstanding and tension. Rather than have a single arbitrator, both parties may prefer the establishment of an arbitration board. The board may be established on a tripartite basis with a company and union representative, as well as the third neutral chairman, whose decision represents the balance of power. Such an arrangement makes it more certain that the chairman will have before him adequate representation for both sides of the dispute. As a further alternative, an arbitration board may be made up entirely of public representatives with the majority vote of the board determining the award.

Why has arbitration grown so popular in recent years? In our earlier chapters we stressed that man flees from uncertainty and if this is so, why should a device, aptly described by George Soule's phrase as " the peaceful uncertainty of arbitral settlement " be so popular? The answer is again found in the balancing of the cost of disagreement arising from a stalemate to the cost of arbitration. It is not that either party looks to arbitration for a *compromise* solution, but rather for vindication for the position they have taken. It is precisely because one can never be certain which way the decision may go that both parties support the process. Each side usually has ample confidence in the merit of its case and is generally convinced that any objective observer would have to support its position. Needless to say, both sides cannot be right. It is not surprising, therefore, that the selection of the *ad hoc* arbitrator is often made with a careful examination of the background of that person. Both parties are hopeful of securing an impartial arbitrator " on our side " or one who is neutral but " sympathetic."

The costs of arbitration are usually shared jointly by labor and management, and while the price of this service is modest when set against the cost of a strike or lockout, union spokesmen have sometimes complained that the resulting expenses require that they push only their strongest cases. Because the company can better afford such arbitration expenses, the union alleges that the company has a tactical advantage in grievance settlement, simply because the union is under pressure to minimize arbitration costs.

Prior to the arbitration hearings, it is most important that the arbitrator secure a clear bill of submission outlining the precise nature of his jurisdiction in the dispute. Such statements are designed to " clear out the underbrush " from disputes, to avoid confusion and misunderstanding, and to enable the arbitrator to focus his energies more clearly on the basic issue. The decision of the arbitrator must be complete, definite, and clear. It should be within the bounds of the existing contract and within the bounds of the problem originally presented by both parties. It must, of course, also be within the bounds of the law. If the decision of the arbitrator is to be appealed to the courts, it can only be on the basis of some technical aspect rather than the substantive content of the ruling.

Advantages and Disadvantages of Arbitration

The most obvious advantage of arbitration is that it provides an alternative to a costly strike. Secondly, it can generally be undertaken with a minimum of delay. Thirdly, it is usually an informal device which enables both parties to the dispute to present their cases in a relaxed atmosphere. Both sides can make an appeal to the facts and to the merits of their case. The arbitrator may permit those persons involved in the dispute, as well as their representatives, to be present at all hearings. All parties are generally able to cross-examine the others regarding the facts of the case in order that the arbitrator may get as clear a picture as possible. A final advantage is that arbitration is relatively inexpensive, even though complaints are sometimes voiced that an arbitrator may earn a hundred dollars " for a few hours' work."

Set against these advantages are several disadvantages. First, it may be that the alternative of arbitration will weaken the process of genuine bargaining over a dispute. Either union or management, and even both, may prefer to build their case before an arbitration panel rather than attempt to resolve their differences themselves. As we noted earlier, the enthusiasm for such arbitration is likely to be stronger with the party having less economic bargaining power. Arbitration may be the lazy man's out from hard bargaining. A second disadvantage is that often it requires that the arbitrator possess considerable technical skill and background so that he can understand the implications of the dispute. The inexperienced arbitrator, even though objective, may inadvertently reach a decision which both labor and management would agree was foolish. The damage done by the " bull in the china shop " may be serious.[16] The requirement that the arbitrator have technical skill may minimize this difficulty, but it is often difficult to find individuals sufficiently familiar with the history and unique problems of the plant and its personnel.

A third criticism is that arbitration is becoming increasingly cumbersome, technical, legalistic, and expensive.[17] There has been a rising tide

[16] Paradoxical as it may seem, Kurt Braun points out that the possibility of an adverse decision by an arbitrator operates as a " positive force in favor of careful and deliberate effort by both parties to conform to the agreement. The agreement to arbitrate therefore acts as a deterrent to either union or management irresponsibility in contract administration." (*Op. cit.*, p. 47.) This suggests then that the " cost " of unfavorable arbitration decisions may be an impelling reason for sincere bargaining just as the " cost " of a strike encourages peaceful settlement.

[17] Isadore Katz, general counsel for the Textile Workers of America, criticized the arbitration process in no uncertain terms before the 1951 conference sponsored by the American Arbitration Association and the National Academy of Arbitrators. He pointed out that the individual worker is bewildered by and suspicious of arbitration proceedings " that move more and more away from the realities of the mine, mill and factory and further and further into the field of technical legal proceedings. . . ." Katz points out that when the worker arrives at the arbitration proceeding, " he finds a strange, and if not hostile, at least an exasperating world, peopled by lawyers or facsimiles thereof. . . . We find the worker appearing before an arbitrator whose distance from him must be measured in light years. . . ." Often the arbitrator himself does not seem willing to focus discussion on the original issue: " We find the arbitrator peering out from the apertures of the agreement at two lawyers who are arguing as to whether they should be there in the first place. The

of protests against the judicial nature of the arbitration proceedings; the loss of the informal element represents the loss of one of the greatest advantages of arbitration. By introducing formal court procedure, arbitration becomes a " trial by judicial combat," and it goes without saying that the more elaborate the legal proceedings, the greater will be its expense.[18]

This issue provides us with a logical point of departure for a discussion of standards in arbitration decision-making because much of the analysis about standards evolves from one's conception of what the arbitration process is or should be.

Standards in Arbitration: The Judicial Approach

Arbitration is viewed from two conflicting, but not necessarily opposite, viewpoints. On the one hand, it is considered a natural extension of collective bargaining, and in this sense the arbitrator is justified in " mediating " solutions to the difficulties during the hearings themselves. This would be tantamount to the judge recessing a case for a private conversation in his chambers to see if a settlement could not be established without resort to a court ruling. Many arbitrators have had considerable success with this technique and thus stress the advantages of combining mediation with arbitration. Some consider this method hazardous, for it may befuddle the participants and have no sanction in the bill of submission.

The second view of arbitration is that it is a quasi-judicial process, and the mediation and arbitration functions should not be entangled or confused. In line with this approach, it is reasoned that the arbitrator must

question becomes: Is or is not the matter arbitrable and, if it is arbitrable, has the Statute of Limitations outlawed the grievance or has the grievance been properly reduced to writing at the second step of the grievance procedure and duly endorsed at the third step by the chief steward? " The arbitrator himself may be caught in the legal maze being woven by the lawyers: " The arbitrator is constantly reminded that he shall not trespass on contract clauses, and that if he should, a court will swiftly eject him." As if this were not enough: " The arbitrator's opinion is not directed at the immediate participants but is cast in the form of a report to a higher body, with an eye to publication in one of the unofficial reporters . . ." " Challengeable Trends in Labor Arbitration," *The Arbitration Journal*, Vol. 7, No. 1 (1952), pp. 16–17.

[18] Samuel P. Hayes, Jr. agrees that " Voluntary conciliation and arbitration lay an important stress on informality and on the absence of legalistic emphasis on precedent, hair splitting argument, and discussion of eternal ' rights ' and ' principles.' Lawyers are often explicitly prohibited by the agreements from taking any part in the proceedings! " Hayes then quoted Pigou's observations (from his *Economics of Welfare*, London, 1932, p. 422): " . . . technicalities and lawyers should not be admitted before the Board. Such a policy — apart altogether from the saving in cost and time — tends to reduce to a minimum the appearance, and hence, indirectly, the reality of the opposition between the parties." For a somewhat contrasting viewpoint which emphasizes the judicial nature of the arbitration process, see Frances Keller, *Arbitration In Action* (New York, Harper & Bros., 1941).

regard the "contract as king" and make decisions which involve only an interpretation of contract provisions. By such a device a code of common law is built up which will guide future situations and eliminate many disputes over contract interpretation. Each award then serves as a precedent, not only to the company but to the entire industry (or even economy). Supporters of this view often point out that an arbitrator's decision may be thrown out by the courts if it is not consistent with the contract terms. The arbitrator's function, then, is to be a law-interpreter and not a lawmaker.[19]

However attractive this approach may be, several difficulties are immediately apparent. First, if arbitration over interests or over terms of a new contract are involved, there is no existing constitution to serve as a guide. Secondly, the contract itself may be contradictory in certain respects, so that the task of the arbitrator is to select one of two conflicting provisions. Thirdly, more frequently than not the contract is silent or makes only an oblique reference to the issue involved. Such silence or ambiguity leaves the arbitrator with tremendous discretion, and by a strict application of the legalistic approach, he may be literally at sea without a rudder. In a few instances the contract specifies that if the arbitrator should face a dispute that is not covered by the contract terms, the dispute should be returned to the participants for renegotiation.

A further refinement of this approach is to stress the "intent" of the parties in drawing up the contract. Here again, intent is a rather nebulous concept. First, the contract provision may have been deliberately framed in vague terms out of fear that an attempt to particularize its content would make the difference of opinion explicit and delay contract settlement. The arbitrator inherits the dispute at a later date, and the conflict in intent must then be resolved. Needless to say, few participants to a dispute are happy with the arbitrator's interpretation of their "intent" if that interpretation has permitted the arbitrator to make a decision unfavorable to them. A further defense of this approach is suggested, however, with the argument that the arbitrator should maintain his legalistic approach, but interpolate legislation to fill in the gaps of the contract. Kurt

[19] Wayne L. Morse explains this viewpoint rather clearly. ". . . arbitration is a judicial process. The arbitrator sits as a private judge, called upon to determine the legal rights and economic interests of the parties. . . . The principle of compromise has absolutely no place in an arbitration hearing . . . an arbitrator should not take judicial notice of anything which is not presented by the parties in the record of the case. . . . argument, no matter how persuasive, unsupported by evidence and facts, is of little value to an arbitrator. . . . Too many arbitrators still try to apply the principle of compromise in their decisions. . . . I am satisfied that if we followed a less technical and formal system of procedure in our cases, it would be impossible to confine the arbitrator's decision to the record made by the parties. . . . An arbitrator is bound by the language of a contract, and he has no right to reform or amend it. . . ." From "The Scope and Limitations of the Arbitration Process in Labor Disputes," *Proceedings*, International Longshoremen's and Warehousemen's Union, Third Annual Convention (April 6, 1940).

Braun explains, " It cannot be said that they [the arbitrators] are less qualified to explore and to write down the developing law than a parliament, particularly when they include experts, as they always should." [20] This returns us to our original point that the larger purpose of arbitration " is to establish a new, now non-existing body of common law.[21]

Apart from these problems arising from the inadequacy of the contract, several other criticisms are leveled at the strictly legalistic approach. First, the legal mind many apply concepts of logic and legal philosophy not compatible with harmonious labor-management relations. Uniformity and consistency may be attractive to the logician, lawyer, or professor, but they are hardly attractive in arbitration if they provide decisions which upset or disturb further labor-management relations. The use of precedent and the evolution of a common law may pose a deceptively simple panacea for industrial disputes: those close to labor-management relations (as well as those experienced in arbitration) caution that the complex of circumstances changes rapidly from time to time and from industry to industry, making it unwise to lean heavily on precedent.[22]

Several students of arbitration have stressed the hazards of legalism. Professor Willard Wirtz states that " if the parties can find a mutually satisfactory basis for realizing a particular problem, it would be obviously unfortunate if anything in the contract should be considered a bar to settlement on that basis." Lois MacDonald found that arbitrators themselves feared that " lawyers are too legalistic in their thinking and tend to overlook the spirit of the agreement and the dynamics of labor relations." [23] Aaron Horvits raises the question: " Was not arbitration intended as a relief from the absolutism associated with legal principles — with emphasis on the facts, the equities, and the agreements involved and not on legal dogma? " [24] In an even more pointed criticism, Herman Cooper complains that " the whole subject of arbitration and arbitrators needs re-examining in order to stay the rapid process of hardening of the arteries which is giving us judicial, if not judicious, pronouncements instead of practical solutions. . . ." [25]

[20] *The Settlement of Industrial Disputes* (Philadelphia, Blakiston Co., 1944), p. 120.

[21] As described by Ludwig Teller, *Management Functions Under Collective Bargaining* (New York, Baker, Voorhis & Co., 1947), p. 348.

[22] For an interesting discussion of this problem and the results of a survey of the attitudes of several nationally famous arbitrators, see Paul Prasow, *An Examination of the Role of Arbitration Principles in an Emerging 'Industrial Jurisprudence,'* an unpublished Ph. D. dissertation for the Department of Economics, 1948, University of Southern California.

[23] Both of the above quotations are found in Edgar L. Warren and Irving Bernstein's study, " The Arbitration Process," *Southern Economic Journal,* Vol. XVII, No. 1 (July, 1950), p. 22.

[24] " An Appraisal of Arbitration: An Arbitrator's Viewpoint," *Industrial and Labor Relations Review,* Vol. 8, No. 1 (October, 1954), p. 87.

[25] " An Appraisal of Arbitration: A Labor Viewpoint," *Industrial and Labor Relations Review,* Vol. 8, No. 1 (October, 1954), p. 85.

As the above controversy suggests, there is hardly uniform support of the judicial approach. However, one of the major points in its favor is the even greater difficulty for securing a common principle for arbitration if the contract itself is not to be the sole standard. In this context it is interesting to note that many students of arbitration do not recommend that the arbitrator state the reasons for his decisions. In most state arbitration laws such explanations are not required, nor can they be demanded by litigation. The usual reason for this viewpoint is that the decision may be right, but the reasoning supporting it, wrong. This indicates the problem of finding standards, criteria, or principles to guide the arbitrator. The fact is, of course, much more serious if the arbitrator is assigned the task of settling outstanding differences that exist in the negotiations of a new contract.

Standards in Arbitration: *The Nonjudicial Approach*

Three propositions generally arise in discussion of arbitration standards: (1) The arbitrator must advance his solution in terms of some "principle"; (2) the arbitrator must advance a solution with which both parties can live; (3) the arbitrator must avoid a simple "split the difference" approach. Unfortunately, all of these may not be consistent one with the other, for if an arbitrator avoids splitting the difference (because of his aversion to compromise), he may still render a decision with which neither party can live. Paradoxical as it may seem, a real hazard arises when the arbitrator projects a decision on the basis of his private philosophy without appreciating that his decision may create more problems than it solves. In other words, the arbitrator cannot isolate himself from the reality of the need for a workable solution.

As a case in point, let us assume that an arbitrator has been called in to resolve a wage issue during contract negotiations. The company has offered 5 cents and the union insists on 10 cents. Any number of economic standards might be advanced to reach a decision, including changes in the consumer price index, the company's ability to pay, changes in labor productivity, wage comparisons with other plants, and so on. Combinations of these standards by any weighting device, or the use of any one of these alone, may not necessarily provide a settlement that is within the 5- to 10-cent range. It is obvious that the settlement must lie somewhere within the gap between the two parties, but isolated instances have existed where arbitrators have denied the relevance of such bargaining to establish their own figure outside of this range. Similarly, situations occasionally develop where a solution to a dispute is "rigged" by both labor and management. Because of factionalism within the union or within management, it is necessary that the decision appear to be that of an arbitrator rather than one reached by mutual agreement. Could an arbitrator in good conscience consent to such a prearranged solution to a dispute if this solution did not appear consistent with his own philosophy?

Much of the discussion over standards arises from the allegation that arbitration involves simply a mechanical " split the difference " calculation. The hazards of this procedure are apparent enough. The integrity of the arbitrator is likely to be questioned and the arbitration process itself is undermined.[26] But more than this, it will encourage each party to the dispute to establish artificial positions on exaggerated claims in order that the split of the difference may be more favorable. In addition, any party to a dispute sincerely seeking a solution by making concessions is immediately placed in an unfavorable position, for the final concession will be the jumping-off point for the " split the difference " calculation.

The word " compromise " is loaded with unfavorable connotations, especially in arbitration. According to Kurt Braun, " as a rule there is no place for compromise in the awards. . . ."[27] But in defense of the fact that most decisions do fall somewhere between the expectations of management and labor, Tracey H. Ferguson explains: " No word has been abused more than the word ' compromise.' . . . Merely because an arbitrator's award falls within the middle of the levels suggested by the parties does not mean that for that reason the award is a compromise. . . ."[28] Even so, the expectations of the parties cannot be neglected, for these patterns determine labor-management harmony in the post-decision period. Much to the point, Aaron Levenstein aptly characterizes the arbitration decision-making process: " The arbitrator knows very well that his decision is based on a hundred subtleties of economics, social philosophy, psychology and pure hunch. . . . All of which add up to his estimate of what will best further a continuing more harmonious relationship between the contenders." [29]

Thus, the arbitration process involves consideration of both principle and reality, both the power of contending groups as well as their expectations.[30] Probably the dominant consideration is that decisions must min-

---

[26] For further discussion, see Lois MacDonald, " The Selection and Tenure of Arbitrators in Labor Disputes," *New York University First Annual Conference on Labor* (New York, Matthew Bender & Company, 1948), pp. 158-159.

[27] As quoted by Harold W. Davey, " Hazards in Labor Arbitration," *Industrial and Labor Relations Review*, Vol. 1, No. 3 (April, 1948), p. 389.

[28] *Op. cit.*, p. 84.

[29] "Some Obstacles to Reporting Labor Arbitration," *The Arbitration Journal*, Vol. 1, No. 4 (new series, Winter, 1946), p. 426.

[30] As Samuel P. Hayes, Jr., explains: " Just as most legal decisions are compromises based upon the relative strength of the disputants and elaborately supported by selected precedents and reasoning, purporting to show the consistency and applicability of legal ' principles,' so also conciliation and arbitration result in compromises that fairly closely represent the believed relative bargaining strength of the parties concerned and the relative importance to them of the point at issue. Where this is not true (as, for instance, where one side believes itself stronger than it really is), con-

imize disaffection between labor and management, or be one that is most conducive to future harmonious relations. The decision, in other words, must attempt to provide some reasonable *modus vivendi* between disputants.[31] Irving Bernstein puts the point this way: " The arbitrator is obliged to consider not only the general standards of wage determination but also the parties' relative bargaining power. If he fails to do so, he may well undermine his basic function — keeping the peace." Acceptability and workability must be paramount considerations, for " a rejected decision is no decision at all. . . ."[32]

The decision-making process in arbitration reveals again the facility and feasibility of buttressing any " practical " decision with the logic of economic theory as well as references to the public welfare. Such principles may be viewed as the " logical defenses of private purposes " or " the rearrangement of private prejudices," but they do perform an essential role in convincing each side of the reasoning behind a decision. In Feis's often-quoted words " The lack of any widespread understanding of the possible principles which might be used in setting wage disputes, and the strongly held opinion that no set of satisfactory principles can be devised, have certainly been obstacles to the peaceful and constructive settlement of disputes. When men do not see any principle on which they can agree, it is much easier to disagree."[33] Certainly this is not a problem confined alone to arbitration, but mirrors the larger difficulties created by conflict within our society as well as the even greater difficulties arising between nations.

The arbitration of disputes has, as one would expect, a long history. Arbitration was used during Aristotle's time and even more extensively under Roman law. In the United States, New York set up an arbitration law in 1829; Maryland established one in 1870. Permanent arbitration boards were set up in Massachusetts and New York in 1836. Today, all states except South Dakota have established some type of arbitration machinery. The need for arbitration became more obvious in those industries where disputes disrupted the entire economy, and it is not surprising, therefore, that early government legislation on industrial disputes should be found in the railroad industry. Let us look at this area of law briefly.

ciliation and arbitration break down and there is resort to direct action." From *Psychological Study of Social Issues in Industrial Conflict: A Psychological Interpretation*, edited by G. W. Hartman and T. M. Newcomb, 1939.

[31] As the authority David L. Cole explains, " Certainly in contract-making disputes his (the arbitrator's) principal aim is to find a sound solution on which the parties may build a stable relationship, and not to say who is technically right or wrong." David L. Cole: " Arbitration — Whose Responsibility? " *Proceedings* of the Industrial Relations Research Association, 4th Annual Meeting (Boston, December, 1951), p. 153.

[32] From his study, *Arbitration of Wages* (Los Angeles, University of California Press, 1954), pp. 5–6.

[33] From H. Feis's study, *Principles of Wage Settlement* (New York, H. W. Wilson Co., 1924), pp. 1–2.

Arbitration and the Railroad Industry

The Arbitration Act of 1888 provided for two methods for settling disputes in the railroad industry that interrupted interstate commerce — (1) voluntary arbitration (but no provision was made to enforce the decisions of a tripartite arbitration board) and (2) investigation. Under this latter provision, the President of the United States had authority to appoint a three-man commission to investigate disputes, with the United States Commissioner of Labor as the chairman of the committee. These provisions of the law were never used, except for the appointment of an investigating committee to explore the circumstances surrounding the Pullman Strike of 1894. This law was replaced with the Erdman Act in 1898, placing emphasis on conciliation and mediation, with the Commissioner of Labor and the Chairman of the Interstate Commerce Commission serving as mediators. If such mediation should fail, then the commissioner should attempt to have the dispute submitted to a tripartite arbitration panel whose decisions, in turn, would be binding on both parties.[34] In 1913 the Newlands Act was passed, providing for a permanent Board of Mediation and Conciliation made up of three members appointed by the President. The government seized the railroads in 1916 because of a threatened strike, and when these were returned to private operators in 1920, provision was made for establishing the United States Railroad Labor Board. This again was a tripartite board but appointed by the President. The recommendations of this board were not enforceable and were often disregarded.

The Railway Labor Act of 1926 laid the foundation for dispute settlement as known today. Two boards deal with disputes. The National Railroad Adjustment Board is composed of thirty-six members, eighteen selected by the carriers and eighteen by the national organizations of the employees. The awards of this board are final and binding except insofar as they contain a money award. If a deadlock exists on the board, it must select a neutral person, known as a " referee," to sit with the division and make an award. The second agency in the Railway Labor Act is the National Mediation Board, composed of three members appointed by the President with the advice and consent of the Senate. This board, in turn, has a staff of mediators to assist it in its services. The mediation board is available to parties for disputes related to changes in pay, rules or working conditions not adjusted by the parties in conference, or disputes not referable to the National Railroad Adjustment Board, and in other situations where a labor emergency exists. The prime function of the Media-

---

[34] Between 1906 and 1913, 61 cases were settled by the mediation and conciliation provisions; 26 of the cases were settled by mediation alone; 10 by mediation and arbitration; and 6 by arbitration alone. All the awards were fully complied with except one. *Prentice-Hall Labor Course* (New York, Prentice-Hall, 1949), par. 3022, p. 3013.

tion Board is to mediate the dispute, and if this should fail, to encourage the parties to submit to arbitration. If the parties refuse to arbitrate the dispute, the Board would notify the parties that its mediation efforts have failed, and for thirty days the status quo must be maintained. If arbitration is agreed to, a tripartite arbitration board is set up. Both parties are compelled to abide by the arbitration award unless both parties agree in writing to revoke the decision. If the mediation and arbitration efforts fail to settle the dispute, the President may then appoint an Emergency Board to investigate the dispute and report to him. Again, for thirty days after the creation of the fact-finding board, no change in the relations between the parties can take place unless by mutual agreement.

The railroad industry thus has at its disposal fairly elaborate machinery for peacefully settling disputes. As we have seen, legislation provides for the combination of mediation, investigation, and the creation of a "cooling-off" period. While such railroad legislation has often been held up as a model, it also reveals the shortcomings of government intervention: the cooling-off periods often becoming "heating-up" periods. Disputes are more frequently reaching the final "fact-finding" stage, one might suspect as part of the bargaining tactic. The fact-finding court of *last* resort becomes the court of *first* resort, undermining sincere collective bargaining.

> The National Mediation Board has complained about a growing trend among employers and union to get through collective bargaining and mediation in a hurried and perfunctory manner assuming no chance of settlement by these procedures and hastening referral of disputes to a Presidential board of investigation. . . . [it] has strongly emphasized that such extensive use of emergency provisions prevents the law from working as intended, and it has exhorted both railroad management and labor to re-awaken to their statutory responsibilities.[35]

The Compulsory Arbitration Process

When the public grows impatient with the number of strikes taking place, proposals for compulsory arbitration usually receive fresh attention. However, compulsory arbitration is one of the few proposals that both labor and management unite in resisting. What are the pros and cons of this process?

The advocates of compulsory arbitration often point to the costs of strikes. They represent a loss of wages to labor, a loss of sales and income to management, and a loss of real income through the decline of production for the public. It is also stressed that the consolidation of bargaining means that disputes are no longer isolated local disturbances, but major industrial catastrophes. It is no longer safe to let management and labor

[35] As noted by Braun, *op. cit.*, p. 114.

fight it out. Finally, if power is to be the arbiter of disputes, why not invoke public power rather than permit the private coercive power of labor and management to run rampant?

But the weight of criticism against compulsory arbitration is greater than the arguments for it. Basically, the compulsion to submit a dispute to a third party may seriously modify the bargaining process. Neither party would feel it imperative to resolve disputes as long as they realized that continuing differences would result in arbitration. It is significant that a minority report on the Taft-Hartley bill indicated that requiring fact-finding in national emergency disputes with recommendations would be tantamount to compulsory arbitration. The report contained the significant observation.

> Labor and management are unanimous in their condemnation of compulsory arbitration. . . . Motivating them all is the conviction that compulsory arbitration would mean a significant and undesirable extension of government control into an area where such extension may spread to traditional management functions of supervision, prices and profits. Labor justly fears that compulsory arbitration means the cutting down of freedom of the working people. Compulsory arbitration and free enterprise are incompatible. A free enterprise system is founded upon a system of free collective bargaining.[36]

The public demand for arbitration is strongest, of course, in those disputes which are considered to create national emergencies. Actually, though, how serious are such strikes? [37] It is true that particular groups of people suffer a hardship because of strikes, but whether this hardship is serious enough to attempt to outlaw strikes is doubtful. As Ching points out, "Economic warfare must be looked upon for what it is, namely a manifestation of free people competing with each other as vigorously as they can for objectives, which may appear to be in conflict, but which oftentimes result in common good. We must be on guard against any moves which would tend to change it." [38]

We can say that the compulsory arbitration method is exposed to all the hazards of voluntary arbitration with the essential difference that neither party has the opportunity to escape them. Compulsion would weaken, and perhaps cripple collective bargaining; [39] it would encourage

---

[36] National Labor Relations Board, *Legislative History of the Labor Management Relations Act*, U. S. Government Printing Office, 1948, p. 393.

[37] For commentary, see Cyrus Ching, *Review and Reflections: A Half Century of Labor Relations* (New York, B. C. Forbes and Sons Publishing Co., 1953), p. 103.

[38] *Ibid.*, p. 111.

[39] Boris Shiskin, economist for the American Federation of Labor, declared: "The very existence of courts of last resort breeds disputes and prevents their settlement at the source. When you have a court of last resort, no management or labor representative worthy of his salt would have any inducement to resolve the trouble when and where it starts. No, he would be prompt to demonstrate that he, too, was entitled to the recognition, publicity and prestige of carrying his controversy all the way up

disputes; it might turn collective bargaining issues into political issues. The decisions of the industrial courts might reflect the political sentiment of the population controlling the tenure of the courts rather than the economic issues facing the workers and management.[40] As Boris Shiskin observed, " There is no superior wisdom that can prescribe better solutions by remote controls stemming not from knowledge and experience but from ignorance of the multitude of details which enter into the conduct of business and every-day life of workers." [41] Walter Reuther has expressed similar sentiment: "Labor, as well as management, is opposed to compulsory arbitration because we do not believe it is desirable or practical in a democratic society to place in the hands of a third party, to whose selection labor and management have not agreed, the power arbitrarily to fix wages, hours, or working conditions. Such a measure would be a long step toward the creation of a super-state that would limit to an increasing degree the rights of individual citizens." [42]

It appears that compulsory arbitration will only be accepted during periods of national emergency when both labor and management are willing to sacrifice their freedom to strike and lockout. It has had more success in other nations, probably because of the greater willingness of both parties in these countries to accept third-party decisions.[43] The free enterprise spirit in America probably does much to discourage its application here. Each party usually enjoys the illusion that greater success can be achieved by utilizing every technique and weapon in the bargaining process to maximize its gains. Even if this expectation proves wrong, we still cling to the freedom to make fools of ourselves, rather than have the government make fools of us.

Fact-finding

Closely related to compulsory arbitration is the process of fact-finding. Boards may be set up to secure the " facts " from which recommendations

to the highest tribunal." Town Meeting, *Bulletin of America's Town Meeting of the Air* (January 9, 1947).

[40] Supreme Court Justice Frank Murphy explained: "My objection to compulsory arbitration is that it is neither feasible nor practical. . . . Labor and capital, having placed their fate in the hands of courts and judges, would become active contestants for the control of government." Address before the National Conference of Social Work, May 28, 1837. Samuel Gompers also wrote that "The only real effect [of compulsory arbitration] is to . . . make wage earners dependent upon political agency to carry industrial problems into politics. . . ." *Labor and the Employer*. In his *Seventy Years of Life and Labor* (New York, E. P. Dutton & Co., 1925), Vol. II.

[41] *Op. cit.*

[42] " Industrial Relations," Dartnell Corporation, Chicago, Illinois, and quoted in *Compulsory Arbitration* (Chicago, Industrial Relations Division of the National Association of Manufacturers, August, 1951), p. 8.

[43] For an interesting account of compulsory arbitration in Great Britain, see Jean Trepp McKelvey, "Compulsory Arbitration of Labor Disputes in Great Britain," *The Arbitration Journal*, Vol. 7, No. 1 (1952), pp. 31–38.

may or may not be made. The Taft-Hartley Act of 1947 provides for the appointment of a fact-finding board by the President of the United States, which reports to him on the nature and causes of the national emergency conflicts. This committee does not, however, make any recommendations for the settlement of the strike, even though President Eisenhower suggested that the law be modified to permit such recommendations. Such fact-finding is generally associated with a " cooling-off " period. It is assumed that labor and management may be able to give more sober consideration to the need for agreement, and the gathering of facts will serve to pacify the outraged participants suffering exaggerated notions of injustice. If recommendations are made, these are usually backed by the moral suasion of public sentiment. Labor and management fear fact-finding for just this reason. It may be a veiled form of compulsory arbitration and therefore a threat to collective bargaining. Of course, fact-finding is subject to limitations and problems raised by the conciliation and arbitration method. The fact-finder may not have sufficient insight into operating experiences to offer sound recommendations. Each party may fear the recommendations suggested by fact-finding, especially since usually neither has any voice in the selection of the fact-finding commission. While, as we noted above, it was feared that a strong public reaction in support of fact-finding recommendations would mean that fact-finding would be tantamount to compulsory arbitration, public indifference to findings would greatly weaken the process. Obviously some optimum of public response is required, and this response will be conditioned by the number of times that the process is used. A final difficulty arises for those appointed to the fact-finding board, for they must sort out and arrange facts in some meaningful relationship. " It may be laboring the obvious to emphasize that if there are no accepted criteria for the determination of the question at issue, a knowledge of the facts alone cannot be expected to settle it." [44] A further limitation is that facts are, for the most part, static records of historical experience. They cannot anticipate future developments, and it is in the future that both labor and management must live under the contract being negotiated.

[44] Bryce M. Stewart and Walter J. Couper, *Fact Finding in Industrial Disputes* (New York, Industrial Relations Counselors, 1946), p. 47.

15

Principle and the
Bargaining Process

The argument that we should make efforts to avoid an international armaments race — for the simple reason that it might culminate in mutual destruction — has often been applied to the power accumulations of domestic pressure groups. Thus in domestic relations, too, the appeal is made that " reason " should intervene: militancy should give way to cooperation. Those swords represented by the coercive influence of domestic power blocs should be hammered into ploughshares. This argument will always be persuasive, but its success depends on the willingness of pressure groups to embrace common principles or standards.

Standards for guiding economic behavior can be derived by study of religions, philosophies, systems of jurisprudence, or with reference to the basic social and psychological needs of man. But more often than not, any principle that is proposed must also meet the acid test of its " workability " or be examined in terms of its economic impact. Thus, the economist is often called upon to advance standards for economic behavior because of his presumed insight into the complex mechanism that our economy represents. While most economists display engaging modesty in their reluctance to become outspoken advocates of any single economic principle, they are willing to contemplate possible repercussions that may follow from society's acceptance of particular standards. In this chapter we have selected the wage issue as a small cross-section of this much larger problem and will catalog and speculate briefly on some of the more important standards that have often been advanced for wage adjustments.

At the outset we should not be overoptimistic about uniform acceptance of any single standard for wage adjustments or even a combination of these. Power and principle are always carefully balanced by labor and management at the bargaining table. Kurt Braun expresses a conclusion typical of those students of wage policy: " In a free economy, it appears impossible to set up an objective, all-inclusive, and generally accepted code of economic justice and equity and, according to the view of many, it would be undesirable to do so, if it could be done." [1] As a Senate Committee on Education and Labor explained: " Prudence forbids any attempt by the government to remove all the causes of labor disputes. Disputes about wages, hours of work, and other working conditions should continue to be resolved by the play of competitive forces." [2]

We noted in our previous chapter that interest in wage standards has been made necessary by the degree of imperfection of competition coexisting with high levels of labor employment. In an imperfectly competitive market individuals have a degree of discretion over wage and price adjustments. If, in this setting, the fear of unemployment or overproduction does not exist, the momentum behind wage and price increases may be substantially augmented. If fear is not to be a stabilizing influence, substitutes for fear must be found in economic principles.

Standards are important at both national and local levels. In times of national emergency, for example, the government usually finds itself in the unenviable position of adjudicating the terms of agreement between labor and management. Needless to say, the rationale for government decisions must meet the test of public approval or the general requirements of equity and justice. In a peacetime economy, too, government intervention is obvious in the establishment of minimum wage rates, the determination of benefits that unemployed workers receive and other forms of social assistance, the application of standards for wage scales for government employees, and so on. And within each private company, too, wage standards are equally important. Our previous discussion of arbitration and mediation indicated the need for agreement on principle before these processes can operate effectively.

Multiple Functions of Wages

Before reviewing several wage standards it is important to appreciate that wage adjustments provide several basic functions within our economy and that none of these functions can safely be neglected in subscribing to a wage standard. First, wages are important as income or purchasing power for the worker. Secondly, they represent a major cost element to management. Thirdly, wage adjustments often control the effectiveness of labor recruitment: high wages are often necessary in a tight labor market if new workers are to be attracted to a particular industry. Relative wage adjustments, therefore, have some influence on labor mobility or the more general allocation of the labor resource. Fourthly, the wage-price ratio for the particular employer may determine the operating revenues of the firm. Company profits in turn often deter-

---

[1] *Labor Disputes and Their Settlement* (Baltimore, Johns Hopkins Press, 1955), p. 37.
[2] National Labor Relations Board, Senate Report, 573, 74 Cong. 1 sess. (1935), p. 2, and quoted by Braun, *op. cit.*, pp. 37–38.

mine whether the firm can afford capital expansion or technological innovations to reduce per unit labor costs. However, the wage-price ratio
for the economy as a whole may determine the general distribution between total consumption and total investments. Imbalances between the
expansion of either of these latter variables may cause serious dislocations
and unemployment. In a more general context wage adjustments must
be appraised in terms of their price or inflation effect, and here the ultimate wage rate increase may be cushioned by changes in labor productivity as well as changes in product prices. They may also be appraised
in terms of their employment effect. The "cost" adjustment of wages
must be set against the "income" effect. The theoretical issues implicit
in these relationships are reserved for discussion in Section V, but we cannot escape tentative consideration of them in our contemplation of the
adjustments of wage standards.

In effect, the outcome of any discussion of appropriate wage standards
often reflects one's view of the basic function of wages. As one might
suspect, the values of both labor and management change as do economic
conditions. This shift reflects an adjustment in bargaining strategy. During periods of rising prices and stable productivity, for example, labor is
as interested in cost-of-living adjustments as management is interested in
productivity adjustments. But if prices are stable and productivity is increasing, both groups "switch sides" in the argument. The difficulty of
securing a uniform wage standard equally acceptable at all times and to
all persons is suggested by Lloyd Reynolds' observation that "ethical
considerations cut in both directions. From the standpoint of relations
with workers, it is not ethical to pay too low a wage. From the standpoint of relations with other employers, however, it is not ethical to pay
too high a wage."[3]

Use of the Consumer Price Index for Wage Adjustments

The criterion that wages be related to changes in the cost of living is
probably the most controversial of all standards for wage adjustments,
and it is one that inevitably gains national attention when prices and living costs are in motion.[4] This standard focuses attention on the real wage

[3] *The Structure of Labor Markets* (New York, Harper & Bros., 1951), p. 160.
[4] W. S. Woytinsky, in a survey of 52 unions, representing 11,523,000 members, found
that the wage criterion considered most important during the 1947–1948 negotiations
was changes in the cost of living. The total of responses to his survey was broken
down in percentage terms and weighted in proportion to the union membership represented by the response. He found that cost-of-living changes were mentioned 84.2
percent of the times, productivity 20.3 percent, standard of living 16.0 percent, profits
9.9 percent, comparison with other occupations or industries 4.9 percent, comparison
with other localities 1.7 percent, and "other" 5.6 percent of the time. Because some
responses indicated more than one criterion, the total is greater than 100 percent
(p. 73). This emphasis, of course, reflected the then current inflation. A breakdown

income of the worker or what a person can buy with his money income. Estimates of changes in the consumer price index are made monthly for the whole economy and show changes in prices of a given quantity of goods usually purchased. The effect on living standards of these price adjustments can then be determined (in only an approximate manner) by calculating the ratio of labor earnings to the consumer price index. The approach strips away the "monetary veil" that presumably obscures the effect of both inflation and deflation on earnings. In recent times labor has shown considerable interest in such price movements so that the "money illusion" is becoming less and less of an illusion. Changes in living costs are also observed carefully by housewives. They are given prominence in the press and often spark national political debate and general economic speculation.

In a slightly oversimplified sense, if wages are adjusted only in proportion to changes in living costs, the wage earner suffers no decrease (or increase) of real earnings. The suggestion that living standards should be stabilized has antecedents in the status society of the Middle Age. Because of the importance of real wage measurements, let us briefly recapitulate some of the landmarks in the development of the consumer price index.

Historical Development and Applications of Cost of Living Escalation. Studies were made of various industrial prices by the Bureau of Labor Statistics (BLS) as early as 1888–1890. In 1901–1902 a survey was made of living costs for 22,000 families, and following this survey, the Bureau of Labor statistics began the regular compilation of retail food prices, although no single national index was developed for food costs. During World War I a more comprehensive index became necessary, for it was essential to have some standard to measure the wage levels necessary to attract workers into industrial centers where living costs had mushroomed upward. A study of consumer expenditure patterns for 12,000 families was undertaken, and living costs were then calculated for 32 cities. It was not until 1921 that a national index was published. Local surveys were then made of consumer expenditure patterns. In the early thirties several members of the President's cabinet requested that the American Statistical Association survey the cost-of-living index, as then computed, to determine its accuracy. The committee so formed made recommendations which culminated in a comprehensive family expendi-

---

of management attitudes, in terms of the total 88 companies responding, found that 80 considered the cost of living in 1947–1948 negotiations, 40 considered wages, etc., of other firms in the industry; 39 considered wages, etc., of other firms in the area; 28 considered increases won by certain big unions; 25 considered the earnings position of the company; 20 considered the effect on price of product; 12 considered strength of union or a strike threat, and 6 considered changes in productivity (p. 84). *Labor and Management Look at Collective Bargaining* (New York, Twentieth Century Fund, 1949). These data are reproduced in Gitlow, *Wage Determination Under National Wage Boards* (New York, Prentice-Hall, 1953), pp. 64–65.

ture survey of 14,000 families in 42 cities. A revised index was then available by 1940. With the increased interest in living costs during the war crisis, authority was given to publish living costs for 34 cities monthly, rather than quarterly, and to accelerate the publication of data. As mobilization intensified, new problems were introduced in calculating living costs. With prices allegedly frozen, some retail merchants would report the frozen or official price rather than the prices they actually charged. It was impossible to record the degree of black-market activity, the reduction in the number of sales conducted by merchants, changes and deterioration of quality of product, the disappearance from the market of new cars, and the absence of high quality or low-price merchandise. The BLS again requested that the American Statistical Association appoint a committee to study the index. A six-man committee was appointed under the chairmanship of Frederick C. Mills of Columbia University. The committee concluded that the index was a " trustworthy measure of changes in prices paid by consumers for goods and services " and as " an acceptable approximation to recent changes in living costs." [5]

Meanwhile the War Labor Board was finding its defenses against price and wage increases inadequate and in July 1942 evolved the "Little Steel" formula for stabilizing wages. Since January 1, 1941, the cost of living had increased 15 percent, and it was decided that the 15 percent should be the permissive (but not mandatory) maximum for wage adjustments for those workers who had not received a 15 percent wage increase in the interval. The government index thus acquired new political and economic significance, and it soon became a target of strong union criticism. On October 22, 1943, President Roosevelt asked Chairman William H. Davis of the War Labor Board to appoint a tripartite committee to investigate the index to determine whether changes should be made in it. The committee was unable to agree on the Mills report, and the two labor-union representatives on the committee, George Meany of the AF of L and R. J. Thomas of the CIO, issued their own report on the index in January 1944. It alleged that the index understated the increase in living costs by at least twenty index points.[6] Because this tripartite committee could not come to any agreement, Davis appointed a technical committee headed by Wesley C. Mitchell to advise him on the reliability of the index. Mitchell's committee made several suggestions to improve the index and made the " informed guess " that the index was between three and four points too low. Interest in the index did not end with the cessation of hostilities. Between June 1946 and the summer of 1948 the index shot

[5] " Consumers' Price Index," *Hearings* before a Subcommittee of the Committee on Education and Labor, House of Representatives, 82d Congress, House Document 404 (May, 1951), Appendix, p. 22.

[6] For a detailed analysis of this controversy, see Kathryn Smul Arnow, " The Attack on the Cost of Living Index," Committee on Public Administration Cases, No. 3 (Washington, Thomas Circle, 1951).

up 30 percent, and in May 1948 the AUW–GM agreement was made which tied the consumers' price index to wages. Thus the validity of the index became a lively issue in collective bargaining. As Ewan Clague testified, if we assume a one-point change in the index raises wages by one cent an hour, and with close to 3 million workers tied to this index (as of May, 1951), a one-cent per hour wage increase may reflect itself in a $20 a year wage increase, which applied to 3 million workers can mean a wage increase of $60 million.[7] Congress, in the spring of 1949, provided funds for a three-year program for improving the index, but the Korean war began in June 1950 before the project was completed. Because of the acknowledged inadequacy of the old index, an interim adjustment was made, followed soon after by the "new" consumer price index.[8]

A new surge of interest in cost-of-living wage escalation developed during the Korean crisis. The scare buying at the beginning of this conflict produced a sudden spurt of inflation from June 1950 to September 1951, and there was a sixfold increase in the use of such escalation in contracts. In the twelve-month interval after September 1950 the coverage increased from 800,000 workers to 3 million workers. Transportation, mostly railroads, accounted for 44 percent of the workers covered by such contracts, with another 38 percent accounted for by metalworking, particularly the automobile and agricultural machinery industries. In

[7] "Consumers Price Index," *Hearings, op. cit.*, p. 29.

[8] This interim adjustment revised city population weights, made correction of the rent index for the "new unit bias," added some new items to the pricing, and revised a group of weights of some commodities in the market basket. Twenty-five items added to the budget included frozen peas, strawberries, and orange juice concentrate, canned baby food, group hospitalization payments, home permanent-wave refills, and television sets. The comprehensive revision of the index was completed January 1953. For details on this revision, see "The Consumer Price Index: A Short Description of the Index as Revised, 1953" BLS Bulletin (January 1953). Further information is available in BLS Bulletin No. 699, Changes in Cost of Living in Large Cities in the U.S.; BLS Bulletin No. 966, "Consumer Prices in the U.S. 1942–48"; and the *Report to the President's Committee on the Cost of Living* (Washington, Office of Economic Stabilization, 1945). See also Lazare Teper, "Observations on the Cost of Living Index of the Bureau of Labor Statistics," *Journal of the American Statistical Association*, Vol. 38 (September, 1943). The new index is based on the 1947–1949 = 100 rather than on the previous base period 1935–1939. The retail index in the spring of 1957 was 197 or 97 percent higher than the 1935–1939 base, but calculated on the new base year, the cost of living was 118 or 18 percent higher than 1947–1949. In the new index over 300 items are priced (200 were prices in the "old" series, 225 in the "adjusted" series). Ninety food items are included (compared to 60 in the "adjusted" index and 51 in the "old" series). The weights were determined from the 1950 study by the BLS of 91 cities. Because of budget limitation, the index is calculated only for 20 large cities; while prices for small cities are used in the national average, these are not published separately. One can convert the index point on the old scale to the index point of the new scale by the following ratio:

$$100.0/167.2 = 0.5980861 \text{ (for the large cities combined).}$$

See H. M. Douty, "The Growth, Status and Implications of Wage Escalation," *Monthly Labor Review*, Vol. 76, No. 2 (February, 1953), pp. 126–129.

1951, 80 national and international unions had negotiated such agreements. Further impetus came with the policy of the Wage Stabilization Board to permit the operation of escalator clauses adopted on or before January 25, 1951. Ultimately, the board permitted workers to bargain for wage increases as long as these did not outstrip changes in the consumer price index. Today the Bureau of Labor Statistics has a record of over 100 formulas for computing cost-of-living indices and relating these to wage adjustments. Usually floors and ceilings are incorporated in the contract, the floors being more popular of course with the union and the ceilings more popular with management.

Technical Difficulties in Constructing the Consumer Price Index. This brief survey of the development of indices points up some of the conceptual and statistical problems related to its use. First, peoples's buying habits change through time, and it is impossible for the government to make month-by-month changes in its weighting to take account of these adjustments. Secondly, it is difficult to define the market basket typical for all citizens. It must be appreciated that the cost of living will reflect the living cost for those that buy the market basket of goods that is priced in the index. If one consumes a disproportionately large quantity of one commodity, his living cost is likely to vary from that estimated by the government.[9] In addition, the index is not calculated for every city or every area in the United States. Indeed, the coverage of the index has been reduced in recent years, and it can often be argued that the national average does not reflect regional conditions. An additional difficulty is that of finding an appropriate base year for the index. Frequently the intensity of percentage adjustments will depend on the base year selected. A further difficulty is taking into consideration quality changes, such as the improvement in the new car models and other features from year to year. The physical unit of production does not remain constant from year to year. In addition, there is usually about a six-week time lag in the survey of living costs and the final tabulation of the national average. Such a lag may provide some difficulty if costs are changing rapidly in the interval. Because of these many problems, the BLS often stresses that its index is not a " cost-of-living " index, but a " consumer price index." It measures only the *prices* of a given market

---

[9] This consideration may be of paramount concern during a war period when the government chooses to subsidize those commodities which are heavily weighted in the index. For example, milk production was subsidized in England, but not beer production. If one drank beer rather than milk, his " cost of living " probably increased much more rapidly than that of the milk-drinking populace. It was suggested that since the total of taxes received from the low-income families in Britain was roughly equivalent to the subsidies they received, these taxes and subsidies both could be canceled with no resulting hardship whatsoever. This overlooks the discretionary impact of taxes — with those " poor " people who were smoking and drinking heavily paying high taxes, with those tax revenues going to subsidize milk and orange juice consumption.

basket of goods, not changes in the total amount families spend for living or changes in the direction of that spending.

Advantages of Consumer Price Index Escalation. The prime advantage is, of course, that it stabilizes real wage rates. If living costs and wages move together, the real income of the worker is stabilized, assuming there has been no change in the total hours worked or intervening unemployment. This accounts for labor's interest in escalation during a period of runaway inflation, when labor usually has difficulty in pacing price changes with wage increases. It gives some protection to labor during the contract period, a consideration particularly important for contracts extending for more than one year. While labor is not satisfied with only stability of its real income, the cost-of-living adjustments provide a useful foundation upon which to build further demands. Because escalation provides for flexible adjustments rather than a "once and for all" adjustment, it permits contract terms to be extended. The 1950 five-year UAW–GM contract with its cost-of-living and improvement factor escalation provided a half decade of peaceful relations in the auto industry.

From the viewpoint of the economy as a whole, the general adoption of a cost-of-living plan tends to solve the most serious problem created by inflation: the redistribution of real income from those who have fixed incomes to those who have flexible money incomes. If inflation cannot be stopped, should we not then make all incomes as flexible as all prices? [10]

It can also be reasoned that the source of cumulative instability in our economy is an imbalance that initially develops in the cost-price structure. If wages lag behind prices during an inflationary period, windfall profits may excite management to overinvestment, aggravating the inflationary problem and inevitably causing the collapse of prosperity when such overinvestment is realized. Similarly, if wages expand too rapidly, such pressure will reduce profit margins, leading also to a general depression. The distortion of price cost ratios is important to all theories of the business cycle. It is possible that with escalation, these distortions may be dampened or minimized. With a price inflation, for example, wages will tend to follow prices in proportion. With both variables moving together, there is less danger that runaway pessimism or runaway optimism will develop. We may, in effect, stabilize the *relative* positions of costs to prices.[11]

[10] A contributor in the British *Economist* (undoubtedly writing with tongue in cheek) builds up an effective case for this proposal. See "Agenda for the Age of Inflation" (August 18, 1950; August 25, 1951; and September 1, 1951) and "The Economist's Reply" (September 8, 1951).

[11] No less an authority than Alfred Marshall suggested we might enjoy greater stability if the government published a regular index of changes in consumer prices ". . . and then nearly all wage arrangements, but especially all sliding scales, should be on that unit. This would by one stroke make wages and profits more stable, and at the same time increase the steadiness of employment." Preface to L. L. Price, *Industrial Peace* (London, Macmillan and Co., 1887), pp. xx–xxi.

Disadvantages of Consumer Price Index Escalation. As convincing as these arguments may be, there are also several difficulties related to the use of escalation wage adjustments. It is clear that *if* the price level is stabilized, such escalation will provide for stability of wage rates. But can we be certain that prices will be stabilized? Of course, during a period of military crisis the government usually establishes a system of price controls, and escalation can then minimize the danger of wage pressure. In a peace-time economy government and banking authorities can pursue rigorous anti-inflation monetary and fiscal policies which can, in turn, stabilize the price structure. However, in this context, stable prices lead to stable wages; stable wages do not necessarily lead to stable prices. Unless effective monetary and fiscal controls are in operation, cost-of-living escalation alone cannot solve the problem of inflation. With escalation it is clear that individual employers may find it possible to escape the incidence of paying higher wages simply by raising their prices more rapidly than the consumer price index. With wages tied to the cost of living, employers may, by this device, be able to accumulate windfall profits (which, incidentally, the workers would not be able to share). As long as the market can support higher prices, the individual employer may gain more through higher prices than he loses through higher wages. Is not, then, cost-of-living escalation an open invitation to inflationary price policies?

In addition, the major components to the cost of living are food and housing expenditures but neither of these directly reflect manufacturing or industry price structures. Thus, disturbances to the wage structure could develop apart from the industry's ability to absorb those changes. An upward shift in farm prices, for example, might burden industry with higher wage costs which they are unable to pass on to consumers. This may lead to unemployment or hardship for industry. Or the reverse may develop: The decline of agricultural prices may lead to " windfall " profits for industry. Unless agriculture, housing and rent costs move somewhat sympathetically with the balance of industrial prices, distortions can develop in industry cost-price structures.

Another facet of this formal interrelationship of prices to wages is the very real possibility that, while the national average of living costs represents all consumer prices, it reflects no single product price. Certain manufacturers and employers may find the market will not absorb price increases which are proportionate to the cost of living, whereas other manufacturers may be eager to impose price increases, knowing the market will support them. With the infinite variation in demand elasticity for various products, those employers with highly elastic demands for their products may be embarrassed by the " going pattern " of price and wage increases.

It is possible, however, that such escalation may prevent a recession from developing in a cumulative manner into a full depression. Many employers point out that if they could be given some cost relief when consumer demand softens for their products, they might be able to avoid the layoff of workers. The cost-of-living escalation arrangement, if it does not have too high a floor, might provide that essential degree of flexibility in the wage structure at a critical moment. In another sense, however, the escalation arrangements might encourage cumulative price and wage cuts. Generally production and employment decisions are made on the basis of anticipated consumer demand. If a wage-price deflation has begun, the feeling may develop that a cumulative deflation is in the offing. As prices drop, so do wages. Prices pull down wages, and wages in turn pull down prices. In such a situation employers may defer expenditures on new plant equipment, on hiring labor, on extending production so that they may enjoy minimum costs when the expansion is undertaken. A " once and for all " cut of wages is more likely to encourage the immediate expansion in the level of employment. Cumulative price cuts may encourage producers to defer immediate plans for expansion.

During a depression it is possible that the use of escalation may somewhat dampen the pace of economic recovery. Often the lag of money wages behind prices, which results in the growth of profit volumes and business, makes possible a buoyant rate of expansion. If wages were tied to the cost of living during a recovery, there would be less opportunity for windfall profits and the stimulus these give to recovery. Indeed, one of the major problems of the depression is that real wages have grown very high, but only for those who still have jobs. It would be unfortunate to freeze real wages at high levels for this would then make the recovery all the more difficult. John Maynard Keynes was inalterably opposed to such escalation, probably because in his analysis of the labor market employment could only be expanded in the short run by decreases of the real wage rate.

An additional criticism of the escalation arrangement relates to its lack of general application. Why should labor alone enjoy the protection of parity between income and living costs? The question reflects the sentiment that we should all live a little dangerously in our capitalistic system. During wartime, however, the question of equality of sacrifice looms large in the public mind and use of cost-of-living escalation is very controversial in this setting. During World War II, for example, some unionists charged that the major defect of the government index was that it did not include, as a part of living costs, personal income taxes. It is clear that if taxes were incorporated in the index, labor could escape the burdens of government expenditures, as well as the consequences of inflationary forced savings during a war crisis. But why should labor alone deserve such protection when it is not available to the rest of society? [12]

Unions often regard the use of escalation with skepticism. First, it may be a two-way street. While labor appreciates the protection against inflation, it finds it difficult to accept decreases in money income. Labor is not organized to maintain stability of real earnings but to increase these. Further, the gains that workers receive, when cumulated, are often substantial, but the incremental gains are, taken by themselves, very modest. There is nothing dramatic or exciting about piecemeal benefits. Labor leaders may find that such mechanical or automatic wage adjustments tend to reduce their functions (and importance) in the eyes of the rank and file.

If the price level is lowered because of an increase in production in the economy, it would hardly seem sensible (or feasible) to lower money wages also. To cut wages because of the growth of productivity may indeed undermine the prosperity of the economy. A dangerous imbalance may then develop between per unit labor costs and prices, between wages and sales, between consumption and investment.

Use of Ability to Pay for Wage Adjustments

This standard is probably one of the most relevant in collective bargaining because management very often takes the position that it cannot pay labor the funds which the company has not earned and cannot earn. Frequently management will calculate before negotiations the dollar volume represented by union demands, and then indicate that the revenues of the company are inadequate to support the new wage bill. Unfortunately, this argument is used so frequently that union negotiators often discount its importance. Today it is often viewed as part of the bargaining ritual, but when it is apparent to all that no tactical bluff is involved, the union then faces the very difficult question as to whether to defer its wage demands, or perhaps even meet the company's request for a wage cut.

[12] As Carroll R. Daugherty wrote, cost-of-living adjustments ". . . are repugnant to my conception of the public interest and it offends my sense of social equity for any group to be especially favored at a time when the country as a whole must make sizeable sacrifices as we prepare to defend ourselves against the threat to our way of life. I feel very strongly that these sacrifices should be shared fairly by all groups." From "Wage Rate of Control Standards," *Problems in Business and Industrial Mobilization*, Bureau of Business Research, Bulletin No. 11 (Bloomington, Indiana University, September 1951). Keynes expressed his sentiment towards cost of living escalation in his *How to Pay for the War:* "A demand on the part of the Trade Unions for an increase in money rates of wages to compensate for every increase in the cost of living is futile, and greatly to the disadvantage of the working class. Like the dog in the fable, they lose the substance in gaping at the shadow. It is true that the better organized sections might benefit at the expense of other consumers. But except as an effort at group selfishness, as a means of hustling someone else out of the queue, it is a mug's game to play." (New York, Harcourt, Brace & Co., 1940, pp. 6–7.)

The difficulty associated with the ability-to-pay criterion is that the controlling factors of the ability are *future* sales and costs. Obviously, information about the future is imperfect for both labor and management, but it is likely that management will feel that it is better to be safe than sorry in committing itself to high costs. The consequences of errors of optimism may be disastrous.[13] It is likely that should company sales prospects become a factor in negotiations the history of the company in dealing with labor will have considerable effect on the weight union representatives give to them. If management has generally been sincere in its statements, the union may accept " on faith " the company outlook for the coming year.[14]

If we adhere only to the ability-to-pay standard, wages become, in a sense, the residual claimant on the company income stream. But labor may not always be inhibited by the smallness of existing profits in formulating its demands. If wages are increased, management can, in the union view, initiate an efficiency drive or even lay off some of the allegedly "nonproductive " front-office personnel.

From the economic viewpoint, there are two problems related to the ability-to-pay argument. On one side it is reasoned that wage increases should follow the productivity of labor, where such productivity reflects itself in high revenues for the company. Because of varying profits for various industries, however, the wage structure is likely to become highly distorted. These distortions have an economic function: to attract labor from low-profit, low-wage firms to the high-profit, high-wage firms. On the other hand, paralleling wage movements with profit movements may not provide the industry with the necessary surplus for capital expansion. If management is not allowed to enjoy the full benefits

[13] In Reynolds' study of the larbor market from 1946–1948, he found that " the dominant considerations were the profit prospects of the company and the wage changes currently being made by other companies in the area " (*op. cit.*, p. 156). He also points out that " There are two starting points for management reasoning on ability to pay. The first is the conception of a ' normal ' or ' safe ' rate of profit. This is invariably expressed as a percentage of sales, but the percentage regarded as normal varies with the circumstances of the industry. . . . The other starting point is the income statement for the most recent accounting period, usually a calendar quarter. . . . The estimate of prospective sales volume is particularly strategic. A marked drop in volume can very quickly push a plant below its ' break-even point.' . . . Some of the larger companies in the area set up sales and production budgets for a year in advance, but little reliance is placed on figures beyond the quarter immediately ahead." (P. 163.)

[14] Of course, the union negotiators may never know when the company is bluffing. One union leader points out that he takes a cue by the subconscious gestures of the company representative. When he begins to drum his hands on the table, he knows that he has reached the breaking point and has probably secured all that the union can without a strike. Another union leader explains that when the company representative gets up and starts pacing the floor and mumbling to himself, he knows the breaking point is near. As we noted in our previous chapter, often the union and company both will refuse to make any compromise until the very last moment in order to make certain that they have secured the best possible concession.

of those profits due to the application of the ability-to-pay standard, management may have little ability to expand production. Labor may be attracted to the industry because of high wages, but management may be deprived of the means to expand because of relatively stable profits.

A further problem is that profits are notoriously unstable over time. In industry it is often feast or famine. Labor has not yet learned to appreciate the need for wage cuts when profits decline. Indeed, unions argue that such wage flexibility would shift the incidence of industry insecurity to the labor force, a risk which it is management's function to assume. But labor cannot have it both ways. If profits are the reward for success, are not the lack of profits the punishment for failure? Labor can hardly ask to share only in success and never in failure. Of course, in reality, labor usually does secure advances in the general wage level if the company is enjoying general economic prosperity.

Additional problems arise when one attempts to define profits. Ability to pay may be related to a number of different concepts and measurements of profits. Company policy for retaining earnings, for setting up contingency reserves, for expanding capital, for declaring dividends, for accumulating inventory, and so on, affect the immediate profits of the company. Should profits be considered those which exist before or after taxes? Disagreement can easily develop over the appropriate profit statistic.

Use of Productivity for Wage Adjustments

Productivity standards relate the adjustment of wages to changes in labor productivity. Labor productivity can be measured in two general senses: the ratio of the *value* of labor's output divided by man-hours of input and the ratio of the *physical* volume of labor's output divided by man-hours of input. It should be noted that the use of man-hours as the denominator of the ratio does not prove that labor alone is responsible for the volume or value of output. Indeed, the numerator of this ratio may be changed by alterations in plant capital, improvements in methods of production, increases in the efficiency of supervision, changes in market demand, in fact on a whole host of factors independent of labor effort. The labor productivity ratio is more useful than the capital productivity, land productivity, or management productivity ratios simply because man-hours of labor is a more homogeneous factor than any of the other contributors to the production process.

Productivity calculations can be developed for the economy as a whole, for particular industries, for single firms, for single departments, and for individual workers. All of these ratios have been used at one time or another as justification for wage adjustments. Before we survey briefly the advantages of each of these standards, it might be remembered that the use of a *value* productivity ratio moves closer to considerations of the firm's ability to pay than does consideration of the *physical* productivity ratio. An increasing index of value productivity is more likely to be associated with expanded profits than an increasing index of physical productivity. Changes in the volume of output can conceivably be associated with inverse changes in the value of total sales. A high volume of production or high labor productivity might create, for example, an overproduction of goods, causing a marked decline in the market value of each unit of output, and hence less profits and less ability of the company to meet a wage increase.

The Case for Distributing Productivity Gains by Price Cuts. It is sometimes reasoned that wages need not increase with expanding labor productivity, for labor will enjoy the increases of real income through the decline in the price structure productivity gains make possible. This has the advantage first, of distributing the benefits of productivity gains to the total society rather than to the organized pressure groups. However, labor may object that such a method spreads too thin the benefits that particular labor groups might otherwise enjoy. Furthermore, unions often doubt that prices will decline. Stable wages and growing productivity result in a decrease in per unit costs, and in the absence of price cuts the difference goes to management in higher profits rather than to the consumers in the form of lower prices. Competitive pressures, in other words, may not be sufficiently strong to force prices down. Especially with the " oligopolistic " nature of many key industries, a few large producers may be reluctant to lower prices for fear that all competitors will do likewise. In addition, a deflationary policy, if it is realized, may discourage purchasing by consumers. If prices are assumed to be decreasing month by month, many consumers may be encouraged to defer purchases until they have reached their lowest level. This may act as a drag on economic activity. Finally, from the union viewpoint such wage stability reduces the need for union organization. Suppose it be assumed that workers benefit from price cuts imposed by employers, rather than through wage increases negotiated by unions. Could unions be expected to support a program which would eliminate one of their most vital functions, or subscribe to a process which might strengthen the ties between labor and management at the expense of the ties between labor and the union?

The Use of the National Productivity Index. A second alternative is to adjust wages with changes in national income. Gains of 2.5 percent per year may appear modest, but in twenty-five years or so incomes will double under such an arrangement. This has the advantage of minimizing inflationary pressure arising when wage demands exceed productivity. But again it is true that particular firms may enjoy gains of productivity which exceed the national average. If their workers are tied to an improvement factor related to the national average, such firms can then enjoy a windfall profit which their work force cannot tap. But on the other hand, if an individual firm cannot keep pace with the national pattern of production, it may find itself forced to the wall. Labor will then have to decide whether to deliver a sudden death blow to the company, or perhaps prolong the agony by abandoning the national average arrangement. This plan might cause marginal firms, then, to become bankrupt, and create some social problems for regions having only one industry with low productivity. It might encourage the growth of large industry if it is found that large-scale industry has the advantage of higher labor productivity.

The Use of Industry and Company Productivity Indexes. The third alternative is to relate productivity adjustments on the basis of industry experience. This method is subject to limitations when a marginal firm cannot keep pace with industry productivity gains. A further problem introduced by this arrangement is the wide distortion of the wage structure that could develop. The patterns of labor productivity vary considerably from industry to industry, and such divergencies might create pressures and problems both for companies and management. A further difficulty is that productivity adjustments vary considerably from year to year, from department to department, from plant to plant. Such variability, besides causing distortion of the wage structure, would create a certain instability of earnings which labor could hardly appreciate. As noted before, upward flexibility is fully endorsed; downward adjustments are accepted very reluctantly.

Carrying the productivity argument to its logical conclusion reintroduces the question of the use of incentive or piece rates in industry. Under incentive pay plans the total earnings of the worker vary directly with his own output. Each additional unit of production provides an additional measure of income, and the variability of production thus reflects itself in earnings. Such a plan is likely to stabilize the per unit labor costs for management, as well as provide labor with fairly attractive earnings. The controversy between labor and management over the use of incentive pay has a long history. Labor's objections usually are in terms of the fear that when earnings become high, management will cut the rate; that production standards are set too high; that interruptions in production are caused by management carelessness; that arbitrary and unscientific devices are developed by management engineers for setting rates; that tremendous distortions develop within the wage structure affecting the morale of the work force. Considerable bitterness can develop within the work force as workers vie with each other for jobs with loose rates. Tension and jealousy often develop because of the high earnings of particular workers; sometimes the low-earning workers attempt to sabotage the productivity of high-earning workers. Such a setting is not conducive to the labor solidarity upon which the union movement must sink its foundation.

Use of Wage Comparisons

Wage differentials continue to characterize the intra- and inter-labor market wage structures.[15] This fact has led many labor students to the conclusion that the equilibrium mechanism of the labor market has " broken down." Under competitive conditions and with adequate mobility, it was thought that wage differentials should be narrowed. However, it is probably more correct to look for the explanation of such differentials in the pace and tempo of demand adjustments, rather than in the sluggishness of labor force allocation. The fact that the dog (wages) chasing the bicycle (economic demand) never catches up with the bicycle cannot be taken as evidence that the dog has ceased chasing the bicycle.

While wage differentials perform a vital economic function (however imperfectly), they also provide important social and political by-products. As we have indicated earlier, the worker tends to view his own economic welfare not alone in terms of the absolute level of his real income, but in terms of the comparison of his wage level with those around him. Thus, those differentials made necessary and justified by basic economic forces may nevertheless produce explosive responses from the work force itself. The worker does not always review " economic conditions " in appraising existing wage differentials, especially if his wage level suffers by such comparisons. As Arthur Ross has pointedly observed, " . . . concepts of equity and justice . . . move in a different orbit from supply and demand." [16]

Let us look at the economic orbit first. Wage differentials provide the labor force with signposts for mobility. While studies indicate that labor is not as mobile as the orthodox economists presumed it to be, we have supported the proposition that labor is interested in income maximization and, other things being equal, would be willing to move in the interests of improving its economic status.[17] Wage differences in effect mirror changes in consumer preferences, changes in labor productivity and so on. They reflect the dynamic nature of economic activity.

Let us now superimpose the worker's concept of equity on this highly fluid setting. First, labor generally supports the proposition of " equal pay for equal work." In attempting to translate this principle into prac-

[15] For one study indicating the persistence of interindustry wage structure differentials, see Donald E. Cullen, " The Interindustry Wage Structure: 1899–1950," *American Economic Review*, Vol. XLVI, No. 3 (June, 1956), pp. 353–369.

[16] " Wage Determination Under Collective Bargaining " *The American Economic Review*, Vol. XXXVII, No. 5 (December, 1947), p. 798.

[17] Such movement is discouraged by the attachment the worker has to his community but more important, by the uncertainties attached to " new " jobs compared with the relative certainties of his old job. The calculation of the relative advantages of movement involves calculation of the *future stream* of income payments quite apart from the *present level* of income.

tice, it is necessary to establish uniform job descriptions. Even if job descriptions are uniform, there is no certainty that those working in each job are performing only the described functions. Thus, at the outset, it is difficult to establish a uniform job classification for making direct comparisons. Secondly, a whole host of economic factors may make such uniformity unworkable. Productivity, price, and profit adjustments vary considerably from firm to firm. The relative supply and demand for labor also varies within each labor market. Thus, a uniform wage for each job classification may not be feasible. For example, a small employer in a rural labor market may be paying the " going wage " for labor in that industry. A second employer producing a different product enters the same labor market and pays a higher " going wage " for labor in his industry. The two standards of equity now clash, not because one is more correct than the other, but because two employers undertake labor recruitment in the same market with different wages. Should the first employer violate industry practices in order to compete with the pattern being established within the community labor market?

In summary, the notion of equal pay for equal work may have to be stretched to cover many practical difficulties facing management. Not the least of these difficulties is the fact that many employers are unable to meet uniform wage adjustments, even though wage adjustments must be uniform if the wage structure is to be kept " in line." Such uniformity can be more readily supported by those industries enjoying rapid increases of labor productivity, consumer demand, and capital utilization, but it works a serious hardship in declining industries. Any national wage board utilizing the comparative criterion must remember such problems. As one student of wage policy points out, " The arbitrary elimination of these differentials by administrative fiat would tend to halt the flow of capital to excess labor market areas, forcing labor to move to the areas of capital concentration, with consequent intensification of the unevenness with which capital and labor was distributed over the entire nation." [18] Stated in slightly different terms, uniformity of wage adjustments would permit growing industries to grow at a more buoyant rate and encourage " sick " industries to experience a more sudden death. Whether such mercy killings can be justified depends on one's value orientation, and more specifically on whether one is employed in the industry or firm being eliminated.

It should be appreciated that the comparison standard for wage equity provides both labor and management with a bottomless pit of ratios — some favorable and others unfavorable. Again, as Arthur Ross has rightly stressed, " Equitable comparison links together a chain of wage bargains into a political system which displays many of the characteristics of an

[18] Abraham L. Gitlow, *Wage Determination Under National Boards* (New York, Prentice-Hall, 1953), p. 39.

equilibrium relationship." [19] But psychological disequilibrium is more common than equilibrium. While Ross explains that to the individual worker "it is an affront to his dignity and a threat to his prestige when he receives less than another with whom he can legitimately be compared," there is little to determine what comparison is "legitimate." [20] Even the highest paid worker can find some source of dissatisfaction if he explores and broods over a sufficient number of wage comparisons. This, of course, is just another way of suggesting that the American worker is never satisfied.

Use of Consumer Budgets and Wage Adjustments

The consumer budget refers to the market basket of goods and services that a family must command in order to achieve a minimum standard of living. Such standards have been developed by the government and by private research agencies. They provide a basis for claiming a wage adjustment if it can be established that workers' incomes are so low as to deprive them of basic necessities.

The task of defining a minimum standard is both awkward and difficult. Several methods have been employed: First, one can survey existing families throughout various income ranges and determine the pattern of expenditure for each income range. Then one can establish arbitrarily that level of expenditure which is minimal (in terms of the goods actually being purchased) for each income level. Secondly, one can ask people what they think they "ought" to enjoy as a minimum standard of living. This of course introduces an aspirational element into the calculation. Thirdly, it is possible for a committee of experts — nutritionists, housing authorities, and so on — to determine the minimum standards that people need. Such standards can, of course, be defined without making the judgment that these should be universally applied. However, the determination of a minimum standard in this technical sense inevitably carries with it the implication that this is a goal that families ought to enjoy.[21] The Heller Committee for Research in Social Economics pro-

[19] *Op. cit.*, p. 798.

[20] *Ibid.*, p. 799.

[21] The traditional breakdown in terms of the technical appraisal of family needs is: (1) Poverty Level, (2) Minimum of Subsistence Level, (3) Minimum Health and Decency Level, (4) Comfort Level. For analysis of content, see Millis and Montgomery, *Labor's Progress and Problems* (New York, McGraw-Hill Book Co., 1938), p. 64. Ernest Dale stresses the psychological aspects by breaking down standards in terms of (a) the standard necessary to maintain life, (b) the standard to preserve morale, and (c) the standard that protects status and makes advancement possible. See his *Sources of Economic Information for Collective Bargaining* (New York, American Management Association, 1950. The Bureau of Labor Statistics describes a city worker's family budget to provide a modest but adequate level of living for a four-person urban family. In determining the specific list of items considered necessary for a modest but adequate level of living, scientific standards were used, when available,

vides budget studies of living costs for the San Francisco executive, white-collar worker, and wage earner. In its analysis the " commonly accepted standard of living " is the sum of those goods and services that public opinion currently recognizes as necessary to healthful and reasonably comfortable living.[22] In determining which items should be included in the budget, the committee applies the test to determine whether the item is purchased by more than 50 percent of the economic group for whom the budget is designed.[23]

The minimum consumer budget is an average. Like all averages, it attempts to represent all families, but in reality may not represent any single family. Both the BLS and the Heller budgets operate on the assumption of a four-person family unit. The BLS budget assumes that the father is the only income earner and has a housewife, a son of 13 in high school and a daughter of 8 in grade school. Major criticisms of this statistic stress that it operates from the erroneous premises of (a) a single breadwinner and (b) a larger than average family size.[24] Census data for March, 1950, indicated that 25.4 percent of households had 2 persons in the labor force, 5.9 percent had 3 persons in the labor force, and 2.1 percent had 4 or more persons in the labor force, making a total of approximately one third of household units with more than one person in the la-

as a starting point. The largest expenditure group — food — was based on nutritional requirements recommended by the National Research Council combined with preferences of consumers, as observed in studies of family expenditures. The standards for housing were those established by the Federal Public Housing Administration and the American Public Health Association. Eunice M. Knapp, " City Worker's Family Budget for October, 1951," *Monthly Labor Review* (May, 1952). For further discussion, see Chapter 3, pp. 53–55.

[22] *Quality and Cost Budgets for Three Income Levels: Prices for San Francisco* (Berkeley, University of California, September, 1949), p. 3.

[23] Jules Backman has pointed out that this test tends to inflate the final budget total. Tastes and spending habits vary among families. The 50 percent standard makes it possible to include items the consumption of which many families may deliberately forego in order to satisfy some other desire. Jules Backman, *The Heller Budget in Wage Negotiations, Studies in Personnel Policy*, No. 82 (New York, National Industrial Conference Board, 1947), p. 4. Of course the method may also deflate the total in the sense that a large number of items may be purchased by no more than 50 percent of the people, and these would be excluded by such a test.

[24] The BLS is, of course, fully aware of the limitations of these data. As Ewan Clague, Commissioner of Labor Statistics, has emphasized: " The four-person families whose heads comprised 9 percent of the labor force had a variety of compositions. In some cases the mother was the earner in the family because the father was disabled, in other cases, the four-person families were mainly adults, etc. It is impossible, because of limited amounts of data, to tell precisely what portion of the American families in 1940 are like those represented by our budget. Since the budget-type four-person family . . . is something of an American ideal, it was chosen as the kind of family for whom the budget should first be developed. It is clear, nevertheless, that this budget-type family represents a relatively small portion of the country. Great caution should be used, therefore, in applying this budget to all families or even to all families of four persons." Statement before the Western Subcommittee of the Joint Committee on the Economic Report, December 16, 1947, and quoted in Gitlow, *op. cit.*, p. 85.

bor force.[25] The median number of related persons in each family in March 1950 was 3.2.[26] The ratio of breadwinners to dependents can be derived in another way, by calculating the ratio of the work force to the population. In 1956 the population of the United States was approximately 167 million. The total employed was approximately 66 million, meaning that there are 1.53 persons not in the labor force for every person in the labor force. This ratio is, of course, much lower than the 1 to 3 used in the BLS consumer budget.[27] Obviously, it has the appeal of the living-wage doctrine, for labor should not be expected to subsidize those employers unable to provide a living wage. The logic of this point of view may be more impressive to the national office of the union than to the worker who may, as a consequence of implementing this policy, lose his job. Social workers point out that substandard wage payments produce by-products of poverty, crime, juvenile delinquency, and slum conditions. They create a whole series of indirect costs which the community must assume. Labor also points to the vast area of unfilled demand on the part of the low-income groups as the most promising area for solving the allegedly perennial problem of overproduction. The poor have the desire to buy, but not the ability. By giving higher income to those in the lower-income scale, everyone will benefit. The CIO research department's study titled " Maintaining Prosperity " pointed out that:

> Even after a general rise in American living standards over the last two decades, average family incomes are still far below the level considered adequate for city families by the budget studies of the U. S. Department of Labor. . . . Who can speak of exhausting the need for new housing when, according to the 1950 Census, 10 million out of 35 million occupied non-farm dwellings in the U. S. were

[25] "Marital and Family Characteristics of the Labor Force in the U.S. March, 1950" *Current Population Reports*, No. 29 (Washington, Bureau of the Census, May 2, 1951), p. 3. During 1955, the wife was working in 28.7 percent of all families. See *Current Population Reports, Labor Force*, Series P–50, No. 62 (Washington, Bureau of the Census, December, 1955), p. 15.

[26] Bureau of the Census data, reproduced in *The Economic Almanac: 1951, 1952, The Conference Board Business Fact Book* (New York, National Industrial Conference Board), p. 163. In order to minimize the difficulty of calculating budget costs for varying family sizes, the Bureau has worked out approximations that may be based on such data. Taking the 4-person budget as 100 percent, a 2-person family would require 66 percent of the 4-person family cost, a 3-person family 84 percent of the 4-person family cost, a 5-person family 114 percent, and a 6-person family 128 percent.

[27] Sumner Slichter made similar calculations for 1946, finding the ratio of the labor force to total population of 1 to 1.42. But he estimated that about 10 million wage earners had no dependents, and making allowances for only those families who had dependents, he found the ratio to be about 1.76 dependents for each wage earner. Slichter also points out that the number of persons who work part time or at some time during 1946 may have reached over 70 million, and this too would decrease the burden of dependents. *Basic Criteria in Wage Negotiations* (Chicago, The Chicago Association of Commerce and Industry, 1947), pp. 13, 14.

found to be substandard, and 3 out of every 4 farm homes were listed as dilapidated or lacking running water or private toilets or baths? . . . In January 1953 over 40 percent of our wired homes had no vacuum cleaner, over 88 percent had no electric freezer, over 95 percent had no electric or gas clothes drier, food waste unit, electric dishwasher or air conditioning equipment. . . . Almost all of the 31 percent of the spending units without mechanical refrigeration in early 1952 were lower income families . . . In 1951, 8 percent of all spending units bought new automobiles, but while 30 percent of those earning over $7,500 bought a new car, only 4 percent of the units with incomes of $2,000 to $2,999 undertook to purchase a new one. Surely there is a great potential market for housing and consumer goods — non-durable, as well as durable — if purchasing power can be lifted by a substantial rise in family income.[28]

[28] Report by the Committee on Economic Policy, CIO Department of Education and Research, Stanley H. Ruttenberg, Director (undated), pp. 23–24.

16

The Impact of the Union

There is complete agreement that the rapid growth of labor organization has altered the basic structure of our economic system. However, there is little agreement whether the effect of unionism has, on balance, been beneficial or destructive. Has it handicapped economic growth, discouraged private investment, caused inflation, caused unemployment, raised labor costs? We cannot, in this chapter, answer these questions conclusively nor even review every phase of the conjecture and controversy each raises. We shall attempt, though, a brief summary of some of the more important effects of union growth on private investment, production, the distribution of income, and the wage level. Our analysis will, for the most part, be deductive. One cannot prove that unions have discouraged private investment simply by comparing data on investment before and after union organization: correlations do not prove or disprove causal relationships. Of course, deductive analysis has its pitfalls too. The statement, " all other things being constant " is a frequent and necessary point of departure for theoretical and deductive analysis, but in our dynamic economy other things are *not* usually constant. We must remember too that the union, while certainly a most important force in our economic life, is not the *sole* force. The union reacts on many economic variables and is conditioned in turn by these same variables.

Unions and Private Investment

Unions often argue that wage pressure provides an important stimulus to private investment. Let us review the basis for such reasoning. The level of production is determined by the degree of specialization within our economy, and the degree of specialization, in turn, is limited by the size of the market. Mass markets make possible mass production. Production cannot proceed without consumption any more than can profits be enjoyed without wages. In the union view the stimulus to industrial growth in America is not explained so much by the courage and foresight of the adventuring entrepreneurs, but rather because unionism has helped sustain, through wage demands, a high degree of purchasing power. By such reasoning the poverty of any nation as rich in natural resources as America is caused only by the poverty of the buying power of the mass of its population.

Wage increases thus serve as a force pulling forth new investments, but they may also serve as a force to push technological change.[1] As wage costs are increased, employers are encouraged to search for labor-saving devices. If wage increases become general, the less efficient employer is put under tremendous pressure to discover and develop new economies in the production process. In 1923 Samuel Gompers noted in the *American Federationist* the correlation between technological change and wages.

> Some years ago I had occasion to travel in the southern states, and there I saw in the middle of the rivers colored men who were dredging with buckets and long poles. They were getting 20 and 30 cents a day. Wherever men are cheap, no machinery is used in industry or any other way. It is only when men are dear and wages are high that machinery is brought in.[2]

If labor is cheap, management will reason that it is uneconomic to devise and purchase labor-saving machinery. However, the facility for establishing technological changes may be lessened when the need for such change is most compelling. If the employer has his back to the wall by ever-increasing labor costs, he may be in a poor position to locate venture capital to implement technological changes. But again, labor is likely to feel that if the impulse to efficiency exists, management will find a way.

The cost incidence of such wage adjustments will depend, of course, on the proportion of wages to total costs. Where this ratio is high, management will be sensitive to demands for wage adjustments. And it is likely that the ratio of labor costs to total costs will be higher where the degree of capital invested per worker is smallest. It is in the industry that has already established a large capital base that wage adjustments are more readily absorbed, often by even further improvements in production techniques. The fact that wages tend to be higher where capital investment per worker is high than where the capital ratio is low poses the interesting issue: Are wages high because investment is high, or is investment high because wages are high?

As we noted earlier, one of the important yet difficult, aspects of analyzing the motives behind investment is that these decisions involve a

[1] This proposition has received support from many conservative economists. J. W. F. Rowe indicated that if unions kept wages " a trifle above " the current marginal productivity equivalent, the greater is "the stimulus to organization and invention." *Wages in Practice and Theory* (London, G. Rutledge and Sons, 1928), p. 229. Similarly, J. R. Hicks has indicated that wage pressure will "induce investment," especially in labor-saving technology. See his *Theory of Wages* (London, Macmillan and Co., 1932), p. 125.

[2] "Accept the Machine – Organize the Workers," *American Federationist* (September, 1923), pp. 719–721.

projection of future market conditions. While there are undoubtedly innumerable determinants of business optimism and pessimism, let us speculate on the possible effects of union organization on investments.

Let us assume that union organization is exerting continuing wage pressure. If the employer then anticipates ever-increasing wage costs, he may be encouraged to invest today on the assumption that he is not likely to experience relief of high labor costs in the future. Current investment is thereby stimulated. If the wage pressure is associated with a favorable income or market demand projection, such optimism will also encourage current investment. But again it must be remembered that while the projection of both expanding costs and revenues may stimulate the impulse for current investment, the anticipation of ever-increasing costs may reduce the ability for such investment.

If we make the alternative assumption that union organization will be weakened in the future and characterized with reduced wage pressure, the employer may defer capital expansion in anticipation of cheaper labor costs. However, two factors may weaken the incentive for such future investment; market demand may sag because of anticipated decreases in labor earnings, and employers will be less anxious to introduce expensive mechanization if stability of wage costs does not justify the displacement of men with machines. Clearly, the potential effect of union organization on investment is complicated and controversial. In general, two pressures are set in motion as a result of union wage demands — the pressures of cost and of income. Both may encourage investment expansion, but management is more likely to reason that only expanding consumer income provides an incentive to investment, while higher labor costs are often a deterrent. Even this latter deterrent is weakened when labor-saving technology is established in order to relieve the pressure of expanding labor costs.

Union interest in fringe benefits and guaranteed wage provisions may also affect investment decisions by affecting the volume and direction of money flows into the money market. Many companies have charged that the postwar union demands for pensions would seriously drain the company of that supply of venture capital so necessary for the dynamic growth of American industry. However, funds for pensions, insurance, and guaranteed annual wages, and the like, have not been kept idle, but are invested. They represent, in effect, a new source of institutional savings contributing to the capital growth of industry. Furthermore, as labor's income increases, the labor force itself provides an important source of savings for industry. The tremendous accumulation of funds by private insurance companies further suggests that the general public rather than the very wealthy alone is providing industry with its venture capital. Union success in increasing labor's distributive share does not, therefore, necessarily imply that capital expansion will run aground on the reef of inadequate savings. The persons doing the savings will be different, but the volume of savings forthcoming may not be seriously diminished. It may even increase.

It should be noted, too, that labor in America is not only pro-capitalism, but pro-capital. Labor leaders appreciate that society needs high investment. In a statement typical of such sentiment Walter Reuther declared:

> We don't want to smash automatic machinery. In fact, we couldn't, but we can encourage better machines and processes. The problem is to gear such machinery so as to create economic abundance for the people. These improvements can prove to be a blessing only if the fruits of industrial progress are shared equitably among the various economic groups of the population. If this is done, the rising productivity of the national economy can make possible improved conditions of living — increasing both output and leisure — while providing a base of economic strength for the free world.[3]

In the final analysis both labor and management appreciate their interdependence and their mutual dependence on the efficiency of the production process. Unreasoning conflict can only result in the ultimate and permanent injury to both. With enlightened cooperation, the union need not be an obstacle to private capital formation.

Investments and Union Restrictionism. Apart from these considerations of the capital market, in what respect does union organization reduce investment and production? First, workers often have resisted changes when they involve a rearrangement of production methods. Behind the resistance to change is labor's fear of unemployment. Philip Murray stated it thus:

> Classical economic pronouncements about the automatic reabsorptions of displaced workers by private industry, whether true in the long run or not, are just so much dribble to the men and women who are deprived of their accustomed way of making a livelihood. These pronouncements can be classified with the myths of the nineteen twenties that no intelligent person can have faith in today, in view of the striking failure of our economy in the last ten years to reabsorb the victims of technology. . . . I say to the leaders of industry to keep your economic theories in textbooks. So far as the workers of this great nation are concerned, they want to know only one thing. When do they get jobs? [4]

The hostility of this statement reflects the serious difficulty technologically displaced workers had in securing re-employment in the thirties.

The impact of wage increases on the savings-investment process is highly speculative, but contract provisions restricting technology are

---

[3] As cited in the *Progressive*, Vol. 19, No. 5 (May, 1955), p. 4.

[4] *Technological Unemployment*, Steel Workers Organizing Committee, Publication No. 3 (April, 1940), pp. 35–40, and quoted in E. W. Bakke and C. Kerr, *Unions, Management and the Public* (New York, Harcourt, Brace and Co., 1948), p. 542.

concrete and on occasion, effective. Gordon F. Bloom explains, ". . . in the future, growing union efforts to safeguard the jobs of individual union members and to preserve the *status quo* will probably act as an overall brake on the pace of technological advancement. . . ." [5] But the defense mechanism constructed by the union reflects the intensity of their fear of unemployment. Continuing experience of high employment will do much to dissolve and discredit those work rules designed to " make the job last."

Many of the work rules now existing in labor-management contracts reflected the acceptance of the " lump of work " theory by labor in previous decades. This theory argues that there is only so much work that can be done. Any technology which permits an increase in the pace of production simply increases the threat of unemployment. It is unfortunate that union pressure for such rules is intensified at the very time when unemployment is high and business conditions are depressed. Union policies which discourage technology often compound the problems of depression and unemployment rather than solve them.

Union Wage Pressure and Industrial Research. Technology is rooted not only in the availability of investment funds and the inclination to use them, but also on pioneering research. In an effort to determine the impact of union wage pressure on this " grass-roots " developmental stage of technology, Gordon F. Bloom undertook to survey the directors of research in fifty industrial concerns.[6] He found that research expenditures did not correlate directly with union growth, for expenditures greatly expanded in the twenties, while unionism declined during that decade. Furthermore, directors of research, for the most part, denied that wage pressure was an impelling reason for their activities. The funds allocated for research are built up from the bottom rather than down from the top and depend primarily on the number of promising ideas with which the staff can work. He also found that wage pressures had not induced a change in the direction of research. It might be thought that research would be confined to labor-saving innovations rather than new-product innovations during periods of high-wage pressure, but such was not the case, for the proportion of funds for new products was steadily increasing. Bloom's research findings led him to conclude that " On the whole, there is little empirical evidence to suggest that wage pressure substantially affects the total volume of industrial research expenditures." [7]

Before accepting the conclusion outright, let us look at some of the reservations — the bulk of which is developed by Bloom — to his own conclusion. First, economies in the use of labor may not be the defined

[5] "Union Wage Pressure and Technological Discovery," *American Economic Review* Vol. XLI, No. 4 (September, 1951), p. 617.

[6] *Ibid.*, pp. 603–617.

[7] *Ibid.*, p. 611.

function of the research department, but may absorb the energies of the industrial engineering or other company department. Secondly, the plant using new technology may not pioneer the development of technology. The problems of high cost are transmitted to research firms, who in turn attempt to capitalize on such difficulties with their innovations. Thirdly, the growing interest in product development and improvement rather than in labor saving may simply be a disguised way of absorbing wage increases. When industry offers a high-quality product, price increases may not produce substantial reductions of purchases. The company may then be better able to shift the incidence of wage pressure on to the consuming public. And finally, as Bloom points out, steady wage pressure as well as a sharp increase in labor costs " will bring orders from management to speed up experimentation and get into production as rapidly as possible. Thus wage pressure may increase the effective rate of discovery by shortening the average period of gestation of invention." [8] On balance, *both* industry costs and industry revenues determine the feasibility of mechanical innovation. When both indexes are moving upward together and show no sign of leveling off or turning down, the pressures for technology are usually persuasive.

Unions and Production

Related to but not identical with the issue of investment is union policy affecting plant production. Again, it is difficult to generalize about the ultimate impact of union policies on individual worker motivation, but industrial sociologists have undertaken to examine the influence that group decisions have on individual labor productivity. The union may formalize or institutionalize group decisions and thus exert a pervasive influence on labor behavior.

Individual Motivation and Production. Let us look first at individual motivations and productivity. Daniel Katz has pointed out that: " People are more effectively motivated when they have some degree of freedom in the way in which they do their work than when every action is prescribed in advance. . . . If the ego motivations of self-determination, of self-expression, of a sense of personal worth can be tapped, the individual can be more effectively energized." [9] Unfortunately, today many of the

[8] *Ibid.*, p. 616.

[9] " Morale and Motivation in Industry," appearing in, *Current Trends in Industrial Psychology* (Pittsburgh, University of Pittsburgh Press, 1949), pp. 159–160. Helen Marot observed in 1920, " A system that requires mastery over other men's ability robs the industry of the common desire of those who are working to promote it; it robs the industry of the discipline which men get in the testing out of their ideas; it leaves a mass of undigested ideas in the minds of men, which are sure to fester because there is no opportunity to discover whether they are good or bad; it creates issues which have no functional value." " Production and the Preservation of Initiative," *The Annals,* Management and Production, No. 180 (September, 1910), p. 17.

processes of industrial change have tended to increase the division of labor to the point where individual workers feel they are but small cogs in the complex of mechanically powered production processes. The link between productivity and pay is not clearly established in the worker's mind.

It was Frederick Winslow Taylor who did much to publicize not only the inherent laziness of man, but that compulsory laziness induced by group norms. If such inefficiency could be overcome or if labor could only be motivated to provide a " fair day's work," the resulting increase in production could provide substantial benefits for everyone. Taylor could see little value in union organization, for unions seemed more interested in quarrels over the appropriate distribution of the product than in increasing its size. The union, he feared, simply encouraged the resistance of labor to higher productivity.

It is becoming increasingly evident that group attitudes — whether organized or not — are probably the most important determinant of total group production. This may not always be true where the shop is small and where there is a close identification of labor with management, or where the job is largely machine controlled. But in many situations the work group itself determines the production norm, and it is a brave individual who attempts to exceed that norm. As Solomon Barkin points out, " The level of application [of workers] is basically conditioned by social mores and customs and prevailing practices and group pressures rather than by individual job satisfactions." [10]

The Special Case of the " Rate Buster." Not all workers blindly accept the group norm regarding production standards. Rate busters do exist, and certainly many a worker is still inclined to believe that his future economic status rests squarely on his own productive ability rather than on the coercive power of his union. But the rate buster is more inclined to be the exception than the rule. In a modest study of a work group of 300 men, Melville Dalton examined nine men who had consistently exceeded the group's informal production ceiling. Needless to say, the nine men were little appreciated by the rest of the work group: " Look at Richeter over there! He's so damned worried about how much bonus he's going to get that he can't act like a human being. I wouldn't be in the shape he is for an extra thousand a year." Another worker commented: " Now you take that son of a b—— over there — the incen-

---

[10] " The Relations of Productivity to Morale " Discussion (Madison, Industrial Relations Research Association, 1951), p. 83. Samuel Stouffer, in his *The American Soldier: Combat and Its Aftermath* (Studies in Social Psychology in World War II, Vol. II, Princeton, Princeton University Press, 1949, pp. 139-149) found that " the soldier's will to fight does not stem from his perception and acceptance of strategic generalized goals; rather, it reflects his need to protect his primary group and to conform to its expectations." Similarly, the production goals of the individual worker are probably determined in large part by the expectations of his work team.

tive system made him what he is. He'd cut the working man's throat for a nickel. I've told him to stay the h—— away from my machine and not to speak to me because I'd feel insulted. I value my fellow worker's opinion above the dollar." [11] The reactions of the rate buster, and his opinion of the rest of the work force, were equally violent:

> I want to send my girl to school, and as long as I can make the money to do it, I'm not lettin' a d—— union stop me. A lotta these guys think a union will get them big money for doin' nothing. Well, I joined to shut them up, so I'll make as much as I can. They're always puttin' pressure on the inspectors to get my work rejected, but I'll get by. Sometimes I think this is the d———— country in the world. If you need a little help, everybody runs from you; if you make a little money, everybody's down on you. Well, they can stay down on me.[12]

It would, of course, be unwise to generalize about highly productive workers in America in terms of nine rate busters in one small plant, but this study indicated that eight of the nine rate busters were Republicans (from a group made up of 70 percent Democrats); eight read the *Chicago Tribune* (a paper that is strongly laissez-faire and isolationist); all but one came from northwestern European lineage (Germany, Sweden, and the British Isles); all came from middle-class families; all but one were Protestant; most came from rural families where "solitude, hard work, and production were essentials of life." Success was, in other words, equated with work.[13]

What steps can the union take to control technical changes designed to increase output? The union may demand contract provisions which require that the company notify labor in advance of all planned changes in production methods. The union may even insist on contract provisions which regulate management's right to incorporate innovations. This latter proposal is more likely to be resisted than the former, for it may jeopardize management's ability to manage its business in an efficient manner. Today, secure and "enlightened" union leadership is more likely to support management drives to increase efficiency even when they involve adjustments within the work force. The union is likely to feel that man-

[11] "The Industrial 'Rate Buster': A Characterization," *Applied Anthropology*, Vol. 7, No. 1 (Winter, 1948), pp. 7, 10.

[12] *Ibid.*, pp. 10–11.

[13] As Dalton summarizes his study, "Despite his restricted social life and extremely individualistic behavior, the rate buster is not personally disorganized. He has a set of standards valid to himself. His adherence to them may make him a problem to the work group, but not to himself. He rebels against authority of the work group, but not that of the social order, the competitively derived success values which are the same as his own. There is no uncertainty or confusion in his behavior. His impulses are channelized and guided by clear-cut images and goals. He is maladjusted only in the sense that he is a microcosm of *laissez-faire* thought in occupational contact with workers of a collectivistic outlook." *Op. cit.*, p. 18.

agement is operating in good faith if it makes conscientious efforts to reduce the hardships arising from technological change. The basic difficulty, as noted earlier, is that neither the union nor the work force can always translate the efficiency of the particular job to the income paid for that job. Union leaders often suspect that greater efficiency is more likely to mean higher profits rather than higher wages.[14]

Union-Management Cooperation and Productivity. To suggest, as have some authors, that the only area of interest between unions and management is mutual survival is an exaggeration. In discussions of total production, for example, it is apparent that both parties have a vested interest in greater industry revenues. High living standards and employment security cannot be secured from a firm about to collapse any more than one can squeeze blood from a stone. Unions are not blind to this reality.

Management has often attempted to establish the harmony of interest between labor and management in greater productivity by establishing wage incentive standards. Such a method of wage payment rests on the assumption that labor has strong pecuniary motivations. A further device to encourage labor interest in productivity is profit sharing. Under many of these provisions workers still fear that they are being manipulated by management for management's own self-interest, that they must be most cautious in expanding output lest they will fall into a management " trap," *viz.*, end up working at a more rapid pace of production with a tightened piece rate.

A further device that appeals to both the pecuniary as well as non-pecuniary labor motivations is the establishment of joint labor-management cooperation committees. Such committees gained widespread attention following the parliamentary report of the Whitley Committee of the House of Commons during World War I in Great Britain. Whitley Councils were recommended to secure the joint participation of labor in plans to increase labor productivity. When labor had the opportunity to cooperate, it was felt labor would have little reason for destructive militancy. But what should be the role of the union when invitations are extended to the labor force to consult with management in the solution of mutual problems?

At first the AF of L was rather lyrical in its support of such cooperation committees: " It is more than collective bargaining that is required. In sending up its voice for a great constructive democratization of industry Labor is not asking for a chance to *get*. Labor is asking for a chance to *give*. There will be enough for *all* when it comes to getting." [15] But the

---

[14] For discussion see Robert L. Hahn and Nancy C. Morse, " The Relations of Productivity to Morale " (Madison, Industrial Relations Research Association, 1951), p. 76.
[15] *American Federationist* (May, 1924), p. 401, and cited by Neil Chamberlain, *Collective Bargaining* (New York, McGraw-Hill Book Co., 1951), p. 426.

conjunction of the establishment of such committees with management's open-shop offensive soon changed enthusiasm to fear. The decline of union influence and membership in the twenties led union leaders to suspect that such committees were being offered as an alternative rather than as a supplement to unionism. Soon committees were considered a "snare and a delusion" leading to the "semi-serfdom of labor conditions."[16]

The hazards of such cooperation seemed apparent enough to unionists. Management usually dominated committee deliberations. Worker representatives might even be appointed or "recommended" by management and could not make recommendations from a position of strength. In reality, the committee findings were only recommendations which could easily be neglected by management. The worker was being "consulted," not asked to formulate policy. And if the committee should become concerned with such vital issues as wage payments, it would then usurp or undermine the authority and role of independent unionism. While greater labor productivity would be forthcoming when management pursued policies sanctioned by worker "consent" rather than when labor worked under management coercion, such consultation must not impair independent unionism. In an early study of this problem, Paul Douglas concluded that such cooperation committees could never substitute for independent unionism: "The interest of the workers can ultimately be protected effectively by an organization of the workmen themselves to resist the pressure for lower wages and sweated conditions brought to bear upon them through the market structure. . . ."[17]

In spite of stormy union resistance the idea of cooperation has never died. Two conditions encourage its growth: during a national crisis when appeals of patriotism encourage both labor and management to subsume sectional and partisan arguments for rapidly expanded output; and when particular employers or industries face an economic crisis and are threatened with immediate bankruptcy. During the thirties, for example, three unionists of unusual ability, Clinton Golden, Joseph Scanlon, and Harold Ruttenberg, championed the notion that labor could improve its economic status by assisting management in meeting and solving its economic problems. The Steel Workers union was one that stressed the advantages of such cooperation, and following the blueprint of the "Scanlon plan," attempted to assist many companies in difficulties. Such cooperation was contingent upon mutual trust and respect between labor and manage-

[16] For an interesting account of American Federation of Labor Policies during the twenties, see Jean Carol Trepp, "Union-Management Cooperation and the Southern Organizing Campaign," *Journal of Political Economy*, Vol. 41, and her later monograph, Jean Trepp McKelvey, *A. F. L. Attitudes Toward Production: 1900–1932*, Cornell Studies in Industrial and Labor Relations, Vol. II.

[17] "Shop Committees: Substitutes for or Supplement to Trade Unions?" *Journal of Political Economy*, Vol. 29, No. 2 (February, 1921), p. 100.

ment, the complete sharing of information between parties, the guarantee of employment security for all employees who might be affected by economies in production, and the assurance that labor would " share equitably " in all benefits gained by production economies. Such cooperation accomplished amazing reductions of costs and undoubtedly " saved " many companies from failure.

During World War II, the War Production Board urged the establishment of such cooperation committees to insure greater output. From 3,000 to 5,000 such " win-the-war " production committees were established with mixed success. The organization of such committees rapidly decreased following the war.

There can be little doubt that unions can make substantial contributions to productive efficiency, but one of the most serious obstacles to continuing cooperation is the deep-seated suspicion that all economies simply result in larger profits rather than larger wages. Such committees have, in the past, developed successful policies to cut down industrial accidents, improve the quality of production and eliminate wastes, reduce absenteeism and lateness, cut down labor turnover, and so on.

Various degrees of levels of " consultation " may be developed. The union may be used by management as a device for communicating information to the work force, sometimes referred to as simply " information-sharing " cooperation.[18] If the union is by-passed in the communications of management to the labor force, it will very likely interpret such strategy as an attempt to undermine the union. On the other hand, " a union does not exist solely for the purpose of adding another link to the communication chain within a plant." [19] A second and more involved stage is " problem-solving " consultation. Here the union is advised of the problem and invited to suggest solutions for such problems. Between these two forms is " status-protection " consultation, through which the com-

[18] In more recent times " communications " has attracted considerable attention as a device for securing greater worker cooperation. As a case in point, C. A. Mace describes some of the basic reasons for labor's resistance to change: " No one is strongly predisposed to change as such — to all and every possible change — and no one is resistant to all and every change. Everyone resists some changes. Hence it is not surprising that an organization concerned with the promotion of desirable changes may itself be highly resistant to suggestions that it should change its own methods of effecting its purposes." The difficulty is not in the blind rejection to all change, but rather the lack of appreciation of the usefulness that such changes provide. The problem is not that we resist change, but resist understanding the advantages that change may bring: ". . . a large measure of the resistance to change lies in the resistance to communication — the refusal, the disinclination, the incapacity or the simple failure to receive a message. . . . Despite plausible evidence to the contrary, men are not always implacably opposed to the acceptance of information to their own advantage, information, that is to say, which would contribute to the satisfaction of their wants and their needs." " Resistance to Change," *Occupational Psychology*, Vol. 27, No. I (London, January, 1953), pp. 23, 27.

[19] As noted by Robert Dubin, " Union-Management Co-operation and Productivity," *Industrial and Labor Relations Review*, Vol. 2, No. 2 (January, 1949), p. 199.

pany keeps the union informed of all major plans in order that the union will understand and appreciate the background for company decisions. As Robert Dubin explains, " The union is given an opportunity to review a proposed plan of action in order to protect whatever interests the organization may feel are involved. . . . the union does not review the action as though it were acting in the position of management. . . . Management does not figuratively take the role of the union and ask itself how the decision ought to be made from the union's standpoint." [20]

Such committees will always be attractive to those who believe in the role of reason rather than conflict in labor-management relations. Unions cannot lightly reject the role of cooperation. William Green succinctly stated this viewpoint: " We come preaching the doctrine of cooperation and good-will. . . . We are reasonable men and women, reasonable in our outlook on life and reasonable in our conclusions. . . ." [21] But in the absence of a specific and agreed-upon formula for distributing increments of production — as are congealed in various piece-rate plans and variations of the Scanlon plan — labor is still likely to be lukewarm to those admonitions that the union actively support management's efficiency drives.

Unionism and the Equality of Income Distribution

The old cliché that " the rich get richer and the poor get poorer " has had to be revised in the light of statistical evidence to the contrary. The distribution of income is usually revealed by a Lorenz curve, which shows the cumulative proportion of total income received by cumulative proportions of the population.[22] The inequality of income distribution plays a critical role in our economic development and few economists, regardless of political orientation, seriously advocate complete income equality. However, potent pressures for greater income equality continue to operate in our society. In the context of unionism, one of the greatest incentives for wage pressure is the publicity given to the enormous incomes earned by isolated individuals. As noted earlier, such earnings create the illusion that skillful bargaining can provide substantial wage increases for the total work force.

It is difficult to establish any direct connection between union pressure and the trend toward greater equality of income distribution. Probably tax policies of the government are more significant a force than union wage pressure, for income taxes cannot be readily shifted. The progressive nature of tax rates is one of the most widely known facts of our

[20] *Ibid.*, p. 200.

[21] Quoted in Trepp, *op. cit.*, p. 616.

[22] For a graphic Lorenz curve presentation of the narrowing of income distribution over time, see Selma F. Goldsmith, " Statistical Information on the Distribution of Income by Size in the United States," *American Economic Review, Proceedings,* Vol. XL, No. 2 (May, 1950), p. 329.

economic life, probably because of the frequent criticism that these rates approach confiscatory levels for increments of income. In 1929, 513 individuals reported to the Bureau of Internal Revenue that their incomes exceeded $1 million annually with the average for the group about $2.5 million. By 1939 only 44 individuals had an income over $1 million with an average of $2 million each. In 1948, 149 persons were again above the million dollar level but the average was down to $1.7 million per person. Needless to say, the per capita income for this group *after taxes* dropped more rapidly than the average before taxes.[23] Certainly the " millionaire " group does not represent a substantial portion of our population, either in numbers or total income earned. In 1948 their aggregate of income after taxes was only about 1/20 of 1 percent of the national income.

Further evidence of the secular decline of income going to the richest portion of the population has been developed in recent times. If we follow Kuznets' [24] data from 1913 to 1948, we find that the top 1 percent of the nonfarm population accounted for 15.9 percent of the income in 1913 and was close to this level at 14.8 percent in 1929. But from 1929 a downward trend in this share became evident. By 1939 it was 12 percent. The decline was accentuated during and after World War II; by 1948 it was 8.8 percent of the national income.[25] In Kuznets' own words, ". . . in the distribution of income among families (excluding individuals), the shares of the two lowest quintiles rise from 13½ per cent in 1929 to 18 per cent in the years after the second world war; whereas the share of the top quintile declines from 55 to 44 per cent, and that of the top 5 per cent from 31 to 20 per cent." [26]

Kuznets suggests several factors which may account for this greater equality of income, but most of these are not directly related to union influence. As noted above, government taxation, including inheritance taxes, generally involves transfer payments from high- to low-income groups. Secondly, inflation tends to reduce the real value of fixed price securities. Thirdly, dynamic economic technology hastens the obsolescence of older investments and unless the wealthy are quick to adapt their investments to young industries, they may find their income diminishing. Fourthly, the changing job requirements in a rapidly expanding economy require that labor be paid increased wages. Entire segments of the labor

[23] These data are continued in Geoffrey H. Moore's study, " Secular Changes in the Distribution of Income," *American Economic Review, Proceedings,* Vol. XLII, No. 2 (May, 1952), p. 527.

[24] Simon Kuznets' definitive study, *Shares of Upper Income Groups in Income and Savings* (New York, National Bureau of Economic Research, 1953), has prompted considerable discussion in this area.

[25] From Table 116 in Kuznets' study cited above and reproduced in Daniel Creamer's study, *Personal Income During Business Cycles,* National Bureau of Economic Research (Princeton, Princeton University Press, 1956), Table 24.

[26] "Economic Growth and Income Inequality," *The American Economic Review,* Vol. XLV, No. 1 (March, 1955), p. 4.

force enjoy upgrading because of the new demands of industry. And the reduction in the " swarms " of unskilled workers competing for limited job opportunities provides greater opportunity for raising the lower end of the income scale. It is probably in this latter category that unionism is a force behind income redistribution, for the union simply makes explicit that bargaining power found in relative labor scarcity.[27]

Unions and the Distribution of Income

The appropriate distribution of the product of industry is a more controversial issue than problems related to the responsibility for creating the product. To labor, " the uneconomic distribution of the national income is the fundamental cause of most of our economic ills," [28] and many union leaders stress that the " prime objective of collective bargaining is the redistribution of the proceeds of production. . . . Organized labor's obligation to its members is to pursue wage increases until . . . the national income is distributed equitably and stays so distributed." [29] Distribution theory represents a battleground for conflicting economic philosophies. But more than this, the apportionment of distributive shares has often been employed as a standard to measure the effectiveness of union wage drives. A high level of real labor income is a necessary, but not sufficient condition for such union success. Workers must also receive a " fair share " of the value-productivity of industry. Economists have always been interested in the forces accounting for income distribution, and in recent decades the conviction has gained ground that some " optimum " combination of profits to wages (and counterpart balance of investment to consumption) would be necessary to sustain maximum employment and economic growth. It is not surprising, therefore, that the economists' arguments have been " used " by partisans interested in the distributive process. Distribution which permits high profits, savings, and investment is considered by management most conducive to economic growth; and a high distributive share to wages is, in the union viewpoint, the key to such growth.

[27] For a discussion on how the Kuznets data may actually overstate the reduction of inequality, see Robert J. Lampman, "Recent Changes in Income Inequality Reconsidered," *The American Economic Review*, Vol. XLIV, No. 3 (June, 1954), pp. 251–268. William J. Fellner also notes that ". . . undistributed corporate profits have increased relatively to personal income. If undistributed profits are regarded as constituting income for the shareholders, the income share of the top groups may not have changed much before taxes." "Significance and Limitations of Contemporary Distribution Theory," *American Economic Review, Proceedings*, Vol. XLIII, No. 2 (May, 1953), p. 492, *note*.

[28] Mathew Woll, *Labor, Industry and the Government* (New York, D. Appleton Century Co., 1935), p. 146.

[29] Clinton S. Golden and Harold J. Ruttenberg, *The Dynamics of Industrial Democracy* (New York, Harper & Bros., 1942).

One of the most startling facts in labor market analysis is the relative constancy that wage payments represent, when taken as a proportion of national income. In 1939 John Maynard Keynes observed that "the stability of the proportion of the national dividend accruing to labour was one of the most surprising, yet best-established, facts in the whole range of economic statistics, both for Great Britain and for the United States," [30] and he felt that it was somewhat of a miracle that this should be so. Figure 12 reflects alternative proportionate shares that can be calculated to measure labor's share of income, and indicates the general stability of this index.

Let us glance at the composition of data from which the three indices in Figure 12 are derived. The first ratio reveals the total of wage and salary receipts, as a percentage of total personal income. We see in Index I a rather steady increase in the distributive share of income going to labor, with a more substantial increase in labor's distributive share in the twenty-year period from 1909 to 1929 (from 49.7 percent of total personal income in 1909 to 61.8 percent in 1929) than in the succeeding twenty-year interval. Labor's distributive share was 65.3 percent of total personal income in 1949.[31] The second index on Figure 12 reveals the total of private employee payments over private gross national product. Because gross national product is an inflated measure of income, the proportionate share labor receives is, as a consequence, reduced. This index reveals a more remarkable degree of stability in the trend than does our first index. The third index in Figure 12 is confined only to the distributive shares in manufacturing. Here wage payments are compared to value added or income originating in the manufacturing sector alone. Value added represents the net contribution of an industry to the gross national product.[32] Here again we see a surprising degree of constancy in the trend of this ratio. In 1899 the ratio was 40.7 percent, and 48 years later, it was 40.6 percent, or only 0.1 percent lower in 1947 than in 1899. The absence of short-run fluctuation may, however, be attributed to the fact that these ratios are plotted only for Census years.

General Influences on Labor's Distributive Share. A glance at Figure 12 suggests that the mushroom growth of unionism since the mid-thirties has not produced any upheaval in distributive shares. This observation does not, however, disprove the thesis that unionism has no

[30] "Relative Movements of Real Wages and Output," *Economic Journal*, Vol. XLIX (1939), pp. 48–49.

[31] Data for this index and the statistics cited above are taken from Daniel Creamer's study, *op. cit.*, Appendix A, Table A–2, p. 120.

[32] To avoid double counting in calculating the total income generated by the manufacturing sector alone, it is necessary to determine the value that each manufacturer *adds* to the production process, or subtract from the final value of the manufacturing process the value of the raw materials and goods and services purchased from other enterprises in the production process. Purchased goods, components and energy are therefore subtracted from the total sales value of the product.

FIGURE 12. Alternative Indices of Labor's Share of Aggregate Income

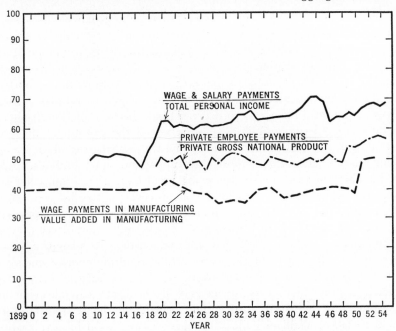

Source:

Index 1 (solid line): Data from 1909 to 1951 reproduced from Daniel Creamer, *Personal Income During Business Cycles,* National Bureau of Economic Research (Princeton, Princeton University Press, 1956), p. 120. Data from 1952 to 1956 derived from *Statistical Abstract of the United States, 1956* (Washington, Department of Commerce, 1956), p. 294.

Index 2 (dot-dash line): Data from 1919 to 1948 contained in Woytinsky and Associates, *op. cit.,* Table 29, p. 67. Data from 1949 to 1955 contains the government sector, and thus the series from 1949 on is not comparable with the earlier years. This data derived from *Statistical Abstract of the United States, 1956, op. cit.,* pp. 293, 295.

Index 3 (dashed line): Census of Manufactures. Data from 1899 to 1947 contained in W. S. Woytinsky and Associates, *Employment and Wages in the United States* (New York, Twentieth Century Fund, 1953), Table 30, p. 68. Data from 1947 to 1953 contained in the *Statistical Abstract of the United States, op. cit.,* p. 791.

effect on distributive shares. It is impossible to determine what the distribution of income " would have been " in the absence of union pressure. We cannot rewrite history in the conjunctive.

It is often presumed that an increase in labor's wage rate or earnings will automatically provide labor with a larger share of the national product. But this is not necessarily true. First, the increase of either wage rates or earnings may be associated with a decrease in employment which can, on balance, reduce the total of the wage payments labor receives. Other things being equal, this would reduce the proportion of income labor receives. Secondly, while wage earnings and the wage bill may both increase, labor's share will not increase if the income going to other groups increases even more rapidly.

There are several long-run forces at work which one would suspect would alter distributive shares. In a predominantly agricultural society the proportion of income devoted to wage payments would be small, but as the industrialization process permeates all society, one would expect the ratio of wage payments to increase simply because the proportion of wage earners has increased. In the advance stages of industrialization, however, the ratio may tend to decrease again because of the change in the occupational responsibilities of society and the growth in the proportion of payments to support and extend the capital structure.[33]

The relative rates of growth of both capital and labor do much to determine distributive shares. If, following rapid industrialization, labor becomes the bottleneck to the production process, the market mechanism would tend, under reasonably competitive conditions, to increase the distributive share going to labor. However, the utilization of each factor is a function of its cost, and its cost a function of its availability. Stated in somewhat different form, the scarcity (and resulting expensiveness) of labor will induce labor-saving innovations while the relative scarcity of capital (resulting in its expensiveness) will encourage capital-saving innovations. This substitution effect will depend on the relative costs of capital to labor. William Fellner believes that a reasonable explanation can be found for the constancy of distributive shares in terms of such substitution.

> . . . if relative labor shortage induces primarily labor-saving innovations and vice versa, then in the long run the shifts in the labor-productivity functions are unlikely to get very much out of line with the shifts of the capital-productivity functions. Or if, as is likely to be the case, a relative shortage in some factor tends to develop because of different rates of growth in the various factor supplies, then technological progress will lead not to approximately equal shifts but to offsetting shifts in the various productivity functions.[34]

In effect, if labor scarcity (relative to capital) leads to high wages and a high distributive wage share, this will set in motion two forces — an influx of the labor service, diluting the premium return to labor, and the development of labor-saving innovations. When distributive shares get " out of line," these compensating forces begin to operate.

[33] Opposing this trend is the movement up the occupational ladder of individual workers who still retain their labor force status. Their earnings (and hence the proportion of wage payments received by labor) thus increase. Such vertical mobility of labor is common today and can affect changes in distributive shares. For discussion of how qualitative changes in labor force utilization affect the wage structure see M. W. Reder, "The Theory of Occupational Wage Differentials," *American Economic Review*, Vol. XLV, No. 5 (December, 1955), pp. 833–852.

[34] For further discussion, see his "The Theory of Income Distribution," *American Economic Review, Proceedings*, Vol. XLIII, No. 2 (May, 1953), p. 491.

Market Considerations and Labor's Distributive Share. What influence does the union have on distributive shares? In most instances changes in the level of wage rates are associated with changes in employment in the same direction. Hence, more often than not, increases in money wages increase the take-home pay for labor. But will management be forced to absorb the wage increase out of *its* distributive share? In some cases management may find it possible to shift a portion of the incidence of the new wage cost on to the public in the form of higher prices. Obviously changes in the denominator of our equation produce changes in the *proportion* of income labor receives. Since industry income is subject to many random market forces, it is difficult to generalize about changes in industry income related to changes in wages.[35] If industry incomes increase in proportion to wages payments, labor's distributive share may remain constant. On the one hand, if the public's demand for industry output is highly elastic, management will have little opportunity to raise prices without experiencing a decline of income. If, on the other hand, the demand for the firm's output is less elastic, the more successful will be the firm in shifting the incidence of the higher wage rate. In a less static sense, the ultimate effect of a wage rate increase on distributive shares depends on whether the economy is generally expanding both in terms of production and prices. If all prices tend to be increasing or if monetary and fiscal authorities are following an " easy- " rather than a " hard-money " policy, it is likely that wage increases may not cause any significant redistribution of income in labor's over-all share.

Paradoxical as it may be, it is likely that substantial increases in the share of income going to labor will be associated with a decline in the wage bill and a more rapid decline of industry revenues. During a recession wage costs are likely to be more rigid than income, and this rigidity forces the redistribution of income in labor's favor. During a period of inflation, on the other hand, wages may lag behind prices, and labor's distributive share may decline.[36] With prosperity unions are strong and usually vigorously pursue wage increases. General wage pressure to-

[35] For further discussion, see E. H. Phelps Brown and P. E. Hart's analysis in, " The Share of Wages in National Income," *Economic Journal*, Vol. LXII, No. 246 (June, 1952), p. 253.

[36] As E. H. Phelps Brown and P. E. Hart explain this situation, " We could . . . suppose . . . that at different times the generality of firms have a different ability to maintain or raise profit margins. When trade-union strength raises wages, at one time firms may be unable to raise prices proportionally, but at another they can ride the punch, and raise their prices so as to maintain their profit margins. . . . if the unions are strong they can squeeze profits between rising wages and market controlled prices; if they are weak, the market will keep prices down to the resultant level of costs so that profits do not rise. . . . if the trade unions are strong they can only push the whole cost and price structure up with them, and profits keep pace with wages; if they are weak, profits may draw ahead of wages. . . . " *Ibid.*, pp. 269–271. Strength and weakness is a function of business trends as well as fiscal and monetary policy.

gether with easy money policies will serve to pull up prices, and in turn give management relief from the labor-cost pressure. Strange as it may seem, the more general the wage increase and the more effective it is in increasing labor's take-home pay, the more likely it is that this will not cause a permanent redistribution of income in labor's favor.

This discussion suggests how tenuous any conclusion must be that purports to explain the ultimate effect of union bargaining power on distributive shares. Obviously, the movement of prices is an important element in this analysis. If prices are stable, uninhibited bargaining will probably increase labor's distributive share.[37] If, on the other hand, wages are controlled and prices are free to find their competitive level, it is likely that labor's distributive share would decline. The stability of labor's share in the face of a wage increase does not prove stability of labor's living standard. It may indicate only the success that management has had in shifting the burden of the wage increase to the general public. Labor, as a pressure group, may be on the whole better off while other groups within our economy, especially those on relatively stable money incomes, may be worse off.

Unionism and Labor's Distributive Share. We may attempt to untangle the influence that unions may have had on the distribution of income by categorizing industries as being unionized or nonunionized and then determine whether there has been a significant difference in the wage income ratios for the unionized and the nonunionized sectors. In Figure 13 we have provided an index of the ratio of wage and salary payment (including supplements) to "income originating" in four industrial sectors, characterized as having little unionization. These include Wholesale and Retail Trade, Services, Agriculture, Forestry and Fisheries, Finance, Insurance, and Real Estate. Indices for each of these are combined into a single index by ratios weighted to give a total index for this category, with the weighting of these in terms of the national income originating in each sector in 1951.

The second index in Figure 13 is the weighted average of wage/income ratios for five major industrial sectors which have had more or less active unionization.

We see that the ratios of wages to income tended to increase sharply during the recession for both union and nonunion sectors. This seems to suggest that the rigidity of wage costs, together with the decline of

---

[37] The International Labour Office study on this problem indicates that " Theoretically, labour's real income could rise without an increase in productivity if price policy is successful in preventing prices from rising as quickly as money wages, so that labour's share of national income is increased. The record with respect to labour's share of national income during war and transition is not clear." For international comparisons of distributive shares and analysis, see Chapter VII, " Wages and the Price Level " of *Wages: General Report,* from the Agenda of the 31st session of the International Labour Conference in 1948, San Francisco.

income, was an important cause for the increasing labor share during the depression period, with the union having only relatively modest influence in accounting for a higher wage income ratio in the union sector. During the World War II period the union ratio tended to increase more rapidly than the nonunion sector, but after 1948, the nonunion ratio pushed above the union ratio. Surprisingly enough, in 1955, the proportion of income going to the so-called unionized sector was eight full in-

FIGURE 13. The Ratio of Wage and Salary Payments (Plus Supplements) to Income Originating in the Unionized and Nonunionized Sectors of the Economy, from 1929 to 1955

Base: 1929 = 100
Sector Components Weighted by Income
Originating in 1951

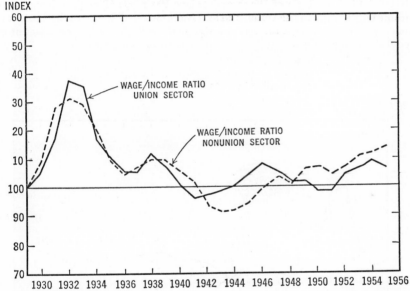

Note: The Union group includes manufacturing, mining, transportation, construction, and communications.
  The Nonunion group includes finance, agriculture, forestry and fisheries, and service and trade.

dex points below the ratio going to the nonunion sector. Throughout most of this period, however, the two indices follow a remarkably similar path. It is also surprising that in the "normal" statistical base years of 1937, 1941, and 1948, the union and nonunion indices are not only close to their 1929 base, but very close to each other. This seems to suggest that in "normal" periods (loosely defined as the absence of runaway inflation or deflation) union wage/income ratios are likely to approximate those in the nonunion sector, union wage pressures notwithstanding.

The force of unionism may partly explain this discrepancy. During a depression unions resist the " backward step " of accepting wage cuts; they further implement make-work practices to increase both employment and the wage bill, even though industry revenues are declining. The growth of the union sector ratio during World War II may, in part, be explained by the shift of labor into these unionized sectors at the expense of the service sector. The additional costs of overtime work and shift differentials probably added to the wage bill of the union group more than it did to the nonunion group. The price control program also was more effectively applied in the union sector. Such activity as real estate, services, finance, and insurance in the nonunion sector did not lend themselves to effective price regulation.

FIGURE 14. The Ratio of Wage and Salary Payments (Plus Supplements) to Income Originating in the Unionized and Nonunionized Sectors of the Economy, from 1929 to 1955, with the Income Originating Reduced by the Amount of Federal and State Corporate Income and Excess Profits Taxes

Base: 1929 = 100
Sector Components Weighted by Income
Originating in 1951

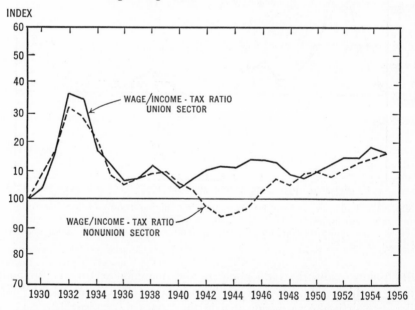

While the union, on the basis of this analysis, has not been successful in increasing its distributive share when compared to the nonunion group, it is still possible that unionized labor is better off than it would have been in the absence of union pressure, although these conclusions remain strictly conjecture. It is likely, however, that whatever pressures are exerted on employers in unionized industries, these effects are not isolated and confined to those industries alone. Nonunion employers undoubtedly feel that it is wise to " keep in step " with the current pattern of concessions being given to unions, simply to avoid unionization. Indeed, nonunion employers may be anxious to do somewhat more for their employees than union employers in the interests of keeping the union out.

One of the more effective ways of changing the distribution of income is through the direction of government tax policy. If account is made of wage/income ratios for the union and nonunion group above by deducting Federal-State Income and Excess Profits Tax Liability from each industry making up the average, it is found that the differences in the distributive shares between the two groups tend to narrow. As can be seen in Figure 14 "After taxes," the union provides a slightly larger share of remaining income for its workers than nonunion employers.

This analysis is not conclusive in that it cannot prove or disprove union influence. Furthermore, the student must regard all data with some caution for indices calculated over time usually reflect changes of industrial classification and other extraneous details: By altering the weighting of indices, working with different terminal years and so on, surprisingly different conclusions may result.[38]

Unionism and Earnings

The analysis of union influence on wage earnings cannot be confined to aggregate data alone, for the index represents both union and nonunion pressures. Several attempts have been made to establish categories in industries, again in terms of the degree of unionization, to determine if differences in the earnings record exist. One early attempt by Paul Douglas compared earnings in six organized and eight unorganized industries, and he concluded that:

> During the nineties, and the early years of the present century, the unionists were able to secure for themselves appreciably higher wages and shorter hours than the mass of the workers, and this absolute ad-

[38] As a case in point, see Harold M. Levinson's study, "Collective Bargaining and Income Distribution," *American Economic Review, Proceedings*, Vol. XLIV, No. 2 (May, 1954). With a slightly different " package " of union and nonunion industries, and with the application of three " correction factors " (including the device to untangle interindustry shifts in revenue from intraindustry revenue adjustments). Levinson points out that labor's distributive share in the union sector increased some 16.2 percent from 1929 to 1952 while labor's share in the nonunion sector increased by only 1.4 percent (p. 309). See also his earlier monograph, *Unionism, Wage Trends, and Income Distribution: 1914–1947* (Michigan Business Studies, Vol. 10, No. 4, Ann Arbor, University of Michigan Press, June, 1951, Chapter 4) for somewhat different conclusions. An interesting discussion of this problem is contained in the *American Economic Review* cited above, with excellent papers by Clark Kerr, " Trade Unionism and Distributive Shares "; Martin Bronfenbrenner, " The Incidence of Collective Bargaining "; and Levinson's article cited above.

vantage has continued down to the present day. Part of this differential was undoubtedly due to the superior trade skill of the unionists, but there seems no good reason to doubt the fact that part of it was also due to the added bargaining powers which collective bargaining brings.[39]

Douglas found, however, that after 1914 the rate of increase of wages in the nonunion manufacturing industries paced those for the union manufacturing industries. "The evidence seems to indicate that when labor organization becomes effective, it yields very appreciable results in its early stages, but that thereafter the rate of gain enjoyed by its members tends to slow down to a speed which does not appreciably exceed that of the non-union industries." [40] In more recent times, Arthur Ross reached similar conclusions with somewhat more refined data. Ross pointed out that a certain bias could be introduced to such comparisons since the union wage data reflect earnings for the more skilled workers, with initially higher wages. The calculation of percentage changes creates, therefore, a tendency to understate the increase of wages for the high-wage groups. On the other hand, calculations of these increases in terms of dollars and cents (rather than percentage) tends to understate the increase of income for the low-wage groups. Ross attempts to overcome the difficulty by observing the percentage changes for various "wage classes." He found some correlation between the weighted averages of percentage increases of hourly earnings for various wage classes from January, 1933 to January, 1945. His findings provoked a fresh wave of research and analysis in this area.

A more comprehensive study of such influences was undertaken by Harold M. Levinson, who analyzes a thirty-three-year period from 1914 to 1947.[41] From 1914 to 1920 he found little distinct influence exerted by unions. The second interval from 1920 to 1923 covers the period of the sharp recession midway in 1920, and suggests that the union was much more successful in resisting downward wage cuts than were nonunionized workers. While the twenties was characterized as a period of declining union influence, the union groups secured wage increases higher than those of nonunion workers. And in the depression interval of 1929 to 1933 the union sector seemed better able to resist wage cuts, although in all instances wages declined for both union and nonunion workers. On balance, the data suggest that the union was successful in advancing wages to higher levels than might have otherwise been possible if labor was organized and that the union was also relatively successful in resist-

---

[39] Paul Douglas, *Real Wages in the United States, 1890–1926* (Boston, Houghton Mifflin Co., 1930), p. 562.

[40] A. M. Ross, "The Influence of Unionism Upon Earnings," *The Quarterly Journal of Economics*, Vol. LXII (February, 1948), pp. 263–286.

[41] Levinson, *Unionism, Wage Trends and Income Distribution, 1914–1947, op. cit.*

ing wage reductions. Levinson found that after 1933 there was little association between the degree of unionization and wage increases. In effect, the nonunion industries were in a " catching-up " period. In 1934, in particular, nonunion labor received extraordinarily large wage increases. "From 1933 to 1934, the unorganized workers obtained increases approximating 16 per cent, as compared to a 5 per cent increase for the union trades. From 1934 to 1937, the non-union laborers gained an additional 21 per cent, in contrast to only 11 per cent for the organized groups. . . ." [42] It is surprising that at the very moment in history when unions enjoyed tremendous power and influence, the relative wage differential advantage accruing to the union sector should appear to diminish. Levinson concludes "On the basis of these figures . . . it would be extremely difficult, if not impossible, to demonstrate any significant correspondence between the rise of union strength from 1933 to 1947 in the manufacturing and extractive industries and the rate of increase in straight time hourly earnings during that same period." [43]

Interest in this problem continues to gain momentum, and controversy has developed over both the methods that can best untangle union from nonunion influences, as well as conclusions that can be legitimately derived from data. The question has been raised: Might not high wages enable union organization just as much as union organization enables high wages? Other students stressed the correlation that could be established to labor productivity and union wage adjustments, with the implication that the economic force of productivity was probably a more important force in wage determination than the political " bargaining power " of unionism.[44]

In a later study Arthur Ross and William Goldner modified Ross's earlier thesis, with a new approach to the problem. Turning to Paul Douglas's thesis described above, they postulated that " New unionism (that is, unionization) has been a source of relative wage advantage during the 1933–46 period, whereas continuing unionism has not." [45] Analyzing those industries which were less than 40 percent organized in 1933, they found that the cent per hour increase in straight-time hourly earnings increased more rapidly where unionism had grown most rapidly. As one might suspect, this research has hardly settled the argument.

[42] *Ibid.*, p. 54.

[43] *Ibid.*, p. 62.

[44] For analysis of the productivity argument, see John T. Dunlop, "Productivity and the Wage Structure," in *Income, Employment and Public Policy*, H. L. Meltzer and others (New York, W. W. Norton & Co., 1948); Joseph W. Garbarino, "A Theory of Interindustry Wage Structure Variation," *Quarterly Journal of Economics*, Vol. LXIV, No. 2 (May, 1950); Richard Perlman, "Value Productivity and the Interindustry Wage Structure," *Industrial and Labor Relations Review*, Vol. 10, No. 1 (October, 1956).

[45] "Forces Affecting the Interindustry Wage Structure," *Quarterly Journal of Economics*, Vol. LXIV, No. 2 (May, 1950), pp. 254–281.

In more recent times, John E. Maher investigated differences in wage rates (rather than earnings) between union and nonunion industries and concluded that " for the industries and occupations considered, there are no significant differentials between the rates of workers in union and nonunion plants." [46]

Our discussion in this chapter has revealed the complexity of any analysis which purports to establish the impact of the union on investments, innovations, production, distributive shares, and hourly earnings. If any conclusion can be reached, it is only that one must be cautious in holding too dogmatically to any single assertion about the over-all impact of the union. The influence of unionism cannot be easily measured. And when measurable, forces cannot be readily untangled from those environmental circumstances affecting union policy and those being affected by it. Our data suggest only that we have scattered islands of information located in a very large ocean of ignorance.

[46] " Union, Nonunion Wage Differentials," *The American Economic Review*, Vol. XLVI, No. 3 (June, 1956), p. 352.

IV

The Public Interest and Industrial Relations: A Review of Labor Legislation

IV

17

Labor Law: The Search for Rules of the Game

The controversial area of labor legislation and court-made law reflects the basic elements of the clash of economic interests in society. Rules have evolved in common law, in legislative enactments, in judicial construction of the enactments to achieve certain objectives — protection of traditional entrenched "rights," furtherance of the general welfare, protection of the freedom assumed to be the legal and economic birthright of citizens, and facilitation of peaceful co-existence of labor and management. Often these rules have been conflicting in their import; and their concrete application to specific situations has often produced different concrete results.

Conditioning Forces and Early Labor Legislation

Let us recall some of the underlying notions and assumptions from which have evolved the rules controlling employer-worker relations. Were we to dogmatize any basic notion embodied in the law of labor, the assertion would be that all men are free and independent and that there must be embodied in the constitutions and laws means of protecting these rights of freedom and equality. But what does freedom imply?

The concept of freedom was cast in cultural perspective by Professor Franz Boas when he wrote:

> Freedom is a concept that has meaning only in a subjective sense. A person who is in complete harmony with his culture feels free. . . . Obedience to a ruler, law, or custom is not exacted but rendered freely. For this reason, the concept of freedom can develop only in those cases where there are conflicts between the individual and the culture in which he lives. The more uniform the culture, that is, the more intensely all the individuals of a community are subject to the same customs, the stronger will be the feeling of lack of restraint. . . . The individual, on account of the lack of knowledge of diverse forms of thought and action, cannot form by himself the con-

cept of something new, not intimately connected with the range of his experience and, therefore, the possibility of a free choice does not exist.[1]

Freedom, therefore, represents not only the freedom *from* restriction on physical movement and physical expression, but as a corollary, involves also the freedom *to* perform acts. And in this latter context, it involves awareness of possible alternatives to present procedures. Conceivably if a person enjoys no knowledge of alternative ideologies or political forms or knows of no alternative to his present cultural environment, he may consider himself free within his own culture or within his own value orientation.

Dominant nineteenth-century economic philosophy postulated that justice was accomplished when individuals had self-help opportunities, uninhibited by government restrictions. In this setting the collective organization of labor seemed irreconcilable with individualism and free enterprise. Legal tenets approved competitive and individual bargaining in the market place, but group organization forced revision of judicial and legislative assumptions. Regulation and control appeared to be necessary to deflect the direction of economic pressures or to cushion society from the impact of group bargaining.

Recapitulation of some of the basic legal notions permeating public policy with respect to the objects and methods of labor combinations and to legislative attempts to regulate them will shortly be in order, but such recapitulation may advantageously be prefaced by brief mention of some of the forces conditioning and shaping labor law. Legislation reflects — although often imperfectly — the social point of view. The social point of view, in turn, reflects the underlying needs of the economy and the state of its development.[2] Because the American economy was undergoing industrial change in the nineteenth century, the weight of legal opinion both sanctioned and encouraged those circumstances conducive to the rapid growth of a free economy. Of what significance was this to organized labor? To pre-industrial America the pressure of consumption against a limited income could only reduce the pace of industrial development. Could or would the union movement reconcile itself to this fact?

[1] Franz Boas, "Liberty Among Primitive People," in *Freedom: Its Meaning*, edited by Ruth Nanda Anshen (New York, Harcourt, Brace & Co., 1940), pp. 51, 55, and cited by David Bidney, "The Problem of Freedom and Authority in Cultural Perspective" from the 12th Symposium on the Conference on Science, Philosophy and Religion, titled *Freedom and Authority in our Time*, edited by Lyman Bryson, Louis Finkelstein, R. M. MacIver, and Richard McKeon (New York, Harper & Bros., 1953), p. 289.

[2] As Karl Polanyi has rightly observed, "The fate of classes is much more often determined by the needs of society, than the fate of society is determined by the needs of classes. . . . The 'challenge' is to society as a whole; the 'response' comes through groups, sections, and classes . . ." *The Great Transformation* (New York, Farrar and Rinehart, 1944), p. 152.

Labor could not always understand why low consumption need be a pre-condition for economic development and responded with mixed emotions to the constant pressure for high profits, high savings, and high investment, especially when these increased at the expense of wages. The problem of dividing up the jointly created product could command attention only after there was something to divide.

A second conditioning factor, more social than economic, was the outlook of the judiciary. While the legislative bodies provided the frame of labor legislation, it was the courts that painted the picture.[3] Courts have been unwilling to view current facts except in terms of legal principle, and these principles were, more often than not, rooted in traditional classical economics.

As we shall see in Section V, individualism and laissez faire were the essential doctrines of economic orthodoxy, and these concepts left an enduring imprint on the judicial and legislative outlook. Among the classical economists, David Ricardo explained that "Like all other contracts, wages should be left to the fair and free competition of the market, and should never be controlled by the interference of the legislature."[4] And in America, the courts concluded that legislation designed to increase the power of labor would be "insulting to their manhood and degrading, to put them under guardianship, to create a class of statutory laborers and to stamp them as imbeciles."

The history of labor legislation and its judicial interpretation reveals, then, the preoccupation of legislative bodies and the courts with competitive norms. Freedom was often considered to be synonymous with competition. Thus, the "yellow-dog" contract was legal, for the employer had the right and freedom to require that labor sign such a contract, just as labor had the right and freedom not to sign. The justices reasoned: "In all such particulars the employer and the employee have equality of right, and any legislation that disturbs that equality is an arbitrary inter-

[3] Benjamin N. Cardozo explains in *The Nature of the Judicial Process* (New Haven, Yale University Press, 1932): "There is in each of us a stream of tendency, whether you choose to call it philosophy or not, which gives coherence and direction to thought and action. Judges cannot escape that current any more than other mortals. All their lives, forces which they do not recognize and cannot name have been tugging at them — inherited instincts, traditional beliefs, acquired convictions; and the resultant is an outlook on life, a conception of social needs, a sense in James' phrase of 'the total push and pressure of the cosmos,' which, when reasons are nicely balanced, must determine where choice shall fall. In this mental background every problem finds its setting." (Pp. 14–15.) There is little doubt that the judiciary has, on balance, been influenced by conservative economic philosophy which found it difficult to justify the organization and activities of unions. As another law student has written, "The rights of labor are determined quite as much, if not more, by the social and economic philosophy of the judges as by so-called immutable principles of the law. In other words, legal theory is shaped to fit economic and social facts as the judge sees them." Alpheus T. Mason, *Organized Labor and the Law* (Durham, N.C., Duke University Press, 1925), pp. vii–viii.

[4] David Ricardo, *Principles of Political Economy*, Chapter 5, Section 7.

ference with the liberty of contract, which no government can legally justify in a free land." [5]

The Conspiracy Doctrine

Before the enactment of modern legislation the conspiracy doctrine, together with the doctrine of restraint of trade, dominated the attitude of the courts toward collective action on the part of labor. These concepts evolved for the most part from court decisions with their origin in the attempt to protect individuals from capricious litigation or false testimony given in malice. As Dean Roscoe Pound has described the application of the doctrine: " It has been said that the common law will not help a fool. But equity exists to help and protect him. It is because there are fools to be defrauded and imposed upon and unfortunates to meet with accidents and careless people to make mistakes that we have courts of equity." [6]

In such common law, the conspiracy doctrine had its origin. It is not surprising that the somewhat nebulous and always flexible common law doctrine of conspiracy could be used to attack "imperfections" in the mechanism of free competition. Judicial and public policy evolved from the simple proposition that a number of persons acting in combination possess power for wrongful accomplishment not possessed by individuals. This power of combined number, in turn, afforded logical basis for a number of principles: that when men combine to accomplish a wrongful end, the mere combining is itself unlawful; that purposes lawful in the case of an individual are not necessarily lawful in the case of a number acting in concert; that when an illegal plot has been formed, all the conspirators are responsible for the acts of any one of them; that every act done in pursuance of a conspiracy is illegal; and that a conspiracy may obtain if the means used by the members of the combination are unlawful, even though the lawfulness of the purpose is conceded. In the application of these principles court decisions gradually congealed into a body of precedent. It was a short step to apply the doctrine against groups whose activities appeared coercive or damaging to an expanding economy. The doctrine of conspiracy had crystal clear implications for union organization.

The conspiracy doctrine was first applied in the United States in the Mayor's Court of Philadelphia in the famous case of *Commonwealth* v. *Pullis* (The Philadelphia Cordwainers' case, 1806). In this case the eight defendants were charged with conspiring to raise wages and coercing their employer to maintain a closed shop. The court charged that the defendants agreed they "should and would endeavor to prevent by

[5] *Adair* v. *United States*, 208 U. S. 161, 175 (1908).
[6] "Liberty of Contract," *Yale Law Journal*, Vol. XVIII (1909), pp. 454–487.

threats, menaces and other unlawful means . . . other workmen and journeymen in their occupation from working except at certain large prices and rates set by them for their future work, to the great damage and prejudice of others. . . ." The analysis of the court in this case provided an example of the problems that arise when noncompetitive elements are introduced into the labor market. Employers were injured by labor conspiracy because they lost the volume of business that might otherwise have been enjoyed if a union had not organized a " turnout " or a strike. In this 1806 case the employer estimated that because of his high labor costs, together with the turnouts, he lost $4,000 in business per year. The court also reasoned that labor's freedom to apply coercive power to determine wages would serve to inflate prices, and this in turn would obstruct commerce:

> If he [an employer] makes a large contract for goods today, for delivery at three, six, or nine months hence, can he calculate what the prices will be then, if the journeymen in the intermediate time, are permitted to meet and raise their prices, according to their caprice or pleasure? . . . It is impossible that any man can carry on commerce in this way. There cannot be a large contract entered into, but what the contractor will make at his peril. . . . What then is the operation of this kind of conduct upon the commerce of the city? It exposes it to inconveniences, if not to ruin. . . .[7]

In a later conspiracy case of *Commonwealth* v. *Carlisle* (1821) attention was drawn to the need to examine the *intent* of union organization. Reasoning by analogy, the court pointed out that " if a number of persons should combine to establish a ferry, not from motives of public or private utility, but to ruin or injure the owner of a neighboring ferry, the wickedness of the motive would render the association criminal." Thus, by analogous reasoning, " if the bakers of a town were to combine to hold up the article of bread, and by means of a scarcity thus produced, extort an exorbitant price for it, although the injury to the public would be only collateral to the object of the association, it would be indictable. . . ." In summary, the courts feared that through collective organization labor acquired the power, and often had the intent, to inflict harm on the employer. Whether intentional or not, such injury raises the question of the legality of the workmen's combination. In the 1821 case, it is true, the court did point out that " A combination to resist oppression, not merely supposed but real, would be perfectly innocent. . . ."[8] But few courts generally regarded employers as the oppressors or aggressors in labor-management relations. The efforts of labor to exact high wages, to impose union- and closed-shop conditions on their employ-

[7] Cited by Sidney C. Sufrin and Robert C. Sedgwick, *Labor Law: Development, Administration Cases* (New York, Thomas Y. Crowell, 1954), p. 31.

[8] *Ibid.*, p. 37.

402 *Labor Law: The Search for Rules of the Game*

ers were in judicial contemplation, "aggressive" rather than defensive measures.

Adverse effect upon the public weal was also recognized. Again, in the Cordwainer's case:

> . . . as the journeymen declare they will not work at certain wages . . . they, if persisted in, would put the whole body of the people into their power. Shoes and boots are articles of the first necessity. If they could stand out three or four weeks in winter, they might raise the price of boots to thirty, forty, or fifty dollars a pair, at least for some time, and until a competent supply could be got from other places.[9]

Thus, the cost incidence of the wage increase would be shifted to the public leaving "the pockets of the whole community to the discretion" of the union workers.

The courts often expressed concern that the conspiracy of workers would corrupt workers by reducing their incentive to excel in their trades; it would deprive labor of its essential freedom to join or not to join a union. It would result in the redistribution of income from the public to organized pressure groups; it would reduce the competitive advantages of employers so organized and reduce the commerce in the community; and it might well delay the capacity of commerce to expand. Clearly, such organization seemed inconsistent with prevailing notions of economic and political freedom.

These early American applications of the conspiracy doctrine have been examined in some detail because the basic precepts of the doctrine were mighty forces in determining the limits of labor's permissible self-help efforts. Rather inevitably, however, as time passed modifications by judicial restatement of the doctrine took place, and the factors responsible for such modification are fairly apparent. Some cognizance had to be taken of such realities as increasing organization in nonlabor segments of economic life, the development of large-scale production, the corporation, the employers' association, and the not infrequent cases in which a combination did not have greater power than a single person. In time, the mere fact of combination no longer seemed adequate to serve as a starting point in decisions condemning the activities of laborers in controversy with employers.

These modifications took various forms. A distinction was made by some courts between "motives" and "intent," the former being an ultimate object and the latter an immediate intent of the combination. Motive had no causal influence upon the lawfulness of a combination; only the intent had legal significance. But the distinction between motive and intent had to be a somewhat arbitrary one, and it still left the courts with the burden of ascertaining what was *the* purpose in a group of inextricably

[9] Sufrin and Sedgwick, *op. cit.*, pp. 31–32.

interwoven purposes. Other courts drew a distinction between *malice in law* and *malice in fact*, the former determining legality and consisting of intentional infliction of injury without justification. The question before the courts, therefore, was whether the workers had "just cause" for seeking to attain certain ends and resorting to certain actions to effect their attainment. However, the evaluation of the just-cause criterion was necessarily subjective, capable of yielding diametrically opposite conclusions as to the lawfulness of specific objects and types of conduct.

Still other courts abandoned the attempt to probe into the motives of workers acting in concert and placed their emphasis upon the means used. The modifications of the early pure and simple version of the conspiracy doctrine led eventually to less restrictive court action. In the clarifying *Commonwealth* v. *Hunt* decision of 1842 (4 Metcalf 111, 45 Mass. 111) the extreme position that combinations seeking to raise wages were unlawful *per se* was definitely rejected and the tests of motive and means were recognized as the controlling ones. "Without attempting to reconcile all the cases, . . . a conspiracy must be a combination of two or more persons, by some concerted action, to accomplish some criminal or unlawful purpose, or to accomplish some purpose not in itself criminal or unlawful by criminal or unlawful means." After *Commonwealth* v. *Hunt* the history of American labor law was a steady accumulation of instances in which the line was drawn between purposes and acts permitted and those forbidden.

A union, prior to this decision, might be prosecuted for any one of three reasons: (1) when the means to accomplish its ends were illegal; (2) when the means may be legal but the ends were not; (3) when the means and the ends were illegal. The court finally reached the conclusion that certainly not all the purposes of union organization should be condemned: "Such an association might be used to afford each other assistance in times of poverty, sickness and distress; or to raise their intellectual, moral and social condition; or to make improvements in their art; or for other purposes." But should the workers have the freedom to strike and perhaps deprive other persons of employment to implement other goals of the union? This was the more thorny issue, but the court rose to the occasion with another analogy:

> Suppose a class of workmen, impressed with the manifold evils of intemperance, should agree with each other not to work in a shop in which ardent spirit was furnished, or not to work in a shop with any one who used it, or not to work for an employer, who should, after notice, employ a journeyman who habitually used it. . . . It seems to us, that as the object would be lawful, *and the means not unlawful*, such an agreement could not be pronounced a criminal conspiracy.[10]

[10] As cited in Sufrin and Sedgwick from the case of *Commonwealth* v. *Hunt, op. cit.*, p. 39, italics added.

The court further explained that the evaluation of union techniques must " depend altogether upon the force of the word ' compel,' which may be used in the sense of coercion, or duress, by force or fraud. It would therefore depend upon the context and the connection with other words, to determine the sense in which it was used in the indictment." This indicates that one must examine the specific acts of the union on a case by case basis to determine its legality, and suggests simply that " If [the association] is to be carried into effect by fair or honorable and lawful means, it is, to say the least, innocent; if by falsehood or force, it may be stamped with the character of conspiracy." [11]

A union, it was held in the Hunt case, is legal and a legitimate form of organization if the means it employs are legal and if the ends it is seeking are legal. But just what were legal ends and legal means? The question was, for the most part, unanswered. We are left with: " It just depends. . . ." Justice Oliver Wendell Holmes once wrote of this " just cause " theory: " The ground for decision really comes down to a proposition of policy of rather a delicate nature concerning the merit of the particular benefit to themselves intended by the defendants and suggests a doubt whether judges with different economic sympathies might not decide a case differently when brought face to face with the same issue." [12]

The Strike and Public Policy

The strike, organized labor's most potent economic weapon, has frequently been held to be unlawful on the ground that it was the means of furthering a conspiracy. In numerous cases courts ruled that strikes were the means of effecting trade restraints and therefore violative of the Sherman Antitrust Act. At this point a few words about the court reasoning and rules propounded with respect to strikes are in point.

If we view strikes as simply the collective decision of all workers to walk off the job, strikes have been lawful in almost all jurisdictions; but this definition of a strike fails to suggest all its component elements. There is an antecedent formulation of demands, an agreement to cease work if the employer does not yield. It is in these components that the substance of unlawfulness has been found. If the primary end to be achieved by the employer's yielding has been the advancement of the legitimate interests of the workers, and if the methods have not been threatening, coercive, or judicially unpermissible for other reasons, the strike has been lawful; if the object was malicious or the methods judicially unpermissible, or both, the strike has been unlawful. Lack of sufficient proximity of interest on

[11] As cited in Sufrin and Sedgwick, *op. cit.*, pp. 40–41.
[12] " Privilege, Malice and Intent," *Harvard Law Review*, Vol. 8, 1894, p. 114, quoted in Millis and Montgomery, *Organized Labor* (New York, McGraw-Hill Book Co., 1945), p. 505.

the part of the strikers, in addition to the character of the objects and methods has been another reason why strikes have been held to be unlawful.

In its concrete application, the test of the lawfulness of the objects and methods has led to different rulings about the same kinds of conduct.

> Whether the purpose for which a strike is instituted is or is not a legal justification is a question of law to be decided by the court. . . . To make a strike a legal strike, the purpose of the strike must be one which the court as a matter of law decides is a legal purpose of a strike, and the strikers must have acted in good faith in striking for such a purpose.[13]

The lawfulness of methods has been to no small extent a product of what has seemed to the judicial mind to be logical deductions and inferences rather than the mechanical application of absolute criteria.

It is, however, possible to enumerate the types of strikes (classified according to object or purpose) that frequently were held to be unlawful and those generally regarded as being lawful.[14] Strikes for higher wages or against reduction in wages, for shorter hours or against increase in the length of the work day, and strikes concerning apprentice regulations, shop rules, safety and sanitary conditions generally have been held to be lawful. On the other hand, the various species of sympathetic strikes, strikes to prohibit employers from working on the job, those to compel them to continue manufacturing operations, those aimed at forcing the hiring of more men at given operations, and those to force apportionment of work during slack seasons have come within the category of the generally or frequently unlawful. Likewise, in some jurisdictions strikes to impose fines on employers for their alleged violation of trade agreements, those (prior to the legislation of the 1930's) called to thwart efforts of employers to require individual nonunion contracts of employment from their employees, and those to extort money or to do damage to a business have been held to be unlawful. The declaration of unlawfulness in the case of such strikes has stemmed from application of the general tests of whether rights more legally weighty than the right to strike were being violated.

Organized Labor and the Injunction

For those whose property or property rights (as conceived of by the courts) have been damaged or are threatened with damage by the illegal activities (as conceived of by the courts) of labor combinations, the writ

---

[13] In *DeMinico* v. *Craig*, 207 Mass. 593 (1911).

[14] This enumeration omits strikes held to be unlawful on the basis of federal or state statutes, such as those alleged to violate the Sherman Act or certain provisions of the Taft-Hartley Act.

of injunction was developed as both a preventative and remedial expedient. Damage suits have, of course, often been brought against union officials, union members, and unions as entities. However, such suits were often found unsatisfactory, as many of those sued were likely to be financially irresponsible, making recovery of damages both uncertain and difficult. The petition for injunctive relief — particularly beginning in the 1870's and 1880's — became a preferred method.

An injunction may be defined as a restraining order, issued by an equity court, requiring specified or described persons to refrain from certain acts. Justification arises from the fact that irreparable injury to property or property rights (for which there is no adequate remedy at law) is threatened. One implication in the underlying theory of the injunction was, therefore, that it could be issued only because the damage feared was irrecoverable. It should not apply to crimes against which other restraints and remedies existed in the statutes. In the United States, however, the injunction was many times extended to cover criminal acts where the injury to property or property rights, arising from such acts, was assumed to be irreparable. In such cases the courts issued injunctions on the theory that they were protecting property rights and that the criminal act and the act threatening the irreparable injury happened to be identical. Edwin E. Witte, one of the leading students on injunctions, has explained that injunctions are " . . . ordinarily negative in character, prohibiting the commission of specified acts under the pain of punishment for contempt. Their purpose is preventive; and in theory at least, they are designed primarily for the protection of property." [15] If an injunctive order is not obeyed, the party enjoined may be held in contempt of court and fined and/or jailed.

While the injunction is centuries old — going back in one form or another to the Romans — it has been applied to labor controversies only since the early second half of the nineteenth century. State courts issued injunctions in the 1880's. The legislation regulating and limiting the use of this instrument, a matter discussed later in this volume, is an important segment of labor law, but here attention will be focused upon some of the more general issues related to what organized labor has called " government by injunction."

The Pullman Strike of 1894 first demonstrated and advertised the great efficacy of this instrument. When Eugene V. Debs and his relatively young American Railway Union gave support to employees of the Pullman Company, a complaint was filed charging the union, Debs, and sixteen other individuals with a conspiracy to interfere with and restrain regular transportation and the mails. An injunction was issued restraining the defendants " from in any way or manner interfering with, hindering,

[15] *The Government in Labor Disputes* (New York, McGraw-Hill Book Co., 1932), p. 83.

obstructing or stopping" any of the business of the railroads entering Chicago or of any trains carrying United States mails or engaged in inter- state commerce. When the injunction was not obeyed and the boycotting action by the railway union did not cease, federal troops were sent into the Chicago area. Violence and bloodshed developed. With the strike continuing, the federal court in Chicago summoned a grand jury and charged that the strike represented an insurrection against the state. Leaders of the union, including Debs, were indicted on criminal conspir- acy charges, and a second indictment was issued for the arrest of Debs and three other leaders for contempt of court for violating the injunction. While the charge of criminal conspiracy against Debs was not pursued, the contempt charges for violating the injunction were prosecuted, and Debs was sentenced to six months in jail. Debs declared that " the ranks were broken, and the strike was broken up . . . not by the Army and not by any other power, but simply and solely by the action of the United States Courts in restraining us from discharging our duties as officers and representatives of the employees. . . ." [16]

The exact number of injunctions that have been issued is not ascertain- able, owing to the fact that the majority came from lower courts whose decisions are not reported in any series of law reports. Witte found record of 508 cases in the federal courts and 1,364 in the state courts prior to 1931, approximately 98 percent being issued to give relief to the employer and 2 per cent to give relief to the union.[17] As the law has stood in the United States, the following have been grounds for the issuance of injunc- tions: unlawful strikes, unlawful boycotts, unlawful picketing, damage to physical property, restraint of interstate commerce, expending of strike funds when the strike has been for an unlawful purpose, disturbing non- union shops where nonunion contracts have been in use, inciting to strike where the complainant has alleged (and the court has agreed) that the strike would be of unlawful character, the holding of meetings and other means of organization, and in a few cases to restrain workers from leaving their work, as in strikes on the railroads, street car systems, and other pub- lic utilities. In addition, the Attorney-General has petitioned for injunc- tions to protect the public interest, and in national emergencies (after appointment and recommendations of a fact-finding board) it is now in- cumbent upon this official to seek an order maintaining the *status quo* for a limited period of time. Originally, when a complaint was filed, the complaint alone could be considered an adequate basis for the judge to determine whether or not he should issue a temporary restraining order. In an emergency the judge might issue such an order without notice to the persons whose actions were being enjoined. Obviously, the petition for the injunction could be highly prejudiced, deceptive, or misleading;

[16] Elias Lieberman, *Unions Before the Bar* (New York, Harper & Bros., 1950), p. 41.
[17] Witte, *op. cit.*, pp. 84–85.

temporary restraining orders were, nevertheless, issued to maintain the *status quo* in a dispute. Following a restraining order, however, a hearing was held, at which time both parties to the dispute had the opportunity to testify and to submit affidavits. A temporary injunction could then be extended until the trial, when opportunity would be given to hear both sides of the dispute. On the basis of such evidence, the judge could convert a temporary injunction into a permanent injunction.

Increasing opposition to the issuance of injunctions in labor disputes had various bases. Injunctions issued to restrain " unlawful " activities frequently prevented labor organizations from seeking to conduct their normal objectives. Both labor and management were often deprived of the right to disagree, a right essential to the development of compromise agreements. In many cases — especially in view of the uncertain state of the law of labor in the past — the injunction restrained employees from doing lawful things. Furthermore, when management secures an injunction, the public may take it for granted that the union is guilty of illegal behavior, thereby strengthening public support of management. And if the injunction is not obeyed, the union faces contempt citations. Regardless of the justice of the injunction, prosecution for contempt will certainly undermine sympathy for the cause of the union. The public seldom sympathizes with anyone operating on the " other side " of the law. When strikes were broken in consequence of an injunction, this only served to strengthen the feeling of many workers that the law provided remedies for employers but not for organized labor. Since exhortation of fellow workers, supervisors, and the public generally, to refuse to obey a court order constituted contempt of court, it was frequently difficult for workers to do anything but obey the court order.

Historically, few injunctions have been converted from the temporary restraining order to the permanent injunction because of the expense and the delays of the litigation and the fact that most disputes have been resolved before a permanent injunction can become an issue. Unions have felt that they have not had the resources to hire the legal staff necessary to fight an injunction, and even if they are prepared to fight to the bitter end, the issue may have been lost before the various stages of legal litigation have been resolved. If the restraining order itself seems unfair, the prosecution of union leaders for noncompliance appears all the more unreasonable. The fact that labor often feels that the resort to the courts is an unfair management tactic to begin with may incite further agitation and resentment. Such frustration often has created a new set of obstacles to peaceful labor-management relations. It is not surprising that union leaders have in the past characterized the injunction " as the most perfect and modern strike-breaking agency there is on earth." As John Mitchell explained, " No weapon has been used with such disastrous effect against trade unions. . . ."

Several additional issues arise from the use of the injunction. First, the injunction originally may deny the party enjoined of the right of trial by jury, although statutory modification and court practice have for years moved in the direction of permitting jury trial. It was the responsibility of the judge alone in the equity court to determine the merits of the case, and this same judge could impose the injunction, cite the enjoined party for contempt if the injunction was not obeyed, and then establish the punishment for disobedience. Does he not then assume the responsibility of the judge, jury, and executioner? This is particularly serious if one doubts the objectivity of the judge. Charles O. Gregory has suggested that while there was often evidence of imminent violence or unlawful conduct, " too many judges got into the habit of making findings of actual or threatened violence and other specifically unlawful conduct where nothing of the sort had occurred or was imminent." [18]

Two points should be remembered in this connection: The equity court is preventative, while the distinguishing feature of the trial court is remedial. Thus, it is of the essence of equity court proceedings to anticipate the possible damage that might be incurred if injunctive relief were not granted. Obviously, these decisions may necessarily be speculative so that the outlook of the judge may be a controlling factor. Second, it is obvious that the social and economic predilections of the judges will provide a frame of reference to the judge regarding the merits of the case, and he is more likely to be sympathetic to the problems of management than he is to the problems of the union.[19] Also, attempts to define, even temporarily, the proper scope of union behavior creates a whole host of problems which the courts cannot attempt to resolve. Originally, injunctions were rather sweeping in their scope, enjoining any and all persons who might be, say, participating in a strike and all who might give encouragement to such strikers. In this setting, could a restaurant or barbershop be then cited for contempt if it posted a sign indicating that they would not serve " scabs "? Or did a church violate a blanket injunction when it provided free meals to workers who were defying the injunction by continuing to strike? The problem was dramatized in the railway shopmen's strike in Kansas in 1922, when the courts prosecuted merchants for posting signs

[18] *Labor and the Law* (New York, W. W. Norton & Co., 1946), p. 100.

[19] It is also sometimes charged that the injunctions represent a new area of labor legislation in the sense that they define the rules of the game, and these rules are not sanctioned by any legislation and may indeed actually conflict with existing legislation. This, of course, is more often the exception than the rule, but it raises some awkward problems in specific instances, especially for a union which is caught between what it regards as legal behavior in terms of existing law, and yet enjoinable behavior in terms of the equity court. Fred Witney in his book, *Government and Collective Bargaining* (Philadelphia, J. P. Lippincott Co., 1951) has observed, " Experience has shown that . . . the injunction procedure has declared unlawful many labor union activities which legislative bodies have not outlawed . . . Through its power to issue injunctions, the judiciary literally enacts legislation." (P. 49.)

in their windows declaring: "We are for the striking railroad men 100 per cent." The issue was joined by William Allen White, editor of the *Emporia Gazette*, who advertised "We are for the striking railroad men 49 per cent." He declared that he would raise the percentage a point each day that the Kansas courts violated the constitutional right to freedom of speech.[20]

The Sherman Antitrust Act: The Unions and Anti-Monopoly Legislation

Most students agree that the Sherman Antitrust Act of 1890 was aimed basically at the growing power of corporations reflecting the "trust-busting" spirit of Congress. Whether the legislation was intended to apply to labor is not made clear by the law itself, but in common law labor combinations had been subject to the restraint of trade interdiction and Section 1 of the act declares: "Every contract, combination in the form of a trust or otherwise, or conspiracy, in restraint of trade or commerce among the several states, or with foreign nations, is hereby declared to be illegal." The Supreme Court later held that the records of Congress indicate that efforts were made by some legislators to exempt farmers and laborers from the act, and since "all these efforts failed, so . . . the act remained as we have it before us . . . and it includes combinations which are composed of laborers."[21] The Sherman Act could be enforced by criminal prosecution by the government, by an injunction suit of the government, or by damage suits by persons who could prove that they had been damaged as a result of violations of the act. In the Danbury Hatter's case — one of the most important in the annals of American labor law — the Supreme Court specifically affirmed application of the act to the activities of labor, held to be irrelevant the fact that the means used by the Hatters' Union (a strike at the Danbury plant and a nation-wide boycott of retail venders of Loewe hats) did not interfere with the physical movement of the commodity in interstate commerce, and established that individual members of labor organizations could be sued for damages arising from violations of the act. What was the background for this decision?

This important Danbury Hatters' case did for the Sherman Act what the Pullman case had done for the injunction. The Brotherhood of United Hatters of America had attempted to secure closed-shop arrangements in all hat-manufacturing firms. By 1902 only about 6 percent of the firms had not yet agreed to such contracts. One of these was the Loewe and Company firm. The union initiated a boycott of the Loewe products, placing the name of the firm on the "We Don't Patronize" list in the American Federation of Labor newspaper. Pamphlets were distributed

[20] For discussion of this case, see Lieberman, *op. cit., p.* 135.
[21] Decision of the Supreme Court in *Loewe* v. *Lawlor*, 268 U.S. 274 (1908).

alleging that the firm maintained a 12- to 15-hour day, with wages of about $13 a week.

Two actions were initiated by the company. First, a common law conspiracy was charged against the union and its members, claiming damages approximating $100,000, and another action was taken in the U.S. District Court for violations of the Sherman Antitrust Act, claiming damages for $240,000. The homes and bank accounts of 248 members of the union were attached. The courts ruled in favor of the company and the award of $252,130 in damages to the company, placing the homes of 186 workers in jeopardy. Because the union did not have the money to pay the fine, it appealed to the American Federation of Labor, which declared a " Hatter's Day " with each AF of L member asked to contribute an hour's income to pay this fine. This case encouraged the politically neutralist Gompers to agitate for further legislation to undo the damage of adverse court decisions. Labor's slogan, quite understandably, became: " The Sherman Law: Amend it or End it."

Non-Sherman Act cases were also important. In 1907 the Court ruled that the section of the Erdman Act of 1898, prohibiting discharge of employees because of trade-union affiliation, was in contravention of the Fifth Amendment.[22] In 1898 the Erdman Act provided for conciliation and mediation facilities and, if these failed, for arbitration of a dispute in the railroad industry. This act also contained a provision which prohibited yellow-dog contracts. In April 16, 1906, the United Mine Workers struck at the Hitchman Coal Company for a wage increase, and after six weeks the strike had failed. The company would rehire employees only on condition that they worked as individuals without a union contract. The United Mine Workers sent Thomas Hughes into the area to see what might be done to re-establish a union in the area, but the Hitchman Company took steps to block his organizing efforts. The company insisted all workers sign a yellow-dog contract, and then secured an injunction prohibiting the United Mine Workers from using " argument, reason and persuasion " or from " talking to " Hitchman employees or attempting to persuade them to become members of the union. It was not until December, 1917, that the Supreme Court ruled on this case. The Court held that a contract not to join a union during employment was valid, that the effort to get workers to join a union was equivalent to inducing them to violate their contract with the employer, and that injunctive relief was the proper remedy. The Court explained that the employers were as free to formulate the provisions of their contract as the workers were free to reject them. In a slashing attack on this decison, Thomas Reed Powell of Columbia University pointed out that " The common law left the employee free to join a union. It left the employer free to decline to hire members of a union. In some upper conceptual chamber these two com-

[22] *Adair* v. *United States,* 208 U.S. 161.

mon-law liberties may dwell together in amity. In actual life they conflict." [23] Powell further pointed out that the decision was tantamount to
declaring that unions may organize men only if they do not, in that process, interfere with the employer's " undoubted legal and constitutional
right to run its mine nonunion." [24] The essence of the Court's doctrine
was to be found in the words, " the right of a person to sell his labor upon
such terms as he deems proper is, in its essence, the same as the right of
the purchaser of labor to prescribe the terms upon which he will accept
such labor from the person offering to sell it."

Labor's campaign for " emancipation " from the injunction in labor disputes was accelerated when, in the Danbury Hatters' and other cases, activities of labor combinations were brought within the purview of the
antitrust laws.[25] Having failed by 1906 to secure the relief sought, the
American Federation of Labor that year made injunction-limitation legislation one of its chief demands in the congressional elections. Both political parties in 1912 pledged legislation defining the position of labor combinations under the antitrust laws and limiting the power of courts of
equity to restrain labor organizations from pursuing their ordinary objectives. In a number of states, also, bills were introduced phrased largely in
the language of the Federal Clayton Act of 1914. Finally, in October,
1914, President Wilson signed the Clayton Amendment to the antitrust
laws.[26]

Section 6 of the Clayton Act,[27] hailed by Samuel Gompers (along
with Section 20 and the other provisions of the act) as labor's " magna
charta," was construed during the years following 1914 to have changed
not substantially the liability of labor combinations under the antitrust
laws.[28] " Lawful " and " legitimate " meant what they had meant prior to

[23] "Collective Bargaining Before the Supreme Court," *Political Science Quarterly*,
Vol. XXXIII (1918), pp. 396–499 and also reproduced in J. R. Commons (ed.), *Trade
Unionism and Labor Problems* (Boston, Ginn and Co., 1921), p. 645.

[24] *Ibid.*, p. 659.

[25] Among the many historical sketches of efforts to legislate with respect to the
labor injunction, see Frankfurter and Green, *op. cit.*

[26] 38 Stat. L. 731.

[27] Section 6, still on the statutes of the United States, reads: " The labor of a human
being is not a commodity or article of commerce. Nothing contained in the antitrust
laws shall be construed to forbid the existence and operation of labor, agricultural, or
horticultural organizations, instituted for the purpose of mutual help and not having
capital stock or conducted for profit or to forbid or restrain individual members of
such organizations from lawfully carrying out the legitimate objects thereof; nor shall
such organizations, or the members thereof, be held or construed to be illegal combinations or conspiracies in restraint of trade, under the antitrust laws."

[28] As late as 1941 the Supreme Court, in a decision delivered by Justice Frankfurter,
rehabilitated what many had regarded as the original purport and congressional intent
of the Clayton Act (*Hutcheson* v. *U.S.*). In this decision the court practically said
that judicial interpretations of the act had thwarted the intent of Congress and that
the Sherman Act of 1890, the Clayton Act of 1914, and the Norris-LaGuardia Act
of 1932 should be viewed as " an interlacing whole."

enactment of Section 6 of the Clayton Act; unions were not *per se* violations of the law, and the old conspiracy doctrine was, in the purport of court rulings, subject to the same tests as theretofore. Likewise the Supreme Court interpreted the anti-injunction provisions of the act, found chiefly in Section 20, to have been merely declaratory of court-made law.

The reading of labor legislation prior to 1930 cannot but impress the student with the hostility of Congress and the courts in framing and interpreting labor laws. Perhaps it is only because the pendulum has swung so far the other way toward the more " liberal " interpretation of legitimate union behavior that the decisions in previous decades seem so patently biased in favor of management. But, as we noted earlier, the temper of society changed under the impact of the depression of the thirties, and even the judiciary itself must have questioned the wisdom of leaning heavily on an old-fashioned economic philosophy. The depression left deep imprints on the government and the courts, and with the shift in the public temper, the Congress was willing to experiment with new rules for labor-management relations. The courts indulged such experimentation. As one student observed, even the Supreme Court justices read the election returns.

18

Liberalism in
Labor Legislation

The intellectual climate of the depression years of the 1930's, as almost everyone knows, engendered greater public tolerance of the purposes and policies of organized labor and reversed somewhat the middle-class disposition to regard unions with moral indignation and economic suspicion. Reflection of this changed public disposition in federal and state legislation probably was inevitable.

The Norris-LaGuardia Act

The most far-reaching anti-injunction legislation enacted in the United States is the Norris-LaGuardia Act, approved by the President on March 23, 1932. This measure, while amended in some respects by the Labor-Management Relations Act of 1947, proved itself capable of practically sweeping from the federal courts the strike injunction. It was designed to effect a substantive change in the law of contracts and to confer immunities from injunctions that, prior to its enactment, were denied on the ground of infringement upon liberty or property rights. The measure was predicated upon the theory that lower courts are creations, not of the Constitution, but of Congress. No court of the United States has jurisdiction to grant any restraining order or injunction in cases growing out of labor disputes "except in strict conformity with the provisions of this Act."[1] An industrial dispute is broadly defined: parties to an industrial dispute are "persons who are engaged in the same industry, trade, craft, or occupation, or who have direct or indirect interests therein, or who are employees of the same employer, or who are members of the same or an

[1] Defined in the act as any court of the United States whose jurisdiction has been or may be conferred or defined or limited by act of Congress, including the courts of the District of Columbia. This excluded the Supreme Court, which derives its power not from act of Congress but from the Constitution.

affiliated organization." [2] The provisions of this important legislation should be summarized briefly.

" Yellow-dog " contracts are declared to be contrary to public policy and unenforceable in law or in equity in any federal court.[3] No court of the United States may issue temporary or permanent injunctions except upon a finding, based on testimony in open court, that (1) unlawful acts have been threatened and will be committed unless restrained, or have been committed and will be continued unless restrained; (2) substantial and irreparable injury to the complainant's property will follow; (3) as to each item of relief granted, greater injury will be inflicted upon the complainant by denial of relief than will be inflicted on the defendant by the granting of relief; (4) evidence establishes the absence of any other remedy at law; and (5) testimony has been established beyond reasonable doubt that public officers charged with the duty of protecting the complainant's property are unable or unwilling to furnish adequate protection. The significance of these procedural provisions was far reaching. The first of these conditions noted above still left with the courts the question of what was an unlawful act, but the courts, viewing the statement of public policy of the law as well as its other sections, construed the limitation so as greatly to limit the issuance of injunctions. The second provision above, while in itself merely restating the old theory of the injunction, when taken in conjunction with the third, now explicitly recognizes the union's stake in the issues of industrial controversy. The fourth condition cited above has had to be considered in the light of the provision elsewhere in the act, and particularly Section 8, which states that the employer must have utilized, as part of the other remedies available, existing machinery for negotiation and arbitration. Equally important, the legislation discouraged placing upon courts of equity the task of protecting employer property rights by requiring that before issuance of an injunction, the court must have found public officers to be unwilling or unable to furnish adequate protection. These procedural provisions are, moreover, integrated with the various immunities from injunction. No federal court has jurisdiction (Section 4) to restrain the following acts, "whether done singly

[2] The purpose of this broad definition was, of course, the circumventing of the kind of constructions that had been placed upon the Clayton Act of 1914. Two results ensued from the restrictive interpretations placed upon the 1914 law: the act did not affect disputes involving persons other than parties to the employment relation in which the dispute arose, and secondly, suits in the name of the government of the United States to restrain interstate commerce could be withdrawn from the operation of the act.

[3] Section 3. Later Supreme Court decisions sustaining the unfair labor practices of the Wagner Act of 1935 (301 U.S. 1–147) made the Norris-LaGuardia type of approach to the yellow-dog contract (denying it the protection of the injunction) unnecessary. The Wagner Act prohibited discrimination against employees because of union affiliation or activity, and this provision could hardly be construed to exclude one of the chief instruments of discrimination, the yellow-dog contract.

or in concert" in any labor dispute: ceasing or refusing to perform any work or to remain in any relation of employment, giving publicity to the existence of, or facts involved in, any labor dispute whether by advertising, picketing, patrolling, or any other method not involving fraud or violence, or peaceful assembly and persuasion; paying to any person involved in a labor dispute any strike or unemployment benefits; aiding by lawful means any person participating in or interested in any labor dispute who is being proceeded against in any court; peaceful assembling; and advising or notifying any person of an intention to do any of the things described in the foregoing immunities.

Following 1932 the courts had two statutes to guide their decisions: the Sherman Act and the Norris-LaGuardia Act. But these acts were not altogether consistent with each other, and the gap between them was not completely bridged by the Clayton Act. Mr. Justice Black, delivering the opinion of the Supreme Court in the Allen Bradley Case in 1945, seemed well aware of this problem.

> We have two declared congressional policies which it is our responsibility to try to reconcile. The one [the Sherman Act] seeks to preserve a competitive business economy; the other [the Norris-LaGuardia Act] to preserve the rights of labor to organize to better its conditions through the agency of collective bargaining. We must determine here how far Congress intended activities under one of these policies to neutralize the results envisioned by the other.[4]

To avoid the judicial interpretation of what Congress *meant* to establish by the legislation, the Norris-LaGuardia Act carefully (in Section II) spelled out the intention of Congress.

In summary, it can be seen that by adopting a very broad definition of a labor dispute, the Congress was attempting to implement the provisions of the Clayton Act and, literally, to widen the perimeter of legitimate trade union activity. Unions could apply pressure not only on a single firm, but on the entire industry, and the union itself need not necessarily be represented within the firm to which it is desiring to extend its influence. Furthermore, the unenforceability of the yellow-dog contract meant that labor could no longer be coerced, under the pressure of economic circumstances, to sign such a contract. Several procedural limitations were incorporated on the issuing of injunctions; hearings must take place before the court; the defendant must be given the opportunity to challenge the allegations of the complainant; if a temporary restraining order is issued, it must expire within five days; the injunction must be specific and name those persons or parties enjoined.

[4] *Allen Bradley Co.* v. *Local Union No. 3, International Brotherhood of Electrical Workers*, 325 U.S. 797, 65 S. Ct. 1533, 89 L. Ed. (1939).

Implications of the Norris-LaGuardia Act

What were the effects of this brief but clear policy statement by Congress? The door to more liberal treatment of labor before the courts pushed open so suddenly that certainly many — including unions themselves — must have been somewhat startled by the implications of the new viewpoint. One of the first crucial tests of the anti-injunction legislation developed in the case of *Senn* v. *Tile Layers' Protective Union*. During the depression Paul Senn found that work in his plastering trade was slack, so he turned to the craft of tile laying, forming a partnership with another man and hiring a third worker. The three men began a small contracting business, doing all the work themselves. The Tile Layers' Union, weakened by the depression, began a drive to organize the industry, and insisted that the Senn Company sign a contract with the union. But the contract stipulated that the owners could not perform any journeymen's work. Obviously the company could hardly be supported by the one worker and Senn refused to sign. The union then began picketing any site where the trio worked with the sign: " Let the union tile layers install your tile work." Senn felt he would be bankrupted if the picketing continued, but also bankrupted if he signed the union contract. He sought injunctive relief, but the circuit court for Milwaukee refused him the injunction. On appeal to the Wisconsin Supreme Court, the application was also denied. The case finally reached the Supreme Court in March, 1937, and the Court decided that the picketing was peaceful, that the proposals put to Senn by the union were, in view of existing economic conditions, reasonable; that such peaceful picketing was but an exercise of free speech. Finally, they reasoned Senn had no property right in his employment that was necessarily protected by the Constitution. The situation reveals the painful conflict between the drive of the union to capture as many job opportunities as it can for its members and maintain union standards within the industry, and the hardship this may create for employers. Another test of anti-injunction legislation developed with the Lauf case. In this case the plaintiff, owner of five meat markets, refused to recognize the AF of L Butchers Union. None of Lauf's thirty-five employees belonged to the union. The union began picketing the shops, and the Court issued an injunction because the pickets were not employees of the company. The Supreme Court reversed the lower court, concluding that a labor dispute within the meaning of the Norris-LaGuardia Act did exist.

The flexibility of the Norris-LaGuardia Act was further demonstrated when, in Washington, D.C., a grocery company opened a branch in a Negro section and refused to employ Negroes. A group titled the New Negro Alliance (established to reduce racial discrimination) began to picket the store with signs reading: " Do your Part. Buy Where You Can

Work. No Negroes Employed Here." An injunction was granted by the lower court, but the Supreme Court decided that this picketing could not be restrained, as it grew out of a labor dispute. It could be construed as a conflict between persons seeking employment and employers.

The benefit of the Norris-LaGuardia Act to union activities can hardly be exaggerated. Until the passing of the Taft-Hartley law of 1947, secondary boycotts were held legal by the courts and could not be enjoined unless evidence existed of fraud or violence. The courts also held (prior to Taft-Hartley) that strikes and picketing to enforce the closed shops could not be enjoined even in cases where the picketing was organized by workers who were not employed in the company involved.

Unions and Recent Sherman-Act Decisions

Some of the more restrictive constructions placed upon the Sherman Act have been recorded in the preceding chapter, but the immunities conferred by the Norris-LaGuardia Act, just summarized, gave organized labor reason to believe that the long-sought " exemption " from operation of the antitrust statute had been achieved. Some of the Supreme Court decisions since 1932 reveal the extent to which this is true.

Prior to 1940 many of the members of the Milk Wagon Drivers' Union, an organization of about 5,000 members, were employed to deliver milk in company trucks, but in the face of competitive pressures a " vendor system " had developed, in which an individual contractor owning his own truck would buy milk from the dairy, and sell it to retail stores. Unsold milk under this system could be returned to the dairy for the full purchase price. Retail stores buying milk in the vendor system enjoyed slight cost advantages and were able to reduce their price to customers, with consequent reduction in the volume of sales for those retail stores still receiving deliveries by the traditional union employee and a parallel reduction in employment of union members. The attempt to unionize the vendors having failed, the union in 1934 began picketing the cut-rate stores. In 1938 a petition was requested for injunctive relief on the basis that the picketing restrained interstate commerce and that the union was involved in an unlawful secondary boycott, designed to sustain the traditional high price of milk rather than simply to unionize the vendors. In the opinion of the Court, after a survey of the alleged abuses of the injunction, Justice Black concluded that ". . . one must agree that the committees and the Congress made abundantly clear their intention that what they regarded as the misinterpretation of the Clayton Act should not be repeated in the construction of the Norris-LaGuardia Act. For us to hold, in the face of this legislation, that the federal courts have jurisdiction to grant injunctions in cases growing out of labor disputes, merely because alleged violations of the Sherman Act are involved, would run counter to the plain mandate of the act, and would reverse the declared purpose of the Congress." The dismissal of the injunction was affirmed.

A second significant decision was that reached in the *United States* v. *Hutcheson* case, where a dispute developed because the Carpenters Union charged that they should have been assigned the job of installing and dismantling machinery in the Anheuser-Busch property in St. Louis, rather than workers belonging to the International Association of Machinists. The Carpenters Union not only called a strike, but began picketing the company as well as the Gaylord Container Corporation, which had leased an adjoining property from the Anheuser-Busch Company, and two construction companies performing contracts with Anheuser and Gaylord, resulting in a jurisdictional problem complicated by a secondary boycott. In its decision the Supreme Court held that the Norris-LaGuardia definition of a labor dispute precluded application of the Sherman Act; thus the union could continue its activities. The Clayton Act, the Sherman Act, and the Norris-LaGuardia Act, Justice Frankfurter observed, have to be read as " an interlacing whole," and the implication was strong that the congressional intent in the Clayton Act had been thwarted by the Supreme Court decisions construing it.

In another significant decision rendered in the Apex Hosiery Case (of 1940), further trade union freedom from restraints under the Sherman Act was established, and emphasis of the Court shifted to the effects of trade union activities upon commodity markets and prices. Efforts were made to organize the plant of the Apex Hosiery Company in Philadelphia, and a stay-in strike, something clearly unlawful under Pennsylvania law, developed. The company sued under the Sherman law, alleging that the union had prevented the shipment of over $800,000 in hosiery, 80 percent of which was scheduled to be moved out of the state. The lower courts awarded triple damages to the company with an award over $700,000. Several other companies began to take immediate legal action against their unions for damages unions had inflicted on them. However, the Supreme Court reversed the decision and reasoned that it was only natural for unions to attempt to eliminate nonunion competition. This intent does not justify prosecution under the Sherman law: ". . . an elimination of price competition based on differences in labor standards is the objective of any national labor organization. But this effect in competition has not been considered the kind of curtailment of price competition prohibited by the Sherman Act." All strikes involve some diminution in the flow of commerce, so that if one took a narrow interpretation in persecuting restrictions of interstate commerce, the courts would of necessity challenge the legality of all strikes. The Apex Company's output represented about 3 percent of the national output of silk stockings, and there was no evidence to suggest that the intent of the union was basically to restrain interstate commerce. Such restraint was rather the unhappy by-product of its legal goal of standardizing conditions for labor within the industry. Justice Stone stated that the object was simply " to compel the company to accede to the union demands " and the interruption of commerce " was not intended to have and had no effect on prices of hosiery in the markets." C. O. Gregory explains, " By 1940, after the *Apex* decision, speculative lawyers began to wonder if there were really *any* normal labor union practices that might be regarded as violations of the Sherman Act . . ." [5]

There remained, however, an area in which the Sherman law might be applied, an area suggested by Justice Felix Frankfurter in his majority decision in the Hutcheson case. In this case, it will be recalled, the Court refused to declare the actions of the Carpenters Union illegal, reasoning in effect that if the boycott initiated by Hutcheson was nonenjoinable under the Norris-LaGuardia Act, it automatically became lawful under even the Sherman Act. But Justice Frankfurter added a significant exception: " So long as a union acts in its self-interest and does not combine with non-labor groups, the licit and illicit under Section 20 are not to be distinguished by any judgment regarding the wisdom or unwisdom, the rightness or wrongness, the selfishness or unselfishness of the end of which the particular union activities are the means." The import seemed to be that if the unions conspire with management to control the market, the public might suffer and such an alliance between labor and management would be regarded within the purview of the Sherman Act.

This "special case" of union-management combination did confront the Court in the *Allen Bradley Company* v. *Local No. 3, IBEW* in 1945. In this case Local 3 of the International Brotherhood of Electrical Workers had organized the large bulk of production and installation electricians employed in the New York area and had made contracts with contractors specifying that they would install only equipment that had been assembled by their workers. This of course eliminated " outside " competition of non-New York electrical products. Several out-of-state manufacturers initiated legal action against the union, charging violation of the Sherman Act. In delivering the majority opinion of the Supreme Court, Justice Black held that the combination among the three groups — union, contractors, and manufacturers — became highly successful from the standpoint of all three, and that some New York manufacturers were, as a consequence, able to sell their goods at an artificially high price in New York (with the controlled supply) and at lower prices outside of the state.

> We think Congress never intended that unions could, consistently with the Sherman Act, aid non-labor groups to create business monopolies and to control the marketing of goods and services. . . . the " purposes of mutual help " can hardly be thought to cover activities for the purpose of " employer-help " in controlling markets and prices. . . . the primary objective of all the anti-trust legislation

[5] *Labor and the Law* (New York, W. W. Norton & Co., 1946), pp. 268–269.

has been to preserve business competition and to proscribe business monopoly. It would be a surprising thing if Congress, in order to prevent a misapplication of that legislation to labor unions, had bestowed upon such unions complete and unreviewable authority to aid business groups to frustrate its primary objective.

Holding that the union activities did violate the Sherman Act, the Court concluded that " It [Congress] intended to outlaw business monopolies. A business monopoly is no less a monopoly because a union participates, and such participation is a violation of the Act."

It is not very helpful to suggest, as was done in the Apex case, that unions were still subject to the Sherman Act to " some extent not defined " nor does the sharp boundary between legal and illegal union behavior in the Allen Bradley case remove all uncertainty. The attempts, for example, to prove or establish collusion between corporations in the pattern of price leadership common today have not proved very successful, and it is equally possible that wage-price patterns may evolve from habit or custom rather than explicit agreements between unions and management. Applying the Sherman Act to labor-management "collusion" poses issues as thorny as its application to imperfect competition in the field of corporate control.

The National Industrial Recovery Act

Among the early New Deal experiments to mitigate the cumulative price deflation and its by-products of overproduction, business failures, and mass unemployment was the National Industrial Recovery Act of 1933. This legislation provided business groups with the opportunity to negotiate price codes to stabilize the effects of competition. Section 7(a) of this provision had considerable significance for unionism, for it provided that " employees shall have the right to organize and bargain collectively through representatives of their own choosing, and shall be free from the interference, restraint, or coercion of employers of labor, or their agents, in the designation of such representatives or in self-organization or in other concerted activities for the purpose of collective bargaining or other mutual aid or protection." The section following the first comma was taken verbatim from the Norris-LaGuardia Act and was, of course, designed to buttress the case for noninterference in the collective bargaining process. However, this provision goes much further than the earlier legislation, for it provides the freedom for workers to organize not only without interference of the government, but now without interference from the employer. The government was now moving from its position of being a " disinterested " or neutral observer of labor-management relations to giving positive protection to unions from employers. The section further stated that " no employee and no one seeking employment

shall be required as a condition of employment to join any company union or to refrain from joining, organizing, or assisting a labor organization
of his own choosing and that employers shall comply with the maximum
hours of labor, minimum rates of pay, and other conditions of employment, approved or prescribed by the President."

In spite of the seriousness of the economic crisis, several management
groups had serious misgivings about the wording of Section 7(a). James A.
Emery of the National Association of Manufacturers suggested that workers should have both the freedom to organize and the freedom *not* to bargain collectively. John L. Lewis was among those to quickly condemn
management's sudden concern for the freedom of labor, and he suggested
that when the steel companies had refused to hire union members, the
companies had denied labor this freedom of choice which management
now held so important.

In order to implement the provision of the act, a National Labor Board
was created, made up of three employer and three employee representatives, presided over by an impartial public chairman. Soon twenty regional
boards were established. The Board enjoyed early success in advancing
the " Reading Formula " to settle controversies based on the recognition
issue. Through this formula, all strike action must be called off, all workers must return to work without prejudice, and an election would then be
held by the National Labor Board to determine the collective bargaining
representative. By 1934, however, several companies began to challenge
the authority of the Board to make these decisions. The Weirton Steel
Company refused to allow their workers to vote on whether they desired
to be represented by an outside union. President Roosevelt then issued two
executive orders in 1934, giving the Labor Board explicit power to conduct elections to determine the collective bargaining representatives, and if
any employer should refuse, the case could be referred to the Compliance
Division of the National Recovery Administration and/or the office of the
Attorney General. But the most that the government seemed prepared to
do was to withdraw the " Blue Eagle " from those firms challenging the
ruling of the Board, and even within the ranks of the NIRA, several individuals doubted that the " majority rule " of the Reading Formula should
be binding on all workers. The prestige of the Labor Board was further
weakened on March 25, 1934, when President Roosevelt intervened to secure a peaceful settlement of a dispute developing in the automobile industry. Two months later a district court ruled that the Weirton Steel
Company could not be compelled to participate in representation elections ordered by the National Labor Board.

There was obviously considerable confusion regarding both the constitutionality of the NIRA and the intent of the Congress in Section 7(a).
Employers, for the most part, doubted that any significant concession had
been given to labor, other than the fact that employers should tolerate the

desire of workers for collective representation before management. Naturally, many employers felt that a company union would be preferable to an " outside " union, and a union influenced or even controlled by the company would be preferable to one that had completely independent status. Consequently, from 1933 to 1935 many of the heavy industries established such company unions.

Any hope that the NIRA might survive was settled with the Schechter decision handed down by the Supreme Court in 1935. In determining the constitutionality of the NIRA, Chief Justice Hughes (delivering the opinion of the Court) simply pointed out that the constitution did not provide the federal government with authority to regulate the details of commercial activity for the economy, regardless of the desirable results that might arise from such regulation:

> It is not the province of the Court to consider the economic advantages or disadvantages of such a centralized system. It is sufficient to say that the Federal Constitution does not provide for it. . . . without in any way disparaging this motive [of maintaining adequate purchasing power for recovery], it is enough to say that the recuperative efforts of the Federal Government must be made in a manner consistent with the authority granted by the Constitution.

Just when the liberal provisions of Section 7(a) seemed doomed by the Supreme Court decision, the foundation for even more liberal labor legislation was being created by the Congress. In the spring of 1934 Senator Wagner of New York State regarded existing NIRA labor provisions inadequate and proposed extended revisions. His proposals for reform were received with considerable agitation, and out of the controversy, Public Resolution No. 44 became law in 1934. The National Labor Relations Board created under this provision did much to expand the " common law " of decisions of the NIRA National Labor Board.[6] Wagner had been

---

[6] This " early " NIRA board had ruled that employers should be restrained from discriminatory practices, including the discharging or demoting of employees for their activity within the union, or threatening in any way to discriminate against workers who had supported the union. The Labor Board also ordered the reinstatement of workers (often with back pay) if they had been so discriminated against, even though it was difficult, of course, to prove such discrimination. An election was held to determine the representation of the work force, with both the company and outside union represented on the ballot. During a strike workers on strike were eligible for voting, as were the nonstriking workers. But workers hired since the strike began were not entitled to the vote. The Board also reasoned that the majority principle would apply — that is, the majority of those workers voting would determine the representation for all the workers, and that the employer is required to bargain in good faith with such labor representatives. The National Labor Relations Board created under Public Resolution No. 44 proceeded to expand the common law of the earlier Board. This Board confined itself to the readjustment of rights rather than serving as an agency to adjudicate or resolve disputes. This represented an important distinction, for the Board was trying to isolate itself from the enormous area in which honest differences between labor and management existed. The Board

named by President Roosevelt as the chairman (representing the public) on the National Labor Board, and it is not surprising that, as the Board found it difficult to gain compliance for its common law, Wagner should propose explicit legislation to minimize this difficulty. Even before the Schechter Poultry decision, Wagner's new legislation was before the Congress.

The National Labor Relations Act

The overwhelming victory of the Democratic party in November, 1934, gave further encouragement to reform legislation, and Wagner began pulling together what he considered to be the most essential elements for an effective labor law. Any new law must state clearly the intent of the legislation, the role of the National Labor Relations Board in enforcing the law (and have adequate teeth to make the law respected). The Board itself must be made up of public representatives rather than a tripartite board, since the major function of the Board was not to settle disputes but to enforce the rights of both labor and management under the law. Wagner felt that the Board must be established outside of the Department of Labor to avoid political influence. On June 5, 1935, the President signed the bill reflecting these principles. The Wagner or National Labor Relations Act had become the law of the land.

Section I of the new bill stated the economic philosophy upon which the legislation was rooted: the inadequacy of purchasing power in the hands of the workers arose because of unequal bargaining power between labor and management. This inequality led, in turn, to the obstruction of interstate commerce as well as to industrial unrest. By 1934 the purchasing power theory was gaining substantial prestige, and it was hoped that relating this doctrine to interstate commerce would provide a rationale sufficient for the Supreme Court to support such legislation. Harry A. Millis, one of the three members of the first National Labor Relations Board, testified that the legislation would restore balance to the economy and supported the philosophy of the act: " In order that the strong may not take advantage of the weak, every group must be equally strong." [7] He further complained that company unions had grown like weeds. Strengthened unionism could lead to high wages and more equality in the distribution of income. This, then, would stimulate consumption and strengthen

---

wanted to confine its activities only to the interpretation and enforcement of existing legislation. It was conceived that the Board would be in a sense the " Supreme Court " with more quasi-judicial than mediation or arbitration functions. This Board gave further precision to the concepts of unfair labor practices of employers, affirmed the majority rule principle, and began to evolve policies for defining appropriate bargaining units.

[7] As quoted by Bernstein, *The New Deal Collective Bargaining Policy* (Berkeley, University of California Press, 1950), p. 101.

the motive for investment, while reducing the dangers of an industrial miscarriage arising from excesses of savings.

Industry was very much alarmed by the Wagner Act, but ironically the Schechter Poultry decision probably did more to assure the passage of the legislation than any other single event. First, Congress believed that some substitute legislation was necessary when the NIRA program fell to the ground; some action was required to fill the vacuum. Secondly, the reasoning of the Court induced many employers to believe that, if the NIRA was unconstitutional, certainly the Wagner Act too would be found unconstitutional. It has even been suggested that many Congressmen supported the Wagner Act, anticipating that it would be declared unconstitutional by the Supreme Court. In this way the courts, rather than the legislature, would be declared the villains frustrating liberal social legislation. But the support given to the bill far surpassed the expectations of even Senator Wagner, and employers responded with a mixture of disbelief and hope that the Supreme Court would once again rise to the challenge to protect America and its institutions from the " dangerous experiments " of the New Deal Congress.

Two months after the Wagner Act was passed, the National Lawyers' Committee of the American Liberty League, made up of fifty-seven prominent lawyers, announced its unanimous verdict that the Wagner Act was unconstitutional. This statement of legal sentiment was widely circulated throughout the country and did a great deal to undermine the public's confidence in the permanence of the legislation. And as the employers' confidence that the law would be declared unconstitutional increased, so did their resistance to unionism. It was estimated that from the summer of 1935 to the spring of 1937, organizational and recognition strikes represented some 50 percent of the total of all strikes. Unfortunately many of these disputes were characterized by violence and bloodshed.

The situation that led to the test case of this act developed in August, 1934, when the Amalgamated Association of Iron, Steel and Tin Workers attempted to organize a local in the Jones & Laughlin Steel Company's Aliquippa plant. The company had established a company union and was determined to resist the outside union's efforts to organize their workers. Thirteen employees were fired for minor infractions of regulations, although it seemed clear to everyone that the basic intent of the company was to eject this core of workers that had been most active in supporting the drive to establish the outside local. Charges were filed with the National Labor Relations Board alleging that the thirteen men were discriminated against because of their union activities. The NLRB hearings established that the company was dealing in interstate commerce, shipping about $47 million of steel annually, and that the company owned facilities and mines in other states. The company had systematically terrorized those men attempting to organize the plant, including beating, arresting, and fining one union organizer, having their company police shadow other union officers, refusing use of their halls or even open lots within the company town for union meetings. With this and other evidence gathered, the Board ordered that the company cease and desist these acts and ordered that the men be reinstated with back pay. The company refused, and the Board then petitioned to the Federal Circuit Court of Appeals for the enforcement of its order. Consideration of the case by the Supreme Court followed President Roosevelt's triumphant re-election and his special message to Congress in the Spring of 1937 proposing the reorganization of the Supreme Court.

The decision of the Supreme Court was certainly one of the most momentous in the history of organized labor. On April 12, 1937, in a 5 to 4 split of voting, the Supreme Court upheld the constitutionality of the Wagner Act. The majority reasoned that the federal government was entitled to legislate in the area of labor-management relations because of the commerce clause within the constitution. And further, it was not necessarily the source of the obstruction to interstate commerce which should control such federal jurisdiction, but the effect upon commerce that local obstruction might have. Chief Justice Hughes, speaking for the majority, further explained:

> We are asked to shut our eyes at the plainest facts of our national life and to deal with the question of direct and indirect effects in an intellectual vacuum. . . . When industries organize themselves on a national scale, making their relation to interstate commerce the dominant factor in their activities, how can it be maintained that their industrial labor relations constitute a forbidden field into which Congress may not enter when it is necessary to protect interstate commerce from the paralyzing consequences of industrial war?

Furthermore, the Supreme Court observed that the company did not even trouble to deny that they had discriminated against the workers because of their union activities, but rested their case on the argument that the Wagner Act itself was unconstitutional. The courts reasoned that the right to organize was a fundamental right just as employers had the right to organize their own business with their own officers and agents. Such rights did not invade the constitutional rights of management. The courts also accepted the reasoning of Senator Wagner that the establishment of the union may be a necessary precondition for industrial peace. Nor was the delegation of power by Congress to the National Labor Relations Board an unauthorized extension of such Congressional authority, for the court system existed to protect any aggrieved party from the arbitrary application of Board power.[8] Congress had, in the Wagner Act, virtually or-

[8] Following the court decision, the Jones & Laughlin Steel Company agreed to acknowledge the Steel Workers' Organizing Committee as the exclusive bargaining agent for their workers, if it secured majority support in a National Labor Relations

dered employers to stop resisting the spread of unionism, telling them that the desire of their employees to organize was none of their business and to keep their hands off.[9]

The Wagner Act in Operation

Rather than attempt to summarize all phases of the Wagner Act, we shall attempt only to outline briefly some of the major highlights of that legislation. Employees were granted the right to form or join unions and to implement that right. The act described five specific unfair labor practices which were now illegal. Employers violated the law if they interfered with, coerced, or restrained workers in exercise of their rights to collective bargaining. Employers could no longer hire professional spies, indulge in union espionage, bribe workers into dropping union activities, or threaten them because of such activities. Employers could not hire strikebreakers for purposes of provoking violence or creating fear in the minds of striking workers. The act outlawed company-dominated unions. Evidence of such domination might arise from the company providing the union with funds, advising the union in the nomination of officers, providing the union with newspaper space, bulletin boards, company automobiles, stenographic services, office space, free use of company halls, refreshments, and other facilities. The employer could not fire a worker because of union activity nor refuse to hire a worker because of his membership or interest in a union. Employees filing charges of unfair practices before the NLRB cannot be discharged for that reason. Furthermore, the employer is required to bargain collectively with representatives of his union, and even if a strike should develop, the employer must remain willing to meet with the representatives of the workers. Of course, the requirement to bargain in good faith does not in any way require the employer to accept demands of the union.

The employer was required to bargain only with the majority representatives of the employees. The majority rule was applied in the determination of the bargaining representative, but one of the thorniest issues confronting the Board was the designation of the appropriate bargaining unit. Establishing wide boundaries for the voting unit would emphasize the industrial rather than the craft basis for union organization and tend to consolidate power in the hands of fewer unions. It has the advantage of administrative simplicity and reduces the hazard of jurisdictional disputes.

Administratively, the National Labor Relations Board was made up of three members, appointed by the President with the approval of the Senate. Each was appointed for a 5-year term with a salary of $10,000 per year.

Board election. The vote was more than 2 to 1 for the outside union, and the existing company union then merged with the S.W.O.C.

[9] Gregory, *op. cit.*, p. 224.

Regional offices were again established to administer the law and service each geographical area of the country. Each regional office is headed by a regional director and includes a staff of field examiners. The field examiners, for the most part, investigate charges and recommend action to both labor and management and the regional director. Actually, the large bulk of the work of the Board is accomplished by the informal recommendations of the Board (and regional offices) rather than through formal hearings. If an employer refuses to comply with the recommendations of the regional director or rejects the complaints of that director, a formal hearing will be held, with a trial examiner representing the Washington office of the National Labor Relations Board. Both sides to the dispute may be represented by attorneys, call witnesses, and submit documents. The trial examiner will make an intermediate report, and if this, too, is rejected, the case will be appealed to the NLRB in Washington. Again, a formal hearing is undertaken, and when the NLRB issues its decision, the party accused may challenge the decision by appealing to the federal courts. The final arbiter is the Supreme Court of the United States.

In representation cases, most frequently the field examiner will appraise the proportion of workers who have joined the union and compare this with the payroll of the firm. He may recommend that both the company and union forego the formality of a ballot if the evidence is convincing that either the majority of the workers are already in the union or if only a minority of the workers appear interested in union representation.

Congress left to the National Labor Relations Board the task of defining the " majority " support given to a union, to determine whether the union should be certified by the board as the official bargaining agent. Originally, it was thought that the majority support would be established when more than 50 percent of those voting desired union representation, although the Board tended later to the position that certification would be forthcoming only if the majority of workers decided to vote. Thus over 50 percent of the workers should vote, and over 50 percent of those voting should support the union if a union were to be certified. The Board then faced a new problem when a company, refused the right to have its own company-dominated organization listed on the ballot, exerted pressure to discourage workers from voting. While the large majority of those workers who did vote supported the union, only a small proportion of workers did vote. In this case the NLRB refused to certify the union. Following this case, however, the Board decided that the majority of workers need not vote, but a substantial number should. In some cases, certification has been granted with only 20 percent of the eligible voters casting their ballots.

19

Union Power and
Legislative Restrictions

The frustrations of the depression had jolted the American public to the point where it was willing to sanction legislation to facilitate the organization of labor. However, it was not until the decade of full employment of the forties that economic circumstance gave real force to the legal rights labor acquired during the depression. At the beginning of World War II the number unemployed was approximately equivalent to the number of workers who had joined unions, but with the enormous expansion of demand for war material in the forties the indexes of unemployment and union membership quickly moved in opposite directions. Through labor legislation management had faced " enforced conversion " to the collective bargaining process, but it was during the period of full employment that the significance of these rights became fully appreciated.

It was the realization of union power during and immediately following World War II that led to a substantial change in the attitude of the public toward unionism. During those years when the union movement was sweeping forward with ever-increasing peaks of membership and influence, anti-union sentiment seemed to find a new source of strength. Hegel was catching up with unionism and out of the conflict evolved a new synthesis, a new *modus vivendi*. In order to fully appreciate the forces behind this change of public sentiment, we shall in this chapter attempt to blend together those elements of our more recent political and economic history with recent labor law.

Pre-World War II Union Successes

The first few months of 1937 proved to be eventful in union history. In Michigan, the sitdown strike in the General Motors plants provided a much-publicized test of union power. John L. Lewis gave vigorous and dramatic leadership to the strike, counting heavily on the willingness of President Roosevelt to support labor in return for labor's support of his re-election the year earlier. Following several weeks of tension, with the constant threat of violence arising from the use of the state militia, on February 11, 1937, General Motors capitulated and decided to recognize the union as the bargaining agent. This was followed shortly with the recognition by the Carnegie-Illinois Steel Corporation of the Steel Workers Organization Committee. Soon after the balance of " Big Steel " agreed to union recognition. By April 6 of that same year Chrysler signed a contract with the United Automobile Workers, and six days later the Supreme Court announced its momentous decision validating the Wagner Act. The split between the CIO and the AF of L gave further impetus to the growth of union membership, with the CIO absorbing many of the now outlawed company-dominated unions and pressing vigorously to widen the organization of the several mass-production industries. The AF of L, sensitive to the growing successes of the CIO, embarked upon its own organizational campaigns with renewed intensity.

The public still regarded labor as the underdog in the labor market. Senator La Follette's subcommittee revealed the extent to which large corporations were stockpiling arms in private arsenals and this served to reinforce the public's conviction that corporations were not sympathetic to unionism. La Follette found that General Motors had spent close to a million dollars in an 18-month period for labor spies, with four sets of spies hired, each operating independently of each other. The Republic Steel Corporation was found to be the largest single purchaser of tear and sickening gas, and in 1938 its arsenal was estimated to include 552 pistols, 64 rifles, 245 shotguns, 143 gas guns, 1,325 rounds of rifle ammunition, 58 gas billies, 2,707 gas grenades, 4,033 gas projectiles, and 5,784 shotgun shells, together with other equipment.[1] Senator La Follette observed that the arsenals were adequate for a small war, and the public sensed the continuing militancy of corporate resistance to unionism.

While union membership and influence were expanding rapidly under the aegis of the Wagner Act, strangely enough unions were not satisfied with the operations of the act. The American Federation of Labor was particularly aggrieved, for it felt that the craft basis for union organization was being discriminated against in the decisions of the National Labor Relations Board in defining rather broad limits for the appropriate bargaining agent. And conversely, when the Board declared that craft units represented the appropriate bargaining unit, the CIO charged discrimination against it.

Labor in a War Economy

With growing international tension abroad, both the AF of L and CIO took an isolationist position, reasoning that the issues did not involve

[1] As cited by Joel Seidman, *American Labor from Defense to Reconstruction* (Chicago, The University of Chicago Press, 1953), p. 17.

America and fearing that intervention would subject labor to new hardships and possibly government controls. When France fell in June, 1940, a reappraisal of America's position indicated that intervention might be necessary. The AF of L grew particularly concerned, but John L. Lewis, as head of the CIO, pursued a more isolationist position. Lewis's stand was probably, in part, conditioned by his open break with President Roosevelt. By January of 1940 Lewis openly opposed the re-election of Roosevelt to a third term, declaring that even if the Democratic convention was " coerced or dragooned into renominating him, I am convinced that, with the conditions now confronting the nation and the dissatisfaction now permeating the minds of the people, his candidacy would result in ignominious defeat." [2] Lewis's viewpoint apparently did not reflect that of the CIO membership which regarded Roosevelt as the friend of labor. But Lewis was prepared to challenge Roosevelt directly, and in October declared: " I think the re-election of President Roosevelt for a third term would be a national evil of the first magnitude. He no longer hears the cries of the people. . . ." Lewis then explained that if labor should re-elect Roosevelt, " I will accept the result as being the equivalent of a vote of no confidence, and will retire as president of the C.I.O. at its convention in November." [3]

Officials within the AF of L were pleased with this contest, for it seemed that Lewis might be cutting off his own nose to spite himself. With this rebel no longer holding the key office of the CIO, the prospects for labor unity would increase. As the AF of L publicist Philip Pearl exclaimed: " We cannot . . . suppress our delight that the entire nation is now discovering for itself what we have been shouting from the housetops for years — that John L. Lewis is just as honest, just as sincere and just as loyal as a rat." [4] While Lewis did step down in the November, 1940, convention of the CIO, it was not without further blasts at his many critics. To the charge that he had nurtured within the CIO the activities of Communists, he retorted:

> Those who infest the columns of the public press with their vile fulminations, saying that the policies of the C.I.O. are conceived and endorsed, and supported, and encouraged, and administered by Communist philosophy, or Nazi philosophy, or Fascist philosophy, or any other philosophy, they lie in their beard and they lie in their bowels. And that remark goes for Old Lady Green.[5]

And to the suggestions that attempts be made to unify the CIO and AF of L because of the growing military crisis and the need for domestic har-

---

[2] As cited by Seidman, *op. cit.*, p. 33.
[3] *Ibid.*, p. 34.
[4] As cited by Seidman, *op. cit.*, p. 35, from Philip Pearl, "Facing the Facts," *American Federation of Labor Weekly News Service* (October 29, 1940).
[5] As quoted by Seidman, *op. cit.*, p. 38.

mony within the ranks of organized labor, Lewis replied: "We have explored every proposition . . . Explore the mind of Bill Green? . . . I have done a lot of exploring in Bill's mind and I give you my word there is nothing there." [6]

As international tensions mounted, the National Defense Advisory Commission was organized, with Sidney Hillman of the Amalgamated Clothing Workers representing organized labor. Hillman proved to be a loyal friend of Roosevelt's and provided a much needed link between the government and the labor movement. Again, however, the AF of L felt inadequately represented because Hillman's union was one of those that had defected from the ranks of the AF of L to establish the CIO. In December, 1940, the Office of Production Management was established to expedite defense production, and Hillman was given a key post in that agency.

Month by month, as the European war mounted and grew more ominous for Western democracies, Americans began to sense that the personal security of their nation was dependent upon the speedy expansion of output. Public annoyance and concern over industrial strife increased out of all proportion to the actual number of strikes taking place. But as prices and profits started upward in the face of rapidly expanding government and consumer demand, unions sensed an opportunity to share in the windfall profits accumulating to management. Company officials were, however, reluctant to commit themselves to a high plateau of costs on the basis of what might well be a temporary expansion of revenues. This long-run possibility dictated a policy of resistance, and industrial conflict took an upswing. The growth of industrial strife created a hostile mood in Congress. Measures to curb the "irresponsible" behavior of the labor movement were proposed in increasing numbers.

The Success and Failure of the National Defense Mediation Board

In order to head off impending repressive labor legislation, on March 19, 1941, Roosevelt established by Executive order the National Defense Mediation Board. This board operated on a tripartite basis, with three public members, four employer and four labor representatives. Its task was to resolve those disputes affecting the national welfare that could not be resolved by the Conciliation Service, should that dispute be referred to the Board by the Secretary of Labor. Both labor and management promised to cooperate with the Board. In its ten months of operation the Board settled 96 of its 118 cases without difficulty and ran into serious trouble in only two cases from management and two cases from labor. In slightly more than half of its cases strikes were already in progress.

The tripartite structure of the NDMB had the advantage of giving both

[6] As quoted by Seidman, p. 38.

labor and management a sense of participation in the solutions affecting them, and this undoubtedly served as a safety-valve on labor-management tensions. In turn, the tripartite structure appealed to the average man as a fair way to resolve disputes. Unfortunately, the fact that neither labor nor management representatives could be compelled to remain as members of the board, gave, in effect, each group the " veto " power. As we shall see, labor's protest and resignation from the board ended its service to the country. A further difficulty in the operation of the Board was that the public and labor representatives were not presumed to be working full time on the job, and the conflicting responsibilities of both labor and management representatives undoubtedly added tremendous burdens to the participants. The all important question of enforcement of the decision of the Board was not clearly established, although it was assumed that the prestige of the group would force voluntary compliance. In the few cases of noncompliance the government seized the plants involved in the dispute, and thus the mediation function came pretty close to compulsory arbitration. Chairman of the Board, William H. Davis, was among those rather unhappy about the vague enforcement aspects of Board decisions: " The combination of mediatory and recommendatory power of a vaguely compulsory nature in a body without statutory authority raised practical problems of great moment to the public." [7]

The issues confronting the Mediation Board became increasingly difficult, especially disputes involving the union security issue. A compromise solution to union security disputes developed in the giant Weyerhoeuser Company lumber camp in Snoqualmie Falls. Here the union was as determined to win a union shop as was the company to deny it. The Mediation Board suggested the compromise maintenance-of-membership clause, a provision which would permit the individual worker to join or not join the union. All workers had an " escape " period of some fifteen days in which to make up their minds. If they should elect to join the union, they would be required to maintain that membership during the life of the contract, whereas they might join the union at any time during the contract. But workers electing not to join the union could not be induced or coerced into membership. Chairman Davis supported this compromise between an open and closed shop by pointing out that no one was compelled to join a union: " It has been suggested that this clause does restrict the worker's freedom of action in some measure, because when he has joined the union he cannot get out. But . . . this is in reality a restriction which he has chosen to impose upon himself; and self-imposed restriction is the essence of freedom." [8]

Several cases before the Mediation Board resulted in government seiz-

---

[7] As quoted in George Taylor, *Government Regulation of Industrial Relations* (New York, Prentice-Hall, 1948), p. 99.

[8] As cited by Seidman, *op. cit.*, p. 63.

ure. The Federal Shipbuilding and Dry Dock Company, a subsidiary of
the United States Steel Corporation, refused to accept the recommenda-
tion for the maintenance-of-membership clause for the union, and this
plant was operated by the government beyond the lifetime of the National
Defense Mediation Board. The Air Associates Company of New Jersey
was also seized when they rejected the Mediation Board's recommenda-
tion that they return earlier strikers to their job.

One of the more significant disagreements arose in the North American
Aviation plant in Inglewood, California, in June, 1941. It was alleged that
the Communist element within the United Automobile Workers union
had encouraged the defiance of the local of the Mediation Board to end
their strike. The national union urged acceptance of the Mediation Board
proposals, but the local remained recalcitrant. Finally President Roosevelt
ordered over 2500 troops into the plant with fixed bayonets to disperse
the pickets and open the plant. Tempers had grown taut and the public
feared that the Communist element within the union was attempting to
sabotage the defense effort. Immediate changes were incorporated into the
draft laws so that striking workers in essential industries would lose their
deferred status. Many labor leaders were startled at the swift and determined use of military power to crush the strike, but the public was growing increasingly nervous about irresponsible and " subversive " union behavior.[9]

A further serious dispute developed in the coal mines. The United
Mine Workers demanded a union contract in all bituminous coal mines
that were operated by the steel companies. Over 95 percent of the workers in these mines were already members of the United Mine Workers
Union, but John L. Lewis decided that the time was ripe to reinforce and
complete union representation by securing a union-shop contract. Lewis
called a strike in September (in spite of the pleas of President Roosevelt to
continue operations) and a second walkout in October. The Defense Mediation Board finally decided against granting the United Mine Workers a
union shop on a 9 to 2 vote, with the CIO representatives Philip Murray
and Thomas Kennedy dissenting. Following this decision, both CIO members resigned from the board. A storm of protest arose from the press and

[9] Since the nonaggression pact between Germany and Russia had been signed, the
Communist party line in America was that the conflict between Germany and England (and her allies, many of which were already defeated) represented a struggle
between rival imperialist nations. Ironically, just five days after William Z. Foster had
described how the Inglewood strike reflected the " resentment among millions of
workers at being forced to pay for a criminal war to which they are opposed," the
German army began its sweep across the Russian frontier. William Z. Foster quickly
reversed his field, declaring " To the question of how far should we go in the struggle against Hitler, the answer must be an emphatic – ALL THE WAY! " Now, in
Foster's words, any person who attempted to keep the United States out of the war
was spreading pro-Hitler propaganda. (The quotations are drawn from Seidman, *op.
cit.*, pp. 48–51.) The new support received from the Communist element within the
union movement was hardly comforting.

the public, denouncing the "headstrong and insane" leadership which John L. Lewis represented. Even within the ranks of labor and especially within the American Federation of Labor, the feeling grew that John L. Lewis was overplaying his hand. Public agitation could lead only in one direction: repressive labor legislation. Roosevelt, by this time, had become completely antagonized by Lewis's tactics and declared: "I tell you frankly that the Government of the United States will not order, nor will Congress pass legislation ordering a so-called closed shop." But the mine workers were only willing to return to work when Roosevelt promised to appoint a special board of arbitrators whose decision on the issue would be binding. Needless to say, this procedure did much to undermine the prestige of the Mediation Board, which had presumably already resolved the issue. In the tripartite arbitration board, public representative John R. Steelman of the United States Conciliation Service voted with the labor member, John L. Lewis, against the company member, Benjamin F. Fairless, to support the union-shop provision. John L. Lewis had won the battle, but it appeared that he might lose the war. The public was annoyed that Lewis had flaunted the government and the Mediation Board and had disregarded the pressing need for greater production. Representative Howard W. Smith of Virginia, sensing this rising anti-labor sentiment, proposed a bill containing a thirty-day cooling-off period before a union could strike in a plant working on a defense contract, forbidding strikes except after a majority vote by workers by a secret ballot, prohibiting strikes in defense industries for the closed shop, providing that unions guilty of illegal strikes would lose their rights under the Wagner and Norris-LaGuardia acts, and outlawing jurisdictional strikes and boycotts affecting defense contracts. On December 3, 1941, the House voted to support this bill by 252 to 136. If it were not for the events that took place on the mid-Pacific Islands four days later, this bill would certainly have become law.

America Becomes Involved in World War II: the Creation of the War Labor Board

Following Pearl Harbor, the public united with a single dedication: to prove that Japan now had the lion by the tail. The invectives against the "insane leadership" of the labor movement were now saved for the leaders of the Japanese and German war machines. Labor and management spontaneously pledged uninterrupted production, and President Roosevelt moved swiftly to consolidate such sentiment by calling a labor-management conference on December 17, with twelve labor and twelve management representatives attending. This group pledged that strikes and lockouts should be abandoned during the duration and that a War Labor Board should be appointed to assist in peaceful dispute settlement.

The principle of tripartism of the National Defense Mediation Board was continued in the National War Labor Board, appointed January 12, 1942. The Board was made up of twelve members, four representing the public, four management, and four labor. Again, following the precedent of the Mediation Board, the War Labor Board agreed that it would be necessary to rely heavily on the direct negotiations of both parties to a dispute, but if settlement could not be secured, the dispute could be referred to the Board for a ruling. The Board might use the technique of mediation and voluntary arbitration, but the principles guiding settlement would depend again on the merits of each individual case. It was hoped that a body of common law would evolve from this case-by-case method which would facilitate the settlement of disputes once precedents had been established. Even during this period of national emergency, it was feared that the attempt to evolve preconceived "principles" (around which each dispute would have to be solved) would prove an enormous task, and would lead to controversy and excessive delay.

As one might expect, the thorniest issue confronting the new War Labor Board was that of union security, and again the maintenance-of-membership provision was advanced as a compromise between open-shop and closed-shop demands. The details of this provision evolved from case to case, with the Board first taking the position that they would not certify the maintenance-of-membership provision unless a majority of the workers would voluntarily indicate their willingness for such a clause. It was soon found through referendums taken that the majority of the workers did support the clause. The company representatives on the Board did, for the most part, go along with this provision, although the Board itself refused to apply the security doctrine if the union itself had appeared irresponsible in tolerating or authorizing strikes. Probably one of the most dramatic issues arising from the security issue developed when Sewell L. Avery, head of the Montgomery Ward Company, defied the application of the maintenance-of-membership provision to his employees. He declared he would accept the Board's order only if the President directed him to do so, and when so ordered, declared he would only comply if the contract contained a clause indicating that it was signed "under duress." The Board substituted the phrase "after protest," and the agreement was settled. Avery later gained national fame in connection with his refusal to extend an expired contract with the union, in defiance of the Board's order. The government seized the company's Chicago plant, but when Attorney General Biddle attempted to take over Avery's office and secure the company books, Avery denied him the right to his office. Two soldiers picked up Avery and carried him bodily out of the office. This scene was photographed and given national publicity. As Avery was lifted out of his office, he described Biddle with what were probably the most derogatory words in his vocabulary: " You New Dealer You! " [10]

[10] This situation is described by Seidman, *op. cit.*, p. 148.

Wage Stabilization During World War II

The wage issue soon became a second major area of dispute. There was general agreement that the war could not be fought without sacrifice, but a surprising degree of bitterness developed over the question as to where the ultimate incidence of the costs ought to lie. Generally, labor groups claimed that they were being asked to assume too large a share of that burden, pointing to the large windfall profits accumulating to business and corporations as evidence of this inequity. Labor further claimed the need to stabilize its real living standard by having wage adjustments which would at least compensate for changes in prices. But why should labor's income be stabilized? As the *New York Times* declared, the argument that labor should be able to maintain the living standard it enjoyed January 1, 1941 "defies elementary logic and simple arithmetic" for this would exempt two thirds of the country's income from the incidence of the war, with the war costs being met out of the remaining third.[11] The problem was further complicated when the cost of living index, as it was then called, became an issue in determining real wage rates. Labor charged that the index grossly underestimated the actual costs of living, giving weight to those items which could no longer be purchased, and so on. The Board found that each standard for wage adjustments posed different problems. If prevailing wages became a standard, obviously a slight adjustment upward in any one sector would start a cumulative circle of upward adjustments. Any adjustment to the wage structure could trigger an endless series of wage demands.

In an early wage decision the Board decided that it must give consideration to wage adjustments which would provide an income " compatible with health and decency," that it must provide for adjustments which would not " impede maximum production or war materials," and that wage adjustments should be permitted for the " substandard brackets." While labor could not expect wage adjustments to compensate for changes in the cost of living, the Board suggested that " labor should be encouraged to negotiate through the processes of collective bargaining for fair and reasonable upward wage adjustments as an offset against increases in the cost of living." [12] As the pressure of wages increased, further precision to wage standards evolved in the form of the " Little Steel " Formula. It was estimated that living costs had risen 15 percent from January 1, 1941, to May 1, 1942. In the steel dispute of 1942 the workers had asked for a dollar a day pay increase, but the Board, in calculating the increases in wages since January, 1941, together with adjustments of the cost of living, settled on a 44-cent per day pay award. The Board decided that this

[11] *New York Times*, July 18, 1942, and quoted by Seidman, p. 114.
[12] Majority opinion of the War Labor Board in the International Harvester Company case, 1 War Labor Report 112, 120 (April 15, 1942).

Little Steel decision should represent a line of defense against the growing number of claims for wage increases, and this maximum allowable by the Board soon became the minimum demanded by unions.

A more general defense against the wage-price spiral was clearly in order and in September, 1942, Congress adopted the Economic Stabilization Act, which was designed to stabilize all prices, wages, and salaries on the basis of levels existing on September 15, 1942. The President asked the War Labor Board to administer the wage stabilization program whether issues in the wage stabilization program arose out of a dispute or not. This represented a substantial increase in the responsibilities of the Board, for it was not now basically a dispute settlement agency, but a wage stabilization agency. By Executive Order 9250, wage increases involving a price increase could be approved only with the consent of the Director of Economic Stabilization. Needless to say, labor protested these provisions as placing it in an economic strait jacket. Because of such pressure, permission was again given the Board to permit wage adjustments to correct gross inequities or relieve substandards of living and make other adjustments necessary for the successful prosecution of the war. On April 8, 1943, with the wage level continuing to bulge under the pressure of demands, President Roosevelt issued Executive Order 9328, stripping the War Labor Board of any authority to grant increases on the ground of inequities. It must confine wage increases only to the limit of the Little Steel Formula and for substandard labor groups. This ruling eliminated some 10,000 cases before the Board. Organized labor again protested vehemently. A modifying proposal developed one month later which permitted the Board to establish occupational groups in various labor markets and assign wage rate brackets for each group. The Board was enabled to make adjustments up to the minimum of these rates. This bracket system, soon known as the " bracket racket," encouraged employers (to circumvent the stabilization order in order to maintain their present workers — and secure new ones) to classify workers in artificial job titles. This stabilization measure did much to encourage the development of job evaluation systems. The Board itself felt that extension of wage-incentive devices would also encourage an expansion of output and earnings without any increase in per unit labor costs.

As one might expect, John L. Lewis was not content to remain docile during the war, especially since his clash with President Roosevelt. Lewis rejected the notion that labor should be tied to the Little Steel Formula, declaring: " When the mine workers' children cry for bread, they cannot be satisfied with a ' Little Steel Formula.' When illness strikes the mine workers' families, they cannot be cured with an anti-inflation dissertation." [13] Lewis set his sights on big game and came up with the demand that his men receive an increase of pay of $2.00 a day as well as portal-to-

[13] *United Mine Workers Journal* (February 15, 1943), p. 9.

portal pay. The union had already received their maximum under the Little Steel Formula, but Lewis had charged that, by imposing such a restriction, the government had violated its pledge to treat labor fairly during the emergency, and the union was not therefore bound by the no-strike pledge. The American community could not believe that Lewis would call out the mine workers while the war was at a critical stage, but nevertheless, on June 11, 1943, the strike was called.

The public's uproar was instantaneous, and almost unanimous in its condemnation of Lewis. The angered Congress was eager to approve the War Labor Disputes Act, or the Smith-Connally Act. President Roosevelt declared he would ask Congress to raise the draft age from 45 to 65 so that striking workers might be conscripted into the army. Under such pressure, Lewis ordered his men back to work until October 31. But the damage was done, and the Smith-Connally Act was quickly approved. It gave authority to the President to seize any struck plant, to punish by fine or imprisonment a strike at a plant in the government's possession, required a 30-day cooling-off period following a strike notice in a war plant, and prescribed a strike vote to be taken by the National Labor Relations Board on the thirtieth day after the notice was filed.

A further crisis threatened to develop in the railway industry and was only averted when Roosevelt seized the industry. The steel workers participated in a short strike, and the public became increasingly irritated by the irresponsibility of such acts. Speaking of the steel strike, Secretary of War Henry L. Stimson pointed out the strikes in the week previous represented the equivalent of "nine divisions gone AWOL for one day." Many of the members of the services overseas began to protest against those money-hungry civilians who put their own material interests above those of the discomforts and risks of the combat soldier. Meanwhile, from the viewpoint of organized labor, the Smith-Connally Act provided some dangerous legislative precedents, for the legislation was built on the assumption that most strikes developed through the inspiration of union leadership and would not be supported by the rank and file if a secret strike vote were taken. Actually, in those instances where an election was held, the bulk of voters did support the strike move and often a pro-strike vote strengthened rather than weakened the hands of union leadership. It also created the paradoxical situation where the workers were asked to vote on whether they wished to strike or not at the time when labor had pledged not to strike.

The Postwar Period

Both labor and management were restless under the controls imposed upon them during the war period. Actually, strike data indicate that, taking the entire war period, the man-days lost by strikes was lower than for a comparable period of World War I. The government's appeal for restraint and labor-management cooperation had genuine meaning to both parties, and the cooperative attitude prevalent was reflected by the growth of labor-management cooperation committees. These committees were organized, not as substitutes but complements to the regular union movement, and they were designed to secure labor's cooperation on various measures to increase production and efficiency.

However, as VE and VJ days were celebrated, the depression neurosis or unemployment fears were again revived. Labor, for the most part, reasoned that the only device for sustaining prosperity would be to expand consumer demand as an offset to the decline of government expenditures. Keynes's theory impressed upon the college sophomore as well as the general public that unless total demand was somehow sustained, unemployment would develop. Several competent economists predicted widespread unemployment in the postwar adjustment period.

Because of both labor and management restlessness, it became untenable for the government to continue its wage and price stabilization policies. Labor and management both denied the wisdom of continuing the no-strike, no-lockout pledge, and the stabilization program thus lost much of its support. Obviously, both profits and wages could not advance rapidly simultaneously, but hope springs eternal. The determination of each party to get more accounted for the price pressure in the postwar years.

In November, 1945, President Truman called a labor-management conference which he hoped would evolve principles and machinery around which any major postwar interruption in production might be averted. The President felt that the backlog of demand must first be satisfied through the immediate expansion of consumer goods, and that industrial peace would greatly hasten the readjustment of the economy. The conference failed in its main purposes for both parties rejected any extension of no-strike, no-lockout pledge. However, several constructive recommendations were agreed upon, including the strengthening of grievance machinery in existing contracts and the ultimate settlement of grievances (if necessary) by voluntary arbitration. The conference suggested, too, that the United States Conciliation Service be strengthened, that wildcat and unauthorized strikes be eliminated, and that there should be no discrimination by either management or the union on such basis as race, color, creed, or sex. But the test of power between labor and management was not to be denied.

Walter Reuther headed a hard-hitting drive of the GM employees of the UAW with a sweeping demand of a 30-percent wage increase, alleging that the corporation's profits were so enormous that this could be absorbed without price increases. The company was only more astounded by the sweeping nature of these demands than by the suggestion that the company books be opened for the union to determine the precise ability to pay of that company. The union was denied access to the books, and the union struck in November, 1945. The President appointed a fact-finding board, which recommended a pay increase of 19.5 cents. This was rejected by the company, and the strike continued. After 113 days of striking, the company accepted an 18.5-cent adjustment, and this established a pattern for the rest of the economy. On January 15, 1946, 750,000 steel workers went out on strike when the United States Steel refused President Truman's mediation efforts with the proposal of an 18.5-cent settlement. On January 15, also, 200,000 members of the United Electrical Workers struck together with an equal number of packing-house workers the following day. The nation was dismayed by the quick series of walkouts, and again, congressional wheels began turning in response to the general public frustration. As a capstone to this agitation, John L. Lewis felt it would hardly add to his stature to simply follow the pattern that had been established by other large unions; so he began agitation for a package which would include, besides the wage pattern secured by the steel and automobile settlements, royalties on each ton of coal mined to finance health and welfare services for the miners. When negotiations were deadlocked on April 1, 1946, the miners walked out, but under congressional pressure were persuaded to return to work for a two-week truce. In the interval the government seized the coal mines with Secretary of the Interior Julius A. Krug named to administer the mines. Krug and Lewis after a considerable hassle reached an agreement, largely giving Lewis what he had originally demanded. Before the year was out, however, Lewis again became restless and charged that the government had violated the provisions of the Krug-Lewis agreement. He threatened another coal strike unless further concessions were made. At this point the government prepared for a show-down fight with Lewis. The government charged that the strike was in violation of the Smith-Connally Act and secured a temporary restraining order against all officials of the union and ordered Lewis to withdraw his termination notice for the contract. This Lewis refused to do, and when the coal mines were shut down November 20, Judge Goldsborough issued an injunction against the union which was ignored. He then found Lewis and the United Mine Workers guilty of civil and criminal contempt. The union was fined a whopping $3,500,-000 and John L. Lewis himself $10,000. The union was stunned that the government and the courts would attempt such a frontal attack on it, and with the dreaded injunction. The Supreme Court later validated the conviction, although it reduced the fine on the union to $700,000 if it would purge itself of contempt within reasonable time. The mine workers were ordered back to work. The audacity of Lewis's demands were sowing the seeds for anti-labor legislation again, although of course Lewis was not alone responsible for the unsurpassed total of man-days lost through strike action in 1946.

The Taft-Hartley Act

Pressure for legislative action to curb union power picked up momentum with the victory of the Republican party and its control of both the House and the Senate in the 1946 elections. In 1946 President Truman was able to veto the repressive Case Bill, with the House only five votes short of the necessary two-thirds majority needed to pass the bill over the President's veto. But the 1947 Congress, with its Republican majority and general antilabor sentiment, had both the desire and the ability to overcome the presidential veto. Representative Fred A. Hartley of New Jersey had proposed a highly repressive bill, and it had passed in the House with 3 to 1 support. The Senate committee came up with a much milder Taft bill, and the final bill approved by both houses was much closer to the moderate Taft bill than the Hartley Bill. President's Truman's veto could not save the day for labor, for it was outvoted 331 to 83 in the House and 68 to 25 in the Senate. A new era of labor-management relations was ushered in with the Taft-Hartley law.

Probably no single congressional measure has attracted more controversy than the Taft-Hartley Act. Every invective applied by the organized labor movement since its conception was utilized to describe the disaster this legislation represented for the cause of humanity. The usually moderate leader of the CIO, Philip Murray, probably felt that the English language failed to provide phrases adequate to describe his scorn for Congress's actions when he declared: ". . . the Taft-Hartley bill was conceived in sin; that it was a sinful piece of legislation, and that its promoters were diabolical men who, seething with hatred, designed or contrived this ugly measure for the purpose of imposing their wrath upon the millions of organized and unorganized workers throughout the United States of America." [14] Labor had rejected *any* legislative proposal to amend or in any way alter the provisions of the Wagner Act and this noncompromising attitude on labor's part made the implementation of moderate legislation much more difficult than would otherwise have been the case.

The underlying economic philosophy of the Taft-Hartley law can be reflected in the statement that employees shall have the right to organize ". . . and *shall also have the right to refrain from any or all such activity*. . . ." This provides the fundamental rationale for the bulk of the legislation: The individual employee must have the freedom to determine for himself the nature of the representation he desires, independent of coercive pressure from either the employer or the union. This argument appealed to both employers and the public. The protestations against the act, it has been stressed, come not from the rank and file but only from union leaders, for it is not anti-labor in nature.

[14] Final Proceedings of the Ninth Constitutional Convention of the CIO, 1947, p. 22, and quoted by Seidman, *op. cit.*, p. 268.

The Taft-Hartley Act outlawed the closed shop and other contractual provisions which required the employer to hire only those workers who were members of a union, or contracts that gave preference to union members over nonunion members in the hiring of new workers. Similarly, restrictions were placed on union-shop provisions. A list of unfair labor practices of which a union might be guilty was drawn up, including pressure by a union to force an employer to discriminate against a worker for reasons other than nonpayment of dues to a union. A union could not begin to negotiate for a union security provision unless it had filed all reports regarding its financial status, its organization, salaries paid to officials, and so on. Union leaders must sign a noncommunist affidavit. If the union wanted to negotiate for a union shop, it had to show that at least 30 percent of the workers in the bargaining unit supported the union security provision, and even then it would be necessary for the National Labor Relations Board to conduct an election to determine whether the majority of the workers favor the union shop. Furthermore, the law stated that a union-shop contract would be prohibited if state law restricted such agreements. Such state law would supersede the federal law on this issue. The Taft-Humphrey Amendment of October, 1951, permitted union-shop negotiations without these NLRB elections, for it was found that in over 95 percent of the cases, the majority of workers supported the union in these demands.

In the administration of the act the National Labor Relations Board was expanded from three to five members, and to meet the criticism that the Board served the functions of both prosecutor and jury, the law created the office of the General Counsel. The General Counsel had the task of determining those issues which should be prosecuted, while the Board itself was to serve in the judiciary capacity in appraising cases presented to it. This division of labor was well justified.[15]

After the Taft-Hartley law, the determination of those industries which were truly in interstate commerce (and hence covered by its provision) tended to be somewhat more restricted. This shift conformed to the economic philosophy then gaining ground, and the Board found pragmatic reasons for not becoming involved in cases which were essentially local in character. The responsibilities of the Board were further confined by the narrower definition provided in the act for an "employee." The legislature attempted to resolve once and for all the continuing hassle as to whether supervisory personnel were entitled to the protection of the Wagner Act, by excluding them from the definition of employee.[16] The

[15] But complications arose when the General Counsel presented an extremely individualistic viewpoint regarding the types of cases that should be subject to NLRB hearing. This disagreement was minimized when the original General Counsel resigned, and a basic policy between the Counsel and Board was evolved with his successor.

[16] This group posed definite problems for they were often in the unenviable position

Board still has the difficult task of distinguishing between those foremen with "traffic-cop" functions and those who have genuine responsibilities of hiring, firing, and disciplining workers. Under the provisions of the Taft-Hartley law, foremen's unions are not illegal; they simply secure no protection from the law. An employer is not obligated to bargain with them and following the Taft-Hartley Act, several refused to renew contracts, then expiring, with foremen unions.

Another provision of the law gave recognition to the employer's rights to freedom of speech on the union issue, on condition again that his statement did not contain any threat of reprisal or promise of benefit to the workers for their activities or lack of activity within the union. The National Labor Relations Board had the often difficult task of determining which statements of the employer might be coercive in their nature, and frequently the character of employer statements could only be fully appraised in terms of the environment into which they were projected. The Board originally felt that any hostile statement by the employer tended to intimidate workers, although in later years it adopted a more tolerant attitude toward legitimate employer statements. After Taft-Hartley the Board decided that employers could assemble the labor force on company time and indicate their reasons and opinions regarding union activities.

The law also stipulates that the Board should not act on unfair labor practices that are more than six months old. Furthermore, the act prohibits the board from ordering the reinstatement of a worker if it is clearly established that the worker was discharged for cause — even though he was an active union organizer or member. It was previously felt that some workers would use their union activity as a defense against

of having one foot in two separate camps, having neither the status of management nor the security of labor. When the Wagner Act was passed, the NLRB generally denied to employers the freedom to discharge foremen who joined unions, and on June, 1942, the Board decided that foremen could represent an appropriate bargaining unit with whom employers would have to negotiate. But with a change in the composition of the Board, the decision was reversed in the Maryland Drydock case of May 11, 1943. Employers had grown concerned about the early decision of the Board, reasoning that any tolerance of union growth within the foremen group would place such members of the management and the company itself in a peculiar position. The Maryland decision did not outlaw foremen unions, but merely denied them statutory protection while organized. Such unions continued to grow in spite of adverse decisions, and the foremen themselves were resorting to the use of the strike in order to secure recognition. In the Packard Motor Car case the NLRB on March 26, 1945, again reversed its position in declaring that such unions were entitled to the protection of the Wagner Act. The Packard Motor Company protested the case to the Supreme Court, where the Court supported the National Labor Relations Board. Speaking for the majority, Justice Robert H. Jackson declared that the fact that foremen were employees for purposes of the NLRB "is too obvious to be labored" but the 5-4 division of the Court hardly reinforced his point. It is probably not a coincidence that the decision of the Supreme Court came on March 10, 1947, while the Taft-Hartley issue was being debated on the floor of the Congress and that the legislation deliberately reversed the majority interpretation of the Board and the Supreme Court on this issue.

sloppy workmanship, infraction of company rules, and other misconduct on the basis that the company might have difficulty defending itself against the charge of discrimination against the worker because of his union activity. The Board is determined that union behavior should not be used as subterfuge for inefficient workmanship.

The procedures of the Board in conducting run-off elections were modified. Originally, the Board had decided that if the balloting indicated the following order of popularity: Union A, No Union, Union B, with no category enjoying a clear majority, a run-off between Union A and Union B would follow. Later it was decided that, assuming the same order of preference as above, the run-off election would be between Union A and No Union, and this procedure became mandatory under the Taft-Hartley law. In addition, the Board had pursued the policy of decertifying any union which was not affiliated with either the AF of L or CIO which was found to be company-dominated. Even if this union had purged itself of such dominance, it was not entitled to recognition at a later date. On the other hand, the Board policies to the affiliated unions were different. A dominated union could be decertified temporarily and later recertified if such dominance were purged from the union. The law stipulates that both the affiliated and the nonaffiliated unions be treated equally, and that both be candidates for recertification if such dominance has been eliminated.

The opportunity for the employer to request an election to determine the appropriate bargaining agency — if any — has been liberalized under the provisions of the law, and once an election has been made, a new election may not be held for twelve months. This contributes to the stability of bargaining. Another important provision of the act is to make unions vulnerable to lawsuits if they violate their contracts or if unions indulge in unlawful boycotts or jurisdictional disputes. It was felt that this provision would encourage a rush of lawsuits, but this did not prove to be the case. Furthermore, it was suspected that unions would avoid any " no-strike " provision in their contracts because of their risk of lawsuits, but this has not been the case.

Probably one of the most significant amendments to the Wagner Act was the list of unfair labor practices of which the union could be guilty. It will be remembered that the Wagner Act listed only the unfair labor practices of the employer, and it did not seem to occur to the legislators in 1935 that the union could be guilty of abusive practices. Of the six unfair practices cited in the Taft-Hartley legislation, the first declared that the union must not interfere with either the right of the individual to bargaining collectively, or his right to *refrain* from bargaining collectively. The only exception to this latter provision was where a union security provision had been negotiated, but the freedom to negotiate such a contract, as we noted above, was itself restricted. Such a union shop cannot compel the employer to discharge any worker for any reason other than the fact that the worker may refuse to pay his dues. Another unfair practice is the refusal on the part of the union to bargain in good faith. Again, this was designed to give symmetry to the legislation, for employers had on occasion claimed that labor had flaunted management's efforts to bargain in good faith. It became an unfair union practice to engage in illegal strikes and boycotts. The union could not compel a small employer or self-employed person to join a union, when the economic survival of such persons depended on their independent status. A second illegal purpose for strike and boycott activity would be to try to apply indirect pressure to an employer, or to indulge in secondary strikes or boycotts. This situation arises where Employer A may refuse certain concessions to the union representing the workers employed by A. The union then applies pressure by boycotting Employer B because B is handling A's product. Or the union may induce the employees of Employer B to strike against their employer. It is also an unfair tactic to force or require an employer to recognize an uncertified union. This was designed, of course, to eliminate jurisdictional disputes and the awkward problem confronting an employer when he refuses to bargain with Union B because Union A has been certified. It was also illegal for a union to exert pressure to require an employer to assign work to employees in one craft or union rather than in another craft or union, another issue which had often prompted jurisdictional conflicts within the union movement itself. Furthermore, Congress made it mandatory that the NLRB secure injunctive action against any union violating the first three situations of illegal pressure described above, and of course the unions could be sued for property damage arising out of illegal strike action.

An additional unfair labor practice was the charging of excessive initiation fees by the union. Few cases of such practices have been presented before the Board. It was also an unfair labor practice for a union to " cause or attempt to cause an employer to pay or deliver or agree to pay or deliver any money or other thing of value, in the nature of an exaction, for services which are not performed or not to be performed." This was designed to eliminate featherbedding provisions within the plant, but by a Supreme Court decision, it has not prevented the union from insisting that certain work be performed even if that work is of no value to the company.

Other provisions are more controversial than those already detailed. A case in point is the requirement that the officers of labor organizations be required to file with the Board an affidavit indicating that they are not members of the Communist party or any organization teaching or advocating the overthrow of the United States government by any illegal or unconstitutional methods. While some labor leaders were undoubtedly pleased with the provision in that it facilitated their isolating and eliminating Communist elements from their union, the larger group felt that such a provision operated on the unfair assumption that the union leaders were potentially more likely to be Communists than either employers or the rest of society. Why should this group be discriminated against by the requirement of such an oath, when a Communist employer would be given full protection of the act? Several of the major union officers refused at first to sign such an affidavit on principle; noncompliance on the part of the allegedly Communist-dominated United Electrical, Radio and Machine Workers of America undoubtedly facilitated the efforts of its CIO competitor to attract a large part of the membership away from the left-wing union.

Further requirements were imposed on unions, including the provision that they must file with the Secretary of Labor copies of their constitutions, bylaws, and reports showing salaries of officers above $5,000, initiation fees, and annual financial statements. Such filing undoubtedly encourages the union to follow judicious financial procedures, even though such statements may not reveal every case of misuse of union revenues. Another restriction was the declaration that unions could not make direct contributions to the election of any federal political office. In a test case of this section the CIO and its president, Philip Murray, were prosecuted for endorsing a candidate for Congress in a union paper. The Federal District Court declared the provision unconstitutional but not so the Supreme Court. In the words of one law student: " It [the Supreme Court] agreed that the union could not be prevented from including political endorsements in a regularly published paper of its own under the circumstances of this case, for that would be an interference with freedom of speech and of the press. But it refused to commit itself on such things as paid advertisement and radio time to promote political candidates, saying that the full implications of the provision must be worked out case by case and intimating that it would not be constitutional as applied to certain situations." [17] Such a decision is hardly enlightening for labor, and it has followed the policy of proceeding cautiously in the form of support it provides candidates. Prior to most elections, however, the political loyalty of union leaders is not kept secret from the rank and file. The act also provided that where employers are contributing to welfare funds, this fund must be administered by a joint labor-management board rather than by union representatives exclusively. It provided that neutral persons settle disputes that might arise regarding the disposition of such funds.

Union spokesmen have often charged that the Taft-Hartley law contains union-busting provisions, however obscure at first sight. Traditionally in an economic strike, the NLRB had permitted the striking voters to vote on an issue relating to the representation of the union, along with the strike replacements. But if the issues were on an unfair labor practice

---

[17] Charles O. Gregory, *Labor and the Law* (New York, W. W. Norton and Co., 1949), p. 454.

of the company, only the striking workers were permitted to vote. Under the Taft-Hartley amendments any workers that the employer might hire to replace labor indulging in an economic strike would be entitled to vote *in place of* the striking voters. Unions feared that employers might provoke an economic strike, replace workers with strikebreakers, petition for an election, and in this way have the union decertified. Apparently this technique has not been utilized by management to date, probably because of the continuing high employment situation and the difficulty of finding strike replacements. But some unions still fear that management might resort to this device if unemployment should grow, especially in those plants employing unskilled labor which could readily be replaced with other unskilled labor.

The law also prohibited the compulsory checkoff, requiring that any employee desiring to have the company deduct his union dues for him would have to make such a request in writing to the employer. Even then, the commitment to the checkoff system remains in effect only for one year or the duration of the contract, whichever was shorter. The law also gave greater precision to the task of the Board in attempting to designate the appropriate bargaining unit, the effect of which is to incorporate the " Globe " doctrine into the legislation, or give greater attention to the desire of labor to organize into craft rather than large industrial units. Again, industrial union leaders have charged that the wide application of such a policy would lead to the Balkanization of labor-management relations. The act further provides that an employer is not justified in discriminating against an employee for nonmembership in a labor organization if membership is not available to the employee.

The act also contains provisions designed to minimize the dangers of strikes before both parties have had a chance to participate in the bargaining process. The law requires that 60 days prior to the termination of a contract, both unions and employers must notify each other of plans to terminate or modify the contract. Then, if within a 30-day interval a deadlock in discussions has developed, it is required that the appropriate state and federal conciliation agencies be informed of the deadlock. This 60-day interval prior to the contract termination is called the " cooling-off " period, and if employees strike within the 60-day period, they lose their status as employees under the act.

The same principle of the cooling-off period is applied, with modification, to disputes which imperil the national health or safety. If the President of the United States views a threatened or actual strike in this light, he is authorized to appoint a fact-finding board to determine the points at issue. This board is not authorized, however, to make recommendations about the settlement of the dispute, but simply to bring the details to the President, Congress, and the public. Upon receipt of the fact-finding report, the President is then authorized to seek an injunction to restrain any strike or lockout. This injunction is to provide a 60-day cooling-off period, at which time the Conciliation service will make every effort to secure a compromise agreement from both sides. After 60 days the President has to reconvene the board of inquiry if the dispute remains unsettled, which will make a further report on the progress toward settlement of the dispute, as well as the last offer of the employer. Within 15 days the NLRB must conduct a secret election to determine if the employees will accept this last offer of the employer, but after 15 days, whether the dispute is settled or not, and regardless of the outcome of the vote, the injunction is vacated. If the dispute is still unsettled, the President may then make a complete report to Congress, together with any recommendations he may think are appropriate. This procedure appears rather cumbersome as well as time-consuming, but the problem of settling disputes of national significance is not one that can be easily resolved. The major criticism is that the " cooling-off " period may again become a " boiling-up " period, and that the election provision is built on the assumption that the workers' sentiment toward striking is not always reflected in the leadership of the union. Seldom, however, have these elections found a split in the sentiment of the rank and file and the leadership of the union.

As we noted earlier, unions found it difficult to believe that the Taft-Hartley law was actual reality when it was overwhelmingly approved by Congress. These same leaders further assumed that it would quickly be modified or altered under the pressure which they could exert at the polls. History has proved how incorrect this assumption was, and the consolidated efforts of organized labor to defeat Senator Taft in Ohio proved how many workers are not prepared to embrace the sweeping indictment placed upon this law by union officials. The several attempts to modify the legislation have not been notably successful although there seems to be general agreement that some sort of modification is in order. In July, 1953, Eisenhower had been developing nineteen points for a basis for modification of the Taft-Hartley law, and these were leaked to the press before the President was able to include them in his State of the Nation message. The reaction of the conservative element was immediate in its condemnation of the concessions planned for labor, and labor itself had little praise for such modest and piecemeal concessions. Probably because of this reaction, the President denied that all nineteen points were intended as the basis for legislation, but served merely as a " working draft " for further discussion. President Eisenhower in his message to Congress, January, 1954, finally did suggest several concrete modifications for the Taft-Hartley law, provisions which would eliminate the mandatory requirement for an injunction in secondary boycott cases, exclude construction projects from the secondary boycott prohibition, permit pre-hiring contracts in industries where employment is intermittent, prohibit employers from petitioning for a bargaining election for four months after a strike, extend the non-Communist affidavit requirement to employers as well as unions, and clarify the agency rule under the act so that a union could not be held responsible for an act of an individual member solely because of his membership.[18] These proposals received only lukewarm support and were not enacted into law.

Today, every congressional and presidential representative usually agrees that something ought to be done to modify existing legislation. However, the continuing stalemate probably reflects the sentiment of one part of our population that the Taft-Hartley law did not go far enough in restricting the arbitrary powers of the union and the belief of the other part of the population that it went too far.

[18] As described by Bloom and Northrup, *Economics of Labor Relations*, (Homewood, Ill., Richard D. Irwin, 1954), p. 705.

V

The Economics of Wages
and Employment

20

Mercantile and Classical
Wage Theory

In this, our final section, we are concerned with the economics of the labor market, and more directly with the economics of wages and employment. Our analysis for the most part will be theoretical rather than institutional. Needless to say, our purpose is not to isolate theoretical analysis from the institutional and judicial reality, but rather to indicate the relationship and interreaction of ideas and institutions. Again, we have attempted to provide some historical perspective in the development of "thinking" about the labor issue. Our focal point is the wage issue and those underlying forces which were presumed to elevate labor's living standard. Our following discussion can be subdivided into two compartments: pre-depression and post-depression labor economics. As we shall observe, prior to the depression economists were much more concerned about the capital effects of wage adjustments and neglected the employment effects simply because they believed that the economy was either " at " or " tending to " the position of full employment at all times. The first two chapters of this section thus deal predominantly with orthodox or classical labor economics. The terminating point in the popularity of this analysis was the widespread unemployment that developed in the thirties. We have, therefore, punctuated the chronology of wage theory with a chapter on unemployment, the various forms that unemployment has taken, and the problem it poses for society. With this background, we proceed with a further chapter, reviewing, for the most part, the role of wage adjustments in minimizing unemployment. Our final chapter assumes that the problem of unemployment has been solved. If this assumption is correct, we can be certain that a new set of problems — mainly arising from economic instability — faces society. Paradoxical as it may seem, if Keynesian expedients assure us that we can operate " at " or " close to " the level of full employment, classical or pre-depression labor economics acquires new relevance. Once again, economists are concerned with growth economics and viewing the distribution of income, not in terms of that optimum that can best maintain full employment, but in terms of that combination that can minimize price level inflation and maximize economic growth. We have, in a sense, traveled the full circle.

In this chapter, we shall undertake a brief sketch of the essential principles of classical or orthodox wage thinking. As we noted in Chapter 1 of this volume, the ideas of the economists have paced the change of economic institutions. We shall review the shift in thinking from the mercantile era, when government intervention was considered essential to maintain full employment, to the golden era of nineteenth-century classicism. The liberalism of this century left each individual with the responsibility for his economic welfare. And the welfare of the individual was identified with the greater welfare of the whole.

A Note on the Function of Theory

Before we embark upon this analysis, it is necessary to appreciate the importance of theory to our understanding of labor problems. Abstraction in theory is often necessary simply because of the virtual impossibility of explaining all forces and describing all institutions. Because the real world is so complex, theory is, in a sense, a sort of shorthand. By abstraction we hope to achieve a degree of simplicity which will make the problem-solving process somewhat easier.[1] Of course, theories must be regarded with caution. A conclusion may follow from deductive analysis simply because of assumptions made at the outset. Apart from the obvious hazards involved when we attempt to reduce to simple terms the operation of our complex system, theories are often suspect as the instruments of the " advocateur " rather than of the scientist. This viewpoint is usually derived from the mistaken notion that facts are neutral while theories are not. We must remember Charles Darwin's declaration: " How odd it is that anyone should not see that all observation must be for or against some view if it is to be of any service." [2] Of course, both facts and ideas are necessary to our understanding of the labor market. Facts provide the test for theories, while theories give us a framework for viewing relevant data. Alan T. Peacock has stated it thusly: " Those who still maintain that historical and empirical methods of research should replace theoretical deductions are about as intelligent as those who assert that a rifle can be fired without bullets." [3] Reality and ideas interact upon each other as do facts and theory. In the same way, wage theories and wage adjustments also interact, one with the other.

[1] One economist has observed: "Simplicity merely means knowledge of the true determinants" E. F. M. Durbin, "Methods of Research, A Plea for Cooperation in the Social Sciences," *Economic Journal* (June, 1938), p. 189.

[2] Quoted from Morris Cohen and Ernest Nagle, *An Introduction to Logic and Scientific Method* (New York, Harcourt, Brace and Co., New York, 1934), p. 197.

[3] " Recent German Contributions to Economics," *Economica*, New Series, Vol. XVII, No. 66 (May, 1950), p. 177.

Mercantile Wage Theory

Mercantile doctrine is often popularized as misdirected economics because, first, mercantilists suffered the illusion that if their nation had a favorable balance of trade (exported more goods than it imported), it would enjoy an increase of wealth and because, secondly, they were in error in identifying gold or bullion with wealth. But now the pendulum is swinging toward a more sympathetic treatment of mercantile writing because of the alleged similarity of the " Keynesian " viewpoint to mercantilism.[4]

Mercantilism is generally defined as economic policy which emphasizes the responsibility of the state and overemphasizes the role of precious metals, foreign trade, and abundant populations. Mercantilism represented, in one sense, a continuation of medieval economic thought and yet a reaction to it. The novelty of the mercantile viewpoint was that economic, rather than moral principles, were to guide state policy. The shift was from spiritualism to materialism.

The mercantilists did not subscribe to the belief that man, if left to his individual resources, would advance the wealth of the nation, the theme that was to be developed so successfully by subsequent classical theorists. To mercantilists, national prosperity was not accidental but arose from wise governmental direction. Postlethwayt wrote, if working people are idle " that is for want of being rightly governed." No blame should be placed on the unemployed: " There is nothing criminal on their part . . . they would work if sufficiently encouraged." Mercantilist Malynes also reasoned that unless " policy " was superimposed upon spontaneous human activity, nothing could result except discord and dissension. The viewpoint was probably best summarized by Postlethwayt when he observed that " Art . . . was like a piece of clockwork, which State action must wind up." [5] State direction was required to stimulate international trade too. Francis Brewster wrote in 1702 that " Trade indeed will find its own channels, but it may be to the ruin of the Nation if not Regulated." Petty expressed similar sentiment: ". . . it was not possible to per-

[4] J. M. Keynes found ample merit in mercantile doctrines: " Mercantilists perceived the existence of the problem without being able to push their analysis to the point of solving it. But the classical school ignored the problem, as a consequence of introducing into their premises conditions which involved its non-existence with the result of creating a cleavage between the conclusions of economic theory and those of common sense." (*The General Theory*, p. 350.) The great authority of mercantile doctrine, E. F. Heckscher, points out that writers in this period were concerned with the question: " How does a state become powerful? . . . What should one do to bring it to prosperity and well-being? " Heckscher adds the significant comment: " Even today —or perhaps one should say, once again today — popular ideas in this respect are in the main Mercantilistic." *Mercantilism* (London, George Allen & Unwin, 1931), Vol. 1, p. 26.
[5] These several quotations are taken from E. A. J. Johnson, *Predecessors of Adam Smith* (New York, Prentice-Hall, 1937), pp. 112, 287, 45, 248.

suade Water to rise out of itself above its natural Spring," and Misselden wrote: "Those that trade Without Orders are like unto men that make Holes in the bottom of that Ship wherein [they] themselves are Passenger." [6] Of course, the role of government regulation and control is not foreign to us today, but the principle was so firmly entrenched in mercantile reasoning that it swamped any sentiment for individualism.

Mercantile desires for a favorable balance of trade was not unrelated to interest in the maximum use of the domestic labor force. If more goods are exported than imported, the difference in the trade balance was to be made up by accepting gold in exchange for goods. Such gold would stimulate economic activity within the nation for two reasons. First, it would add to the amount of money in circulation, cheapen the cost of borrowing money, and hence give encouragement to investment activity. It was in this context that Keynes felt the mercantilists had perceived the benefits derived from an "easy" money policy. The increase in the money supply in circulation would quicken the tempo of the production and employment of labor. Investment activity would increase the industrial potential of the nation, adding to its material strength. The second "advantage" of gold imports was of more direct concern to labor. It was presumed that such imports would be inflationary, but inflation itself would stimulate the work force to greater output. Why was this true? Let us examine the assumptions behind mercantile reasoning more carefully.

First, mercantilists believed that the nation could only be wealthy if the mass of the population was fully employed at all times. Unfortunately, though, the individual worker did not enjoy the impulse to work. He was, in their minds, as lazy as he dared be. Such laziness encouraged labor to work only long enough to enable it to enjoy "subsistence" income, subsistence being defined in a physiological rather than psychological sense. How then could men be induced to labor a full day so that the nation itself might become wealthy? If the buying power of, say, four hours' work would provide subsistence for the total day, why should labor work more than four hours? Even today we occasionally hear the lament that prosperity has spoiled the labor force. Labor no longer has the motivation nor the compulsion to work because it can, in effect, afford not to work. In 1697 the mercantile writer Pollexfen declared that "the advance of wages hath provided an inducement to Idleness . . . in a free nation where Slaves are not allowed of, the surest Wealth consists in a Multitude of laborious Poor." [7] Arthur Young, in his tours over Europe and England, became firmly convinced of the positive correlation between the wage rate and idleness. In 1771 he concluded: "Every one but an idiot knows that the lower classes must be kept poor or they will never be industrious." [8] And when he discovered that the riots in the southern coun-

---

[6] Johnson, *op. cit.*, p. 64.

[7] Heckscher, *op. cit*, p. 162.

[8] Arthur Young, *Eastern Tour* (1771), Book IV, p. 361, quoted by Edgar Furniss,

tries during the late 1740's were limited to the best-paid workers, he was more convinced than ever that high wages for labor created more problems than they solved: " The more these fellows earn, the more time and money they have for the ale-house and disorderly meetings." [9] High wages, the mercantilists felt, destroyed the moral fiber of the worker and debased his character by permitting him to disregard his duty and obligation to the state.

By similar reasoning, just as high wages might spoil labor, so would low wages improve labor. And it is in this context that inflation plays an important role. If labor will work only sufficient hours to maintain subsistence, could not more work be secured from the labor force if the subsistence earned per hour were reduced? In other words, if the buying power of the wage per hour were decreased by price inflation, would this not encourage greater interest in work? The answer to this question was generally in the affirmative. David Hume reports common belief that in " Years of scarcity, if it be not extreme, the poor labour more and really live better than in years of great idleness and riot." Josiah Tucker agreed that " if the price of labour is continually beat down, it is greatly for the public good." An anonymous writer explained: " The way to render a people sober, temperate and industrious is to render provisions dear so as to deprive them of any opportunity to be either idle or debauched." [10] Perhaps in its most extreme form, Mandeville summarized this sentiment by observing that the laboring poor " ought to be kept from starving [but] so should they receive nothing worth saving . . . the poor should be kept strictly to Work, and it was Prudence to relieve their wants but folly to cure them." [11] This sentiment has sometimes been called the doctrine of the " utility of poverty " or the " economy of low wages." It was this sentiment that led Mandeville, in his *Fable of the Bees* to lament: " We have hardly Poor enough to do what is necessary to make us subsist." [12] This thesis implies, as we have seen, that if wages are increased, less labor is forthcoming on the market, while if wages are decreased, more will be forthcoming. The supply curve of labor does not, in this sense, slope upward to the right in the conventional manner, but rather slopes upward to the left. The supply curve has been dubbed — for obvious reasons — the " lazy *S* " supply curve of labor.

One of the problems that inevitably arise when one speaks of the ad-

The Position of the Laborer in a System of Nationalism (Boston, Houghton Mifflin Co,. 1920), p. 118.

[9] *Ibid.*, p. 120.

[10] Quotations from David Hume, *Political Discourses* (1752), p. 118; J. Tucker, *Brief Essay* (1750), pp. 46, 132; and Furniss, *op. cit.*, p. 134.

[11] From *Britannia Languens*, Chapter 7, quoted in Heckscher, *op. cit.*, p. 164. In his *Essay on Charity* (1724) Mandeville wrote: "To make the Society happy and People easy under the meanest Circumstances, it is requisite that great Numbers of them should be Ignorant as well as Poor " (*ibid.*, p. 167).

[12] Furniss, *op. cit.*, chapter 2.

vantage of keeping labor poor is, " Who then is to consume the goods that labor is producing? " But it will be remembered that the mercantilists advocated a favorable balance of trade — the exporting of more goods than were being imported — and such exports might postpone or even eliminate the dangers of an overproduction in the domestic market. In summary, the international trade emphasis was related to mercantile labor economics in two ways: The favorable balance of trade would exert inflationary pressures, which would encourage more investment and more employment. It would also solve the problem of depression arising from the inability of the labor population to consume domestic production.

Another facet of mercantile reasoning (which certainly has a counterpart in present thinking) was the concern with unemployment. Mercantilists invariably believed that the foundation for national wealth lay in the size of the population. The number of people represented a vast, but perhaps undeveloped, potential for adding to national wealth. One could not safely trust natural impulses or market forces to provide for the full employment of labor. We have noted the alleged disinclination of labor to work, and many mercantile writers were busy developing government schemes to provide for the full employment of the labor force. Again, the interest in such projects was not to relieve the working class of the hardships related to unemployment, but rather to enrich the nation by the fruits of such labor. Idle workers represented a betrayal of the nation's interest. Most plans envisaged the establishment of government works projects or government workhouses, in which the idle or unemployed would be taught the virtues of labor. Workers who were imprisoned for " crimes " (including the crime of being unemployed) should not be kept idle while serving their terms but should be sent to work schools where they would acquire useful habits of labor and add to the national product by their output. Some proposals provided for workhouses for the children of the poor, so that they too might be encouraged to become part of a thrifty and industrious population. Some writers calculated the value to the nation of such " reclamation " processes. One proposal, advanced by William Temple, was rather unique in that it suggested that children, at the early age of four, be institutionalized.

> When these children are four years old, they shall be sent to the country workhouse and there be taught to read two hours a day and be kept fully employed the rest of their day in any of the manufactures of the house which best suits their age, strength and capacity. . . . there is considerable use in their being constantly employed at least twelve hours a day . . . for by these means we hope that the rising generation will be so habituated to the constant employment that it would at length prove agreeable and entertaining to them.[13]

[13] William Temple, *Essay* (1770), p. 66, quoted in Furniss, *op. cit.*, pp. 114–115.

One writer made a tabulation of the increment of wealth that would be enjoyed by the British nation if all unemployed hands were set to work, a calculation not unlike some made in this country to measure the loss of income and wealth incurred during the depression of the thirties. As one might suspect, many of the mercantile writers were employees of companies operating under charters from the state. The Hudson Bay Company and East India Company were typical of such large trading establishments, and it is not surprising that such employees should write pamphlets which conformed to the interests of their companies. Heckscher has pointed out that the doctrine of low wages " approximates suspiciously close to the tendency to keep down the mass of the people by poverty, in order to make them better beasts of burden of the few; not only *de facto*, but, as we see here, deliberately and with set purpose."

A second reason accounting for the character and popularity of mercantile doctrine was the constant fear the British had of international competition. Since labor costs were a major factor in the production process, the British often pointed to the laboring propensities of European labor — especially the Dutch — as a factor which could undermine her race for dominance in international trade. The Dutch workers were usually described as being frugal, energetic, and skillful, while the British workers were slothful, lazy, extravagant, and often preferring idleness to employment. Unless the problem could somehow be solved, Britain might well lose her struggle to secure international markets.

A third force behind the mercantile interest in workhouse projects and the need for full employment was the difficulty created by the rising tide of population in Britain. Life expectancy was being extended; families were increasing in size. Labor was being displaced from the soil by the enclosure movement, and labor-saving mechanical innovations dramatized even more the growing excess of the labor supply. A floating labor supply drifted about the country in search of employment, and the more obvious and certain their helplessness, the more reckless they became in their desperate search for subsistence. The historian John Wade describes conditions during Elizabeth's reign in England:

> Rogues were trussed up apace . . . there was not one year commonly wherein 300 or 400 of them were not devoured and eaten up by the gallows in one place and another. . . . every part of the kingdom was infested with robbers and idle vagabonds, who, refusing to labour, lived by plundering the peaceable inhabitants; and, often strolling about the country in bodies of 300 or 400, they attacked with impunity the sheepfolds and dwellings of the people. The laws and police were totally inadequate to control these ruthless spirits.[14]

---

[14] John Wade, *History of the Middle and Working Classes* (London, 1833), p. 49. A magistrate of Somersetshire in 1596 affirmed that " 40 persons had been executed in that county in a year for various felonies, 35 burnt in the hand, 37 shipped, 183 discharged; and those who were discharged were most wicked and desperate persons

A fourth element that must be considered in appraising mercantile doctrine was the need for economic development. While distribution theory was not a focal point in mercantile analysis, most writers seemed quite convinced that to the extent wages lagged behind rising prices (and the pressure of a growing population might make such a lag more certain), the greater would be the opportunity for profits, saving, and investment. Capital expansion could be forthcoming only at the expense of domestic living standards. While this need frequently resulted in the crude rationalization that labor must, at all costs, be kept poor, the indirect justification for such poverty was that capital could only be expanded at the expense of consumption.

Classical Labor Economics and the Wages-Fund Theory

The classical theorists, whose body of economic philosophy was catapulted into prominence with the publication of Adam Smith's *Wealth of Nations* in 1776, were certainly much more liberal and humanitarian than previous mercantile writers. In essence, classical theory changed the whole frame of reference for appraising human welfare: the wealth of the nation was considered the total of the wealth of individual members of that nation. This, as we have seen, is in sharp contrast with mercantile reasoning. However, classical writers were not so carried away with their zeal for humanity to the point of becoming sentimentalists rather than realists, and out of their realism emerged the much-maligned wages-fund doctrine.

The wages-fund theory is beautiful in its simplicity. It explains that the per capita income of the work force at any point of time is determined by the consumer goods available and set aside for labor's support. In more simple terms, labor could not possibly consume goods which had not yet been produced, and hence the level of production establishes a very real outside limit for the living standard of the population. But the per capita level of income would depend on the number of claimants for the national product. If the population and work force increased and the wages fund did not, per capita income in real terms would, of necessity, be diminished. If the wages fund expanded more rapidly than the work force, per capita income could be increased. This, of course, was a matter of simple arithmetic. However simple the wages-fund theory, it was not readily embraced by labor, and indeed, was the subject for considerable controversy throughout the latter part of the nineteenth century. While most economists today consider this wage theory dead — and much of its original rigid formulation has been abandoned — it would be an error to assume that its logic is not part of our current thinking.

who never would come to any good because they would not work, and none would take them into service." *Ibid.*, p. 6.

If *today* we cannot eat more than we have produced, what is it then that determines the amount that we can consume in the *future?* Future consumption is, in large part, controlled by the level of present investment. It seemed clear to classical economists that any institution which threatened today's level of investment (such as a union) would jeopardize

FIGURE 15. Alternative Uses of the Income Stream

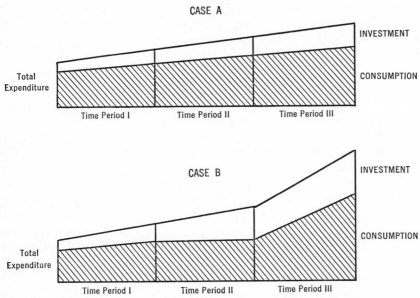

CASE A

Total
Expenditure

INVESTMENT

CONSUMPTION

Time Period I   Time Period II   Time Period III

CASE B

INVESTMENT

CONSUMPTION

Total
Expenditure

Time Period I   Time Period II   Time Period III

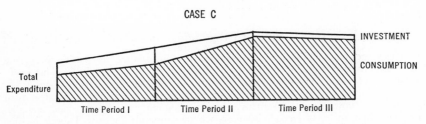

CASE C

INVESTMENT

CONSUMPTION

Total
Expenditure

Time Period I   Time Period II   Time Period III

the future growth of our nation, or at least the prospect for future improvement of our living standard. Thus, wage increases which augmented consumption might satisfy the immediate wants of the labor force, but in the long run they may prove disastrous for the nation. Stated in other terms, a decline in the rate of growth of capital would undermine the size of the wages fund, and hence inevitably labor's own living standard. So convincing was the logic of this argument that when such persons as the French socialist Sismondi protested that " Man must eat in the short run " (whatever the long-run benefits of classical theory) they were considered to be on the crackpot fringe of sound economic analysis.

The pressures created by population expansion in the nineteenth century reinforced rather than destroyed classical reasoning. In effect, the living standards of society would depend upon the race of population with capital expansion, and in England it seemed that capital investment could only expand at the expense of consumption. In the seventy years between 1750 and 1820 the population of England doubled. This upsurge of population growth intensified the pressure for greater output, and this, ironically, intensified the need for higher investments rather than higher consumption.

We may visualize this issue by posing three hypothetical alternatives for the distribution of present income and its effect on future output. In Figure 15, we assume in each case that all resources are fully utilized and divide the total stream of income into either consumption or investment expenditure. In Case A the distribution of income is not disturbed, and it may be assumed that in Period I the distribution is such as to permit a gradual but steady rate of growth of income through time Periods II and III. In Case B it is assumed that wage and consumption levels are stabilized in Period II. The resulting increment of profits permits a more rapid expansion of savings, a growth in turn of investment, and (with the expansion of capital) a greater growth in national income. In Period III both wages and consumption are pulled up by the force of expanding income, an expansion made possible by the abstinence of labor in Period II. But what might happen if labor should organize into unions, and demand premature increases of income in Period II? In Case C we see that the pressure on profits and investment reduces the size of the capital structure, which in turn reduces the productive capacity of industry. Income declines and drags with it the level of wages and consumption.[15] All society suffers.

This analysis runs counter to that underconsumption analysis which

[15] This somewhat simplified scheme ignores, of course, other distributive shares and the possibility that wage income can be used for savings, as well as the fact that profit income can be used for consumption. It is provided in this form only to focus attention on the relationship of the distribution of income between consumption and investment to future growth. Actually, classical economists were concerned that, because of the scarcity of land, living costs would constantly increase. Labor's income could not be reduced by such living cost increases, for it was assumed that labor was already living close to its physical subsistence level. If money wages did not increase to compensate for such increases in the living costs, the size of the labor force would decrease (through starvation) and then money wages would be increased. In this scheme money wages do not represent an increasing share in income, but rather a constant share. With the landowners receiving an increasing proportion of income due to the scarcity of the land factor, profits would be squeezed to minimum levels, limiting the opportunity for capital expansion. It was in this situation that society might represent a "stationary" state. This analysis operates, it will be noted, independently of the issue of labor organization, and is therefore not stressed as part of the *labor* economics of classical theory.

usually assumes that it is possible to expand consumption (and wages) simultaneously with investment (and profits). But with the relatively modest level of output of the nineteenth century, it was easy to believe that one could not simply increase output by increasing wages or consumption alone. The French economist Charles Ganilh observed in 1812: " To suppose that, the more there is consumed, the more is produced, as has been well observed by a modern writer, is to suppose that it is as easy to produce as to consume, that the powers of labour are inexhaustible, and its produce unlimited." [16] Any attempt to expand consumption at the expense of investment, as we see in Case C of Figure 15, will result in less total output: " The wages of labour sink, the population decays, nations are impoverished, and frequently leave no vestige of their existence but the pages of history and the monuments of their ruin." [17]

Labor's criticism of this approach is that the funds accumulating in profits may not re-enter into circulation. The motivations for investment may be undermined by the lag of consumption. However, every classical economist denied that an act of savings would reduce the total of spending. Adam Smith, in 1776 reaffirmed this position by stressing that " What is annually saved is as regularly consumed as what is annually spent, and nearly in the same time too." [18] For over one hundred years this axiom was strongly entrenched in classical thought. Nassau Senior (in 1858) postulates the case of a rich entrepreneur who suddenly decides to abandon all unproductive expenditure and live simply on the bare necessities of life. He then poses this question:

> What should he do with the 10,000 pounds which he would still annually receive? No one supposes that he would lock it up in a box or bury it in his garden. It must increase . . . the whole fund applicable to the use of the rest of the community. If not spent by himself, it *must be lent*, as is done by the miser of the present day, to some other person, and by that person it must be spent productively or unproductively. . . . every man must spend his income, and the less he spends on himself, the more remains for the rest of the world.[19]

Every major classical economist was firmly convinced that not only would savings automatically produce investment, but that investment would in turn, stimulate the demand for labor, and hence augment labor's income. Again, Adam Smith sounded the keynote for classical thinking with his observation that " Wherever capital predominates, industry prevails; wherever revenue, idleness." [20] In effect, he concluded that " capital

---

[16] *An Inquiry into the Various Systems of Political Economy and Their Advantage and Disadvantages and the Theory Most Favorable to the Increase of National Wealth.* Translated from French by D. Voileau (New York, 1812), p. 450.

[17] *Ibid.,* p. 457.

[18] *Wealth of Nations* (London, Methuen & Co., 1925), p. 320.

[19] *Political Economy* (London, Richard Griffin, University of Glasgow, 1858), p. 170.

[20] *Op. cit.,* p. 219.

limits industry " and industry controls the demand for labor. He reasoned that if the capital of the nation remained the same, so would the demand for labor. Ricardo some years later also agreed: " It is not easy, I think, to conceive that under any circumstances an increase of capital should not be followed by an increased demand for labour. . . ." John Stuart Mill also concurred with his own dictum: " The limit of wealth is never deficiency of consumers, but of producers and productive power." [21] And in 1851 John Ramsay McCulloch added: " There are no means whatever by which wages can be raised other than by accelerating the increase of capital as compared with population or by retarding the increase of population compared with capital. And every scheme for raising wages, which is not bottomed on this principle, or which has not an increase of the ratio of capital to population for its ultimate objective, must be nugatory and ineffectual." [22] In substance, all these authorities supported the single thesis: real income could only be increased in the long run — and then only at the expense of immediate increases of consumption.

However, if the prospects for short-run increases in the numerator of the wages-fund ratio are limited, cannot benefits in per capita income be realized by reducing the participants in the denominator, *viz.*, the size of the working population? Unfortunately, the road to labor emancipation seemed blocked here also, for Malthus had developed the widely accepted thesis that population would always tend to outstrip the growth of real income.

So dismal were the prospects that, on the basis of the labor supply considerations alone, many concluded that real wages must always gravitate around the subsistence level. Socialists branded this an " Iron Law " of wages. The logic behind the Iron Law was simply that if income is above subsistence, the labor supply increases, driving the per capita real wage rate down. If real wages drop below the subsistence level, the work force is decreased by starvation, and real income then increases to the subsistence level. Malthus did not believe that the problem of labor poverty could be resolved simply by redistributing the property of the wealthy to the poor; in effect, the wealthy did not possess the ability to solve labor's problem, and hence labor did not have the right to expect that the more wealthy find such a solution.

To Malthus the level of wages was determined by labor itself, or more specifically by the size of the laborer's family. It was possible, however, that the laborer might be induced to have a smaller family if he could enjoy the taste of luxury. The habits and aspirations of labor may be increased, and if the " subsistence " to which labor aspires is not limited to

[21] As quoted by W. B. Robertson, *Foundations of Political Economy* (New York, Walter Scott Publishing Co., 1905), p. 118.

[22] *A Treatise on the Circumstances Which Determine the Rate of Wages and the Condition of the Labouring Classes* (London, Longmans, Brown, Green, and Longmans, 1851), p. 16.

only bare physical subsistence, but includes other comforts considered essential before a large family is created, this may in itself solve the problem. " When habit changed, then one had to admit that there would be a new equilibrium to which wages would adapt themselves." [23]

But other classical writers were not so hopeful as Malthus. James Mill, for one, was not too encouraged that the population size could be reduced by such restraint, a conclusion which Paul Douglas has suggested " befitted the father of a large family." McCulloch, on the other hand, sided with Malthus in expressing a belief that after a wage increase, a stimulus would be given to improved tastes and habits. The process of *desiring* to maintain and improve the living standard may then be cumulative ". . . and as they [labor] learn to form more exalted notions of what is required for their comfortable and decent support, the natural or necessary rate of wages is gradually augmented." [24]

The general emphasis of the wages-fund theory is that employers are protecting the interests of employees in extending that capital, from which will ultimately be drawn the " wages funds " to support labor. There cannot be, therefore, any legitimate clash of interests between labor and management, and it would be foolish for labor to resent the size of management's distributive share.[25] The amounts that management received were put to good use in expanding capital. If management, for example, should receive more than a " fair " share of income over one period of time, nothing could prevent, as a consequence of that, an increase to labor's real income in the future. This point was explained in simple terms in a bestselling volume circulated around 1820, titled *Mrs. Marcet's Conversations on Political Economy*. The book is in the form of imaginary conversations between Caroline, an ingenuous maid, and Mrs. " B," a wise old lady, who naturally does most of the talking. The harmony of interests between labor and management is explained: ". . . the ' rich ' in maintaining and

---

[23] As noted by Maurice Dobb, *Wages* (London, Nisbet and Co., Cambridge University Press, London), 1928.

[24] McCulloch, *op. cit.*, p. 33.

[25] The historian, John Wade, refers to one of Plutarch's analogies to demonstrate the foolishness for the body politic to resent the use to which the income is put, for all parts work together; all are equally important to each other. In Plutarch's story: " It all happened formerly that the several members of the body rose in rebellion against the belly. They thought it hard they should do all the work and receive so little of the reward: the legs carried it from place to place with the easy swing of a sedan-chair, the hands fed it with dainty morsels, the ears cheered it with delicious music; and the eyes, the palates, and the touch, like so many sentinels guarded it from all internal and external injuries. . . ." But the cooperation breaks down when various body parts begin to resent the fact that the stomach seems to gain a disproportionate share of the rewards: ". . . it was intolerable; there was no equality; it was downright aristocracy or monarchy, or worse. Discontent spread rapidly from one member of the community to another, till at last, the whole commonwealth became violently agitated . . . the legs refused to do their office, the eyes put up their shutters, and the arms were suspended in the air; a terrible crisis was evidently at hand, society was on the eve of dissolution." As quoted by Wade, *op. cit.*, p. 165.

employing their capital, advance and support the poor " and she adds:
" it is one of the most beneficent ordinations of Providence that the employment of the poor should be a necessary step to the increase of the
wealth of the rich." [26] The primary proposition that wages depend upon
capital is established for Caroline with the following analogy: A ship-
wrecked crew lands stripped and forlorn on an island where, obviously
enough, they must depend on the native population for "maintenance
and employment." This is the capital which " sets labor in motion " and
enables labor to provide subsistence for itself.

The Decline of the Wages-Fund Doctrine

However willing one may be to accept the arithmetic of the wages-fund
ratio, there were many — especially workers and unionists — who were unhappy with its implications. Labor refused to believe that organized pressure for higher wages would jeopardize the advance of its future living
standards. Of course, the notion that " successful combinations may really
prove to be injurious to the working class " was not inconsistent with the
possibility that labor could really redistribute income (at least temporarily) in its favor. As John Elliott Cairnes explained, " There can be no
doubt at all that under such circumstances well-concerted Trades-Union
action would be capable of achieving success. This, however, does not in
itself establish the wisdom of such policy. . . ."

The argument that labor could redistribute the proceeds of industry in
its own favor co-existed with another not altogether consistent proposition. This was the notion that in the long run, the distributive shares
would remain relatively stable. If this latter proposition be true, the gain
that one group of workers might secure would only result in a reduced
wage share for other labor groups. Cairnes pointed out: " Trade Unions
cannot in the long run materially influence the rate of wages. . . ." Organized labor only benefited at the expense of unorganized labor. As we
have seen, this argument buttressed the application of the conspiracy doctrine in early America. But unions usually rejected the notion that the incidence of all wage pressures was simply shifted to the public in the form
of high prices. If other groups did suffer, was this not the result of management price policy rather than union wage policy?

The second and more sophisticated criticism of the wages-fund doctrine
posed the question: If capital sets labor in motion, what then sets capital
in motion? As we noted, the classical position is that the adequacy of savings and/or profits provides the necessary and sufficient condition for capital expansion, but labor and underconsumptionists deny that the vacuum
created by the decline of consumption will automatically be filled by the

[26] As quoted by Frank Taussig, *Wages and Capital* (New York, D. Appleton & Co.,
1896), p. 187.

expansion of investment. It will be noted that throughout this discussion it is assumed by the classicists that profits and wages, as well as investment and consumption, are in a competitive relationship. But can we not expand *both* profit and wages, *both* consumption and investment simultaneously? It is clear that if we have vast amounts of unused resources that can be rapidly utilized to expand production, this would be true. But classical economists generally operated from the assumption that our economy, if not actually at full employment, was always tending toward full employment. If we move from depression to prosperity, both investment and consumption could expand together out of an expanded national income. And it was during a depression that labor generally advanced the thesis that investment would and could be expanded only if excited by increases in consumption.

Probably much of labor's unrest with classical political economy arose because of the high expectations held out for all society. The hopes of labor had been elevated by the words "Liberty, Equality, Fraternity." The new liberalism stressed the political freedom and economic opportunity for the common man; and as expectations soared, the harsh reality of the real world resulted in considerable consternation and disappointment. Socialists scoffed at the classical economic philosophy. Typical of the socialist viewpoint was that of Sismondi, who concluded that the maldistribution of income caused frequent economic crises in our society. "It is not enough to be hungry in order to buy bread unless there is wherewithal to pay for it. . . . For a man to buy bread, it is not enough to have an income, he must also be able to eat it; now not only is the quantity which the rich eat limited; the quantity of all manufactured production which they can use is limited also. It is not the income of the rich but the income of the poor that must be increased, for the poor are the only purchasers who can add greatly to the extent of the market." [27]

It is surprising that within the camp of economic orthodoxy itself, Malthus advanced several arguments which could be used as part of the artillery against classical theory, and certainly many of his arguments were anticipations of the Keynesian viewpoint. First, Malthus stressed that classical economists should not (in their speculations that in the long run everything will be all right) dismiss the hardships that may exist within the short run. "Theoretical writers [referring to Ricardo in particular] are too apt, in their calculations to overlook these intervals of depression; but eight or ten years recurring not infrequently are serious spaces in human life. They amount to a serious sum of happiness or misery, according as they are prosperous or adverse." [28] Malthus did not deny, like many

[27] From Sismondi's *Political Economy* (London, 1847), as cited by Edmund Whittaker, *A History of Economic Ideas* (New York, Longmans, Green & Co., 1943), pp. 208–209.

[28] From Malthus' *Political Economy*, as cited by H. L. McCracken, *Value Theory and the Business Cycle* (New York, Falcon Press, 1933), p. 121.

Socialist critics, that the private savings and investment process was vital to the economic health of the nation, but feared that society might over-invest because of underconsumption. In an often quoted observation, Malthus declared:

> . . . if consumption exceeds production, the capital of the country must be diminished, and its wealth must be gradually destroyed from its want of power to produce; if production be in great excess above consumption, the motive to accumulate and consume must cease from the want of will to consume. The two extremes are obvious; and it follows that there must be some intermediate point. . . . where taking into consideration both the power to produce and the will to consume, the encouragement to the increase of wealth is greatest.

Malthus further challenged classical theory by suggesting that capital could become redundant if it were not supported by sufficient demand. He did not, in other words, fully agree that supply automatically created its own demand, and the further corollary that capital necessarily ex-panded such demand. Demand might be inadequate because the rich may have the " power but not the will " to spend: such would be a voluntary failure of demand. The poor may have the " will but not the power ": such would be an involuntary failure of demand. He did not believe, in other words, that continuous savings, when pushed to excess, would auto-matically create demand. " In general, demand is quite as necessary to the increase of capital as capital is to demand. . . . they mutually act upon and encourage each other and neither of them can proceed with vigour if the other be left far behind." [29] It is significant that the observations in Malthus' *Principles* received little attention, while his thesis on popula-tion growth became a national issue. Apparently in 1821 society (or at least most of its economists) refused to believe that depressions were in any way related to the inadequacy of consumption.

In the middle of the nineteenth century sentiment began to gain ground that high wages, by stimulating consumption, might not only stimulate investment, but might also have beneficial effects on the worker himself. The ultra-orthodox economist, McCulloch, also had kind words to say on labor's behalf, expressly denying that low wages would impel greater la-bor productivity: " Have the *low* wages of the Irish, the Poles and the Hindoos, made them industrious? . . . or the *high* wages of the Ameri-cans, the English and the Hollanders, made them lazy, riotous and profli-gate? " He insisted that just the opposite has been the case:

[29] As cited by McCracken, *op. cit.*, p. 125. To clarify his position in his discussions with Ricardo, Malthus explained: "All that I mean to say is that no nation can *possibly* grow rich by an accumulation of capital arising from a diminution of con-sumption; because, such accumulation being greatly beyond what is wanted in order to supply the effective demand for produce, a part of it would very soon lose both its use and its value and cease to possess the character of wealth." From *Principles of Political Economy* (Boston, Wells and Lilly, 1821), p. 287.

The experience of all ages and nations, proves that liberal wages are the keenest spur to assiduous exertions. . . . In fact there cannot be a doubt, notwithstanding all that has been said and written to the contrary, that high wages are the most effectual means of promoting industry and frugality among the labouring class. No country can flourish where wages are low: and none can be long depressed where they are high. The labourers are the thews and sinews of industry. . . . They are the foundation of the social pyramid; and so long as the standard of wages continues high this foundation will be solid and secure.[30]

The possibility that high wages could improve the character of labor led to the possibility that a wage increase (in money terms) may not lead to a proportionate increase in per unit costs. If labor lived in better circumstances, had adequate shelter and food, secured more complete rest, the productivity of labor might then increase as rapidly, or even more rapidly, than wages. The British manufacturer, Robert Owen, became so obsessed with the possibility that " investment in men " could produce returns even greater than the investment in machines, that he abandoned his opportunities for private gain to establish a utopian community based on his " new " principle. Robert Owen is often credited as being the father of personnel management because of his principles of human relations.

We see, in effect, that the critics of the wages-fund theory reasoned that supply does not always account for demand, but rather, that demand may account for supply. As early as 1826, Sir Edward West, in his controversy with Ricardo, took the unusual position in suggesting that demand might independently increase supply, but his observations went unnoticed. By following the reasoning of Say's Law of Markets, West concluded:

We might just as well say that the demand for coats depends upon the quantity of cloth as that the demand for labour depends upon the quantity of capital. Though the number of coats cannot be increased without an increase of the quantity of cloth, increase the demand for coats and the price of coats and the cloth will soon be manufactured; so increase the demand for the price of labour and the necessaries which the labourers require will soon be raised and manufactured.[31]

This comes pretty close to saying that if one looks after demand, supply will look after itself. For to West, if labor were allowed sufficient purchasing power, it would not be long before industry responded by increasing production. This is the purchasing power theory in simple form.

Toward the end of the nineteenth century, more and more economists were willing to admit that labor could, through pressure, increase its share

[30] *Principles of Political Economy* (4th ed., 1849), pp. 45–49.
[31] *Price of Corn and Wages of Labour* (London, John Hatchard & Sons, 1826), p. 81.

of income, but the majority still doubted the wisdom of such action. John Stuart Mill stated:

> There is no law of nature making it inherently impossible for wages to rise to the point of absorbing not only the funds which he [the employer] had intended to devote to carry on his business, but the whole of what he allows for his private expenses beyond the necessaries of life. The real limit to the rise is the practical consideration how much would ruin him, or drive him to abandon the business, not the inexorable limits of the Wages-fund.[32]

The outside limit to wage increases was seen in the mobility of capital. But if capital is not mobile, if the capitalist is not ready to quit, it appeared that labor had considerable opportunity to extract additional income from the proceeds of industry. It is of course true that there is a breaking point, for management will not continue to operate indefinitely if it cannot cover its costs. However, in the short run it may be willing to operate at a loss so long as its revenues are sufficient to cover its fixed costs (or those costs which would exist whether the plant were operating or not). The propensity of management to quit will depend on earning opportunities elsewhere as well as the prospects for earnings in the long run. Thus, there is no well-defined wages fund nor even, for that matter, a well-defined wage ceiling. If this be true, the only method for determining the outside limit to the wages fund is through trial and error.[33] The limits are being reached when a wage increase results in a substantial decrease in employment. It is certainly reached when the employer folds his business.

Probably the most outspoken critic of the wages-fund theory was the American economist Francis Walker. He objected to such pronouncements as, " Strikes could not increase the Wages Fund; strikes did not diminish the number of applicants for employment; therefore it was plain as a pikestaff that strikes could not raise wages." [34] He bitterly announced that it " may seem wanton to break such a pretty toy as this; but the fact

[32] As quoted by Alfred Marshall, *Principles of Economics* (London, Macmillan & Co., 1938), p. 825.

[33] In more recent times, the British economist A. C. Pigou has revived interest in the wages-fund theory and reiterates that while ". . . the size of the fund proper to any year does not rigidly determine the amount of the wages flow . . . it does set a ceiling to it. Beyond the amount of the fund it is impossible for any agency, government, trade union or anything else to force up the wages of labour as a whole. They may, of course, force up the wages of a particular group of wage-earners, but that can only be at the expense of other groups." " Mill and the Wages Fund," *Economic Journal*, Vol. LIX, No. 234 (June, 1949), p. 173. Compare to Alfred Marshall's *Principles of Economics* (1938 ed., p. 825), in which Marshall discussed the upward flexibility in wage adjustments and Bronfenbrenner's observations in " Wages in Excess of Marginal Revenue Product." *Southern Economic Journal* Vol. XVI, No. 3 (January 1950), pp. 297–307).

[34] *The Wages Question* (New York, Henry Holt and Co., 1891), p. 144.

is that the wage fund theory is demonstrably false, contrary alike to the reason of the case and to the course of history. . . ." Walker's major criticism of the theory is that labor has a very elastic wages fund because of the elasticity of labor productivity. But he goes further to deny " that if the wage laborer does not seek his interest, his interest will seek him; that economical forces are continually operating to relieve and repair the injuries of labor; and, specifically, that all sums taken in excessive profits . . . are sure to be returned to wages." To Walker it was not true that high profits *inevitably* benefited the work force. Therefore union organization was justified, for organization may be necessary if labor is to secure distributive justice.[35]

Probably the wages-fund theory lost its prestige when the great economist, Alfred Marshall, concluded that the doctrine that the amount of wages was limited by the amount of capital was a statement that could not be defended. " At best it is but a slovenly way of talking." [36] With Marshall no longer willing to defend the wages-fund theory against criticism, few economists seemed willing to contain the rising tide of criticism against it. McCulloch places his finger on the most sensitive issue in which the pro and con of the wages-fund theories were joined. He observes that:

> It does not . . . follow that capitalists would be placed in a really preferable situation were wages to fall and profits to rise. The rate of profit, however important is not the only thing to which they have to look. Security and tranquility are still more indispensable than high profits to the successful prosecution of industrial undertakings. . . .[37]

High profits alone, then, do not provide the sufficient conditions for investment. If this be true, it places labor-management relations in a completely different context, for from this axiom the corollary can be advanced that high wages need not necessarily impede economic progress. Private investment decisions are geared to a multiplicity of considerations, including McCulloch's " tranquility." Business must have both the desire and ability to invest profits, but since investments relate to future prospects for income, the expectations projected by businessmen regarding the future are likely to be controlling factors. By such reasoning, it is possible to advance the argument that unionization can encourage rather than discourage private investment by encouraging rather than discouraging industry prospects for revenues.

[35] Typical of the " fatalism " that Walker was rebelling against was the observation by Arnold Toynbee before a group of workers in England in 1880. Toynbee explained: " You might as well try to make iron swim as to alter the rate of wages . . . wages, like the succession of night and day, is independent of the will of either employer or employed." See Arnold Toynbee, *Wages and Natural Law* (London, Rivingtone, 1887), p. 159.

[36] *Op. cit.*, p. 823.

[37] *Op. cit*., p. 49.

21

Neoclassical Wage Theory

It has often been alleged that the "pronouncements of economists on topical wage questions are so out of touch with reality that they do nothing but harm to the reputation of economic science," [1] and more often than not, this sentiment is "proved" by reference to the sterility of the wages-fund concept of the nineteenth century. While we have joined in criticism of the static nature of this wage theory in Chapter 20, we have noted too the elements of truth it contained. If we view, as did the classical economists, the wages fund as a stock of consumer goods available for consumption at a point of time, the outside limits of this for improvement of labor's living standard is readily apparent. If we view the wages fund as a stream or flow of consumer goods, the *future* output of such goods depends upon the present allocation of productive resources between capital and consumer goods production, and this in turn depends upon the allocation of income between investment and consumption. In this more realistic or dynamic context classical economists were confident that high investments (or low consumption) could not but provide for ultimately higher consumption. In effect, the demand for labor was the "upside-down" demand curve for savings, for the greater the savings, the lower the rate of interest, the larger the number of investments that could be profitably undertaken, the greater the level of production, and hence the greater the demand for labor.

It is in the latter links in this causal chain that neoclassical wage theory made its contribution. In examining more carefully the relationship between investment and the demand for labor, the classical economists hoped to offer conclusive evidence that "capital sets labor in motion," or that an expanded supply curve of savings would result in an expanded demand curve for labor. In this sense, the development of the marginal productivity theory was not a contradiction of the wages-fund theory but rather a logical extension to it.

Before we take into consideration the refinements of nineteenth-century

[1] K. W. Rothschild, *The Theory of Wages* (New York, The Macmillan Company, 1954), p. 7.

wage theory we should remember once again that the pattern of wage and employment adjustments is determined by two forces — the supply of labor (and its related cost) together with the demand for labor. The nineteenth-century economists were not cheered by analysis of the labor market from the supply side, for it seemed evident that population expansion was pressing against limited resources. The long-run labor supply curve seemed fairly elastic or flat, and the hope for improving living standards was seen mainly in the possibility that technology and, through technology, production might somehow expand more rapidly than population. The wages-fund theory thus stressed production more than it did demand, for classical economists seemed to take it for granted that production would generate its own demand, that goods represented the purchasing power for goods, that the basic problem confronting society was not poverty in the midst of plenty (arising from inadequate demand), but poverty in the midst of scarcity (arising from the bottlenecks in the production process). The bottleneck was capital (and in England, land). The superfluous factor was labor.

The marginal productivity theory continued to stress the determinants of the demand for labor, determinants rooted basically in the productivity of labor rather than in the purchasing power of labor. While today such emphasis seems out of tune to students versed in acceleration principles, multipliers, consumption functions, and compensatory spending, the popularity of this approach until the great depression, reflected the needs of an economy in process of industrial development. It was not until the thirties that economists felt the overwhelming need to reconcile the jarring reality of " poverty in the midst of plenty " to a body of economic analysis which had, up until that time, largely precluded any possibility of the insufficiency of purchasing power.

Early Origins of the Marginal Productivity Theory

Like most other economic doctrines, the germ of the marginal productivity theory can be found in early economic analysis. Adam Smith suggested that, among other forces, the demand for labor was determined by the productivity of labor. Even before Smith, a small group of mercantile writers had rejected the then current notion that low wages would stimulate greater labor productivity by suggesting the opposite: high labor productivity would make possible the payment of high wages, and even more heretical, high wages would make possible high productivity. Sir Edward West, as we noted in our previous chapter, indicated that the value productivity of labor was in part determined by the wage level and both wages and productivity could advance together. In 1833 Mountiford Longfield suggested that the demand for labor is " caused by the utility or value of the work which they (the laborers) are capable of performing."

The most explicit statement of the marginal productivity theory has been developed by the German landowner and amateur economist, von Thünen.

On his farm, von Thünen observed that when additional farm hands were added to his fixed plot of land and his fixed capital supply, the productivity of the extra workers tended to decline. He also noted that as more workers were employed, the wage rate for all workers tended to decline, even though the workers previously hired were working as hard as usual. He came to the conclusion that the " wage of labor is the increment which results in a large business from the last laborer." Von Thünen seemed rather perplexed that this should be so, for by such reasoning the wage level seemed determined not alone by the energy with which the worker labored, but rather by the total labor supply. He deflected his attention away from what " was " to what " should be " by developing a law for wage payments. The wage rate should be equal to: (the geometrical average of the amount labor required for subsistence) times (the value of his output).[2] The formal development of marginal productivity was enhanced by the analysis of Philip H. Wicksteed and Léon Walras in Europe and J. B. Clark in America.

The Principle of Diminishing Returns and Marginal Productivity

The four factors of production — land, labor, capital, and management — each receive their own reward of rent, wages, interest, and profit. The reader will recall that economics is usually defined as a study devoted to the way in which people attempt to satisfy allegedly insatiable demands from limited resources. The fact that the economy's resources are usually available in uneven quantities is the key to understanding the forces allocating income. One economy may experience an abundance of labor and a scarcity of capital, as in India today, while another may suffer a scarcity of labor relative to other factors. If all resources were available without limit, total production could proceed in direct proportion to the rate at which ingredients (*viz.*, the factors of production) were poured into the production " mix." But if society (or the individual firm) faces a variable or limited supply of one or more of the factors of production (as is more likely to be the case), total production can be increased, but at a diminishing rate. Society or the firm usually faces diminishing returns. The marginal productivity theory of distribution is built up on this principle of diminishing productivity. We are saying, in effect, that a *disproportionate* (*viz.*, an uneven) combination of additional factors of production results in an increase of total production, but at a decreasing rate.

[2] In arithmetic form the " just " wage is equal to $\sqrt{ap}$ where a is the price of the goods labor must buy for subsistence and p is the value of the worker's product.

Determining Labor's Marginal Productivity

One of the problems that has for years plagued economists — and society in general — is the attempt to determine the output of labor as distinguished from the output of the other factors of production. If we could untangle the contributions of each factor of production to the total output, would it not then be possible to simply reward each in terms of its unique contribution? However laudable this effort may be, it must be admitted at the outset that the marginal productivity theory does not solve this problem for us. However, the marginal productivity theory attempts a " first approximation " of this. The mechanics of this method is relatively simple. If all factors of production are fixed or constant in supply and the labor supply alone is then varied, it is clear that the resulting variations in total production can be related to the variations in labor-force utilization. By comparing changes in total output related to changes in labor force utilization, it is possible to secure a " marginal labor productivity " index. Again, it must be remembered that labor's marginal productivity does not reveal the unique contribution of labor alone. Labor works with other factors of production which, while fixed in supply, nevertheless contribute to the final product. The arbitrary decision to correlate changes in total production with changes in man-hours of employment does not in any way prove that labor alone is responsible for the resulting quotient. An example may make this analysis clearer.

Let us assume at the outset that we have a given plant, with a fixed amount of capital and a fixed managerial staff, and then add units of an assumed homogeneous labor force to the fixed amount of other resources. We can then correlate the changes in total production to the changes in the labor supply. If the plant had no workers whatsoever, total output would be zero. The second worker may produce more than double that of the first worker, and the third worker may account for an addition to the total production which is even greater than the contributions of the second worker. Initially, then, the plant enjoys increasing returns because the relatively scarce labor factor is being applied to fixed capital. But as successively more and more workers are applied to the plant, inevitably the plant becomes overstaffed, so that the additional workers still contribute something to the production process, but not as much as the previous workers did. In such a situation, total production is increasing but at a decreasing rate.

We may now distinguish between total production, average labor productivity, and marginal labor productivity. Once the point of labor saturation is reached, total production increases less rapidly with additional workers. As a consequence, the average productivity of all workers declines. Another way of indicating this is to say that the contribution of the additional worker declines, pulling down the average for all workers.

TABLE 18   Relationships Between the Total, Average and Marginal
Productivity of Labor

(1) Workers	(2) Value of Marginal Productivity (Assumed)	(3) Value of Total Production (Cumulative total of Col. 2)	(4) Value of Average Production (Col. 3) ÷ (Col. 1)	(5) Average Labor Cost (Assumed)	(6) Total Labor Cost (Col. 1) × (Col. 5)	(7) Value of Output *less* Total Labor Costs (Col. 3) − (Col. 6)
0	0	0	0	0	0	0
1	40	40	40	30	30	10
2	60	100	50	30	60	40
3	65	165	55	30	90	75
4	60	225	56	30	120	105
5	55	280	56	30	150	130
6	50	330	55	30	180	150
7	45	375	54	30	210	165
8	40	415	52	30	240	175
9	35	450	50	30	270	180
10	30	480	48	30	300	180
11	25	505	46	30	330	175
12	20	525	44	30	360	165
13	15	540	42	30	390	150
14	10	550	40	30	420	130

The incremental production of the additional worker is the marginal productivity of that worker. These relationships can be seen in Table 18 and
Figure 16. In this hypothetical case, we have assumed that the first, second, and third workers add successively greater amounts to production.
The total then increases at an increasing rate, and the average production
of all workers also increases because the marginal productivity of each additional worker increases. But the fourth worker's additional contribution
is less than that of the third. As we see in Table 18 and Figure 16 the total
productivity increases less rapidly, the average productivity declines some-

FIGURE 16. Average and Total Labor Productivity

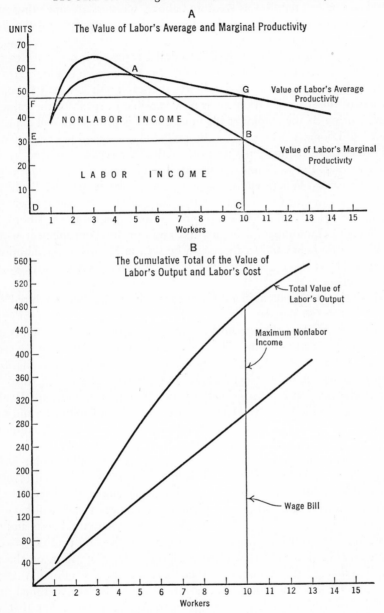

what, simply because the marginal productivity of the fourth worker was less than that of the third worker.

The marginal productivity of labor represents, then, the change in total output induced by the change in the number of workers hired. Can this marginal productivity be isolated and identified as the unique product of labor? Certainly if new workers were not added, this new product would not be created. But as we noted above, workers are operating with the fixed block of capital, and thus the additional output is still the *joint* product of labor and capital.

In order to convert our analysis into dollar terms, it is necessary to calculate the value of the physical output. In Table 18 and Figure 16 we have assumed, for the sake of simplicity, that each unit is worth $1.00, regardless of the scale of output. It is now possible to speak of the value of labor's output. If the employer is to maximize his profits, he will continue to hire additional workers up to the point where the added cost of new labor just equals the marginal revenue or the new revenue created by the added worker. Let us assume an arbitrary wage level of $30 which every worker receives. Where will management maximize its profits? By hiring workers up to point *C* in Figure 16 the value of labor to management (in terms of the additional increment of production) is equal to the labor cost. This level of employment provides maximum profits. Management would not hire workers beyond *C*, for as can be seen in Figure 16 the additional costs would not be compensated for by the additional revenues these new workers create.

Looking at the problem in a different way, if ten workers are hired and each receives $30 per day, the wage bill is $300, or the area *DEBC* on Figure 16-A. Each of the ten workers on an average produces 48 units, for a total of 480 for the group. These are assumed to be valued at $1 each, so that total revenue is $480. The nonlabor income is $480, less the $300 wage bill or $180, or the area *EFGB*. Another way of viewing this is to look at the relationship between the total labor cost and the total value of output as in Figure 16-B. Data here are taken from Columns 3 and 6 of Table 18. By our assumption that management is interested in maximizing profits, management will hire that number of workers that maximizes the distance between total labor costs and total revenue. That point is the same, of course, in Figure 16-B as it is in Figure 16-A. The total revenue and total cost curves are often drawn by management as " break-even " charts to illustrate the effects that changing volumes of sales will have on their income-cost ratios. The break-even point is where total costs and total revenues are equal, or where management receives no profits.

Our analysis thus far has stressed the productivity of labor, on the assumption that we are keeping the other three factors of production stable. We can, of course, use the same analysis to determine the marginal productivity of land, capital, and management. Again, if we assume that we add successive increments of capital to a fixed amount of land, labor, and management, we can correlate the changes of total production to the changes in capital employed, and such changes represent the marginal productivity of capital.

In summary, the marginal productivity theory enables us to relate the value of each additional factor of production to its potential contribution to the production process. One cannot isolate the distinctive contributions of each factor of production, but one can at least guess what the additional contribution of each new worker will be, considering the capacity of the plant and the size of the existing work force. The value of labor's marginal product is the employer's demand schedule for labor.

It can now be seen that the elasticity of that labor demand is determined by the capacity of the plant to absorb larger amounts of workers (without a rapid decline in output per worker) as well as the ability of the market to absorb increasing quantities of the goods being produced without a decline in the per unit value of those goods. If the public will absorb a larger quantity of those goods only at lower prices, the demand curve for labor is for this reason less elastic. Two forces operate to determine the elasticity of this curve then: the diminishing productivity of the worker operating with fixed plant capacity and the diminishing utility of the consumer for larger quantities of the goods produced.[3]

The productivity of labor is one blade of the scissors which cut the pattern for wage and employment adjustments. It must not be assumed that wages always equal the precise value of the marginal product for the last worker hired. Paul Douglas points out in his *Theory of Wages*, " No sensible advocate of the theory claims that it applies with absolute precision, but merely that there is a pronounced tendency for wages to adjust themselves in fairly close proximity to the margin [of productivity]." [4] And J. R. Hicks, the British proponent of marginal productivity theory, further adds that the marginal product is a " regulator " of wages but does not determine their precise magnitude at any moment of time:

> For the marginal product of a man's labor, defined in this way, changes incessantly and wages do not incessantly change. But any such difference if it is maintained for long slowly bends wages to meet the new situation. The forces elucidated by equilibrium analysis are the forces which in nearly every case cause wages to change.[5]

What would happen, for example, if the wage level were below the value of the marginal product for the last worker? The employer would increase his profits if he extended his employment. If wages are above the

[3] Our example above has abstracted from the diminishing utility and imperfect competition in that we assumed that whatever the quantity of goods produced, its value in the market place would be $1. If the value declines as more is produced, the marginal value productivity schedule would have less elasticity or a steeper slope than the *physical* marginal product schedule. We should note too that we are by now assuming that the employer is *interested* in the new value that new employees may generate for the firm. More specifically, we assume that the worker will be hired only if the employer believes the added value of the new worker is greater than his added cost. This is equivalent to saying the employer will hire workers only to the degree that they increase his profits.

[4] Paul Douglas, *Theory of Wages* (New York, The Macmillan Co., 1934), p. 61.

[5] *Theory of Wages* (London, Macmillan & Co., 1935), p. 86.

value of the marginal product, workers would be laid off until the marginal labor cost is equal to the marginal revenue productivity.

Implications of Marginal Productivity Analysis

We are now in a position to indicate some of the further implications of marginal productivity analysis. As we have seen, by our assumption that labor was working with a fixed lump of capital, the output per additional man continued to decline as additional workers were hired. This expansion of employment forced down the wages for all labor and, should the marginal productivity schedule be inelastic, the expanded employment will reduce not only the wage rate but also the wage bill. How then can management absorb an expanding labor force without reducing wages? In the short run management cannot expand its plant capacity, but over time capital growth will alter labor's production function. If management is able to incorporate devices to increase labor efficiency, the production schedule will be shifted to the right. As a consequence, the demand curve for labor is increased, for labor has then grown more valuable to management. Through capital expansion labor may enjoy the benefits of either expanded employment or higher wages, or a combination of both of these. Thus the marginal productivity theory makes explicit what the wage-fund theorists had intuitively felt was true: that capital " sets labor in motion." An act of saving was a necessary pre-condition for expanding the demand for labor.

In this context, we can also see more clearly one of the basic tenets of classical and neoclassical employment theory. In Figure 17 we have drawn the assumed value productivity schedule for the entire labor force. This schedule would, of course, vary considerably from firm to firm, from industry to industry, but for purposes of exposition, we may represent the aggregate demand for labor in terms of a single production function. At point B we draw an assumed band or zone of full employment. It becomes immediately clear that there is a wage ceiling if full employment is to be maintained. If the wage rate should, for any reason, be above A at point C, the margin of unemployment DB will appear. Such a noncompetitive wage may be established by labor because of such factors as uninhibited bargaining or ignorance of market conditions.

Strange as it may seem, unemployment itself is seen as the cure to such unemployment. The unemployed workers, sensing their plight, begin competing for existing jobs, and such competition will force the wage rate down to A. And in this manner full employment is once again secured. It was by such reasoning that classical economists concluded that the labor force always tended toward full employment. If unemployment should exist, it would be temporary to the extent that adjustments are in the process of being made in the labor market. Furthermore, if unemploy-

FIGURE 17. Value Productivity Schedule for Labor Force

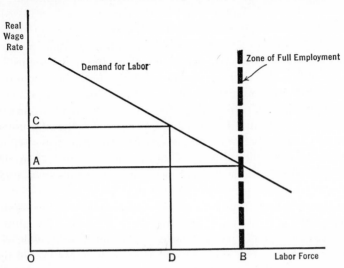

ment exists, it must of necessity be voluntary: Labor has priced its service out of the market. The solution is equally simple: downward adjustments of wages. Because the hardships of unemployment were seen as the cure to unemployment, many of the neoclassical writers looked with stern eyes on social welfare measures which were designed to protect the unemployed worker from the hardships of unemployment. Just as the law of gravity creates stability in the physical universe, so does the prospect that one could price himself out of the market represent the stabilizing force in the labor market, and a force which serves to push labor forward full employment. Needless to say, the thesis that unemployment can be solved by reducing money wages has lost much of its popularity. During the thirties most unemployed workers were willing and able to work at any wage that would provide subsistence for themselves and their families but often they were still unable to find employment.

Criticisms of Marginal Productivity

No topic can split labor economists into two opposing camps more quickly than discussion of the relevance of marginal productivity theory in labor economics. Criticism has gained momentum in recent decades. Generally, critics suggest that the profit-maximizing principle may not be the sole force operating on employer decisions, and hence any mechanism that depends entirely on this motivation collapses. Secondly, union leaders deny any precise wage-employment relationship because of the dynamic character of economic developments. This reflects, in turn, the

criticism that marginal productivity theory is essentially static in that it
assumes " all other things being equal " in order to determine the specific
productivity of a single factor. Thirdly, the theory cannot readily be reconciled with imperfections of competition, discontinuities of production
and cost functions, and " ranges " within which bargaining power operates. Finally, it is argued that the marginal productivity theory cannot
provide us with a determinate solution to the problem of income distribution. General wage adjustments may set in motion a pattern of income
adjustments, which, in turn, affect labor's value productivity and trigger
further wage adjustments. The economy may be in a state of constant disequilibrium.[6] This criticism for the most part, stresses the inadequacies of
static theory in explaining dynamics, and the misleading conclusions that
one might reach on the basis of competitive assumptions of a model designed to describe an imperfectly competitive world.

Attacks on marginal productivity are often made on the assumptions
required of the marginal productivity theory. Following is a typical list of
assumptions, developed by Paul Douglas: (1) Employers are able to measure or estimate added productivity; (2) there is free and complete competition among employers for labor; (3) labor knows its marginal productivity; (4) there is free and complete competition among the wage
earners for work; (5) capital and labor both are mobile; (6) all labor and
capital is fully employed; (7) labor and capital have equal bargaining
power; and (8) laissez faire is a normal condition of the economy.[7] Further assumptions which Hicks considers to be essential to the theory are
(1) the law of diminishing returns, (2) the doctrine of the flexibility of
capital, (3) the conviction that the specific product of a factor is discernible, and (4) the constancy of the short-run supply of labor.[8] Let us briefly
evaluate the substance of some of these criticisms.

Dependence on Diminishing Returns. It is true that if the marginal
productivity of labor is not declining but increasing, the demand curve
for labor slopes upward and varies directly with the wage rate rather than
inversely with it.[9] In such a situation we have a state of disequilibrium,

---

[6] As Rothschild explains, "The theorem of the 'economy of high wages' shows
however, that we cannot assume that productivity is an independent variable uniquely
determining a certain wage level. It is itself a function of the wage level, both cause
and effect of wage changes. Therefore, there is more than one equilibrium position,
and the marginal productivity theory cannot tell us which equilibrium combination of
wages and productivity is the 'proper' one." *Op. cit.,* p. 30.

[7] *Op. cit.,* p. 94.

[8] *Op. cit.,* p. 12.

[9] This point is made by Eveline M. Burns: Under the assumption of increasing returns,
"the unreality of this wage theory is soon apparent. It is then to see that if wages did
approximate to the net product of the marginal worker it would very soon be to the
disadvantage of an employer to engage extra men even though the extra men added
rather more than those previously employed." From her chapter, "Productivity and
the Theory of Wages" contained in *Essays in Economics* (London, Routledge &
Sons, 1927), p. 188.

but the profit maximization assumption requires that employment be extended to the point of intersection of where incremental revenues are matched by incremental costs. It is likely that the employer will be hiring workers in the zone of diminishing labor productivity rather than increasing labor productivity.

Employers Cannot Discern the Value Productivity of Labor. In the real world, all factors of production are often added coincidentally in uneven amounts. In such a situation it is difficult to impute the resulting change of total production to any one of the additional inputs. We cannot readily unscramble the eggs. Eveline M. Burns puts it this way: " The product is an inextricable mixture of the various factors which compose it." John Hobson explained that " it is as futile to find the specific productivity of any one factor of production as it is to determine which leg of a three-legged stool supports the stool." [10] There can be no question that the determination of the potential value of hiring an additional worker is a difficult one to resolve, and it is difficult not only because of the problem of untangling his contribution from that of the other factors of production, but also because the value of output may change from time to time in the future, while the wage rate at which the new worker is paid is not so likely to vary. But we cannot escape the fact that, however difficult the decision is, it is one that *is* made, and made thousands of times each day. If it is true that management desires to maximize its profits, it must constantly be concerned with the question of expanding — or contracting — employment " on the margin."

The Labor Force Is Not Homogeneous. Since all workers are not the same, it is unrealistic to speak of a production function for groups of workers. Hicks points out:

> If the labourers in a given trade are not of equal efficiency, then strictly speaking, they have no marginal product. We cannot tell what would be the difference to the product if one man were removed from employment; for it all depends which man is removed. The only way in which it is possible to overcome this difficulty is to treat each man as a separate factor of production. His interval marginal product is then easy enough to identify — it is the difference which would be made to the total produce of the firm in which he is

[10] Even in the field of literature and philosophy, comments have been made on this point. In Bernard Shaw's *Intelligent Woman's Guide to Socialism and Capitalism* (New York, Brentano Pub., 1928) Shaw explains: " When a farmer and his laborer sow and reap a field of wheat nobody on earth can say how much of the wheat each of them has grown " (p. 21). Bertrand Russell, in his *Prospects of Industrial Civilization* (New York, Century Co., 1923, p. 144) writes: " In an industrial civilization a man never makes the whole of anything, but makes the thousandth part of a million things. Under these circumstances it is totally absurd to say that a man has the right to the produce of his own labor. Consider a porter on a railway whose business it is to shunt goods trains: what proportion of the goods carried can be said to represent the produce of his labor? The question is wholly insoluble."

engaged if his labour were to be removed. That clearly sets a maximum to the wage he can get, and still remain undisturbed in employment.[11]

As we see, Hicks has pointed out the difficulty, but also suggested a solution to it. Undoubtedly workers vary considerably in talent and efficiency and management is greatly concerned about such variation in its hiring and layoff policies. Certainly labor is not a homogeneous product, and while we speak of aggregative labor production functions, the variations of individual efficiency reveal themselves and are vital considerations to management within the scope of any contract commitments it has made with labor. The union negotiation of the standard rate indicates organized labor's desire to minimize management's freedom to make interpersonal comparisons. Individual piece-rate systems as well as merit-rating plans reflect management's ability and desire to differentiate individual worker productivity.

Market Imperfections and Discontinuous Production Functions. A whole host of criticisms of marginal productivity have been inspired by the " rigidities " of the market place, including the oligopolistic character of industry, the immobility of labor and capital, the rigidity of costs, the " lumpiness " of the production process and/or the indivisibility of labor and capital. Perhaps the most outspoken critic in these terms is Arthur Ross, who writes: ". . . in teaching, one cannot help recognize the extent to which it is necessary to talk around the problem and resort to such devices as wages in theory versus wages in practice, upper and lower limits with an unchartered no man's land between, a catalogue of imperfections in the labor market, and so forth. . . ." He is discouraged with the " multitude of rigidities, imperfections, deviations and discontinuities in labor supply and demand " to the point where he wonders if " all the significant forces affecting wages under collective bargaining can be compressed into a supply and demand explanation. . . . So many attacks have been made on marginal productivity theory and so many retreats have been made that we can hardly claim to have a theory at all." [12] Most of these criticisms can be described as " institutional " rigidities to the labor market which obstruct or interfere with the forces of supply and demand.

It must be stated again, however, that the marginal productivity theory is rooted on the assumption that management is motivated to maximize

---

[11] *Op. cit.,* p. 23.

[12] *Trade Union Wage Policy* (Berkeley, University of California Press, 1948), pp. 2, 45. Typical of such criticisms are those of Belfer and Bloom: ". . . The marginal productivity doctrine has swallowed collective bargaining without a second glance at its indigestible contents, with the result that reasoning about the effects of wage increases on the one hand, and of union rules on the other hand, went on in more or less separate compartments with little cross fertilization from the one to the other." " Unionism and the Marginal Productivity Theory " in Lester and Shister, *Insights into Labor Issues* (New York, The Macmillan Co., 1948), p. 239.

its profits. Because there are institutional rigidities, capable of deflecting somewhat the freedom and scope of maneuvers to maximize those profits, we cannot for this reason agree that the employer is less interested in profits or, in our specific case, the incremental contribution of the additional worker. The marginal productivity theory offers a formal explanation of that level of employment which will provide the employer with maximum profits when that employer is confronted with a given labor cost and his own intuitive guess as to what the value of labor's marginal product is. None of this analysis denies that unions attempt to elevate their wages above that level otherwise imposed by the marginal productivity ceiling. Nor does it deny the possibility of a range of "indeterminateness" in labor's production function itself. It is true, for example, that under conditions of oligopoly, wages may be advanced by labor without any resulting loss of employment.[13] It is also true that the inelasticity of consumer demand may enable the employer to shift a large part of the incidence of the wage increase to the public, without any serious decline of sales or reduction of employment. Furthermore, in some cases the production function for labor may be highly inelastic because of the inability of management to combine labor with machinery and plant capacity in any but a unique ratio. In these three cases the employer's demand for labor may, in some range of that schedule, be close to vertical or highly inelastic. Whether the wage rate rests near the bottom or top of this range can only be determined by considerations of labor supply. But to return to our original point, the existence of imperfections, discontinuities, or "lumpiness" in the labor market cannot be taken as proof that efforts to maximize profits are of no consequence. However institutional rigidities restrict management's discretionary power in extending its own profits, such obstacles do not disprove the relevance of marginal theory in explaining that force or, for that matter, in explaining how the force might be obstructed. As Alfred Marshall once explained, ". . . a machine may stop if one of its connecting rods gets out of order, but that does not mean that the driving force of the machine is to be found in the rod."

Static Nature of Marginal Productivity Theory. A key limitation to marginal productivity is that it is essentially static, designed to explain decisions at a point of time. In our society everything is in a state of flux. The real hazard of leaning on marginal productivity analysis, especially for policy conclusions, is that it assumes a given production function. While it is true that management, especially during full employment, cannot readily expand its plant capacity, the volume of spending and hence

---

[13] This is because an employer may be reluctant to raise his prices when he suspects that others in the industry will not raise theirs. He prefers, therefore, to maintain present production and employment levels rather than risk the loss of sales arising from a price increase. In such a situation the wage increase is "absorbed" by other distributive shares or by management profits.

the *value* productivity schedule can shift immediately and in a most erratic fashion. This limitation becomes more apparent when we review the policy decisions for solving the problem of unemployment rooted in static rather than dynamic marginal productivity concepts.[14]

The Neoclassical Solution to the Problem of Unemployment

The marginal productivity theory served as a point of departure for the employment theories of both neoclassical writers and Keynesian theorists. Both felt that at any moment of time, *given the value productivity schedule for labor*, the volume of employment would vary inversely with the real wage rate. The higher the level of wages, other things being equal, the lower the level of employment. The real wage rather than the money wage controlled employment, for the ratio of money wages to retail prices provided a more meaningful index of wage cost to the employer. If a general money wage increase of 5 percent was associated with an increase in the consumer price index of 10 percent, the real wage, or the ratio of money wages to living costs, would be lowered. In a rough sense, so would the ratio of business wage costs to business prices. Employment should, other things being equal, expand.

However, a sharp clash developed among economists during the thirties on the method for reducing real wages. The more conservative economists firmly believed that the situation would soon right itself as long as the government did not intervene to repress unemployment by artificial devices. Let us briefly recapitulate the substance of this classical view.

First, they admitted a small margin of the work force would normally be unemployed because their productivity is below the level of their subsistence. Since labor does not normally work for less than subsistence, the unemployed are a burden for all of society. But most classical economists considered this group to represent only a minor portion of the labor force. A second and more important form of unemployment arises when the demand for labor in general declines. Many employers may hope that the decline in their markets is only temporary and may absorb the decline of sales by reducing their work force (rather than attempting to lower their wages) to maintain some balance between sales and total wage payments. Unionism, while admittedly weaker during a depression, usually forces

---

[14] Most Marxists have rejected the law of diminishing returns as essentially a bourgeois principle. In a slashing attack, Lenin condemned the static nature of this principle: ". . . this is the same as saying that the stopping of trains at stations represents the universal law of steam transport, while the motion of trains between stations is a temporary tendency which paralyses the operation of the universal law of stopping." *Selected Works of Lenin,* Vol. XII, p. 58 and quoted by Ronald L. Meek, "Malthus: Yesterday and Today," *Science and Society,* Vol. XVIII, No. 1 (Winter, 1954), pp. 35–36.

such action because the union resists wage cuts. The employer then can only sustain operations by reducing his payroll. To recapitulate, general unemployment occurs because of the imbalance in the cost-price structure, and the hard task arises of effecting an adjustment of this ratio to eliminate unemployment. To classical writers, the obvious solution was to lower wages. If the wage level is not adjusted, we face the continuing possibility of an " equilibrium " of the economy at a point less than full employment. Stated somewhat differently, if labor insists on pricing itself out of the market, there is no reason why unemployment ever should diminish.

Why is labor unwilling to appreciate this principle of economics? The real difficulty is that the true nature of the developments are often obscured to labor. " The unemployment caused by their [union] policy does not all appear at once but only declares itself gradually. Even if the initial advance was made at a time when the state of trade was neither particularly active nor particularly depressed there would probably still be very little unemployment to begin with." [15]

A somewhat more elaborate defense for the neoclassical position in employment theory was made by the British economist Pigou, who became involved in a series of disputes with Keynes regarding the validity of classical theory. Pigou contended that the classical economists had never held that full employment must exist at all times. The basic tenets of classical theory was simply that while full employment need not always exist, market forces tend to push the economy in this direction. But this tendency will be allowed to operate effectively only in relatively free markets:

> With perfectly free competition among workpeople and labour perfectly mobile . . . there will always be at work a strong tendency for wage-rates to be so related to demand that everybody is employed. . . . The implication is that such unemployment as exists at any time is due wholly to the fact that changes in demand conditions are continually taking place and that frictional resistance prevent the appropriate adjustment from being made instantaneously.[16]

In effect, classical writers assumed that if labor were to accept a reduction of money wages, real wages would also be reduced, and then — assuming a constant demand curve — the level of employment could be increased. However, if a money wage cut is to result in a reduction of real wages, it is necessary that the consumer price index not drop in proportion (or more than) the money wage cut, for otherwise real wages would be unchanged (or even increased). As we shall see, Keynes pounced on this point in his attack on the classical system, denying that prices were in fact less flexible than wages. However, Pigou felt it was unlikely that

[15] Hicks, *op. cit.*, p. 232.
[16] Pigou, *The Theory of Unemployment* (London, Macmillan & Co., 1933), p. 252.

prices would move more widely than wages unless there was a complete financial collapse. "We conclude that, whatever may be *possible* in imaginary circumstances, cuts in money wages will not carry with them proportionate reductions in the price level in any practicable circumstances." [17] To classical economists then, unemployment arose because of the high wage-price ratio and the cost burden this imposed on industry. In August 4, 1933, the London *Times* published a letter written by Pigou which expresses the essence of his viewpoint:

> Under the present social system real wage rates cannot be raised beyond a point without inducing unemployment. Apart from improvements in methods of production and so on, it is impossible both to maintain existing money wages when commodity prices are falling and to raise them parallel to commodity prices when these are rising except at the cost of a large number of people being unable to find work. Since January, 1930, the Board of Trade Index of general commodity prices has fallen some 20 percent; the cost of living index some 14 percent and the index of money wages 5 percent. During this period of heavy depression there has thus taken place a substantial rise in the rate of real wages for persons in employment. I think that we should be frank about this matter. It is, in my opinion, beyond question that this state of things is responsible for the high level of unemployment. Maybe this is an unpopular doctrine. If so, it is the more the duty of economists to announce it. [18]

Some Limitations of Classical Wage Theory

One of the problems related to wage cuts as the solution to unemployment is that it might encourage employers to believe that such a single wage cut is but one of a series of wage cuts. If this is the case, employers might feel that it is wise to wait until wages have reached their minimum level and unfortunately this minimum cannot be recognized as the minimum until it is past. Everyone seems agreed that if wage cuts do promise a solution to unemployment, they should be of a " once and for all " nature and rather substantial. Such reduction might minimize the dangers of cumulative downward cuts and the related delay of employment expansion. [19]

[17] *Employment and Equilibrium* (London, Macmillan & Co., 1941), pp. 85–86. A revised edition of this book appeared in 1952. References cited are from the original work.

[18] As we shall note, Keynes was willing to admit that the cause of unemployment was the high real wage rate or the cost pressure on employers. But Keynes took the position that employers should have price relief rather than cost relief: the very attempt to lower labor costs would be equivalent to moving the piano to the piano stool.

[19] Pigou does not feel that employers will hold back in their employment of labor if successive wage cuts appear imminent: ". . . this consideration is probably less important than it seems to be at first sight . . . in any event it does not substantially affect our main contention." *Employment and Equilibrium, op. cit.*, p. 87.

A further problem related to the reduction of money wages as the solution of unemployment is the rather obvious possibility that such reductions in wage rates will reduce the size of the wage bill, and possibly the amount of purchasing power in circulation. This argument is based on the assumption that the demand for labor is inelastic below the prevailing wage, so that with wage cuts, the wage bill is reduced. Classical writers, while not concerned with the question of demand elasticity directly, seemed to believe that the demand for labor in terms of the real wage was invariably elastic. Pigou, on the basis of deductive reasoning, felt that the demand curve for labor was elastic so that noncompetitive wages would produce substantial unemployment and a reduction of the wage bill. Similarly, reductions in the wage rate would be likely to increase the level of employment and the wage bill.

Finally, if two blades of the scissors — demand and supply — determine the wage and employment pattern, is there any particular reason why one blade should be assigned the responsibility for cutting the pattern that actually exists? *If* supply is held constant, it is true that such variations in wages and employment as actually exist are determined by demand variations. *If* demand is held constant, obviously the supply becomes the determinant of employment. The basic difference between Keynesian and classical theory was whether demand or supply should be kept constant, or indeed, if either should. Classical economists had always assumed that *given a constant demand for labor*, labor's wage rate would determine the level of employment. Keynes's basic criticism was that the wage rate and wage bill were not unrelated to the position and elasticity of that demand curve. A *general* wage adjustment was likely, in other words, to affect (through variations in the stream of purchasing power) the direction and volume of consumer demand, and hence labor demand itself. Wages could not be isolated alone as costs, adjusted up and down a given demand schedule to determine employment, for wages were important both as costs and as income. Pigou was fully aware that the different assumptions between Keynes and classical writers might explain a large part of their disagreement. In an appropriate analogy, he explains:

> When a ship is too low in the water, this effort is a combined result of the weight of the cargo and of the capacity of the ship. If the capacity of the ship is taken as given, the excess weight of the cargo is called the cause; but, if the weight of the cargo is taken as given, the inadequate capacity of the ship is called the cause. In truth, neither of these things taken by itself is the cause, but the maladjustment is removed either by decreasing the cargo in sufficient measure or by enlarging the ship in sufficient measure.[20]

If both demand and supply are considered jointly responsible for the employment pattern, the issue which society must resolve is: Which variable

[20] *Employment and Equilibrium, op. cit.,* p. 27.

can be more *readily* manipulated to change the employment pattern if society is anxious to maintain high levels of employment?

Neoclassical writers are not content to " solve " the problem of the imbalance in the cost-price structure by encouraging or permitting price relief or price inflation. For one thing, such price inflation represents an open invitation to further wage increases, and if full employment is to be maintained, it will only be at the expense of a constantly increasing price level. We have then swapped the problem of unemployment for the problem of inflation. Thus the classical economists fear that the abandonment of the " cost " viewpoint in approaching unemployment and the attempt to solve this problem by working on prices alone is an open invitation to inflation. Once labor groups realize that wage demands do not result in unemployment they are encouraged to pursue even more aggressive wage demands. Inflation is the " father of chaos," and the amount of inflation that would be required to absorb unemployment would grow increasingly substantial. To Pigou and other neoclassical writers, labor must, in the last analysis, " choose between higher rates of wages and lower rates of unemployment." Such a choice is not easy for labor, but if labor is not asked to make it (as in cases where public policy provides the solution with more inflation), society may create more problems for itself than it solves. Unemployment is indeed an evil but society may, in its efforts to find an expedient solution to the problem, create worse evils.

22

The Impact of
Unemployment

Prior to October, 1929, it was generally held that labor determined the volume of its own employment. While labor was not a commodity, it was, nevertheless, necessary to reconcile the price of labor to market reality. Could employers afford to indulge in the sentiment that every worker had the " right " to an income, particularly when that right could not be reconciled to the cold reality of a competitive economy? In reality, labor could be assured employment only if it could promise management a contribution greater than its wage cost. Since the value productivity function was beyond labor's control, it was only reasonable to expect labor to adjust the variable within its control — the wage rate — to maintain employment. In summary, the level of employment was determined by the cost of labor. The cost of labor was determined by labor when it established its " asking " price. The level of employment — and unemployment — were thus determined by labor itself.

As the depression of the thirties deepened, it seemed increasingly apparent to everyone that the unemployed represented a large group willing and able to work, but unable to secure employment. Downward wage adjustments did not appear a promising solution to general unemployment, for those searching for employment asked only for a " job " and seldom about working conditions and wages. It slowly became apparent that the level of employment was determined by the demand for labor's service. This demand, in turn, was determined by the employer's calculation of the need for additional production, a need painfully absent in view of the increasing inventories of unsold goods. The conclusion seemed inescapable that the level of employment — and unemployment — were thus determined by the capacity of the economy to absorb increased production, and more directly by the employer's perception of the need for additional production.

Quite apart from the problem of assigning responsibility for the level of unemployment was the more urgent difficulty that unemployment itself represented to the unemployed. Few if any problems in the labor field acquired and required so much serious attention. Even today, making the job secure is certainly the most important single goal of the union movement. Both the height of the wage rate and the continuity of the flow of wage payments are very important, but on balance, primary consideration must be given to the continuity of the income stream over time rather than its cross-section area at a point of time. Reflecting this concern, unions often justify the need for union membership with the slogan: " The job you save may be your own."

In this chapter we shall first examine the impact of unemployment on the individual and his family together with some of its psychological, sociological, and economic implications. We shall then turn to the various forms of unemployment, including " disguised," " technological," " frictional," " seasonal," " hard-core," and " cyclical " unemployment.[1] We shall then discuss briefly the various methods of measuring unemployment. Understanding the limitations of unemployment data is a prerequisite to any discussion of policies dealing with it. We shall also survey briefly some unemployment data and conclude with some distinguishing features between voluntary and involuntary unemployment. This distinction is one that hits the very nerve center of both our political and economic philosophy. On the one hand, some believe that labor should not be isolated from the reality of market forces. As one general manager explained, " I know workers. I've managed men all my life and they are human like the rest of us; they won't work hard unless they have to." A contrasting view is offered by a minister: " I know workers. They have an innate sense of human dignity and you violate that at your peril." [2] Neither group is actually " for " unemployment any more than they could be for poverty or suffering, but to the former group, tolerating unemployment may be the necessary means to secure the more justifiable and necessary end — the freedom from government intervention or the freedom of the individual to carve out his own economic destiny, for better or for worse.

The Initial Impact of Unemployment on the Workers

The knowledge that one is making a contribution to the productive process in some concrete manner is still very important to labor. As one worker explained to Professor E. W. Bakke: " Now suppose all of us were Yale professors. Where would you get men to do the real work, tell me that? Someone — a lot of someone's, in point of fact, have to be produc-

[1] Such categories, reflecting the causes of unemployment, need not be mutually exclusive, for it is possible for a person to be released from a seasonal industry and at the same time be unable or unwilling to take a job elsewhere. In such a case the unemployment may be considered both frictional as well as seasonal.

[2] Both quotations from E. W. Bakke, *The Unemployed Worker, A Study of the Task of Making a Living Without a Job* (New Haven, Institute of Human Relations, Yale University Press, 1940), p. 3.

ers. It is mighty nice for them to wear out the seat of their pants and get bald-headed a-thinking, but without us fellows they'd starve. We are the *producers.*" [3] It perhaps goes without saying that the satisfactions of being productive are not fully appreciated until the opportunity to be so has been denied the worker. The individual worker wants to feel indispensable not only to his own family and community, but also to his own employer. The foundation for worker satisfaction and security must, in the final analysis, be in his job. It must be derived from the feeling of being needed and wanted, from being a vital cog in the production process.

If these considerations are true, it is immediately apparent how much of a shock being discharged from industry can be. It represents a crushing blow to one's ego, to his self-confidence and self-respect. Workers quite naturally resist the consideration that they are "expendable" and derive little satisfaction from "enforced" idleness.[4] In a broader context, the worker may feel that his total function in society has lost its significance. Whatever his personal valuation may be of his own efficiency, few individuals can face rejection by the labor market without doubting their own intrinsic value.[5]

The Effect of Unemployment on the Family

Perhaps the most disturbing aspect of unemployment is the hardship that this imposes on the family. With high fixed costs, industry is vulnerable to any decline in the volume or value of sales and has, in effect, a high "break-even" point. But labor's "break even" is usually much more obvious and pressing than that of the company's. The family must continue to meet the fixed costs of living.

The initial experience of unemployment is not harmful if it is considered to be only for a short duration. Unemployment benefits often encourage the worker to believe he is getting a "paid vacation." The breadwinner may actually enjoy a new schedule which permits him to get to know his family better. But if the prospects for re-employment fade, the family atmosphere usually changes quickly. While the challenge of unemployment and austerity may act as a cohesive influence on the family unit,

[3] *Op. cit.*, Vol. I, p. 6.

[4] Bakke provides several quotations from the unemployed workers surveyed in the late thirties reflecting the psychological need for employment: " Work is necessary to keep man's mind at ease. . . . It is necessary to keep from going crazy." . . . "What is life without a job? You are nobody." . . . "Work keeps you from feeling like a damn fool." "It's a natural instinct I tell you. Why even rich people work. It *must* be an instinct." *Ibid.*, p. 81.

[5] As Erich Fromm writes in his *Escape from Freedom* (New York, Farrar & Rinehart, New York, 1941, pp. 21–22), " Unless he [man] belonged somewhere, unless his life had some meaning and direction, he would feel like a particle of dust and be overcome by his individual significance. He would not be able to relate himself to any system which would give meaning and direction to his life, he would be filled with doubt and this doubt would eventually paralyze his ability to act – that is, to live."

it more often serves to disturb the equilibrium of family relationships. It may be necessary, as was often the case in the thirties, for the wife to attempt to find some source of income, perhaps by taking in ironing, by providing "room and board," or by working in industry at low pay. In such a situation, the status of the father quickly changes in the eyes of both the mother and the children. The wife may charge that the husband's efforts to secure employment have not been adequate or sincere. The husband, feeling inadequate and insecure, may attempt to reinforce or reassure himself of his status in the family by becoming increasingly severe in his discipline of his children. The humiliation of the breadwinner's position may be further aggravated if the family should find it necessary to borrow funds from relatives. With unemployment compensation depleted, further cash savings are used up, insurance policies are cashed in, durable consumer goods purchased on the installment plan are reclaimed. If unemployment continues, the mortgage may be foreclosed and the family forced to move to a poorer neighborhood. Teen-age children may feel an obligation to quit school to search for employment in order to supplement family income. The corroding effects of unemployment are most apparent when the worker is overcome with his frightful responsibility for his family's plight.[6]

It is impossible to catalog all the hardships created by enduring unemployment, but every facet of human, social and economic relationships is affected. As Dr. W. Searle eloquently testified before a Congressional Committee in 1941:

> I had to see [in the thirties] the terrible corrosion of unemployment at work on individual personality. I saw men grow bitter, others collapse in despair. . . . I saw the frustration of youth and the beatenness of middle or old age. I watched families disintegrate in spirit and body. I assure you gentlemen, what you well know, that this is not just an economic problem. It is a basic moral problem. . . . I am convinced that sustained and involuntary unemployment is not only a frightful waste of human personality — a tremendous indignity — but it is a denial of the fundamental promise of our Nation and its democracy. . . .[7]

[6] In one study of unemployment during the depression of the thirties, the following consequences were revealed by careful case studies. *Financial effects:* Savings used up or no savings; indebtedness to grocers; borrowing money from friends, relatives, and neighbors; borrowing from loan agencies; pawned jewelry; insurance policies lapsed; back payments on houses and mortgage interest; rent unpaid; moving to cheaper quarters; wife goes to work; children go to work; boarders or roomers taken in; living with parents or otherwise sharing a home; charitable relief. *Physical effects* included: food trimmed; milk supply cut down; inadequate clothing; malnutrition; respiratory diseases. *Psychological effects* included: drinking; cruelty toward wife and children; irritation in home atmosphere; juvenile delinquency and other behavior problems; humiliation at receiving relief, and so on.

[7] Dr. Searle, Executive Secretary, Greater New York Federation of Churches, testifying before a Subcommitee of the Committee on Labor, House of Representatives 77th Congress, First Session HJ Res. 59 (Washington, 1941).

In summary, the unemployed worker may be overwhelmed with his sense of inadequacy. He may believe: " I don't suffer from an inferiority complex — I am inferior." Labor service is certainly (to quote the principle of classical economics) the most perishable of all commodities. William Beveridge in his early study of the problems of unemployment in Great Britain observed:

> Casual employment, by demoralising men largely increases its own evils. . . . They work badly; they take the chance of lying in bed now and again since work is always uncertain but will not be made more uncertain tomorrow by the fact that it has not been sought today. . . . There is general agreement that casual employment . . . acts as a trap to catch the unemployed and turn them into unemployables.[8]

Forms of Unemployment

Unemployment may be classified in terms of its causes, incidence, duration, and effects. Let us look at some basic causes. An unemployed worker may, of course, be unemployed for a number of reasons, and our analysis of separate causes of unemployment should not obscure the fact that these forces often overlap. We should keep in mind also the basic distinction between voluntary and involuntary unemployment. Voluntary unemployment arises where a worker elects to be idle, when he willingly and knowingly rejects those expedients that he must follow if he is to secure employment. Involuntary unemployment arises when the worker is anxious and able to work, not only at existing wage rates but at lower wage rates, and is unable to secure a job. Generally it is only the latter form of unemployment that represents a serious problem, for if a worker elects to be idle, it is his responsibility to bear the consequences of that decision. Unhappily, the line distinguishing those workers who are voluntarily and involuntarily unemployed is not precise, either conceptually or statistically.

Disguised Unemployment. Disguised unemployment is unemployment within employment. The worker is " at work," but at a job much below his training and experience. Or he may be working on a part-time basis and is able and anxious to secure full-time employment. In either situation the aggregate unemployment percentage does not reflect this form of unemployment. It represents, in effect, the imperfect allocation of labor.

Such an imperfect allocation of resources can arise for numerous reasons, but most important is the loss of production made necessary because of a decline of business activity. In addition, labor may be imperfectly utilized because of discrimination against particular groups, because of inade-

[8] *Unemployment, A Problem of Industry* (New York, Longmans, Green and Co., 1912 edition), p. 108.

quate and unequal education and training opportunities for particular workers, or because of managerial ignorance of labor skills and labor ignorance of management needs. When the labor market is tight, or when management is unable to secure as many persons as are necessary, every effort will be made to utilize effectively every worker. On such occasions there is then economic as well as moral justification for not discriminating against particular labor groups. But when business conditions slacken off, highly skilled workers may be given the opportunity to perform unskilled tasks. The costs of the depression are not accurately reflected, then, in unemployment data alone, for society loses not only the production of those laid-off employees, but production that would otherwise be possible if everyone worked to capacity.

Unfortunately the concept of disguised unemployment, while conceptually clear, is difficult to isolate for measurement purposes. It is almost impossible to define in concrete terms the best allocation of the labor resource, and hence measure the cost of deviations from this.[9] As a case in point, disguised unemployment can arise when workers so fear unemployment that they try to extend their present jobs. How could one accurately measure such costs?

During a depression the displacement of the less skilled workers by skilled workers quickly develops under a seniority system. And if unemployment is extended, even the very skilled workers cast about in search of any job.

> And what kind of jobs did these [unemployed] men finally secure? Trained clothing cutters with years of experience had become gasoline station attendants, watchmen in warehouses, time keepers in steel plants, and clerks in meat markets. Rotary press operators were pressing clothes in tailor shops. Machinists were selling hosiery for mail-order houses. Welding machine operators had become farm hands, and skilled woodworkers were mixing salves for patent-medicine manufacturers. A significant number of men admitted frankly that after some months of loafing, they had taken to bootlegging.[10]

In another study of unemployment in the early thirties the researchers pointed out, "We found mechanics, cabinet makers, shoe makers and the

[9] Because this broader concept of disguised unemployment can cover such a multitude of sins, it has been suggested that disguised unemployment represent "not all deviations from optimal allocation, but only those which are due to cyclical variations in the level of effective demand." (Russell A. Nixon, and Paul A. Samuelson, "Estimates of Unemployment in the United States," *Review of Economics and Statistics,* August, 1949, p. 103.) This approach attempts to meet the criticism that disguised unemployment is too comprehensive a term because it entails all imperfections of human judgment in the allocation of resources.

[10] As explained by Isador Lubin and quoted in the House of Representatives' Study, Subcommittee of the Committee on Labor, 77th Congress, on Establishing an Emergency Economic Advisory Commission and a National Unemployment Commission (Washington, 1941), p. 501.

rest dropping down to the ranks of truck drivers, janitors, watchmen, street cleaners and snow shovelers. Their former skills only made them misfits at manual labor. We soon read of further deterioration caused by accidents, overstrain and exposure undergone in their new work." [11]

It is readily apparent that society faces a serious loss of human skills as workers perform menial tasks and grow less confident in their ability to return to previous skilled work. Such unemployment leaves a permanent scar on the labor force which may only become apparent at a future date. At the beginning of World War II, for example, the United States found itself facing a serious scarcity of technically skilled manpower to handle the tremendous demands for increased production. Undoubtedly high levels of employment in the thirties would have provided America with the higher number of skilled workers at the very time that they were desperately needed.

The attempt to determine just who should be included in the labor force indicates how shadowy or ephemeral the concept of underutilized or disguised unemployment can be. In March, 1942, the Census Bureau decided to experiment by asking those persons who were neither working nor looking for work at the time (normally not considered part of the labor force) whether they would take a full-time job if one should become available in 30 days. If one should count the "yes" respondents as part of the labor force, the number of unemployed workers in 1942 would increase by 1 million.[12] In a Census survey conducted in March, 1948, it was found that of those who were working less than 35 hours in the survey week because of economic factors, 510,000 were classified as " Usually employed part time but available for full-time work." [13] In this sense our unemployment data can easily underestimate the incidence of unemployment within employment and the unemployment outside of the labor force. In recent years [14] the Census has undertaken a breakdown into " economic " and " other " reasons for those working less than 34 hours a week, with those

[11] *Case Studies of Unemployment*, Compiled by the Unemployment Committee of the National Federation of Settlements, edited by Marian Elderton (Philadelphia, University of Pennsylvania Press, 1931), p. xxx.

[12] See *Unemployed Estimates*, Economic Policy Division Series No. 25 (New York, National Association of Manufacturers, April, 1950), p. 4.

[13] "Recent Unemployment Trends," *Monthly Labor Review* (Vol. 70, No. 5 May, 1950), p. 489, foonote 6.

[14] For discussion and data on the proportion of part-time workers who desire full-time employment, see Russell A. Nixon, " Correction of Census Bureau Estimates of Unemployment," *Review of Economics and Statistics*, Vol. XXXII, No. 1 (February, 1950), p. 52, note. In the postwar period the proportion of part-time workers desiring full-time employment (*viz.*, those working part time for economic reasons) reached a peak of 33.8 percent in May, 1949. In September, 1955, it was down to 22.6 percent. In the week of January 6–12, 1957, 16.6 percent of the total labor force worked less than 34 hours, and 3.4 percent of the total labor force worked part time for economic reasons. Thus, slightly more than 2 million workers would probably have preferred full- to part-time employment. For data, see, *Current Population Reports, Labor Force*, Bureau of Census, Series P–50, No. 61 (September, 1955), p. 9, and Series P–57, No. 175 (February, 1957), p. 11.

economic reasons including slack work, material shortages, repairs to plant and equipment and starts or termination of job during the week. Workers laboring part time for these reasons would probably prefer full-time employment. But because those working part time are not counted among the unemployed, unemployment figures tend to obscure the loss to society arising from such part-time employment.

Technological Unemployment. Technological unemployment is unemployment that arises from the substitution of capital for labor. The constant pressure of labor for an ever-higher living standard, reinforced in more recent times by the consolidated power of the organized labor movement, has accelerated the drive for improvement in the methods of production and industrial efficiency.

It may seem rather paradoxical that labor should resist technological change, but such resistance reflects the fact that mechanical change threatens or jeopardizes something very vital to the individual worker: the flow of income at his present job. This response is not confined to labor alone. It is difficult, for example, for a businessman to support tariff reductions if his own business can only survive through the protection that tariffs afford him, no matter how well he understands the advantages of free trade. Similarly, it is difficult for labor to appreciate the inevitable benefits of technological change when its immediate effect is the loss of employment and income. This viewpoint can be seen in the reactions of a technologically unemployed man when confronted with the argument that technological change benefits everyone:

> I went to a lecture up at Yale the other night and the bird what did the talking said as how we didn't have to worry about what the machines did to our jobs. They just made more of them he says. So what? I work for the Water company and they've got machines that do a job in 6 months that it would have taken us a year to do right after the war. So what am I going to do the other six months? Go and make some of those blasted machines? No, I go and listen to a Yale economist telling me I ain't unemployed. Now let's be reasonable about this business, he says. All right, let's be reasonable. Can he get *me* a job making those machines that other 6 months? That's what I'm interested in. Hell, those machines are made in Ohio. Who's going to pay my fare out there and move my family back and forth every 6 months? Now let's be reasonable about this thing, I says, just like he said.[15]

The logic of economic theory indicates that such technological unemployment need not be a " long-run " problem; displaced workers will be absorbed in other industries, especially if they are willing to accept a wage level consistent with their value to other industries. Of course, in many situations, the required flexibility of wage rates and mobility of labor are not forthcoming. Organized labor has often protested that it does

[15] Quoted by Bakke, *op. cit.*, p. 69.

not resist technological change as such, but only having to absorb alone the incidence of technological change. Even the classical economist, John Stuart Mill, observed early in the nineteenth century that " There cannot be a more legitimate object of the legislator's care than the interests of those who are thus sacrificed to the gains of their fellow-citizens and of posterity." [16]

The problem of technological unemployment was succinctly stated by William Green before a Congressional committee in December 14, 1928. Speaking first of the AF of L view, Green explained:

> The American Federation of Labor has never stood in the way of the introduction of machinery. We have invited it. We have felt that machinery relieved drudgery and toil and that its expanded use would help increase the income of the working men and women; and, as a result, it would be a blessing to the great mass of the people.

But then turning to the problem of unemployment, he refers to the " strange situation " confronting the musicians:

> The musicians' unions are grappling now with that very problem through the introduction of the talking pictures. Musicians are being displaced and their organizations are grappling with that problem now. Just think of those men that have become artists, in big orchestras, men who have studied for years, men of genius, who are thrown out, being displaced, through the introduction of mechanical devices — the talking pictures. Among these, it is the skilled people, artists, that are being thrown out. It is a pretty tough thing for a man that is skilled to go down and accept employment at unskilled work, unskilled industry. The artist, the musician, what is to become of him?

Mr. Green did not attempt to answer his own question. It is possible, however, that the lower cost made possible by the artificial reproduction of sound through phonograph records and film sound tracks has increased the total demand for musicians rather than reduced it. However, this long-run possibility does not solve short-run difficulties. For example, the expansion of the television industry today has set in motion a pattern of allied demands for supporting equipment. While total labor demand may not decrease but even increase, the direction in which the demand is extended may not help the worker who has been displaced. In other words, the fact that aggregate demand is not changed even in the short run is of little consolation to the technologically displaced worker if he sees no opportunity for immediate re-employment.

The reabsorption of the technologically unemployed worker depends on a variety of factors, including (a) the adaptability of the worker to new jobs, (b) the mobility of the worker, and (c) the general level demand for labor. During the thirties the low demand for labor undoubtedly complicated and delayed the re-employment of labor displaced by ma-

16 Quoted in Beveridge, *Unemployment: A Problem of Industry*, p. 13.

chines. And the hardship of unemployment probably increases geometrically with the duration of unemployment itself. Technological unemployment may, therefore, be considered less of a problem during a period of high employment, but a rather serious problem when re-employment opportunities are limited.

Frictional Unemployment. No category of unemployment can be so conceptually precise and yet so nebulous when it comes to measurement as frictional unemployment. The following are the usual characteristics attributed to frictional unemployment: It is unemployment between jobs. It is assumed that when a man has lost one source of income, he usually has the opportunity to secure another one. This latter characteristic of frictional unemployment is difficult to test in a quantitative way, for no regular compilation is made of unfilled employment opportunities, and, of course, job openings may require skills or qualifications not possessed by the unemployed. Frictional unemployment does not arise from the lack of general demand for labor. Thus it is sometimes viewed as the margin of unemployment which exists when demand exceeds supply or as "unemployment with inflation." [17] This aspect of frictional unemployment is important, for it is sometimes thought that unemployment reflects inadequate demand for labor, and can readily be solved by measures increasing labor demand. If frictional unemployment is defined as unemployment not significantly reduced by a general increase in the demand for labor, it may require specific rather than general remedies.

Frictional unemployment inevitably becomes a focal point in discussions of unemployment because of the general conviction that it is the necessary by-product of economic efficiency, reflecting the dynamic and changing nature of industrial growth. The initiating impulse for frictional unemployment is the shift in the direction, rather than a change in the quantity, of labor demand. Like technological unemployment, it becomes a problem because workers do not or cannot readily adjust themselves to such shifts in demand. The solution to frictional unemployment is not to be found in preventing changes in demand (for these are rooted in the very important freedom of consumers to buy what and when they want) but rather in increasing the adaptability of labor to change.

Whenever controversy develops about the seriousness of existing employment levels, it is often suggested that existing unemployment levels largely reflect frictional adjustments of a dynamic and expanding economy.

[17] "Probably the best clues as to whether unemployment at any given time is largely frictional can be found in evidence of labor shortages in some parts of the economy or in pressures toward rising prices for the factors of production. Hence over-all appraisal of the general economic situation must be relied upon to determine if the volume of unemployment reported at any given time is essentially frictional in character. It is apparent that the frictional component of unemployment cannot be readily isolated and may vary widely from time to time." Charles Stewart and Loring Wood, *Employment Statistics in the Planning of a Full Employment Program,* BLS and Bureau of Budget, Mimeographed paper, undated, p. 5.

Rather than being a symptom of maladjustment, unemployment is seen, in this context, as a symptom of growth. In its more ambitious form, the argument suggests that economic growth is inherently cyclical, and even cyclical unemployment (as well as frictional unemployment) is simply a manifestation of the dynamic growth characteristics of our economy. The argument contains within it a grain of truth, for certainly an expanding economy is one characterized by constant changes in the direction of total spending. However, it must not be used as a rationalization for all unemployment, for it is simply not correct to identify expanding unemployment with expanding production. On the other hand, because changes are inherent in our economy, some workers will always be " between " jobs. This reality complicates the problem of defining the irreducible minimum of unemployment, as well as that of establishing benchmarks for public policy in the face of growing unemployment.[18]

This difficulty is apparent when one attempts to define full employment. How much unemployment must be tolerated in terms of the inevitable frictions that one finds in our economy? Theodore O. Yntema (expressing a general view) points out that " at the optimum level of employment, the labor market would not be so tight as to prevent the maintenance of a reasonably stable price level. . . . In normal times frictional unemployment would be higher [than during the war] probably from 2 to 5 per cent of the labor force." [19] The National Planning Association had estimated a postwar labor force which made allowances for 1.5 million frictionally unemployed or 2.5 percent of the total labor force. The British *Economist* suggested that unemployment in the postwar transitional period could reach 2.5 percent of the British labor force and still be consistent with its concept of full employment.[20] But more conservative estimates are sometimes advanced in America. Karl T. Schlotterbeck, in a Brookings Institute publication, explained:

> We are inclined to believe that even under generally favorable conditions there would perhaps be out of work on the average over a

[18] As a BLS study explains: " Frictional unemployment, broadly defined, results from the process of entry into the labor force, from voluntary job shifting by workers, and from fluctuations in labor demand among individual employing units when the over-all level of job opportunities is in general balance with the number of workers available for jobs. Although a certain amount of frictional unemployment is a necessary cost of economic progress in a democratic society, the minimum amount of such unemployment is difficult to determine. At any time, it is a function of the adjustments under way in the labor market and of the adaptability of the labor force to changing conditions." " Recent Unemployment Trends," *Monthly Labor Review* (Vol. 70, No. 5, May, 1950), p. 489, a study by Harold Wool and Calman Winegarten.

[19] " Full Employment in a Private Enterprise System," *American Economic Review* (March, 1944), Supplement, p. 107.

[20] National Planning Association, *National Budgets for Full Employment*, Washington, April 1945.

period of years as many as 4 million (7 percent of the total labor force). In the best years — under boom conditions — the level might fall as low as 3 million (5 percent of the total labor force). In other years it might rise as high as 5 million (8.5 percent of the total labor force). Only when the number out of work exceeded 4 million need the employment situation occasion real concern. It should be clearly understood that this total does not represent a permanent army of unemployed — seeking jobs in vain.[21]

The *Monthly Labor Review* analysis of frictional unemployment suggests that " A constantly changing group of unemployed averaging 2 million workers moving between jobs might be compatible with a condition of satisfactory employment opportunity " but cautions that " a particular volume of unemployment should not be defined as frictional unless something is known about the nature and causes of unemployment." In Britain and other countries during World War II unemployment gravitated little above 1 percent of the labor force, much below that proportion usually considered to be the irreducible minimum.

If we consider frictional unemployment as that proportion of the labor force unabsorbed when aggregate demand is expanding more rapidly than aggregate supply (associated with inflation), we distill from the unemployment total those idled because of inadequate demand. To suggest that frictional unemployment varies inversely with the degree of price inflation might lead one to the conclusion that inflation is caused by " inadequate " frictional unemployment. While it is undoubtedly true that belligerent union demands can exert considerable pressure on the price structure, the suggestion that the margin of frictional unemployment be increased to assure price stability is to subvert the economic necessity of frictional unemployment to other purposes. It is one thing to accept such unemployment as the inevitable consequence of free market forces and another to suggest this margin be increased to minimize the dangers of a wage-price spiral.

Conceptually, economists find themselves in one of two camps in attempting to define full employment. One group suggests that a " margin " of unemployment (often loosely defined) is necessary to minimize the recruitment problems of industry, to maintain discipline within the plant, and to reduce the hazard of a wage-price spiral induced by strong wage pressure. The other group suggests that full employment exists only when there are more jobs available than there are workers to fill them. It, therefore, discounts more heavily the inconvenience of inadequate manpower for industry than it does the personal tragedy arising when labor is willing and able to work but unable to find employment. As one might suspect, this latter group believes that only the smallest margin of workers

[21] *Postwar Re-Employment* (Washington, The Brookings Institution, 1943), p. 19, quoted in the *Monthly Labor Review* (Vol. 64, No. 1, January, 1947), p. 7.

should normally be caught between jobs, and this would be possible only when displaced workers had jobs to go to. The former view is indicated in the National Association of Manufacturers statement which complains that " The public does not realize that even in periods of high production there is a *normal* float of frictional unemployment of from 2,000,000 to 3,000,000." [22] Taking the latter view, Russell Nixon complains that this fuzzy and exaggerated conception of what the irreducible minimum of frictional unemployment is often " lulls government policy makers and the public generally . . . into a feeling of false security and inactivity precisely at the stage of initial depression development when corrective measures have the greatest opportunity for success." [23]

It is generally agreed that the frictionally unemployed workers often become unemployed through no fault of their own and are therefore more likely to be involuntarily rather than voluntarily unemployed.[24] Programs to minimize the effect of such unemployment include policies to improve worker skills through vocational training or on-the-job training programs, policies to improve information of employment opportunities elsewhere through the expanded facilities and publicity of employment information service, and a more careful integration of labor market analysis from state to state. Assistance might be given to the worker in the form of a subsidy for travel, especially out of a chronically depressed area when unemployment has been so continuous that labor cannot meet the costs of such mobility.

In summary, the solution to frictional unemployment is not simply to be found in increasing the general demand for labor. This may result in an increment of prices greater than the increment of employment would justify. The problem must often be solved on the regional basis, with more intensive remedies applied to specific areas rather than to the total economy. One thing is certain however: The stronger or more expansive the general demand for labor, the smaller the proportion of those workers represented by frictional unemployment.

[22] *Unemployment Estimates, Economic Policy Division*, Pamphlet No. 25 (April, 1950), p. 1. Prepared by John C. Gebhart, Director of Research. Italics added.

[23] " Correction of Census Bureau Estimates of Unemployment," *op. cit.*, p. 50.

[24] It is possible that the growing demand for labor in a full-employment market may cause an increase in the amount of frictional unemployment because of labor's high voluntary quit rate. This, of course, is not so much a problem of the social welfare of the worker as it is a problem for the economic health of the nation. In a full-employment situation workers may be tempted to window-shop for jobs. William Beveridge explains the need for " organized " labor mobility: " When we give up playing musical chairs with not enough seats [jobs] to go round we don't have a necessity to play general post with enough seats for all but with no one allowed to keep his seat. Mobility of labour does not mean perpetual motion. Mobility of labour means that labour should be capable of moving and ready to move if necessary. Organized mobility means that men do not move if movement is fruitless and do move rapidly and directly to the job when there is a job." *Full Employment in a Free Society* (New York, W. W. Norton & Co., 1945), p. 175.

Seasonal Unemployment. Seasonal unemployment arises for three separate but not unrelated reasons. First, month by month changes in labor force employment are required because of temperature variations throughout the year. Secondly, fashion changes and annual style changes result in a clustering of labor activity within each year. Both of these factors involve adjustments in the number of job opportunities for labor from month to month. Thirdly, seasonal unemployment arises because of the periodic influx of job seekers in the labor market.

In the first case, the seasonal nature of labor force utilization is most apparent in agriculture. Additional hands are required during the planting and harvesting seasons. Similarly, in the Northwest lumber industry layoffs are common in the summer if the forest fire hazard is severe and during the winter too if timber tracts become snowbound. Seasonal unemployment is more likely to be a serious problem in those regions and countries characterized by seasonal extremes of temperatures. In the second case, changes in the styles of clothing within the year cause slack seasons in the needle trades. Retail store sales also follow a seasonal pattern, with a peak at Christmas, and a decline following the holidays. Automobile production too follows a seasonal pattern, with layoffs occurring when the industry retools for newly designed engines and chassis. Further seasonality in employment is found in food-processing plants, which must, of course, package or can the foods at the times they are harvested. In meat packing, also, a burst of activity follows the summer months of stock raising. It is difficult to find any occupation which is completely unaffected by these month-to-month variations in temperature and consumer temperament. Finally, changes in the labor supply — arising particularly when students enter the labor market for employment during the summer months — cause seasonal periodicity to both employment and unemployment indexes.

The Bureau of Labor Statistics has estimated that the "unemployment resulting from seasonal influences alone may vary by about 40 percent within a calendar year — from 20 percent above the annual average in February to 20 percent below in October. For example, when unemployment averages about 2.5 million, changes of one-half million in either direction could be expected as the result of seasonal variations alone."[25] As one might expect, the incidence of seasonal unemployment varies considerably from occupation to occupation, as well as for the sex, age, and race characteristics of the work force. Seasonable variability is more apparent for women than for men, as women often adjust their participation to short-term intervals such as working in the retail trade during the

[25] Herman Travis, "The Structure of Unemployment in Recent Years," *Monthly Labor Review*, Vol. 79, No. 10 (October, 1956), p. 1147. For further data and charts see W. S. Woytinsky and Associates, *Employment and Wages in the United States* (New York, Twentieth Century Fund, 1953), Chapter 24.

Christmas season. There is, too, much more seasonal variation in utilization of the very young and very old as well as for the nonwhite components of the labor force. In a 1 percent sample of unemployed insurance claimants in the United States, it was found that over 31 percent of the claimants were "unskilled" and 25.8 per cent "semiskilled," [26] and it is likely that many of the female, young and old, and nonwhite workers are in these classifications. The incidence of seasonal labor demand arising because of climatic conditions is indicated by the number of insured unemployed in various industries compared to the total number of workers covered by insurance. In the week ending February 18, 1956, it was found that the highest rate of insured unemployment was found in contract construction (15.1 percent) followed with lumber and wood products (except furniture) (9.4 percent), food and kindred products (6.5 percent) and apparel and other finished textile products (5.1 percent).[27]

Is seasonality of employment a serious social and economic problem? It would not be if those seasonally employed in one industry could secure supplementary employment, perhaps in a second seasonal industry, to provide for an adequate year-round income; or if those seasonally employed elect to work only part of the time during the year to supplement family income or for other personal reasons; or if the income secured during the season employed provided income adequate for the year. During a period of general economic prosperity, growth of seasonal employment need not suggest hardship, as many housewives, students, and elderly workers may prefer to work only part time to supplement family income. Sumner Slichter has observed that:

> Seasonal slacks may be one of the *attractions* of the job. The cutter in a clothing factory who has instructions to report back to work at a given time is probably enjoying a vacation which regularly goes with his work and which is one of the attractions of his line of employment. . . . The workers may spend their "unemployed" time in Miami drawing unemployment benefits, as a number of states have found out . . . for many [and probably most] seasonal workers, seasonal unemployment comes closer to being a vacation than true involuntary idleness.[28]

This happy situation is not likely to continue during a period of depression, for labor often finds it difficult to adjust its living standard downward as employment becomes more irregular. Obviously, when employment opportunities and income payments are limited, enforced idleness cannot easily be viewed as an enjoyable vacation.

[26] "Characteristics of the Insured Unemployed," *Monthly Labor Review*, Vol. 79, No. 6 (June, 1956), p. 661.

[27] *Ibid.*, Table I, p. 660.

[28] "Comment on Papers on Employment and Employment Figures," *Review of Economics and Statistics* (February, 1950), p. 75.

Like frictional unemployment, seasonal unemployment does not disappear with a general expansion of labor demand. However, when the labor market is exceedingly tight, there are increased opportunities for seasonally employed workers to dovetail a continuing series of jobs with each other. Furthermore, management has increased incentive to provide year-round employment because of the recruitment problem. It is not surprising, therefore, that during World War II the seasonal pattern for labor employment in textiles, apparel, shoes and furniture disappeared. Following the war, however, seasonal unemployment reappeared. Available data indicate that unemployment is highest where the seasonality of employment is greatest, although the rate at which seasonal unemployment declines with total unemployment depends in large part on the direction of employment expansion.[29]

One of the more cheerful aspects of seasonal unemployment is that many opportunities exist for minimizing it. The Social Security Act of 1935 provided for a 3 percent tax on employer payrolls, but 90 percent of this (or 2.7 percent of the tax) could be refunded to states if they established an unemployment system that would meet certain minimum standards prescribed by the federal government. All states quickly established unemployment systems, and many states have provisions for experience rating. " Experience rating " adjusts the tax each employer pays in terms of the unemployment he creates. The assumption is that those firms who had a stable employment record should not be compelled to bear the burden of unemployment and tax payments created by the irregular employment record of other employers. To the extent payrolls are taxed by the government and to the extent that employers find it possible to pass such a tax on to their customers, the employer and public are required to share at least part of the burden of irregular employment. The National Association of Manufacturers has urged business to increase its efforts to stabilize employment as failure to do so may invite increased government regulation: " Employees are naturally restless on this score, many of them influenced by past unemployment experiences to look to government-imposed plans for security." [30] Fortunately, there are several steps that industry can take to minimize such seasonal labor force utilization. A partial list of measures proposed by the National Association of Manufacturers is indicated in the outline of Table 19. Needless to say, labor, management and the public stand to benefit from the successful application of stabilization measures.[31]

[29] *Monthly Labor Review* (May, 1950), p. 492.

[30] *Employment Stabilization: Industry's Progress Toward Steady Work and Steady Pay* (New York, Industrial Relations Division, NAM June, 1952), p. 10.

[31] For a more detailed discussion of techniques for eliminating seasonal unemployment, see Paul Hubert Casselman, *Economics of Employment and Unemployment* (Washington, D.C., Public Affairs Press, 1955), Chapter 4.

TABLE 19   Methods for Minimizing Fluctuation in Employment

I. *Sales Techniques*
  1. Change habits of customers
     a. Advertising, timing of annual showing of new models or new prod-
        ucts, etc.
  2. Diversification of products
     a. Develop new products with a seasonality which dovetails with ex-
        isting products.
  3. Stimulate " off-season " buying
     a. Price concessions, assured delivery dates, etc.
     b. Provide incentive to salesmen
     c. New packaging at beginning of dull season.
  4. Avoid specialty items, cataloguing products for buying selection from
     standardized articles.
  5. Establish quotas with maxima and minima based on sales forecasts and
     production possibilities.

II. *Production Techniques*
  1. Manufacture for inventory
     a. If not finished article, standardized parts
  2. Defer work for slow periods
     a. Maintenance, clean-up, etc.
     b. Long-term orders and standard items
  3. Sub-contract items which interrupt normal production flow

III. *Employment Techniques*
  1. Centralized employment control
     a. To inventory job requirements and skills available
     b. To govern hiring and layoffs
     c. To effect transfers as needed
  2. Training program
     a. To increase versatility and flexibility of labor force (May require
        union contract changes)
     b. To achieve cooperation of entire management personnel
  3. Utility crews or labor pool
     a. To break " bottlenecks " in production
     b. To fill in during vacation periods and for absentees
  4. Educational activities
     a. To " sell " program to employees
     b. To improve public relations
     c. To improve labor-management relations
  5. Schedule vacations during slow season if production is not stabilized
     or when plant is closed for inventory, repairs, etc.

IV. *Community Stabilization of Employment*
  1. Establish needs by seasons of all community industries. Then transfer
     from slow company to busy company and back again when original
     company becomes busy.

Hard-Core Unemployment. As the name suggests, hard-core unemployment reflects the regional incidence of long-term unemployment.
The national average of unemployment percentages can easily obscure

high-level regional unemployment, and this suggests that national policy must be oriented to local difficulties rather than to aggregate data alone. Because of this qualitative aspect of unemployment data, the government keeps a close check on regional employment trends. If any area has more than 12 percent of its local labor force unemployed, it is classified as a "very substantial labor surplus" area. The federal government has attempted to minimize such problems in granting special tax amortization benefits for new defense facilities that are located in surplus labor areas and in placing government contracts, so far as is feasible, in these areas.

How does hard-core unemployment arise, and in what respects is it different from frictional unemployment? Generally, such spot unemployment arises because of a long-run decline of market demand for the product labor is producing. The resulting decrease in labor demand can arise because of the growth of competition of a foreign-made product of comparable or superior quality; it can arise because of a long-run shift in consumer tastes; and it can arise because local technology has not paced industry innovations, resulting in the obsolescence of plant equipment and noncompetitive production. Probably our best case study of such chronic unemployment is the textile industry of New England. In this area William H. Miernyk attributes the increase of textile unemployment to "competition from the low-wage South, technological change, the loss of export markets, increasing imports, the changing pattern of consumer preferences, and interfiber competition. . . ." [32]

But such hard-core unemployment involves not only a secular decline in the demand for the product, but a marked absence of geographic mobility of labor to new employment opportunities. In a sense, hard-core or depressed-area unemployment is largely a combination of chronic structural, technological, and frictional unemployment.

It goes without saying that the hardships engendered by chronic long-term unemployment are serious and often tragic. But if employment opportunities are limited, why do not the displaced workers shift to new labor markets and acquire new job skills for new jobs? While this is a feasible alternative for the younger worker, the discrimination of industry against those employees 45 years of age and older represents a serious roadblock to such mobility. In the several studies of the adjustments made by New England textile workers it has generally been found that the continuing unemployment of the displaced worker ranged from about 20 to 45 percent, with a much higher incidence of unemployment in the elderly worker. "Many of the older workers who have found nonmanufacturing jobs are doing unskilled and relatively low-paying work as janitors, porters, hospital attendants, and so forth." [33]

[32] "Unemployment in New England Textile Communities," *Monthly Labor Review*, Vol. 78, No. 6 (June, 1955), p. 645.
[33] *Ibid.*, p. 647.

The solution most commonly proposed for meeting this difficulty is to encourage new industry into such depressed areas. While many local industrial development commissions have been established to advertise the availability of manpower in depressed regions, William Miernyk's conclusion, following his study of New England experience, was that " the over-all results have not been impressive." [34] If industry mobility into a depressed area is not always feasible, it may then be appropriate to accelerate efforts to encourage the mobility of labor out of depressed areas. But more than this, additional efforts shall have to be established to retrain workers to new job skills. And even these efforts of retraining together with subsidized mobility to labor-scarce markets will be frustrated if the over-all demand for labor is low, or if management continues to discriminate against those workers who are 45 years of age and older.

Cyclical and Structural Unemployment. Because of the continuing experience of " high " levels of employment, discussion of the cyclical nature of economic growth has lost much of its vogue. Certainly few economists contemplate the repetition of the depression decade of the thirties in the near future. The government's propensity to spend, even in peacetime, provides a floor under total spending to buoy up private spending. Unemployment percentages are carefully observed, and any growing trend of idleness produces immediate political pressure. No government, regardless of its economic philosophy, can afford to appear indifferent about unemployment. The conviction that the government should take vigorous anti-cyclical and anti-unemployment measures has pretty well permeated our personal and national economic philosophy.

In addition to this public state of mind, many built-in stabilizers exist which serve as counterdeflationary forces. The social security program, and especially the unemployment insurance provisions, help sustain purchasing power when unemployment is increasing. The large quantity of liquid assets owned by persons, especially cash savings, appreciate in value with a downturn in prices and such appreciation may stimulate spending. Wider adoption of guaranteed annual wage plans may also serve to prevent a downturn from becoming cumulative.

These considerations do not permit us to ignore, however, those imbalances in our economy that can quickly lead to cyclical unemployment. It is better that the economist be accused of attempting to " solve the last depression " than to be oblivious to the hazards that still face our economy. Few persons enjoy the conviction that our economy will *automatically* produce full employment. Indeed, the very growth and complexity of our industrial mechanism, together with the tremendous increase in the tempo of its operation, compound the difficulties that can quickly develop when any part of that mechanism breaks down. The reality of industrial crisis may never be appreciated until after the fact; it can best be

[34] *Ibid.*, p. 648.

avoided by appreciating those forces which lead to the crisis before the fact.

Unhappily, there are several alternative theories of cyclical fluctuation which lead to opposite or contradictory policy recommendations. If all of the multiple explanations of cyclical variation contain within them an element of truth — as is likely to be the case — this suggests that a policy of cycle control involves the use of multiple techniques: monetary policy, fiscal policy, wage policy, and the like. As we shall see in the following data, the growth of unemployment has represented one of the most costly by-products of uneven economic growth.

Some Unemployment Data

Figure 18 reveals unemployment in numbers and also unemployment as a percentage of the civilian labor force from 1900 to 1956. Prior to World War I the unemployed never totaled more than 2.33 million workers and almost completely disappeared during the peak wartime

FIGURE 18. Estimates of Unemployment from 1900–1956 in Numbers and Percentage of Total Labor Force

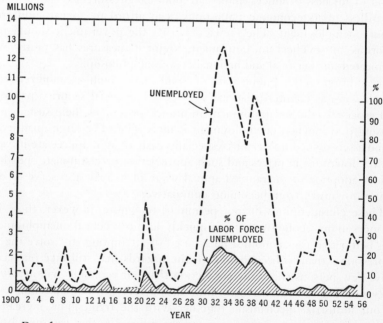

Source: Data from 1900 to 1929 — *Conference Board Economic Record* (New York, National Industrial Conference Board, March, 1940), Table i, p. 78. Data from 1929 to 1940 — *Handbook of Labor Statistics, 1947,* Bulletin No. 916 (Washington, Bureau of Labor Statistics, 1948), Table A12, p. 36. Data from 1940 to 1950 — Bureau of the Census. Data from 1950 to 1956 — *Statistical Abstract of the United Sates, 1956* (Washington, Department of Commerce, 1956).

mobilization from 1917 to 1919. The sharp recession left over 4.5 million unemployed in 1921 with the spectacular total of 11 percent of the labor force idle. But the recession was short-lived, and throughout the twenties the economy enjoyed a fairly high plateau of labor utilization.

As one might expect, the depression of the thirties produced mass unemployment with 13 million workers, or close to 25 percent of the work force, idle in 1933. Not only was the proportion of workers unemployed large, but the duration of the unemployment was equally severe. Taking the average for the 10-year period from 1931 to 1940, in each year close to 10 million persons were unemployed or an annual average of 18.8 percent of the labor force. The economist could no more skirt these frightful statistics than the tongue could skirt the socket of an extracted tooth. In 1938, as unemployment increased again from 7.7 million to 10.4 million, it was a brave soul who could announce that prosperity was "just around the corner."

The all-out mobilization during World War II quickly absorbed the vast reserve of idled workers. While large-scale unemployment had been predicted in the postwar adjustment period, especially because of the anticipated decline of government expenditures, serious unemployment failed to develop. The pre-World War II decade provides an interesting contrast with postwar employment experience.

Unemployment from 1945 to 1956 never reached more than 3.5 million

TABLE 20   Unemployed Persons by Duration of Unemployment 1946–1956

Period	Civilian Labor Force	Total	Per-centage of Civil. Labor Force	Percentage Without Work for			Average Duration of Unemployment in Weeks
				10 Weeks or Less	11 to 26 Weeks	Over 26 Weeks	
1946	57,520	2,270	3.9	na	na	6.2	na
1947	60,168	2,142	3.6	72.5	19.9	7.7	9.8
1948	61,442	2,064	3.4	77.1	17.3	5.6	8.6
1949	62,105	3,395	5.5	70.1	22.3	7.5	10.0
1950	63,099	3,142	5.0	65.6	23.1	11.4	12.1
1951	62,884	1,879	3.0	75.8	17.0	7.3	9.7
1952	62,966	1,673	2.7	78.8	16.4	5.0	8.3
1953	63,815	1,602	2.5	79.2	16.0	4.9	8.1
1954	64,468	3,230	5.0	65.4	24.8	9.8	11.7
1955	65,847	2,654	4.0	65.4	22.0	12.7	13.2
1956	65,913	2,834	4.3	62.8	27.2	9.9	12.9

na: not available

Source: *Statistical Abstract of the United States: 1956* (Washington, D.C., Government Printing Office, 1957), p. 199.

workers and percentage-wise never exceeded the 1949 peak of 5.5 percent of the civilian labor force. The expanding trend of unemployment in 1949 was quickly deflected downward by the outbreak of Korean hostilities, and while unemployment increased to 2.8 million workers in 1954 or 4.4 percent of the labor force, this proportion diminished in 1955.

One qualitative aspect of unemployment data that is most significant is the duration of unemployment for those who are idled. In many instances prolonged unemployment for a small proportion of the population represents a more serious social and economic problem than temporary idleness for a large number of workers. In Table 20 it can be seen that the duration of unemployment tends to increase when the total proportion of workers idled increases. It is generally true that the larger the numbers unemployed, the greater the duration of unemployment for each person idled.

Measuring Unemployment

It is unfortunate that one of the most important parameters of our economic health — the level of unemployment — has been developed by the government only since 1940 and that much of the discussion of the problem of unemployment returns to the basic issue: the reliability of government data. It is, of course, only natural that if public concern is to be raised about unemployment, it should be based on reliable rather than on imperfect data. Much energy is undoubtedly diverted from the discussion of just what should be done about unemployment to the issue, "How much unemployment do we actually have?" The heat of this discussion varies directly with the level of unemployment.

The constant effort to improve and refine our data increases the risk of making historical comparisons of unemployment data over a broad expanse of time. For example, the change in the definition of the "gainfully employed" worker can alter the denominator of the unemployment ratio, leading to rather substantial changes in the percentage of those unemployed. While in recent decades we have less to fear from the noncomparability of our concepts, the data prior to 1940 provides only approximations of unemployment. The estimates of unemployment made during the thirties by various private agencies followed a sympathetic pattern from year to year, but the absolute level of unemployment varied substantially from estimate to estimate.[35]

Prior to 1940, the Bureau of Census enumeration of persons "gainfully

[35] For example in 1929 alone the following estimates were made of unemployment:

Agency	Estimate
American Federation of Labor	1,864,000
Congress of Industrial Organization	1,831,000

employed " included all persons 10 years of age and over who reported a gainful occupation, regardless of whether or not they were then at work or looking for work. This tabulation generally excluded those new job seekers who had no previous work experience.[36]

In 1940 a more accurate unemployment index was developed, in which the " labor force " was substituted for the " gainfully employed worker." The labor force concept was designed to focus attention on the " attachment " and identification of the worker with the labor force in the current survey period. As one student of this problem explained:

> The term " unemployment " can include a variety of concepts. It can have a " condition concept " — that of being without a job. It can have an " activity concept " — that of actively seeking work. It can have a " psychological concept " — that of desiring a job. It can have a " physical concept " — that of being able to do a job. Or it can have a combination of these and other concepts.[37]

As pointed out earlier, this measure does not, therefore, give weight to those persons who are not in the labor force and yet might like to be, for

Agency	Estimate
National Industrial Conference Board	429,000
Robert Nathan	1,752,000
Alexander Hamilton Institute	3,456,000
National Research League	1,250,000
Daniel Carson	1,910,000

Derived from Table 93, Woytinsky and Associates, *op. cit.*, p. 716.

[36] Further distinctions between the total of " gainfully employed " prior to 1940, and the estimates of the total labor force as defined in the 1940 Census included:

(a) *Seasonal workers:* Prior to 1940, if seasonal workers reported an occupation they were included in the labor force. But after 1940, if the seasonal worker was not working and not seeking a job, he was not counted as either being unemployed or employed. He was not counted as part of the labor force.

(b) *New workers:* Persons without previous work experience, but seeking work during the census week were counted as part of the labor force (with unemployed status) in 1940; prior to that time, such persons were probably for the most part not counted as gainful workers.

(c) *Retired and disabled persons:* Prior to 1940, if such persons reported their former occupation, even though unemployed, they were usually counted as " gainful workers." With the 1940 census persons unable to work and retired workers no longer working or seeking work were excluded from the labor force, *viz.*, counted neither as employed nor unemployed.

(d) *Inmates of institutions:* In the 1940 census all inmates of penal and mental institutions and homes for the aged, infirm and needy were excluded from the labor force, regardless of their activity during the census week. In previous census inmates of these institutions were reported as gainful workers if they performed regular work in the institutions.

Historical Statistics of the United States: 1789–1945 (Washington, D.C., U.S. Department of Commerce, Bureau of the Census, 1946), p. 55.

[37] Louis Levine, "Adaptations of the Unemployment Concept," *Review of Economics and Statistics*, Vol. XXXII, No. 1 (February, 1950), p. 65.

the reason that they have not been seeking work. The aggregate figure does not reflect the part-time work carried on by workers who would prefer to work full time. It does not classify the worker as unemployed if he has done any work in the survey period, even though he may have given up his job and be searching for work at the time he is interviewed by the Census Bureau.

The most commonly cited data on labor force growth and the volume of unemployment and its characteristics are contained in the *Monthly Report on the Labor Force*. The data for September, 1956, are provided in Table 21. The definitions of the categories are important, for they explain

TABLE 21　Current Population Reports of the Labor Force

Employment Status: September 9–15, 1956	Thousands of persons 14 years of age and over
Total noninstitutional population	119,047
Total labor force including Armed Forces	70,896
Civilian labor force	68,069
Employed	66,071
Agriculture	7,388
Male	5,490
Female	1,898
Nonagricultural industries	58,683
Male	39,056
Female	19,627
Unemployed	1,998
Male	1,152
Female	847
Not in labor force	48,151

Source: Bureau of the Census, Series P–57, No. 171 (Washington, D.C., Department of Commerce, October, 1956), p. 1.

in large part the behavior of the data included in each category. Let us briefly review those concepts utilized by the Census Bureau in developing such data.

Employed. Employed persons represent those who, during each month's survey week are (1) " at work " — who did any work for pay or profit, or worked without pay for 15 hours or more on a family farm or business, (2) were not looking for work but had a job or business from which they were temporarily absent because of vacation, illness, industrial dispute, bad weather, or layoff with definite instructions to return to work within 30 days of layoff. Also included are persons who had new jobs but had not yet started to work.

The Unemployed. Unemployed persons include those who did not work at all during the survey week and who were looking for work. Also included as unemployed are persons who would have been looking for work except that (1) they were temporarily ill, (2) they expected to return to a job from which they had been laid off for an indefinite period, or (3) they believed no work was available in their line of work in the community.

By combining both those who are classified as unemployed, and those who are " employed " the Census develops its concept of " the civilian labor force." To secure the total labor force, figures on the net strength of the armed forces are added to the civilian labor force. By such method, all persons over 14 who are neither employed nor unemployed by the above definitions are not in the labor force. This group largely consists of persons engaged at home doing housework, young infants, persons in school, retired persons, those permanently unable or too old to work, seasonal workers for whom the survey week fell in an " off " season, and the voluntarily idle. Persons doing only incidental unpaid family work (less than 15 hours) are also classified as not in the labor force.[38]

The census breakdown of the numbers of hours worked provides vital information for those who are concerned about the potential expansion of labor output by expanding part-time employment into full-time employment. The present methods for calculating unemployment are " operational " in the sense that they minimize the difficulties related to the state of mind of the person replying to the questionnaire. As it is, unless individuals volunteer the information that they are really active job seekers, they are not considered part of the labor force. It is not a regular practice for the Census Bureau to ask the so-called " inactive " job seekers why they were not looking for work during the survey week. " It is felt, however, that such an inquiry would lead some people who actually are not in the labor force to rationalize their status in such a way that the enumerators would register them as unemployed workers, and that the resultant overstatement would be greater than the understatement resulting from the present approach." [39]

As a case in point of the statistical hazards in calculating unemployment data, the *Monthly Report of the Labor Force* is usually developed by an interview of 25,000 households throughout the country each month. In January, 1954, the sample of the usual 25,000 households was made in 68 areas covering 123 counties, producing an estimate of 2,359,000 unemployed. At that time the Census Bureau decided to cross-check these sample results with a second survey also covering 25,000 households, but spread over 230 areas containing 450 counties. This second sample indicated that unemployment was around 3,087,000 or an increase of 700,000 over the first estimate. Needless to say, when rising unemployment be-

[38] Definitions derived from *Historical Statistics of the United States: 1789–1945, op. cit.*, p. 56.

[39] Woytinsky and Associates, *op. cit.*, p. 400.

comes a vital issue, the accuracy of the data is important, and news of conflicting data in 1954 sparked considerable controversy about the " actual " as opposed to " estimated " levels of unemployment.[40]

An alternative for determining the trends of unemployment is to survey the aggregate of state unemployment insurance records. These data, which are available from July, 1945, provide an excellent basis for determining the geographical incidence of unemployment and the changes in the employment situation as reflected by the number of new claims being filed with the state agencies. However, the total of unemployed listed by the Bureau of Employment Security is generally less than the total listed by the *Monthly Report on the Labor Force.* This is just as one would expect, for unemployment insurance does not cover agricultural workers, government workers, the self-employed, employees of nonprofit organizations, and in many states, employees of small firms. In addition, a person who has never had any occupational experience does not qualify for unemployment insurance, but he would be counted as unemployed by Census definitions of unemployed. Furthermore, the eligibility requirements and interpretations of various state unemployment plans differ, so that the uneven screening of applicants for relief from state to state is likely to deprive some of unemployment benefits who would be classified as unemployed by the census. And, of course, benefits may be exhausted and claims no longer filed even though the unemployment may continue. Unemployment compensation data are made up of reports from the various state unemployment compensation systems, veterans' unemployment compensation, and the railroad unemployment program. These data may include persons who are claiming partial benefits, and these would be excluded from the census definition of unemployed.[41]

The Personal Incidence of Unemployment

Just as unemployment does not develop uniformly from region to region, so is its incidence not equally absorbed from person to person. We must be cautious of slipping into the circular reasoning that only " marginal " workers tend to become unemployed. In a technical sense, the marginal worker is usually thought to be that employee whose efficiency or value productivity does not warrant his employment at prevailing

[40] For discussion, see "Why Unemployment Estimates Don't Jibe," *Union Labor Report* (March 5, 1954), Part 2. As of May, 1956, the Census surveys 330 areas comprising 638 counties and cities with approximately 35,000 households interviewed each month.

[41] For further discussion see Thomas C. Fichandler, "Unemployment: Its Composition and Measurement," Chapter 32, pp. 400–402, in Woytinsky and Associates, *op. cit.;* Gertrude Bancroft: "The Census Bureau Estimates of Unemployment," *Review of Economics and Statistics,* Vol. 32, No. 1 (February, 1950), pp. 59–65; and Virginia Kyner, "Total Insured Unemployment Estimates: A Criticism," *Review of Economics and Statistics,* Vol. XXXII, p. 4 (November, 1951).

wages. By this standard all unemployed workers are marginal, and by such reasoning one would have to say that in 1933, 13 million workers were " marginal " employees. As we shall see below, there is no compelling reason to believe that the unemployed worker is always the least efficient or inferior laborer.

For the post-World War II period it has been found that the proportion of women unemployed is generally larger than the proportion of male unemployed, although when unemployment increases, generally the unemployment ratio increased more sharply for male than female employees. This latter development may reflect the fact that as women lose their jobs, they withdraw from the labor force. In not actively seeking work, they are not counted as part of the labor force. Men, usually being the main breadearners, cannot so readily retire from the employment search, and thus the proportion of men searching for employment is likely to be higher than the proportion of women looking for jobs. The number of women entering and leaving the labor force is substantially greater than for men. But the fact that unemployment rates *on the average* tend to be higher for women suggests that employers may discriminate against female employees, especially those that are supplementing family income, giving preference instead to the long-term male employee with family responsibilities. Furthermore, women tend to be concentrated in such industries as food processing, apparel, retail trade, service and those semi-skilled occupations characterized with higher unemployment averages.

Age, too, is a factor in unemployment incidence, with the lowest proportion of male unemployed workers being in the central age group from 25 to 44, and relatively low averages also for the 45- to 54-year-old group. While unemployment increases for men over 45, the reverse is true for women. Indeed, the 45–54 female age group has had less unemployment than many other age groups, probably because women of this age are more likely to be the only breadwinner for families and less distracted with family responsibilities.

The young workers, from 14 to 17 years of age, also have a high incidence of unemployment. In 1955 this group represented some 9 million persons and will expand by 1965 to some 14 million. In 1955, 5.3 percent of the students in this group were looking for work and were unable to find it. But, significantly, 13.8 percent of this age group *not* attending school were unemployed. " Because of the possibility of juvenile delinquency among unemployed youths, especially those not attending school, the problem of unemployment for them cannot be measured in terms of economic implications alone." [42]

[42] Herman Travis, " The Structure of Unemployment in Recent Years," *Monthly Labor Review*, Vol. 79, No. 9 (September, 1956), p. 1035. Most of the data for this section are taken from his study. The second part of his analysis is contained in the October, 1956 issue of the *Monthly Labor Review*, pp. 1147–1151.

Unfortunately, racial minorities often suffer an unusually high incidence of unemployment. In 1948 it was estimated that the average unemployment rate for nonwhites was 5.2 percent or about two thirds higher than for the white workers.[43] In more recent estimates, the incidence of nonwhite unemployment (over 95 percent of whom are Negroes) " has typically been from 1.5 to 2.5 times greater than among whites. . . ." [44] In 1955 only 10 percent of the nation's population was nonwhite, but 20 percent of unemployment was accounted for by this group. Again, it might be reasoned that this incidence reflects the fact that the employment of this group is largely confined to industries traditionally having higher rates of unemployment. However, the fact that such persons are often unable to secure employment in trades other than those having intermittent employment is an unhappy commentary on existing prejudice.

Are Only the Least Efficient Workers Unemployed?

Behind the scenes of any discussion of unemployment is the question: Are not those who become unemployed the least efficient workers, and hence in a sense deserving of their plight? There can be no doubt that the majority of employees discharged for " cause " must accept responsibility for their status, but we must not indiscriminately lump together those discharged who refuse to work with those who can and want to work. Since the widespread unemployment of the thirties, the public attitude toward the unemployed has changed considerably, and there can be little doubt that the vast majority of the workers do not prefer enforced idleness to constructive employment. Several studies were undertaken in the thirties to determine the qualitative characteristics of the unemployed.

In Bakke's two-volume work, the conclusion is reached: ". . . out of our six years of attempts to find genuine cases of refusal of jobs with any claim to minimum standards, we have developed a thorough conviction that this state of affairs is so unusual as to be of no real concern for public administration." [45] Few cases were found of workers refusing employment when the employment opportunity was available. Bakke refers to John Smith's admonition to colonial settlers to work:

> I should like to see John Smith lecture a group of men at the employment office in 1940 on " the duty to work." His seventeenth century armour might protect him from physical violence. It would not protect him from the realization that the wrong text had been chosen for the occasion. I have heard sermons on the text preached in drawing rooms, but not at the employment offices or at the factory

[43] For discussion, see "Recent Unemployment Trends" *Monthly Labor Review,* Vol. 70, No. 5 (May, 1950), pp. 485–496.

[44] Travis, *op. cit.,* p. 1036.

[45] *Op. cit.,* Vol. I, p. 369.

gates. The problem for the unemployed gathered there is focused in no unwillingness on their part to fulfill that duty. It is focused in the inability of business and industrial management to offer jobs.[46]

In a more limited study by Ewan Clague and Webster Powell, *Ten Thousand Out of Work*, the writers concluded that:

The great majority of these men [who are unemployed] were by no means marginal workers who would be the first to be laid off and the last to be hired. On the contrary, there is much evidence that they were quite representative of industrial workers generally in stability and earning capacity. Their previous records indicate that, by and large, they had definitely made good as workmen. The trouble was, that they, and perhaps their employers, were engulfed in an economic disaster of the first magnitude, a disaster too great for any individual action to be effective. Under such circumstances no blanket charge of personal responsibility can be laid against these workers.[47]

[46] *Ibid.*, p. 387.
[47] Community Council of Philadelphia (Philadelphia, University of Pennsylvania Press, 1933), p. 26. For similar references in this study see pages 25, 42, 78, and 79.

23

Keynesianism: A New
Philosophy for Labor

The rising tide of unemployment in the thirties paralleled the rising tide of criticism of classical and neoclassical wage theory. In this chapter we shall survey some of these major criticisms, briefly recapitulate the contributions of John Maynard Keynes to wage and employment theory, and review some of the shortcomings of wage policy as an anti-cyclical device.

A Summary of the Classical Position

The frame of reference for conservative wage theory was the marginal productivity theory of distribution. As our discussion in Chapter 21 revealed, changes in total production can, if capital and the other factors are kept constant, be related to changes in the labor input. The change in the value of total production is labor's marginal value productivity, and this represents the employer's demand for labor. We also noted that the productivity of labor is, in a very real sense, determined by the size of the existing stock of the "other" cooperating factors of production. In Figure 19 we have compared two total production functions for labor. In Section A labor employment is expanded with a very limited stock of capital. The consequence of this capital scarcity is reflected in the sagging slope of the total production curve. By contrast, in Section B of Figure 19 a substantial stock of capital exists. Because capital is relatively abundant, the employment of additional workers does not cause the principle of diminishing returns to come into operation so quickly: the total production curve can soar to new heights before the bottleneck of capital drags down the increase of total production. The implications of this comparison are most important for labor, for if the demand for labor is derived from labor's incremental production, the demand for labor in Case B will be much stronger than it is in Case A. This can be seen in the lower part of Figure 19 where we have drawn the demand curve for labor derived from total production functions in both A and B.

FIGURE 19. The Effect of Capital Scarcity on the Demand for Labor

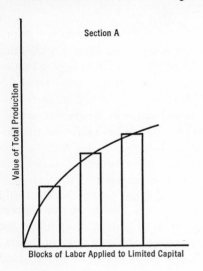

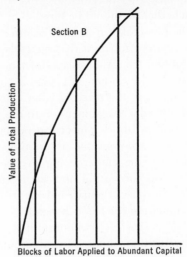

The Demand Schedules for Labor Derived from the Above Production Functions

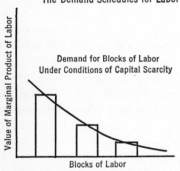

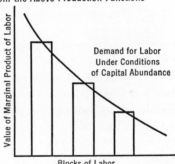

The analysis reveals that the position and elasticity of the demand for labor depend on the availability of the cooperating factors of production. Furthermore, in the classical view there was no reason to believe that substantially large increments of capital could suddenly be made available to labor, and hence there was no reason to believe that labor demand could be substantially or suddenly increased. In summary, the demand for labor depends on the productivity of labor. The productivity of labor depends on the availability of capital. The availability of capital depends on the availability of savings for the investment process. And the availability of such savings depends on the extent to which society can or will collectively abstain from consumption.

The above analysis abstracts, for the most part, from one vital consideration: changes in the *price* of labor's physical productivity. It can be readily appreciated that the incremental labor cost must be weighed against the incremental *value* of the additional worker in determining whether he should be hired. This value of labor productivity reflects both the physical output and the price of that output. In the thirties it was immediately apparent that the collapse of the demand for labor did not arise initially from the collapse of labor productivity (or even from the reduction in the amount of capital available for labor's use) but rather from the collapse in the *price* of labor's output. This sharp reduction in prices introduced a new dimension to the wage problem, for in the thirties any increase in labor's physical productivity seemed only to aggravate the decline in labor's value productivity. In some industries it was necessary to destroy the embarrassing excess of production in order to sustain the demand for output and for labor. What then becomes of the marginal productivity theory and its traditional stress on productivity as the foundation for labor demand?

The classical economists had reasoned that, in a barter economy, the greater the volume of production, the greater then was the buying power of the population in exchanging goods for goods. While certain items might be overproduced, it was impossible to overproduce all goods, for all goods represented, in effect, the demand for all goods. In a money economy the argument became somewhat more complicated, but it was still true that the factor costs in producing goods represented the buying power for those goods. Thus, a natural balance was maintained between those expenditures made by industry in order to produce goods, and those expenditures made by the public in order to consume goods.[1]

But was it not possible that the public may vary its total expenditures, especially if its income was sufficiently high so that it could "afford" not to spend all its current income? If the money not expended does not immediately re-enter into circulation, it is then apparent that the smaller volume of money in the expenditure stream must do the work of the previously larger amount. This is only possible if industry reduces the prices for the products it offers, and price reductions are only possible if costs — and particularly wages — are as flexible as prices. Variations in

---

[1] While such reasoning may appear in error or at best, unrealistic, its impact on economic thinking should not be discounted. For example the contemporary disciple of full-employment policies, William Beveridge, explained in his 1909 analysis of the problems of unemployment that "A rising demand for labour will be no cure for unemployment. . . . It is not a problem of securing a general balance between the growth of the demand for labour and the growth of the supply — for this balance is already secured by economic forces — but one of perfecting the adjustment in detail. . . . All history shows that a rising demand for labour is no cure for unemployment." Beveridge explained, in effect, that "over-production of any one particular thing is possible and not uncommon. Over-production of all things in life is, strictly speaking, an impossibility. The satisfaction of one need is followed by the immediate growth of another; the standard of comfort can and does rise indefinitely." From his study, *Unemployment: A Problem of Industry,* 3d ed. (London, Longmans, Green & Co., 1912), pp. 1, 193.

total spending need not result in variations in total production or employ-ment as long as prices, costs, and wages are responsive to the changing pattern of spending. During the nineteenth century classical economists could not believe that the decision " not to consume " would ever reduce the total level of spending. However, when wholesale interruptions in the circuit flow of spending became a reality in the thirties, classical econo-mists were thrown back on a second line of defense: price and cost flexi-bility that paced the variations of spending could solve the problem of depression.

The diagnosis of the classical solution to unemployment leads inevi-tably, then, to an appraisal of the presumed benefits that arise from wage reductions. Let us briefly sample some of the major elements in the con-troversy as it developed in the thirties.

Lower Wages and Price Policy

Within the framework of the marginal productivity theory, unemploy-ment arises because of an imbalance in the cost-price structure, and, as we have suggested above, the expansion of unemployment in the thirties arose because of the collapse of labor's *value* productivity schedule (or labor demand). Can wage cuts eliminate unemployment? Several possible price repercussions may develop from a money wage cut. First, if money wages are reduced, and if the nonwage earners do not increase their spending to fill in the gap caused by the reduction of labor spending, the price level will be reduced by the amount of the wage cut. Therefore, wage and price relations may be relatively stabilized at a new low level, with no stimulus to employment.[2]

A second difficulty is that one wage reduction may set in motion a pat-tern of expectations of subsequent wage reductions. To the extent that wage cuts reflect themselves in price cuts, both consumers and employers may defer present consumption and employment until prices and wages have reached their " lowest " level. Such expectations represent a serious obstacle to present employment expansion.

Thirdly, if prices do decrease in proportion to the wage cut, not all money incomes decline together. For example, price cuts will result in an increase of bondholder real income at the expense of the business enter-prise. As E. M. Bernstein stated, " if bondholders and stockholders are on

[2] This point is made by R. F. Harrod "Professor Pigou's Theory of Unemploy-ment," *Economic Journal* (1934), pp. 19–32, note p. 23. He explained that there was no compelling reason why the nonwage earners should increase their consumption simply because money wages were reduced. "But if they do not . . . [expand con-sumption] prices will fall by as much as prime costs; they will have no unspent income left over and they will have no subsequent stimulus to expand production." As we shall shortly see, Keynes was to make considerable capital of the notion that price adjustments may follow (or even exceed) money wage reductions in his attack on the classical system.

the whole equally wealthy and equally disposed toward spending and saving, a shift in income from one group to the other would have little or no effect on consumption . . . and the volume of employment after the reduction in wage rates would have to remain at the same level as before." [3] The ultimate effect of the wage and price adjustments will depend on the relative pattern of money income adjustments, or more specifically on the propensity to spend of those whose real income has increased compared with the propensity to spend of those whose real income is reduced. [4]

But what if prices do not decline as much as wages? Is it not possible that the imperfectly competitive or oligopolistic industries might resist price cutting? Might not there be a certain time lag before the wage cuts are translated into a reduction of consumer demand, and might not such windfall profits stimulate investment and employment? [5] It is likely that the price structure cannot be sustained unless the increment of income falling to management is quickly spent. If management has a lower propensity to spend than labor, the redistribution of income in management's favor will reduce spending and cause price deflation, but many economists fear that there will be little motivation for management to increase its investment expenditures even though present labor costs are lower. " As a rule, the other [nonlabor] groups of the society will not begin to spend more until their income has risen, and this cannot occur until production has continued for some time at the old level after the reduction of wages." [6] It is clear that unless those groups enjoying higher real income increase their total expenditures, the consequence of the wage cut will be a decline in over-all spending. In summary, there is not much reason to believe that a stimulated demand will follow a reduction of wages. If prices drop as rapidly as wages, there may be no basic alteration of relative money and price relationships. And if prices do not drop so rapidly, there may be a weakening of motivations to expand investment at the very time when labor's purchasing power is reduced.

Lower Wages and the Interest Rate

The reduction of money wages cannot be isolated from other parts of the economy, particularly the effects this might have on the rate of inter-

[3] "Wage Rates, Investment and Employment," *Journal of Political Economy*, Vol. XLVII, No. 2 (1939), p. 222.

[4] For a discussion of the "opposing influences" on company sales created by a money wage cut, see Ronald E. Walker's analysis, "Wages Policy and Business Cycles," *International Labour Review* (November, 1938), p. 780.

[5] Jacob Viner points to such market imperfections as a basis for hoping that industry profits could be sustained following a wage reduction. See his discussion " Mr. Keynes on the Causes of Unemployment," *Quarterly Journal of Economics*, Vol. LI, No. 1 (November, 1936), p. 160–163.

[6] As explained by M. Mitnitzky, "Wage Policy Today and Tomorrow," *International Labour Review*, Vol. 32 (1935), pp. 358.

est and investment decisions. If prices are not reduced as much as wages are, the increase in savings that accrue to profit recipients would tend to exert a downward pressure on the interest rate and, other things being equal, would encourage a larger volume of investment. But the demand for investment funds is geared to the rate of expansion of consumption, and if the increase in the supply of venture capital is made available for the very reason that consumer demand is reduced, the stimulus to further investment, made possible by cheap money, may be swamped by the discouraging effect on investment caused by declining consumption. In other words, the investor's anticipation of future stream of income payments may be contracted because of present or anticipated declines of consumption. It would seem that, on balance, the position of the demand for investment funds is a more significant determinant of investment levels than the rate of interest.

In an early formulation of the neoclassical position wage cuts were analyzed in terms of the quantity theory of money. In the quantity theory, the total of expenditures MV (money quantity times its velocity) is equal to PT (prices times transactions). Any reduction of wages would involve a reduction of prices, but there was not any reason to believe that the total of money expenditures (MV) should for that reason decline. With price deflation, total money released from the support of traditional purchases was then available to purchase new goods and services. In other words, the price deflation would set in motion an expansion of T, or the total of goods and services for exchange. An expansion of employment followed.

The assumption of stable MV or total spending did not square with the reality of the depression and the argument was modified. With downward wage adjustments, it was then suggested that money income would fall more rapidly than the supply of money; this would increase the real value of liquid assets and would, in turn, serve to increase the real value of savings. With such an increase in real savings, the interest rate would be reduced. From this it was deduced that two stimulating developments would take place. To the extent that the interest rate decreased, more investments could be profitably undertaken. Demand for labor would thus be increased. And to the extent that interest rates went down, the motive for saving would be reduced, and hence the alternative use of funds for consumption would be stimulated. Again demand would be increased. Thus the deflationary force carried with it stabilizing or counter-deflationary forces. To recapitulate, with deflation the real value of existing money stocks is increased, and such appreciation of money's value stimulates investments (via reductions of the rate of interest) and increases consumption (because each dollar will buy more in the consumer market and because the rate of return for making funds available to the investment market is reduced).

How was this more sophisticated theory received? First, it was stressed that the purpose of wage reductions was basically to reduce the rate of interest *via* an increase in the supply of savings. But was not this a rather painful and devious device to reduce interest rates when the same effect might be much more easily achieved by an easy money policy? [7] Furthermore, could we be certain that the lowering of the rate of interest would ultimately reverse the impulse to save? It was presumed in classical theory that the tendency for the rate of interest to decline would "wipe out" any tendency for excess savings. But Keynes introduced the unhappy thought that as the rate of interest decreased, the public's willingness to keep funds idle might actually increase. A decision to reduce spending might not, therefore, increase the availability of funds in the investment market. Deflation may not encourage either additional investment or consumption.

To recapitulate the classical argument, if wages are decreased and prices also fall, there is a decrease in the need for cash to fulfill all the purposes for which money was previously used. Or alternatively, deflation increases the real value of existing money stocks, stimulating savings. This release of funds or appreciation in the value of money stocks leads to a fall in the rate of interest (*unless* it is offset by an increase in the liquidity preference of the public, or the desire of the public to remain as liquid as possible simply because it costs so little to be liquid). The lower rate of interest will stimulate investment (*unless* the prospect of falling prices has weakened the propensity to consume). In summarizing the hazards to this solution to unemployment, A. P. Lerner concludes: "If all the hurdles are crossed, wages keep on falling until full employment is reached. It is important to note that the reduction in the rate of interest is what does the trick. . . ." [8] Other writers referred to the " slender reed " that such a solution to unemployment represented and others to the weak links in the chain of interrelationships. Lawrence Klein also points out that to seek the alleviation of depression by reducing money wages rather than by directly reducing the rate of interest or otherwise encouraging investment or consumption is to abandon the high road for a devious, dark, difficult, and unreliable path.[9]

John Maynard Keynes: The General Attack on Classical Theory

In his brilliant book, the *General Theory of Employment, Interest and Money*, Keynes undertook a frontal attack on the whole structure of clas-

[7] As James Tobin explained, most Keynesians were unimpressed with this argument, indicating that "this shaky line of causation is the only channel through which wage policy can influence the volume of employment." "A Note on the Money Wage Problem," *Quarterly Journal of Economics* (May, 1941), No. 3, p. 508. For further discussion, see A. P. Lerner, "Ex ante Analysis and Wage Theory," *Economica* (November, 1939), p. 442.

[8] "The Relations of Wage Policies and Price Policies," *American Economic Review,* Vol. 29, No. 1, Supplement (March, 1939), p. 165.

[9] *The Keynesian Revolution* (New York, The Macmillan Co., 1947), p. 108–110.

sical reasoning. Keynes's basic proposition was that our society could rest in equilibrium *with* unemployment. If this proposition could be sustained, it had widespread implications for all society, for it would no longer be possible to argue that time would " cure " our economic problems or that there was much sense for society to continue to suffer mass unemployment while it waited for market forces automatically to absorb idle workers. Because of the seriousness of the problem of unemployment in the thirties, Keynes's new book became the growth cone for widespread discussion and criticism.

Keynesian analysis represented a mingling of wage, monetary, and fiscal considerations. The variability of private investment was seen as the trigger mechanism inducing larger fluctuations in total spending. This, in turn, caused fluctuations in the level of employment. While it is possible to construct an independent theory of underemployment equilibrium with reference to the capital market alone, we shall stress here the underemployment of labor arising from forces in the labor market. Of course, labor and capital markets are interrelated. High levels of unemployment in the labor market can be caused by inadequate investment in the capital market, just as the underutilization of capital in the investment market can cause inadequate employment in the labor market. Because of the twofold nature of the Keynes attack on the classical system, let us briefly review his analysis of the capital market — aspects of which have already been suggested in the above paragraphs — before turning to consideration of underemployment in the labor market.

Keynesian Analysis: The Case for Underemployment in the Capital Market

In Keynesian analysis the total level of employment is determined by the total level of spending, and this spending can be broken down into such components as consumption, investment, government, and foreign trade expenditures. Statistically, the percentage variation in private investment has been larger than consumer expenditure variations, and this has led economists to believe that the fluctuation of such private investment may trigger a business crisis and cause depression. The difficulty of maintaining continuously high levels of employment is then seen as the difficulty of maintaining high levels of stable private investment, and through this, adequate levels of total effective demand.

Within the Keynesian model, Keynes reasoned that as society became wealthier, the *proportion* of income that society would spend for consumer goods would diminish. This lag in the growth of consumption to income is called the " consumption function." If income is to increase in any period by $10 billion and consumption increases by $8 billion, the total level of spending (and hence employment) can only be maintained if the $2 billion not consumed finds some other outlet to the expenditure stream. We have noted that classical economists reasoned that all savings would be absorbed into investments, for any increment of savings would force the rate of interest down, making it profitable for investors to absorb these savings. But Keynes feared that during a time of crisis, society may attempt to hold money idle as insurance against the contingencies of the depression or for speculative purposes since money would appreciate in value during deflation. Unfortunately, holding money would also serve to prevent the interest rate from declining. The lower the rate of interest, the more reluctant will be the public to part with liquidity, for the income lost by staying liquid is reduced. Keynes feared that the attempt on the part of society to save more than it was willing to invest could easily act like a boomerang to reduce income. In effect, the decline of income would reduce society's ability to save more than it wished to invest. But more than this, it would reduce the level of employment.

What can be done then to encourage or stimulate private investment? Keynes felt that interest rates should be kept low, so as to give as much encouragement to investors as is possible with the availability of cheap funds. The demand for investment funds — which Keynes called the marginal efficiency (or productivity) of capital — reflects the investor's calculation of the prospects for future earnings from alternative investment prospects. If investors are highly pessimistic, the capital productivity function will obviously sink to very low levels and become inelastic; if they are optimistic about the future, this demand curve will shift to the right and stimulate private investment.

In his analysis of the investment market, Keynes comes close to holding hands with the underconsumption theory. The richer the society, the larger the margin of savings that accumulates. The larger, therefore, is the amount of investment that must be forthcoming if full employment is to be maintained. In effect, Keynes suggested that if we desire to maintain full employment at all times, it may be necessary for the government to supplement private investment by an amount necessary to provide adequate total effective demand. It is often suggested that if the wage earner is inclined to consume a higher proportion of new income received (*viz.*, has a high marginal propensity to consume) and the rich consume a small proportion of their new income (*viz.*, have a low marginal propensity to consume), it would be fruitful for the government to arrange a tax policy which would boost total consumption levels by taking income from the rich and giving it to the relatively poor. Keynes, however, cautioned against indiscriminate increases of consumption, especially at full employment, for these might slacken the pace of industrial development. Furthermore, because socialist agitation always existed because of the scarcity returns going to capital, the way to solve this problem was to make capital abundant, rather than make it scarce.

Keynes's stress on the importance of private investment follows the conservative tradition of the nineteenth century. He further accepted the conservative axiom that in the short run, investments could not be extended unless interest rates were decreased. But in spite of the conservative roots in Keynesian theory, there is much in his analysis that can serve the purpose of those who have ambitious plans for a modified form of capitalism. The argument that the economy would not necessarily provide us with full employment represents one of the most damaging criticisms of classical theory. With Keynesian economics now an important part of every elementary economics text, with Keynesianism becoming in a sense the new "orthodoxy," should the breadlines develop once again, the cause of the plight will be made clear and simple: "lack of effective demand arising probably from inadequate investment." The solution will be equally clear: government spending. It is not surprising that organized labor has had no difficulty in integrating its own economic philosophy to this explanation. Private investment does not decline because of the insufficiency of funds, but because of the lack of incentive to use those funds. Say's Law, "Supply is demand," has now become (if you will) Keynes's Law, "Demand is supply."

Keynesian Analysis: The Case for Underemployment in the Labor Market

We have noted the importance of marginal productivity theory in the employment constructions of classical theory, and Keynes developed his own labor market analysis within this same framework. If Keynes had denied the relevance of marginal productivity, his break with classical theory would have been complete. But he was intent on showing that, even granted the assumptions of productivity analysis, labor could not be certain that the reduction of money wages would provide it with higher levels of employment. It is also significant that Keynes, in this wage-employment context, was much more concerned with the cost effect of wage adjustments than he was with their income effect. This too reflects the conservative point of departure for his analysis, for essentially he was analysing employment determination from the employer's viewpoint.

In Figure 20, Section I, we have summarized the essential feature of classical wage theory discussed above. We see that if (a) money wages are reduced and if (b) prices are stable (or decline less rapidly than money wages), it then follows that after the wage reduction, the real wage rate (c), or the ratio of money wages to prices, is also reduced. On the assumption that the demand for labor is a function of this real wage rate, the level of employment (d) is increased. In Part B, Section I, the demand curve for labor is so drawn, indicating that the reduction of wages from E to F has caused the expansion of employment from G to H. We might also add that classical economists usually assumed that the de-

FIGURE 20

Section I: Classical Reasoning on Wage Cuts

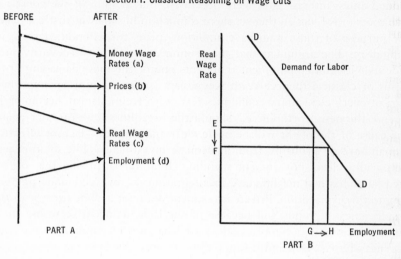

PART A

PART B

Section II: Keynes's Criticism of Classical Reasoning on Wage Cuts

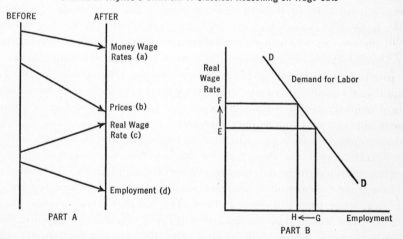

PART A

PART B

mand curve for labor was elastic, so that the wage bill, following a reduction of wages, is increased.

Keynes criticized such classical reasoning. He reasoned that under competitive conditions a reduction of wages would result in proportionate reductions of prices. In such a situation, the real wage rate (or again the ratio of wages to prices) would remain unchanged, and hence the labor cost remained unchanged. Therefore, the level of employment would be un-changed. But even more than this, Keynes guessed that a reduction of money wages might not be associated with constant real wages, but an *increasing* real wage. This situation could readily develop if the reduc-tion of money wages was associated with price cuts and was greater than the money wage cut. The struggle to lower money wages might intensify price deflation as strikes and industrial unrest develop and as employers anticipate a reduction of consumer demand. If prices do go down as rap-idly as wages, the alleged benefits of wage cuts are lost, at least as far as the real-wage employment relationship is concerned. And as can be seen in Section II of Figure 20 the situation becomes even more serious if prices go down more rapidly than wages.

By such reasoning labor can be *involuntarily* unemployed. No longer must all unemployment be voluntary, for in this case labor has lowered its money wage in order to secure a job only to find that its real cost to the employer has increased. Because the determinant of employment is the ratio of money wages to prices, and because labor has not any control over prices, labor has no direct control over the level of employment. Thus it could no longer be alleged that labor could be certain of securing employment by accepting a lower wage. The fault was in the flexible price structure rather than in the inflexible money wage structure.

The advantage of Keynes's hypothesis regarding inverse money and real wage movements was that it was "operational," *viz.*, it could be tested by a study of the direction of actual money and real wage move-ments. Several investigations were undertaken by economists, and these generally revealed that when money wages were increasing, it was likely (in two thirds of the cases) that real wages would also increase. In approx-imately one third of the cases real wages went down when money wages went up. Thus Keynes's guess regarding inverse money and real wage re-lationships was not completely supported. These survey results suggest that one might not be able to decrease real wages by increasing money wages, for, on balance, prices tend to lag behind the increase of money wages.

The most controversial side of this problem is whether a decrease in money wages is actually followed with a decrease or an increase in real wages or real labor costs. Here the evidence suggested that in 50 percent of the cases when money wages were decreased real wages were also de-creased. In the other 50 percent of the instances real wages increased. Again, Keynes "guess" of inverse relationships is not established. But is Keynes's case against money wage flexibility thereby destroyed? We think not, for if one is confronted with the solution to unemployment in downward wage cuts, and there is a fifty-fifty chance whether this will increase or decrease real wages (and decrease or increase employment), he hardly faces an attractive choice. If a pill promises either to cure the patient completely or kill him outright, it is not likely to be a remedy eagerly sought after or widely applied.

If the reduction of money wages was not a successful solution to the problem of unemployment, what was? Keynes felt that price relief for industry would be a more effective device for reducing cost pressure than the attempt to lower costs. We can now see why Keynesian economics has sometimes been branded as a reversion to mercantile theory. In Figure 21, we see that with stable wages (*a*) and with prices that are increasing (*b*), the real wage level (*c*) tends to decrease. Within the same marginal productivity demand curve used by classical theory, the lower real wage permits an expansion of employment. In this situation the ratio of money wage rates to prices is reduced. This means that (all other things being equal) the employer will increase his profits by expanding employment. As we see on the right-hand section of Figure 21, the decrease in the real wage rate (or ratio of money wages to prices) from *E* to *F* makes possible the expansion of employment from *G* to *H*.

FIGURE 21. Keynes's Solution for Unemployment

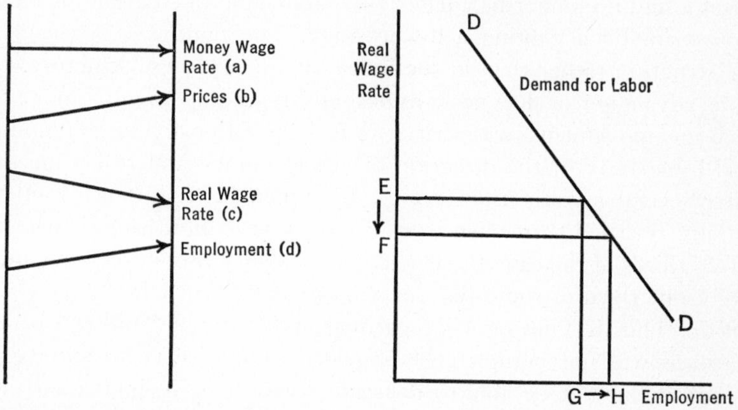

Several problems come to mind in attempting to appraise Keynes's solution to the problem of unemployment. First, it may seem perplexing to the individual worker to understand just why his real wage rate should be reduced in order that more workers be employed. It must be understood, however, that Keynes was speaking of only the "short run" where management was operating with fixed capital and fixed capacity. In this context, the employment of additional workers inevitably runs against the descending ceiling of diminishing physical productivity so that, *given this demand curve,* management cannot profitably expand employment unless real wages are reduced. If we assume that the plant capacity can be readily expanded so that the physical productivity schedule for labor can be shifted to the right, a declining real wage condition would not be a precondition for employment expansion. If such extension of capacity can be made rapidly, the short run is very short, and the need for lower real wage rates much less enduring.

Secondly, many have expressed the legitimate concern that an easy money policy or mild inflation may create problems just as difficult to solve as the problem of unemployment itself. The inflationary pressure arising from the expanding money supply becomes more serious as the economy approaches full employment. When the several studies of money wage and real wage movement revealed that they tended, more often than not, to move together, Keynes was willing to take the best of both worlds by suggesting that the expansion of employment and money wages need not necessarily be associated with dangerous inflation. If industry had widespread unused capacity, per unit costs of labor might be stabilized even while money wage rates are increasing. He wrote:

> In particular the warnings given, quite rightly, by D. H. Robertson of the dangers which may arise when we encourage or allow the activity of the system to advance too rapidly along the upward slopes of the marginal-cost curve towards the goal of full employment, can be more often neglected, for the time being at least, when the assumption which I have previously admitted [of inverse money and real wages] as normal and reasonable is abandoned.[10]

Wage Adjustments and the Income Effect

Thus far our analysis of wage adjustments has concentrated on the wage-price ratio as a determinant of the employer's employment decision, but wage changes involve an income effect as well as a cost effect. The cost effect relates to the cost impact of a wage change while the income effect relates to the change in the total wage bill (and hence labor's purchasing power) arising through the adjustment of the wage rate. The income effect is determined by the elasticity of the demand for labor. If labor demand is elastic, a wage reduction results in a substantial increase in labor employment. If the percentage increase in employment is greater than the percentage decline in wage rates, the wage bill is increased and total labor income is therefore increased. If labor demand has unit elasticity, the proportionate reduction of wages is matched with a proportionate increase in employment. The wage bill remains the same. If the labor demand is inelastic, the percentage reduction of wages is not matched by an equal percentage of employment expansion, and so the wage bill is reduced.

The significance of such income effects may better be understood by reference to Figure 22. Taking the original demand curve for labor as D_1D_1, the wage rate is reduced from A to B. The resulting expansion of employment from G to D does not pace the reduction of wages, and as a

---

[10] "Relative Movements of Real and Money Wages and Output," *Economic Journal*, Vol. XLIX, No. 193 (March, 1939), p. 45.

consequence the wage bill that labor receives is now smaller. The area of wage payments *BCDE* is now smaller than the original area of wage payments *AFGE*. However, on the basis of the favorable cost effect created by the wage reduction, employment is initially expanded. If it can be assumed that such demand elasticity characterizes the labor force, and that there has been a *general* wage reduction, it may be anticipated that total labor purchasing power will as a consequence be reduced. This may ultimately result in a decrease in the position of the demand schedule for labor from D_1D_1 to D_2D_2. It may then cause employment to decline from level *ED* to level *EJ*.

FIGURE 22. The Cost and Income Effect of a Wage Adjustment

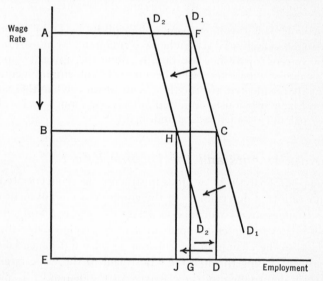

A moment's conjecture will suggest that if the demand for labor is generally elastic, general downward wage adjustments will increase the total purchasing power of labor. Employment will not only expand because of the original reduction of labor costs, but the reinforcing stimulus of expanding purchasing power may further extend labor employment.

Several limitations are inherent in this analysis. First, can a single employer always be certain that he will enjoy expanded markets because he alone has pursued a generous wage policy? When Henry Ford paid $5 a day, could he believe that his own workers would increase their purchases of Ford cars to absorb the cost incidence of the wage increase? This is doubtful. As Pigou suggests:

> Plainly the proportion of any ordinary worker's wage that he spends on the article made by the industry in which he is himself engaged is too small to allow this [income] effect to be other than negligible.

Broadly speaking, the rate of wages paid in any industry, *a fortiori* in any individual firm in an industry, has no effect on the money demand schedule for the commodity that the industry produces and, consequently, no effect on the derived money demand schedule for labour engaged in making it.[11]

One must be cautious, however, in pushing this inference too far: It is true that a favorable income effect produced in Industry A has a beneficial effect on every other industry, but the income effects produced in every other industry will have their beneficial effects on Industry A. In other words, the cost effect in each industry is " locked in " or tied to that industry, while the income effect is exported to all industry. From this it is clear that the cost effect of a wage adjustment in Plant A is more certain than its income effect. This is particularly true if every other firm is not following the pattern set by A, or if A is not following the pattern set by other industries. Thus, a vital distinction must be drawn between reasoning in the particular and reasoning in the general. It is true, as classical economists suggested, that if one takes an individual firm and assumes the demand for labor in that firm remains constant, a wage reduction (whatever the income effect) will often increase employment. But as Keynes pointed out, the constancy of the demand curve was the very issue that had to be resolved. Classical economists had eliminated the problem by simply making the assumption that for the individual firm the income effect must be negligible. However, what is true for the individual firm is not true for the total economy. Thus, the purchasing power theory is rooted in macro or aggregative analysis, in that it reasons that the income effect cannot be neglected because, for the economy as a whole, it is the most important determinant of the position of the demand curve for industry's output and labor's service.[12]

[11] *Lapses from Full Employment* (London, Macmillan & Co., 1945), p. 11.

[12] While it is not vital to our understanding of the labor market, there is some disagreement as to whether Keynes had intended to stress the favorable " income " benefits that might flow from wage increases, or the favorable " cost " benefits that might flow from price increases. On one hand, Arthur Smithies points out that Keynes in 1939 "explicitly repudiated the notion that employment must increase by a lowering of real wages and a movement along a declining so-called general demand curve for labor. In his view employment is increased by raising effective demand, thereby causing an upward *shift* in the demand curve for labor." (As stated in " Effective Demand and Employment," *New Economics* (New York, Alfred A. Knopf, 1947, p. 561). The opposing view is offered by Seymour E. Harris, who suggests that " supporters and detractors of Keynesian economics in the popular press find little support for high wage theories in the *General Theory*. ". . . Undoubtedly Keynes in 1946–7 would object to wage increases which were not related to rising productivity, although he looked with favor upon a rise in money wages in the United States which would tend to bring the supply and demand for dollars once more in equilibrium. Yet he had little to say in favour of rising wage rates; and, as has been noted, was critical of wage inflations which brought to an end expansion in the years 1500–1700." (" Keynes Attacks on Laissez Faire and Classical Economic and Wage Theory," *New Economics, op. cit.*, p. 541.) It is, of course, more important that we appreciate and

The conclusion that one reaches as to the ultimate effect of wage adjustments depends, unfortunately, upon whether one assumes that the demand for labor is elastic or inelastic, and whether the wage change is general or confined to one firm or industry. Table 22 indicates the cost and income effects that arise when the wage change is confined to a par-

TABLE 22   Income and Cost Effects of Wage Changes

Character of Wage Change	Direction of Wage Change	Cost Effect	Income Effect if	
			Labor Demand Elastic	Labor Demand Inelastic
General wage adjustment	Wage rates increased	Unfavorable	Unfavorable	Favorable
General wage adjustment	Wage rates decreased	Favorable	Favorable	Unfavorable
Particular wage adjustment	Wage rates increased	Unfavorable	Negligible	Negligible
Particular wage adjustment	Wage rates decreased	Favorable	Negligible	Negligible

ticular firm, or when it is general to the entire economy and whether demand is assumed to be elastic or inelastic. As we see above, the only occasion upon which wage increases have a favorable income effect (assuming other considerations constant) is when the demand for labor is inelastic and the wage concessions are general. This is the implied assumption of underconsumption or purchasing power reasoning. The classical case for wage reductions, on the other hand, is built on the assumption that if all wages are reduced, the favorable cost effect may be reinforced with a favorable income effect. But again, this will only be true if the demand for labor is elastic. It becomes clear how important the determination of demand elasticity is to these arguments and why underconsumptionists generally believed labor demand to be inelastic above existing wages and classical economists generally believed it to be elastic below existing wages. The labor demand schedule represents a series of *hypothetical* wage employment relationships, and it is unfortunate that such a schedule, which is so vital to the resolution of these issues in wage theory, is so difficult to quantify.

Wage Policy and the Depression

The background discussion of classical and Keynesian wage theories provides us with some basis for appraising the role of wage adjustments

---

understand the impact of wage adjustments both from the wages as cost and the wages as income point of view rather than resolve just what Keynes said or meant to say.

during a depression. Rather than attempt to recapitulate the essential features of alternative theories of the business cycle, we shall view wage adjustments during a depression with particular focus on the alleged advantages of increasing and decreasing wages at that time.

During a depression, prices, money wages, and employment decline. One of the factors contributing to the decline of demand is that unemployment, once created, may cause a cumulative spiral downward in purchasing power resulting in even more unemployment. Wages are not usually as flexible downward as prices, and the resulting imbalance in the cost price structure forces the contraction in the level of employment. Further, additional workers may elect to be unemployed because of declining earning opportunities, the intensified scramble for limited jobs, and the stiffening attitude of employers regarding labor's performance on the job. Some workers are unwillingly squeezed (and others permit themselves to be squeezed with only tacit resistance) out of the employed labor force.

Some will reason that in a depression wage stability serves as a floor under the depressive influence of prices and purchasing power. Such a wage policy imposes a limit on the pessimism of society by " building in " stability of both costs and income and thereby preventing further price declines. On the other hand, some believe that complete wage flexibility is the more intelligent wage policy to follow. If wages, rather than acting sluggishly to the price changes, are kept in proximate proportion to price adjustments, there is less danger of unemployment, and less danger of continuous deflation. Proportionality in wage-price adjustments prevents unemployment from developing.

A number of experiments have been undertaken in adjusting wage levels in an effort to minimize unemployment: " In Germany all wage rates were reduced by 10 per cent in 1931 by a decree of the Brüning government. In the United States under the New Deal the wage rate was increased suddenly in the spring of 1933 by approximately 20 per cent. In France too, the Popular Front government of Blum raised the money wage rate a number of times with sudden jumps." Ordinarily one would expect that sudden changes in wage rates would be associated with a direct effect on employment, but the Dutch econometrician, Jan Tinbergen, concludes that ". . . in none of these three cases could such a change be observed, and this fact would tend to support the belief that the total effect of changes in wage rates on the level of employment is not great." [13]

Most economists, as we noted earlier, are generally skeptical today that a policy of wage reductions will, especially as a single device, solve the problem of unemployment. However, there is still a case to be made about the problems created by wage rigidity. As the British economist, R. G. Hawtry once phrased it:

[13] *The Dynamics of Business Cycles* (Chicago, The University of Chicago Press, 1950), p. 309.

In a sense all the mischief of trade fluctuations arises from the tendency of changes in wages to lag behind changes in the value of
money. . . . If the working classes would accept an early reduction
of wages when a period of bad trade begins, and if the employers
would give an early increase of wages when a period of good trade
begins, not only would the harmful consequences of a trade fluctuation be avoided, but the fluctuation itself might even be prevented. . . .[14]

But another British economist, viewing the wage reductions taking place
in America in the thirties, doubted that such a policy was very effective.

No country has suffered more intensely from the depression than
the United States; and in no other country, and at no other time,
have such wholesale and drastic cuts been made in wages, salaries and
every element of money costs as were made in the United States between 1930 and 1933. The obvious moral of the American experience
is that a general lowering of wage rates serves to accentuate and per-
petuate the vicious circles of depression. . . .[15]

It is significant that the champion of the classical theory, Pigou, in his
memoir on Keynes, pointed out that one of Keynes's major contributions
to our understanding of economics was his criticism of the alleged benefits of wage reductions. As Pigou wrote:

While nobody could ever have formally argued that, because reduction in money wages in a particular industry usually increases employment there, *therefore* a reduction all around would usually
increase employment all around, nevertheless the possible indirect effects of wage cuts upon prices and incomes had certainly not received
adequate attention. Keynes brought this central and very important
matter to the forefront of discussion.[16]

Whatever the theoretical intricacies of the controversy, it is much more
the fashion to sidestep all the economic possibilities today, and point to
the practical impossibility of reducing wages. Unions are so determined
not to take the backward step that it would be nearly impossible for employers to demand or impose wholesale wage cuts. It would be inexpedient for any political authority to recommend that such a wage policy be
accepted by unions.[17]

[14] From *Good and Bad Trade*, 1913, pp. 265 and 266 and cited in A. G. Pool, *Wage
Policy in Relation to Industrial Fluctuations* (London), Macmillan & Co., 1938, p. 92.
[15] From H. D. Henderson's review of Lionel Robbins' *The Great Depression*, *Economic Journal*, Vol. XLV, No. 177 (March 1935), pp. 122, 123.
[16] *John Maynard Keynes* (Cambridge, Printed for King's College, 1949), p. 22.
[17] Writing on the responsibility of the economist to express convictions and all the
"uncomfortable possibilities" confronting society, D. H. Robertson has warned:
". . . I feel sure that if the economist is in too much of a hurry to pose as the complete man — too anxious to show that he is duly sensitive to 'the changed temper of

In summary, there are many theoretical as well as practical limitations to wage reductions as a solution to unemployment. Even the ultraconservative economist, Wilhelm Röpke, has acknowledged the possibility that in a secondary depression the demand for labor may be so inelastic that wage cuts will be of little value:

> In time of enormous mass unemployment, such as accompanies the secondary depression, the rigidity of the wage system can no longer be considered as one of the major causes of depression and unemployment. The elasticity of demand for labour has by then so much decreased that in many cases even a wage approaching zero would not restore the equilibrium of supply and demand on the labour market; cases of a negative wage even are not altogether inconceivable in a period like this.[18]

Pointing up the practical difficulties of wage cuts the ever-poetic John L. Lewis declared in the late thirties:

> All we need now in this country to encompass and insure a complete and most devastating economic, social and political debacle is to reduce the wage structure of this country. I hope that those in this country who are charged with the responsibility of leadership, both in the industrial field and in the financial world and in the area of statecraft, will not permit themselves to be lured to follow this economic will-of-the-wisp price slashing and wage reduction.[19]

Looking at the other side of the argument, it is argued that just as employers may not be able to clear the market of high-priced items, so it is true that workers can also price themselves out of the labor market. The

the age' and has taken full account of what is 'politically and psychologically possible,' he will be in danger of betraying his calling. Twenty-five years ago it needed some spirit on his part to develop the case for deficit financing as a remedy for trade depression without being prematurely silenced by the argument that it would scare the business man and so do more harm than good. Now the boot is on the other foot, and it takes some spirit to state clearly and fairly the case for wage reduction as a cure for unemployment or an adverse balance of payments, or the case for the curtailment of subsidies and the overhauling of social services as a solvent of inflationary pressure, without being prematurely silenced by the argument that nowadays the Trade Unions would never stand for such things. Perhaps they wouldn't; but that is no reason for not following the argument whithersoever it leads. But it is easier flogging dead horses than taming live ones; and some of those who display great retrospective gallantry against the fallacies and obscurantisms of yesterday seem to me somewhat over-hasty to make their peace with those of to-day." ("On Sticking to One's Last," *The Economic Journal*, Vol. LIX, No. 236, December, 1949, pp. 508–509.) Our point here is that Keynesian economics has undoubtedly changed in large part the climate of opinion regarding the efficacy of wage reductions in increasing employment. That fact alone, however, does not prove that either Keynes, or for that matter the general public, is necessarily correct in its belief.

[18] From his book, *Crises and Cycles*, p. 211 and cited by Pool, *Wage Policy in Relation to Industrial Fluctuation*, pp. 143–144.

[19] *The New York Times* (January 26, 1938).

difficulty is basically very simple. One economist presented the case simply:

> General unemployment is in reality to be explained almost in the same way as particular unemployment. In a particular unemployment, provided demand for its product is elastic, more persons can be employed if they will work for less remuneration. In all employments *taken together,* demand is indefinitely elastic, and consequently indefinite numbers can be employed if they do not ask for too high a remuneration. General unemployment appears when asking too much is a general phenomenon.[20]

Why should we develop separate values, one for the product market and quite another for the labor market? Can we allow sentiment to deny or obscure the actual application of the forces of supply and demand in the labor market when their impact is readily admitted in all other markets? The cost benefit enjoyed by employers is certain and immediate if wages are reduced. If prices are not lowered, employers should enjoy a windfall income and, with cost relief, have good reason for expanding employment and output. How else can employment be expanded if not through the optimism of the employer, and how else can optimism be provided if not through profits which the employer enjoys immediately himself? And even if prices are lowered, counterdeflationary forces are immediately set in motion: As Haberler explains the substance of our earlier discussion, ". . . with the fall in prices, existing money hoards rise in real value and, sooner or later, the point will be reached where even the most cautious individuals will find an irresistible temptation to stop hoarding and to dishoard." [21]

Thus, whatever the causes of changes in prices, if proportionality can be maintained in wages, there is less reason for unemployment. Stated in another way, the changing ratio of wages to industry prices may account for the changing ratio of unemployment. Indeed, the French economist, Jacques Rueff, took British quarterly data from 1919 to 1930 of the ratio of wage rates to wholesale prices and compared this to the percentage of insured workers who were unemployed. He found such a tight correlation in the two indexes that he felt he had discovered a new scientific law to explain changes in the level of employment. When the wage wholesale price index increased (reflecting cost pressure on employers), so did unemployment.[22] Was it not reasonable, therefore, to conclude that if sta-

[20] Edwin Cannan, *Economic Journal* (September, 1932), pp. 357–370 and cited by Z. Clark Dickinson, *Collective Wage Determination* (New York, Ronald Press, 1941), p. 355.

[21] *Prosperity and Depression* (Lake Success, New York, United Nations, 1946), p. 403.

[22] *Revue Politique et Parlementaire* (December 10, 1925) and *Revue d'Economie Politique*, Vol. 45, No. 2 (March–April, 1931), p. 211.

bility could be secured in the cost-price structure, so could stability be secured in the employment level?

We have already noted that by the late thirties such sentiment lost a great deal of its vogue, and it became more popular to conclude that if the cost-price structure should be stabilized, it would be much simpler (and probably much more effective) to control volatile prices than attempt adjustments in wages. Fiscal policy, in other words, became the more popular antidepression weapon rather than wage policy.

24

Labor in a
Full-Employment Economy

The case for automaticity and laissez faire was largely discredited by the dual influence of the great depression and the publication of Keynes's *General Theory*. In Chapter 22 we pointed out that the continuing experience of mass unemployment in the thirties created a mood for action. The *General Theory* confirmed what many had already intuitively sensed must be true. That Keynes — the student of Alfred Marshall and a respected academician within the camp of economic orthodoxy — should attempt such a daring and sweeping attack on classical theory reflected the disenchantment of even conservative economists with conservative theories.

Today the impact of Keynesianism is reflected in society's willingness to give the government the responsibility for maintaining high levels of employment. The revolution in our attitudes toward the role of government can be appreciated only when one remembers that in the early years of the depression the American Federation of Labor still opposed unemployment insurance as dangerous government intervention. Today, it is difficult to distinguish any basic difference in the economic philosophy of the Republican or Democratic party on this all important issue.[1] Certainly the conviction is firmly established that the luxury of employment security is one that will not be readily abandoned, and any government which attempts, in the face of mass unemployment, to return to individu-

---

[1] In John K. Galbraith's essay, *Economics and the Art of Controversy* (New Brunswick, N. J., Rutgers University Press, 1955), Professor Galbraith supports this thesis. For example Thomas E. Dewey pointed out that " It must have been a very clumsy Republican who sought to make political capital out of the term 'welfare state'," and added, " Anyone who thinks an attack on the fundamental idea of security and welfare is appealing to the people is living in the middle ages." (P. 76.) And during the 1952 election campaign, General Eisenhower observed that things had now reached the point where "The government does everything but come in and wash the dishes for the housewife." Later, to the delight of all, he was able to produce a pamphlet of the U.S. Department of Agriculture which showed that the government actually advised the housewife on how to wash dishes. Galbraith points out that during the Republican administration, it is significant that no important welfare service has been withdrawn. " Even the pamphlet on how to wash dishes has enjoyed unprecedented popularity and has gone through several more editions." (P. 79.)

als the freedom to solve their own problems, would be committing political suicide. In the last two decades high employment has been correlated with an unprecedented advance of living standards, with an unusual degree of worker discretion in selecting suitable job opportunities, with vertical mobility within the labor force, with home ownership, and with advanced educational and training opportunities to working-class families. The social and psychological adjustments conditioned by this happy state of affairs cannot be jeopardized without immediate repercussions.

There are further reasons for anticipating that high employment will generally characterize our economic future. The needs for additional production are impressive: The more determined is the drive of pressure groups for " more " (drives, we shall see, made more effective by full employment), the more important it is that production expand rapidly to cushion these demands. We can hope that the expanding demand can be paced with the expanding supply only if we continue to fully utilize our resources. In addition, the conflict between communism and capitalism creates further pressures for high employment. The necessity to divert a portion of our national output for defense purposes — and the reluctance of our population to absorb the costs of such defense preparations — indicates that the burden will be less serious the larger is the national income that can be taxed for such purposes. Furthermore, the ideological conflict involves a contest between two alternative methods of economic organization. The contest requires that capitalism perform to capacity.

While it is tempting to catalog the many advantages that arise from high employment (and neglect the several problems this condition creates), in this chapter we shall focus our attention on problems. However, our problem-oriented discussion should not obscure the impressive merits of high employment.

The Cost and Income Approach to Full Employment

In order to appreciate the implications of a full-employment policy, it is necessary to contemplate the question: " Do we want full employment at any cost? " Having looked at both orthodox and Keynesian approaches to this problem, we are in a position to compare the policy implications of each. In Figure 23 we have drawn a demand for labor D_1D_1 and indicated that the level of full employment is OC. Wage rate OA will give full employment. Let us now assume that a union negotiates a wage increase from OA to OE. Assuming a static demand curve, the level of employment is reduced from OC to OD. The question then confronting society is: What if anything, should be done to absorb the unemployed workers from D to C? The orthodox solution is apparent. If wages are again reduced to their competitive level OA, full employment is enjoyed.

In our previous chapters we have noted the political inexpediency of wage reductions. Unions, more often than not, exercise a veto power on wage cuts, and frequently this veto is taken for granted. But if wage rates are not to be reduced, what then is to become of the unemployed? [2]

FIGURE 23. The Effect of Wage Increases on Employment and Labor Supply

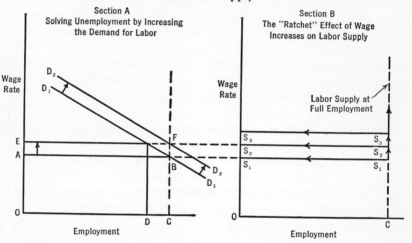

The alternative solution is a shift in the demand curve for labor from demand curve D_1D_1 to D_2D_2. Such a shift may be accomplished by fiscal and monetary policies designed to increase the aggregate of demand for the products that labor is producing, and through such policies, the demand for labor. In our example full employment is restored to level OC at the higher wage level OE. Most Keynesians are convinced that manipulating demand is a much more expedient and effective device for absorbing pockets of unemployment than manipulating supply.[3]

[2] If the union refused a wage reduction, classical economists will still argue that workers are voluntarily unemployed inasmuch as they have permitted their organization to price their services out of the market. The case for voluntary unemployment is less clearly established if the cost pressure arises because of an increase in minimum wage levels by the government. Institutional money wage rigidities still leave the worker exposed to the charge of voluntary unemployment as long as workers are able to change those institutional arrangements. The case is much less clear for legal arrangements which limit wage flexibility. For discussion, see William Fellner, *Monetary Policy and Full Employment* (Berkeley, University of California Press, 1946), pp. 4–5.

[3] While the argument that demand *can* be more readily manipulated than supply has generally won the day, even from such staunch defenders of the classical position as A. C. Pigou (see his *Lapses from Full Employment*, London, Macmillan & Co., 1945), there is not complete agreement that demand *should* be manipulated to absorb cost increases. The Austrian school today has clung tenaciously to the original view. Unemployment, to Hayek, Röpke, and Mises, is simply a symptom of maladjustments in the wage-price structure. The attempt to eliminate unemployment without correcting the underlying sources of the maladjustment is tantamount to denying that the fevered patient is ill by changing the scale on the temperature chart.

Many economists, not completely infected with the Keynesian fever, were a little suspicious of such a deceptively simple solution to unemployment problems for were we not, in a sense, cutting off one end of the blanket and sewing it on to the other in the hope that we would somehow end up with a longer blanket? Could labor actually benefit when the ultimate consequence of its ambitious wage demands was upward price adjustments? Before pointing to the essential " treadmill " nature of such wage and price adjustments it is important to appreciate that workers receiving inflationary wage concessions tend to gain more as wage earners than they stand to lose as consumers. As long as *all* prices do not pace the wage increase, the wage increase provides the pressure group with a substantial increment of real income. Labor cannot be easily discouraged from its drive to gain higher wages by raising the specter of inflation.

The popularity of an easy money policy as a solution to unemployment exposes society to the problem of secular inflation. Secular inflation is defined as the long-run trend of prices upward. This does not mean that prices will rise uniformly each year, or indeed that they must rise every year. When the demand for labor declines, the wage rate is often found to be rigid. In Figure 23, Section B, we see such labor cost structures related to the adjustment of demand adjustments in Section A. At wage level A in Section B the labor force is willing to work at the prevailing wage rate, but no worker is willing to work below this rate. Thus, the labor supply curve is horizontal just below the prevailing wage rate. As full employment is reached at point C, the labor supply curve becomes vertical.[4] Once wage level OE (as in Section B) is established, no worker is willing to work at any rate below this level. The labor supply curve has now shifted upward from horizontal position S_1S_1 to horizontal position S_2S_2. Again, the subsequent increase in the demand for labor at full employment will force wages up to a new level and the labor supply curve quickly adjusts itself to this rate. Wages increase when the demand for labor cuts the vertical portion of the labor supply curve, but the labor supply curve proves to be horizontal in the face of declining demand. In this setting reductions of labor demand do not result in wage reductions, but rather in reductions of employment. The expedient solution to the problem of unemployment is seen in " counterdeflationary " monetary and fiscal policies. The lack of symmetry in wage adjustments leads to the asymmetry in price adjustments. This " ratchet " effect leads to secular inflation.[5]

Before exploring more fully the problems of inflation, let us turn to some of the conceptual problems in defining full employment. We shall

[4] In reality, this curve is more likely to arch upward, becoming more vertical as employment is extended.

[5] This discussion owes much of its substance to Martin Bronfenbrenner's study, " Some Neglected Implications of Secular Inflation" pp. 31–58, in *Post-Keynesian Economics,* edited by Kenneth K. Kurihara (New Brunswick, N.J., Rutgers University Press, 1954).

observe that the inflationary pressure is often a function of the fullness of employment. This definitional problem cannot be neglected when the maintenance of high levels of employment has become an integral part of public policy. While politicians often retreat behind the " amiable wooliness " of full employment (undefined) the definitional problem is serious when unemployment increases. When have we failed to hit our full-employment target? We cannot answer this question if we do not know what or where the target is.

Defining Full Employment: Some Conceptual Difficulties

The term " full employment " is indeed a slippery concept. Some economists consider full employment to exist only when the number of jobs is larger than the number of workers to fill them. A less extreme definition describes full employment as that condition when the number of job openings and the number of workers are equal. In this case a margin of unemployment will always exist because of the ignorance of workers of job opportunities and because of the shifting of labor from job to job. A further definition is that full employment exists when unemployment is anywhere from 3 to 5 (or even 7 percent) of the labor force. Why should we have so many alternative definitions of full employment?

Conceptually full employment can involve the full utilization of all factors of production and not simply labor alone. While we are mainly concerned here with labor employment, it is clear that the full utilization of all resources may pose quite a different problem than the full utilization of the labor. Let us take the case where labor is in relative abundant supply compared to capital and other materials which may support that labor in employment. We have noted previously that the lack of balance in the availability of resources enormously complicates a full-employment program. In India, for example, there are more unemployed workers than there are job holders in the United States.[6] What does a full-employment program involve in that setting? Speaking of the problem of bottlenecks, M. Kalecki observed:

> If the maximum capacity of equipment is inadequate to the available labor, as will be the case in backward countries, the immediate achievement of full employment is clearly hopeless. If the reserve capacities are nonexistent or insufficient, to attempt to secure full employment in the short run may easily lead to inflationary tendencies on large sections of the economy because the structure of equipment does not necessarily match the structure of demand.[7]

[6] In India, the 1956 estimate of unemployment was 68 million. *Time* Magazine (May 28, 1956), p. 32.
[7] " Three Ways to Full Employment," from the *Economics of Full Employment* (Oxford, Oxford Institute of Statistics, Basil Blackwell, 1946), p. 43.

If capital should be the bottleneck in the production process as employment is fully utilized, the relative scarcity of capital would tend to divert income to capital. The production function for labor grows inelastic, and the pressure to extend labor employment involves a reduction of both the real wage rate and labor's distributive share. Because of this possibility, many of those economists who are the friends of labor have cautioned against overextending the drive for full labor utilization. Alvin Hansen has raised the question: "Is there something inherent in the cost-price structure under full employment conditions which produces abnormally high profits? If so, profits could not be tapped by trade-union demand. For such demands, if granted, could only raise both the cost curves and the demand curves, leaving profits largely unaffected." But abnormally high profits are unstable. In Hansen's mind, pressing for the complete utilization of the labor factor may lead to profit inflation and he therefore suggests that with a capital scarcity perhaps labor must choose between accepting high profits to capital or experience considerable unemployment.[8] However, the hazard of profit inflation is considerably reduced if labor is the bottleneck in the production process while capital exists in relatively abundant amounts. In other words, pressing for the full utilization of labor in India would undoubtedly have more destabilizing influence than pressing for full employment in America.

The definition of full employment often reflects the economic philosophy of the person making the definition, and many avoid the problem by simply speaking of the desirability of high, reasonable, or satisfactory levels of employment rather than of full employment.[9]

To appreciate the many facets that a definition of full employment involves, let us sample a few of the expressions of students in the employment field. William Beveridge says full employment exists only when there are always more vacant jobs than unemployed men: "It means that the jobs are at fair wages, of such a kind, and so located that the unemployed men can reasonably be expected to take them; it means, by consequence, that the normal lag between losing one job and finding another will be very short."[10] Edwin G. Nourse explains that "The optimum

[8] "The Cost Function and Full Employment," *American Economic Review*, Vol. 37, No. 4 (September, 1947), pp. 353, 564.

[9] A. P. Lerner, for example, is a little cynical about the motives management may have for tolerating something less than full employment. "To many this [reluctance to define full employment] has seemed to reflect a readiness of management to sacrifice the right of every worker to a job and even the greater profits of full employment, for the sake of maintaining 'factory discipline' by the threat of dismissal — a threat which would be much weakened if alternative jobs were too easy to find." From his "An Integrated Full Employment Policy," in *Planning and Paying for Full Employment*, edited by A. P. Lerner and Frank D. Graham (Princeton, Princeton Press, 1946), p. 187.

[10] *Full Employment in a Free Society* (New York, W. W. Norton and Co., 1945), p. 18.

employment is that level that gives all potential workers the opportunity of employment up to the point at which they value leisure more highly than further goods or services that could be purchased with their labor." [11] An early version of the Murray Full-Employment Act contained the following definition: " The term ' full employment ' means a condition in which the number of persons available to work, lacking work, and seeking work shall be substantially equivalent to the number of unfilled opportunities for productive work, at locally prevailing wages and working conditions for the type of job available and not below minimum standards required by law, and in which the amount of frictional unemployment, including seasonal and other transitional and temporary unemployment, is no greater than the minimum needed to preserve adequate flexibility in the economy." Russell Nixon and Paul Samuelson explain, " Employment is full when individuals work as much as they would be willing to work at a given real wage (or structure of real wages)." [12] The British Oxford Institute Study of the economics of full employment suggests that employment is full when " Everybody who wants to work can find it at established rates of pay. . . ." The British economist Joan Robinson defines full employment as that point at which every impediment on the side of labor to a rise in money wages finally gives way. To her, some point short of 100 percent utilization of the labor force is desirable because of the inflation this latter state will involve. " In general, it may be said that something appreciably short of full employment must be regarded as the optimum." [13] And finally, the British economist Nicholas Kaldor draws our attention once again to the uneven availability of resources as the economy travels toward full employment. Because there is no assurance that land, labor, or capital will exist in equal supply, " the point where the output of a particular industry becomes inelastic is the point where one of these factors is fully employed." [14]

The supply curve of labor, expressed in terms of money wage rates, is likely to be fairly horizontal until the zone of full employment is approached. That is to say, short of full employment there are likely to be more workers willing and able to work at the existing wage rate than there are jobs to be filled. A shift in the demand for labor is not likely to be met with immediate demands for wage increases, and unemployed workers can be easily persuaded to accept employment at " going rates." This suggests, in other words, that the unemployment of labor does not arise from an unwillingness of labor to work *at existing wage rates*, but sim-

[11] As quoted by Benoit Smullyan, " On the Meaning of Full Employment," *Review of Economics and Statistics* (1948), p. 129.

[12] " Estimates of Unemployment in the United States," *Review of Economic Statistics* (August, 1949), p. 102.

[13] From her *Essays in the Theory of Employment* (London, Macmillan & Co., 1937), p. 38.

[14] " Stability and Full Employment " *Economic Journal* (December, 1938), p. 643.

ply because that demand is insufficient to absorb total labor supply at existing rates.

Several quantitative difficulties arise in calculating unemployed data. There is a time lag involved in securing data on unemployment. One economist states that "The pattern of economic relationships is so complex, slow moving, and in some parts obscure, and the data themselves inevitably lag so far behind the events that a corner ordinarily cannot be recognized until several months after it has been turned. . . ." [15] In addition, regional unemployment often arises because of conditions peculiar to single areas so that monetary and fiscal devices available to the government may not solve the regional problem. In a statistical sense, the concept of full employment is a "family name for a whole brood of concepts," the father of which is likely to be statistical expediency rather than economic theory, social philosophy or even government policy.[16]

In summary, if the demand for labor is pushed to the point where it is always in excess of labor supply — to satisfy Beveridge's definition — we then face the continuing problem of labor scarcity. Of course, this does not seriously disturb every economist. Lerner puts the problem this way: "There are a number of minor discomforts which will arise in a full employment economy. It will not be so easy to get men to sweep the streets in case of sudden snow-fall . . . employers will speak of the difficulty of maintaining discipline . . . servants will be hard to get. The movement of people out of sweated industries will mean that some products, like pecan nuts, will seem unduly expensive. . . ." [17] The inconvenience to industry of an insufficient labor supply is hardly as serious a problem as the inconvenience to labor of not having any income. The more difficult problem is not, however, whether industry is inconvenienced — or whether we shall have pecan nuts on our ice cream — but whether we may have a tolerable degree of price stability with full employment.

Wage Pressures and Full Employment: The Cyclical View

Before returning to the problem of secular inflation, let us briefly survey those arguments which indicate that wage adjustments during the boom phase of business prosperity culminate in business crisis and depression. In other words, what substance is there in the argument that a plateau of prosperity could be enjoyed if the economy experienced only "proper" wage adjustments? As one might guess, there are as many viewpoints on this issue as there are theories of the cycle. Rather than at-

[15] Malcolm P. McNair, "Some Practical Questions About the Murray Bill," *Review of Economic Statistics*, Vol. XXVII, No. 3 (August, 1945), p. 114.

[16] For a critical review of the dangers of using employment data, see Clarence D. Long, "The Concept of Unemployment," *Quarterly Journal of Economics*, Vol. LVII, No. 1 (November, 1942), p. 29.

[17] *Op. cit.*, p. 219.

tempt to outline the role of wages during all phases of various cycle theories, we shall examine the role of wage changes during a period of full employment in three cycle theories.

Psychological Theories. Psychological theories of business crisis emphasize the importance of the climate of opinion. The collective state of mind is, of course, conditioned by an infinite variety of factors — some of them " real," or rooted in sound statistical data and actual business experience, and others " nonreal," or rooted in intuitive hunches or speculations. Unfortunately, the state of mind can be influenced by predictions or speculations not necessarily rooted in fact or experience. But whatever the outlook or state of mind, if it is generally accepted, it is likely to justify itself by actual business developments. If the conviction is established, for example, that unemployment is to increase, employers will probably act in such a way today as to realize that expectation. Similarly, if employers become optimistic (for whatever reason), such optimism is likely to result in an expansion of both production and employment and justify the expectation after the fact. In a strictly psychological sense, during a period of rising employment, optimism tends to become cumulative to the point where errors of optimism tend to feed on themselves. When optimism collapses, it gives birth to errors of pessimism.

Studies indicate that employers often show more concern with market prospects than their own wage adjustments when planning future production and employment. It is difficult to measure the psychological incidence on employers that wage increases represent, but it is likely that if a pattern or round of wage increases is developing, the employer will be reasonably certain of his ability to absorb his own cost increment with expanded sales. On the other hand, if a *single* employer is forced to make wage cost concessions, he may have little reason to believe that the market will absorb this cost. Such individual difficulties are not likely to cause a general recession. It must be admitted, however, that all general business decisions must operate through the psychology of the employer so that every business crisis must be viewed as a psychological phenomenon. It is difficult to assign wage increases alone as the primary cause of business recession, although it can operate with other factors (such as a tight money policy) to induce a contraction of business operations.

Underconsumption Theory. This theory is beautiful in its simplicity. All production is motivated by profits. Profit is related to sales, but inadequate purchasing power in the hands of the workers leads to a loss of markets, and in turn to a decrease in employment. Thus an economic crisis is triggered by inadequate consumption. This consumption lag may come about in a number of ways: If money wages lag behind substantial price increases, the real wage rates and buying power of workers and many others in society may be reduced. While windfall profits may temporarily excite further investment, the expansion of output is coincident with the decline of purchasing power. As markets turn sour by the excess production and sagging prices, investment expenditure joins the decline of consumption expenditure. It is this decline of spending — initially caused by the inability of wage earners to consume and followed by the unwillingness of employers to invest — that causes the depression. The rich (and employers) have the ability to spend but not always the desire; the poor (and wage earners) have the desire, but not always the ability. The distribution of income between wages and profits, between consumption and savings, determines whether both consumption and investment will be sustained. The underconsumptionist usually concludes: Look after wages and profits will look after themselves. It is not surprising that management usually supports a very different version of business cycle analysis.

Overinvestment Theories. Some versions of the overinvestment theory stress the " overconsumption " or " lack-of-saving " causes of crisis. It is usually argued that the capital structure can no longer be sustained during the end of the boom of economic prosperity because there has been an interruption of the flow in income supporting the capital structure. The crisis results in " overinvestment " caused by the inadequacy of income to support investments. The income stream supporting the capital structure is represented by the flow of profits, savings, or credit. What obstructs the flow of these revenues to industry?

Various writers emphasize different obstructions. One group explains that during the full employment of the boom phase of the business cycle, aggressive union demands result in higher wage rates. The pressure of these wage demands may reduce profit margins to the point where funds are inadequate to support and maintain the capital of the plant. When this occurs, less of the industrial capital is utilized, resulting in unemployment. The process of production becomes less " roundabout " in the sense that the production of consumer goods now involves less capital and the employment of less labor. The dilemma is created by the competition of consumption against investment or the competition of wages against savings and profits. The theory assumes that savings will automatically enter into investments and that the collapse of investment activity stems not from the lack of desire to invest, but rather from the lack of ability to invest. If it were not for the irresponsible and oppressive wage demands of labor, the difficulty or crisis need never arise.

A second group emphasizes the role of credit. When the banking system offers credit to satisfy business needs, the initial impact of such credit injections is an increase in the price structure. Since costs generally lag behind price increases (especially if there is considerable unemployment), this results in windfall profits. These in turn stimulate the demand for more credit. Paradoxical as it may seem, the banking system may have difficulty in refusing such demands for the banking system is established to meet the " legitimate " needs of business, and the underlying profit expansion justifies the granting of more credit. But satisfying the demand leads to even higher prices, even more windfall profits, and a more intense demand for credit. The cumulative process must eventually be broken for the inflationary pressures grow increasingly serious. When a tight rather than an easy credit policy is followed, private enterprise immediately loses the important source of funds for financing capital expansion. Throughout the boom phase of the cycle the economic process has grown more " roundabout," but this very expansion requires an increasing flow of funds for its support. The contraction of credit signals the withdrawal of such support and this in turn leads to the reduction of employment. Industrial expansion based on injections of credit are built on a shifting foundation, for the inevitable readjustments of credit policy lead to the crisis and the collapse of economic activity.

In both of these versions of the overinvestment theory, the crisis arises, not from the underconsumption of society but generally from its overconsumption; it arises not because of excess savings (reducing the circuit flow of money) but from inadequate savings. It is not unusual for business groups to point out that the drying up of venture capital, through wage pressures, tax pressures, or credit restrictions, threatens the dynamic growth process of American industry. In essence, the protection of the profit-savings-investment flow is claimed to be the best assurance we have for continued high levels of prosperity and full employment.

In summary, one group of theorists believes that the crisis arises because of a lack of venture capital, a lack of profits, and the burdens that union wage pressure impose on management. The other group argues that depressions arise because of excess savings, excess profits, and inadequate investment. It is the lag of consumption, arising because of the lag of wage rates, which undermines prosperity. At least one economist, Kenneth Boulding, has a sense of humor about the diametrically opposed conclusions that evolve from conflicting theories.

> If workers, low-paid, seek to better their lot
> By grabbing some dough from the rich,
> It makes jobs for more workers — or else it does not;
> I cannot be positive which.[18]

Full-Employment Wage Pressures and the Safety Valve of Inflation

Let us agree for the moment that full employment exists only when there are more jobs available for labor than there are workers to fill them. By this definition, we have a seller's market for labor. Let us also assume

[18] *Impact of the Union,* edited by David McCord Wright (New York, Harcourt, Brace and Co., 1951), p. 342.

that the government is determined to maintain full employment " at any cost." Under such circumstances the average worker is not motivated by the fear of being dismissed or fired, for he is likely to appreciate that he can readily secure employment elsewhere. If the impression is firmly established that high levels of employment will continue to characterize the future, this outlook may involve some rather drastic changes in the character and behavior of the labor market.

As we observed above, the stabilizing or equilibrating force on the labor market was the prospect that noncompetitive wages would produce unemployment. Unemployment represents the " gravitational " force which will drive wages back to their competitive level. What would be the consequences if, with ever higher wage adjustments, unemployment is not allowed to develop? Obviously, labor will be less inhibited in its wage demands. The most vital equilibrating force — the prospect of unemployment — is lost or greatly minimized. The classical standard for measuring the responsibility of wage demands no longer exists.[19] The major criticism of full-employment policy is not that it provides labor with the comfort of employment security, but only that such confidence will give rise to wage demands which exceed productivity. If the sum total of all demands (in money terms) exceeds the growth of the national product (in real terms) the imbalance can only be reconciled by an upward increase in the price level. While it is true that everyone cannot enjoy a larger slice of the national income pie when everyone approaches the pie with a larger knife, or that everyone cannot grow richer by picking each other's pockets, as long as the increment of money gains is not equally distributed, the prospects for redistributing the final product by pressure bargaining are fairly apparent.

It has been suggested that inflation represents a lubricant for such income demands and tends to obscure from pressure groups the incompatibilities of their total demands. Since it is apparent that not more than 100 percent of the final product can be distributed, the opportunity for increased money income may at least establish the illusion that having more money makes possible substantial increases of real income. If the government or central bank does not permit an expansion of the money supply to support the aggregate of pressure group demands, the consequence of the cost pressures will be unemployment. With a stable price structure the resistance of management to wage demands will become.more determined. Bargaining will take place in real terms, for the increase of labor's real income is likely to be at the expense of management's real profits. The awk-

---

[19] Of course, there is no reason to single out labor as the only group which might be rather uninhibited in pushing for more income in such a situation. All pressure groups, assured of employment security, are likely to exert greater pressure to enjoy higher income. We shall focus our attention on labor alone simply because labor's decisions have greater impact on the total economy than probably any other bargaining group.

ward realization of the impossibility of distributing more than has been produced can be obscured from all parties by the monetary veil of price increases. An easy money policy may contribute to industrial peace, but it is a peace that is, in a sense, being " bought " by inflation. The dilemma has been put in poetic form by Kenneth Boulding:

> We all (or nearly all) consent
> If wages rise by ten per cent
> It puts a choice before the nation
> Of unemployment or inflation.[20]

The Uneasy Triangle:

The difficulty of reconciling full employment with price stability can be presented in somewhat different form. Society has three desirable goals represented as (1) full employment, (2) price stability, and (3) free collective bargaining. But if, in a fully employed society, income tends to outstrip production, we may simultaneously enjoy only two of these desirable goals. What is the basis for such a conclusion? If we enjoy full employment and price stability, the only way that we can stabilize the price structure is through regulation of the bargaining process. A capitalist-oriented form of such regulation would be to control or even freeze wage levels and let prices find their competitive level; a socialist-oriented form of regulation would be to control or freeze prices and let wages find their level. Whether either or both prices or wages are regulated, such controls destroy the essential features of free collective bargaining. Such regulation can be tolerated during a war period or national emergency, but it is not likely that society would accept such controls as a permanent feature of a peacetime economy.

If we enjoy full employment and free collective bargaining, we sacrifice price stability. This again follows from the implication that wage demands will outstrip production, forcing ever-higher price levels. If, as the third alternative, we enjoy price stability and free collective bargaining, we suffer unemployment. This follows from the assumption that wage demands so narrow profit margins as to force employers to contract their labor force. Such analysis is rather pessimistic, for its logic implies the loss of one of the desirable and essential features of our economic life. But it is built on the basic and unresolved issue: Do wage and other income demands necessarily outstrip production growth? And if so, cannot we tread the narrow path — perhaps the razor's edge — between the chasm of unemployment on one side and that of inflation on the other? That is, cannot we view some optimum level of employment (or some minimum level of unemployment) which provides us with minimal inflation?

Such a hypothetical situation as the relationship of the fullness of employment (or the proportion of unemployment) to price inflation is

[20] *Op. cit.*, p. 79.

FIGURE 24. The Hypothetical Relationship of the "Fullness" of Employment to Annual Price Changes

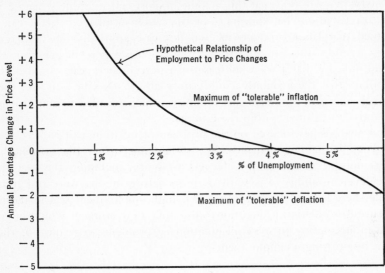

represented in Figure 24. The vertical scale measures the annual change in the price level, expressed as a percentage, while the horizontal scale measures the percentage of the work force unemployed. The line relating unemployment to inflation in Figure 24 is strictly hypothetical, but it suggests that the tighter the employment situation the greater the hazard of inflation. We may, as a society, establish what is considered to be a tolerable degree of inflation or deflation. We may arbitrarily decide a zone of stability exists when the price index increases or decreases no more than 2 percent each year. Assuming that a fairly precise functional relationship exists between inflation and the level of employment, it is possible to determine the "safe" degree of full employment. In our hypothetical case, we are assuming that when unemployment is less than 2 percent of the work force, we face the dangers of inflation. And when unemployment is larger than 6 percent, we face the problem of serious deflation. Study of historical employment price experience may reveal the relationship of employment levels to price instability, but of course it must be appreciated that what has been true for last year will not necessarily be true for next year. Institutions, productivity, and the economic climate change from year to year. It is for society as a whole to decide whether, say, a reduction in unemployment levels from 3 to 2 percent is "worth" an increase in the inflation from, say, 2 percent to 4 percent per year.

The substance of tolerable inflation varies from person to person. Those with fixed incomes could hardly appreciate the deteriorating of their living standards by as much as 2 percent per year. John M. Clark explains: " At 2 per cent annual inflation, a man who at age thirty contributes to a retirement contract destined to yield a stipulated income at age sixty-five will find that this income has lost half its value when he begins to receive it. That appears to be too much shrinkage." [21] If it can be assumed that labor productivity will increase approximately 2 percent per year, and if the safe limit to price inflation is 2 percent per year, this would indicate that a wage increase of 4 percent per year would be the maximum that the economy could safely absorb. Needless to say, there is hardly uniform optimism that unions can be persuaded to confine their demands (and gains) within these limits.

Our analysis has focused on the problem of inflation as it is " created " by group bargaining demands. We should not forget the existence of other multiple causes of price level instability, including the fact that price level instability was with us long before unions were organized. While there is logic in suggesting that high employment sets in motion pressures for inflation it does not follow that a government would be justified in attempting to solve all inflationary problems, regardless of their cause, by creating unemployment.

Some Implications of Secular Inflation

Not all economists are confident that governments will have the courage to resist the demands for easy money in the face of threatened or existing unemployment. The price structure, so the argument goes, must inevitably buckle in any democratic community because the majority of the populace will abandon neither their high employment nor their ambitious income drives. Reder has written of the " monetary totalitarianism " that may be necessary if all power blocs outside the monetary authority are destroyed in order to give force to a policy of price stability.[22] In a similar vein, Bronfenbrenner writes that the " Austrian " solution to instability — including unemployment, wage cuts, tight money, liquidation or " healthy bankruptcy " — is one that no democratic community will tolerate. " A Fascist revolution will be required to put ' Austrian ' economics into effect; a Socialist revolution may be the answer of labor and agriculture to the attempt to do so." [23]

To compound the pessimism, other economists have argued that price stability provides no guarantee that unions will desist in their demands for ever higher wages, and that even resulting unemployment will not deflect such demands. When J. M. Clark suggested that unions may voluntarily adopt a noninflationary wage policy, Milton Friedman replied: " I have

[21] *Impact of the Union, op. cit.,* p. 25.
[22] See his interesting study, " Theoretical Problems of a National Wage Policy," *Canadian Journal of Economics and Political Science,* Vol. 14 (February, 1948), p. 60.
[23] In *Post-Keynesian Economics, op. cit.,* p. 48.

no hope that unions can be persuaded to commit suicide deliberately." [24] The existence of unemployment in the coal industry, for example, has not discouraged the mine workers from pursuing vigorous wage demands, and similarly, the existence of general unemployment may not discourage wage drives. Indeed, those unionists imbued with a purchasing power or underconsumption philosophy will argue that even greater wage demands are necessary in order to " solve " the problem of growing unemployment.

If we live in an age of inflation, its repercussions are not always uniformly injurious. What are some of the alleged advantages of inflation? To the extent that price increases are not wage inspired but credit inspired, they can permit a more buoyant rate of economic growth. If credit is injected for investment rather than consumption purposes, this permits a redistribution of resources away from consumption to investment. If capital expansion is limited to voluntary savings, industrial growth may be limited. Credit injections leading to " forced savings " (or the forced reduction of consumption arising because of price inflation) can be justified in terms of the ultimate benefits of capital expansion.

A further advantage of inflation is that it generally stimulates spending. Such stimulation can, however, become dangerous, especially if the expectation is generally established that in the future price increases will not only continue but accelerate. Such expectations can trigger a rapid increase in the velocity of spending. Indeed, if one considers that the demand curve for labor and production is determined by existing prices as well as by the anticipated changes in future prices, demand is likely to be inflated with each *present* increase in prices. Price increases would then encourage more spending rather than less spending, and the dishoarding of funds (or the increase in the velocity of spending) can easily lead to serious inflation. But if inflation can be confined to modest increments, it can provide a gentle stimulus to production and employment.

Furthermore, inflation is likely to redirect income in the hands of those willing to undertake risk investments. Bond earnings decline, while speculative stock earnings increase. There may then be a more vigorous exploration of investment opportunities.

But inflation poses some genuine problems for society too. It has the effect of redistributing real income from those with relatively stable money incomes to those who are members of pressure groups. It reduces the *rentier* income, which can work a genuine hardship for those institutions relying on bond investments for their incomes. It reduces the living standard of old-age pensioners and all others who have a fixed money income. And, as we have already seen, while it may choke off any tendency to hoard money, such dishoarding may become cumulative, and lead to runaway inflation. As Lenin declared, the best way to destroy capitalism is to debauch the currency. Speaking on this same point, Keynes agreed

[24] See their discussion, *Impact of the Union, op. cit.*, particularly, p. 27, note.

and added that " The process [of inflation] engages all the hidden forces of economic law on the side of destruction, and does it in a manner which not one man in a million is able to diagnose." [25] When inflation arises through government deficits each pressure group within society usually blames the other for the price instability, and the government stands outside the circle of mutual recrimination. In effect, unions argue that they want wage increases to come out of excessively high profits. Management shifts the burden of wage increases to the public with higher prices. But management claims that price policies are no more responsible for inflation than rain can be said to be caused by wet streets. Cost increases have forced the price increases.

Union Wage Policy during Full Employment

Union officials and labor in general are often a little bewildered — and perhaps a little suspicious — of economists who reason that we should cling to the ideals of unfettered free enterprise during a period of unemployment, while in a period of full or over-full employment, they caution against the uninhibited application of union bargaining power. Responsibility of economic behavior then becomes the new by-word, and unfettered free competition is forgotten. Labor is thus confronted with the alternative " Heads you win, tails I lose." [26]

It should be appreciated that the union membership is not likely to be persuaded that the income it gains will necessarily deprive other labor groups of income. Even in a full-employment situation, the purchasing power doctrine is applied: The fear of overproduction can only be minimized by upward wage adjustments, and the responsibility to maintain prosperity by wage increases is even more urgent in a period of inflation. When this writer challenged a group of union stewards in the steel industry over the redistribution of income resulting from the steel union's wage demands, he was met with the not illogical suggestion that he (a) participate more actively in a teacher's union or (b) quit his job as a teacher and become a steel worker. But when reference was made to the fixed-income groups suffering from inflation, such as old-age pensioners (who could hardly organize an effective union), the union officials pointed out that the union movement, more than any other group, was attempting to bring to the public eye the hardships arising from inadequate social security laws. We must remember, too, that the union is not an agency created to educate the rank and file to the virtue of moderation in wage demands.

[25] As quoted by Bronfenbrenner, *op. cit.*, p. 31.
[26] For an excellent discussion of the rationale for trade union behavior, see H. W. Singer, " Wage Policy in Full Employment," *Economic Journal*, Vol. LVII, No. 228 (December, 1947), p. 440.

Union leadership has predicated the union's very existence on the argument that through union organization, labor can secure material gains which would not otherwise be possible. Wage increases, in the union parlance, do not fall from the sky like the gentle rain, but have to be extracted by the coercive and skillful bargaining power of unions. Bargaining is essentially a power play. But many supporters of full employment suggest that given full-employment guarantees, there is no need for such a power play. Indeed, such traditional bargaining can wreck a full-employment program: In Barbara Wootton's oft-quoted words, if full employment were to become a permanent reality it would:

> . . . be a change which would completely do away with bargaining in the present sense of a tussle of economic strength and wits and which would do violence to the fundamental *raison d'être* of the organizations which now make these bargains. Trade Unions and their counterparts on the employer's side, exist . . . to get all they can for their members. They would be turned upside down and inside out, if they renounced this function in favor of the task of helping to regulate wages and conditions of employment in such a way as to match labor supply with the requirements of public plans.[27]

The tradition of unionism and union leadership is one of negotiating a treaty through the effective application of bargaining power. Whether the union is dominated by autocratic leadership or is the model of democratic organization, the immediate interests of both leadership and membership reflect the demand for " more " rather than the demand for " moderation " and " restraint."

Furthermore, each individual union can hardly sense any personal responsibility for aggregate price movements when each separate wage increase represents only a microscopic segment of the total upward push on prices.[28] Fractionalized negotiations tend to obscure the cumulative effect of each individual wage and price adjustment. Some feel, therefore, that consolidating the bargaining process would facilitate responsible bargaining. Consolidated power centers could then observe and appreciate the consequences of their policies. Such consolidation, though, might not, in itself, solve the difficulties we are discussing. One economist states it thusly: " In the past, when the interests of different groups seemed to co-

[27] Barbara Wootton, *Freedom under Planning* (Chapel Hill, University of North Carolina, 1945), p. 113.

[28] Writing on the issue of wage policy, Arthur Ross stresses the difficulty of securing consent to any single wage policy: " How can thousands of separate wage settlements be coordinated? Under our present fractionalized collective bargaining system, this is impossible. Centralized organizations of unions and employers or a public wage control agency might do the job. If wage policy is to be geared into some overriding economic objective, substantial institutional changes will be necessary." From " Comments on the GM–UAW Wage Contract for 1948," *Review of Economics and Statistics*, Vol. XXXI, No. 1 (February, 1949), p. 6.

incide, wage bargaining was sectional. Now that the worker is told that higher wages for him means lower wages for the rest, he is asked to change over to a unified method of bargaining. Unite because your interests clash! " [29]

One danger of such consolidation is that each party may still disregard the consuming public or those nebulous concepts of public welfare. By surrendering in part the discipline of competition to the discipline of power blocs, the public may be more, rather than less vulnerable to abuse. Fritz Machlup has cautioned:

> Particular groups or personalities within the omnibus union would usurp the power and would wield it in their own interest. The likelihood would be too great that the leader of the omnibus union would promote himself to be the all-powerful leader of the union now known as the U. S. A. It is merely a toss up which is the shorter road to serfdom: this one union system of labor, constituting a government of labor by labor for labor, or the syndicalist system of strong industry unions independently and militantly exploiting the less strongly organized or unorganized workers and disrupting the economy through a series of paralyzing strikes.[30]

Integration of bargaining to implement a wage stabilization policy would represent a radical change in the nature of collective bargaining. National wage policy would still have to float on the "sea of external forces" peculiar to each region, each industry, firm, and union. Evolving a sensible national wage policy would be extremely difficult. As labor economist Joseph Shister has observed, "even if collective bargaining were conducted by separate industrial unions on a national basis, each union would still be too small a part of the total labor supply to take into account the direct and indirect effects of its wage policies on the national income and the consequences of variations in this income on its own members." [31]

There is, therefore, ample evidence for pessimism when one anticipates a completely new attitude in collective bargaining in a fully employed society, but there are, too, several reasons for optimism. First, with security of employment assured there would be less reason for restriction of output. Secondly, the continuing experience of prosperity will serve to mellow somewhat the militancy of both labor and management. Both parties will be anxious to appear as reasonable to the public, and the drive for public approval will inevitably require that each party reconcile its

[29] W. Singer, "Wage Policy in Full Employment," *op. cit.,* p. 442.
[30] Fritz Machlup, "Monopolistic Wage Determination as a Part of the General Problem of Monopoly," from *Wage Determination and the Economics of Liberalism* (Washington, D.C., Chamber of Commerce Report, 1947), p. 63.
[31] *Economics of the Labor Market* (Philadelphia, J. B. Lippincott Co., 1949), p. 533.

partisan demands more completely with the public's conception of its own welfare.

In conclusion, we must set against the abundance of advantages and satisfactions that full employment provides for labor and all society, the cold and hard difficulties this condition creates. We must soberly assess the feasibility of Beveridge's maxim that " Bargaining for wages must be responsible, looking not to the snatching of short sectional advantages, but to the permanent good of the community." [32] The success of such a policy depends on society's ability to agree on both the substance and means to that " permanent good " of the community. Full-employment supporters have rightly stressed the need for evolving some principle or formula that would be acceptable to labor, management, and the public. They have sincere faith that such an assignment is not beyond the wit or the wisdom of man.

In reality, we shall probably meet these difficulties by adopting flexible standards for spotting and controlling damaging inflation and damaging unemployment. Undoubtedly a modest degree of inflation is preferable to a high degree of unemployment, but it does not necessarily follow that we must have one or the other in the extreme. We may stride somewhat awkwardly with one foot in each world or zigzag between both hazards.

Any analysis of the problems created by continuing full employment must undoubtedly leave the student seriously pondering whether the benefits of full employment are worth the risks, whether we are not swapping one set of problems for another. There can be little doubt, however, that the fear and reality of unemployment has been the dominant force shaping policy and behavior in the labor market. It, in large part, accounts for the growth of unionism. Even today, it does much to explain the belligerence of unions who prepare endlessly their defense mechanisms against the next onslaught of declining business activity.

We speak rather glibly of freedom and of labor's right to employment without fully appreciating the content of correlative responsibilities. But certainly the fear of unemployment is one that is well worth attacking, for freedom in a society in which one's income is in constant jeopardy is certainly a perversion of the term. One economist contends that:

> The conception that freedom means the unrestricted opportunity to move in any direction or to stand still, as caprice may dictate, is a modern and calamitous delusion, the falsity of which can only be concealed by prosperity. A castaway on a desert island, hunting gull's eggs for his food would not count his freedom from interference as liberty.

Fortunately, in America labor's opportunities have not long been frustrated in this respect, for the abundance of resources and the flood of ma-

[32] Beveridge, *op. cit.*, p. 23.

terial wealth have created an economy in which freedom has real significance. However, it is a freedom that labor will constantly endeavor to increase, as it strives to reduce the possibility of any threat to that vital stream of money income so necessary for its dignity, and indeed for subsistence itself.

Epilogue

Many writers undoubtedly aspire to write an epilogue which provides the key to unlock the unsolved mysteries in previous chapters. And yet, as one grows increasingly aware of how limited our present understanding of our economy is, these few final pages often develop into a semi-philosophical treatise in which the author gingerly confides to the reader a few of his private values. Or, if it is suspected that those values may already be too apparent to the reader, the author may instead catalog those conclusions which are presumed to enjoy universal significance. However, even here further contemplation leads to a dwindling list of such immutable truths. A third alternative is to recapitulate some of the major unresolved issues analyzed in earlier chapters. This we shall undertake in the following pages.

Individuals cannot isolate themselves from the stream of life any more than they can disregard society's values. For the most part, we are not happy as " outsiders," and are usually anxious to integrate with the group, to bask in the warmth of public approval, to fulfill the expectations of those around us. Society may take notice of the nonconformist, but it seldom loves him.

Whatever foundations exist for the individual's need for a sense of relatedness, rootedness, a sense of identification, and integration with groups in this social and psychological dimension, the effectiveness of group action in the economic sphere is even more convincing. And it is this latter reality which provides the fulcrum around which every argument on the merit of labor organization must turn. The fact that group organization does not square with the norms of classical competitive theory produces one of the most important — and yet unresolved — issues of our time.

This is not to suggest that individualism has not made tremendous contributions to the advance of our material welfare, or that individualism as an ideology is dead today. Yesterday's Horatio Alger has become today's Cash McCall, and many still believe in the opportunity for self-made success. It is only when such ambitions are frustrated that the individual is prone to construct a new value-orientation to explain the reason why, after working for say ten years, he has not been promoted to the front office where his true potential could be realized. The rationale for the lack of advancement is not difficult to establish: the opportunities for success are not distributed equally. When environmental circumstances seem to limit the chance for such individual advancement, the motivation for overcoming obstacles is very much weakened.

It is in this context that the union idea evolves: The conviction is established that there are economic difficulties which cannot be successfully overcome with any but a group effort. Needless to say, the need for this " problem-solving " form of unionism varies inversely with the seriousness of the problems confronting the worker. There is, for example, less impelling reason for union organization in a high-employment situation. But conditions which exist today may not exist tomorrow, and the justification for union organization arises out of this uncertainty of the future. As we have previously noted, in a depression management may be willing but quite unable to sustain its enlightened personnel policies. Ironically, the survival of the fittest employer may involve the survival of that employer who is rather ruthless in his treatment of labor.

Related to the problem of pressure group organization is the philosophical issue of justifying the purposes of that group. Adam Smith provided the convincing rationale that what was good for each was usually good for all. This same axiom has been translated to read: What is good for the group must be good for the economy. Today we still cling rather desperately to this concept of enlightened self-interest as the justification for almost all our behavior. It must be remembered, however, that in the Smithian context, the consequence of this force was the expansion of total output. In a fully employed economy, however, the drive for " more " may result in the redistribution of a given product, rather than a rapid increase in its size. Such income redistribution that does arise has moral as well as economic implications. However, most economists attempt to skirt these moral implications in the name of maintaining a " neutral " or " scientific " approach to economic issues. Undoubtedly many of our best scientists still cling hopefully to the assumption that they can isolate themselves from the many serious moral problems of our time by maintaining that division of labor traditionally established in the study of moral and non-moral issues. But these same persons can (and on occasion do) offer intelligent moral pronouncements and allegiance to the scientific method should not inhibit their expressions of what " ought " to be. Such pronouncements should be more common and extended beyond the point where — to use the analogy given us by Lionel Robbins — the botanist is permitted to have views of his own on the layout of gardens. We can join with Robbins' statement that " Propositions involving the verb ' ought ' are different in kind from propositions involving the verb ' is.' " [1] But when he adds that ". . . it is difficult to see what possible good can be served by not keeping them separate or failing to recognize their essential difference," we reply that morality and scientific investigation cannot be safely compartmentalized.

[1] For discussion, see *An Essay on the Nature and Significance of Economic Science*, 2d ed. (New York, The Macmillan Co., 1940), pp. vii, ix, 150–151.

Because of the problems created by group organization, it is not surprising that the union movement is becoming a focal point for antimonopoly discussion. No longer is the union organization characterized by its fragility; it is a major force in contemporary society. Even though we have noted the difficulty of measuring the impact of that force, this should not obscure the fact that it is, nevertheless, a pervasive influence.

But we should not assign to the union movement all the major problems confronting society. First, many of the abuses which are imputed to the union movement are more properly imputed to human nature. In the great depression there can be little doubt that employers, trapped by circumstances beyond their control, shifted as best they could the burden of this plight to the worker himself. Workers went begging for jobs and literally " jumped through hoops " in their desperate effort to maintain a livelihood. The immediate peril facing industry gave employers an unanticipated windfall of bargaining power. The union emerged as an institution to minimize the indignities caused by the disorderly scramble of labor for limited job opportunities.

In a full-employment economy, on the other hand, the situation is reversed, with jobs begging for men. The " tragedy " is that workers are often able to provide less than a fair day's work, and yet they dare management to make an issue of it. In this latter setting, it is not surprising that the union movement is often charged with corrupting a labor force which otherwise would be willing to work to capacity. However, a distinction must be made between the source of labor motivation and its manifestation. The union serves as a connecting rod, making explicit the workers' attitudes. Blaming the union for the deficiencies of human nature is tantamount to blaming the thermostat for the temperature provided by the furnace. In reviewing the very substantial problems facing industry in a full-employment economy many of the difficulties arise, not because of the limitations of union institutionalism, but because of the limitations of human nature.

To what extent is it true that unions exercise monopoly control over the labor market? Union monopoly generally implies control over the labor supply so that the wage rate can be controlled by varying the quantity of labor service introduced into the market. Union ability to control the aggregate of labor supply is obviously limited. First, unions have not organized as much as one third of the labor force. And secondly, because the union cannot usually prevent its unemployed members from searching for employment, it cannot " remove " the excesss supply from the market.

But unions do not generally attempt to control the wage rate through reductions in labor supply. Rather they negotiate a standard wage rate for each job classification, and the labor supply adjusts itself to this administered rate. To the extent that this rate is " noncompetitive " (or results in unemployment), the numbers seeking employment at the going rate is greater than those securing jobs. The restrictive force of unionism manifests itself through the reduction of labor demand rather than through the reduction of labor supply. Even here, however, the growth of unemployment often poses a serious limit on the extent to which unions can raise wages. There is only one goal that is more important to the work force than high wage rates, and that is employment itself.

A further problem arises in considering the labor monopoly issue. Even in a competitive society it is not possible to visualize the existence of as many employers as there are employees, or for that matter, *always* as many job opportunities as there are job applicants. Individual bargaining, in this context, can hardly be considered equal. The individual worker can threaten management with the loss of perhaps as much as 1 percent of the employer's labor supply by withholding his labor service; but in that same process he losses 100 percent of his income. It is true, of course, that under conditions of full employment, all workers may have more freedom to secure alternative employment opportunities than employers have freedom to secure alternative sources of labor supply. But even here the bargaining power of the *individual* worker is usually extremely limited.

Finally, the application of anti-monopoly statutes has always proved a difficult task, for it is not enough to state that labor-management relations must remain competitive. Specific rules have to be framed by the legislature to guide the anti-trust division and the courts. It is not difficult to imagine that, just as corporations have advertised that they were being prosecuted by the government " for charging low prices," so might the union under indictment complain that it was being prosecuted for attempting to stabilize industry conditions.

We have stressed throughout the job consciousness of the American labor movement. It is this security-minded approach of the union that is often singled out for attack by those (including university professors with tenure) who want the rest of society to " live dangerously." It is indisputable that as consumers we all desire change, not only with an ever-expanding level of personal consumption but also with variations in the direction of our personal expenditure. But as producers we are not equally willing to absorb the incidence of such change. Here again, however, the resistance is not to change but to the insecurity associated with change. It is rather unfair to suggest that labor desires " secure poverty " to " insecure advancement," for such a dichotomy suggests that security systems must necessarily frustrate growth. Is this necessarily true? Workers will undoubtedly encourage automation when they are given assurances that this will reduce the burden of their tasks, provide them with opportunities to learn new skills, and increase their earnings. As we have noted earlier, it is not enough to establish that *after the fact* such automation will benefit everyone when the individual worker fears *before the fact* that he might lose his job. Obviously, the resistance to change can be greatly minimized as management offers firm commitments to labor regarding the new role it can play in expanding output. We need not then indulge in head-shaking about the " secure, stratified poverty " which is sometimes alleged to be the goal of our labor movement.

The organized labor movement in America is still firmly wedded to " pure and simple " or " bread-and-butter " goals. Neither workers nor union leaders are groping for a new ideology or searching out a blueprint for a new utopian society. Aspirations are limited to the deep freeze, the latest model car, the new home, or the extended vacation with pay. While some may argue that such single attention to acquisitive goals is morally indefensible, labor is usually willing to take the chance that an increment of money income can be complementary to (rather than inconsistent with) cultural and spiritual enrichment. Without doubt the notable success labor has had in selling to the American public this essentially conservative philosophy has made possible the survival and growth of unionism.

It is precisely because of this conservatism, though, that we face many of the economic problems today. Industry revenues may not always support wage demands. To state the point in another way, production may not always expand as rapidly as our aspirations for consumption. As we noted in our earlier chapters, wage adjustments are related in an intricate way to consumption, profits, and investment. In the past it has been thought that an imbalance in the consumption/investment or wage/profit proportions gave rise to depressed conditions. But in more recent years, with the continuing experience of high employment, economists are more interested in the consumption/investment ratio in terms of an " economic growth " context rather than in terms of a " cyclical unemployment " context. In this growth context, if unions pursue wage policies (or if the government pursues a tax policy) which sharply reduces the revenues flowing to industry stock and bondholders, the ability of industry to sustain investments with reduced venture capital may be undercut, and the long-run pace of economic growth hindered. There is not convincing evidence to suggest that unions have had sufficient power to accomplish (at least by economic pressure) the redistribution of income in their favor that they desire. But should such a redistribution in fact be possible, either by economic or political means, society must then balance its desire for a high current level of consumption today with its desire for a rapid pace of industrial growth tomorrow.

Marxists have claimed that in a capitalist society the relating of the issue of current distributive shares to the pace of future industrial growth makes explicit the class conflict within the capitalist economy. Labor will never believe — as the argument goes — that profits can benefit the worker and hence can never willingly accept an expansion of management's distributive share in the interests of capital expansion. Similarly, the Marxists argue, in a communist society with capital owned by the state, such an issue becomes merely a contest between the present and the future, and contains no basis for class conflict within the communist society. This argument oversimplifies the issue in two respects: First, labor in our society is willing to permit management a fairly constant proportion of the national product for, whether labor realizes it or not (and probably it does not), labor has absorbed a surprisingly constant share of the national product. Secondly, the contest of the future over the present exists in all societies, regardless of their economic organization. The political instability within contemporary Russia and her satellites may, in no small way, be related to the inability of the people freely to determine the proportions of present income they can consume. If this has not produced a clash among the classes in Russia, it has apparently produced a clash among the bureaucrats who must make this decision.

In general summary, the study of labor problems does not encourage one to be dogmatic in his assertions about major labor issues, for these problems mirror the painfully complex economic and moral issues confronting society. It is not enough to condemn labor organization as the sole villain on the scene when such organization is but one manifestation of group activity typifying every phase of our life. Still, one cannot escape the emotionalism which surrounds most labor issues. This emotionalism is not easily dispelled by an appeal to the facts, especially when the facts themselves are so tentative and flexible. And yet, from a methodological viewpoint, the basis for understanding labor issues is not to be found in pursuing only those works which massage one's existing prejudices, but in a careful surveillance of the terrain of opposing concepts. Furthermore, because labor issues are inextricably bound up with the problems facing all society, it is not generally safe to compartmentalize the analysis of labor disputes, or treat the problems arising from labor organization as a " special case " requiring unique solutions. The raw material out of which most of society's problems evolve is the fact that gross national appetites expand more rapidly than our gross national product. As we have seen, it is difficult for individuals and groups to accept responsibility for expanding the size of that product when it is both conceptually and practically impossible to untangle the specific contributions of various groups to the final product. These problems arise then because our aspirations are infinitely expansible; the solution lies in the hope that human nature is infinitely perfectible.

We must, in other words, tolerate the existing limitations of human nature and yet hope for ever-higher standards of behavior. We must have faith that through society the conflicting standards of power and principle can ultimately be reconciled. This task is not one that need tax the wisdom of the intellectual, but rather one that challenges the substance of human nature itself. It is not a question whether the academician is clever enough to propose solutions, but rather whether the " average sensual man " will have the patience, tolerance, and forbearance to add new dimensions of social interest to his ingrained concept of self-interest. The Spanish writer, Unanumo, thinking of Goethe's dying words, " Light, light, more light," declared passionately, " No, warmth, warmth, more warmth; for we die of cold not of darkness. It is not the night that kills but the frost." [2]

[2] As noted by Stephen K. Bailey "Political Elements in Full Employment Policy," *American Economic Review*, Proceedings, Vol. XLV, No. 2 (May, 1955), p. 350.

Index

Aaron, Benjamin, 175, 180n, 188
Ability to pay, concept in wage determination, 59, 254, 359–361
Acquisitiveness, 84–90, 214, 543, 568–569; *see also* Economic man; Motivations
Adair v. *United States*, 400, 411
Adamic, Louis, 314
Aged, the, economic problems of, 40–41; labor-force participation of, 40–42, 508–509; proportion of, 39–40; retirement or employment of, 40–42; self-support of, 40–41
Agency shop, 276
Agrarianism, 104; *see also* Evans, George Henry
Alger, Horatio, 80–82; *see also* Class consciousness
Allen Bradley Co. v. *Local 3, IBEW*, 416, 420–421
American Federation of Labor (AFL, AF of L), 163–165; history of, 109–111, 411; membership of, 142, 143; political activities of, 115, 189–191; rivalry with CIO, 117–118, 160–163, 430–432; *see also* AFL–CIO
AFL–CIO, structure of, 160–171; political activities of, 192–194
American Liberty League, National Lawyer's Committee, 425
American plan, 114
American Railway Union, 112; *see also* Debs, Eugene V.
Anarchism, 107–108
Annual earnings, 61–62
Annual improvement factor, *see* Productivity, factor in wage determination
Annual wages, *see* Employment stabilization; Guaranteed annual wage plans
Antitrust laws, *see* Monopoly; Sherman Antitrust Act
Apex Hosiery Co. v. *Leader*, 419–420
Apprenticeship, as requirement for union membership, 173
Arbitration, 330, 335–345; compulsory, 345–347
Arbitration Act (1888), 344
Archibald, Katherine, 84
Arnow, Kathryn S., 353

Automation, 94; and manpower needs, 48, 282–288; *see also* Technological unemployment; Technology
Avery, Sewell L., 436

Back-to-work movements, 325
Backman, Jules, 331n, 367
Bagby, Wesley S., 286
Bailey, Stephen K., 569
Bakke, E. W., 297., 492n, 493n, 498, 518
Balance of trade, favorable, 458
Balkanization of bargaining units, 244, 246; *see also* Bargaining units
Bambrick, James J., 143, 150, 159, 173, 174, 179
Bancroft, G., 40, 516
Bargaining, collective, *see* Collective bargaining
Bargaining in "good faith," 246–248, 323
Bargaining power, determinants of, 242, 301–307; equality of, 329–330; *see also* Collective bargaining; Strikes
Bargaining units, 230–235; under labor boards, 242–246, 445, 448
Beck, Dave, 134, 183
Belfer, Nathan, 159n, 484n
Bell, Daniel, 78, 129, 138–139, 140n, 181, 182
Bentham, Jeremy, 21
Bernstein, E. M., 523–524
Bernstein, Irving, 122, 124, 126, 127, 139, 340, 343, 424
Berry, George, 177–178
Beveridge, Sir William, 495, 499, 503n, 522n, 547, 561
Birth rates, in America, 37–39; in foreign countries, 49–51
Black, Justice Hugo, 416, 418–419
Bloom, G. F., 484n; and Northrup, H. R. 186
Boas, Franz, 397
"Boring from within," 184–186; *see also* Communists
Bortz, Nelson M., 42
Boulding, Kenneth, 552, 554
Boulwareism (Lemuel R. Boulware), 325–326
Bourgeoisie, 197–199; *see also* Class consciousness; Communists; Marx, Karl